THE FORGING OF THE
AMERICAN EMPIRE

☆☆☆☆☆

THE FORGING
OF THE
AMERICAN
EMPIRE

SIDNEY LENS

☆☆☆☆☆☆☆☆☆☆☆☆☆☆☆☆☆☆☆☆☆☆☆☆☆☆☆

THOMAS Y. CROWELL COMPANY

NEW YORK / ESTABLISHED 1834

204589

L.C. Card 74-158710
ISBN 0-690-31309-8

1 2 3 4 5 6 7 8 9 10

☆☆☆

OTHER BOOKS BY THE SAME AUTHOR

☆☆☆

Left, Right and Center

The Counterfeit Revolution

A World in Revolution

The Crisis of American Labor

Working Men

Africa—Awakening Giant

A Country Is Born

The Futile Crusade

Radicalism in America

Unions and What They Do

Poverty: America's Enduring Paradox

The Military-Industrial Complex

To the Children of Vietnam,
Who Are Being Murdered and Maimed
by My Government—
and Yours

ACKNOWLEDGMENTS

I'd like to thank four academic friends for having read this manuscript and given me of their wisdom: D. F. Fleming, Staughton Lynd, Thomas Steiner, and Howard Zinn. The contributions of my lovely wife, Shirley, cannot be catalogued, but they merit more than an expression of affection in this cold print.

Isolated paragraphs in the last two chapters have appeared in another book of mine, *The Military-Industrial Complex*, published by Pilgrim Press and the National Catholic Reporter in 1970.

CONTENTS

1	THE MYTH OF MORALITY	1
2	FORGOTTEN ALLY	15
3	FALLEN STAR	40
4	ON TO CANADA	62
5	PICKING THE SPANISH BONE	87
6	MEXICO FOR AMERICANS	99
7	TRANSCONTINENTAL CONQUEST	111
8	THE BRAVE BRAVES	135
9	COMMERCE FOLLOWS THE FLAG	149
10	THE FLAG FOLLOWS COMMERCE	169
11	SUBDUING THE BANANA REPUBLICS	195
12	THE FINE ART OF VANDALISM	217
13	THE BIG LEAP	236
14	THE WAR BEFORE THE WAR (I)	275
15	THE WAR BEFORE THE WAR (II)	292
16	AGAINST FRIEND AND FOE	313
17	GLOBAL IMPERIALISM	333
18	THE ECSTASY AND THE AGONY	366
19	CLOSING THE CIRCLE	395
	SELECTED BIBLIOGRAPHY	437
	INDEX	453

THE FORGING OF THE
AMERICAN EMPIRE

☆☆☆☆☆

☆☆☆☆☆

1

☆☆☆☆☆

THE MYTH OF
MORALITY

The United States, like other nations, has formulated a myth of morality to assuage its conscience and sustain its image. The United States, we are told, has always tried to avoid war; when it has been forced to take the military road, it has seldom done so for motives of gain or glory. On the contrary, its wars were fought only for such high principles as freedom of the seas, the right of self-determination, and to halt aggression. In thought, as in deed, the United States—so the myth goes—has been antiwar, anti-imperialist, anti-colonialist. It has not sought an inch of anyone else's territory, and the few colonies it acquired were treated with kindness and liberated as quickly as circumstances permitted.

Sophisticated Americans admit that in the course of two centuries their nation has been guilty of some cruelties and excesses—as in driving the Indians westward—but these are usually dismissed as unfortunate aberrations. By and large, according to the myth, the United States has religiously respected the rights of other peoples to determine their own destiny: it has always been sympathetic to revolutionaries fighting for genuine independence; it has always refrained from interfering in the internal affairs of other nations, large or small, powerful or weak. More than any other great nation it has been guided by a selfless concern for those less fortunate.

America the benevolent, however, does not exist and never has existed. The United States has pilfered large territories from helpless or near-helpless peoples; it has forced its will on scores of nations, against their wishes and against their interests; it has violated hundreds of treaties and understandings; it has committed war crimes as shocking as most; it has wielded a military stick and a

1

dollar carrot to forge an imperialist empire such as man has never known before; it has intervened ruthlessly in the internal life of dozens of nations to prevent them from choosing the leaders they did want or from overthrowing, by revolution, the ones they didn't. And contrary to the myth, the urge for expansion—at the expense of other peoples—goes back to the beginnings of the United States itself. If the appetite for imperialism did not emerge fully matured, it nevertheless grew concomitant with opportunity and a sense of burgeoning power.

As early as 1778, Samuel Adams, leader of the left wing of the Revolution, proposed to his compatriots that they set their sights beyond the thirteen original colonies toward the acquisition of Canada, Nova Scotia, and Florida as well. "We shall never be upon a solid footing," he said, "till Britain cedes to us what nature designs we should have, or till we wrest it from her." According to his cousin, John Adams, Britain would always be "the enemy of the United States, let her disguise it as much as she will" so long as she held these territories. "The unanimous voice of the continent is Canada must be ours; Quebec must be taken." The weight of these declarations was not that the Canadian people necessarily wanted to be incorporated into the Union, but that the *United States* needed the province for its own purpose. That purpose, as expressed by Samuel Adams, was to prevent Britain from disturbing "our peace" and from diffusing "mischief and poison through the states."

Contradictory as it sounds, leaders of a new republic fighting an expansive overseas empire felt they were destined to establish an empire of their own. George Washington referred to the United States in March 1783 as a "rising empire." Thomas Jefferson wrote in 1786 that "our confederacy must be viewed as the nest from which all America, North and South, is to be peopled." He prayed that the Spaniards would hang onto their colonies long enough "till our population can be sufficiently advanced to gain it from them piece by piece." Meanwhile "we must have" some of their territories around the Mississippi—"this is all we are as yet ready to receive." The Americans believed that in furtherance of the "great law of self-preservation" nature had given them a special right to expand. They were, like the ancient Israelites, a "chosen race," representing a higher societal order, carrying progress wherever they went. They were not trampling on other people, they were opening up new vistas for them; to be part of the United States was a privilege, not a yoke. Thus, after the Louisiana Purchase, when many people in New Orleans expressed dissatisfaction with being joined to the United States, Jefferson sent troops to keep order, and American officials from the nearby Mississippi Territory proclaiming that "Nature designed the inhabitants of Mississippi and those of New Orleans to be one single people. It is your peculiar happiness that nature's decrees are fulfilled under the auspices of a philosopher [Jefferson] who prefers justice to conquest. . . ." Having struck this note of sympathy and fairness, the American officials warned that while Jefferson "is careful of your happiness, he will not permit you to destroy it by obstructing *our* rights." (Emphasis added.) This same dual approach was taken toward the Indians. Many American leaders were genuinely concerned about the welfare of a million natives, living in the wilderness, but the nation as a whole felt it had a special mission in clearing the continent which must not be impeded by the "backward" red men.

If the lines between self-preservation and aggression were blurred in the early days, it became evident in subsequent decades that the acquisitive instinct rather than national security dominated American policy. Acquisitiveness was never unchallenged, but it was never vanquished either, and indeed became more fervid with success. The desire for Spanish territory in Latin America underlay the naval war with France in the 1790's, and the desire for Canada and Florida, the War of 1812. The war against Mexico in 1846–48 was a brazen expression of territorial lust, for by now it was obvious that no European power threatened U.S. "self-preservation." The invasion of Mexico was undertaken under the interesting doctrine of "manifest destiny." It had been stated tentatively by John Quincy Adams in 1811: "The whole continent of North America appears to be destined by Divine Providence to be peopled by one nation, speaking one language, professing one general system of religious and political principles, and accustomed to one general tenor of social usages and customs." This thesis was repeated in stronger form in 1845 by an editor named John L. O'Sullivan, who wrote about the "fulfillment of our manifest destiny to overspread the continent alloted by Providence for the free development of our yearly multiplying millions." President James K. Polk put the theme into magnificent practice by overrunning Mexico.

A half century later, when the "rising empire" stretched from the Atlantic to the Pacific and expansion could proceed only in a different form, Theodore Roosevelt elaborated a variation of Manifest Destiny. It is not true, he said in his annual message to Congress in 1904, that the United States "feels any land hunger." Any nation in this hemisphere that is "stable, orderly, and prosperous . . . can count upon our hearty friendship." But if it is guilty of "chronic wrongdoing"—for instance, defaulting on its loans—then the North

American colossus, "however reluctantly," has the right to "the exercise of an international police power." Under the self-proclaimed Monroe Doctrine, according to Roosevelt, it was imperative for the United States to defend small nations from seizure by European powers, as well as to defend them from themselves. "It is our duty towards the people living in barbarism to see that they are freed from their chains."

Roosevelt's "big stick" policy was obviously crass. The national leadership soon found that there were methods other than permanent occupation of an underdeveloped country to gain control over it. William Howard Taft adopted "dollar diplomacy." Woodrow Wilson, who followed Taft, announced on the one hand that the United States would "never again seek one additional foot of territory by conquest," and then, through his Secretary of State, Robert Lansing, declared that "the Caribbean is within the peculiar sphere of influence of the United States." To bring order to that "peculiar sphere of influence" Wilson dispatched troops to Haiti, the Dominican Republic, and Mexico, forcing them to bend to Washington's wishes. They did not have to be converted to outright colonies to do America's bidding; temporary occupation, or just the threat of it, was enough. "It is a paradox," writes Albert K. Weinberg in his *Manifest Destiny*, "that the aggrandizement of American empire in the twentieth century has not taken place principally through territorial expansion." The "acquisition of sovereignty over land is no longer the only or most expedient way to the substantial control which may be called empire." In due course the United States, following this principle, became guardian and master of the twenty Latin American republics in the western hemisphere, tuning them to its own pitch. If it was not old-style colonialism, it was not less effective.

With World War I the United States began to assert its right to world leadership. Unfortunately, "leadership" is often just a mask of imperialism: when the United States impinges on the sovereignty of other nations or peoples, forcing weak states to select governments that are its virtual puppets, that is control and domination, not leadership. By such techniques the United States soon forged an unbounded empire. By being a nonbelligerent for more than two years before entering World War I, it was able to accumulate the capital and expand its industrial machine so as to seize markets from both the defeated as well as the victorious powers. By sending troops to Russia (along with thirteen other countries) in 1918–20, and by granting loans to Europe, it slowed the momentum of the Communist revolution and saved the established capitalist order to which it now offered leadership from possible dissolution. Two decades later it repeated the process, but on a grander scale. It emerged from World War II—again having hung back for two years—as the undisputed manager of the non-Communist world, its chief prop, protector, and policeman.

To many people America's policies after the second great war seemed the very antithesis of imperialism. The United States gave the Philippines its independence, actively opposed colonialism in the Dutch East Indies, and made available scores of billions of dollars in grants and loans to literally dozens of nations. On the surface at least this did not appear to be selfish self-interest, nor was it easily visible how the sovereignty of other nations was being breached. Modern imperialism, however, differs perceptibly from that of the past. It does not center around a single act such as the nineteenth-century occupation of India by Britain or Algeria by France. In an era of national revolution, with dozens of countries winning independence, this old-style imperialism is no longer possible. It would require millions of troops and incredible sums of money, and even then—as the experiences in Algeria and Vietnam have shown—might not be successful. Modern imperialism therefore must rely on a variety of techniques. It is a complex *process* that combines economic, political, and military means. Aid—grants or loans—is given to foreign governments on condition that they retain the so-called free-enterprise system and take down the barriers to American trade and investments. Aid is given with explicit and implicit conditions that soon make the client government a dependency of the United States. This is even more true of military aid. The Pentagon trains and supplies dozens of armies, and transforms them into satellite military establishments. These satellite establishments also defend the "American system," fighting their own people when they try to make genuine revolutions—as in China, Guatemala, Iran, Cuba, and Brazil, for instance—and overthrowing governments that turn toward neutralism and break with the "system." Supplementing these military efforts is the largest instrument of international subversion that has ever been forged by any great power, the Central Intelligence Agency. Covertly, it interferes in the internal affairs of dozens of countries almost daily, seeking to mold them to the "American way," and paying for and organizing one counterrevolution after another. Between the Pentagon and the CIA, American imperialism intervenes in the domestic life of many nations on an almost regular basis. One unit of the Air Force, called the Special Operations Force, has made secret forays, according to Donald Robinson in an article for *Parade* (January 31, 1971), in twenty-eight countries. The famed Green Berets doubtless have an even more impressive record.

The new formula for imperial control did not exclude direct military intervention. When other methods have failed and when satellite military establishments have been incapable of defending satellite governments, the United States has sent in its own forces—as in Lebanon, Korea, the Dominican Republic, Vietnam. Generally, however, it relied on economic and military assistance and pressures to carry out its objectives. This, plus the massive navy it built to rule the seas, and the hundreds of major bases in every corner of the world, has been the complex mechanism for America's global imperialism. If it differed from the old forms, it was no less effective—on the contrary. It is no exaggeration to say that it molded all of what is called the "free world" into the American pattern, beneficial to the interests of the American establishment.

II

In unguarded moments national leaders have frankly conceded that the underlying purpose of their diplomacy and wars has been economic aggrandizement. Senator Henry Cabot Lodge put it pithily in March 1895: "Commerce follows the flag." In 1914–15, Secretary of State William Jennings Bryan argued for absolute neutrality to keep America out of the European maelstrom—including the withholding of loans to Britain, France, and Russia. But his successor, Robert Lansing, in taking the opposite line, pointed out to Wilson that from "December 1, 1914, to June 30, 1915, our exports exceeded our imports by nearly a billion dollars," and within the next six months would show a favorable balance of another billion and three quarters. If Britain and her allies are not permitted to borrow from American bankers, said Lansing, they "will have to stop buying and our present export trade will shrink proportionately."

Dean Acheson, Undersecretary of State in 1944, defined American purposes in the second war much as Lansing did in the first war. Stability at home, he told a congressional committee, was impossible without adequate markets abroad. "We have got to see that what the country produces is used and is sold under financial arrangements which make its production possible." The government, he urged, "must look to foreign markets." After the war the enormous expansion of American military bases and military power was accompanied by an equally sensational expansion in trade and capital export. Long-term investments abroad, $11.3 billion in 1940, were $13.7 billion in 1945 and $70.8 billion in 1965; commercial exports were $4 billion in 1940, $10.5 billion in 1945, and $27.5 billion in 1965. By checkmating the Germans in two wars, and by taking advantage of the crisis of its own allies at the end of hostilities, the United States fostered a handsome economic and political expansion of its own. It may simply have been good fortune that in "defeating the Kaiser" or "destroying Nazism," the United States was also able to gain an advantage against Britain and France. But in the process of gaining this advantage it evolved what Senator J. William Fulbright was to call an "arrogance of power," an ultimatistic attitude of "do it our way or else."

At any rate, the United States has fashioned an empire more formidable than any of the past. It has graduated from the territorial imperialism of the nineteenth century to the limited imperialism of the early part of this century, and finally to the present global imperialism. In this long annal there has seldom been a year when American troops were not fighting on someone else's soil. Senator Everett Dirksen on June 23, 1969, entered into the record a list of more than 160 military ventures by the United States, from the "undeclared naval war with France" 1798–1800, to Vietnam. According to the well-known army historian William Addleman Ganoe, the country was involved, during its first 148 years, in 110 military conflicts and 8,600 battles "with a consequent casualty list, totalling approximately 1,280,000 men." Quincy Wright puts the figure somewhat higher, 9,000 battles from 1775 to 1900, and Francis B. Heitman somewhat lower, 3,292 engagements for the army and 1,131 "distinct episodes" for the navy—plus the capture of "some 4,000 merchant vessels." From 1865 to 1898 alone, records Colonel R. Ernest Dupuy, the American army "fought no less than nine hundred and forty-three engagements against the Indians—running the gamut from skirmishes to pitched battles—in twelve separate campaigns, to say nothing of a score of other disconnected bickerings, to insure that this national expansion should become fact."

III

Despite this record, the myth of morality has persevered in the United States more tenaciously than in most nations because of five fortunate circumstances:

(1) The imperialism of the United States, as already indicated, has differed in form, though not in objectives or results, from that of Britain, France, Germany, Italy, and Japan.

(2) The United States has always fought against minor powers with inconsequential military might or great powers which were enervated or preoccupied elsewhere.

(3) Its total casualties have been exceptionally small compared to those of other nations.

(4) Its tradition was antimilitarist until a quarter of a century ago.

(5) It has always had vocal antiwar and pacifist minorities.

American imperialism began to construct an overseas empire in the old way, occupying certain lands much as Britain occupied and made colonies out of India and Kenya. But if found that Cuba, for instance, could be dominated through the Platt Amendment—granting the *right* of unilateral intervention—as effectively as through occupation; that Paraguay could be held as an American sphere of influence by training a satellite military establishment; that a combination of pressure for an open-door policy and economic and military assistance could make Iran an American vassal state. The United States, a latecomer to modern imperialism, had to find other ways to dominate weaker nations—and it did, with an effectiveness at least equal to that of Britain or France.

No nation has been more fortunate in the choice of enemies—at least until recently—than the United States of America. They have either been so weak that they needed only a slight push to drop into oblivion—the native Indians, Tripoli, Spain, Mexico, Filipino nationalists, the banana republics—or so involved with other adversaries their energies were divided. The United States fought Britain twice; each time Britain also was at war with a more serious enemy —France. The United States took up cudgels against France while France was embroiled in the Napoleonic Wars against most of Europe. The United States engaged Germany twice when she was already debilitated by two years of hostilities with England, France, and Russia. To put it bluntly, the colossus of the western hemisphere has fought either midgets with limited capacities, or giants that had one hand tied behind their back.

Good luck in choosing the right enemy at the right time not only helped transform a fledgling republic into a giant empire but had the bonus effect of sparing American lives. In its nine major wars, from the War of the Revolution to Vietnam, approximately a million Americans were killed, four fifths of them in the Civil War and World War II. The Soviet Union, by contrast, lost six times as many soldiers on the battlefield in World War II alone, and Germany three times as many. Wars that achieved enormous political objectives for the United States have taken a surprisingly small toll in lives. According to the Department of Defense, 4,435 soldiers perished while fighting in the Revolutionary War—which established an independent nation. Just 1,733 battlefield deaths and 11,500 "other deaths"—from disease and accident—were the cost of victory over Mexico, which incorporated one half that nation into the United States. Fewer than 400 men were killed at the front during the Spanish-American War, though another 2,061 died from other causes. Each death, to be sure, was final for the man who perished, but for the nation as a whole these were remarkably small payments for significant territorial and political benefits. This fostered the false conviction that the United States was not a warlike nation, that expansion came about primarily through other—just and pacific— means.

Another boon to the myth of morality has been the modest size of America's armed forces, and the tendency—until World War II—to demobilize most of the troops after hostilities. On June 2, 1784, after the War of the Revolution, Congress ordered all soldiers discharged from service, except "twenty-five privates to guard the stores at Fort Pitt and fifty-five to guard the stores at West Point, with a proportionate number of officers," none above the rank of captain. And though military men strove avidly thereafter to build a sizable standing army, the number of officers and men in its ranks in 1845, on the eve of the Mexican War, was a mere 9,000, and as late as 1904, a relatively small 53,000. Not long before World War II the armed forces numbered only 139,000. i

This opposition to militarism has strong roots in the American heritage, related in large measure to the fear of military dictatorship. As early as 1638, John Winthrop, the governor of Massachusetts, warned that it would be dangerous "to erect a standing authority of military men which might easily in time overthrow the civil power." The Declaration of Independence castigated an English king who "has kept among us, in times of peace, standing armies without the consent of our legislatures" and who "has affected to render the military independent of and superior to the civil power." The colonists did not shun military activity when necessary, but instead of a standing army (and mercenaries) they relied on citizen soldiers whose martial activities were episodic to farming. The famed Minutemen of the early Revolutionary period were young citizens ready to drop the farmer's plow for a gun "at a minute's notice." Older men were assigned to "alarm companies," to be mobilized for action only as occasion demanded. The concept of a militia was very much different from that of professional troops. And while Washington did command a national army in addition to the militia, libertarian American tendencies asserted themselves sturdily once hostilities ended. Less than six months after General Washington had resigned his commission and returned to Mount Vernon, the

Continental Congress stated its philosophy in unencumbered terms: "Standing armies in time of peace are inconsistent with the principle of republican governments, dangerous to the liberties of a free people, and generally converted into destructive engines for establishing despotism." Such fears had been confirmed in 1782, when Colonel Lewis Nicola proposed to Washington that he lead a military coup and install himself as king—a suggestion which the general vehemently rejected.

The antimilitarist mood was so strong that political leaders had to pay obeisance to it even when urging a regular army. When Washington, for instance, asked Congress for four regiments of infantry and one of artillery—a total of 2,631 men—"to awe the Indians, protect our trade, prevent encroachments," he conceded in advance that "a *large* standing army in time of peace hath ever been considered dangerous to the liberties of the country." His only justification was that a "few troops" would be "safe." Congress, however, did not agree. The only concession it made to those of military bent was to order the Secretary of War to raise from the militia of New York, Pennsylvania, Connecticut and New Jersey a contingent of 700 men to guard the western posts against Indians. The Constitution did, it is true, authorize a standing army, but James Madison in defending the provision subsequently made the same sort of apology as Washington. An army on a small scale, he said, "had its inconveniences," whereas on "an intensive scale its consequences may be fatal." Clearly, for most of the founding fathers military preparedness was a dangerous drug, to be taken in small doses at best.

In addition there has always been, in the annals of America, some sentiment opposed not only to militarism but to war per se. If many who were hostile toward standing armies nonetheless endorsed specific wars, there were others who took issue with both. They ranged all the way from philosophical pacifists like Noah Worcester, Henry David Thoreau, and A. J. Muste, to nonpacifists who were critical of the particular war at hand, such as Daniel Webster, Grover Cleveland, Robert M. La Follette, George W. Norris, Wayne Morse, George McGovern, Eugene McCarthy. Long before there was a United States, John Woolman denounced war as a grab for riches. "The rising up of a desire to obtain wealth," he wrote, "is the beginning. . . ." Anthony Benezet, another Quaker, was opposed even to the Revolutionary War because it killed off "creatures originally formed under the image of God. . . ." His explanation of the causes of war sounds like a blend of Freud and Marx: "War is the inseparable union between the sensual and malignant passions; war protracted to a certain period necessarily compels peace; peace revives and extends trade and commerce; trade and commerce give new life, vigor and scope to the sensual and malignant passions, and these naturally tend to generate war."

After the Revolution, many of the founding fathers expressed weighty concern on the subject. At the behest of the Massachusetts Legislature, Samuel Adams drafted a letter of instructions to members of the United States Congress from his state, bidding them to find means so "that national differences may be settled and determined without the necessity of war, in which the world has too long been deluged, to the destruction of human happiness and the disgrace of human reason and government." Benjamin Franklin wrote in 1783 that "there never was a good war or a bad peace." In another letter he commented that "All wars are follies, very expensive and very mischievous ones. When will mankind . . . agree to settle their differences by arbitration? Were they to do it even by the cast of a die, it would be better than by fighting and destroying each other."

George Washington, in a letter to the Marquis de Chastellux in 1788, took issue with "young military men" who want to sow the seeds of war. Jefferson recoiled with "horror at the ferociousness of man." Will nations, he asked, "never devise a more rational umpire of differences than force?" "Peace," he said on another occasion, "is our passion. . . . We prefer trying *every* other just principle, right and safety, before we would recur to war."

Each generation and each conflict has had its own antiwar brigades. The Jeffersonians opposed the naval war with France; New Englanders, the war against Britain in 1812; Whigs generally, the war against Mexico; Democrats, the war against Spain in 1898; a handful of independents in both houses of Congress, World War I. Concomitantly there was the agitation of an enduring pacifist movement. Noah Worcester, secretary and founder of the Massachusetts Peace Society early in the nineteenth century, proposed a Congress of Nations and arbitration of international disputes by a world court as substitute for the sword. William Ladd, the Harvard-educated sea captain who turned Congregational minister, ascribed the causes of war to the "many men in this country, and more in Europe, [who] get their living and acquire splendid fortunes by war. . . ." The Massachusetts Legislature in 1844, after condemning war as an institution, suggested "arbitration as a practical and desirable substitute. . . ." The Free Soil Party, whose members later merged with the Republican Party, recommended in their 1852 program "the introduction into all treaties hereafter . . . of some provision for amicable settlement of difficulties by a resort to decisive arbitration." A year later the Senate Committee on Foreign Affairs passed a similar resolution. Elihu Burritt, the self-educated blacksmith who organized an international conference for peace in 1848, had a more radical antidote—a general strike by workers of all the industrial nations. "This, then," he wrote, "is the alternative: either a congress of nations for simultaneous and proportionate disarmament, or an organized strike of the workingmen of Christendom against war, root and branch."

In 1890 Congress adopted a resolution calling on the President to negotiate bilateral treaties for arbitrating disputes "which cannot be adjusted by diplomatic agency," and a treaty embodying this principle was actually concluded between Lord Pauncefote of Britain and Secretary of State Richard Olney in 1897. It failed to get the necessary two thirds in the Senate by a slim three votes. A year later the nation was at war with Spain—but against mixed opposition that included former President Grover Cleveland, the financier Andrew Carnegie, Mark Twain, and later the Anti-Imperialist League. World War I was bitterly denounced by leaders of certain ethnic minorities such as the German-Americans, and by the Socialists, "Wobblies," and Anarchists.

Clearly, the antiwar strain in American life has been so deeply implanted that many have considered it the predominant one. Taken together with the other factors—the character of the enemies, the low number of casualties, antimilitarism—it has reinforced the myth of morality, the myth that America wants no one else's territory and religiously respects other nations' sovereignty.

IV

Yet, the overwhelmingly stronger strain has been expansionist and martial. Americans boast that they have never lost a war, and they have justified intervention and expansion on the grounds that it made their nation "great." So enamored has the nation been with its military victories that of the thirty-six presidents it has elected up to Richard Nixon, ten were military heroes—Washington in the War of the Revolution; Jackson and Harrison in Indian campaigns and the War of 1812; Taylor and Pierce in the Mexican War; Grant, Hayes, and Garfield in the Civil War; Theodore Roosevelt in the Spanish-American War; Eisenhower in World War II. By contrast, there has never been a labor leader, a clergyman, or a physician in the White House, though they have been more numerous than military leaders.

There has been a certain intoxication with "strength" and self-righteousness in the American saga that has more than counterbalanced antimilitarism and pacifism. To be "strong," it is felt, is to be "great," and America in its own eyes has always been the "greatest." Thus any people or nation absorbed into the United States or aligned with it as a sphere of influence, should—it is believed—be happy with the relationship. Strength, war, greatness, expansion— these are inherent facts of life, and their spokesmen have combined the myth of morality with a definition of man as war-prone. "Until the Gospel shall have extensively corrected the hereditary depravity of mankind," John Jay wrote to pacifist Noah Worcester in 1817, "the wickedness resulting from it will, in my opinion, continue to produce national sins and national punishments; and by causing un- just wars and other culpable practices, to render just wars occasion- ally indispensable." According to the outstanding theorist of imperi- alism, Admiral Alfred T. Mahan, the expansionist instinct is rooted in the "moral obligations" of a great nation. Another theoretician of this bent, "General" Homer Lea, ascribed it to nationhood itself.

Lea, a Denver-born hunchback who gained his title "General" by fighting with the revolutionist Sun Yat-sen in China, insisted in *The Valor of Ignorance,* published early in the twentieth century, that "the prolongation of national existence" is based exclusively on the ability to make war. A great nation cannot avoid war, since it is in- herent to its existence. Its only alternatives are: "Wars—Victory—a nation. Wars—Destruction—dissolution. . . . As manhood marks the height of physical vigor among mankind, so the militant suc- cesses of a nation mark the zenith of its physical greatness." As soon as a nation stops expanding its starts to decline. Thus the strength of a society is in its "military vigor." Its "ideals, laws and constitutions are but temporary effulgences. . . ." The United States, Lea argued, "has been built up from the spoils of combat and conquest of de- fenseless tribes" and it must now continue "this irrepressible expan- sion" against nations which have a military ability equal to or in ex- cess of its own. Once it stops doing so its death is inevitable, for "a nation that is rich, vain, and at the same time unprotected, provokes wars and hastens its own ruin."

Lea, who was toasted by the Hearst press and was paid the du- bious honor of having Adolf Hitler plagiarize a few paragraphs of his book for *Mein Kampf,* expressed in the sharpest terms the other side of the American ambivalency, that despite the need for a moral stance, conquest and war were mandates of nature. Lea offered as proof of this thesis that in the 3,400 years before his book was pub- lished there were only 234 years of peace. "Nations succeeded one another," he pointed out, "with monotonous similarity in their rise, decline and fall. One and all of them were builded by architects who were generals, masons who were soldiers, trowels that were swords and out of stones that were the ruins of decadent states."

If few American leaders would state it so boldly this essentially has been the American experience. In the *realpolitik*, as contrasted with verbiage, the byword has been aggressiveness. The same Washington who wrote the Marquis de Chastellux denouncing "the waste of war and the rage of conquest," a decade later ordered Generals Arthur St. Clair and Anthony Wayne to fight the Indians in Indian country. A few years after leaving office he was supporting the naval war against France and aligning himself with Alexander Hamilton in a grander scheme, to seize Spanish possessions west and south. Jefferson, who opposed the naval war with France, nonetheless was urging a naval blockade—an act of war—against the Barbary States as early as 1784. He himself ordered hostilities against Tripoli during his administration and supported the war against England in 1812 under the Madison administration. This same dichotomy between word and deed was equally pronounced in Polk, McKinley, Wilson (who ran on a slogan that he kept the nation out of war), Franklin Roosevelt (who ran on a similar slogan two decades later), and the five post-World War II presidents.

Each act of aggrandizement in the American chronicle has been valiantly camouflaged in the rhetoric of defense. The War of 1812 was a "defense" against British impressment of American sailors. The innumerable wars against the Indians were a "defense" against their rampages and violations of treaties. The war against Mexico was a "defense" of Texas and a necessary measure, in the words of Secretary of State James Buchanan, "to hold and civilize Mexico." The Spanish-American War was fought to avenge the sinking of the *Maine*. The two world wars were waged to save the world from the Kaiser and Hitler—and for democracy. In Korea and Vietnam the United States, according to Harry Truman and Lyndon Johnson, was "defending" helpless small powers against Communist aggression.

The myth of morality, however, wears thin against the aggregate of history. For even a cursory look suggests that American policy has not been motivated by the desires and needs of other peoples but by its own concept of "the national interest." That national interest, as conceived by the leaders and establishments of the United States, has pivoted around such mundane things as land, commerce, markets, spheres of influence, investments, or strategic threats from other nations that might threaten land, commerce, markets, spheres of influence, investments. Almost universally, America's primary concern has not been moral, but imperial.

☆☆☆☆☆

2

☆☆☆☆☆

FORGOTTEN
ALLY

Ten weeks after George Washington was inaugurated in 1789, the masses of Paris stormed the Bastille, inaugurating an era of revolution which leveled kings, aristocracies, and clerical orders like proverbial tenpins. Three years later, as the French Revolution moved steadily to the left, France and the monarchs of Austria and Prussia became embroiled in war, and in February the following year, after Louis XVI was guillotined, the circle of war widened to include Britain and Spain. By 1793, a debilitated France stood alone against almost all of Europe, with no allies except—potentially—the young republic overseas which she had helped to gain independence a decade previously.

The French Revolution and the war that followed it were to have a fateful and unanticipated effect on the United States.

"In no part of the globe," wrote John Marshall, "was this revolution hailed with more joy than in America." Most Americans saw it as an extension of their own experiment in liberty and republicanism, a triumph for common aspirations. They danced in the streets, wore cockades like the French, addressed each other as "citizen," and forced officials to dispense with such honorifics as "Sir," "Honorable," and "Excellency." They exulted with every success for their counterparts in Europe; when news came of Doumouriez's victory against the royalists at Valmy there were wild demonstrations here. In Boston the marchers carried French and American flags, shot off cannon, and roasted a one-thousand-pound ox in a great barbecue. New Yorkers, rallying to the newly formed Society of the Sons of St. Tammany, staged parades and toasted each other in saloons. When Louis XVI was executed there were more demonstrations; in Philadelphia, the dead King was guillotined in effigy dozens of times a day for weeks. When an innkeeper in the same city hung a picture of Marie Antoinette on his door, the Jeffersonians forced him to paint a streak of red around her neck and daub her clothes with splotches of blood. King Street in New York was renamed Liberty Street and Royal Exchange Alley in Boston was changed to Equality Lane. Small children in Philadelphia taunted aristocratic families by singing the *Marseillaise* outside their windows, and extreme republicans called for immediate war against Britain in conformity with the treaty of alliance made with France in 1778.

The spark from France also ignited political fires in the American hustings. Beginning in 1792, the same type of militant farmers, laborers, and intellectuals that had rallied to Samuel Adams' Sons of Liberty two decades before started to form Democratic Societies and Republican Clubs in all fifteen states, modeled on the Jacobin Clubs of Paris. For them the French Revolution and the American Revolution had a common destiny. They knew that the cry for liberty had already been squelched in Poland by the monarchial federation. They believed that if freedom were to be snuffed out in France, there would be little hope for democracy in the United States.

In America, the French Revolution precipitated a bitter class division and rekindled the dream of empire by the upper-class faction. "At no time in our history, with the exception of the period during the convulsions of the Civil War," writes historian Nathan Schachner, "was there as sharp a cleavage and as furious a hatred among the component parts as in these years." While Republicans rejoiced for the French Revolution, Federalist editors called them "filthy Jacobins," "anarchists," "frog-eating, man-eating cannibals." A Puritan clergyman, according to Charles and Mary Beard, "proposing to go beyond verbiage, called for a war on France so that the Federalist administration could destroy its critics at home"—an idea that also occurred to Alexander Hamilton, spokesman, as he made it clear at the Constitutional Convention, for the "rich and well-born." Timothy Dwight, President of Yale, cynically demanded: "Shall our sons become the disciples of Voltaire and the dragoons of Marat; or our daughters the concubines of the Illuminati?" Rich merchants, whose trade with France's enemy, Britain, constituted almost seven eighths of America's foreign commerce, and old Tories who had consorted with British officers during the Revolution, eagerly denounced France. In this state of internecine bedlam setting conservative Hamiltonians and radical Jeffersonians against each other, evoking street demonstrations and violence, bitter polemics in and out of Congress, and a small uprising in Pennsylvania called the Fries Rebellion—in this backlash, one wing hoped for the extension and fulfillment of the democratic impulse, the other for its suppression and the imposition of a neoaristocratic government. One wing prayed that America would join France, or at least not impede its efforts; the other maneuvered the United States into a naval war against its former ally and hoped to widen the conflict into a war of conquest.

The conservative goals were not attained, but the measures taken by the Hamiltonians to bring them about were significant. They revealed instincts for conquest that would become more pronounced as the nation grew stronger and its elites more domineering. There were three features to the crisis that make it a tale worth recounting:

First, the easy manner with which the American government regarded its treaty obligations—to be honored when useful, to be circumvented or renounced when they weren't. The treaty with France, for instance, which made her an ally in the Revolutionary War, was reduced to a dead letter.

Second, the gap in credibility. The small war with France was waged ostensibly over French spoliations of American shipping, but from 1797 through 1799 Hamilton plotted a full-scale war, not only as a reprisal for shipping grievances, but as a vehicle for seizing Louisiana, the two Floridas, and parts of Latin America from Spain. This true purpose was not confided to the public; indeed, it was camouflaged.

Third, the relationship of war to repression. The Alien and Sedition Acts, passed in the heat of "preparedness," were the first legislative measures in American history designed to stifle dissent.

II

Back in the bleak days of 1777, when General Washington expected his army to "starve, dissolve, or disperse" unless "some great and capital change takes place," American emissaries in Paris pleaded with the government of Louis XVI to join the United States against Britain. The sympathetic French, always happy to see their ancient enemy tormented, secretly sent munitions, clothing, and some money; and when the Americans had shown their mettle by capturing Burgoyne's army at Saratoga, accepted the offer of an alliance. The compact was cemented by two treaties, adopted almost exactly as Benjamin Franklin wrote them, pledging both nations to fight side by side until Britain recognized American independence.

France also dropped her claim to Canada, thereby paving the way for its incorporation into the new Union as a fourteenth state. In return the United States "guaranteed the present possessions" of France in the western hemisphere "from the present time and forever. . . ." It was an unambiguous arrangement committing both nations to do for each other what allies are supposed to do, and its duration for certain aspects—such as defense of France's eleven islands in the West Indies—was an unequivocal "forever."

When word of the agreement reached Washington's disheartened soldiers at Valley Forge on May 6, 1778, they enthusiastically sent off salvos of artillery and shouted "Long live the King of France!" Washington had never seen, he later said, "such unfeigned and perfect joy." In fact this was a turning point in the war, for while France's military effort in the early phases was not particularly distinguished, its navy, engineers, and troops contributed decisively to the American victory at Yorktown in 1781, which caused Britain to sue for peace. "Without the French alliance and the liberal loans of the King," comments naval historian Gardner W. Allen, "the fortunate outcome of the war must surely have been impossible; and gratitude to France was a universal sentiment in America." The venture cost France $280 million—not an inconsequential sum at the time—for which she received in the ultimate settlement two pieces of marginal real estate, Tobago in the West Indies and Senegal in Africa. But if the material rewards were meager there was at least the satisfaction, after losing four wars to England in the previous century, of having won this one.

Ten years later the shoe pinched on the other foot. France was now in a "war of all people against all kings," which was to last almost uninterruptedly for twenty-two years. Moreover, the initial years, 1792–93, were especially difficult ones. The nation was wracked with internal dissension, its crops failed, its manufacture and commerce were paralyzed, its shipping bottled up, and most of its Caribbean islands seized by the British navy. Guadeloupe, one of the West Indies group, was recaptured and served as a base of operations for French cruisers and privateers, but the republic needed additional harbors in the western hemisphere to refit its vessels and dispose of its prizes of war, and it desperately required American foodstuffs. This was obviously the moment for repaying the promissory notes of the 1778 treaties.

To secure American aid and amity, the Gironde regime in Paris dispatched to Philadelphia a vain, handsome, and eloquent minister, Edmond Charles Genêt. Barely thirty years old, he proved as inept as he was audacious, but Citizen Genêt did have some tempting offers to make. He had been advised by superiors that France would not be averse to rewarding the United States with the Floridas and perhaps Canada, if it would support a planned French campaign into Louisiana, Mexico, and other Spanish colonies. The possibility of reinvigorating the alliance of 1778, however, never came up seriously, for on April 22, 1793, Washington proclaimed a policy of neutrality; in the meantime Genêt was bumbling about the United States as if it were his own land, alienating, finally, even the sympathetic Jefferson. Perhaps he was intoxicated with the reception at Charleston—where his ship strayed—and the titanic welcome he received during the five-and-a-half-week trip to the capital. He did not wait to present his official credentials, before issuing four commissions to privateers to prey on English commerce—and by the time he concluded his mission, he had outfitted 14 such ships with 120 guns. The raiders succeeded in capturing 80 enemy vessels, taking many of them to American harbors, much to the discomfiture not only of Hamilton, who was predisposed against revolutionary France, but of Secretary of State Jefferson, who felt it was a glaring infringement on U.S. sovereignty. Genêt also enlisted George Rogers Clark, hero of the rout of the Shawnee Indians at Chillicothe, Ohio, in 1782, for a grand scheme of recovering Louisiana. American crowds continued to shout themselves hoarse for Genêt, and continued to urge an alliance with France. As many as ten thousand people gathered daily in the streets of Philadelphia to damn Washington for his policy of neutrality, and some editors went so far as to publish woodcuts of the dignified general being guillotined. Pro-French juries, called on to try French marauders, freed them despite clear violations of American law. Genêt nonetheless had gone too far and in August, when he failed to obey an order by Jefferson to hold a prize of war in port until a legal opinion could be issued, he was declared persona non grata.

The Genêt debacle, however, though it injured the Republican cause, was not decisive in reorienting the American government from an alliance with France to a virtual alliance with Britain. Other pressures were at play, for while there seemed to be unity between the Hamilton and Jefferson wings on sending Genêt home, the ultimate objectives of the two were poles apart. When word of war between England and France reached the United States in April 1793, Washington hurried back to Philadelphia, where Treasury Secretary Hamilton had already prepared for him a list of thirteen problems to discuss. The most important question of course was what to do about the 1778 treaties. In Hamilton's view they were inoperative because they had been made with a king, now executed.

How then, he asked, could they apply to a rebel government that was not the expression of a "free, regular, and deliberate act of the nation"? Jefferson rejected his rival's reasoning as casuistry, insisting that treaties were made with nations not with the specific men who rule them. But while he recognized Philadelphia's obligation to honor the treaties, Jefferson eschewed war, suggesting instead that Washington wait until France formally called on the United States to uphold its side of the 1778 bargain. For the moment he proposed, like Hamilton, a policy of neutrality, though it was "a disagreeable pill to our friends." Washington was happy to oblige with a Neutrality Proclamation—in which the word itself was not used so as not to offend Jefferson's sensibilities.

Thus, in the opening gambit of the crisis a tenuous unity was achieved between a radical leader who was trying to prevent war and a conservative who was well aware that public opinion was overwhelmingly against him and had to be carefully manipulated. In the process the treaties with France lay in limbo.

III

Alexander Hamilton, a leading figure in the events of the 1790's, was a man of magnificent abilities. Only thirty-six at the time of the Neutrality Proclamation, he was five feet seven inches tall, slim and straight in stature, handsome, elegant in dress, a ladies' man— sometimes bedeviled by scandal—and a proponent of the "rich and well-born" from the top of his red head down to the toe of his white silk stockings. Whatever there was in the United States of a ruling class, an establishment, a power elite—call it what you will— Hamilton was its mentor.

Born on the island of Nevis in the West Indies, the future Secretary of the Treasury was reared under difficult circumstances. His father went bankrupt and deserted his common-law wife. His mother died when he was only eleven, leaving him to the care of maternal relatives. His opportunities for education were meager, for he went to work in a countinghouse almost immediately, but he was a bright and poised youngster who read avidly on his own. For some reason he developed a love of things military early in life; "I wish there was a war," he wrote dreamily before he was thirteen. An article he composed about a hurricane commended Hamilton to patrons who sent him to the colonies on the mainland for schooling. He prepared for college in Elizabethtown, New Jersey, then went on to King's College (Columbia) in New York. By the time he was nineteen he was enrolled in Washington's army, where he won the general's respect for his canny insight into political problems and an ability to express complex issues in perceptive prose. At twenty he was a lieutenant colonel, assigned to Washington as private secretary. He served during the war with distinction, both with pen and with sword. At Monmouth he fought recklessly and had a horse shot out from under him. At Yorktown, after being relieved at his own request of secretarial work, he led the troops that made the initial breach in the British position and paved the way for a resounding victory.

The Revolution had by no means sated Hamilton's appetite for military glory. In 1794, as temporary Secretary of War, he rode with twelve thousand militia to suppress the so-called Whiskey Insurrection in four western counties of Pennsylvania. It is recorded that on those rare occasions when he drank too much he sang a song not unlike "Praise the Lord and Pass the Ammunition":

> *We're going to war, and when we die*
> *We'll want a man of God near by,*
> *So bring your Bible and follow the drum.*

Though domineering, impatient, and sometimes insulting, Hamilton was so impeccably honest, profound, and clearheaded that he made enemies and admirers in equal proportions. All of his talents were mobilized for the single goal of creating a nation in an aristocratic mold—or as aristocratic as practical politics would permit. At the Constitutional Convention, where he served as a delegate from New York, Hamilton favored the selection of a chief executive who would hold office for life, appoint all state governors, and have the irreversible right to veto all legislation. Without the title of king, such an executive could say with Louis XIV, "*L'état c'est moi.*" Hamilton also campaigned for an upper house of property owners, similarly with life tenure. As one of the first exponents of the "art of the possible" in American politics, he was forced to give ground on these aristocratic notions, but he continued to guard the interests of the "rich and well-born" throughout his life. It was Hamilton, as Secretary of the Treasury, who funded the national debt, making it possible for nascent capitalists to accumulate capital, while refusing to redeem the continentals, which were widely held by the poor. It was Hamilton, too, who wrote the famous report on manufactures which among other things extolled the virtues of child labor. To Washington he confided in 1794 that he had "long since learned to hold public opinion of no value." He distrusted the common man, as the common man distrusted him, and he saw in the victory of the revolutionists in France a menace not only to Europe but to his own class at home. As a private citizen practicing law in New York after he had retired from the Treasury in January 1795, he truly believed that the American Jacobins were preparing an immediate revolution, and along with many others of like mind he joined the twenty-man armed bands that patrolled each ward at night. A series of suspicious fires convinced him that the Republicans were ready to burn down the city as the opening act of tearing down the government.

An alliance with France was unthinkable for Hamilton, then, for two reasons: first, that it would cut off his merchant friends from the one market that sustained them—Britain—and second, that it would encourage American radicals to seize the reins. The logical consequence was to seek a *modus vivendi* with Britain, thus initiating—as it worked out—a train of events leading to the breakdown of relations with Uncle Sam's first ally, and, ultimately, to war. Hamilton had no blueprint by which these developments would ensue, for he, like Jefferson, knew how weak was the young republic and how urgently it needed peace to stabilize itself. But each step suggested itself from the previous ones until the idea grew with Hamilton and his associates that a war against France might lead to significant expansion into Latin America—at the expense of France's ally, Spain.

IV

The neutrality that Washington proclaimed in April 1793 alienated France but did little to impress the British. Theoretically there existed an international principle that "free ships make free goods"— that neutral vessels headed for the ports of belligerents were not to be disturbed unless they carried munitions or other war supplies. London, however, had no patience for such niceties. Under a number of orders in council forbidding trade with the French West Indies, she seized hundreds of United States vessels headed in that direction—at least 478 up to the time Uncle Sam and John Bull became informal allies.

Two other items inflamed public opinion against Britain. One was the impressment of many hundreds of American sailors for service aboard admiralty ships. Hapless seamen from the States on layover in British ports, or on captured American vessels, who could not prove they were American citizens were unceremoniously seized and put to work on British ships under harsh conditions. Another major irritant was the refusal of Britain to relinquish posts in the Northwest Territory. By the Treaty of Paris (1783), His Majesty's government ceded to the United States all land east of the Mississippi River. A decade later, however, the English still occupied Detroit, Fort Erie, Niagara, and five or six other forts, and continued to exercise authority over all the inhabitants in these areas. To add fuel to the fire, they were arming Indians in the occupied territory and scheming to establish an independent Indian state to act as a barrier against U.S. westward expansion.

Jefferson protested to London on all these matters, but the powerful British were disdainful of their former wards. In November 1793 they proclaimed a new and more severe order in council, and when their depredations continued at an accelerated pace, American sentiment reached a peak of fury. James Madison introduced a resolution to impose heavy duties on English commerce, and Congress actually voted a one-month embargo on outgoing ships. There were obviously more reasons, in these early years of the crisis, to go to war with the British than with the French. But Hamilton was determined to come to an understanding with the former mother country. At the suggestion of Hamilton's friends, Chief Justice John Jay (Hamilton himself was ruled out as too much of a pill for the Republicans to swallow) was sent to London for just that purpose in the spring of 1794—with a memorandum of instructions written by the Secretary of the Treasury. Hamilton undercut Jay's bargaining power, it was subsequently learned, by leaking information to the British ambassador in Washington about discussions in the cabinet. With this and other handicaps bedeviling him, Jay returned, after nearly a half year of talks with foreign minister Lord Grenville, with a pact so humiliating that it was debated by the Federalist-controlled Senate for eighteen days in secret. It was approved only after a particularly obnoxious section, Article XII, prohibiting American vessels from carrying sugar, molasses, coffee, cocoa, and cotton anywhere in the world, was stricken.

Jay had been instructed to demand unrestricted opening of the West Indies to American trade, but agreed to limit such trade to small American vessels of seventy tons or less. He was unable to end the practice of impressing American sailors, and though he secured from the British a promise to pay for ships and wares illegally captured, he failed to win acceptance for the basic principle that "free ships make free goods." The British might now pay for what they seized, but they would not stop seizing. The sore point of debts owed by Americans was resolved in John Bull's favor, to be adjudicated by a joint commission of the two countries not under the jurisdiction of favorable U.S. courts. Southerners, who owed three quarters of the debts, were outraged. On the other hand, Grenville refused categorically to indemnify the Southerners for Negro slaves carried off during the Revolution. The only features of the treaty worth crowing about were that it did not include the plan for establishing an Indian satellite state—on this Grenville relented—and it did include a commitment to evacuate the British forts in the Northwest by June 1796. Some historians, Samuel E. Morison, for instance, believe that this latter provision more than compensated for the setbacks because it "preserved the peace, secured America's territorial integrity, and established a basis for Western expansion." But at the time a majority considered that the debits far outweighed the credits in the treaty. Jay was burned in effigy in dozens of places. Signs in Boston read "Damn John Jay! Damn every one who won't damn John Jay!" Washington himself was not immune. If history has memorialized him as the "father" of his country, he was often called—in the hectic days of 1795–96—the "stepfather." And he was assailed, as he himself put it, "in such exaggerated and indecent terms as could scarcely be applied to a Nero, a notorious defaulter, or even to a common pickpocket." Hamilton, now a private (though influential) citizen, was hit in the mouth by a stone and forced off the platform as he tried to defend Jay's treaty.

As was to be expected, the treaty caused a severe deterioration in relations with France, for though it specifically stated that treaties with other countries were not contravened, France regarded it as a rapprochement with Britain and a cancellation both of neutrality and of the old pacts with Louis XVI. When its details became known in Paris, stern decrees were reimposed against U.S. shipping, and in the following year there was a sharp increase in the sinking or capture of American ships by French marauders. The French also recalled their ambassador in Philadelphia and told Charles C. Pinckney, the American minister in Paris, to leave or be arrested.

The Hamiltonians, however, had achieved their purpose. Through their machinations, the former enemy was now friend; the former ally, an embittered adversary.

V

With the furor over Jay's mischief ringing in his ears, Washington decided not to run for a third term, and in 1797, after delivering a historic farewell address urging his countrymen to "steer clear of permanent alliances," retired. His successor, Vice-President John Adams, was a man of integrity and intelligence, but at sixty-one he had few close friends in politics, and was patently lacking in charisma. Though he shared with Hamilton an aversion to the "rabble," he had little love for his fellow Federalist, and joined with his schemes at first as much by accident as by intent. Because of his wife's fragile health and her dislike of Philadelphia society, Adams was away from the capital 385 days of his four years in office, and during that time the cabinet played a more formidable role than it might have otherwise. That cabinet, naïvely carried over in toto from the Washington administration, included in its three top posts men who revered Hamilton. Secretary of State Timothy Pickering, Secretary of War James McHenry, and Secretary of the Treasury Oliver Wolcott consulted the "King of the Feds" on all major decisions. Through them Hamilton was for a number of years the guiding force of the government, although he himself was not officially a member of it.

Relations with France were the darkest cloud hanging over the Adams administration as it began its work. The fortunes of war in Europe had now turned in favor of the Gallic revolutionists, and the rate of spoliations of American shipping was ominous. Secretary Pickering reported that in the year from July 1796 to June 1797, French cruisers had seized 316 American vessels. New England merchants who had forborne making war threats against England in similar circumstances a few years back reacted vigorously this time. Extremists in the Federalist camp, such as William Smith and Uriah Tracy, called not only for immediate war but played with the notion of a secession by the North from the Francophile South.

Hamilton, though not yet ready for hostilities, delivered himself of some of the most venomous rhetoric of his career. "The man who, after this mass of evidence, shall be apologist of France, and the calumniator of his own government," he wrote, "is not an American. The choice for him lies between being deemed a fool, a madman, or a traitor." But since there was a "very general aversion to war in the minds of the people of this country," Hamilton was still content to play the diplomatic game. Before Washington retired, Hamilton had suggested a peace mission to Paris; he now urged it—through his cronies in the cabinet—on Adams. Thus it was that in May 1797 Adams appointed two Federalists, Pinckney and John Marshall, and one Republican, Elbridge Gerry, as a commission to negotiate a treaty of commerce and amity with the French foreign minister, Charles Maurice de Talleyrand. They arrived in Paris five months later, to a lukewarm reception. Talleyrand let them cool their heels for months before receiving them officially. Instead they were approached by three mysterious figures—whom they referred to as X, Y, and Z in their dispatches. "XYZ" solicited a $10 million loan for their country and "something for the pocket"—a bribe of $240,000 for leading French officials. The offer was rejected by Pinckney with the famous rejoinder "No! No! Not a sixpence!" And when word of the bribe request reached home it was greeted with the howl "Millions for defense, but not one cent for tribute." Even the Jeffersonians were nonplussed.

For Hamilton, however, it was manna from heaven. Even before the diplomatic efforts aborted, Adams had asked his cabinet for suggestions on what to do next. The three cabinet members under Hamilton's influence thereupon consulted him secretly, and the sage of New York came back with a proposal for "mitigated hostility." If France failed to come to terms, the United States, he said, should renounce all treaties with her, arm its merchant ships, build a sizable navy, and recruit a standing army. As the commander of that standing army he suggested George Washington, with himself as inspector general—second in command. Having moved from neutrality to rapprochement with England, the King of the Feds now urged preparing for war. After a considerable amount of manipulation—and resistance from Adams—Hamilton won his coveted assignment as inspector general, and plans were laid to add 16,000 men to the existing army of 3,500, authorize an additional 20,000, construct 20 sloops for a new department of the navy, float a war loan, and institute wartime taxes. The standing army, even if it had no other use, would deter the American Jacobins and if they took the road to revolution, crush them. Hamilton also initiated a propaganda campaign to prepare public opinion. Writing under a pseudonym in the *Commercial Advertiser*, he referred to France as "the most flagitious, despotic, and vindictive government that ever disgraced the annals of mankind . . . a volcano of atheism, depravity, and absurdity. . . ."

Resigning his lucrative law practice, the former Treasury Secretary now headed for the glory road of military adventure. Unbeknownst to Adams, the man who had written as a boy, "I wish there was a war" was planning something much grander than naval defense, directed primarily against Spain, which in the meantime had changed sides in the European conflagration. "It is a pity, my dear sir, and a reproach," Hamilton wrote War Secretary McHenry, "that our administration has no general plan." Such a plan, he said, should be formulated without delay. "Besides eventual security against invasion, we ought certainly to look to the possession of the Floridas and Louisiana, and we ought to squint at South America." He visualized himself as the effective head of 40,000 troops, protected at sea by a dozen British frigates, marching toward the annexation of territories many times the size of the original thirteen states.

If war were now inevitable, Hamilton wanted it to be a major one not simply for defense but to add territory to the "rising empire." To a friendly senator, he wrote in the autumn of 1798, that when war was finally declared "our game will be to attack where we can. France is not to be considered as separated from her ally [Spain]. Tempting objects will be within our grasp." Reaffirming this thesis in January 1799 he commented that "if universal empire is still to be the purpose of France, what can tend to defeat that purpose better than to detach South America from Spain. . . ."

To aid in this conspiratorial undertaking Hamilton depended on two men, General James Wilkinson—whom history has confirmed was a spy for the Spaniards—and a Venezuelan revolutionary named Sebastian Francisco de Miranda. Miranda had a checkered career in the Spanish army, having fought with it against the Moors, as well as in Cuba, but later being imprisoned for insubordination. Thereafter he nursed ambitions to liberate his country from Spain and in 1784 came to America to discuss his plans with Hamilton and General Henry Knox. Though he received a friendly hearing, nothing came of the project then; Miranda moved on to the continent, joined in the French Revolution, was elevated to general, then tried for treason and acquitted. In 1798 he was discussing with Rufus King, the American minister to London and a friend of Hamilton's, a refurbished version of his scheme for liberation. He suggested an alliance of the English-speaking nations in which London would supply the cover ships and the United States the invading troops. King, in touch with Hamilton about these glorious dreams, was impressed by them, and though there is some evidence to show that Hamilton's ardor for Miranda eventually cooled, the original plan seems to have been to include him. After Wilkinson and Hamilton had taken New Orleans, they would join with Miranda in a campaign against Spanish possessions in the Caribbean and South America. A letter by Hamilton to King in August 1798 indicates that the inspector general may have changed his mind about Miranda, but not about the project. "With regard to the enterprise in question, I wish it very much to be undertaken, but I should be glad that the principal agency be the United States—they to furnish the whole land force if necessary. The command in this case would very naturally fall upon me, and I hope I shall disappoint no favorable expectation."

VI

Hamilton had good reasons to be optimistic, for in the fateful year of 1798 the martial mood captivated Americans; it was only a question of how far the twig could be bent. France had issued a new decree ordering its men of war and privateers to confiscate all ships carrying any kind of supplies to Britain or other enemies. In this state of affairs American sentiment turned itself around. Instead of lyrical parades on behalf of the French Revolution, the streets rang with the cries of the war hawks. Twelve hundred young people in Philadelphia marched toward the home of President Adams, cheered by large crowds as bands blared military music. The President, savoring perhaps his most prestigious moment, met them in military dress, a cockade on his head and a sword at his side, and proceeded to castigate the French Revolution. Later in the evening some of the youths attacked the home of a Republican editor, Benjamin F. Bache. On May 9, a day set aside by Adams for fast and prayer, Bache's dwelling was again desecrated and the statue of Benjamin Franklin defiled with mud. It was open season on Republican editors; Bache, for instance, was viciously attacked in his office—his attacker was released by the courts with a fifty-dollar fine. Vice-President Jefferson was sneeringly serenaded at his home by young people in uniform to the tune of "The Rogue's March." A new patriotic ditty, "Hail Columbia," was sung at the theaters to the beat of tom-toms as citizens shouted "War, war, war!"

While the nation lapsed into an intemperate mood, an undeclared war was already under way. President Adams advised Congress in March 1798 that peace could not be achieved "on terms compatible with the safety, the honor, or the essential interests of the nation." He therefore authorized merchant vessels to arm themselves and fire in self-defense. Along with provision for a much enlarged army and wartime taxes, Congress—despite Republican control of the House —established a separate Navy Department and arranged for a flotilla of naval vessels. Three frigates, the *United States, Constellation,* and *Constitution,* all launched in 1797, were fitted for war, five more purchased from private merchants, and many others built in booming naval yards. By the end of the year there were fourteen men-of-war on the high seas guarding merchantmen, seizing French ships, and sometimes seeking out the enemy's men-of-war for battle. All told, the American flotilla was expanded to 45 vessels, manned by a navy of 700 officers and 5,000 sailors, and hundreds of armed merchantmen. As wars go it was a small affair. By prearrangement, the British navy protected ships headed to Europe, the American fleet defended both its own nationals and those of its informal ally in the Caribbean. In the two years of the naval war with France it seized 85 prizes "not counting recaptured vessels and small boats." It did not often seek out enemy frigates for full-scale battle, but in the few engagements of this kind it acquitted itself quite well—losing only one vessel with 14 guns, the *Retaliation*, to a much superior force of two French frigates with 80 guns. In taunting the French the Americans also managed to give some help to the black revolutionary Toussaint L'Ouverture, who was resisting their rule in Haiti. For all this effort, the dollar costs were surprisingly small—$6 million.

VII

The true costs, however, went beyond dollars—to an attempted suppression of democracy itself. The hysteria on the streets, matched by lurid outpourings in the Federalist press, laid the groundwork for a campaign of repression. The nation was led to believe that invasion of the United States was imminent. Thus William Cobbett, editor of *Porcupine's Gazette*, wrote an engaging scenario of how Negro slaves would be armed against their white masters, and how French guns bought in the West Indies would soon be used "for Virginia and Georgia." "Take care," he warned, "take care you sleepy southern fools. Your Negroes will probably be your masters this day twelve month and your matrons and young girls will be defiled." Another Federalist sheet, the *Gazette of the United States*, stridently cautioned that "our time, though delayed by the great projects of France in Europe . . . will certainly come, when we are to be invaded by a body of their troops, who are expected to be joined by their friends among us, our Jacobins." Whether the hawks believed their own propaganda is not clear. One of them, retired Federalist Fisher Ames, called the "sage of Dedham," urged Secretary Pickering in July 1798 to "wage war, and call it self-defense." It was necessary to do so, he said, because average citizens "reluct at offense" and "yield much, far too much, for peace."

The extreme Federalists, rewarded at last with a foreign enemy largely of their own making, now set to work cutting to size the "traitors" at home. Even Hamilton was taken aback by the ferocity of their antidemocratic measures. The Naturalization Act raised from five to fourteen years the residence requirement for those applying for citizenship. The Alien Enemies Act, on the order of the McCarran Act after World War II, empowered the President to arrest, jail, or exile any alien of an enemy state—an invidious threat to the twenty-five thousand Frenchmen in the United States, some of whom immediately chartered a ship to take them back to France.

The most oppressive of the four bills were the Alien and Sedition Acts. Under the Alien Act the President was granted authority to order any alien he adjudged "dangerous to the peace and safety of the United States" out of the country. Fortunately, the bill, directed primarily against the radical-minded United Irishmen, who were refugees from British terror, was enforced only against two Irish writers. But Federalists were boasting in the taverns of New York that they would soon send the Republican leader of the House, Congressman Albert Gallatin, back to the home of his forefathers, Switzerland.

The Sedition Act, a virtual blueprint for authoritarianism, caused greater consternation. Under its strictures it was a "high misdemeanor," subject to a two-thousand-dollar fine and jail up to two years, for anyone to publish "false, scandalous and malicious writing" against the government, Congress, or the President. Anyone opposing enforcement of federal law or advising "insurrection . . . or combination," was subject to stiffer terms, up to five years and five thousand dollars in fines.

The Sedition Act (like the Alien Act) had a time limit of two years and was permitted to lapse when Jefferson became president. But while in force it sowed considerable mischief. Twenty-five persons were put in the dock; ten Republican journalists or printers were convicted. Thomas Cooper, editor of a backwoods newspaper in Pennsylvania, was given six months for this "dangerous" passage in one of his essays: When Adams "entered into office . . . even those who doubted his capacity thought well of his intentions. Nor were we yet saddled with the expense of a permanent navy, or threatened, under his auspices, with the existence of a standing army. Our credit was not yet reduced so low as to borrow money at eight percent, in time of peace." For similar critiques, James Thomas Callender received nine months in jail and a two-hundred-dollar fine. The longest prison term—four years—was assessed against David Brown, for seditiously persuading fellow New Englanders to erect a liberty pole with a sign reading:

> No Stamp Act, No sedition, No Alien Bills,
> No Land Tax, downfall to the Tyrants of
> America, peace and retirement to the
> President, Long Live the Vice President
> and the Minority.

Nor was the reign of repression confined to the judicial scene. Typically, four men, including the editor of the Republican *Aurora* in Philadelphia, were set upon and beaten by a gang while circulating a petition urging repeal of the Alien Act. None of the attackers were arrested, but the victims were sent off to jail charged with precipitating a seditious riot. Jacob Schneider of *The Reading Adler* reported that troops under a captain named Montgomery "came to my printing office on Saturday last . . . like a banditti of robbers and assassins; they tore the clothes off my body, and forcibly dragged me from my house. . . ." Montgomery ordered the editor given twenty-five lashes on "the bare back," a fate he escaped when other soldiers intervened. Vigilantism was accompanied by spying on prominent Republicans. Vice-President Jefferson, visiting the home of a friend, apologized for being late because he had been "watched in the most extraordinary manner" and was forced to take a circuitous route "to elude the curiosity of his spies."

How far matters would have gone if the intolerance had continued is a matter of conjecture. The Jeffersonians, taken aback at first, were able very soon, however, to regain their composure and mount a counterattack. In September 1798 Jefferson retired to his sanctuary in Monticello to draft a series of "resolves" for passage in anti-Federalist states. In essence they said that the federal government had preempted the powers of the states in passing the Alien and Sedition Acts and that they were therefore "altogether void, and of no force." The eighth and ninth "resolves" were ominously reminiscent of Samuel Adams' strategy during the American Revolution, since they called for establishing a "committee of conference and correspondence" in each state to consult with each other for joint action. Only Kentucky and Virginia passed the "resolves"—in watered-down form—but it is not difficult to imagine them moving toward secession if Hamilton had had his way in enlarging the war and the repression had widened.

Another sign of the hardening schism was the so-called Fries Rebellion or House-Tax Rebellion in the eastern section of Pennsylvania. The war party in the government, headed for battle and desperately trying to recruit a volunteer army—without much success incidentally—needed loans and taxes to shore up its financial ramparts. An attempt to borrow $5 million from Federalist bankers provoked a conflict of conscience between the bankers' allegiance to country and allegiance to profit. Though they cherished the war spirit as avidly as Hamilton, they refused to make the money available unless the interest rate was raised from 6 to 8 percent. Business was business. The $2 million direct tax on land, houses, and Negro slaves, however, fared better since it fell on the common citizen. It hit an embarrassing snag nonetheless among the German-speaking citizens in five Pennsylvania counties.

The leader of the "rebellion" was a middle-aged vendue crier—auctioneer—who had sired ten children, and was without education, but who spoke with "rude eloquence," had steady black eyes "as keen as the eyes of a rabbit," and a pleasant disposition. John Fries had fought in the Revolution and had supported Adams in the 1796 election, but he was now disillusioned. He believed that if he could mount a resistance to the new taxes there would be ten thousand rebels in Virginia ready to join the crusade. The tax itself was not large—twenty cents to a dollar for most households, depending on the value of their property, and fifty cents for each slave. It was the principle of the thing, however, and the good burghers of Bucks, Northampton, and three other counties, abetted by sympathetic militia, held meetings, damned the Tories, shouted for liberty, and refused to pay. In due course, after local assessors had been chased from a number of homes, the federal marshal and twenty deputies moved in, and—not without difficulty—made eighteen arrests. On hearing of the incident Fries and 140 poorly armed men marched on the tavern where the prisoners were incarcerated and rescued them. This was the "Fries Rebellion." No one was killed or wounded, but government authority had been flaunted and the President was afraid the idea might become contagious. On March 12, 1799, Adams himself issued a proclamation decrying the mass conspiracy "to defeat the execution of the laws for the valuation of lands and dwelling houses." Thousands of militiamen were ordered mobilized —two thousand from New Jersey alone—and hundreds actually sent into the rebel area to seize the subversives. Fifteen men, including Fries, were charged with treason, fourteen with lesser crimes. Fries, tried twice, was convicted and sentenced to death—though pardoned by Adams in 1800 when tempers simmered down.

VIII

Fortunately, while the contending sides were berating each other, the President was having second thoughts about the undeclared war. It occurred to him at long last that he was not the master in his own house, that decisions both in the administration and in Congress were emanating from the brain of Alexander Hamilton. He learned also that the image of an intractable France, brought back by the two Federalists on his first commission, was strongly overstated.

Envoy Gerry, the Republican, had stayed behind after his associates left and in due course had been rewarded by an interview with Talleyrand. The French foreign minister denied that his government had in any way been associated with the lurid XYZ bribery proposals and expressed a firm interest in resuming diplomatic relations with the United States. Further, as a good-will gesture, the

French government issued a decree requiring its privateers to put up a money bond that would be forfeited if they engaged in unauthorized seizures of American vessels. Gerry's report, needless to say, was a traumatic shock to the war party, and even more so was the news, as Americans living in Paris also confirmed, in notes sent home, that the French government wanted no war with its recent ally. Lafayette wrote his old hero, Washington, offering to come to Philadelphia to explain the misunderstanding, and Talleyrand sent a message to Adams, whom he had met years back, suggesting that a new start be made.

Gerry's report was supplemented by an irrepressible Quaker physician, Dr. George Logan, who made a trip to France, on his own, in search of peace. Logan was no fly-by-night fanatic but a well-to-do citizen on intimate terms with the most noted men in America. At his estate in Stenton, near Philadelphia, he had entertained the Washingtons and, on innumerable occasions, his close friend Jefferson. Having conceived of the private peace project, Logan paid his debts, sold two parcels of real estate to finance his trip, and fortified himself with letters of introduction from Jefferson and the Chief Justice of the Supreme Court of Pennsylvania. Slipping away from a Federalist committee of surveillance which dogged his footsteps, he boarded a neutral ship for Hamburg, and thence, after more harrowing adventures, betook himself to Paris. Talleyrand received the Quaker "with great politeness," but little encouragement. However, the chief of the Directory, Merlin, responded with more than politeness. As a token of his desire for amicable relations with the United States, he issued an *arrêt* to lift the embargo on American ships and to free American sailors being held in France. Every important figure Logan talked with in Paris assured him that war with the United States was "unthinkable."

Logan was severely castigated when he returned home. William Cobbett proposed that he be put in the pillory, together with his subversive wife. Washington received him coolly. Secretary of State Pickering told him: "Sir, it is my duty to inform you that the government does not thank you for what you have done." And Congress passed a law—the Logan law—prohibiting private citizens from engaging in diplomatic relations with a foreign state.

But Logan's report, coming on the heels of Gerry's, and additionally confirmed by similar information from the American minister to Holland, William Vans Murray, convinced Adams to make another try at negotiations. The Federalist hawks cried "treachery" but Adams by now was convinced he had strayed too far. He had authorized a standing army but "this damned army," he said, "will be the ruin of this country." Taxes were being "liberally laid on"—a stamp tax, a salt tax, an increased carriage tax, a tax on land and dwellings, on slaves, on imports—but they would not be enough for full-scale war. And with the tightening of the financial noose, Adams feared that the government would be plunged to bankruptcy before he finished his first term. Increasingly he was distressed by the disloyalty of the three key members of his cabinet, who owed their first allegiance to Hamilton, not to himself. Public opinion too had taken a turnabout. Despite the repressive laws, four thousand citizens in Pennsylvania signed petitions against the Alien and Sedition Acts, and Republican editors, despite the legal restrictions, continued to clamor for peace. It was time to call a halt.

Without consulting a single member of his administration, therefore, in March 1799 Adams nominated Murray as minister to France. The hawks were chagrined. They forced the President to compromise for a commission of three instead of Murray alone, and Pickering deftly used one pretext after another to hold up the commission's passage. In due time, however, it departed and arrived in Paris just as Napoleon Bonaparte was replacing the Directory as the ruler of France. The First Consul, having thrashed the Austrians once more and at a peak of his glory, wanted peace with the Americans but not at any price. He offered to pay for French spoliations, provided that the United States recognize the recently abrogated treaties of 1778. He would pay up only if the Americans agreed to reconstitute the alliance. If they were not ready to go that far, he said he would agree to a lesser pact in which the two nations would treat each other's commerce equitably and return captured vessels, but little more. The U.S. commission, unwilling to fashion an entangling alliance, and unwilling to come home empty-handed, accepted the second offer.

This pact of 1800 had the effect of bursting Hamilton's bubble. He found himself at the head of an army with no one to fight. Louisiana, Mexico, the Floridas, had slipped from his grip like a greasepan. He had expressed a willingness—indeed a prayer—"to subdue a refractory and powerful" Virginia when it made a "test of resistance," but the Virginians had refused to oblige. His friend Washington died in December 1799, his allies in Adams' cabinet were dismissed one by one. With the termination of the undeclared war, the President also put an end to the standing army, as well as to Hamilton's command. And very shortly the Federalist Party itself would fall into hard times—from which it would never recover—as Jefferson and Aaron Burr defeated Adams and Pinckney in the election of 1800.

Good sense somehow had prevailed, and not a minute too soon. Had the conflict not been terminated the United States would not have secured the massive Louisiana Territory in 1803. "The convention of 1800," writes Gardner W. Allen, "did not furnish a satisfactory solution of the questions at issue between the two countries, but it put an end to hostilities which, if they had continued, would doubtless have made impossible the acquisition of Louisiana." While negotiations and ratification—concluded in July 1801—were under way, Napoleon had administered another defeat to the Holy Roman Empire and the European powers had agreed to a respite in their hostilities. As part of the division of the spoils, even before the fighting terminated, Paris prevailed on Madrid on October 1800 to retrocede Louisiana to France, in return for a more lucrative piece of real estate in Italy, either Tuscany or Etruria. The Spaniards, who were recovering only a third of what it cost to administer Louisiana, were delighted with the prospect, provided Napoleon agreed not to relinquish the territory to a third power. On October 15, 1802, all the details were ironed out and His Catholic Majesty put his imprimatur on the arrangement. Seven months later, however, Napoleon sold the tract of 828,000 square miles to Jefferson for $15 million. The heavy cost of suppressing the black rebellion in Haiti (1794–1804) had disposed the French dictator to give up plans for an empire in the western hemisphere in favor of concentrating on the Old World.

Thus, as Edward Channing points out, the talks in Paris that ended a limited war and prevented a major one turned out to be "one of the most fortunate bits of negotiation that ever took place." Had Hamilton had his way the territorial results might have been very much less favorable, and the United States might have exploded into a civil war that would have ruptured it.

IX

Not long after the naval war with France, the United States became enmeshed—from 1801 to 1805—in another naval war, with Tripoli. American motives here were impeccable: to secure freedom of the seas and put an end to piracy. Though the war with Tripoli was an insignificant affair, with few casualties and little opposition at home, its story is worth retelling because this was the first time that an American administration practiced what was to become commonplace in the twentieth century—war by subversion. Uncle Sam sponsored, organized, led, and paid for an internal revolt against a recognized regime.

The Barbary States—Tripoli, Morocco, Algiers, and Tunis—were a group of maritime provinces that had long been part of the Ottoman Empire. At one time or another all the European nations that traded the Mediterranean paid tribute to the Barbary States in order to avoid piratical seizure of their merchantmen. The thirteen colonies in America, as fiefdoms of Britain, were covered by His Majesty's arrangements and for the most part suffered only minor harassment. With independence, however, the United States was no longer shielded by the British flag and its shipping difficulties became more serious. It was not long before America was paying bribes, like the rest, to assure safety for its ships. Thus, a treaty was negotiated with Morocco in 1786 at a bargain price of $10,000 in gifts plus $20,000 nine years later when it was ratified. The other three Barbary States did better. The Dey of Algiers received a million dollars in 1795, half of it for ransoming American captives, plus annuities every two years. The Pasha of Tripoli settled for $56,000 and the Bey of Tunis for $107,000. What with other emoluments, it was costing the United States $100,000 annually, according to historian Marshall Smelser, to secure immunity for a hundred ships working the Mediterranean.

The trouble with Tripoli began in 1801 when its thirty-one-year-old pasha, Yusuf Karamanli, decided he had been overly generous and demanded an additional $250,000 indemnity, plus $20,000 a year. This was too much for recently installed President Jefferson. Through his consul at Tunis, William Eaton, he declared a blockade and dispatched three frigates and a schooner to Tripoli with orders to burn or sink pirate vessels that challenged American merchantmen. Simultaneously, unbeknown to the President, Karamanli had declared war on the United States. What ensued was a sputtering series of engagements with no decisive results. U.S. sailors captured a few enemy ships, destroyed others in port, bombarded the city, but could not deliver the coup de grâce. Hostilities were brought to an end only through a daring adventure in subversion.

William Eaton, the man who conceived this plan and won Jefferson's Secretary of State Madison's assent to it, was one of those incredibly determined people who find it difficult to retreat either in personal relationships or in war. Born in Woodstock, Connecticut, in 1764, he ran away from a large middle-income family to join Washington's army at the age of sixteen. Poor health forced him home, but in a short time he was back in the armed forces and served as sergeant until April 1783. In the following years Eaton pursued an education in classical languages, turned deeply religious, enrolled at Dartmouth, opened a private school, was appointed clerk of the House of Delegates in Vermont, and in 1792 came full circle by reentering the army, this time as a captain.

Serving under other people, however, was not Eaton's forte; the friendliest of biographers describes him as "offensive and impetuous." He quarreled with his adjutant general, was court-martialed for a "misunderstanding" with another commanding officer, and was arrested in 1796 on charges of disobeying orders, keeping bounty money, maltreating horses, and defrauding soldiers of their rations. Though freed by the court, his commandant put him in prison anyway. Finally the State Department rescued Eaton from the army and in 1797 appointed him consul to Tunis. The change in jobs, however, altered neither Eaton's militancy nor his taste for conspiracy. It was through him that the blockade of Tripoli was proclaimed, and it was through him that the plan was hatched for using one brother to topple another. What Eaton proposed to Secretary of State Madison was to "foment a revolution in Tripoli" in order to replace the fractious Yusuf with his older kin, Hamet.

Yusuf was certainly an unmitigated rogue. At the age of twenty he had murdered his eldest brother, Hasan, and in 1796, when his father died, had seized control of the army while Hamet was away and installed himself as pasha. To make sure that there was no trouble from Hamet he kept his family hostage in Tripoli. The only question for the United States was whether it had the right to overthrow foreign rogues when this suited its purpose.

Jefferson and Madison clearly had misgivings on the subject. The Secretary of State conceded that "it does not accord with the general sentiments or views of the United States to intermeddle in the domestic contests of other countries. . . ." But he justified it in the end on the grounds that since this was a "just war" it would not be "unfair" for the United States to turn to its "advantage the enmity and pretensions of others against a common foe." The principle of nonintervention became a victim to the principle of "just war," and Eaton was ordered to proceed with the project in 1803.

Like so many such ventures the pacification of Tripoli had features of high comedy to it. The would-be monarch, Hamet, was in hiding near Alexandria, Egypt, and Eaton first had to find him and overcome his timidity with promises and bribes. He also exacted from Hamet a promise to repay the costs of the expedition out of $20,000 in tribute to be levied afterward on the Swedes, Danes, and Dutch. Having hurdled this obstacle, the American consul assembled a nondescript army of seven U.S. marines, a few midshipmen,

40 Greeks, a handful of Germans, Englishmen, Italians, Spaniards, and Levantines, as well as a contingent of Arabs—400 men in all. As the motley army marched across hundreds of miles of Libyan desert toward a strategic city named Derna, everything that could go wrong, did.

Turkish soldiers arrested some of Hamet's followers, who had to be ransomed by Eaton. The caravan of 190 camels, rented at $11 apiece from Sheik il Talib, had a disturbing facility of dwindling away in the dark of night. At Marsa Matruh the Arabs went on strike and had to be pacified with a payment of $673. Hamet himself proved so cowardly that Eaton had to withhold food from him before he would proceed. Time and again there were small mutinies, and both rain and hunger delayed the "revolutionary" army. Finally, however, Eaton's band made contact with two American warships in the Gulf of Bomba, replenished its supplies, and launched an assault on Derna. Once again Hamet had to be spurred with promise of $2,000, but the city fell under Eaton's heroic attack—during which he was wounded—and Hamet was installed in the governor's palace, awaiting the next drive, to the capital, Tripoli, itself.

With victory now in sight, however, the conspirators suddenly were left in the lurch. The wily Yusuf, seeing the handwriting on the wall, sued for peace and was greeted by a favorable response from the authorities in Washington. While Eaton and Hamet were planning strategy, Colonel Tobias Lear, U.S. consul general in Algiers, hastened to the scene and negotiated a pact whereby Yusuf was permitted to retain his throne on the pledge that American ships would no longer be molested by his pirates. The pasha's feelings were assuaged by a ransom payment of $60,000 to win the release of 300 Americans in his custody; simultaneously 100 Tripolitans were set free by the United States, without ransom. For his toils and tribulations the unfortunate Hamet received only the assurance that his family would rejoin him within four years.

The attempted subversion ended in a miasma of recrimination. Eaton denounced the settlement as dishonorable. Senator Timothy Pickering condemned Lear's agreement as "the basest treachery on the basest principles." Others, however, argued that Yusuf undoubtedly would have murdered the 300 Americans had hostilities continued. "I have seen many of the officers that were prisoners," Secretary of the Navy Robert Smith wrote in September 1805. "All say positively that if Lear had persisted in refusing paying ransom for them, peace would not have been made and they would all have been certainly massacred." To confound matters, many of the prisoners themselves scoffed at the idea that their lives had been in jeopardy.

Implicit in this debate, as in so many others that were to occupy the nation, was where legitimate grievance ended and illegitimate lust began. The United States engaged in the war with Tripoli for what was, by current international standards, a "just cause"—to keep the sea lanes open. Yet before it was over there were men like Eaton who saw in it the prospect of empire. Had Hamet been installed in Yusuf's throne by American arms, it is conceivable that the republic might have established the first "protectorate" in North Africa—a task which actually fell to France a quarter of a century later when it seized Algeria. Because America resisted such blandishments in Africa and Asia for a long time, it gained the reputation of being "anticolonialist" and "anti-imperialist." But it is possible to explain America's restraint on the simpler—and more realistic —thesis that it was still far too weak and too poor for expansion very far from home. Adventure in the old hemisphere could come only after consolidation of a base in the New World.

3

FALLEN STAR

An instinct for acquiring new domain was well developed in the United States from the outset. If it was curbed during the naval wars with France and Tripoli it was only because the cost seemed intolerable. A sixth sense evidently warned Adams in 1798–99 that while he might win territorial booty in a full-scale engagement with France and Spain, the price might be national disintegration. The same sixth sense must have warned Jefferson to call off hostilities with Tripoli, before they became an albatross around the American neck. In both instances, therefore, the federal government confined itself finally to limited, and essentially defensive objectives.

No such restraints, however, inhibited relations with the Indians. Here the aggressive intent was both obvious and flagrant. There is no escaping the conclusion that the United States repeatedly attacked the natives and divested them of their lands simply because they had the misfortune to stand across the path of empire.

From 1790 to 1915, according to a War Department compilation, the United States engaged various tribes in fifty-two wars. That they were not all minor skirmishes is indicated by the losses of General Arthur St. Clair in a single day during the first such war. On November 4, 1791, 630 American soldiers were killed and 280 seriously wounded—a toll much larger than suffered by the United States in any twenty-four-hour period during the Vietnam War, and one seventh as many as died in the eight years of the War of the Revolution. The war against the Seminoles in Florida, from 1835 to 1842, cost the United States $20 million and 1,500 lives—a considerably larger number than died on the battlefield during the Spanish-American War. Within a few hours in June 1876, Crazy Horse's braves surrounded and killed 265 American officers and men under Colonel George A. Custer—one sixth as many battle deaths as in two years of the Mexican War. But while the Indians were able to inflict severe punishment on occasion, winning many individual battles, they were in the long run too weak and disorganized to ward off the white man's advance.

Through war, bribery, and military pressure, the United States forced 200 tribes to sign 363 treaties, ceding enormous stretches of territory. Invariably the treaties began with sentiments for "permanent peace and friendship," as if two equal parties were entering into amicable and voluntary agreements. But as historian Dan E. Clark has observed, "it would be difficult, indeed, to find a land cession made by the Indians entirely of their own volition." A compendium made by Charles C. Royce shows that from 1784 to 1894 the tribes surrendered no fewer than 720 small empires. But the Treaty of Greenville in 1795, a dozen tribes yielded almost two thirds of what is now the state of Ohio, plus land in Indiana and Michigan. By the Treaty of Vincennes in 1803, the Kaskaskia Indians ceded half the territory of Illinois. By the Treaty of Fort Clark in 1808 the Osage relinquished an area between the Arkansas and Missouri Rivers which now comprises half the state of Arkansas and two thirds of Missouri. And so on.

II

It is estimated that when the first Englishmen colonized Jamestown 800,000 natives lived in the area north of the Rio Grande, 200,000 of them in the territory of the original thirteen states. The European nations which descended on Indian domain, in their usual casuistic fashion, elaborated a subtle rationale for their seizure of a hemisphere. Because they were "Christian" and "civilized," said the Europeans, they enjoyed the "right of sovereignty" over the lands they claimed. They were people of a higher order endowed by the Creator with special rights. They conceded, however, that the Indians were entitled to an untampered "right of occupancy." In the Proclamation of 1763, after the French and Indian War, for instance, the British pledged that the red men would "not be molested or disturbed in the possession of such parts of our dominions and territories" that had not "been ceded or purchased by us. . . ."

Some colonists—Roger Williams, William Penn, and Benjamin Franklin, to name a few—religiously respected Indian prerogatives. Of Penn's treaty with the Delaware tribe—negotiated under an elm tree near Philadelphia—the philosopher Voltaire later wrote that it was "the only treaty which was never sworn to and never broken." For six decades the whites and natives of Pennsylvania lived together without bloodshed. On the other hand, William Bradford considered the red men "little otherwise than the wild beasts" and Cotton Mather called them "miserable savages" who had been "decoyed" hither by the devil. Hardly a year passed without a skirmish with the natives, and at least four such conflicts in colonial times could be classed as wars—that with the Pequot Indians in 1637, with the Wampanoag in 1675–76, with the Cherokees of South Carolina from 1760 to 1762, with the Ottawas and their allies in the Ohio Valley from 1763 to 1766.

The same polar differences in attitude toward the Indians was evident after independence. The frontiersmen who pushed into Kentucky immediately after the Revolution contended that "the only good Indian is a dead Indian." Washington's Secretary of War, Henry Knox, however, unequivocally agreed that "the Indians being the prior occupants, possess the right of the soil. It cannot be taken from them unless by their free consent, or by the rights of conquest in case of a just war." Though he did not define "just war" he recommended that the President enter into "treaties of peace with them, in which their rights and limits should be explicitly defined, and the treaties observed . . . with the most rigid justice, by punishing the whites, who should violate the same."

Washington himself also warned against permitting whites to settle in native territory. In a letter to Congressman James Duane, September 7, 1783, he wrote: "To suffer a wide extended country to be overrun with land jobbers, speculators, and monopolizers, or even with scattered settlers, is in my opinion inconsistent with that wisdom and policy which our true interest dictates." It was, he said, "pregnant of disputes both with the savages and among ourselves, the evils of which are easier to be conceived than described." The land grabbers, he cautioned, would inevitably involve the government "by their unrestrained conduct, in inextricable perplexities, and more than probably in a great deal of bloodshed." According to historian D'Arcy McNickle, these "were the views of most men, in or out of Congress, who were not intent on profiting out of Indian lands." Many of them, including Washington, recognized the debt owed to tribes, such as the Oneida and Tuscarora, who had fed starving American troops at Valley Forge when whites refused to provide them corn and grain because Washington did not have the money to pay. "If these Indians," said the Revolutionary general, "had been our enemies instead of our friends, the war would not have ended in American Independence."

Similar sentiments were expressed repeatedly. The Ordinance for the Government of the Northwest Territory (July 13, 1787) reaffirmed that the "utmost good faith shall always be observed towards the Indians, their lands and property shall never be taken from them without their consent. . . ." Jefferson expressed the hope that if the Indian were encouraged to abandon hunting and fishing in favor of agriculture and domestic manufacture, he would soon find the wisdom to peaceably exchange what he "can spare and we want [land], for what we can spare and he wants, the arts of civilization." Chief Justice John Marshall, in three decisions from 1823 to 1832, acknowledged the "unquestionable" right of Indians "to the lands they occupy" and to untrammeled self-government in their areas.

The red man was obviously not without friends among the whites. Some suggested a separate Indian state coequal with the other thirteen. The sixth article of the Treaty of Fort Pitt, negotiated with the Delawares in 1778, provided "that friendly tribes might, with the approval of Congress, enter the Confederacy, and form a State, of which the Delawares should be the head." An agreement with the Cherokees seven years later contained a similar section, and periodically men like the Reverend Jedidiah Morse and the half-breed Creek chief, Alexander McGillivray, revived such proposals. It was an idea, records Professor Annie H. Abel, that was "advocated at intervals for more than a hundred years."

The wars against Indians won approval that was far from universal. For instance, in the midst of the first war, in January 1792, more than a third of the members of Congress who voted on the subject declared that the war had been "as unjustly undertaken as it has since been unwisely and unsuccessfully conducted; that depredations had been committed by the whites as by the Indians; and the whites were more probably the aggressors, as they had frequently made encroachments on the Indian lands, whereas the Indians showed no inclination to obtain possession of our territory, or even to make temporary invasions until urged to it by a sense of their wrongs." The congressmen noted that while the warriors had defeated American troops and could have marched unchecked on Pittsburgh, they desisted.

Despite such expressions of sympathy, however, the basic pattern of relations with the Indian were set not by moral rectitude, but by economic determinism. The American people, doubling their population every generation, had no patience to wait for the natives to sell them acreage. Instead they flooded Indian territory in a great tidal wave and then, through war and treaty, forced the aborigines to cede their lands. As of 1775 only 5,000 whites, mostly of French origin, lived in the Mississippi Valley outside New Orleans. Fifteen years later the number had swelled to 110,000 and by 1800, 377,000. By 1830, according to the U.S. census, there were 937,000 whites in Ohio; 348,000 in Indiana; 157,000 in Illinois; 687,000 in Kentucky; and 681,000 in Tennessee. "In short," comment Charles and Mary Beard, "within 40 years after the heavy migration began, the western territory acquired more inhabitants than the original 13 colonies in a century of development." The introduction of the cotton gin and spinning machinery, which increased cotton exports from 200,-000 pounds in 1791 to 40 million pounds in 1803, whetted the appetite of Southerners for more land westward—and if the Creeks, Cherokees, or Choctaws were in the way, so much the worse for them. The discovery of gold on Cherokee land in northwestern Georgia (July 1829) drove frenzied Georgians into the treaty-protected areas, and though President John Quincy Adams sent troops to defend the natives, President Andrew Jackson, who followed Adams, removed the soldiers and left the Cherokees and other tribes to the tender mercies of the whites. When in a subsequent court test Chief Justice Marshall ruled with the red men, Jackson commented derisively: "John Marshall has made his decision. Now let him enforce it."

The right of Indian occupancy was a casualty of the white man's quest for land; concurrent with the grandiose expressions in favor of "peace and friendship," there evolved a policy of "divide and acquire"—divide the Indians from each other, and take over their holdings piece by piece. In October 1787 Governor Arthur St. Clair of the Northwest Territory was instructed by Congress to "defeat all confederations and combinations among the tribes. . . ." He reported with obvious relish some months later that "I am persuaded that their general confederacy is entirely broken." The federal government was even prepared to buy lands, but by exacerbating tribal differences, through either war or bribery, it hoped to get them for the proverbial song. Commissioner H. Dearborn, for instance, was ordered by the War Department in 1807 to pay no more than "two cents per acre" for land purchased from the red man. "I presume," wrote the Secretary of War, "it will not be necessary to exceed one cent an acre"—this at a time when the government was selling land to its own citizens for $1.25 and $2.00 an acre. Chiefs of the Ottawa, Potawatomi, and Chippewa tribes, ordered to Chicago in 1821 and heavily lavished with whiskey, found themselves five million acres poorer, for which they received a total of $45,000—less than a penny apiece.

The justification for much of this brigandage was that the Indians were nomadic hunters who had no use for all that land. But as Governor Patrick Henry of Virginia once observed, the first holdings taken over by the whites were invariably the cleared fields which Indians had sown for decades. Moreover, the most advanced red men fared no better than their brethren. The Cherokees, for instance, had attained by the 1820's a fair degree of what is euphemistically called "civilization." They invented an alphabet of eighty-six characters, and began publishing a newspaper, the *Cherokee Phoenix*. A white theological graduate, Elias Boudinot, who traveled through their territory, was surprised that "they have advanced so far and so rapidly in civilization." In addition to tens of thousands of domesticated cattle, horses, and swine, they boasted 762 looms, 1,488 spinning wheels, 172 wagons, 2,948 plows, 10 sawmills, 31 gristmills, 8 cotton machines, 18 ferries, some public roads, and 18 schools. "In one district there were, last winter," another report read, "upward of 1,000 volumes of good books." The Cherokees promulgated a written constitution, very much like the American, with a bicameral legislature, a chief executive, a supreme court, and a set of statutes. Their elections were described by a missionary as possessing "nothing of that intrigue and unfairness which is to be seen at elections in some of the civilized states." Whites in the area enjoyed equal rights with their hosts, except that they were not allowed to run for office. And to round out the picture, Christianity was the official religion.

But Christian or not, civilized or not—and despite sixteen treaties holding their existing territory sacrosanct—the Cherokees were unceremoniously uprooted and, according to historian Irvin M. Peithmann, "herded like cattle into concentration camps and stockades by the military in preparation for their long journey to their new homes in the Indian Territory [Oklahoma]." Along the trail—which the Indians called "Trail-Where-They-Cried"—4,000 of the 17,000 died of cold and hunger.

All of this was in accord with the principle enunciated by Andrew Jackson in 1817 that "treaties with the Indians" are "an absurdity not to be reconciled with the principles of self-government." The United States, he said, could not be bound by written pacts with a savage race; if it needed the land for its own people, "self-government" dictated that the land be taken and the savages removed. It was in Jackson's administration that the Indian Removal Act of 1830 was passed. Between him and his successor, Martin Van Buren, more than 125,000 natives were evicted from their homes and sent across the Mississippi. Even there they failed to find the security promised them. Typically, the Creeks, Cherokees, Seminoles, and Choctaws, driven out of Georgia, Florida, Alabama, and Mississippi into what was considered semi-useless land in the Arkansas Territory, were told that "as long as the grass grows and water flows, it is to be yours." In 1866, however, these tribes were forced to cede half their holdings as a bailiwick for other tribes, and in 1899 part of this area too was preempted, this time for white settlement. Eight hundred thousand acres of Cherokee land in the southern section of Kansas was seized by a single railroad through means that the governor of Kansas himself described as "a cheat and a fraud in every particular." But nothing was ever done to reverse the cheat and fraud.

During Jackson's two terms alone the natives were forced to sign 94 treaties ceding territory; those tribes which resisted were put down in eight "little" wars. From 1853 to 1856 the Indians put their hand to 52 treaties, yielding another 174 million acres. During the decade of the 1850's the United States was engaged in 18 additional little wars with the natives. Each time they were assured that this was the last land grab. Yet from 1887 to 1934, when the Indian problem was seemingly "solved," the red men were divested of another 90 million acres. Most of what remained was unfit for the agriculture that American leaders had told them was their salvation.

III

To recount the story of all these wars and treaties would be an exercise in redundancy. The pattern is monotonously similar: whites settle on Indian lands, Indians challenge the settlers, incidents and massacres occur on both sides, the U.S. army is called in for direct military action or to force a new treaty on the Indians. The red men fight heroically, win many battles, but in the end lose every war. Tragedy compounds tragedy, for it would be wrong to say that all the whites were land robbers or gross speculators. Most were running away from their own poverty on the eastern seaboard—the bankrupt Revolutionary soldier, the harassed immigrant, the exploited tenant, the unemployed laborer. If there were speculators growing rich, there were also poor palefaces driven by one despair into another.

It is well, therefore, to view the drama of the Indian wars, which stretched through the nineteenth century, not as a chain of individual events but through the human eyes of victims and victimizers. Symbolic of this enduring conflict were two men with great popular followings, one of whom was to become the seventh president of the

United States, Andrew Jackson, and the other a Shawnee chief named Tecumseh, who was to die on a lonely battlefield in 1813. The paths of these men never crossed, for Jackson's fighting was done in the South against Creeks and Seminoles, while Tecumseh's campaigns against the Americans took place in the North. But they represented the militant extremes in the United States for a century or more, the one seeking to expand his nation toward the south and west, the other seeking to unify disparate tribes into a red man's confederacy that would check this expansion.

Andrew Jackson, third offspring of parents who had migrated from Northern Ireland, was born in a backwoods settlement of South Carolina in 1767. Tecumseh, whose name means Falling Star, or Meteor, in the Shawnee tongue, came into the world a year later, fourth of seven children sired by a secondary war chief named Puckeshinwa. Premature death dogged both families. Jackson's father strained himself picking up a log and died a few days before Andrew was born. His brother Hugh died of heat prostration and fatigue in the course of a battle against the British in Georgia. A second brother, Robert, contracted smallpox and died after being confined in a small jail by the British. His mother perished the same year, 1781, victim of a plague, while nursing American prisoners. At fourteen the agile, slender Andrew—who had already served a brief hitch in the Revolutionary army and manifested the tempestuous courage for which he would become famous—found himself without immediate family, though not without resources. His mother had been left a two-hundred-acre farm; his uncle, James Crawford, was well-to-do; and he himself inherited three or four hundred pounds sterling from a merchant uncle in the old country—his opening stake in a long and adventurous career that led to the White House. He was an American success story.

Peering behind this saga of a self-made man, however, Jackson's exploits were not all that exemplary. His schooling was episodic and casual, primarily because he preferred gambling and women. On one occasion, when his fortunes had run down and he needed money to pay his landlord, he bet his horse against two hundred dollars on one throw of the dice—and won. In Salisbury, North Carolina, he read law with Spruce Macay who described him as "the most roaring, rollicking, game-cocking, horse-racing, card-playing, mischievous fellow, that ever lived" in the area. He was "the head of the rowdies hereabouts. . . ." But after being admitted to the bar he attached himself to John McNairy, a young man of an influential family, and when McNairy was designated judge of the Western District of North Carolina he appointed his friend Jackson prosecutor. In September 1788, accompanied by a Negro girl he had bought for two hundred dollars, Andrew Jackson joined the first group of migrants along the Cumberland Road moving into what is now Tennessee, but was then the outer reaches of North Carolina. In Nashville, after having saved his party from attack by Cherokee warriors who resented the trek over 180 miles of their land, and after killing a panther, Andy Jackson was at the seat of his destiny. At age twenty-one, with the twenty-six-year-old McNairy on the bench, the future president earned his legal spurs by representing creditors against debtors—the rich against the poor; within a month he won seventy writs of execution against the latter and enough good will with the upper classes to establish a lucrative private law practice on the side. In the next few years he became a large landowner, much of his acreage acquired in lieu of legal fees. His holdings were so large, according to biographer Marquis James, that he "had only a rough idea of how much . . . he owned or laid claim to. Much of it he had never seen." And, it might be added, much of it really belonged to the Cherokees. When Jackson went to Philadelphia in 1795 to dispose of 98,000 acres of land, he was advised by John Overton, with whom he owned 50,000 acres in partnership, to be "canded [sic] and unreserved" about the fact that this land was "without the Treaty of Holston"—the 1791 agreement with the Cherokees which took some land from them but set firm boundaries to the territory they were allowed to keep. What Jackson was selling was, at least in part, Indian domain; and he could do it only because the local authorities, without authorization from the federal government, had conducted still another foray against the Cherokees and forced them into submission. Thus land with clouded title that had been bought for a dime an acre would eventually go up to five dollars an acre, and men like Jackson—still in his twenties—would become rich selling it.

To his dying day Jackson would not concede any rights to the Indians. He was indignant when Washington threatened to use the regular army against whites who settled on native holdings. He was impatient about negotiations or compromises with the Indians: "Why do we attempt to hold treaty with them?" he once asked. And his sense of gratitude to individual warriors was something less than exemplary. In the war against the Creeks, a Cherokee chief named Junaluska saved Jackson's life by driving a tomahawk into the skull of an attacker. Many years later, when the general had become president, Junaluska went to plead with him against removal of his people. Jackson dismissed him with a curt "Sir, your audience is ended, there is nothing I can do for you." For a man who loved fighting and military glory the way to "treat" with Indians was by "toughness," and this was the principle which guided him throughout his life. In due course "Old Hickory"—a nickname given him by his men "after the toughest thing they knew"—became a congressman, a senator (at age thirty-one), and a general. When he was called on to lead 2,500 troops in the war against the Creek Indians (1813–14), he had just been severely wounded in a shootout with two American officers, and doctors were thinking of amputating his left arm. But the prospect of fighting the natives inspired him to cry out from his sickbed: "The health of your general is restored. He will command in person." After he had conquered the Creeks he forced them to surrender half their domain, 23 million acres, or approximately a fifth of what is now Georgia and three fifths of Alabama. When the warriors pleaded for mercy, Jackson told them that their lands lay across "the path that Tecumseh trod. That path must be stopped. Until that is done your nation cannot expect happiness, mine security."

This was the man who enforced the policy of Indian removal, a man who in other respects was regarded as the tribune of the lower classes, who challenged banks and bankers—but was absolutely remorseless in dealing with the red men.

IV

The most formidable fighter against the American system of conquest, typified by Jackson, was an oval-faced warrior with sprightly step and brilliant white teeth, who, according to William Henry Harrison, might have founded "an empire that would rival in glory Mexico or Peru," if he had not lived in "the vicinity of the United States." There was little about Tecumseh that fits the stereotype made famous by Wild West movies. He was a nondrinker and he invariably advised his followers not to buy the whiskey sold them by white traders at sixty cents a gallon. He held no innate prejudices against whites; he was in fact brought up with a white boy six months his junior, Stephen Ruddell, who had been captured and adopted by his family. Later he fell in love with a sixteen-year-old white girl, Rebecca Galloway, and would have married her if she hadn't demanded that he leave his tribe. Though he killed many white men in battle he never permitted his warriors to burn or torture prisoners. He had witnessed such an incident when he was seventeen, and was appalled by the practice. Tecumseh was a fine hunter and a courageous fighter, but even more—again contrary to Hollywood stereotype—an excellent orator, negotiator, and statesman.

Tecumseh's Shawnee parents migrated to the Northwest Territory, then called Indian country, in the middle of the eighteenth century. The Shawnees were a nomadic tribe, small in number—never more than two thousand—but related to tribes of greater consequence, such as the Delawares, Wyandots, Potawatomies, Miamis, Illinois. They had drifted south after a dispute with the Iroquois, returned north, and dispersed to various parts of Ohio, Indiana, Illinois. The group that included Tecumseh's father, Puckeshinwa, alighted in Old Chillicothe on the Scioto River in Ohio, and during the French and Indian War fought with the French against the English on the theory that the former wanted only to trade with them while the latter (and their colonists) wanted their land. It was for his role in this engagement that Puckeshinwa became a minor war chief. A few years later his famous son was born near the Mad River in a cabin made of saplings and surrounded by cornfields.

As a young man, Tecumseh imbibed a body of folklore and glorified history that gave him pride in his people. According to the Shawnee legend of creation, the Master of Life, an Indian, had fashioned the Shawnee out of his brain, the inferior British and French out of his breast, and the even more inferior "Long Knives" of Virginia and Kentucky out of his hands. The favored people, brought from the darkness to the Great Island of North America, were colored red by the Master of Life, whereas the imperfect ones from across the Stinking Lake—the Atlantic—were colored white. The hero of Tecumseh's generation of Indians was Chief Pontiac, who had formed a confederation of Ohio tribes to resist the English and their colonists after the defeat of France. Though Pontiac failed to drive the whites back across the Alleghenies and had to take sanctuary in Spanish-held St. Louis, he did weld together the Algonquin family, plus the Senecas, for a concerted effort. He gave youngsters like Tecumseh, whose whole life was affected by white penetration, a dream to follow.

If American youth like Jackson saw its destiny in the mysterious West, Indian children saw it in checking the white incursion. Theoretically the interior was sealed off to colonial penetration by an edict of the British Crown. But in fact the Earl of Dunmore, governor of Virginia, was making grants to speculators and veterans of the French and Indian War in violation of instructions from London. And hunters like Daniel Boone were pushing into Kentucky, killing off the Indians' food supply of deer and buffalo at an alarming rate. Though it was only a trickle by later standards, sturdy pioneers in some number were already loading their families and belongings on flatboats, and floating them down the Ohio in search of the beautiful tomorrow. With equal determination, the Shawnee and other Algonquins tried to halt the invasion of their region. Waiting in canoes at a bend in the river, the Indians would fall on the migrants, seize their property, kill their menfolk—often after torture and burning—and either adopt the women and children into their tribes or hold them for exchange. South of the Ohio they attacked with small raiding parties, giving no ground and expecting none. After a considerable period of these disturbances Lord Dunmore, at the head of 2,000 militia, marched against the Indian villages in Kentucky and Ohio, and at Point Pleasant, West Virginia, inflicted enough casualties (suffering heavily himself) to cause Shawnee Chief Cornstalk to sue for peace. It was in this Lord Dunmore's War, in which the Shawnee yielded their claim to holdings south of the Ohio, that Tecumseh's father, Puckeshinwa, was killed. The time was 1774, two years before the Declaration of Independence; the future leader of the Indian confederation was then six years old.

When the Revolution broke out on the eastern seaboard in 1775–76, most of the Indians joined the British. On purely political grounds their interest meshed closely with that of the Americans, for they too were nationalists fighting for independence. But the Americans were expansionists who coveted Indian lands, while the British no longer had settlers to occupy Indian regions and were committed to the establishment of an independent Indian state in the Northwest. Once again, then, the braves stood watch on the Ohio and sent forays into Kentucky, destroying towns on the Licking River, killing settlers in the Ohio Valley. When he was ten, Tecumseh was elated by the sight of Daniel Boone and thirty other Kentuckians, brought into Indian country as prisoners of war. (The wily Boone, however, escaped a few months later.) When he was twelve he was forced to hide in the woods with his younger brothers as George Rogers Clark, a Virginian, destroyed their town, Piqua, scalped seventeen of its people, and laid waste to every house. Before he was fourteen, Tecumseh was already attached to the war party of his adored elder brother, Cheesekau, hoping to inflict a coup de grâce on the Americans. The Indians formed a confederation of many tribes, including the Cherokees, and attacked Boonesborough. In November 1782, however, as the last land battle of the Revolutionary War, Clark led 1,100 riflemen against the Shawnee and laid waste to five of their villages in the Chillicothe area.

For young Jackson in North Carolina, American victory meant

grandiose opportunity; for young Tecumseh, it was a disaster. Of the
nearly 900,000 square miles of the United States in 1783, more than
half was Indian country, but the Indian was being squeezed out of
it remorselessly. Though Congress assured the red men that the
Ohio was theirs, the flatboats and settlers floated down the river in
ever increasing numbers toward places like Marietta and Cincinnati.
The federal government warned whites repeatedly not to transgress
on Indian lands, even threatening—in 1786—to destroy their homes.
Still later, Washington instructed Generals Arthur St. Clair and Josiah Harmar to forcibly remove white squatters. But the whites remained and spread out, paying little heed to the red man's rights.
Once again, therefore, as when the British ruled the country, the
desperate Indians retaliated with ambushes, pillages, and raids.
From 1783 to 1790, according to John Frost, 1,500 men, women, and
children were killed or taken prisoner by the braves, 20,000 horses
were stolen, and "an immense number of farms and plantations were
desolated."

Tecumseh, as a Shawnee teenager, was one of those assigned to
intercept the flatboats. He acquitted himself skillfully, like the other
youth. Then, after a long trip with his brother Cheesekau to Indiana, Missouri, and southern Illinois, he returned in the late 1780's to
the rebuilt town of Piqua just as war was breaking out with the
Americans. More mature now, and a veteran of buffalo hunts (he
broke his thigh in one, but it mended well), he led warrior bands
that helped inflict disastrous defeats on General Harmar in 1790 and
General St. Clair the following year. As part of a punitive
expedition—the federal government alternated between trying to
buy Indian land cheaply and sending out troops to inflict punishment on recalcitrant tribes—Harmar had set out from Fort Washington (Cincinnati) with 320 regulars and 1,100 militia to bring the
Miami to their knees. Much too confident, the general and his forces
were badly mauled; nearly 200 were killed. St. Clair, an inept and
overbearing officer despised by his 1,500 militiamen, suffered even
greater humiliation—losing, as already noted, 630 dead and 280 seriously wounded.

Following these events, Tecumseh began conducting raids against
white frontiersmen in Ohio and Kentucky, and when called on by
the Cherokees and Creeks, took a group of 30 Shawnee warriors to
the outskirts of Nasville to harry settlements in that region. It was
during one of these engagements that his brother Cheesekau was
mortally wounded, the first of four brothers who were destined to
die for Indian nationalism. Tecumseh buried the body, took his beloved kin's place as the leader of the Shawnee warriors in the south,

and for a number of months guided them in assaults on whites in what is now Tennessee, Mississippi, Alabama, Georgia, and Florida. He returned to Ohio in time to defend the Northwest from "Mad Anthony" Wayne, and again—as 1,400 warriors fought vainly against 3,630 Americans—enhanced his reputation for boldness and bravery. It was at the peak of this encounter that a second brother was lost.

Lost also was the war. Mad Anthony Wayne, impetuous and egotistical but thoroughly competent, had undertaken the campaign in 1793; after a year of hostilities in which he far outnumbered his enemy, he thoroughly defeated the Ohio natives. In June 1795, a thousand vanquished warriors and chiefs of twelve tribes met with Wayne at Greenville, Ohio, and after two months of argument and badgering by the moderate chiefs, ceded away almost two thirds of Ohio and sixteen strategic sites, such as Detroit, Chicago, Toledo, Peoria, Vincennes. In return the victor gave the Indians $20,000 in commodities and the promise of $9,500 a year.

V

A defiant Tecumseh, already a fighter of some repute, refused to attend the Greenville conference, and when its terms were announced became the focal point of opposition to Blue Jacket and other chiefs who had signed away their heritage. He was now twenty-seven years old, slightly under six feet tall, a handsome man with expressive hazel eyes and a resonant voice, highly respected among his peers as a warrior and scout. It became his task to regroup his people for the next round of a long battle.

Defeat, of course, bred dissension and dissolution among the vanquished during the decade after Greenville. The older village chiefs who lived near the white man's forts became pliant tools for the Americans and were easily debauched by alcohol. They and their people traded away their possessions for firewater and wasted away in a morass of self-pity, completely demoralized by the shattering of their world. The many disaffected warriors and the younger chiefs, on the other hand, moved west, determined on further resistance. It was these disgruntled elements who gave the outspoken Tecumseh their loyalty and chose him as their spokesman and primary chief.

In the decade that followed, the Shawnee warrior could only bide his time, for in the backwash of failure the momentum was with the Americans. An uneasy truce prevailed in the Northwest as the federal government built a string of forts to augment its police power, and in 1800 established rudimentary administrative machinery for

biting off another part of the red man's domain—Indiana. The following year, a young man of twenty-seven, William Henry Harrison,
who had served as an aide to Wayne and had married the daughter
of a land speculator, was designated as the first governor of Indiana
Territory. Harrison soon began to force treaties on the Indians and
extinguish their land titles. And as the Indians became further disillusioned they united behind Tecumseh in the most significant of all
Indian efforts to forge a nation.

It was during this winter of defeat that Tecumseh's strategy became finalized. As a political rallying point he promoted a concept
of collectivism, which held that Indian lands were not owned either
by individual people or individual tribes but in common by *all* the
tribes. In a subsequent meeting with Harrison he insisted that this
collective ownership was the rule "at first, and should be now—for
it [the land] never was divided, but belongs to all. No tribe has a
right to sell, even to each other, much less to strangers. . . . Sell a
country! Why not sell the air, the clouds and the great sea, as well
as the earth? Did not the Great Spirit make them all for the use of
his children?" Any treaty between an individual tribe and the
United States was, in Tecumseh's view, null and void, since it
flaunted the tradition of indivisible joint ownership. Oddly enough,
the United States had taken the same position relative to the Northwest Territory in 1785–87, when it extinguished the claims of individual states and assigned the whole area as the domain of the central government.

Tecumseh's means of defending the dogma of collectivism—and
independence—were similar in many respects to those adopted by
Samuel Adams in the 1770's, namely the development of a sense of
national unity and the involvement of the populace through broad
participation. Pontiac had been satisfied, four decades back, simply
with a military campaign to drive the whites back east. In his confederacy the social structure of the red man was untouched. But
Tecumseh argued that military defense must be supplemented, and
thereby strengthened, by popular rule. In Tecumseh's confederacy,
power would rest not with the chiefs but with a broadly based congress of warriors. Those who were asked to fight should have a say
in how their society was governed—a thesis very similar to that of
"no taxation without representation."

To weld his people into a single union Tecumseh faced a much
more formidable job than Sam Adams. With the primitive state of
communication in the back country and the vast number of tribes,
the only way to win allegiance for the confederacy scheme was
through personal contact. Even Harrison marveled at the Shawnee's

tenacity in making those contacts. "No difficulties," he reported, "deter him. For four years he has been in constant motion. You see him today on the Wabash, and in a short time hear of him on the shores of Lake Erie or Michigan, or on the banks of the Mississippi, and wherever he goes he makes an impression."

He traveled through the Northwest, went south to see the Creeks, Cherokees, and Choctaws, even crossed the Mississippi westward. With a couple of dozen warriors at his side he would dance for an assemblage of thousands of tribesmen, then address them on the subject at hand. Typically, as in one speech to the Osage, he would say: "Brothers, we all belong to one family; we are all children of the Master of Life . . . we must assist each other to bear our burdens. . . ." He pictured the white people as "feeble" ingrates who had come to the red man's land with little talent for helping themselves. "Our fathers," said Tecumseh, "commiserated their distress and shared freely with them whatever the Master of Life had given his red children. They gave them food when hungry, medicine when sick, and gave them grounds that they might hunt and raise corn." But the whites were "like poisonous serpents. . . . At first, they only asked for land sufficient for a wigwam; now nothing will satisfy them but the whole of our hunting grounds, from the rising to the setting sun. . . . The white men despise and cheat the Indians; they abuse and insult them; they do not think the red men sufficiently good to live." Tecumseh served notice that "my people . . . are determined on vengeance; they have taken up the hatchet. . . . If we all unite, we will cause the rivers to stain the waters with their [the white men's] blood." And he concluded with the warning that "if you do not unite with us, they will first destroy us, and then you will fall an easy prey to them. They have destroyed many nations of red men because they were not united, because they were not friends to each others."

Concomitant with Tecumseh's efforts at political unity, another brother, Laulewasika—"The-Man-with-the-Loud-Voice"—gave the movement a religious and ethical tenor. In 1805 Laulewasika was designated medicine man by a council of four tribes, and like the man he succeeded assumed the title "the Prophet." He was then thirty-six years old, an indifferent hunter, but impetuous and a passionate speaker. His right eye had been lost in an accident, and over the socket he wore a handkerchief, which together with the wide golden hoops hanging from his ears and the turban on his head, gave him a striking appearance. Much of the Prophet's witchcraft and predictions were simple skulduggery. In June 1806, for instance, after learning from whites of an impending eclipse, he proclaimed to his Indians that he would cast a dark shadow over the sun, and of course won their awe when the eclipse took place and he "prevailed" on the Master of Life to make the sun reappear a few minutes later. His teaching that whites would be paralyzed fighting Indians was another bit of nonsense, but the "miracles" and "predictions," spread by the Prophet's agents to tribes as far away as the Missouri River and central Canada, laid the ground for inculcating the Indian with a sense of pride.

At Greenville, Ohio, where the two brothers erected a large frame meeting house and five dozen cabins for visiting warriors, and later —in 1808—at Tippecanoe, Indiana, the Prophet preached a simple message. Indians, he told his followers, must reject the white man and his works, and return to their ways. They must eschew whiskey, wear Indian dress only, and purge themselves of all alien habits. The Master of Life, he said, had ordered that they respect their elders, and treat with tenderness the weak and the helpless. When they had adopted this mode of living, the Master of Life would again fill the forests with game—now being killed off by the whites—and give the Indians the strength to oust the Americans from their territory. For a people that had suffered harsh defeat these were magnetic words to rouse them from lethargy. Reinforcing his sermons on racial separatism, the Prophet sometimes applied hard muscle to those who opposed his brother's plan for confederation. Not a few chiefs who were pliant to the Americans were denounced as witches' agents, put on trial in flimsy proceedings, and executed. Though Tecumseh himself sharply dissented from this practice, it went on anyway.

The Prophet's preachings and Tecumseh's trips attracted thousands to the banner, widening the schism between the races. The whites, meanwhile, continued to push the frontier westward, moving from Ohio into Indiana. Harrison, by arranging questionable treaties with the weak and older chiefs, had extinguished title to 48 million acres of Indian land by 1809. Even Jefferson was alarmed by his aggressive policies; that year the War Department ordered Harrison not to enter into treaties with the Indians unless the "chiefs of all the nations who have or pretend a right to these lands should be present." But the frontier was a long way from Washington, and Harrison's own predilections coincided with those of the 20,000 settlers in southern Indiana and the steady stream augmenting their number. In September 1809, at Fort Wayne, the governor entered into still another pact with the chiefs. After plying them with large amounts of firewater he divested them of three million acres in central Indiana for the bargain price of $7,000, plus annual payments of

$1,750. Much of the area belonged to tribes that were not even represented at the conference.

This new cession enraged Tecumseh, not only because some of the Shawnee's best hunting grounds were included, but as another example of weak chiefs traitorously giving way to greedy whites. He declared the cession void and a thousand warriors gathered at Prophet's Town in the spring of 1810 ready to defend the ceded area from efforts of whites to settle it. In a historic meeting between Tecumseh and Harrison near Vincennes, the Shawnee chief reminded the governor that "the states have set the example of forming a union among all the fires [states]—why should they censure the Indians for following it? . . . You endeavor to prevent the Indians from doing what we, their leaders, wish them to do—unite and consider their land the common property." The governor replied that Tecumseh actually had no right to discuss the problem of Indiana since the Shawnee home was in Georgia. To the charge that the Americans were despoiling the red men of their land, Harrison blandly responded that the United States had always been "fair" in its dealings with the Indians. At one point Tecumseh shouted "He lies!" and Harrison grabbed for his sword. It was a prophecy of things to come.

There is no question that Tecumseh expected and prepared for hostilities, but he sought to postpone the final accounting until his confederation was a reality. He had been warmly greeted on his tireless journeys by some tribes, but rebuffed by others; and there was still work to be done. Another factor affecting his strategy was the tense situation between the United States and Britain, engaged again in a serious dispute over shipping spoliations and impressment of sailors on the high seas. As Tecumseh's forefathers had accepted support from France against England in the 1760's, so the Shawnee leader was now willing to accept aid and an alliance with Britain against the Americans. "Brothers," he told his followers, "our Great Father over the waters [Britain] is angry with the white people, our enemies. He will send his great warriors against them; he will send us rifles, and whatever else we want. He is our friend, and we are his children." In his talks with friendly tribes, Tecumseh discussed specific logistical problems: how many guns were needed, how many warriors, where they would mobilize, how they would be supplied, where they would launch their attacks.

The war began prematurely from Tecumseh's point of view. Operating on the thesis that the best defense is an offense, Harrison demanded that the leaders of Prophet's Town at Tippecanoe surrender a few Potawatomis accused of killing white men in Illinois; when his request was turned down, he mobilized 1,000 troops at Vincennes to march on Tippecanoe. Tecumseh was on another trip south, seeking converts for confederation. Had he been present, he later said, he would have avoided battle at any cost, for the one thing he deplored most was an isolated engagement that had no relation to a long-term plan. The Prophet, however, smelled glory. Convinced that the enemy numbered only a few hundred men, he ordered a surprise night attack on Harrison's nearby camp but was unable to pierce the lines of a contingent that proved to be much larger. Harrison's casualties were 62 dead and 127 wounded; those of the Prophet, though never verified, probably half as many. Nonetheless, failure of the attack left the initiative with the white governor, who promptly burned the town to the ground and emerged with a reputation as an Indian fighter that three decades later—under the slogan "Tippecanoe and Tyler too"—would place him in the White House.

When Tecumseh returned home early in 1812, Indian bands, seeking to avenge Tippecanoe, were engaged in the kind of sporadic raids against white settlements and uncoordinated engagements that their leader shunned. The defeat, aside from forever eclipsing the Prophet as a major Indian figure, set back the cause of confederacy by discrediting its spiritual leader. Unity, if it was to be welded at all, now could come only as a result of a larger conflict; for in June that year the United States declared war against Britain and Tecumseh's cause became indissolubly associated with that of the British. The British pledged that should they win, the original Indian country north of the Ohio would become an independent nation. Armed with this promise, the Shawnee chief again sallied forth to recruit for his confederation, and was successful this time in winning the support of the powerful Sioux across the Mississippi, the influential Wyandots, the Potawatomis, and, after his initial military successes, many others.

If the Indians were not the decisive factor in the War of 1812 they were quite important, especially in the early stages of hostilities; each side tried to woo them. At a large council meeting called by the Americans at Fort Wayne, Tecumseh defied his hosts, twice breaking peace pipes offered him, and urged the Indians "to form ourselves into one great combination and cast our lot with the British. . . ." This was, he said, "a chance such as will never occur again," for if the British "again get the mastery of all North America, our rights to at least a portion of the land of our fathers would be respected by the King." If they lost, "the remnants of the different tribes . . . will be driven toward the setting sun." Fired by these words, young warriors joined Tecumseh's banner and marched off with him to Fort Malden across the river from Detroit to give their allegiance to the British. His runners spread out far and wide to enroll thousands of others in the same cause, and though they fought under separate, instead of coordinated, leadership, they caused severe disruptions for the Americans from Canada to Georgia.

Tecumseh himself, at the head of 1,000 to 3,000 braves, proved in the next year both his courage and his genius as a strategist. In July 1812 U.S. Major General William Hull, a hero of the Revolutionary War, crossed over from Fort Detroit into Canada with 2,500 men, expecting little opposition. But Tecumseh harried his communications south of Detroit and inflicted on three of Hull's companies—in the words of biographer John M. Oskison—"the most disastrous defeat of American troops since St. Clair's fiasco of November 1791." Then in mid-August, the Indians and a few hundred men under Major General Sir Isaac Brock attacked Hull in Detroit. While Brock shelled the fort, Tecumseh and his men crossed the river in canoes for the main assault. After a short battle, Hull raised the white flag in one of the most humiliating defeats the American army was ever to suffer. It was a defeat for which Hull was subsequently court-martialed and sentenced to death—though the sentence was vacated by President Madison. Tecumseh's career was at its peak when he entered Detroit to reassure the Americans that they would not be massacred. "A more sagacious man or a more gallant warrior," General Brock wrote of him, "does not, I believe, exist." From near and far now Indian chiefs rallied to the common banner with Britain.

Fort Dearborn (Chicago) was captured by the Potawatomis, Fort Wayne was under siege, and Tecumseh's dream of confederation was as close to fruition as it would ever be. In the fall he visited the South once more, and though there is no record of his conversations with the Creeks it is obvious that his plea made an impact: the Creek Confederation was soon embroiled in a war in the South that cost the United States some millions of dollars and large numbers of casualties.

The tide of victory continued to swell in the months that followed. In January 1813, a combined force of Indians and whites under British Brigadier Henry Procter overwhelmed one of Harrison's generals, James Winchester, killing 400 and capturing 500, including the general himself; only a couple of dozen managed to escape. Three or four months later Tecumseh ambushed a force of 866 Kentucky troops near Fort Meigs on the Maumee River, killing about 500 and capturing 150 more. It is interesting that though he furiously hated the Americans, when some of his men began to kill the captives—20 were slaughtered before he learned of the affair—Tecumseh hit one of his Indians with a sword, grabbed another, and stopped the massacre. At this point, Procter might have struck a decisive blow at the Americans and perhaps modified the course of the war if he had continued the seige of Fort Meigs. But he was petulant, indecisive, and, unlike Brock, unable to get along with the Shawnee chief. He rejected the Indian's suggestion to continue the siege, even though the American force inside was seriously enervated.

While the British command had changed for the worse, the American command was immeasurably improved as William Henry Harrison took the reins. The Americans had at least 100,000 men of military age to draw from in Kentucky and Ohio; the British had no more than 15,000 from the white population of Upper Canada. Tecumseh urged Proctor to attack before the Americans could be mobilized, but the general remained timid and hesitant.

Meanwhile, in September 1813, Commodore Oliver Perry defeated the British fleet on Lake Erie, opening it for rapid communication and movement of troops by the Americans. Tecumseh again demanded that Proctor take a stand, but the British commander decided to retreat and fight only at a "favorable" position. He seemed to have little idea of what to do next. As his heavily laden wagons and boats moved into the interior at the excruciating pace of a few miles a day, Harrison's force of 2,500 men were landed by Perry's ships and moved forward at what was then an express speed. On October 3, with the Americans at his heels near McGregor's Creek on the River Thames, Proctor left his command to carry his wife and daughter to the safety of an Indian village twenty miles away. On his return he assigned Tecumseh's forces to the front lines while his own moved to the rear. Here, on October 5, 1813, in a fierce battle that lasted only twenty minutes, the brave Shawnee, already wounded in the arm the day before, fought his last battle. Outnumbered three to one, he knew death was imminent. He removed his sword, symbol of his status as brigadier general in the British army, and instructed an aide: "When my son becomes a warrior . . . give this to him." Tecumseh's body was secretly buried, and with his death the dream of Indian confederation faded.

A year later, Andrew Jackson with 2,000 troops at his command, including such future luminaries as Ensign Sam Houston and hundreds of friendly Creeks and Cherokees, attacked a force of warriors under half-breed chief Billy Weatherford (Red Eagle) at a place called Horseshoe Bend on the Tallapoosa River. He was determined, said Jackson, not only to defeat the "Red Sticks" but to "exterminate them"; and he was as good as his word. "The slaughter was greater than all we had done before," recorded Old Hickory's friend Brigadier General John Coffee. "We killed not less than eight hundred and fifty or nine hundred of them, and took about five hundred squaws and children prisoners." Some 557 bodies were counted at the bend alone. On August 9, 1814, Jackson forced an unhappy band of thirty-five Creek chiefs to append their names to a document which gave the Americans 23 million more acres, about three fifths of Alabama and one fifth of Georgia.

Sixteen years later the hero of this war, Jackson, was ensconced in the presidency busily removing tens of thousands of Indians westward under the powers granted him by the Indian Removal Act.

☆☆☆☆☆

4

☆☆☆☆☆

ON TO CANADA

The Indian wars, in which Tecumseh perished and the Creeks were shattered by Old Hickory Jackson, were part of a broader engagement which was variously called Mr. Madison's War, the Second War for Independence, or—most often—the War of 1812. It was a war fought under the slogan "Free trade and sailors' rights," signifying—presumably—that its goal was to affirm certain maritime freedoms denied Americans by Great Britain. Oddly enough, however, the states that had strong maritime interests not only opposed the war, but opposed it so fervidly that toward the end some of their leaders called for secession from the Union. Every member of Congress from Connecticut, Rhode Island, and Delaware voted against hostilities, as did eleven out of thirteen in New York and eight out of fourteen in Massachusetts. On the other hand, Western and Southern states, with no shipping industries and no ships being seized by the British, favored the war. Every single congressman from Tennessee, Ohio, South Carolina, Kentucky, and Georgia voted for the war resolution, which passed by 79 to 49 in the House and 19 to 13 in the Senate—indecisive majorities, considering how one-sided war votes usually have been.

Clearly the motives for Mr. Madison's War were more complex than they appeared on the surface. If freedom of the seas were the single or even the primary reason for waging hostilities, there were as many, or nearly as many, good reasons for fighting France as Britain. Both powers were ravaging American ships, the British having seized 917, the French 558, and Madison himself evidently gave serious thought to fighting both. An amendment to add France to the war declaration failed in the Senate by a narrow 18 to 14 vote.

"The Devil himself," said Nathaniel Macon of North Carolina, "could not tell which government, England or France, is the most wicked." The opposition Federalists in Congress asked pointedly "if honor demands a war with England, what opiate lulls that honor to sleep over the wrongs done us by France?" Charles Prentiss, a Massachusetts poet, put the question in political rhyme:

If England look askance, we boil with rage;
And blood, blood only, can the wound assuage;
Yet, whipt, robbed, kicked, and spit upon, by France;
We treat her with greater complaisance.

Whatever the immediate cause of Mr. Madison's War, there is no doubt that a large and influential faction sought territorial aggrandizement from it, and that if the United States had won a clear victory, it would have attached Canada and the Floridas to the Union. Ten days after the declaration of war in June 1812, former President Jefferson wrote, in obvious anticipation of imperial gain, "Upon the whole I have known no war entered into under more favorable auspices. Our present enemy will have the sea to herself while we strip her of all her possessions on this continent." The "cession of Canada," he proposed, "must be a *sine qua non* at a treaty of peace." Five weeks later, in a letter to Colonel William Duane, he was even more specific: "The acquisition of Canada this year, as far as the neighborhood of Quebec, will be a matter of mere marching, and will give us the experience for the attack of Halifax the next, and the final expulsion of England from the American continent."

Another focus of expansionist attention was the two Floridas, East and West, both of which included a growing number of émigrés from the United States. At the time, they belonged to Spain, East Florida covering approximately what is now the state of Florida, and West Florida the strip along the Gulf of Mexico from Baton Rouge in the west to the Perdido River in the east. Americans had long considered that these two territorial morsels must eventually become part of the Union. Many years before, Jefferson had outlined a scenario for the acquisition of these and other parts of the Spanish empire, in which the American population advance would do the work of an army. "Our confederacy," he wrote, "must be viewed as the nest, from which all America, North and South, is to be peopled." For the time being it was well that such territories remained under Spanish rule, since the United States was not yet ready to absorb them. "Those countries," Jefferson observed, "can not be in better hands. My fear is that they [the Spaniards] are too feeble to hold them till our population can be sufficiently advanced to gain it from them piece by piece." If Jefferson eschewed war more than most American leaders—at first anyway—he did not eschew territorial expansion. He anticipated that when the trees were heavily laden with American fruit, Spain would be happy to sell them.

West Florida, which had been traded back and forth between Britain, France, and Spain, was infiltrated by émigrés from the Carolinas and Georgia, greatly diluting its French and Spanish population. Baton Rouge was almost wholly Anglo-American. Under the vague terms of the Louisiana Purchase of 1803 it was assumed by Jefferson that West Florida had been included, and by France and Spain that it had not. For a time some members of Jefferson's cabinet—except for Albert Gallatin—considered using military force to seize not only West Florida but Texas, or if not both, Texas alone. Nearby garrisons were ordered to strengthen their forces and be on the alert.

So matters stood until Napoleon's rampaging armies entered Spain and Bonaparte in 1808 installed his brother Joseph as monarch of the Iberian state. Since Spanish loyalists and Britain continued to challenge French rule, the indeterminate state of affairs was an opportunity for revolutionaries from the Spanish empire in the western hemisphere to try and throw off the shackles. In Mexico, Father Miguel Hidalgo organized a popular revolt that ended with the rout of 100,000 poorly armed rebels and demonstrators at Guadalajara. The Anglo-Americans in West Florida, encouraged by friends across the border in the United States, did better. On July 1, 1810, American settlers and adventurers initiated a rebellion which culminated in September with seizure of the Spanish fort at Baton Rouge and a Declaration of Independence by the "Republic of West Florida." The Bourbon flag was torn down and a blue woolen one with a single silver star run up in its place. A "very considerable force" in the lower part of West Florida, which opposed independence, was dissuaded from taking action by the undisguised threat from Mississippi's militia. On October 27, while the rebels were discussing what terms to ask for in negotiations for statehood with the United States, Madison issued a proclamation extending U.S. authority over West Florida up to the Perdido. Troops took possession of a small area between the Mississippi and Pearl Rivers, waiting the next move in the drama.

When the boundaries of the state of Louisiana were set in 1812, they included the occupied area of West Florida; the remaining portion, from the Pearl to the Perdido, was assigned as a county to the Mississippi Territory. Having gobbled up—de facto though not yet de jure—West Florida, Madison asked for and received authority to take East Florida on the theory that otherwise it might be seized by Britain. Thus it was that the appetite for Canada in the north was balanced by an equal desire to acquire the Floridas in the south. That these were not underground notions whispered among friends in private but bellowing cries heard loud and often is attested to by some of the writings and statements made in that period. "Where is it written in the book of fate," asked the Nashville *Clarion* on April 28, 1812, "that the American republic shall not stretch her limits from the Capes of the Chesapeake to Nootka Sound, from the Isthmus of Panama to Hudson Bay?" Richard M. Johnson of Kentucky avowed that he would "never die contented" until Britain was expelled "from North America, and her territories incorporated with the United States. . . . The waters of the St. Lawrence and the Mississippi interlock in a number of places, and the great Disposer of Human Events intended those two rivers should belong to the same people." That this beneficence from the Disposer of Human Events might have favorable economic consequences as well was emphasized by Congressman Peter B. Porter of New York. Since exports from Quebec alone, he said, were nearly $6 million a year, "we should be able in a short time to remunerate ourselves for all the spoliations she [Britain] has committed on our commerce."

The conquest of Canada from England at a time when Canada was defended by only 4,500 regular troops, and of the Floridas from Spain at a time when Spain was reeling in disarray, seemed so effortless a task that it inevitably suggested itself to influential Americans. "I trust I shall not be deemed presumptuous," said Henry Clay —the nation's leading war hawk—in February 1810, "when I state that I verily believe that the militia of Kentucky are alone competent to place Montreal and Upper Canada at your feet." Major General Andrew Jackson of Tennessee offered the President a trained militia of 2,500 men and gave his solemn word that, if commissioned, he would have them at Quebec in ninety days. Brigadier General George Mathews had occupied a section of East Florida before the War of 1812 began. It was a simple flight of fancy then to visualize the quick capture of these outposts and to consider their acquisition a valid purpose for making war. None of these stalwarts, it should be mentioned, suggested that Canada and the Floridas might determine for themselves whether to affiliate voluntarily with the United States, or to establish themselves as independent nations.

According to a resolution passed by the Massachusetts Senate: "The war was founded in falsehood, declared without necessity, and its real object was extent of territory by unjust conquests. . . ."

II

Like the naval war with France, the War of 1812 was a spin-off of events in Europe. During the long period of hostilities in the Old World, a tenuous peace prevailed for two years; but it was shattered on May 18, 1803, when Napoleon Bonaparte declared war on Britain. In doing so he unleashed a storm that battered Europe for more than a decade until he himself was safely incarcerated on St. Helena. Only thirty-three, and with an incredible string of victories already behind him, Napoleon dreamed of storming the last bastion, England, to make himself supreme master of the civilized world. Had he succeeded, events in America would have taken an entirely different course. He miscalculated, however. The island stronghold was defended by almost a thousand warships and 120,000 sailors. By 1805, after Lord Nelson's victory over the French and Spanish fleets at Cape Trafalgar, Britain was unchallenged master of the seas, safe from invasion. Simultaneously, as 180,000 of Napoleon's troops delivered a crushing blow against Austria and Prussia at Austerlitz, France became supreme on land. The war lapsed into a stalemate between a shark and a tiger, neither able to deliver the coup de grâce.

For the United States, the world's leading neutral shipper, the travail of Europe translated itself into an economic bonanza. "The whole situation," observes economic historian Harold U. Faulkner, "was remarkably similar to the early days of the First World War, 1914–1917, when the United States as the great neutral profited from supplying foodstuffs to the warring nations." Britain, unable to supply the West Indies during hostilities, was forced to suspend the Navigation Acts, which limited trade in the colonies to its own ships. This gave New Englanders access to a rich market. France, too, relaxed restrictions over its Caribbean empire. This was also true insofar as commerce with Europe was concerned; so that with relations suspended between the two enemies, American carriers filled the gap, supplying increased amounts of foodstuffs and other wares to both. The magnitude of American prosperity may be gauged from the fact that American tonnage engaged in foreign commerce grew from 124,000 in 1789 to 810,000 by 1807; the corollary statistic on exports was $21 million in 1792 to $108 million by 1807.

Canny Yankee shippers found ways to avoid embargoes and restrictive decrees much as their forefathers had done before the Revolution. The British, for instance, had promulgated a rule back in 1756 that trade prohibited in time of peace, such as that between the West Indies and Europe, would not be permitted in time of war. But the Americans designed a subterfuge called the "broken voyage." Sugar, by way of example, was taken on in the French West Indies, brought to an American port, unloaded for a time, then reloaded and re-exported to a European harbor under French control. As Marshall Smelser records, "the increase in tonnage and value of exports had no parallel in history. Grain and land prices rose similarly; sales to the West Indies built credits in Europe to pay for British manufactures; southern exports remained level, but the re-exporting maritime states almost quadrupled their shipments."

There were, of course, humiliating by-products to this prosperity. On the high seas His Majesty's navy seized American vessels on charges of unneutral behavior, and took them before prize courts which decided whether to hold the ships and confiscate their wares. Even when the American carriers were adjudged guiltless they had to pay certain court costs and sometimes lost the services of their crews. Moreover, British warships contemptuously treated the port of New York as if it were a London suburb, entering its territorial waters, searching vessels, and impressing seamen. This last practice was particularly abasing since it amounted to nothing less than international kidnapping. With all that, prices were so high and profits so lush that, despite the loss of some ships, wounded feelings were easily assuaged. There was certainly no feeling of crisis in the United States.

As of 1805, however, each of the stalemated opponents—and their allies—decided that the course of victory lay in trying to strangle the other economically. Since France could not defeat Britain at sea and Britain, as yet, could not defeat France on land, the way to win, each felt, was to choke off the other's trade. Britain blockaded ports under French rule, hoping thereby to starve its rival into submission, and the French responded by closing European ports to English wares—a sort of boycott to deny the enemy his markets. It was hoped this would force John Bull to close his factories, throw his workers on the streets, and succumb to depression and internal dissolution. The United States of course was a pivotal factor in this game, for if its ships delivered British goods to France or American foodstuffs to England unhindered, economic strangulation was impossible. It was necessary, therefore, to impose restrictions on the Yankees, and each side in the ensuing years did it with increasing severity. In July 1805 a British court, in the celebrated case of the *Essex*, ruled that a "broken voyage" trip would be considered a "continuous voyage" and the vessel subject to seizure unless the shipowner could prove that he had imported the goods into the United States in good faith and paid a duty on them. In effect this cut the ground from an important source of evasion. In November 1807 England tightened the vise a little further by orders-in-council that henceforth neutral ships would have to stop in Britain and pay a fee before being permitted to go on to French or French-controlled ports. Napoleon retaliated with the Milan Decree, declaring that any neutral vessel that sailed to England or its colonies was prey to seizure by French privateers. It was—in theory at least —an impossible situation for Yankee shippers. If they stopped off in London or even permitted themselves to be searched by an English frigate, they were subject to seizure by the French; and if they sallied forth to French-controlled ports without first paying tribute to His Majesty, they were liable to be nabbed by the other side.

Not unexpectedly, as in all such instances, neutral America cried out that freedom of the seas was sacrosanct and should not be abrogated in favor of the selfish interests of any single nation. When the *Essex* decision was handed down, protest demonstrations took place in the United States and the *Salem Register,* speaking what was on many minds, commented that "never will neutrals be perfectly safe till free goods make free ships or till England loses two or three naval battles." James Madison presented a seventy-thousand-word document to Congress—of "massive unreadability," according to Smelser—showing that the Rule of 1756 was "immoral." From the English—and French—points of view, the materialistic Yankees were thinking only of base profits. Both London and Paris considered themselves leaders of progressive coalitions against the other side's tyranny, and could not understand why the United States would not sacrifice a few million in trade to assure their particular victory. Didn't the Americans realize, asked a British lawyer, James Stephen, in an 1805 pamphlet, "that the subjugation of England would be fatal to the last hope of liberty in Europe," and that the United States itself would be in jeopardy from France should England fall? "The neutral powers," he wrote, "can subsist without this newly acquired commerce; but Great Britain cannot long exist as a nation, if bereft of her ancient means of offensive maritime war." Moreover, there was something fraudulent in the Yankee pose of neutrality, since re-exports to France were in effect a "war in disguise" by the United States.

London also had a rationale for the impressment of thousands of American sailors which conformed snugly to its own interests. Unable to secure enough volunteer sailors, England sent out press gangs, on land and sea, to seize any Britisher with enough bone and muscle to work a ship. It was not a new practice; it is said in fact to have occurred sporadically over four hundred years. British sailors worked for low wages (seven dollars a month) under abominable conditions and were therefore prone to jump ship, especially in American ports, where monthly wages were three or four times higher. According to Lord Nelson, in the first stage of the war with France before temporary peace in 1801, there had been no fewer than 42,000 maritime deserters. Twelve British ships were unable to sail from Norfolk in 1804 because their seamen had taken off for better positions. A standard technique for a disaffected English sailor was to flee his ship while in port, buy fraudulent American naturalization certificates—called protection papers—and sign on with an American vessel at more favorable wages. If the U.S. government did not entirely encourage this system, it did nothing to stop it. One enterprising American lady was said to have in her home a cradle full of "protection papers," for sale as low as a dollar each. According to a British claim in 1809, two thirds of the 60,000 men in the American merchant marine were deserters carrying these fraudulent certificates. With a navy that required 120,000 men and a commercial fleet that needed 120,000 more, the problem of deserters was obviously a serious one for His Majesty's government. It might have been solved by raising wages, but such an approach did not appear auspicious to Tory-minded English entrepreneurs.

Instead press gangs, like commissioned locusts, pounced on able-bodied subjects wherever they could be found, and impressed them. Off the American coast, as well as on the high seas, British frigates stopped American vessels to divest them of English sailors. H.M.S. *Leander* in 1806 often held up a dozen or two dozen Yankee merchantmen at one time off the New York coast pending search. By far the largest portion of sailors impressed were Englishmen, but the Crown was not too squeamish about snatching an American here and there, especially if he had no papers and could not prove nationality, or—more perniciously—if he was a naturalized American citizen. The British did not recognize naturalization, insisting that once a Britisher, always a Britisher. An Irish-American with a brogue, who pronounced "peas" as "paise," might be unceremoniously hauled away as a British subject. All told, it is estimated that 6,000 to 10,000 U.S. citizens were impressed, many of whom died in service. According to Lord Castlereagh in 1811, only 1,600 Americans had been illegally seized.

On June 22, 1807, a U.S. frigate, the *Chesapeake*, was hailed by the British frigate *Leopard* ten miles out of Norfolk. The American captain, thinking he was being stopped to take aboard a packet of letters for Europe, sensed no problem. But when he was asked to submit to search and refused, the *Leopard* fired three broadsides at the hapless *Chesapeake*, killing three and wounding eighteen. English seamen thereupon boarded the American ship and hustled off four alleged deserters—the object of their search. Of the four, it turned out, three were Americans who had previously been impressed, and only one a genuine British citizen—who was eventually court-martialed in Halifax and hanged from the yardarm of his own ship. The reaction to this incident in the United States was furious. Elbridge Gerry reflected American sentiment when he said that "a state of warfare" was "preferable to such a state of national insult and degredation." According to historian Thomas A. Bailey, "not since the XYZ days had the American people been more united on an issue." Madison, in a letter to Monroe, noted that "war is proclaimed at every meeting, or rather by every mouth, which is not British." Had Jefferson willed it there would have been war then, instead of five years later.

In 1807, however, the Republican President was still intent on peace, just as he had been in the crisis with France a decade before. He was not a pacifist—as was proven by the war with Tripoli—but he nurtured the hope that further territorial largesse would fall into American hands as Louisiana had done, through purchase or negotiations, not war. Moreover, he was still aware of the internal weaknesses of the adolescent republic, beset by sectional and class differences, troubles with the Indians, and separatist tendencies. The responsibility of knitting a *United* States weighed heavily upon him.

The threat of separatism, though not often remembered today, was no idle one. For example, Brigadier General James Wilkinson of Kentucky served as a secret Spanish agent for twenty years after 1787, during which time he was paid two thousand dollars a year for spying on his country and plotting the detachment of Kentucky and trans-Appalachia from the nation. As late as 1807 the Spanish minister in Washington, the Marquis de Yrujo, reported to Madrid: "Wilkinson detests his present government, and the separation of the Western States has long been his favorite plan. . . . [He] is entirely devoted to us." Senator William Blount of Tennessee intrigued with the British in 1797 to disjoin the Southwest, and, though expelled from the Senate by a vote of 25 to 1, was chosen by his fellow Tennesseans as president of their upper house. Extremists in the Federalist camp, such as William Smith and Uriah Tracy, talked of secession by the North in the hectic 1790's, and when Louisiana was added to the country in 1803 and Ohio admitted to statehood, "separation" again became a live issue in New England. Senator Timothy Pickering and other leaders of Massachusetts and Connecticut, fearing that the balance of power was running against their section of the country, talked of establishing a Northern Confederacy of New England and New York, divorced from "the corrupt and corrupting influence and oppression of the aristocratic democrats of the South." Vice-President Aaron Burr, who decided to run for governor of New York after being dropped from the Republican ticket in 1804, offered to become the confederacy's president if successful in his state campaign. A year later, the same Burr—after killing Alexander Hamilton in a duel at Weehawken, New Jersey—entered into new intrigues with the British minister to sever Louisiana and perhaps the Mississippi Territory from the United States. None of the plots succeeded, but they testify to the fragile character of the Union at the time, and explain to some extent why Jefferson was hesitant about making war.

But if not war, what then? The President's initial response to the *Chesapeake* incident was to order all British ships from American ports. Months later, at his request, Congress passed the famous Embargo Act, which prohibited Americans from exporting any goods to a foreign nation either by sea or by land. U.S. shipping was limited exclusively, except under special permit, to American coasts, and then only if the shipowner gave bond he would not take his cargo overseas. Jefferson reckoned that since nearly half of England's imports and a third of its exports were destined to and from the United States, economic coercion would force His Majesty's government to mend its ways. Officially exports fell from $108 million in 1807 to $22 million in 1808, and tens of thousands of seamen found themselves unemployed. In defending the policy, one of Jefferson's supporters, Senator William Branch Giles of Virginia, argued that if the embargo had not been instituted the European belligerents would have seized $100 million worth of American merchandise and $20 million worth of its ships, as well as impressed thousands of its seamen. According to Giles, "the embargo laws have saved this enormous amount of property, and this number of seamen, which, without them, would have forcibly gone into the hands of our enemies, to pamper their arrogance, stimulate their injustice, and increase their means of annoyance."

Be that as it may, Britain did not yield to the pressure, for it found alternative supplies and markets in Latin America, Turkey, and elsewhere. Moreover, its 1808 crops were so astonishingly good that its reliance on American foodstuffs diminished apace. Equally important perhaps, American shippers evaded the embargo wholesale. Illicit trade moved into Canada either by land or on large rafts guarded by armed men—in defiance of state militia and revenue officers, many of whom cheerfully accepted bribes to look the other way. Another device was to secure licenses from state governors to ship flour along the coast, then set the ship sailing toward Europe. The governors, wise in the ways of the world, issued these papers with abandon, and sometimes at unseemly profit. Every other technique, from forged papers to midnight sailings from obscure inlets, was employed to evade the law. Not a few entrepreneurs who engaged in foreign commerce fared as well as—or better than—before the embargo.

Nevertheless, the embargo was immensely unpopular with the general public. Not only were the wharves and boatyards of New England reduced to minimal operations, but the farmers inland were badly hurt. "In 12 hours after the news of the Embargo," reported a Virginia planter, "flour fell from $5.50 to $2.50 at this place, and tobacco . . . and everything in proportion, and God only knows the results." With curtailed exports, planters and merchants suffered severely; many were forced into bankruptcy, even as their barns and warehouses filled with produce. By the end of 1808 the country was gripped with a self-imposed depression, and in New England, town meetings were calling for secession. In February 1809 there were serious plans afoot to call a New England conference, in the spirit of the Kentucky and Virginia resolves of a decade back, to unilaterally "nullify" the embargo. By now all the state governments of New England were in Federalist hands (in 1807, only Connecticut had been) and many a Republican in that area was disaffected with Jefferson's policies. On March 1, 1809, therefore, just three days before the sage of Monticello left office, Congress decided to repeal the ill-fated legislation in favor of a more moderate form of economic coercion—the nonintercourse act. Under the new bill foreign trade was reinstated, with the single proviso that American ships take no wares to ports in Europe under British or French control. This was modified the following year by a strange law called Macon's Bill No. 2, which reopened intercourse with the two warring states, but offered the carrot that if either repealed its hostile decrees against the United States, Washington would suspend trade with the other.

Historians differ sharply as to whether economic coercion could have worked—if the American people had been more patient. Samuel Eliot Morison concludes that it was Jefferson's "greatest mistake. It altered the policy of Britain or of Napoleon not by one hair, it failed to protect the American merchant marine, and it convinced many good people that the Virginia Dynasty was bound to be Napoleonic." On the other hand, there were a number of occasions when it seemed that either Britain or France would come to terms with Washington, which leads Louis Martin Sears, in his book on the embargo, to conclude that it "came near enough to success to vindicate its sponsor as a practical statesman." Diplomatic expert Thomas A. Bailey observes that "the cumulative effect of economic coercion did contribute to the repeal of the Orders in Council. In the end Jefferson's policy triumphed; but America was not patient enough to reap the benefits." Jefferson himself was convinced that Congress had been "driven by treason [the threat of civil war in the North]" to retreat "from the high and wise ground we had taken. . . ." In any case, as it turned out, war was much more costly than embargo, and quite as unsuccessful.

III

Despite the embargo, the Democratic-Republican candidate, James Madison, was elected president in 1808—though by a much smaller electoral margin than Jefferson had received four years earlier. Madison, described by Washington Irving as "poor Jemmy . . . a withered little apple-john," was in his late fifties, short in stature (five feet six inches), an old veteran of Revolutionary days, erudite and scholarly like his two predecessors, but lacking spark. He was indefatigable, he slept little, often waking to jot down an idea for a memorandum; he was unusually clearheaded in private discussion, yet devoid of the ability to communicate with the public. He was a poor speaker, thin-voiced, and much too detached from gut-level politics to maintain effective control over his party or his nation. Among his assets was a pretty wife, the former Dolly Payne Todd, a Quaker, eighteen years his junior, whom he had married at age forty-three. Dolly Madison achieved a certain popularity of her own with "harvest suppers" at the White House and her elegant clothes, but it was far from enough to make her husband a public hero. "Poor Jemmy" in many respects was cast for the same role as John Adams, caught between the war hawks on the one hand, and the Federalists and Quids—peace Republicans—on the other.

Madison, like Jefferson, was committed to the policy of economic coercion, and within six weeks after being inaugurated seemed to have found a formula for making it work. Eagerly entering into negotiations with David Erskine, the British minister to Washington, who was married to an American, Madison signed what he thought was a firm agreement for reestablishing normal relations. While the *modus vivendi* ignored the issue of impressment, it won a pledge that Britain would rescind its orders-in-council in return for America continuing nonintercourse with France. "Great and Glorious News," read an extra of the New Hampshire *Patriot.* "Our differences with Great Britain Amicably Settled"; and six hundred Yankee vessels took off for London on the appointed day when the agreement was to go into effect—only to find it was a false alarm. Erskine, it seems, had exceeded his instructions and was repudiated by his superiors; a distraught Madison, chafing at what he later defined as a "mixture of fraud and folly," could do naught else but reimpose the restrictions on trade with England.

Having failed to come to terms with the British, the next suggested step was to make peace with Napoleon. The French Emperor, like the British ministry, felt he had little to fear from the paper colossus overseas. In March 1810 he issued his Rambouillet decree confiscating $10 million worth of American ships and supplies in his ports. Five months later, however, seeing an opening in Macon's Bill No. 2 to drive a wedge between London and Washington, he let it be known that "His Majesty loves the Americans." As proof of his new affection, Napoleon had his foreign minister, the Duke de Cadore, send an ambiguous missive to the American minister stating that after November 1 decrees against neutral shipping would be automatically revoked—"it being understood that the English are to revoke their orders-in-council." Madison was so captivated by this prospect for resolving differences with the French that he issued a proclamation on November 2 giving Britain three months to repeal its orders-in-council or see the reintroduction of nonintercourse. Once again Madison was gulled by a foreign potentate, for while he kept his side of what he considered to be a bargain, Napoleon imposed new duties on U.S. trade and ordered all American ships that had arrived after an early date in 1809 seized and sold.

In this indeterminate state of affairs—despite a significant improvement in exports, imports, and foreign-trade tonnage—war fever in the United States continued to rise. If it was directed more against London than Paris it may be because by now Napoleon was occupied with his campaign against Russia, finding little time to concentrate on Uncle Sam, while Britain loomed as a direct, tangible threat to American independence. It was arming Tecumseh's Indians in the West, and with its all-powerful navy seemed determined to reduce the United States to nothing more than a protectorate. On May 16, 1811, the American navy, in a moment of glory, avenged the *Chesapeake* incident of four years earlier. The *President,* a 44-gun frigate, attacked His Majesty's 20-gun corvette

Little Belt, killing and maiming 32 English sailors. But this did not calm the storm, for by now matters were drifting toward war without a single immediate incident—such as Pearl Harbor or the sinking of the *Maine*—to spark it. By now, too, the brash call was being heard more frequently: "On to Canada."

IV

In many minds, the invasion of Canada and the Floridas was simply a good strategy for countering Britain's control of the seas. These were the obvious places to strike for a nation which lacked a credible navy. The advantage of taking Canada, said a Richmond newspaper, "will not accrue so much from the tenure of them as a conquest . . . but from the very important consequences which their loss will occasion to the British." Others, however, lusted for new domain, pure and simple. Either way, the Canada-Florida mood was fed by a new generation of Republicans mounting the stage, who were at once more egalitarian and more nationalist than their predecessors. Henry Clay of Kentucky, leader of the hawks, was in his early thirties; John C. Calhoun of South Carolina, in his late twenties. Felix Grundy of Tennessee, Peter B. Porter of Buffalo, New York, and Richard M. Johnson of Kentucky were all relatively young men. Five or six of the new Republicans, including Clay and Calhoun, roomed in the same boardinghouse, where they plotted together the steps by which America should be brought to battle. Hostile to Britain, generally pro-French, these men manifested the spirit of what was called Young America—independent, prideful, aggressive. And though they shared a democratic philosophy 180 degrees removed from that of the late Alexander Hamilton, they exhibited an instinct for expansion that matched or exceeded his.

Among these men, whom Josiah Quincy called "young politicians with their pin-feathers unshed," the guiding spirit was unquestionably a debonair lawyer from Kentucky, variously called "Gallant Harry of the West," "the Cock of Kentucky," "the Judas of the West," "the Western Star." Henry Clay, one of a large brood sired by a dignified but undistinguished Baptist minister, was born in April 1777 and brought up in a section of Hanover County, Virginia, picturesquely called "the Slashes." His father died when Henry was four, leaving the mother with a 464-acre farm and eighteen slaves— not much by the standards of planter aristocracy, but enough for modest comfort. A few years later the widow married a kindly gentleman from Richmond who took a keen interest in his stepson. The boy had only three years of formal education at the log school in the

Slashes run by a drunken Englishman, but this was not too unusual for the backwoods those days. At fourteen, the tall, thin youngster with a long neck, blue eyes, light hair, wide mouth, and awkward gait was apprenticed to a retail store in Richmond. With the help of his stepfather, he then moved into the clerk's office of the High Court of Chancery; a few years later, after joining the attorney general's office to study, he emerged with a law degree.

With little more than this license in his pocket, Clay, now twenty, joined his mother and stepfather on the trek to Lexington, then the metropolis of Kentucky. With two thousand residents, black and white, Lexington, apart from being an "industrial" center, was considered a cultural mecca, "the Athens of the West." Here the Western Star quickly established his reputation as a great criminal lawyer, his fluent tongue and knack of finding rapport with a jury saving one accused murderer after another from the death penalty. Every now and then he filled in as prosecutor and on one such occasion argued for the execution of a slave who had killed his overseer under extreme duress. Had it been a white man, Clay admitted, he would have been freed on the theory of justifiable homicide, but since he was a slave whose duty it was to submit, he was properly charged with murder. Clay later regretted this decision to prosecute. He also defended Aaron Burr in November 1806 on the charge of organizing the planned invasion of Spanish territory, and secured his acquittal —another deed he lamented. But this was part of his nature. He was a relatively easy-going man, with supreme self-confidence. Not unnaturally he had married into the blueblood family of Colonel Thomas Hart, and what with his own practice and managing his father-in-law's legal affairs, was able to invest in land, business enterprises, and horses. He loved to gamble heavily, play the ponies, chase women, and drink wine.

Friends called Clay "flexible," enemies called him "opportunist." On the whole, however, he was a fervid Jeffersonian democrat. He championed the gradual emancipation of slaves and the democratization of state government. He castigated the Alien and Sedition Acts before a large audience and was carried off on the shoulders of enthusiastic listeners. He was, in other words, made to order for Western politics in the early days of the republic. Elected to the Kentucky legislature in 1803, he was appointed to a short term in the United States Senate only three years later when he was three months under the legal age of thirty. New Hampshire's Senator William Plummer described Clay at this time as a "man of honor and integrity," but also "a man of pleasure, fond of amusements. He is a great favorite with the ladies; is in all parties of pleasure; out almost

every evening; reads but little. . . . He is a man of talents; is eloquent; but not nice or accurate in his distinctions. He declaims more
than he reasons."

In 1810 Clay was again appointed to an unexpired term in the
Senate, distinguishing himself with an impassioned defense of President Madison's proclamation of October 27, 1810, claiming West
Florida for the United States. If Spain's ally, Britain, were to declare
war on the young republic as a result of this seizure, Clay hoped
"that all our hearts will unite in a bold and vigorous vindication of
our rights." Not long thereafter, the Cock of Kentucky, elected to the
livelier House of Representatives, was placed in a more favorable
position for "vindication of our rights." When the Twelfth Congress
assembled in November 1811, almost half the members of the House,
61 of 142, were, like Clay, serving their first term. Of these new men,
9 were Federalists, a few peace Republicans—Quids they were
called—but 30 were determined war advocates. With saucy imper-
tinence the hawks elevated Henry Clay to the speakership of the
House, replacing an old Revolutionary War general, Joseph B.
Varnum, who had moved up to the Senate. To bypass old and experienced hands for a young newcomer was unprecedented, but Young
America was expressing its misgivings of those who still sought diplomatic solutions. Some of its stalwarts favored seizure of the Floridas, others of Canada, and still others of both, but there was a
general unanimity among them for rearmament, war, and conquest.

Seldom has any political force been so frank about its war aims.
As early as February 1810, Henry Clay, while protesting that "no
man wants peace more than I," noted the advantages of ousting
Britain from Canada and extinguishing "the torch that lights up savage warfare." Is "it nothing," he asked, "to acquire the entire fur
trade connected with that country . . . ?" "This war, if carried on
successfully," said Felix Grundy, "will have its advantages. We shall
drive the British from our Continent. . . . I therefore feel anxious
not only to add the Floridas to the South, but the Canadas to the
North of this empire." The seizure of West Florida, consummated in
the fall of 1810, whetted the appetite for booty elsewhere. "To me,
sir," said an eager member of the House from New Hampshire, "it
appears that the Author of Nature has marked our limits in the
south by the Gulf of Mexico; and on the north by the regions of
eternal frost." The *National Intelligencer* of November 28, 1811,
noted that "the country around Lake Ontario is almost everywheres
[sic] extremely fertile, particularly that part which lies at the western end and on the Niagara River. Perhaps this is excelled by no
part of the world." Making its point stronger in February 1812, the

same paper commented drily: "All agree that Canada must be ours.
. . ." If incorporated into the Union it would soon hold "a larger
population than the present population of the United States." There
were, to be sure, endless lands in the prairies across the Mississippi,
but these were considered unhealthy and they lacked water for
drinking, or timber for log cabins, fences, and firewood. Canada, on
the other hand, though inhabited by a sparse 310,000 people (as
against 7 million in the United States), was rich in these resources.
A few ambitious souls even cast eyes beyond the Floridas and Canada. "Behold the empire of Mexico," cried a Nashville writer. "Here
it is that the statesmen shall see an accession of Territory sufficient
to double the extent of the republic." Charles and Mary Beard comment that "if the whole program could be carried into effect, the
'new United States' of which Clay spoke would include the continent of North America."

This was the direction of affairs as the Twelfth Congress assembled. In the speaker's chair Clay was dignified and composed, but
he surrendered the chair frequently for florid presentations of his
personal aggressive views and he used his power to pack committees
with hawks. The all-important nine-man Foreign Relations Committee, chaired by Peter B. Porter, included five war advocates. David
R. Williams, Langdon Cheves, and Ezekiel Bacon, all on the martial
side, were placed at the head of committees on Military Affairs, the
Navy, and Ways and Means. Congress convened on November 4,
1811, just three days before William Henry Harrison pushed the
Prophet, Tecumseh's brother, into oblivion. Shortly thereafter
Grundy announced that the Committee on Foreign Relations would
soon recommend war, and Peter Porter issued a report on November
29 listing all the futile efforts to have Britain repeal its orders-in-
council. Soon a bill was passed authorizing enlargement of the
7,000-man army to 35,000 regulars—with bounties of $16 a head
and a promise to each soldier of 160 acres of land on discharge—and
the President was also given the power to recruit 50,000 volunteer
militia. The navy, so impossibly uncompetitive with the British, was
voted only $300,000 to repair three frigates, but it was assumed that
armed privateers would take up some of the slack by preying on
English ships. In March, resolutions carried to tax the states $3 mil-
lion and solicit loans of $11 million more. That same month, adding
fuel to the fires, President Madison published the indiscreet correspondence between an American spy for the British, John Henry,
and Sir James Craig, governor general of Canada. Among the
fourteen letters, for which the chief executive had paid $50,000, was
one of February 6, 1809, which speculated that "if the Federalists of

the Eastern States should be successful in obtaining that decided influence which may enable them to direct the public opinion, it is not improbable that . . . they will exert that influence to bring about a separation from the general Union." In that likely event, said Craig, Britain wanted to be quickly informed as to "how far . . . they [the Federalists] would look up to England for assistance, or be disposed to enter in a connexion with us." Even though the names of the Federalist leaders were deleted by Henry, the missives created a sensation, confirming for many that Britain would not rest content until she had dismembered the Union.

Simultaneously there occurred a comic-opera invasion. The Madison administration, having added West Florida to its laurels in 1810, secretly instructed Brigadier General George Mathews to take East Florida—if the governor or other local authorities were so disposed. The people, however, were disinterested in becoming part of the United States, if only because as a Spanish colony their trade was booming. In the face of embargoes and nonintercourse, Amelia Island near the Georgia border had become a major shipping center from which and to which hundreds of vessels smuggled produce and lumber. Had there been a vote, it is unlikely that Floridians would have yielded their prosperity to the nebulous glories of Union. But Mathews did not wait to ascertain the opinion of either officialdom or the populace. He forced the town of Fernandina to surrender on threat it would be bombarded by U.S. ships, then imposed a sympathetic Floridian, William Craig, as governor, and at the head of new volunteers from Georgia, he marched toward the capital, St. Augustine. Here, however, the campaign bogged down. Had the war with Britain begun by this time, it is possible that Congress would have authorized continuation of the effort. As it was, a bill offered by Grundy, empowering Madison to take the territory, passed the House but failed in the Senate, where the war fever was not yet at the same pitch. Under the circumstances Madison was embarrassed by Mathews' adventure; the seventy-two-year-old and virtually illiterate general was repudiated, and the captured land relinquished.

The Mathews mishap, however, was only a small setback for the hawks; each week the cry for war grew by a few decibels. In April Congress clapped a ninety-day embargo on trade with England. On June 1, 1812, having waited for a last-minute word from London indicating a change in position, Madison sent his war message to Congress. In it the emphasis was placed on the impressment of sailors by His Majesty's government and the abridgment of neutral shipping rights, as well as the incitement of Indians. The vote, though carefully manipulated by Clay in the House, was, as already indicated, not overwhelming. And had the President or Congress known of developments in London at the time, it might have been even narrower—or it might have been defeated. For on June 23, Foreign Secretary Lord Castlereagh suspended the hated orders-in-council for a year, and optimistic British shippers immediately dispatched $20 million worth of cargo to the United States. Due to the communications lag, this news did not arrive in Washington until August.

Whether earlier information of the suspension would have tipped the scales toward peace is speculative, for there was a welter of motives for going to war. The depressed price of farm commodities had conditioned those in the western and southern regions to see war as a panacea. Thus the *Lexington Reporter* of December 10, 1811, on learning of the plans of the war hawks, exulted that "our government will at last make war, to produce a market for our Tobacco, Flour, and Cotton." For others there was, as John Randolph of Roanoke, leader of the Quids, pointed out, "that rich vein of Tennessee land, which is said to be even better on the other side of the lake than on this." It was, he said, "agrarian cupidity, not maritime right [that] urges the war. Ever since the report of the Committee on Foreign Relations came into the House, we have heard but one word—like the whip-poor-will, but one eternal monotonous tone— Canada! Canada! Canada!"

V

In the mythology that sustains the American ego, the United States has never lost a war. But if wars are fought to achieve specific political objectives, the War of 1812 was a total and monumental failure. The peace treaty concluded at Ghent, Belgium, on Christmas Eve 1814 contained no provisions prohibiting search and seizure of American ships or impressment of American sailors. Nor did the United States gain any new territory. Though Canada had only 4,- 500 regular troops originally, Henry Clay's optimism about how easy it would be for the Kentucky militia to take it proved foolhardy. So did the naïve prediction by John C. Calhoun "that in four weeks from the time a declaration of war is heard on our frontier, the whole of upper Canada and a part of lower Canada will be in our power." Canada remained British. And though the Floridas were partly overrun by American forces, some of the posts seized had to be given up after hostilities were over, and it was not until 1819 that an enervated Spain finally yielded this part of its empire. A case can be made that the Indian menace was checked, that manufacturing was stimulated by the British blockade, that the nation won greater economic independence from Britain, but these results were probably inevitable anyway, and in any case they were not the substance of the war aims.

There were, of course, heroic moments in the war to fatten national pride. As the British fleet bombarded the defenders of Baltimore during the night of September 13–14, 1814, Francis Scott Key, a prisoner on one of the British ships, seeing the flag still aloft over Fort McHenry "by the dawn's early light," composed "The Star Spangled Banner." There was Captain Oliver H. Perry's victory in Lake Erie and the seizure of many enemy ships, despite England's naval superiority, by the 526 American privateers. There were Harrison's exploits against Tecumseh and Jackson's against the Creeks; and there was Jackson's capture of Pensacola and his great success in the battle of New Orleans, January 1815, some days after the peace treaty had been negotiated at Ghent. The dying words of Captain James Lawrence after a nine-minute duel between his *Chesapeake* and the English warship *Shannon*—"Don't give up the ship; blow her up"—became a byword for the American navy.

But to compensate, there were equal or greater moments of distress and humiliation. In the first land war since the Revolution—except for engagements with Indians—the army on the whole acquitted itself very poorly. Five attempts to gain a foothold in Canada during the last half of 1812 were disastrous. Governor William Hull of Michigan Territory retreated in disarray after crossing into Canada from Detroit, and in August 1812 surrendered his army. Shortly thereafter Major General Samuel Hopkins confronted a mutiny in his 4,000-man Kentucky militia; when he asked for 500 volunteers to move on Canada, not a single man stepped forward. On the eastern side of Canada, Captain John E. Wool, after having beaten Tecumseh's friend General Brock, was himself surrounded and captured when a few thousand New York militia declined to come to his aid. In November Brigadier General Alexander Smyth carried his army across the Niagara on boats, encouraging them with such statements as "tomorrow will be memorable in the annals of the United States," but losing his nerve as he surveyed the Canadians on the opposite bank, called off the battle and came back again. Major General Henry Dearborn, another aged chieftain, reached twenty miles above Plattsburg on his trek toward Montreal, when his militia refused to budge another inch. A year later General James Wilkinson's campaign fared only slightly better, and shortly thereafter the British burned Buffalo and Black Rock, and seized Fort Niagara, which they held until the end of the war. Even on sea the successes on the American side were far out of perspective. The

United States might revel in the naval victories of Captain Isaac Hull and his *Constitution* or Captain Stephen Decatur's capture of His Majesty's frigate *Macedonian,* but these were of trivial consequence for the British. The Royal Navy was losing less than 1 percent of its effective fleet, while the midget U.S. navy was being reduced by a fifth.

Indeed, until Napoleon abdicated in April 1814, the war in America was a small sideshow for the British. News of its declaration rated only a few obscure paragraphs in popular London magazines, and it was only when the threat to Canada became serious and after the first American triumphs at sea that it began to attract due attention. Henry Goulburn, later a British negotiator at Ghent, recorded in his diary that "the declaration of war was unexpected. The Canadas in common with other colonies had been denuded of troops to supply a large force in Spain." Until it could pay more serious attention to the western hemisphere, Britain contented itself with defending Canada, clapping a blockade on American ports (though exempting New England until April 1814), and small raids. Such measures could not win a war but they did contain it temporarily. By early 1813 Chesapeake Bay became unsafe for shipping, and Decatur's vessels were locked in at New London for the duration. Foreign trade in 1814 slumped to 11 percent of what it had been in 1811, though illegal commerce made the figure higher. With Britannia ruling the waves, its forces occupied a hundred miles of coast in Maine—without challenge from the thousands of men of military age in that district—and landed small parties of 100 or 150 men elsewhere to steal, burn, and create general havoc.

All of this was distressing enough to a war-hawk faction that had anticipated a cakewalk to conquest. It turned from distress to humiliation when Britain could finally concentrate on the American upstart. In August 1814, General Sir George Prevost, reinforced by 10,000 veterans from overseas, marched on Plattsburg to relieve pressure on Canada. It was an unsuccessful effort, but, as a diversion, 4,000 English troops were sent into the Chesapeake Bay area to destroy a flotilla of gunboats and attack Washington and Baltimore. For the first and only time in America's history since the Revolution, its capital fell into the hands of a foreign power. Dolly Madison's dinner was still on the table at the Executive Mansion on August 24, 1814, when the British occupied the city. Two English generals ate the meal, while President Madison fled across the river, and the enemy proceeded to burn down the White House, the Capitol, the Department buildings, and the office of the *National Intelligencer.* The Patent Office was saved by a plea from its chief, Wil-

liam Thornton, that it was the repository of information needed by
the world at large as much as the United States. But Americans
themselves set fire to the Navy Yard and its ships to keep them from
the British. Next day, a rainstorm doused some of the flames, and
the British withdrew to their transports to prepare for the next assault, on Baltimore. Here they met stiffer resistance and were forced
to withdraw, but the Washington raid had been enough to bolster
their spirits for a long time.

VI

On the home front the War of 1812 created deep fissures that again
approached the outer boundaries of national disintegration. The opposition centered in New England and the Middle States, and while
the Federalists and peace Republicans were by no means an overwhelming majority even there, they left an imprint on every phase
of the war. The regular army, for instance, was never built up to
even half its authorized strength. Fifty thousand one-year volunteers
were authorized but only 10,000 were recruited. The militia, time
and again, proved useless. Only 7,000 out of a potential 95,000
turned up for the defense of Washington. At a critical moment,
when the capital was being razed, Massachusetts—with 70,000
well-trained militia—and Rhode Island and Connecticut, withdrew
their forces from federal command and entered into a pact of mutual defense. The New Englanders made it clear repeatedly that
while they would defend their own territory they would not supply
forces for an invasion beyond their borders. A proposal by Monroe
in 1814, when it seemed as if the war would go on indefinitely, to
conscript 100,000 *regular* troops, was watered down in the Senate to
a draft of 80,000 for two-year terms in the *militia,* and further modified in the House to one-year terms. An amendment by New England's Daniel Webster to reduce it to six months failed by a single
vote. "Where is it written in the Constitution," Webster demanded,
"that you may take children from their parents and compel them to
fight the battles of any war in which the folly or the wickedness of
Government may engage it?" The lower house in Massachusetts
called on people to form a "peace party" throughout the country. "If
your sons," it said, "must be torn from you by conscriptions, consign
them to the care of God; but let there be no volunteers except for
defensive war."

Money, like men, was similarly withheld from the national government. Treasury Secretary Albert Gallatin, though empowered to
raise $11 million in loans, was able to lure out of hiding only $6 mil-

lion, of which a mere million came from rich New England. The war loan of 1814, $10.9 million, had to be sold at a 20 percent discount; even then only $377,000 was raised in Massachusetts. Despite the usual bleatings about heavy taxes, deposits of paper money in 33 Massachusetts banks skyrocketed threefold from June 1810 to January 1814—and gold even more—yet little of this largesse was loaned out to the federal government. Hezekiah Niles, of *Niles' Weekly Register,* asserted that while the British people were willing to spend $25 per capita on their wars, it was "contemptible" that Americans were unwilling to put out $2 per capita.

Even worse, Yankee merchants continued to do business with the enemy as if nothing were amiss. They delivered beef and flour to Canada, accepting British bills of exchange for their provisions, which in turn were sold openly in Boston at a one-fifth discount. "Supplies of the most essential kinds," Madison complained in a special message to Congress on December 9, 1813, "find their way not only to British ports and British armies at a distance, but the armies in our neighborhood with which our own are contending, derive from our ports and outlets a subsistence attainable with difficulty, if at all, from other sources." According to Henry Adams, who examined Canadian archives, New Englanders even provided some specie to pay British troops.

The mood of the United States was understandably grim toward the end of 1814, with the war going poorly, bankruptcy facing the Treasury, a danger of British-sponsored secession in the Mississippi Valley, and a more significant threat of secession from New England. In the negotiations with American emissaries at Ghent, the British demanded that the United States give up a large area of the Northwest as a buffer state for the Indians. It would include one third of Ohio, two thirds of Indiana, and almost all of what is now Illinois, Wisconsin, and Michigan. In addition the United States was asked to cede that portion of Massachusetts now in British hands (part of the future state of Maine), yield certain fishing prerogatives gained in the peace pact of 1783, and abandon military and naval stations on the Great Lakes. The toughness of the British stand, when it became known, exacerbated the defeatist mood in America. The Boston *Repertory* urged "physical force" to stop the war, a proposal that Henry Clay denounced as simple treason. Senator Timothy Pickering, of the extreme Federalist wing, wrote to John Lowell that "if the British succeed in the expedition against New Orleans— and if they have tolerable leaders I see no reason to doubt of their success—I shall consider the Union as severed. This consequence I deem inevitable. I do not expect a single representative in the next Congress from the Western States."

The climax of moves that might have led to secession or civil war came with the Hartford Convention, which assembled nine days before a settlement was reached in far-off Ghent. The twenty-six men who gathered at the State House in Hartford—official representatives from Massachusetts, Rhode Island, and Connecticut, and from local groups in Vermont and New Hampshire—were older and more prudent than many whom they represented, but their report implied a threat of civil war in the future if they did not get their way. Except in case of "absolute necessity," they said, it was wrong to plan for "a severance of the Union . . . especially in time of war." They felt however that "the time for change is at hand." The Convention issued a document which in effect was a manifesto of autonomy for the commercial states. Without mincing words it said that these states were in danger of being ruined by the farming sectors of the South and West, and that drastic constitutional modifications were needed to repair the balance. The Convention urged that the states rather than the federal government assume control over the armed forces from their own areas, and retain "a reasonable portion of the taxes collected within the said States." To reduce the power of the planter states it was urged that slaves be excluded from the computation of residents (each slave was then counted as three fifths of a person in determining how many congressmen and electoral votes a state was entitled to). Another demand called for a two-thirds vote—instead of a majority—for passing on the admission of new states, declaring an embargo, or entering into war— except in cases of *direct* invasion. Finally, the Convention insisted that the states "separately or in concert" should be "empowered to assume upon themselves the defense of their territory. . . ." In other words a New England Confederation would decide for itself when and how to engage in war. This arrangement, if it would not have severed the Union, certainly would have decentralized the nation to the point of impotency. In effect, what New England was now demanding was something similar to what the Republicans asked for in the 1790's in the Virginia and Kentucky Resolves—the right of each individual state "to interpose its authority" against the federal government.

Though the tone of the report was moderate it left the impression that if nothing were done to assuage the resentments of New England, further steps—of a more dire nature—would be taken at a second meeting scheduled for Boston next June 15. Indicative of the militancy—as well as inaccuracy—in some quarters was the comment of the *Boston Sentinel* while the Convention was in progress: "New England is unanimous. And we announce our irrevocable decree that the tyrannical oppression of those who at present usurp the powers of the Constitution is beyond endurance. And we will resist it." A small town in Massachusetts, anticipating Thoreau's thesis on nonpayment of taxes, vowed not to remit any monies to the national treasury. At the time, says Henry Adams in his history of the war, the federal regime "had not five hundred effective troops [in Massachusetts] and if the Convention chose to recommend that the State should declare itself neutral and open its ports, no one pretended that any national power existed in Massachusetts capable of preventing" it.

Again, as in the 1790's, good fortune more than good sense intervened to save the United States from internecine conflict. Britain, it turned out, was bluffing. Enervated by a quarter of a century of war, it withdrew its offensive proposals step by step—though it did not yield to American demands on shipping and impressment—and a peace treaty was consummated on December 24, 1814. For all practical purposes the status quo ante bellum prevailed, with all outstanding differences to be negotiated further. In London, Hart Davis in the House of Commons congratulated the government for having achieved its objectives "to resist aggression and to support our maritime rights." There were misgivings on the part of others, however, that Britain had yielded too much. In the United States, though the casualties were light (2,260 dead, 4,505 wounded), there was a universal sense of relief. The vote for peace in the Senate was 35 to 0. The relief was so pervasive that the Republicans, who had been responsible for the war in the first place, gained most in popular esteem for having ended it, while the Federalists, who had opposed the war, fell into severe decline. Under the circumstances there was no follow-up to the Hartford Convention. The republic survived, though the war was lost.

☆☆☆☆☆

5

☆☆☆☆☆

PICKING THE
SPANISH BONE

In the classic model of imperialism, old empires, like old generals, fade away and new ones are built around their tombstones. It was the decline of the Mogul empire which made it possible for England to acquire India, and the decline of the Ottoman empire which laid the basis for British domination of the Mideast. Similarly, for the United States it was the dissolution of the Spanish empire that was the single most important spur to American expansion in the nineteenth century.

At the dawn of that century, 70 percent of what is now the continental United States belonged to Spain. Had the Iberian kingdom retained its vitality it would have closed a ring around the fledgling republic stretching from the Oregon Territory in the Northwest, south into California, New Mexico, and Texas, east into the Louisiana Territory, and south again into the Floridas. In other words, the United States would have been limited up to the Mississippi River in the West and to the Floridas in the South. But during and after the Napoleonic Wars the Iberian monarchy shook with palsy and as the empire in the western hemisphere slipped from its hands, the foundation was laid for an American empire. Louisiana, by a circuitous route, came to the United States through purchase; West and East Florida through conquest and diplomacy; part of Oregon —again by a circuitous route—through negotiations; Texas, New Mexico, and California through war against Spain's former colony, Mexico. All this territory was incorporated directly into the Union, much as the Russian Tzars incorporated Siberia or the Ukraine into their nation-state, or the dynasties in China swallowed Tibet. Beyond that, however, there were eighteen republics, carved out of the dismembered Spanish body (plus Brazil, originally Portuguese, and Haiti, originally French), which in due course and after a century of manipulation became an undisputed and highly lucrative North American bailiwick. Here the process of "acquisition" was more subtle, since the United States did not affiliate them to the Union or dispatch troops to permanently occupy them. But with the aid of the Monroe Doctrine, aggressive diplomacy, a war with Spain in 1898, economic penetration, and innumerable interventions and threats of intervention, the American Leviathan converted these countries into a vast sphere of influence controlled by the United States much as the old British colonies were by Britain. All told, the decimation of the Spanish empire resulted in the enlargement of the American empire in this hemisphere from less than 900,000 square miles in 1790 to more than 10 million square miles—including spheres of influence—today.

II

The Spanish holdings in the New World originally were incomparably larger and richer than England's thirteen colonies. As the early bird of western colonization, Spain ruled four kingdoms—New Granada, Plata, Peru, and New Spain—stretching from Buenos Aires to Vancouver, populated by six times as many people as the Anglo-American colonies on the eastern seaboard. The four kingdoms annually produced 64 million gold pesos of precious metals, and as Waldo Frank has observed, constituted the richest empire Western man had yet known. Spain's star began to fall, however, after its armada was defeated by Britain's navy in 1588; and the process of decline was exacerbated by the Napoleonic Wars. In 1808, Bonaparte deposed King Ferdinand VII and installed his own brother Joseph as monarch of the decaying kingdom. The Spanish monarchy fought back by establishing a Council of Regency and allying itself with England. But while a junta—first at Seville, then on an island—tried its hand at resistance, the homeland could not be rescued from Napoleon for some years.

This disarray in Iberia was the signal for a hundred and one revolutionaries in the New World to raise the cry of independence. Sebastian Francisco de Miranda, the same radical conspirator who had sought to enlist Alexander Hamilton in his schemes a decade before and had recruited 600 men from New York's Bowery for an abortive raid on his native Venezuela in 1806, returned home to become generalissimo of the army in Caracas. By his side was the heroic Simón Bolívar, who would eventually fight 200 battles for Latin

American freedom. Up north, in New Spain (vaguely from the top of Central America into northwestern Canada), Father Miguel Hidalgo led Indians and mestizos (of Indian and Spanish heritage) in an unsuccessful uprising that demanded not only independence but land for the landless. After his execution in 1811, another popular padre, José María Morelos, renewed the rebellion and was similarly captured and executed in 1815. The defeat of Napoleon of course freed Spain for a more systematic campaign against the revolutionaries, but faced with turmoil at home, including a short-lived military revolt, as well as continuing and enlarged opposition in the colonies, Spain finally relinquished all its major holdings in America, except Cuba, before 1825.

This was the setting for U.S. expansion in the ensuing decades. While the ancient Goliath faltered, Uncle Sam might have intervened to help the Spanish-American insurgents hasten the pace of liberation. But, contrary to future claims that American intervention has always been in the cause of freedom, Washington's leaders neither aided the rebels to any substantial degree nor placed obstacles in the path of Spain. Instead, disregarding political sympathy or ideological identity, the United States took advantage of the weakness of Spain and then of its ex-colonies, to fatten its own hide. To be sure there was a general fondness for the revolutionaries, who seemed to be following the American example of 1776.

Henry Clay called the wave of uprisings a "glorious spectacle of 18 million people, struggling to burst their chains. . . ." Nashville citizens, at a public dinner, toasted "the patriots of South America," and damned anyone "that would wrest from them the standard of liberty for which they have so nobly struggled." George Washington's family in Mount Vernon sent Simón Bolívar a picture of the late President and a lock of his hair as a memento of affection; and Washington's friend, the Marquis de Lafayette, stated on behalf of the family that "of all men living, and even of all men in history, Bolívar is the very one to whom my paternal friend would have preferred to send this present." "I am satisfied," wrote Secretary of State John Quincy Adams to President Monroe in August 1818, "that the cause of the South Americans . . . is *just*." But beyond sheltering a few rebel privateers, the United States did very little to help the revolutions south of its border. When Clay in 1818 proposed that the United States tender diplomatic recognition to the regimes fighting for independence, Adams opposed it and the House defeated it by a vote of 115 to 45. Helping the colonial people, Adams feared, might offend imperialist Spain, and offending Spain might prejudice negotiations then under way for acquiring East Florida. Taking the "middle" course, then, Adams, with an able assist from Old Hickory Jackson, used the hemispheric distress to take the first bite out of the Spanish empire and add another 72,003 square miles to the U.S. domain.

III

Secretary of State Adams, perhaps the most brilliant figure ever to hold that post, was the son of the second president of the United States and was destined himself to become its sixth president. Since he was so close to the center of events, his *Weltanschauung* was strongly conditioned by them. As a child, not yet eight, clutching the hand of his Calvinist mother, Abigail Adams, he had watched the battle of Bunker Hill and seen the blood flowing in the cause of independence. Three years later his father took him to France, on the diplomatic missions that helped crown the American victory. Such experiences created in young John Quincy a patriotic fervor of high intensity. This was united with a moralist approach gained from his mother. "Adhere to those religious sentiments and principles," she had written him when he went abroad, "and remember that you are accountable to your Maker for all your words and actions." Though Adams would later shed his Calvinism to become a free-swinging Unitarian, these strictures on moral rectitude were seared into his psyche—at least where political issues were concerned.

He was, of course, well educated, a graduate of Harvard, conversant in six languages, a keen student of mathematics—and withal a young man attracted to actresses and wine. George Washington appointed him minister to the Netherlands in 1794, and three years later, at thirty, he filled a similar post in Prussia for his father. At thirty-five he was in the U.S. Senate, the only Federalist in that body who approved of Jefferson's purchase of Louisiana. This indeed was strikingly in character, for no man was ever so determined to drive European colonialism from this hemisphere, or to extend U.S. influence over the two western continents. He believed with a passion that God had selected the United States as the leader and civilizing agent for the New World. "The whole continent of North America," he said in 1811, "appears to be destined by Divine Providence to be peopled by one nation, speaking one language, professing one general system of religious and political principles. . . ." During Jefferson's second term, Adams again broke ranks with the Federalists by voting for the embargo—an act which cost him his seat in the Senate. By this time, however, he had become a close friend of James Madison, who selected him as minister to Russia and then later as one of the commissioners in the negotiations at Ghent, which ended the War of 1812. When Monroe, last of this Virginia line, became president in 1817, he chose the tenacious but often irascible Adams as his Secretary of State.

One of the Secretary's first tasks was to initiate discussions with the Spanish minister in Washington, Luis de Onis, for the acquisition of East Florida. Both Spain and the United States had just emerged from the torments of unsuccessful wars. But while the United States recovered its poise, wafting on a wave of self-confidence and nationalism, the Iberian monarchy was enervated by revolution from within and without, its three-century hold over Spanish America finally loosened by Bernardo O'Higgins, José de San Martín, Simón Bolívar, and other patriots. De Onis and his government were engaged in a rear-guard action to save whatever pieces they could, while Adams, flaming with a new North American nationalism, was trying to chip away whatever was available—the Floridas, Texas, Oregon, what have you.

Fortunately for Adams, the Spaniards still nurtured hopes of subduing the South American insurgents and were therefore willing to pay a price to secure their rear. Having withdrawn troops from East Florida to battle the rebels, and having lost effective control over West Florida in the American raids of 1810 and 1813, the Iberians could make a virtue out of necessity by trading off these pieces of real estate for peace with Uncle Sam. De Onis put forth only two conditions: that Washington relinquish its claim to Texas and that it withhold recognition from the Latin American revolutionaries. Adams argued that the future Lone Star State had in fact been included as part of the Louisiana Purchase, but the thesis was so tenuous that the Monroe cabinet ordered him to retreat. Texas, he thereupon conceded, belonged to Spain. The question of recognition, however, proved more troublesome. Apart from the fact that Americans, including Adams, generally favored the rebels, it was important for the United States to come to terms with them as soon as possible if it intended to challenge England for South American trade. There were now only two independent countries in the western hemisphere—Haiti and the United States—but there would soon be fifteen or twenty; to alienate the others in advance might prove embarrassing as well as costly. Adams refused to prejudice lucrative possibilities in the future for quick annexation of East Florida, which he felt must fall into Washington's lap under any circumstances. Moreover, he was so certain an enervated Spain would have to yield substantial ground that he kept the diplomatic pot boiling by injecting a new issue: Spain must surrender its title to the Pacific Northwest as well as the Floridas. This, too, de Onis was ready to accept, for the Northwest, like Texas, was still of nebulous value. He refused to trade, however, unless he could receive assurances that Washington would not recognize and aid the South Americans.

At this point in the protracted proceedings, diplomacy blended with military force—some of it in the comic-opera fashion typical of those days of buccaneers and filibusterers. In June 1817 an adventurer named Gregor MacGregor, with the support of businessmen from Baltimore, "liberated" Amelia Island near the Georgia border from Spanish control, then left to recruit reinforcements. While he was gone the island outpost and its port, Fernandina, were seized by another adventurer, Louis Aury, once an associate of the pirate Jean Lafitte, and "incorporated" into the Mexican republic. President Monroe, unwilling to see any part of East Florida go to anyone else, and seeing an opportunity to exert pressure on the Spanish monarch, thereupon ordered the American navy to seize the island and hold it "in trust."

Simultaneously there was some trouble with the Seminole Indians, which served as a pretext for going further. The Seminoles, who lived on both sides of the Florida-Georgia border, refused to vacate lands that American authorities said had been ceded by the Creeks in 1814, after their defeat by Andrew Jackson. Even more, they flaunted American power by offering their Florida sanctuary as a haven for runaway Negro slaves and disaffected Indians. To force the Seminoles into submission, Major General Edmund P. Gaines was instructed by Washington to attack them north of the border and if necessary pursue them into Florida. In the inevitable brawls that followed, some white settlers were scalped, and forty U.S. troops ambushed and killed on the Apalachicola River. Finally Secretary of War John C. Calhoun ordered Old Hickory Jackson to "adopt the necessary measures" to put an end to the disorders. Though his instructions were vague, they included limits placed on General Gaines, namely that there was to be no molestation of the fortified posts at St. Augustine, Pensacola, and St. Marks.

For the hero of New Orleans, however, pursuit of the Indians was merely an opening salvo for seizing East Florida. "Let it be signified to me through any channel . . . that the possession of the Floridas would be desirable," he wrote, "and in 60 days it will be accomplished." Moreover, it would be done "without involving the government"—in other words by pretending that Jackson was acting on his own. Subsequently there was a heated dispute as to whether the Tennessee general had received such a signal, but in the meanwhile he had gone his merry way. In April 1818 he overran the fort at St. Marks, one of the three military posts still available to the Spaniards, replaced its flag with the Stars and Stripes, and carried off two Englishmen, Alexander Arbuthnot and Robert Ambrister, whom he executed on the charge of aiding the Indians.

Arbuthnot was a seventy-year-old merchant from Nassau, well known for generous and fair treatment of the Indians; Ambrister was a young lieutenant of the Royal Colonial Marines whose girl friend was waiting in London to marry him. To hang two foreigners on someone else's soil, especially when there was no declaration of war, was of course highhanded to an extreme—and doubly so in the case of Ambrister, since a court-martial had reversed itself and ordered him imprisoned for one year and given fifty lashes. But Jackson, not known for his sense of tolerance to "Indian-lovers," refused to accept the court's second verdict, and had the young man put to death anyway. "I hope the execution of these two unprincipled villains," he wrote, "will prove an awful example to the world" and to Great Britain that they must not "excite an Indian tribe to all the horrid deeds of savage war." Far from being penitent, even while the British were speaking of reprisals, Old Hickory only lamented, as he later stated, that he had not hanged the Spanish governor as well. Within a few weeks every important post in Florida, except St. Augustine, was under Jackson's thumb, and late in May, after a march through the jungle, the general seized Pensacola, took over the royal archives, removed the Spanish governor, and installed one of his own colonels to rule the province. Henceforth, he announced, "the revenue laws of the United States" obtained in Florida.

The Jacksonian foray, as might be expected, caused anger and anguish in many places, including London, where the newspapers universally denounced the United States and damned Jackson as nothing less than a murderer and tyrant. Back in Washington, Secretary of War Calhoun called for a court-martial, or at least a reprimand, for the aggressive general, who had exceeded his authority and exhibited an embarrassing strain of brutality. A Senate committee began an investigation, and Henry Clay in the House reminded all and sundry that "ambitious projects" of this kind had "overturned the liberties of Rome." At a four-day meeting of the cabinet only Adams defended Jackson's activities, with the strange rationale that since Spain had failed to effectively police its colony Jackson was entitled to take whatever measures he saw fit. But if the general was unpopular with cabinet officers and such, his stock with the popular mass, especially in the West and South, again pyramided upward.

"Old and young speak of him with rapture," reported *Niles'*

Weekly Register. Resolutions in Congress condemning Jackson's execution of the two Englishmen, the slaughter of Indians, and the "unconstitutional seizure of Pensacola," were voted down by healthy majorities after a twenty-seven-day debate. Another resolution—also designed as a prick at the Tennessee militarist—prohibiting "the invasion of foreign soil, without authorization of Congress, except in fresh pursuit of an enemy," was defeated 112 to 42. Adams and Jackson had correctly calculated that in the eyes of America, victory was its own justification. An illegal raid in defiance of the U.S. Constitution itself, tainted as well by brutal excesses, was applauded only because it gave Americans a sense of national power.

Be that as it may, Jackson's venture achieved its purpose. Minister de Onis hurried back to Washington from a brief vacation in Pennsylvania, to demand "prompt restitution of St. Marks, Pensacola, Barrancas, and all other places wrested by General Jackson from the Crown of Spain." For good measure he asked for indemnities and punishment of Old Hickory. In response, President Monroe, implicitly affirming the illegal character of the raids, did order all the Spanish forts evacuated. But Adams was now able to speed the diplomatic process. With characteristic audacity he demanded that Spain either place adequate police forces in Florida to hobble the Seminoles or "cede to the United States a province, of which she retains nothing but the nominal possession. . . ." In February 1819 de Onis agreed to give up title to the Floridas, as well as Spanish claims to the large and unknown territory of Oregon. Previous demands that Washington withhold recognition from the South American revolutionaries were dropped, and all that Adams was required to pledge in return was surrender of a questionable title to Texas. The history books say that the United States paid $5 million for these areas, but in fact the payment was made to American citizens in justification of their claims against Spain. The Senate ratified the conquest unanimously, and the public acclaimed Adams' diplomacy with unabashed enthusiasm.

Concurring in that estimate many years later, a recent biographer, Walter LaFeber, concludes that "Adams' shrewdness in dealing with Onis, his audacity in supporting Jackson, and his foresight in demanding the claims on the Northwest coast, are unsurpassed in American diplomatic annals."

Minister de Onis had a different and more biting evaluation of both Adams and the Americans. Ruminating on his career in the United States some years later, he observed that "the Americans . . . believe that their dominion is destined to extend, now to the Isthmus of Panama, and hereafter over all the regions of the New

World. . . . They consider themselves superior to the rest of mankind, and look upon their republic as the only establishment upon earth founded upon a grand and solid basis, embellished by wisdom, and destined one day to become the most sublime colossus of human power, and the wonder of the universe."

IV

More important than even the Transcontinental Treaty of 1819 in laying the foundations for the American empire was the proclamation of the Monroe Doctrine in December 1823, as a result of the vigorous efforts of John Quincy Adams. The demise of the Spanish empire, virtually completed by then, posed certain problems for the hemisphere. The liberated nations were not likely, in the beginning at least, to stand on their own feet, independent in fact as in name. They could be, under certain circumstances, subjugated by another power or powers and returned to the status of colonies. The Monroe Doctrine was aimed at preventing this alternative. The United States, at this stage in its history, could not possibly have converted the vast expanses of Latin America into a "sphere of influence" for itself. The best that it could hope for, and then only with England's help, was to prevent others from doing so. If the United Sates "could exclude further European penetration as Spain's authority collapsed," writes historian William Appleman Williams, "then [it] would remain as the predominant power in the hemisphere." In placing limits on what other powers might do, Uncle Sam was laying claims on the future of Latin America.

By 1822 Spanish hopes for reconquering its empire in the New World had diminished to the vanishing point. Five years earlier San Martín had marched from the province of La Plata across the Andes to defeat the royal army at Chacabuco near the Pacific. O'Higgins had established an independent Chile, Bolívar was fomenting revolution in the Orinoco valley and forging the Republic of Great Colombia, which included the present states of Venezuela, Colombia, Panama, and Ecuador. A revolt in Spain itself in 1820 accelerated the pace of Spanish disintegration and gave the insurgents a second wind. In 1821 the liberated states of Argentina and Chile came to the aid of Peru; a year later, when the forces of San Martín and Bolívar converged at Guayaquil there was only one Spanish military contingent in the field and it surrendered soon thereafter. At approximately the same time a mutiny of Spanish troops at Vera Cruz forced the Spanish viceroy to grant independence to Mexico and Central America. Surveying the situation in March 1822, there-

fore, Monroe could state that the five new nations of Latin America
—La Plata (Argentina), Chile, Peru, Colombia, and Mexico—were
"in the full enjoyment of their independence." The only important
colonies remaining in the hemisphere, apart from Canada, were
Cuba and Brazil.

Having gained their independence, however, the new nations
were now in danger not only of internal disintegration (which
would soon become endemic for most of them) but of being reconquered or overrun by other European forces.

After the defeat of Napoleon, the great monarchial states of Europe had formed themselves into a loose, reactionary coalition,
under the guiding hand of Prince Clemens von Metternich of Austria, whose major purpose was to sustain the status quo. They had
already shown their claws during the wave of revolutions that broke
out in Naples, Greece, Portugal, and Spain during 1820–21. The
Austrians suppressed the Italian uprisings quickly and vigorously.
France invaded Spain in the spring of 1823 to unshackle it from a
liberal constitution and to restore the acerbic Ferdinand VII as absolute monarch. The Holy Alliance, operating on a nineteenth-century version of the domino theory, was determined to smash at revolution wherever it reared its head. By the summer of that year,
therefore, there was talk of a meeting in Paris, at which, according
to high rumor, the powers would underwrite an expedition by Franco-Spanish forces to recolonize Latin America.

President Monroe, Adams recorded in his diary in November
1823, was alarmed "far beyond anything that I could have conceived
possible, with the fear that the Holy Alliance are about to restore
immediately all South America to Spain." Adams himself considered
the threat a "fearful question," first because an Alliance victory
would create in its wake a great military ring by European powers
around the United States, thereby inhibiting expansion to Texas,
Cuba, and other points; and second because it would cut off a potential for enlarged commerce. In one of his state papers, Adams
noted that trade with the Colombian Republic, most of which originated with the war for liberation, could be considerably expanded
because "as navigators and manufacturers, *we* are already so far advanced in a career upon which *they* are yet to enter, that we may,
for many years after the conclusion of the war, maintain with them
a commercial intercourse, highly beneficial to both parties, as *carriers* to and for them of numerous articles of manufacture and foreign produce." Henry Clay was certain that within fifty years American traders would occupy the same position "in relation to South
America . . . as the people of New England do to the rest of the

United States." He foresaw large mercantile profits in that area, as well as an outlet for western agriculture. All of this depended, however, on restraining the Holy Alliance—a task for which the United States was unequipped.

Fortunately for Monroe, Adams, and the other American leaders, a nation that was capable of checking the Alliance, Great Britain, had common interests with them—at least up to a point. The British had withdrawn from Metternich's bloc because it threatened to upset the traditional European balance of power. They also saw in the Holy Alliance a menace to vested interests they were rapidly accumulating in Latin America—trade, mining concessions, contracts to float loans for the new republics. Should the area be recolonized, Britain's substantial economic lead would go by the boards. In August 1823, therefore, foreign secretary George Canning asked the American minister in London, Richard Rush, to query his government about joining with London to bar a Franco-Spanish expedition to South America. The message was relayed to Monroe, who immediately consulted his predecessors, Madison and Jefferson, both of whom strongly advised acceptance. The question of cooperation with England, wrote Jefferson, was "the most momentous which has ever been offered to my contemplation since that of Independence. . . . With her then, we should most sedulously cherish a cordial friendship."

Had it not been for John Quincy Adams there might not have been a declaration known as the Monroe Doctrine. Nationalist from head to toe, suspicious of England, he wanted no arrangement in which the United States seemed to be subservient to its former mother country. "It would be more candid," he told a cabinet meeting, "as well as more dignified, to avow our principles explicitly to Great Britain and France, than to come in as a cock-boat in the wake of the British man-of-war." He, of course, favored a declaration denying to European powers the right to further colonize in the western hemisphere, but he objected strenuously to Canning's proviso that Washington (and London) also be bound by that prohibition. Had Washington accepted London's suggestion for a joint statement, it could not in the future have taken Texas or California or Cuba without violating that understanding and currying war with the British.

Adams was convinced that for the time being at least the United States did not have to rely on the British navy since the Holy Alliance was only making noises. "I no more believe," he said, "that the Holy Allies will restore the Spanish dominion upon the American continent than that the Chimborazo will sink beneath the ocean."

The Secretary's persistence carried the day; America disregarded Britain's offer of a joint declaration and went ahead on its own. On December 2, 1823, President Monroe, in a message to Congress, *unilaterally* proclaimed the doctrine that had been outlined by Adams. It stated "that the American continents, by the free and independent condition which they have assumed and maintain, are henceforth not to be considered as subjects for future colonization by any European powers." Europeans might hold those colonies in the New World already in their possession, but seize no others without incurring American wrath. The United States in turn pledged, in a sentence long forgotten, "not to interfere in the internal concerns" of Europe. It was a bold step, for as everyone knew, Monroe had no navy capable of enforcing the proclamation. Only the British fleet could do so, and while Americans congratulated themselves that they had placed a barricade against colonialist ambitions, Latin Americans generally understood that it was Britannia's navy that stood between them and the Holy Alliance.

The Monroe Doctrine was neither a domestic law nor an international treaty. It was simply a self-serving declaration by a single nation, enforceable in no court, that it would not tolerate certain actions in this hemisphere by European states. What was important about it, therefore, was not its original strictures but the *uses* to which it was put later on. It had been proclaimed in 1823 in order to foreclose intervention in Latin America by Europe. It subsequently became a justification for intervention by the *United States*. It was assumed, somehow, that the self-proclaimed Doctrine gave the United States a *legal* right to police the whole hemisphere.

Perhaps anticipating this development, the *Boston Advertiser* asked: "Is there anything in the Constitution which makes our Government the Guarantors of the Liberties of the World? of the Wahabees? the Peruvians? the Chilese? the Mexicans or Colombians?" The same question, rephrased, would be asked many times by pacifists and antiexpansionists, not the least by opponents of the Vietnam War 142 years later.

6

MEXICO FOR AMERICANS

A major catalytic agent in America's territorial imperialism during the nineteenth century was the pioneer who wended his way south and west, beyond the nation's boundaries. In the vast, relatively unpeopled area of northern Mexico and the Pacific Northwest, the settler was followed by the flag, much as in later days the flag would follow commerce. Anglo-American communities, living under foreign rule, became pockets of resistance to their host governments, and instruments for secession, to join the United States—as in the Floridas. True, this was not the central purpose for which most settlers originally emigrated into the Floridas, Texas, and Oregon— what they wanted was free or cheap land. But circumstances and culture conspired to make them vehicles for Uncle Sam's territorial aggrandizement.

The early leaders of the republic did not anticipate this development; indeed they did not foresee that Americans would emigrate to any large extent. Even before the Louisiana Purchase, which doubled the American domain, Jefferson was of the opinion that the existing territory provided "room enough for our descendants to the thousandth and thousandth generation." He was wrong: hardy pioneers moved beyond the national frontier, especially during economic depressions, and established communities far outside Washington's jurisdiction. How to relate to those Anglo-American communities in foreign lands was bound to be a problem. Should the United States try to absorb them through purchase of their provinces or through military conquest? Should it permit them—even help them—to be assimilated into the culture of their hosts? Should it encourage them to become independent sister republics? The

Jeffersonians—at least in theory—leaned toward this third solution. When the nation laid claim to the Pacific Northwest, for instance, Jefferson expressed the hope that this territory would become "the germ of a great, free and independent empire on that side of the continent." President Monroe, in similar vein, considered that his government was simply trustee for the area, preserving it from the British until such time as it became strong enough to be an independent, sovereign nation. In the interim he expected the Oregonians to grant commercial and naval privileges to Washington, but he hoped —as he said in a draft of a message he read to his cabinet in 1824 —that Oregon "would necessarily soon separate from this Union." The Jeffersonians succumbed to the passions of expansion insofar as Canada and the Floridas were concerned, but elsewhere they visualized the formation of parallel and independent republics. They placed limits on the march of empire. Even Senator Thomas H. Benton of Missouri, a close friend of Jackson, believed in 1825 that the Rocky Mountains were adequate as the "everlasting boundary" for the United States. Almost no one at the time would have gone to war for such paltry items as Oregon, California, or New Mexico.

But the steamship and soon the iron horse were making the world smaller, and bad times—especially after the depression of 1837— were drawing new pioneers into areas considered barren or inaccessible before. As one congressman from Indiana put it, there was an "American multiplication table" at work. In the Oregon country, for instance, there were barely 500 American trappers, tradesmen, and farmers in 1841, but four years later there were 5,000. Thousands followed the 2,020 miles of the Oregon Trail from Independence, Missouri, through the newly discovered South Pass in the Rockies, thence to the Northwest. And with the flow of immigrants, eyes widened and ambitions fattened. By a treaty with Britain in 1818— renewed in 1827—the Oregon country was jointly occupied by the two countries, though most of the 700 Englishmen lived above the 49th parallel and almost all the Americans lived below it. By 1843, ignoring the Jeffersonian prescription to form a "sister republic," the American immigrants designed for themselves at Champoeg a "compact of government," as a prelude to incorporation into the United States. The following year the Democratic Party in the States proper carried a plank in its platform stating "that our title to the whole of the Territory of Oregon is clear and unquestionable; that no portion of the same ought to be ceded to England or any other power. . . ." With a fair number of settlers in the area, the Jacksonian Democrats —successors to the Jeffersonian Republicans as clarions of the lower classes—widened their sights. Senator Benton, who two decades earlier would have settled for the Rockies as an "everlasting boundary," now urged the emigrants to "go on and carry their rifles." "Thirty thousand American rifles in Oregon," he said, "will annihilate the [British] Hudson's Bay Company, drive them off our continent, quiet their Indians, and protect the American interests. . . ." A popular speaker, quoted by a New Orleans newspaper, warned the British that Americans had "licked" them twice and could do it again. "Nothing would please the people of the entire West half so well," said the *Illinois State Register* of May 9, 1845, "as a war with England. . . ." In words reminiscent of Henry Clay and the war hawks of 1812, John S. Chipman told Congress on January 14, 1846, that "Michigan alone would take Canada in 90 days; and if that would not do, they would give it up, and take it in 90 days again." A feeling of power permeated the air, reflected in such statements as the one by Congressman Robert Winthrop that the Rockies "are mere molehills. Our destiny is onward." Or the one by Senator David R. Atchison of Missouri: "The march of empire is westward; nothing will, nothing can check it."

The doctrine of imperialism that emerged in the era of Jacksonian democracy followed a simple logic: wherever there was an American pioneer, or likely to be one, it was the "manifest destiny" of the United States to incorporate that territory into its own. John L. O'Sullivan, cofounder of the *Democratic Review* and of the New York *Morning News,* made the term famous when he wrote of "our manifest destiny to overspread the continent allotted by Providence for the free development of our yearly multiplying millions." "Yes," he wrote in the *Morning News* of February 7, 1845, "more, more, more! . . . till our national destiny is fulfilled and . . . the whole boundless continent is ours." American settlers would fan out far and wide, and with the aid of the U.S. government, replace the Spanish-speaking people of Mexico and other nations just as it had replaced the Indians. According to O'Sullivan's *Democratic Review:* "The process which has been gone through at the north, of driving back the Indians, or annihilating them as a race, has yet to be gone through at the south." The *American Review,* another expansionist sheet, visualized the Spanish-Indian people and cultures wasting away in the wake of an American advance.

Oddly enough, among the most sanguine exponents of endless expansion were such writers as William Cullen Bryant, Walt Whitman, Ralph Waldo Emerson, and historian George Bancroft. Whitman, then in his mid-twenties, considered such expansion not as an intrinsic evil but as a reform. It was a measure to ease the pain of depression by offering haven to defeated farmers; it would result not in misery or bondage but in "the increase of human happiness and liberty."

O'Sullivan's sheet had no patience with those who raised "cobweb tissues," such as the rights of Spanish-Americans due to prior discovery and settlement of their lands. The United States, it claimed, had the superior right that Providence had consigned it to develop "the great experiment of liberty and federative self government. . . ." This is "a right such as that of the tree to the space of air and earth suitable for the full expansion of its principle and destiny of growth. . . ." The Hartford *Times* (July 24, 1845) put it somewhat more mundanely when it argued that the United States was entitled to California because the Mexicans were too inept and slothful to develop it, whereas the Americans would make it a paradise.

There was no rebutting these arguments—unless one could talk with Providence directly. Americans had a right to settle beyond their borders because they were a chosen people; the United States had a right to take territory from other nations because it was its destiny, by the will of God, to spread happiness far and wide.

II

One of the fulfillments of Uncle Sam's manifest destiny was in northern Mexico, where it began, as in East Florida and Oregon, with transborder migration. Spanish law excluded Anglo-Americans from Spanish colonies, but starting in 1800, sturdy Yankees, disregarding the law, planned a number of filibustering expeditions. Philip Nolan that year assembled 21 armed men at Natchez and stormed into Texas. Former Vice-President Aaron Burr was far more ambitious; he laid plans to detach Louisiana, conquer all of Mexico, and proclaim himself emperor. Fortunately or unfortunately, the plans never bore fruit. In 1812 a former lieutenant in the American army, Augustus Magee, teamed up with a liberal Mexican who had fought with Father Hidalgo, to lead 3,000 filibusters—850 of them gringos—into New Spain, and succeeded temporarily in capturing Bexar (San Antonio). In 1819 James Long, aided by a Mexican refugee, massed a force of 300 men, seized the town of Nacogdoches, and proclaimed the "Republic of Texas." All these efforts, and others, failed to gain permanent footholds. But the filibusters were a common breed in the early nineteenth century—the "hardy, restless, and lawless" pioneers, as O'Sullivan called them, who tried to establish private empires of their own in relatively unoccupied areas.

On the heels of the filibusters came a mixed breed of contractors and farmers, determined to establish stable communities, as well as unconscionable adventurers who in many cases were just one step ahead of the sheriff. They were able to emigrate because in 1821 the Spaniards finally relaxed their rules limiting immigration to Spanish Catholics, and opened the doors of Texas to North Americans. The viceroy of New Spain issued a grant to Moses Austin, a beguiling Connecticut Yankee who had made and lost fortunes in dry goods and mining, to settle 300 Anglo-American families. The members of the colony, by the conditions of the grant, were to convert to Catholicism, if they were not already Catholics, and pledge allegiance to the Spanish monarchy. Before the agreement could be implemented, unfortunately, the elder Austin died, but his son, Stephen F. Austin, went ahead with the task and in December 1821 founded the town of San Felipe de Austin. It was a fateful event in U.S. history.

Meanwhile, the suspended revolution of Father Hidalgo erupted anew and what was formerly New Spain, a colony of the Iberian monarchy, became independent Mexico. At its birth Mexico was as large as the United States, comprising not only its present borders but California, Nevada, Utah, New Mexico, Arizona, Texas, and sections of Wyoming and Colorado. There was certainly room for more inhabitants, and fortunately for Austin and other *empresarios* who followed, Mexico decided to continue the policy of its former mother country. Just before his regime was overthrown in 1823, General Agustín de Iturbide decreed a colonization law that was extremely generous. In return for bringing in 200 settler families, each of which was to receive 177 acres of farm land or 4,428 acres of grazing land, the *empresario* himself was granted 354 acres for agriculture and 66,000 for grazing.

Within the next few years some 20,000 Yankees crossed the border to acquire a homestead in northern Mexico, more people in fact than had settled there in the three previous centuries. Most were simple folk with no ultimate purpose beyond earning a better living. But there were among them some—soon to play a major role in secession—who swept across the Sabine, as Marquis James records, "with schemes in their heads and guns in their hands—fleeing justice, fleecing Indians, gambling in land and promoting shooting scrapes called revolutions." In this group, largely clustered in the Redlands, as East Texas was called, were such figures as the Bowie brothers, Louisiana slave smugglers for whom an eighteen-inch hunting knife was named; David G. Burnet of Ohio, an associate of Miranda; Davy Crockett, the famous backwoodsman; and many other unruly men who hoped to duplicate Jackson's feat in East Florida. Some had come with Aaron Burr and Long. A few had been associated with the pirate Jean Laffite. For such men Mexican law was inoperative. When the governor, for instance, canceled the agreement with an *empresario* named Hayden Edwards because he refused to recognize the land titles of absentee Mexicans, Edwards recruited 200 men in December 1826, seized Nacogdoches, and proclaimed the short-lived independent "Republic of Fredonia."

This, then, would have been a difficult lot for any government to assimilate, but doubly so for a new nation whose governments were toppling like tenpins. The thirteen English colonies and later the United States had been able to absorb motley contingents of Swedes, Germans, and other non-English-speaking Europeans because they created a moderately strong government and some sense of cohesion. Mexico, however, had neither an adequate army nor police (or priesthood, for that matter) to produce loyalty in the hinterlands. As a consequence, Texas became nothing more than a transplanted community clinging to its previous mores, resisting assimilation. Instead of waiting for a priest to marry them, for instance, young Texans entered into "provisional marriages," and when a priest did finally arrive they refused to be "remarried" or accept baptism for their children; they often drove the *padre* out of town. Instead of Spanish the Texas children were taught English in their elementary schools, and those who went on to higher education usually were sent to the States. A Mexican commissioner, Don Manuel de Mier y Terán, who toured Texas in 1827, reported that as he moved north from Bexar he noted "that Mexican influence is proportionately diminished until on arriving at this place [Nacogdoches] . . . it is almost nothing."

Ironically, the most combustible issue between the "freedom-loving" North Americans and the government of Mexico was that of slavery. The 1827 constitution of Coahuila and Texas—united by Mexico into one state—emancipated all future children of slaves and forbade immigrants from bringing in any more black servants. The Anglo-Americans, however, with an assist from officials willing to wink an eye at the practice, circumvented the law by signing "contracts" with their slaves—perpetuating their bondage—before bringing them across the borders. When President Vicente Guerrero issued a decree in September 1829 to make the abolition of slavery effective everywhere in the nation, Texas had to be exempted because, as the commander on the frontier explained, "he could not hope to see such a decree obeyed unless it should be enforced by a larger military force than he then had."

By 1829 it was clear to the Mexicans that their experiment was a failure and that unless they took stringent measures, the province of Texas would slip from their grasp. They were convinced that the

North American settlers were being encouraged and abetted both by kindred spirits above the border, who applauded such ventures as the "Fredonia" revolt, and by the federal government in Washington, whose persistence in trying to acquire Texas raised alarming suspicions. John Quincy Adams had reluctantly renounced claims to the future Lone Star State in the 1819 treaty with Spain, but Senator Benton—whom Charles and Mary Beard call "the agricultural imperialist of Missouri"—cried out that "I will never accept" the renunciation. Henry Clay similarly denounced this provision of the agreement, and Andrew Jackson called for action to "get the Texas country back . . . with peace and honor." When Adams became president he offered Mexico the grand sum of a million dollars for the province—the biggest bargain, had it been approved, since the Dutch bought Manhattan for twenty-four dollars. For the Mexican nationalists this was a gratuitous insult.

Jackson, who succeeded Adams, was equally clumsy and transparent. He dispatched to Mexico City a swashbuckling land speculator, Anthony Butler, whom he later confessed was a "scamp" and a "liar." Sam Houston, a Jackson protégé, referred to Butler as a "swindler and gambler." But Butler was authorized to pay $5 million for Texas—another effrontery that raised hackles on Mexican skin—and when ordinary purchase seemed impossible, asked Jackson for half a million dollars to hand around in bribes to induce Mexican officials to sell. Though Old Hickory did not accede to this proposal, he sent Butler back to Mexico City, after a visit home, to put in a bid not only for Texas but for California as well. When this mission also failed, Butler impudently suggested that the President apply force to seize some of the desired territory. This was too much even for Jackson, who for internal political reasons dared not to be too forward about his territorial ambitions; he promptly had the "scamp" recalled. The effect of such continuing machinations, however, was not lost on either the sensitive Mexican governments or their people. They were certain that Washington would not rest until it had dispossessed them of their land, either through a shadowy purchase or a secretly supported revolution.

Alarmed, then, by events inside and outside, the Mexicans decided on stern measures to save their domain. Mier asked his government to enforce antislavery measures, send in adequate military forces, and colonize Texas with communities of Mexicans. A decree of April 1830, attacking the source of the problem, forbade further immigration from the United States. It prohibited "emigrants from nations bordering on this Republic" from settling in "territory adjacent to their own nation." Squatters were expelled, and contracts with American promoters who had not fulfilled their obligations canceled. An especially controversial action involved customs duties. By a law of 1823 the naturalized Yankee colonists had been exempted for seven years from paying tariffs on the imports that came by sea from New Orleans and other points in the United States. When the law expired the Mexican government refused to renew it, thus forcing the Anglo-Americans either to pay duties like other Mexicans or to do their trading at inconvenient Mexican centers hundreds of miles away.

With each measure, resistance mounted. Adventurers in the Redlands, in the time-honored fashion of Americans since John Hancock, conducted a sizable smuggling business to evade the customs taxes, and when challenged by the authorities engaged them in small skirmishes. In October 1832 and again in April 1833, Texans held conventions and made demands on Mexico City to lift the ban on immigration, reform the import laws, separate Texas from Coahuila, and grant a constitution for Texas modeled on that of the United States. Before long there was a Committee of Safety in operation, reminiscent of a similar body during the American Revolution, as well as a volunteer militia ready to ward off the Mexican army. Before long too, there were the inevitable "instances" propelling two incompatible forces toward total rupture—such as the capture in 1835 of a young Mexican officer by 40 Anglo-Americans, while trying to put back into operation a customhouse at Anahuac, or the refusal of citizens at Bexar to give up a six-pound brass cannon. When General Antonio López de Santa Anna scrapped the prevailing constitution in favor of a centralized system which abolished states' rights, the Yankee settlers responded by forming a government of their own and an army under the command of the onetime governor of Tennessee, Sam Houston.

III

Definitive as all this appears, it would be wrong to assume that the Anglo-Americans were involved in a giant conspiracy to divorce Texas from Mexico. On the contrary, a good majority, even at the eleventh hour, still hoped for an accommodation: a motion to secede, made at the November 1835 Consultation, was voted down by a lopsided margin. The range of Anglo-American opinion covered a spectrum from Stephen Austin, leader of the "peace party," to Sam Houston, one of the guiding forces in the "war party." Indeed the attitudes of these two leaders reflect the undercurrents pulling Texas in opposite directions. Austin, a resolute and patient man, had never wavered in his loyalty to Mexico; he was convinced that the two peoples could find a common ground. When Hayden Edwards formed the "Republic of Fredonia," Austin mobilized a sizable force to help the Mexican army put down the rebellion. Whatever his differences with Mexico—on the advisability of abolition, on joining Texas with Coahuila, on trying to enforce the Catholic religion—Austin felt an overriding obligation to his adopted country. He was a good friend of Mier and worked closely with him in trying to iron out differences. The conference of Texans held in 1833 sent him to Mexico City to negotiate with Santa Anna and for a brief interlude it seemed that he might achieve a *modus vivendi* on all points except separation of Texas from Coahuila. On the way home he was arrested, ostensibly because he had previously written a letter urging his friends to declare Texas a separate state. But it is noteworthy that even from prison he advised conciliation; he was evidently convinced that the liberal elements in Mexico would eventually prevail and make a fair arrangement with the Anglo-American. When he returned home after eighteen months in the dungeon, he still nursed the hope that war could be averted and union sustained.

Houston was a man of another stripe: he had come to Texas with the specific idea of detaching it. He was certainly a more dynamic figure than Austin, with a far more colorful career. Washington Irving described Houston as "a tall, large, well-formed, fascinating man," six foot two in height, with brown hair and light complexion, who usually wore Indian clothes and was "given to grandiloquence" and a "military mode of expressing himself." He had been brought up in Tennessee, and had run away from the tedium of a clerk's job at age fifteen to live among the Cherokees in the eastern part of the state for almost three years. Though he developed an affection for Indians in general and the Cherokees specifically, he fought with Jackson against the Creeks during the War of 1812, and later served as a subagent to supervise the removal of Cherokees to barren Arkansas. He quit in 1818 because Secretary of War John C. Calhoun questioned his integrity and rebuked him for wearing Indian clothes; then he turned to the practice of law in Nashville, and rode this hobbyhorse into the political arena. After four years in Congress, representing the Ninth District, and a term as governor of Tennessee—elected with the aid of Jackson's machine—he left again for Cherokee country, determined to do something sensational for himself, his mentor (Jackson), and his country.

What Houston had in mind was nothing less than to conquer an empire for his old chief. He would seize Texas—the "New Estremadura," as he called it—perhaps all of Mexico, and while expanding the frontiers of the United States earn a fortune of two million dollars for himself. Presumably he would enlist the Cherokees in his venture; he also intended to recruit several thousand men on the Atlantic seaboard, each to pay thirty dollars as seed money to a common fund. These plans were never put into practice, perhaps because Jackson himself discouraged them; but after a trip to Washington in which he spent night and day discussing a "Florida coup in Texas" with some of Old Hickory's associates, Houston borrowed five hundred dollars from the President personally, and in December 1832, after riding 1,000 miles on a horse, arrived at the scene of operations. At Bexar he told the Indians about his plans, implying that he had a "confidential" understanding with the American President; at Nacogdoches his fame was already so well established he was unanimously elected a delegate to the April 1833 convention. From then until he led his forces to the grand military victory that won independence for the Lone Star Republic, he never flagged in his intention to accouple the New Estramadura to the United States.

The wand of history seems to have rested on Houston's shoulders, carrying even Austin onto the magic carpet of independence. For in late February and early March 1836 there occurred one of those events which sometimes galvanize a whole people. Determined to rout the gringos and establish firm military control over the province, Santa Anna, at the head of 3,000 troops, marched toward the San Antonio River where he surrounded a force of 188 men under Lieutenant Colonel William Barret Travis, holed up in a fortified mission building called the Alamo. The uneven battle raged for twelve days, ending on March 6 with the massacre of every single man under arms, including the remarkable Davy Crockett, who entertained his fellow soldiers with his violin as the enemy crept nearer. Only the wounded wife and daughter of a lieutenant, who had taken refuge in the church, were spared to tell the tale. Three weeks later Santa Anna, who had vowed not to take any prisoners, wreaked his wrath on a force of 400 men, most of them recent volunteers from the United States. Three hundred were slaughtered at Goliad after they had surrendered.

With the Mexicans shouting "exterminate to the Sabine," with scores of terrified Yankee families racing for the border, with many towns burned or abandoned, including San Felipe, and with the Texas government in flight, it seemed as if the issue would be settled in favor of Mexico once and for all. But Santa Anna was overconfident, and on Thursday, April 21, Sam Houston with a force of

780 men attacked the Mexican contingent of 1,200 at San Jacinto while they were enjoying afternoon siesta. Shouting "Remember the Alamo," the Texans killed 600 and captured all but 40 of the rest. Next day Santa Anna himself was taken in the tall grass near the battlefield and was saved from lynching only by Houston's personal intervention. A month later the cagy Mexican dictator, who had an inordinate knack of convincing others of his sincerity, signed two treaties ending the fighting, withdrawing the troops, and promising recognition of Texan independence. When freed, however, Santa Anna promptly repudiated his understanding—leaving the issue hanging for a dozen years. Legally, it didn't really matter, because under the Mexican constitution only Congress had the right to approve treaties, and it vehemently rejected this one. Though a state of war continued, Texas operated in fact as an independent nation— the Lone Star Republic. At its first regular election in September 1836, Houston, the hero of San Jacinto, was elected president. A concurrent plebiscite showed 6,000 Texan voters in favor of annexation to the United States, only 93 against.

The revolution in Texas undoubtedly reflected the sentiments of the majority—there were 30,000 Americans in the state, as against 3,500 native Mexicans, 14,000 Indians, and 5,000 slaves—just as the secession of the Southern states in 1861 reflected the sentiments of that area. But in the United States the North was able to reconquer the South; in Mexico the central government, apart from being inept, always had to consider the possibility of intervention by its northern neighbor. President Jackson resolutely wanted the territory—though, as will be seen, he was prevented from annexing it because of the slavery issue. His aides hoped for "a Florida coup in Texas," and rank-and-file Americans, even some who opposed annexation, felt warm kinship for their brothers across the Sabine.

When the fighting erupted in 1835–36, mass meetings were held throughout the United States and companies of volunteers—such as the one slaughtered at Goliad—were recruited from as far away as New York and Pittsburgh, to "fite or dye" for Texas, as two sympathizers from Maine put it. "Americans to the rescue," cried the New Orleans *Bee*, in urging citizens of that city to respond to Houston's call for help. Not all the volunteers came to Texas out of high idealism; they were lured by bounties of land offered by the Texas government to those who would take up arms in its behalf. A wag in Alabama, through which one of the volunteer companies passed, told a crowd that the slogan "Texas and liberty" ought to be changed to "Texas, liberty, and *land*." In addition to many hundreds of recruits, sums of money were subscribed and weapons were sent to General Houston, including the only two pieces of artillery he used at San Jacinto—made and paid for by the citizens of Cincinnati. Clearly a Texas defeat or a massacre of Texans might inflame public opinion in the United States to the point where troops would be sent across the Sabine to rescue the Texans.

Jackson did, in fact, order General E. P. Gaines to the Mexican border, ostensibly to protect fleeing North Americans from hostile Indians. Gaines was on the eastern bank of the Sabine, not too far from San Jacinto, when Houston was demolishing Santa Anna's army. Whether he would have intervened if Houston had lost the engagement is one of those hypothetical questions for which there is no definitive answer. But that summer Gaines did occupy Nacogdoches, across the border, on the pretext of defending American lives. And at least one historian, Nathaniel W. Stephenson, has concluded that "had the battle of the San Jacinto proved a rout for the Texans . . . it is as nearly certain as anything unproven ever can be that Jackson would have stalked in between Santa Anna and his prey."

American support was obviously important for the Texan cause. Whether it was decisive, however, is almost irrelevant, for there would have been no "Texas problem" in Mexico to begin with without the spillover of population from the United States. Nor would the ultimate "solution," annexation, have taken place without the surge of expansionism under Tyler and Polk.

7

TRANSCONTINENTAL CONQUEST

Few men in American history had had so strong an instinct for imperialist expansion as Andrew Jackson. It is ironic, therefore, that much as he wanted to incorporate Texas into the Union in 1836, he was unable to do so. The Lone Star Republic was all wrapped up on a silver platter, its people clamoring for admittance into the United States, yet Old Hickory was forced to tread warily.

This must have been all the more galling for him because Texan independence hung by a thread.

Sam Houston's victory at San Jacinto was sensational and for the time being the Mexican army was quiescent, but it was not reasonable to assume that a new nation with only 30,000 Anglo-American citizens could hold out indefinitely against Mexico, which had seven million citizens to draw from. Henry M. Morfit, assigned by Jackson to survey the situation, concluded that if the Lone Star Republic were to survive it would not be because of its own strength but because of the "weakness and imbecility of her enemy." Texan leaders, in Texan style, might talk grandiloquently about conquering New Mexico and all the land to the Pacific, but for the moment their cupboard was bare, their army weak and disorganized, and their general situation, according to Houston himself, "desperate."

Once the fervor of identification with the rebels had worn off, therefore, American leaders became coyly hesitant. To absorb Texas meant to inherit its war with Mexico, and since Jackson had only barely extricated himself a few months before from a possible war with France over a trivial issue of spoliation payments, this was no glowing prospect. Moreover, while an incursion into Texas would pose no insuperable military problems, pursuing the Mexicans toward their capital would be no cakewalk such as Jackson's invasion of East Florida a couple of decades back had been. The thin American army of a few thousand troops could be expanded by large numbers of volunteers; still it would have to cross rugged mountains and arid deserts to find its quarry, and would be engaged over an expanse dozens of times bigger than East Florida. When war did break out finally a decade later, the job proved easier than expected; but for the moment it loomed large in many minds, especially since the Mexican army was almost five times as numerous as the American, and—even more—because there was the possibility of intervention by Britain or France, both of whom were anxious to place barriers against Uncle Sam's march westward. Should either one of them join with Mexico, the United States would have a much bigger task on its hands than it bargained for.

None of this might have inhibited Jackson but for the fact that the issue of annexation became hopelessly intertwined with that of slavery. The Southern states were just then beginning to realize that the 1820 Missouri Compromise was working against them. There was only one slave territory left—Florida—waiting to be admitted as a state, whereas there were three free territories—Wisconsin, Minnesota, and Iowa—whose applications would soon be on the agenda. For the South annexation of Texas would be a boon, since almost as its first act it had adopted a constitution legalizing slavery. On the other hand, the North, just beginning to seethe with abolitionist agitation, and also concerned about the national balance of power, was also aware that annexation would tilt the scales against the free states. Senator Thomas Morris of Ohio, originally a fervid supporter of Texas, lost his ardor for including it in the Union because of the slavery issue. John Quincy Adams, now a congressman after having lost his bid for a second term as president, castigated Jackson for trying to introduce slavery in a region where Mexico had abolished it. Annexation was simply a scheme, he said, to plunge the nation into war, on behalf of the slaveowners. Benjamin Lundy, the redoubtable Quaker abolitionist who at one time hoped to plant free colonies in Texas, published a brochure entitled "The War in Texas; a Crusade against the Government set on foot by Slaveholders."

Even the unofficial minister from the Republic of Texas, William F. Wharton, could see that the issue was bound to "agitate this Union more than did the attempt to restrict Missouri, nullification, and abolitionism, all combined." The division within the country and within the Democratic Party that already existed would be greatly exacerbated by a debate on the subject, and Jackson's hope of promoting the "Little Magician," Martin Van Buren, to the presidency might collapse. If Jackson had been able to pull an "incident" out of his sleeve, such as an "attack" by Mexico against Gaines's troops on the border or an Indian massacre below the Sabine, he might have united the nation for war. But in the absence of such an overt act, the best Jackson could do was to secure recognition of the Lone Star Republic—an act he postponed until his very last day in office, March 3, 1837. After San Jacinto he subscribed personal funds for Texas and he quietly encouraged Wharton to lay claim to all of northern Mexico as far as the Pacific; yet beyond that he dared not go.

His successor, Van Buren, was even more cautious, coldly rejecting the formal request to negotiate a treaty of annexation. The Democratic majority had, in the meantime, been whittled to the point where Speaker James K. Polk was reelected in the House by a scant thirteen votes. Furthermore, the terrible economic panic of 1837 had overtaken the United States, and many a businessman who might have been willing to pay higher taxes for an expansionist war in other circumstances now looked at the prospect with dire foreboding. In December that year, after a prominent abolitionist, Elijah Lovejoy, had been lynched by a mob in Illinois, the antislavery forces took the initiative by introducing a resolution condemning plans to annex Texas. For six months during 1838 the members of both houses raged in polemics, pro and con, until Adams talked the subject to death in a memorable filibuster lasting over three weeks.

The Texas regime, thoroughly disenchanted by now, withdrew its request for admission to the Union in October 1838, and for the next five or six years drifted on an alarmingly erratic course, boldly aggressive at times, at others running to the British for succor. In 1841 Texan President Mirabeau B. Lamar sent a force of 270 men across six hundred miles of desert to seize Sante Fe, New Mexico. The half-starved contingent arrived on the scene, was captured without firing a shot, and was ignominiously clapped into jail. The following March, it was Mexico's turn for an offensive; its army suddenly swept into San Antonio and other towns, seized some booty, and returned home. A similar foray in September by 1,200 troops yielded prisoners and more booty. None of this, of course, was decisive, but it left the issue hanging and forced the Texans to seek protection.

In the absence of U.S. support, one alternative was to climb under the umbrella of Great Britain. London, naturally, needed little encouragement since an independent Texas would act as a buffer to Washington's territorial ambitions. Moreover, it would relieve England of its total reliance on the United States for cotton. Unfortunately, Britain was impaled on the same spike as Washington. It had freed its West Indies slaves in 1833 at a cost of $100 million paid to the slaveholders, and its public, though anxious to see Texas' position fortified, would not support a slave state that had torn loose from a free one. The best that England could do for its potential ward, then, was to recognize the Lone Star Republic in 1842 and effectuate a temporary cease-fire between Texas and Mexico in 1843.

What followed this small effort at mediation sheds little credit on Washington's motives. In the White House at the time was John Tyler of Virginia, a nondescript Whig who had run for vice-president in 1840 on the ticket with William Henry Harrison—the military hero who had subdued Tecumseh and the Prophet. In the wake of depression, "Tippecanoe and Tyler too" were able to overwhelm the dapper Van Buren. But Harrison died of pneumonia only a month after the inauguration, and soon thereafter Tyler, in a patent political mistake, vetoed a favorite piece of Whig legislation, calling for a second U.S. bank. He promptly became a president without a party—certain to be bypassed at the next nominating convention. In these circumstances the Texas annexation issue seemed to the man from Virginia a made-to-order ladder for climbing back into public esteem.

Southerners just then were distraught at the cozy relations between Britain and the Lone Star Republic, mostly because they feared that the schemers in London would convince Texas to give up slavery. A carefully planted report by one of John Calhoun's friends, Duff Green, that Britain would indemnify Texan slaveholders if slavery were abolished, caused consternation on the banks of the Potomac. According to Tyler's Secretary of State, Abel P. Upshur, this was the opening gambit of a dark plot by the Londoners to disestablish slavery throughout the continent, thereby strengthening the competitive hand of England's sugar and cotton industries in Asia and the Caribbean. Wily old Albion would also build a wall against Washington's expansionism running from Canada and Oregon in the North to a Texas republic in the South that was simply a British satellite. The result, according to Upshur—an ultraslavocrat —would be severe pressure on the Southern states also to abolish human bondage.

There was never definitive proof of Britain's "plot" to disrupt the United States, but it gave Upshur a handle with which to renew talks of annexation. There was now an enemy at the gates, Great Britain, threatening to destroy America's economy, reestablish colonies and protectorates, and—in Upshur's lurid picture of events— even seize Cuba in payment for Spanish debts. Sam Houston, once again ensconced as president of the tenuous Lone Star Republic, had already withdrawn a second offer to be annexed earlier that year, but at Upshur's request cautiously agreed to talks. Negotiations began in October 1843, were quickly concluded, and a tentative treaty, subject to ratification—signed in April 1844. Unfortunately for Upshur, the treaty ran into Henry Clay's steamroller in the Senate. Of the 29 Whigs—the majority party—all but one voted against the pact, and of the 23 Democrats, 8 spurned the agreement despite a letter from retired Andrew Jackson urging annexation. The issue carried over to the 1844 presidential elections—and some strange maneuvers in the postelection period.

II

When the news was flashed to Washington by telegraph that James Knox Polk had been nominated for president by the May 1844 Democratic convention in Baltimore, cynical Whigs demanded, "Who is James K. Polk?" Polk was not as unknown as the question implied: he had served in the House of Representatives for seven terms, from 1825 to 1839, had been its speaker for two years, and had been governor of Tennessee for one term. Both in and out of Congress he had been a chief spokesman for Old Hickory Jackson, his views meshing so closely with those of his mentor that he was nicknamed "Young Hickory." But Polk, it is true, was no front-runner. He lacked the magnetism of a Henry Clay or the color and charisma of a Jackson. As Allan Nevins describes him, he was "an honest, conscientious, and limited man, who was incapable perhaps of the highest moral elevation, but was certainly also incapable of deceit and double-dealing. . . . He was a man to command respect, but neither liking nor awe." In other circumstances he would have made a good cabinet member or chief presidential aide, perhaps a vice-president. His own sights did not go beyond that: on the masthead of his newspaper, the Nashville Union, was a slogan urging the nomination of Martin Van Buren for president, and James K. Polk for vice-president. But Polk was propelled to a loftier pedestal, and he became one of those accidents of history who leave a greater imprint on events than was intended for them.

Young Hickory, oldest of ten children, was born in Mecklenburg County, North Carolina, in November 1795. His grandfather Ezekiel, a colonel in the Revolutionary War, had received a land grant in the western section of the state—soon to become Tennessee—and later had purchased additional holdings. Had it been up to him he would have migrated to his land in 1795, but it took a full decade to convince the rest of the family—including Polk's father, Samuel—

that this was the land of promise to which they ought to betake themselves. Finally, in 1806, they acceded to his wish, and though conditions in Tennessee were still rustic, were soon able to carve for themselves a stable and prosperous niche, so that young James never knew the economic adversity that plagued so many of his contemporaries.

James was almost eleven when his family settled in the valley of the Duck River. He was handsome, with gray eyes, dark hair, and clear features, but small in stature, frail, and evidently neither suited for nor interested in becoming a farmer. His parents taught him the three R's and indoctrinated him with the Jeffersonian principles they themselves believed in as religiously as the Ten Commandments. But his formal education—after a brief and unhappy stint as a store clerk—did not begin until he was seventeen. After three years at the University of North Carolina, where—as one magazine later put it—he "never missed a recitation, nor omitted the punctilious performance of any duty," he came home to read law in the office of one of Jackson's close friends, Felix Grundy. By the time he had hung up his lawyer's shingle in 1820, his family was in solid circumstances, having built a sumptuous brick home in Columbia, and though it remained Jeffersonian in philosophy was already part of the Tennessee establishment.

Three years later—prodded by the girl he would soon marry, Sarah Childress—Polk entered politics, winning a seat in the state legislature, where he voted to send his hero, Jackson, to the U.S. Senate. After a single term, he moved on to the House of Representatives in Washington, and at the age of thirty began a new career noteworthy for its populism. He plunked for a bill turning over federal lands to Tennessee, the sale of which would be used for a free public school system—a radical idea at the time. He advocated an amendment abolishing the electoral college in favor of direct balloting for the presidency. And when, in 1828, Old Hickory—having been denied the presidency four years before by a deal between Clay and John Quincy Adams—was finally chosen chief executive, Polk became his chief spokesman in the "war" against the United States Bank. He served in the all-important post of chairman of the Ways and Means Committee, became Speaker of the House, after an initial defeat, then in 1839 yielded to Jackson's plea to run for governor of Tennessee and retake the state from the Whigs. It was on this occasion that Felix Grundy attached the sobriquet Young Hickory to Polk, in order to emphasize his kinship with Jackson. Polk did win the governorship, by 2,600 votes, but lost to the Whigs next time around. As the 1844 party conventions opened in 1843–44, therefore, he was in virtual oblivion politically. President Tyler, the Democrat who had turned Whig to run with Harrison in 1840, offered him the secretaryship of the navy, but he rejected this because it would take him out of the running for vice-president. Instead he endorsed Van Buren—as did Jackson—and waited hopefully for the Little Magician to call on him to accept the second spot on the ticket.

The long shadow of Texas and the related issue of slavery, however, changed the preconvention outlook decisively. There was a hint of trouble for the established politicians when a new party, the Liberty Party, met in August 1843 to nominate James Gillespie Birney on an antislavery platform. But the steamrollers of Whig Henry Clay and Democrat Martin Van Buren seemed to be meeting little opposition. Both men were opposed to immediate annexation of Texas, and both evidently had agreed to remove the issue from the campaign by sidestepping it. "Annexation and war with Mexico are identical," Clay wrote in his famous Raleigh letter published in the *National Intelligencer* of April 27, 1844. "I certainly am not willing to involve this country in a foreign war for the object of acquiring Texas." Van Buren, much to the discomfiture of Southerners in his party, came out with an identical position—that annexation might lead to war, that it would be costly to assume Texan debts estimated at $3 to $13 million, and that the matter might best be postponed to a more propitious occasion. Polk, on the other hand, came out with a firm declaration for "immediate *re*annexation" of Texas (presumably because it had already been ceded in the Louisiana Purchase) as well as for taking all of Oregon. Both were justified, he said, because the United States must never "permit Great Britain or any other foreign power to plant a colony or hold dominion over any portion of the people or territory of either." It was this forthrightness on annexation that won him the nomination.

Clay's statement helped to cement his position with the Whigs, who on May 1 nominated him by acclamation. But for Van Buren, opposition to annexation was a catastrophe, losing for him the support of his old friend Andrew Jackson. Old Hickory, manipulating events from the Hermitage back home, urged fellow Democrats to choose James Knox Polk, and in due course, after Van Buren was unable to win the necessary two-thirds vote, Polk was nominated unanimously on the ninth ballot. It was the first time a "dark horse" had been chosen as candidate for the presidency, but if it healed disunity in the Democratic Party, it intensified disunity in the country. A South Carolina newspaper called for an immediate meeting of Congress to either "admit Texas into the Union, or to proceed peaceably and calmly to arrange the dissolution of the Union." A mass meeting in New Orleans threatened to incorporate the Lone Star Republic into Louisiana if it were not done by the United States. And on the other side, in Vermont, the legislature resolved that annexation "if effected, will be a virtual dissolution of the Union. . . ."

There were other issues in the campaign, of course, including the tariff, fiscal policy, and Oregon, but Texas and slavery held the spotlight. The Democratic platform called for the "*re*annexation" of Texas and the "*re*occupation" of all of Oregon up to "fifty-four forty." Public sentiment had so crystallized in favor of expansion by this time that "fifty-four forty or fight" and "reannexation" of Texas carried Polk into the White House. If Clay was by far the more popular figure, Polk had on his side the more popular cause. Even so it was the minute vote for the Liberty Party and Birney that torpedoed Clay's ambitions. The abolitionist polled a scant 62,300 ballots, as against 1,337,243 for Polk and 1,299,062 for Clay, but they were enough to deprive Clay of New York and Michigan, without which Polk would have lost by 146 to 129 electoral votes.

Polk, at forty-nine, was one of the youngest and strangest figures ever to become chief executive. He made few friends, he considered social occasions a waste of time, he lacked a sense of humor, and was so calm and courteous that he seemed to have no feelings. He was neither brilliant nor bold, but on the other hand he did not resort to circuitousness or machination. He believed that presidents should serve a single term in office, and whether he could or could not have been elected a second time, he made himself unavailable. Prim and stiff, he approached the issue of expansion with a remarkable steadfastness that rallied the nation to its "manifest destiny."

Historians differ as to whether Polk intended to plunge his nation into the thicket of war at the very outset, or whether events simply pushed him in that direction. Those most charitable to Polk point out that he sent John Slidell on a mission to Mexico to iron out differences peaceably, and that he retreated completely from "fifty-four forty or fight" in relation to Oregon. But the argument is more rhetorical than real, for Polk was intent on acquiring an enormous parcel of land for the United States—Texas, Oregon, New Mexico, California, if possible Mexico itself—and it was all but inevitable that somewhere along the way a spark would ignite. Like any other rational head of government, Polk preferred to gain his objectives through diplomacy, but he understood full well that the next step after diplomatic failure was war.

III

The urgent territorial issues before Polk as he took office revolved around Texas and Oregon. Insofar as the latter was concerned, the British were decidedly unreceptive to tedious demands such as "fifty-four forty," showing no inclination to clear out of the upper part of Oregon country just because it had been proclaimed in a Democratic Party platform. The influential London *Times* commented that "the territory of Oregon will never be wrested from the British Crown, to which it belongs, but by WAR." Lord Aberdeen, British foreign secretary, seconded these sentiments, though in proper diplomatic phraseology. Winning Oregon up to the Alaska border obviously would take a little doing.

As for Texas, the prospects looked better since part of the problem had already been resolved by President Tyler in the interim period between election and inauguration. Tyler had been unable, it will be recalled, to secure ratification of a *treaty* of annexation, which required a two-thirds vote of the Senate. Asserting now that the elections had been a mandate for incorporating Texas, he took the circuitous and constitutionally dubious route of putting before Congress a joint resolution which required only a simple majority of the two legislative bodies. In vain did opponents point out that there was no popular mandate, that the combined antiannexation ballots for Clay and Birney were greater than for Polk. But in the end, after much casuistry and a barrage of amendments and amendments to amendments, Texas became the twenty-eighth state of the Union. Tyler signed the joint resolution on March 1, 1845, three days before he turned over the reins to Polk. There remained now only two problems: to make the annexation palatable to Mexico—through negotiations if possible, through war if necessary—and to fix the final boundaries of the twenty-eighth state.

Historically, the Nueces River, 130 miles north and east of the Rio Grande, had been considered the border of Texas. It had been so set by Spain in 1816 and reaffirmed in all official maps of the ensuing period. Austin, Jackson, Senator Benton, Van Buren, and Calhoun at one time or another had also accepted this as the outer limit of the province. After independence, however, the wide-eyed Texans, when they weren't wildly laying claim to more than half of Mexico, as their Congress did in 1842, or talking of an "unlimited" territory to the Pacific, officially set their boundary at the Rio Grande. Polk was only too happy to endorse this ukase. According to President Anson Jones of Texas, Polk secretly proposed a military campaign not only to the Rio Grande, but beyond into Matamoros. The American chief executive desired, he said, that "when Texas was finally brought into the Union, she might bring a war with her; and this was the object of the expedition to Matamoros, as now proposed." The tragedy in all this is that Mexico, despite her formal position against annexation, would probably have accepted the loss of Texas as a *fait accompli,* provided she did not have to suffer the additional humiliation of losing the territory beyond the Nueces.

For Polk, however, the frontier issue was linked to a broader concept of expansion that included California and New Mexico as well. Quite early in the game he confided to Secretary of the Navy George Bancroft that California ranked high on his order of priorities, and the secretary, taking the hint, ordered Commodore John D. Sloat to occupy the Pacific province should hostilities break out over Texas. Polk, of course, was ready to purchase California, as Jackson had been years back when he ordered Butler to put in a bid for it. But if purchase was impossible, intrigue and revolution were the second line of aggression. Special instructions went out to the American consul in Monterey, California, in October 1845, advising that while "the President will make no effort and use no influence to induce California to become one of the free and independent states of the Union, yet if the people should desire to unite their destiny with ours, they would be received as brethren. . . ." That Washington was not averse to helping the process along is evident by the expeditions undertaken by a young army lieutenant, John C. Frémont —husband of Senator Benton's daughter, Jessie—who by strange happenstance was on the scene a year later when a small group of Americans raised the Bear Flag and proclaimed an independent Republic of California. Though ostensibly involved in scientific exploration, Frémont in fact was engaged in activity similar to that of Jackson in East Florida and Houston in Texas.

Admittedly upper California was no great boon to Mexico. Settled by the "intrepid Franciscan" Junipero Serra in 1769, its population in 1845 was a mere 10,000 whites, of whom 800 were Americans, plus 15,000 Indians. Communication was abysmal—it was 1,500 miles from the Mexican capital and nearly impossible to reach by land. Occasionally a ship arrived with instructions from the central government, but contact was minimal and political rule little more than a farce. The income from duties collected at Monterey (one of the four tiny towns in its confines) was less than $100,000, most of which disappeared before it reached Mexico City. There were virtually no police or courts, no schools, newspapers, or regular postal services. In 1836 some of the citizens, abetted by Americans and other foreigners, had raised the cry of independence, expelled the few Mexican troops, and established a native government under three local—and feuding—leaders. Seven years later Santa Anna sent a force to straighten out matters, but these troops too were driven out by February 1845.

If California was a liability to Mexico, it offered stirring economic prospects for venturous Americans. As early as 1796 a New England merchantman made the two-hundred-day trip around the Horn, up along the Pacific Coast, and into the small harbor of Monterey. By Spanish law, foreigners were forbidden to trade in the area but scant attention was paid to such technicalities, as numerous ships followed in the wake of the pioneer. They sold beads, gunpowder, cotton, and rum in exchange for furs, then went on to China, where they sold the furs, returning home with oriental wares. The profits were alluring: one Yankee shipmaster realized $22,400 in Canton for otter skins which cost $1,100 in California; another exchanged a few hundred yards of cheap textiles for peltries that brought $7,000 in China. Yankee shippers, typically, dropped anchor and rode inland on horseback to buy hides at approximately $2 apiece. Often it took them a year or eighteen months to fill their ship, but it was a prosperous business with great potential. So too was the American whaling industry, composed of 650 vessels in Pacific waters, valued at $20 million and employing 17,000 men.

There was as yet no easy overland route by which American farmers could settle and exploit the lush lands of the Sacramento Valley, but in 1841 John Bidwell opened a path westward by leading a small party on a harrowing six-month trip that began in Missouri and ended in the promised land with participants at the edge of starvation. Another group, five years later, trying to duplicate the original feat, endured even worse hardship and many deaths, yet in due time a path was chiseled across the mountains to the Pacific El Dorado. Long before this trek would become commonplace, an American representative in Mexico City, Waddy Thompson, described California as "the richest, the most beautiful, the healthiest country in the world. . . . The harbor of St. [San] Francisco is capacious enough to receive the navies of all the world, and the neighborhood furnishes live oak enough to build all the ships of those navies."

To permit such a rich land to remain in the limp hands of chaotic Mexico or, worse still, to fall to Britain or France, seemed immoral to Polk. Jackson had tried to buy San Francisco Bay for a half million dollars in 1835. Daniel Webster had offered to compromise with Britain on the Oregon issue in 1842 if London would apply pressure on Mexico to sell California. And that same year a zealous naval officer, Commodore Thomas Ap Catesby Jones, hearing what he thought was solid information about war between the United States and Mexico, set sail for California, captured Monterey, and boldly proclaimed the province's annexation to the Union—only to give it up the next day when he learned of his mistake. It was now Polk's turn at bat. "The interests of our commerce and our whale fisheries on the Pacific Ocean," Secretary of State James Buchanan wrote to the American consul at Monterey, "demand that you should exert the greatest vigilance in discovering and defeating any attempts which may be made by foreign governments to acquire a control over that country." The prospect of a British take-over was not entirely fantasy—in fact Mexico offered it to London a month after the Mexican War began—but whether this or America's economic desires constituted a legitimate license for Polk seizing California is another matter. The bogey of foreign lust always seemed to extenuate American lust in the minds of American expansionists.

At any rate, a potpourri of issues—California, New Mexico, Texas, the boundary, Oregon country, and a small matter of $2 million in claims owed by Mexico to U.S. citizens—all were linked into a single drama, with the results in one place affecting those elsewhere. Mexicans, for instance, nursed vain hopes that Britain would go to war over Oregon and then join them in the defense of Texas, New Mexico, and California against a common enemy. Polk's diplomacy therefore was aimed at keeping the potential allies separate. In the spring of 1845 he dispatched a special agent to Mexico City in the hopes that diplomatic relations could be restored and the interrelated disputes over Texas, its boundary, and the old claims, settled. The agent, William Parrott, reported that the government of Jose Herrera was receptive, and in September the President assigned to the delicate task former Louisiana Congressman John Slidell, who was fluent in Spanish. The plenipotentiary was authorized to pay $25 million—and if necessary $40 million—as well as the few million in American claims, if the penniless Mexican government would agree to a boundary at the Rio Grande and to cession of California and New Mexico. Slidell arrived in Mexico City in December 1845, but, contrary to expectations, was never able to enter into negotiations with either Herrera or the military group under General Mariano Paredes which overthrew him. The citizens of Mexico were so bitter against the United States that it was political suicide for any regime even to contemplate an arrangement with Uncle Sam. "Be assured," Slidell wrote Polk, "that nothing is to be done with these people until they have been chastized."

Meanwhile a concurrent game was being played out relative to Oregon. Back in 1818 the United States had rejected an offer to divide the territory with Britain, and had instead agreed to a ten-year treaty for joint occupation. The treaty was renewed in 1827 and was to remain in force indefinitely until one or the other party gave a year's notice to cancel it. On three occasions Britain indicated a willingness to split the country in two, but differences over a stretch of territory between the 49th parallel and the Columbia River (two thirds of the present state of Washington) prevented agreement.

Oregon per se was of only secondary importance to the expanding British empire. Only 700 Englishmen lived above the 49th parallel and the Hudson's Bay Company's earnings of a half million a year from buffalo skins and other furs were of small significance compared to what John Bull might lose in a war with Uncle Sam. It could hardly offset the loss of the American market in manufactures or the cutoff of cotton imports needed for Birmingham's textile mills. Furthermore this was a time when the government in London was beset by agitation over the corn laws and harried by a potato crisis in Ireland which would soon reach famine proportions. Britain, then, was realistic enough to recognize the need for compromise, especially since Americans were flocking to the Northwest in droves—3,000 in 1845 alone. But while she was ready to talk about a *modus vivendi* she would not be humiliated by ultimatums.

The Democratic Party platform of 1844, calling for "reoccupation" of Oregon and "fifty-four forty or fight," seemed precisely like an ultimatum to the British. Polk, in his inaugural address, speaking in a heavy downpour with few people able to hear his thirty-minute address, reemphasized America's "clear and unquestionable" title to all of Oregon—unleashing jingoistic sentiments in many parts of the country. "*Oregon is ours,*" cried the Washington *Madisonian,* "and we will keep it, at the price, if need be, of every drop of the nation's blood." But despite all the bombast, Polk was a realist too. It is a cardinal rule of politics to avoid fighting two wars at one time. Thus it was that after protracted negotiations, in which Polk spoke alternately soft and hard, an agreement was worked out in June 1846 very much along the lines suggested by John Quincy Adams many years before and repeated by John Calhoun in 1844. Oregon country was divided along the 49th parallel, the northern part going to Britain, the southern to the United States. Despite the fiery pledge of "fifty-four forty or fight," the prospect of one war at a time was evidently enough.

IV

The war that Young Hickory concentrated on was with the weaker of the two adversaries, Mexico. Step by step he manipulated that nation into hostilities with an adroitness worth the envy of most of his predecessors. "It is impossible to conceive of an administration less warlike, or more intriguing, than that of Mr. Polk," wrote Senator Thomas Hart Benton a decade later. "These were men of peace, with objects to be accomplished by means of war. . . . They wanted a small war, just large enough to require a treaty of peace, and not large enough to make military reputations. . . ." Under the classic concept that aggression must be camouflaged in defensive rhetoric, Polk painted the United States as the aggrieved party, its offers for negotiations spurned, its hope for peace rejected.

In fact, however, the President had long been prepared for a military solution. General Zachary Taylor, who commanded the first division at New Orleans, had been ordered into Texas in the summer of 1845, and had established camp at Corpus Christi to await developments. On January 13, 1846, the day after Polk learned that Slidell's mission had aborted, Taylor was given the fateful instruction to take the left bank of the Rio Grande—what is now the American side—occupying it on March 23, and pointing his cannon ominously across the river at the Mexican settlement of Matamoros. Before long Taylor was building a fort, later to be known as Fort Brown, to emphasize American determination to hold the region. Viewed in the best light these were provocations; viewed realistically they were acts of war, since the disputed land is conceded by the vast majority of historians today to have been part of the Mexican state of Tamaulipas.

For Polk, however, the shoe was on the other foot; there was nothing precipitate in this action. After hearing a report by Slidell, he told his cabinet and recorded in his diary that "we had ample cause of war, and that it was impossible we could stand in status quo, or that I could remain silent much longer. . . ." So far the only affront to the United States had been the refusal of Mexico to receive an emissary, Slidell. Yet it raised hackles with the hawks, who cried out against the "insult" to American "dignity." Every grievance that could be dug up about insults to the flag, mistreatment of American citizens, seizures of American property, was used to inflame sentiments; and for good measure the jingoists warned that the United States could tarry no longer, lest Britain or France take steps that would endanger "American security."

On May 9, 1846, Polk held a crucial session with his cabinet and suggested that Congress be polled for a declaration of war. The only pretext at hand was that Mexico had refused to negotiate, an obviously thin pretext that could satisfy only those with inflamed passions. One cabinet member, Secretary of the Navy (and historian) George Bancroft, had misgivings; he would be happier, he said, if the government would wait for Mexico to commit the first "act of hostility." This would reinforce the stance of defensiveness and patience, and of course weld the American people behind their government. As luck would have it, such an incident had already occurred and would be reported to Polk that evening. In distant Texas General Taylor and his 3,900 men had been asked by General Pedro de Ampudia to retire from the Rio Grande to the Nueces—and had refused. Instead, a week later Taylor blockaded the river to prevent two Mexican ships from supplying Matamoros, threatening the town with starvation. On April 24 the Mexicans (now led by General Mariano Arista) responded by dispatching a force across the river, killing and wounding 16 Americans, and capturing the rest of a contingent of 63 dragoons.

This minor skirmish proved a windfall for Polk. Instead of a flimsy pretext he could arouse American patriotism with a story of a brazen "attack" against innocents. The message he sent Congress claimed that "after reiterated menaces, Mexico has passed the boundary of the United States, has invaded our territory and shed American blood upon American soil. . . . As war exists . . . by the act of Mexico herself, we are called upon by every consideration of duty and patriotism to vindicate with decision the honor, the rights, and interests of our country. . . ." By any standard this was a masterpiece of historical distortion. It glossed over the fact that the boundary issue was at best a subject of controversy, and it implied —contrary to intelligence reports by Taylor himself—that the Mexicans were preparing a general offensive, when in reality they were in a defensive stance trying to lift a small but irritating blockade.

Nevertheless a veritable Niagara of patriotism engulfed the country. If the division before had been intense, the House now voted for war by the overwhelming margin of 174 to 14, and the Senate by 42 to 2. Many an oppositionist, who would later regain his courage, feared to be counted on the side of peace, lest he be charged with treason. Senator John A. Dix of New York wrote Van Buren that he would have liked to vote against "the Texas fraud" which violated "every just consideration of national dignity, duty and policy," but he knew it would be labeled "high treason" and he was forced therefore to "desist." Garrett Davis of Kentucky charged that "it is our own President who began this war," but amid taunts and out-cries he voted for the war declaration anyway. John C. Calhoun was willing to vote men and munitions for the invasion but could not bring himself to approve the preamble of the resolution, which laid the blame on Mexico. It would be, he said, like plunging "a dagger into his own heart, and more so." His motion to strike the preamble lost in the Senate by 28 to 18. When Congressman Columbus De-lano of Ohio, an abolitionist who stood against Polk, denounced the war as "unholy, unrighteous, and damnable," Stephen A. Douglas of Illinois demanded: "Is there not treason in the heart that can feel, and poison in the breath that can utter, such sentiments against their own country, when forced to take up arms in self-defense, to repel the invasion of a brutal and perfidious foe?"

Four months previously the New York *Herald,* sensing a new tem-per in the land, had written that approval for the doctrine of annex-ation was astounding. People were "puzzling their brains to find out new countries to annex." It was the "stepping stone to popularity . . . to invent some new annexation scheme." By May the expansion-ist fury was irrepressible. "Mexico or death," read placards in New York. "For Mexico; fall in!" was the slogan on a recruiting banner in Indianapolis. Congress authorized a call for 50,000 volunteers; 300,-000 men responded. In Illinois the quota of three regiments of 1,000 each was instantly met, while thousands more pleaded to be en-rolled. If enthusiasm in the older states was subdued—only 13,000 volunteered in the original thirteen states—it was uproarious in the Mississippi Valley, where 49,000 rallied to the colors, all hoping to "revel in the halls of the Montezumas."

A few courageous souls resisted jingo pressures. Senator Thomas Corwin of Ohio shouted that "If I were a Mexican I would tell you: 'Have you not room in your own country? . . . If you come into mine, we will greet you with bloody hands and welcome you to hos-pitable graves.'" Congressman Joshua R. Giddings, of the same state, called the venture "a war against an unoffending people, with-out adequate or just cause, for the purpose of conquest; with a de-sign of extending slavery; in violation of the Constitution, against the dictates of justice, humanity, the sentiments of the age in which we live, and the precepts of religion which we profess. I will lend it no aid, no support whatever. I will not bathe my hands in the blood of the people of Mexico. . . ." But these were men spitting against the wind. America was consumed with inverted idealism and a mys-tic justification for aggrandizement.

V

That Uncle Sam was neither defending his honor nor his territory, but attacking that of someone else, became evident immediately. Secretary Buchanan proposed to Polk that he insert a sentence in his war message disavowing any intent "to acquire either California or New Mexico or any other portion of the Mexican territory." But the President coldly spurned such suggestions. Though "we had not gone to war for conquest," he told his cabinet, "yet it was clear that in making peace we would if practicable obtain California and such other portion of the Mexican territory as would be sufficient to indemnify our claimants on Mexico, and to defray the expense of the war which that power by her long continued wrongs and injuries had forced us to wage." The victim was to pay the victimizer a territorial fee for the privilege of being conquered!

The pragmatic Polk matched words with actions. Within a few days orders went forth to Colonel Stephen W. Kearny to invade New Mexico, seize Santa Fe, and move on to California. The doughty colonel quickly outfitted an army of 1,500 men at Fort Leavenworth and was on his way to Santa Fe. The town fell without a shot being fired, giving Kearny control over an area inhabited by 80,000 Mexicans, and releasing him—after a governor had been installed—for duty westward. Meanwhile things were also going well on the Pacific Coast, where Commodores Sloat and Robert F. Stockton and the "scientific" explorer, Captain Frémont, teamed up for a more eventful campaign. In June and July Frémont's forces fought a few engagements and lent a hand with the absurd "Bear Flag Revolt," appropriately declaring California independent on July 4. Simultaneously Commodore Sloat seized Monterey and occupied the San Francisco area and Los Angeles. Again, the whole province fell under the American yoke with hardly a shot being fired.

Subsequently, however, both in New Mexico and in California the Yankee officers were in for some surprises; in both places the natives broke out in rebellions that had to be suppressed with bloodshed. Near the end of September, Stockton in San Francisco was brought the sensational news that all of Southern California had rebelled; unbeknown to the commodore the American garrison, after a week of fighting, had surrendered to the rebels. The natives held most of the interior towns and were ready to move on the disorganized American forces on the coast. Had Kearny not arrived to the rescue in December and defeated the popular forces at San Pasqual and

San Diego, the situation might have been dire. These two victories, in which Kearny lost a third of his effectives and was himself wounded, paved the way for the final American advance. Stockton with a motley group of 500 men, and Frémont, from another direction, moved on Los Angeles, putting down riots against American rule. On January 12, 1847, Frémont negotiated the Treaty of Cahuenga, which ended resistance and gave Polk his great prize, California.

In New Mexico a state of placidity endured until December, when a Mexican plot to rise up and kill all Americans in the region was discovered. Colonel Sterling Price, the military commander who had relieved Kearny, immediately instituted stern repressive measures but was unable to find the ringleaders of the projected revolt. In January 1847 the rebels struck, killing Governor Charles Bent and other government leaders, and mutilating their bodies. It took Price two weeks of whirlwind operations to smash the rebels and level their stronghold at Taos. The action, however, was decisive so that for the duration of the Mexican War there was no further resistance in New Mexico. Thus, within eight months, Polk's legions had completed the thrust to the Pacific and the United States was now richer by more than a half million square miles.

The main theater of war, of course, was along the Rio Grande and in Mexico proper. Early in June, with Matamoros safely in his hands, General Taylor began the trek toward Monterrey, a city of 15,000 that was considered the strategic strong point of northern Mexico. In his mind, as in others, the defense of Texas' alleged borders was to be accomplished by conquering Mexico, or at least large portions of it, and forcing a humbled nation to accept a dictated peace. After a three-day battle in late September, "Old Rough and Ready" Taylor gained the first major leg of this goal, as General Pedro Ampudia surrendered at Monterrey. The Rinconada Pass across the mountains was now open for an American advance and before the end of the year almost all of northeastern Mexico was under U.S. rule. Polk could, at this point, have ordered an overland campaign toward Mexico City, but he was unhappy with Taylor's growing popularity and decided therefore to change both strategy and commanders. The job was first given to sixty-four-year-old Senator Benton of Missouri, then to dandyish Winfield Scott of the regular army, whose boastful arrogance was likely to keep him from gaining a large following. Scott's plan was to seize Vera Cruz by sea, then march to Mexico City. Early in March, then, the navy landed Scott and his army of 12,000 men three miles from the port city. From here, with the aid of men who would leave their mark on history fifteen years later—Robert E. Lee, George B. McClellan, and Ulysses S. Grant—Scott's forces moved on to Churubusco, where in August they won a resounding—though costly—victory. A month later, on September 17, the conquerors finally reached the halls of the Montezumas, and as Mexicans watched from the treetops, Scott and his "doughboys" marched through the city toward the central plaza. Unless the Mexicans decided to wage guerrilla war from the hinterlands, the fighting was now all but over, the arena of action shifting from the military to the diplomatic front. The United States had paid a price of 1,721 killed in battle or from wounds, plus 11,-550 from disease and other causes—a modest cost, as wars go, for so great a victory.

VI

But back home in the meantime, despite the military success, Polk's opposition was as fervidly on the march as Scott's soldiers in distant Mexico. After the first wave of jingoism had spent itself the Whigs, North and South, caught second wind and took to the offensive. The group was not homogeneous, being divided into the "conservatives," who castigated Polk because he had deceived the country and manipulated it into an aggressive war, and the radicals, who feared that conquest in the South would advance slavery. Among the former were men like Daniel Webster and businessmen such as Nathan Appleton, who were known as the Cotton Whigs because they had ties with the cotton community in the South. The radicals were led by inspired abolitionists such as John Quincy Adams, Charles Francis Adams, Charles Sumner, and were referred to as the Conscience Whigs. The Democrats too embraced a significant minority of abolitionist radicals, such as Preston King of New York and David Wilmot of Pennsylvania, as well as old Jeffersonians like Albert Gallatin and some of Calhoun's followers.

Once the hysteria began to abate, the voices of opposition became more persistent. In terms that were to be heard 120 years later during another unpopular war, Whigs castigated Polk for exceeding his authority. "This war is a nondescript," cried Congressman Robert Toombs of Georgia during the 1846–47 session. "We charge the President with usurping the war-making power . . . with seizing a country . . . which had been for centuries, and was then in the possession of the Mexicans." Caleb B. Smith of Indiana insisted that Polk had invaded land "to which we had no manner of claim whatsoever" since Texas "never had owned one inch of territory beyond the Nueces." The opponents who feared being dubbed "treasonous" in May 1846 were less than a year later charging their President with war crimes. Some were proposing that Congress refuse to authorize monies for continuing hostilities. Joshua R. Giddings of Ohio accused the army of planting "itself in the midst of Mexican cornfields" and killing "unarmed peasants" as well as raping Mexican virgins. Charles Hudson of Massachusetts claimed that the war had been pursued solely "in order to give the South a perpetual preponderance in the councils of the nation." Columbus Delano called upon Congress to vote down requests for war matériel even though this would buttress Polk's charge of "aid and comfort" to the enemy. Delano conceded that "Congress should exercise the right of refusing supplies with wisdom and candor and not in a spirit of factious opposition." But he felt it must be done nonetheless "for the country's welfare, and because to do so is truly to sustain the honor and glory of the nation."

The center of opposition was New England where the Massachusetts Legislature passed a resolution branding the United States as an aggressor and conqueror, and called on "all good citizens to join in efforts to arrest this war." Daniel Webster, leader of the conservative Whigs, asserted that the President, by giving instructions to General Taylor to proceed to the Rio Grande, had in fact wheedled the nation into war in violation of the Constitution. What, he asked, "is the value of this constitutional provision, if the President of his own authority may make such military movements as must bring on war?" New England newspapers, as well as the New York *Evening Post* and the Washington *National Intelligencer,* decried the invasion of Mexico because, they said, it would inevitably set up a permanent military aristocracy. Sixty-seven Whigs in the House voted against the first appropriations bill, and Calhoun asserted that the war was destroying America's reputation for "justice, moderation, or wisdom." "In the early stages of our Government," Calhoun said, "the great anxiety was how to preserve liberty; the great anxiety now is the attainment of mere military glory."

Had Polk attempted to impose a draft in order to recruit soldiers, there is no doubt that the crescendo of opposition would have been much greater. It reached, in fact, far beyond Congress, reflecting the bitterness of intellectuals, pacifists, reformers, abolitionists, and average citizens. Charles E. Sumner spoke for the pacifist and antislavery opposition, which endured throughout the war, when he told Bostoners in an 1845 oration that "in our age there can be no peace that is not honorable, there can be no war that is not dishonorable." And pacifist Elihu Burritt organized meetings of workingmen in New England to denounce the annexation of Texas "because it would be giving men that live upon the blood of others, an opportunity of dipping their hands still deeper in the sin of slavery." Workingmen's groups in New York, Boston, and Lowell, Massachusetts, held meetings to urge withdrawal of American troops "to some undisputed land belonging to the United States."

The war was also condemned by poet James Russell Lowell in his famous *Biglow Papers:*

> *They jest want this Californy*
> *So's to lug new slave-states in*
> *To abuse ye, an' to scorn ye,*
> *And to plunder ye like sin.*

Henry David Thoreau wrote in his classic *Essay on Civil Disobedience* that "when a sixth of the population of a nation which has undertaken to be the refuge of liberty are slaves, and a whole country is unjustly overrun and conquered by a foreign army, and subjected to military law, I think that it is not too soon for honest men to rebel and revolutionize." Thoreau urged his fellow citizens to withhold war taxes from the government, and spent a night in Concord prison for his own refusal.

The babble of protest did not end even after Scott's amazing victory. On December 22, 1847, a young congressman from Illinois, Abraham Lincoln, introduced a resolution demanding that the President inform the House "whether the spot on which the blood of our citizens was shed" was not in fact the territory of Spain until the Mexican revolution and, since then, Mexican. A month or two later Representative Hudson went further with a resolution that the American army be withdrawn to "the east bank of the Rio Grande," that no indemnities be assessed against Mexico and that the boundary be placed somewhere between the Rio Grande and the Nueces. The measure was defeated three to one, but 41 Whigs voted for it. In January 1848, when the peace treaty was already being negotiated, Congressman George Ashmun tacked an amendment to a bill voting thanks to General Taylor, which said that the war had been "unnecessarily and unconstitutionally begun by the president of the United States." Though it was not included in the final bill, it momentarily carried by 82 to 81, with a future president, Lincoln, voting aye. A couple of weeks later Lincoln again denounced Polk's arguments as being "from beginning to end the sheerest deception." The President's "mind," he said, "taxed beyond its power, is running hither and thither, like some tortured creature on a burning surface, finding no position on which it can settle down and be at ease." The war was now twenty months old; when would it end, he wanted to know.

There was sound reason for opposition fears, because in the interim the appetite for conquest, once whetted, had grown remorselessly. Until the fall of 1847 most expansionist sentiment rested on acquiring, in addition to Texas, only upper California and New Mexico. Beginning in October 1847, after Scott's military victories, however, responsible newspapers, political figures, generals, and members of Polk's cabinet began to set their sights much higher. "It is a gorgeous prospect," wrote the New York *Herald* on October 8, 1847, "this annexation of all Mexico. It were more desirable that she should come to us voluntarily; but as we shall have no peace until she be annexed, let it come, even though force be necessary at first to bring her. Like the Sabine virgins, she will soon learn to love her ravishers." Even the *National Whig*, an opposition sheet, spoke of annexation of all Mexico to assure "peace and quiet." General Taylor did not go so far but for a time suggested incorporation of all the enemy's territory east of the Sierra Madre mountains—a sentiment shared by Secretary of State Buchanan, who said that the better elements in Mexico "dread nothing so much as the withdrawal of our army." The New Orleans *Picayune* trotted out the old chestnut about Mexico's being likely to "fall into the arms of a European dynasty" if American troops withdrew. Secretary of the Treasury, Robert J. Walker, perhaps the most sanguine expansionist in the cabinet, urged seizure of the whole Mexican nation. Sentiment seemed to be crystallizing for Senator Daniel S. Dickinson's resolution that "true policy requires the Government of the United States to strengthen its political and commercial relations upon this continent by the annexation of such contiguous territory as may conduce to that end, and can be justly obtained." Senator Lewis Cass of Michigan, soon to be a candidate for the presidency, noted that "to attempt to prevent the American people from taking possession of Mexico, if they demand it, would be as futile in effect, as to undertake to stop the rushing of the cataract of Niagara."

A diplomatic accident, however, conspired against the all-Mexico movement and sent its aspirations plummeting. Polk, as already noted, had not wanted a big war, among other reasons because it might make a hero out of Taylor or some other general. He still hoped that some Mexican leader would sell the coveted territories before it was too late. Accordingly he issued instructions on the very day war was declared, May 13, 1846, to let the peripatetic Santa Anna, then in exile, filter through the American blockade to his homeland—on the promise that he would accede to American terms once he again assumed power. As usual, Santa Anna betrayed his benefactor, and instead of urging settlement, aroused his countrymen to resist the invader.

Undaunted, after Scott had landed in Vera Cruz, Polk tried another ploy. He was much concerned at the time over opposition within his own party by Calhoun against large scale conquests in Mexico. The idea occurred to him then of trying to end hostilities in the shortest possible time by sending along with Scott's army an emissary empowered to negotiate a settlement on the spot, whenever it was propitious. Polk would have preferred Buchanan for the job but he could not spare the Secretary of State for the months needed at the front. The choice fell therefore to the chief clerk at the Department, a capable but unknown figure named Nicholas P. Trist, who had served at varying times as Jackson's secretary and consul to Havana, and was related by marriage to Jefferson. What followed was one of the most curious affairs in American diplomacy. During the first few months Trist and Scott, the latter feeling that the mission undermined his own authority, did little more than exchange insulting letters with each other. Eventually there was a reconciliation during which secret contact was made with Santa Anna—who demanded a million-dollar bribe, $10,000 of it immediately. Though the $10,000 was paid out, nothing came of the preliminary talks, and in October 1847, Trist's efforts obviously having misfired, he was called home. Despite the official recall, however, the plenipotentiary decided to stay on. He sent a sixty-five-page letter to Polk giving the reasons for his defiance, then set about trying to find someone to negotiate with. When Santa Anna abdicated, such an opportunity presented itself. After protracted talks with the government that succeeded Santa Anna, Trist signed a treaty at Guadalupe Hidalgo on February 2, 1848, along the lines of Polk's original demands. For $15 million and assumption of the few million in claims by American citizens, title was confirmed to California and New Mexico, and the boundary of Texas set at the Rio Grande. Nothing was mentioned of annexing all Mexico, or that region up to the mountains.

Confronted with a *fait accompli,* Polk was in an unhappy dilemma. Many of his closest followers urged him to reject the treaty and Buchanan insisted that he hold out for all of Mexico east of the mountains. Polk noted in his diary that "if the treaty was now to be made, I should demand more territory, perhaps to make the Sierra Madre the line. . . ." On the other hand he was mindful of the fact that Mexico in that circumstance might continue to resist and if he turned down the Trist treaty Congress might refuse him money and manpower to continue the war. Thus the Treaty of Guadalupe Hidalgo was submitted by Polk to Congress and duly approved, adding to the United States an area greater than France and Germany combined. Five years later, when the United States was contemplating building a transcontinental railroad, James Gadsden, a Southern railroad man, was selected as minister to Mexico and was able to purchase for $10 million additional sections of Arizona and New Mexico. By now there was little fight left in the Mexicans.

From a territorial point of view, then, the Mexican War of 1846–48 was a mammoth success. But it sped the onrush of the War Between the States thirteen years later. Had there been "no Mexican War," writes Samuel Eliot Morison, "there would have been no Civil War, at least not in 1861." The addition of new lands inevitably reopened the subject of slavery expansion. Three months after the war started, Congressman David Wilmot tacked an amendment to a bill providing $2 million to bribe Santa Anna (back in power), stating that in any new territory "neither slavery nor involuntary servitude shall ever exist." The Wilmot Proviso failed in the Senate, but two years later the issue came up as to whether slavery should be permitted in Oregon, where it was already forbidden, as well as in California and New Mexico. A compromise was worked out setting up territorial governments in all three but granting only to Oregon the right to determine whether it would tolerate slavery or not; the other two were expressly forbidden to act on the subject. Early in 1848, however, the famous California gold rush began, and the following year as tens of thousands converged on the region to make their fortunes, Californians held a convention, drafted a constitution —unanimously outlawing slavery—and declared themselves a legitimate state of the Union. Southerners reacted by calling a Southern Convention, which like the Hartford Convention of 1814 was potentially a first step toward secession. In 1850 Henry Clay appeased battered feelings on all sides by his patch-up compromise, which admitted California as a free state, set up territorial regimes in New Mexico and Utah—without resolving the slavery issue—and introduced a harsh new fugitive slave law to appease the South. The compromise was adopted, but as Calhoun pointed out in the debate, "the cords that bind the States together" were snapping rapidly. The issue of slavery having been fiercely reopened by the acquisitions from Mexico, it was only a matter of time before the balance of power would change and the United States drift to civil war.

8

THE BRAVE
BRAVES

On June 26, 1876, Lieutenant Colonel George A. Custer and 264
hardy troops of the Seventh Cavalry rode into a trap at the Little
Big Horn River in Montana from which none was to escape alive.
The incident, memorialized in history and cinema as "Custer's last
stand," is symptomatic both of the fury with which the Indians resisted their final subjugation from 1849 to 1892, and of the bold ad-
venturism of Americans, who meant to dominate the continent at
whatever the cost.

Custer, then thirty-seven, is believed by many historians to have
nursed presidential ambitions not unlike those of William Henry
Harrison of Tippecanoe fame. Called "Long Hair" by the Indians,
he had acquitted himself with such distinction as a cavalry officer in
the Civil War that he was hailed as "the boy general" and awarded
a gift of the table on which General Grant drafted the terms of surrender. Lean, six feet tall, with heavy shoulders that belied his 165
pounds, a magnificent horseman, brilliant marksman, second in his
class at West Point, and daringly self-confident, he earned his spurs
after the war as an unmatched Indian fighter. In November 1868,
when certain chiefs repudiated a treaty removing them south of the
Kansas Territory, Custer attacked a village near the Washita River
and killed 103 Indians within an hour, including their chief, Black
Kettle. After setting fire to the homes Custer was informed that the
people he had attacked were not the malcontents but friendly Cheyenne Indians; nevertheless he called his foray "a great and gallant
victory for our beloved country." In a sense, of course, it was, for the
clearing of the red man from the Great Plains and the mountains be-

yond the Mississippi to make way for gold prospectors, settlers, and the railroads had become national policy.

It would be wrong to imply that no one in Washington—or on the frontier, for that matter—cared about the plight of the Indian, or that expansionism proceeded entirely in a mood of venality punctuated by deliberate massacre. There was in fact a benign and paternalistic aspect to American imperialism, as there was to French, British, and other imperialisms. Just as President Polk would have preferred peaceful purchase of California to war, so most of his successors would have preferred a resolution of the differences with Indians through treaties, annuities, and training of the red man for agriculture.

An Indian fighter like General Philip H. Sheridan might cry that "there are no good Indians but dead Indians," yet President Rutherford B. Hayes could admit to Congress in 1877 that "many, if not most, of our Indian wars have had their origin in broken promises and acts of injustice on our part." To atone for the broken promises he recommended "conscientious fulfillment of all engagements entered into" with the natives, as well as the opening of schools, supply of cattle and agricultural implements, and whatever other aid was necessary "to bring them under the control of civilized influences." Behind this paternalism, however, was an implicit faith that the victim would accept his victimization gracefully, that having been shown the virtues of the white man's culture he would embrace it enthusiastically and give up the hunting lands and other rights he had been promised in some 360-odd treaties. But paternalism was at best a leaky dike, for it did not deal with the true problem, namely that Americans were just too impatient to respect another people's rights.

The white men, often recent immigrants, intoxicated with dreams of land or gold, and the railroads, cutting across the continent in search of a lush profit, would not wait. They occupied land allotted to the Indian by sacred treaty, despoiled his hunting grounds, killed off his food supply. Fifteen million buffaloes which roamed the plains and were the main source of food, clothing, and other necessities for various tribes were systematically destroyed by white hunters—some of whom killed more for sport than for food—and by railroad scouts who shot the ungainly animals to supply meat for the laborers. William F. Cody earned the sobriquet "Buffalo Bill" for killing 4,280 animals in a seventeen-month period as a five-hundred-dollar-a-month contractor for the Kansas Pacific railroad. The workers toasted him with a song:

Buffalo Bill, Buffalo Bill,
Never missed and never will,
And the company pays his bill
Buffalo Bill.

Francis Haines estimates in *The Buffalo* that during the peak years of the great slaughter, 1872–74, more than 6.3 million of the animals were killed, 5.1 million by whites. This was an unparalleled disaster for the plains Indians, whose lives and culture depended on the wild herds.

There were, it is believed, 225,000 Indians in the new Western country. Since seven hundred miles of it was desert and the plains were believed to be inhospitable to agriculture, it was generally assumed that white Americans would infiltrate the area at a slow pace, leaving the red man undisturbed. The West, however, exploded with a series of discoveries which offered many a road to quick riches. Late in 1848, gold was found near Sacramento, California, and soon the "Forty-niners" were descending on the former Mexican province in the greatest gold rush ever known. Overnight San Francisco mushroomed from a few buildings to a metropolis of 20,000, and the population of California itself, formerly known for its sleepy Spanish missions and a few thousand citizens, grew to nearly 100,000 by 1850. Eight years later, shortly after the economic depression of 1857, gold was also found in Colorado and 100,000 people crossed the plains determined to reach "Pike's Peak or bust." Around the same time the Comstock Lode in Nevada began to yield what would amount to $145 million worth of gold and silver ore in the ensuing decade. This was followed periodically by other strikes. Each led to boom towns, such as Virginia City, Montana, which grew to 10,000 within ninety days—wild and lawless, with every third or fourth hut a saloon.

Another force conspiring to squeeze the Indians out of their hunting grounds, into controlled and curtailed reservations, was the railroad. To the 35,000 miles of track in existence in 1865 was added another 122,000 by 1887. Four years after the Civil War the construction crews that had begun the Union Pacific westward from Omaha, and the Central Pacific eastward from Sacramento, met fifty miles west of Ogden, Utah, and sent word over the telegraph that the United States was now joined transcontinentally by the great iron horse. Other lines followed, heavily subsidized by the federal government through land grants, such as the 130 million acres given free to four Western railroads—three times the size of New England

—and causing friction with the Indians through whose territory some of the tracks had to be laid. Concurrent with the railroad came the cattle merchants, who, in the year 1871 alone, drove more than 600,000 head northward from Texas to the Canadian border, each herd with picturesque cowboys taking it to a stockyard or railway depot. The receding frontier filled with the clouds of dust made by tens of thousands of hooves, as well as the battle cries of Indians whose land was being invaded. Finally, after 1870, when T. C. Henry of Abilene successfully sowed winter wheat in the plains, the so-called desert began to bloom and, as James Truslow Adams observes, "the Indian and the cowboy were both doomed."

The cowboy, of course, found other employment. The Indians, "with no country on earth to which they can migrate [and] in the midst of a people with whom they cannot assimilate," as a congressional committee on Indian affairs reported, fared horribly. Incessant removal from one area to another, as the white man decided he needed them, resulted in pressures of many kinds. Formerly distant tribes, now closer together, quarreled over hunting grounds or women, and engaged in battles against each other which might have been avoided, such as those between Crow and Sioux. Some despairing tribes or bands gave up the fight and lived on government reservations supervised by government agencies; they were regarded by Washington as "friendlies." Finally there were the "hostiles," determined to defend their way of life at any price—the "wild" Indians who would not succumb—who retaliated against abuse and were the spark that ignited a spate of painful military conflicts. From the Mexican War to 1892, there were, by official War Department compilation, thirty-four wars with Indian tribes. The list of single engagements with various bands from 1868 to 1882 alone comprises no fewer than a hundred well-filled pages. In five years during the 1870's, a single regiment under General George Crook participated in ninety-seven skirmishes with the Apache. If Custer was making his last stand at the Little Big Horn River it was only an episodic setback for Americans on the road to total victory, whereas the single successes of the Indian warriors were simply the final gasp of a defeated people.

II

The Sioux chiefs who inflicted the ultimate penalty on Custer—most notably Sitting Bull and Crazy Horse—reflect the tragedy of a beleaguered race. They were patriots in the tradition of Tecumseh—

though less adroit politically—trying in vain to defend their country from men they considered invaders.

The Sioux, who next to the Algonquins were the most numerous stock north of Mexico, were hunters and corn growers who settled originally in Minnesota near the headwaters of the Mississippi River. According to one version their name derives from the French word *nadouessioux*—enemies—though by all accounts they were quite hospitable to whites during the seventeenth and eighteenth centuries. They were not a cohesive people, being divided into three great families—the Yanktons, the Tetons, and the Santees—with many bands and groupings below that. They called themselves Dakotas (pronounced Lakotas by the Tetons and Nakotas by the Yanktons) to signify that they were "allies," or "many in one." In the late seventeenth century the Tetons began to move west toward the Missouri River, where they made the acquaintance of the horse and became excellent riders. Around the time that Jefferson was writing the Declaration of Independence, one band, the Oglala, arrived at the beautiful Black Hills of South Dakota, which were to figure prominently in Custer's last stand. A half century later, at the behest of the Rocky Mountain Fur Company, which engaged them in trade, many Sioux emigrated to eastern Wyoming along the North Platte River, so that at the time of the Mexican and Civil Wars the tribe stretched out over a vast area from Minnesota to Montana. At first the United States government was content to leave their members undisturbed, since white migration was still concentrated east of the Mississippi. In 1815 and 1816, three treaties were signed with Sioux bands pledging "perpetual peace" and promising there would be no request for land cessions beyond what had already been granted England, France, and Spain in the past. Four more pacts were negotiated in 1825, again assuring that the Sioux domain would remain intact.

The difficulties began in 1830, when a treaty signed at Prairie du Chien gave Uncle Sam millions of acres between the Mississippi and Des Moines Rivers for next to nothing, followed by another in 1837, which extinguished the Indian title between the state of Missouri and the Missouri River. Even so, if the first few treaties, with their promise of annuities, agricultural instruments, education, and supplies of iron and steel, had been carried out to the letter, "there would have been living today among the citizens of Minnesota," writes Helen Hunt Jackson in her classic *A Century of Dishonor*, "thousands of Sioux families, good and prosperous farmers and mechanics. . . ." Instead, however, the government kept extinguishing

Indian titles—"for the purpose of making room for our emigrating citizens." Treaties entered into in 1841 divested Sioux bands of another half million acres, and another treaty in 1851, under which the federal government agreed to pay eight or nine cents per acre for an area in Minnesota larger than New York State—35 million acres— pushed the Sioux out of that part of the country forever. In fact, by a complicated financial arrangement, Washington paid less than two cents per acre for this rich land, while 8,000 Indians had to remove themselves to a reservation lacking timber and being much less desirable in every respect.

III

The famous Sioux leader Sitting Bull was born in South Dakota during the early 1830's just as this process of land preemption was beginning. The only son of a Hunkpapa Sioux chieftain, he was called "Slow" until he was fourteen, when he defeated an Indian enemy in a fight with *coup*-sticks and thereupon won from his father the more prestigious name Sitting Bull. He was well built but not handsome, careless of dress, good-humored, and popular with women. A white missionary lady described him as having "some indefinable power which could not be resisted by his people, or even others who came into contact with him." Frank Grouard, a white mailman whose life was saved by Sitting Bull after he was captured by two Indians in November 1869, says that during the three years he lived with the chief his name "was a 'tipi word'" for all that was generous and great. The bucks admired him, the squaws respected him highly, and the children loved him. He would have proved a mighty power among our politicians—a great vote-getter with the people." It was for these human qualities as much as for his bravery as a warrior that Sitting Bull was elevated to chief, then head chief of the Northern Sioux, Cheyenne, and Arapaho.

It says something about the tenor of the times that most of Sitting Bull's early military exploits were not against Americans, but against other Indians—such as the Crows who had killed his father. In fact, the chief's first real skirmish with American troops did not occur until 1864. He was not one of the "peace party" chiefs friendly to the whites, but neither was he phobic about them. In the summer of 1872, while he was engaged in another fight with the Crows, for instance, an American commission surveying land for the Northern Pacific traveled six thousand miles back and forth in Sitting Bull's plains without being bothered once. Later in the year, when U.S. troops trespassed along the south bank of the Yellowstone River, clearly Indian territory, Sitting Bull rode out to meet them, and while episodic shooting was still going on calmly dropped his gun, walked toward the soldiers, sat on the grass, and smoked a pipe, in an effort to allay tempers and end the fracas. If, then, as the political leader and medicine man of his people, he turned his camp in the buffalo country into a rallying ground for the "hostiles," it was not out of ingrained hatred for the Americans, but because of the foreign advance.

The background of Sitting Bull's trusted lieutenant Crazy Horse was much different. Born a decade later in the same Black Hills of South Dakota, he saw much more action against the whites—if only because there were more of them in his part of the country. His father—also called Crazy Horse—was an Oglala medicine man, the adviser and confidant of his band; his mother, who died when he was a youngster—leaving the family to be brought up by an aunt—was sister of the renowned Brule chief Spotted Tail. Slender, of medium height, and so light in complexion that Americans at Fort Laramie considered him a captive white boy, Crazy Horse was a quiet and exceptionally serious man. When he went into battle he painted white spots on his face, let his hair hang loose without traditional feathers, and dressed in a white buckskin shirt and leggings.

Crazy Horse's antiwhite feelings were molded in part by his father's biases and in part by his own experiences on the frontier. At Fort Laramie the elder Crazy Horse watched "friendly" Indians trading with whites, buying liquor, and debauching themselves in drink, knifing quarrels, and shootings. He dreamed of a great leader who would unite the Sioux against these denigrating influences and strike back against the whites, who grew more arrogant as their numbers along the Oregon Trail increased. Occasionally he was heartened by the small warrior bands who threatened to stop the cavalcade of covered wagons moving westward and seize the horses. But almost invariably the pliant trade chiefs—the "friendlies"—such as Conquering Bear—restrained these bands.

The younger Crazy Horse gained a graphic insight into these complicated relationships long before he had become an active warrior. When he was nine, in 1851, he attended a meeting of 10,000 Indians at Fort Laramie, where the American Superintendent of Indian Affairs offered the red men annuities for fifty-five years if they would grant safe passage on the Oregon Trail to white migrants. It was an acceptable deal and worked well for three years. But in 1854, while the natives were anxiously waiting for blankets, food, and other provisions due them as part of the annuities, a dispute over a cow shattered the peace. The cow either wandered away from a Mormon wagon train or was spirited away by an Indian, who promptly shot and skinned it. When the commander at Fort Laramie summoned Conquering Bear for an explanation, the chief offered to pay ten dollars for the animal; the owner demanded twenty-five dollars. Thereupon Second Lieutenant J. L. Grattan, a West Point graduate, took thirty men and two howitzers to the Brule village to seize the offending warrior. After a brief parley through a drunken interpreter, Grattan and his men began shooting into the tepees, killing the friendly chief, Conquering Bear, as well as some women and children. The warriors responded in kind and before long, Grattan and every one of his men were dead, except for one mortally wounded soldier who crawled back to the fort. The incident caused all the Sioux, including the Brule, with whom young Crazy Horse was traveling, to desert camp, head north, and vow vengeance for their dead. Simultaneously, in Washington, the federal government vowed to teach the red devils decent manners, and in September of the following year Colonel William S. Harney, an old Indian fighter with experience against the Seminoles in Florida, descended on the Brule camp where Crazy Horse was living and demanded that the Indians surrender those who had killed Grattan. When they denied knowledge of the affair, Harney ordered his men to shoot and within minutes eighty-six Indians were dead and a considerable number of women and children taken prisoner. Crazy Horse fortunately was off on the plains that day chasing a stray horse, but the sight of dead and wounded when he returned filled him with a hatred of the white man that he never relinquished.

The Civil War, occupying so much of Washington's energies, should have muted the conflict between the federal government and the Sioux. In fact, however, the invasion of Colorado and Minnesota by miners and settlers caused new and ever fiercer outbreaks, continuing on and off for a quarter of a century. During 1862, another delay in annuity payments brought latent feelings to the surface and resulted in what is known as the Sioux Uprising, or the Minnesota War. Five thousand hungry Indians gathered at Yellow Medicine, Minnesota, to pick up $72,000 in annuities needed to buy food. As the weeks passed, with the gold shipment still held up, the Indians were forced to eat roots to stay alive. A white trader taunted them with such remarks as "let them eat grass"; they subsequently murdered him. Finally the younger braves forced Chief Little Crow, who at first argued against fighting the whites, to attack the 40,000 settlers who had encroached on their lands. On August 17, 1862, the Upper Sioux killed 800 settlers—many recent German and Scandinavian immigrants—and destroyed millions in property. It was a horrible act of retribution that ended when General Henry Sibley defeated the Indians and a military court condemned 306 of them to death. President Lincoln commuted 268 of these sentences to prison terms, but the day after Christmas the other 38 were hanged at Mankato, Minnesota.

In due course, small incidents or minor misunderstandings led to a wave of Indian wars and massacres unparalleled in American history. In August 1864, violence broke out along the Oregon and Santa Fe Trails as Indians harried the greatly increased white traffic. The territorial governor of Colorado issued a call for citizens to "kill and destroy" the unconquered natives wherever they found them, and two volunteer regiments of cavalry were pressed into service for that purpose. The Cheyenne Indians sent word to an officer named Colonel J. M. Chivington—a former Methodist minister—that they wanted peace, but the colonel told the intermediary he was on the warpath. Again, more attacks, by Cheyenne, Sioux, Apache, Arapaho, Kiowa, with hundreds of miles of land devastated. When 700 Cheyenne, under chiefs Black Kettle and White Antelope, came to Fort Lyon to give up half their weapons—keeping the other half for hunting—Chivington responded with a surprise foray against their village at Sand Creek in which 300 women, children, and men were slaughtered. The incident repelled even so notorious an Indian fighter as Kit Carson, who called Chivington "a dog" and a "coward" for killing squaws and papooses. "When we white men do such awful things," he said, "these poor critters don't know better than to follow suit." Nearly four years later a congressional committee, after listening for 72 days to 30 witnesses, concluded that the event "scarcely has its parallel in the records of Indian barbarity— men, fleeing women, and infants were tortured in a way which would put to shame the savages of interior Africa."

The Sand Creek massacre naturally sparked another assault on white settlements along the South Platte River, one in which Crazy Horse and his Northern Oglalas led the way. Six thousand Indians devastated ranches and government stockades in western Nebraska and Wyoming. With the Civil War about to end, federal troops were diverted to Fort Laramie to retaliate against the Indians, but their expedition was a failure. Crazy Horse distinguished himself during these battles by decoying the enemy into traps and by hit-and-run fighting. He was awarded a leather shirt and put in charge of his band.

Having failed to subdue the Indians, the federal government sent out peace commissioners to find some way of protecting the railroad and opening new trails to the gold mines of western Montana. In the ensuing years this was to be the pattern: wars alternated with peace commissions, treaties, misunderstandings, and more wars. The clash of white and Indian interests is expressed in its most naked form by the events leading to Custer's last stand.

At Fort Laramie in 1868, the Sioux signed a treaty accepting transfer to reservations, in return for which they were guaranteed, in perpetuity, half of South Dakota and Wyoming and a fourth of Montana. But the Northern Pacific Railroad, now completed through Bismarck, again initiated surveys through Sioux lands without bothering to purchase the right-of-way or have the government buy it. In 1872 Sitting Bull's and Crazy Horse's followers held a great sun dance, went on the warpath, and forced the railroad to abandon its efforts. A year later Crazy Horse and Custer fought a number of bitter battles in the Yellowstone Valley in which the Indians were forced to retreat, enabling the railroad to complete its surveys. In 1874 Custer led another expedition, 1,200 men, into the Black Hills of South Dakota for the purpose of protecting the railroad construction crews. While advancing Custer let it be known that there was gold in the hills and urged prospectors to form parties to move into the area behind his troops. The region was soon deluged with 15,000 mining hopefuls, including characters such as "Wild Bill" Hickok of Deadwood fame, and the United States demanded that the Paha Sapa, as the Indians called it, be promptly ceded. Even Custer recognized that the Indians had little choice: "If I were an Indian," he wrote, "I would certainly prefer to cast my lot . . . to the free open plains rather than submit to the confined limits of a reservation, there to be the recipient of the blessed benefits of civilization with its vices thrown in."

At a meeting of 20,000 natives in September 1875, some chiefs demanded $70 million for the hills; one chief proposed that it be paid for with enough Texas steers to sustain his people for seven generations. The peace commissioners offered $5 million. In December, as tensions grew, the Interior Department advised Indians that those who did not move to the reservations by January 31, 1876, would be deemed "hostile" and dealt with accordingly. General George Crook, who had conducted a campaign to drive the Apache into reservations in the Southwest, was assigned the same task in the North. A band of Northern Cheyenne and some Oglala announced they would move to the reservations in March that year, but the zealous Crook attacked their village anyway, turning the mood of compliance into one of resistance. Instead of leaving for the reservations, young braves joined Crazy Horse and Sitting Bull in the North.

In June the great Sioux medicine man held another sun dance, cutting 100 tiny pieces of skin from his arms and looking into the sun until he fell to the ground. This was interpreted as an omen of American troops invading Indian land—and so it turned out to be. Toward the middle of that month Crazy Horse and 1,000 Oglalas moved to the Rosebud River to halt the invasion, and there fought a furious preliminary battle that preceded the one on the Little Big Horn. On July 26, 2,500 braves under Crazy Horse, Gall, and other lieutenants of Sitting Bull finally surrounded Custer and destroyed his forces to the last man. Thus ended the first phase of the punitive expedition by Uncle Sam's troops.

The Americans, however, could lose a skirmish but muster enough forces to win the war. In the fall they returned, this time pushing the Sioux steadily backward. The army occupied all the agencies, promising not only to continue the campaign against the "hostiles," but threatening to deny food to the "friendlies" unless they agreed on behalf of the whole Sioux nation that the Black Hills, as well as unceded areas in Wyoming and Montana, be turned over to the national government. This clearly violated the treaty of 1868, which required a three-fourths vote of all male Indian adults before any changes could be made, but the provision was blithely disregarded. Washington had enough soldiers in the field by now to impose its will, and though Sitting Bull held out until February 1877, he was defeated and forced into exile in Canada. He remained there until 1881, returned to the States, was confined a couple of years at Fort Randall, traveled with Buffalo Bill Cody's Wild West Show in 1885 as a curiosity for ogling crowds, was arrested late in 1890 for allegedly dancing the forbidden ghost dance, and killed by an Indian policeman while being taken into custody.

Crazy Horse met his death more quickly. In December 1876 he took his weary braves to the Tongue River in eastern Montana, where he sent nine emissaries with a white cloth to discuss surrender with Colonel Nelson A. Miles. Five of the nine were promptly killed by the Americans. A few weeks later Miles discovered Crazy Horse's hiding place, but despite a five-hour attack during which the Indians ran out of ammunition, he was unable to capture his quarry. Fighting, however, was now out of the question; in May Crazy Horse accepted the promise of General Crook of a separate reservation for the Oglala and turned himself in along with 800 of his warriors. A few months later, after a number of misunderstandings which led Crook to believe that Crazy Horse was again plotting war, the Sioux chief was surrounded by eight companies of cavalry and 400 Indian auxiliaries. As he realized he was being imprisoned he tried to wrench loose, and was killed by a guard with a bayonet. He died at the age of thirty-five at Fort Robinson, Nebraska, eulogized even by his enemies as "one of the bravest of the brave and one of the subtlest and most capable of captains."

IV

The resistance of the Indians, as Crazy Horse and Sitting Bull proved so graphically, was fierce but uncoordinated. They were excellent rifle shots and highly mobile, able to attack or fade away at will, and relatively unhampered by problems of transport and supply. As fighting men they were easily equal to their adversaries. "Had they been able to unite," writes Samuel Morison, "they might have tired out the United States (as white resistance to reconstruction was doing in the South). . . ." But no Tecumseh arose after the Civil War to guide them toward unity or imbue them with a central purpose.

Each Indian chief who fought back was heroic in his own way. Chief Joseph of the Nez Percé in the Northwest engaged 5,000 American troops and led them on a chase over 1,300 miles of mountains and plain, killing and wounding 300 in eleven isolated battles. Though outwitting his far better equipped adversary, Joseph's original band of 200 braves shrank to 87, half of them wounded. He gave himself up on October 7, 1877, along with his warriors and 330 women and children, though he was only a small distance from safe asylum in Canada. Chief Cochise of the bellicose Apache in the Southwest, and his successor, Geronimo, fought the Americans intermittently for twenty years. But each chief and each tribe fought by itself, falling eventually to superior numbers and firing power.

Thus the Indian removal policy that had begun a half century before in the East was continued by the federal government in the West. Each discovery of gold or rich land added an incentive for the white man to squeeze the red man out of his designated area. The Crows and the Blackfeet were driven out of their reservations in Montana; the Utes out of Colorado. With the discovery of gold in California, the 100,000 natives were reduced in the next dozen years to 35,000. The Nez Percé were forced to clear Wallowa Valley in Oregon and move to the Lapwai reservation in Idaho, when gold was discovered near the Salmon River. All of this was justified on the theory that it was a law of nature—progress—for an inferior culture to give way to a superior one.

There were men and women in the federal government and among the citizenry who deplored the removal policy, but their best efforts resulted only in a policy of paternalism which in the end deprived the Indian of still more of his land. As a result of the recommendation of the Indian Peace Commission, established by Congress in 1867, the absurdity of making treaties with the tribes was abandoned in 1871. Pacts were still concluded, but thereafter they were called "agreements," and they required approval by a simple majority in both houses of Congress, rather than two thirds in the Senate. Individual men like General Francis A. Walker, whom President Grant appointed Commissioner of Indian Affairs, tried valiantly to lighten the burden of their wards. Walker built schools, opened new reservations for defeated tribes, and provided rations where the game was exhausted. But even he recognized, as he stated in his report of 1872, that all this was unavailing: "Every year's advance of our frontier takes in a territory as large as some of the kingdoms of Europe. We are richer by hundreds of millions, the Indian is poorer by a large part of the little that he has. This growth is bringing imperial greatness to the nation; to the Indian it brings wretchedness, destitution, beggary."

A surge of conscience stirred the intellectual community in the late 1870's and the 1880's. In 1879 Indian Commissioner G. W. Manypenny published *Our Indian Wards*, an erudite analysis of the need for reform in the Department of the Interior. More shocking to the public was Helen Hunt Jackson's *A Century of Dishonor* in 1881. Mrs. Jackson, a friend of Horace Greeley and Nathaniel Hawthorne, and married to a wealthy banker, sent a copy of her work to every member of Congress with Benjamin Franklin's words inscribed in red on the cover: "Look upon your hands! They are stained with the blood of your relations." Such exposés of the treatment of the Indians produced some changes, but they didn't work out as Mrs. Jackson, Manypenny, or other friends of the red man had anticipated.

The federal legislature in 1887 passed the Dawes Act, which was supposed to lift the Indian up the ladder of civilization by dividing his reservations into individually owned homesteads. Lobbying for the bill were such organizations as Indian Rights, and religious groups which felt that private ownership would transform the Indian into a self-respecting citizen capable of defending himself. Under the act the President of the United States was empowered to break up a reservation when he felt that was the natives' wish. Each family would be given 160 acres, the unallotted remainder to be bought by the government, sold to whites, and the money placed in trust for the whole tribe. In a single year after allotment began in 1891, Indian acreage shrank by an eighth. Congress then passed another law permitting the red men to lease their homesteads; the results were a disaster. The Indians, without knowledge of such intricacies as private property and rent, were easy prey for the whites. They expected to live on the rents, but in one instance after another they leased their holdings for a dime an acre to white real estate syndicates, which in turn rented the land to individual white farmers for one or two dollars an acre. Out of the allotments of 140,000 acres taken by the Omaha and Winnebago in Nebraska by 1898, for instance, 112,000 were leased out, much of it illegally. It was impossible to live anything approaching a decent life on the remainder. Indian holdings, in the fifty years after the allotment system was introduced, fell from 138 million to 48 million acres. An Indian commissioner, quoted by Samuel Morison, justified the loss of timberlands by the red man on the theory that "as the Indian tribes were being liquidated anyway, it was only sensible to liquidate their forest holdings as well." Some of the tribes were spared the tribulations afforded by the Dawes Act; the Five Civilized Tribes, for instance, were "punished" for having supported the Confederacy during the Civil War. But many who were transferred to Oklahoma Territory were cajoled into selling millions of their new acres. By the turn of the century there was no fight left in the red man.

Crazy Horse, Gall, Sitting Bull, Chief Joseph, Cochise, Geronimo, and many others were—from the Indian's point of view—great patriots defending their ancient cultures and prerogatives. With their defeat the United States finally had forced into acquiescence an internal enemy small in numbers but proud and defiant. Imperial America now stretched from the Atlantic to the Pacific without opposition from either European powers or the Indian "hostiles" who had resisted their incursion for more than a century.

9

COMMERCE FOLLOWS
THE FLAG

On the evening of February 15, 1898, the *Maine,* a second-class battleship dispatched to Havana three weeks before, blew up in the harbor, killing 260 American seamen and sparking a war from which the United States would emerge as a modest colonial power. The Philippines, Guam, and Puerto Rico, wrested from Spain and from native rebels, amounted to less than 120,000 square miles and fewer than 10 million people; and if Cuba, which became a protectorate by virtue of the war, is added to the list the respective figures are 165,000 square miles and 13 million population. Nevertheless the Spanish-American War was a historical dividing marker of great significance. It was a climactic moment, both for the Cuban *insurrectos,* who had unfurled the banner of revolution against Spain three years before, and the Northern Colossus, which now passed from old to new forms of imperialism. This was the first war for the conquest of *non*contiguous territory, the first one in which Uncle Sam was both imperialist *and* colonialist, the first one in which concerns for trade and foreign investment outranked concern for land.

It is axiomatic that the foreign affairs of a nation reflect the thrust of its domestic affairs, more particularly the wishes of its domestic elites. The man on the street, the average citizen, admittedly is mobilized behind the elites, who cater to his sense of national pride, manifest destiny, and the like; but it is the men of power—above all economic power—who give a society its internal direction, and as a consequence, its external one. This is not, needless to say, a simple phenomenon to describe since the nation is a crucible of innumerable and conflicting interests, even among its elites. It is understandable, for instance, why a Louisiana land speculator with small holdings but ready cash might lobby for a war with Mexico to annex nearby Texas, while a land speculator in New York with large holdings and little cash might oppose such annexation on the ground that it offers other outlets to land-hungry New Yorkers, thereby depressing his prices. A manufacturer of munitions might welcome a war, whereas a manufacturer of consumer goods might see it only as an additional tax burden.

Nonetheless, overall, America's expansionism has been oriented by the specific wants of its dominant elites—or coalition of elites—at specific times. When the nation was launched its main industry was agriculture, a pursuit which occupied nine out of ten of its citizens —most of the rest being involved in commerce. Wealth was to be made in land or in shipping, and the men of power pushed for both domestic and foreign policies that favored those interests. Given its proximity to enormous bodies of land, the United States embarked in its first century of existence on a program of *territorial* imperialism. While Britain, France, Spain, Portugal, and Holland, each confined to close quarters in Europe, were forced to express imperialist drives by hedgehopping to Asia, the Americas, and later Africa, the United States—like Russia—could expand contiguously. It bought Louisiana, seized the Floridas, conquered the Indian country, took more than half of Mexico and a section of Oregon, and tried— though in vain—to capture Canada. In all this the primary economic objective was land, for the speculator, the plantation owner, the farmer, the miner, the railroad, and indirectly for the benefit of banker and merchant. The agrarian interest was then the predominant one and while not all presidents agreed with Jefferson that farmers were America's "most valuable citizens . . . tied to their country . . . by the most lasting bonds," they nonetheless saw the destiny of the nation in terms of agricultural and related development.

An interesting feature of this first phase of American imperialism was its anticolonialism. The territory north of the Ohio River and west to the Mississippi, which was deeded to the United States by the treaty of 1783, could have been converted into a dependent colony by the founding fathers, but they chose to give it the same status as the original thirteen states. Under the Northwest Ordinance of 1787, the territory was to be divided into three to five potential states, and once any of these had attained a population of 60,000 it would be admitted to the Union "on an equal footing with the original states in all respects whatsoever." The same type of disposition was made for the states carved out of the Louisiana Territory, the former Spanish and Mexican possessions, and the Oregon Territory.

None were reduced to the level of colony. Indeed, had the United States tried to make them into dependencies the result would have been catastrophic, for there was no way of policing such great areas against secession and revolution; they could be held together only by the fervidity of nationalism, which the United States generated in remarkable abundance. England could hold India together with the aid of rajas, maharajas, zamindars, and other native elites, and Egypt with the aid of the pashas, all armed by the British to uphold "law and order." But there were no feudal lords west of the Alleghenies that the United States could align, even if it wanted to, to its governmental machine. Had Uncle Sam tried to make a colony out of Texas, the republic would never have adhered to the Union. Even nationalism was a loose cement to hold the nation together, as first one section then another threatened to secede, from 1790 on, and actual secession, in 1861, brought in its wake the worst bloodshed America has ever suffered. In any event, by tradition, by necessity, and by choice the United States abjured colonialism while pursuing imperialism.

This was a formula suited for an agricultural nation which needed few raw materials from abroad to stoke its factories and, as yet, was under no great pressure to find markets for surpluses of manufactured goods. The cotton, tobacco, wheat, minerals, animals, and other crude products sent overseas were shipped to the advanced countries of Western Europe; and U.S. imports, 50 percent of which were manufactures, came essentially from the same place. The United States as yet needed no colonialist mechanisms—such as an occupation army—to pry open the doors of other nations to sell its products. Moreover, though it manufactured almost $2 billion worth of goods as of 1860, it was still weak and uncompetitive in this field, and required relatively few raw materials from abroad to feed into its industrial plant. It had yet to feel the glut of surplus products and surplus capital that propelled other nations to imperialist ventures. In fact its balance of trade was usually adverse—imports exceeding exports—and it was only the fact that the U.S. had become the world's largest gold producer after 1849 that this adversity did not lead to economic difficulties. The flow of capital was *to* the United States, with foreign holdings here rising from $222 million in 1853 to $1.5 billion by 1869.

The Civil War laid the basis for a drastic alteration in America's economic structure. It liberated industrial capitalism from restrictions imposed by the slavocratic South and gave it an incredible momentum. The 140,000 factories in 1860 had grown to 355,000 by 1890, and where domestic manufacture was less than $2 billion in the earlier period, it skyrocketed 500 percent, to $9.5 billion, by 1890. Another set of statistics is even more revealing of the trend: from 1850 to 1900 the population of the United States tripled, from 23 to 76 million, the value of agricultural commodities went up apace, from $1.6 to $4.7 billion, but products of the manufacturing industry zoomed from a mere billion to 11.5 billion. Previously fourth or fifth in the scale of world manufacturing, America had moved to first, already fabricating twice as much goods in its plants as Great Britain and about half as much as all of Europe. Of utmost significance by this time was the change in composition of exports, away from agriculture toward manufactures. Of $445 million in products shipped abroad in 1870, about 80 percent was agricultural commodities and only 15 percent came from factories. By 1900, with exports nearing $1.4 billion, the agricultural percentage had fallen to 61 and that of manufactures had risen to 32. "By 1900," writes economic historian Harold U. Faulkner, "industrial development in the United States had advanced to the stage where there was an excess of manufactured products and minerals for export, and this, furthered by the impetus of the Spanish-American War, drove American capital and products into foreign markets." For a decade or two after the Civil War the growing internal market was sufficient to absorb the mountains of products coming out of grim factories. But in the final two decades of the century this was no longer adequate, and the preconditions were at hand for a new imperialism seeking commercial markets and sources for raw materials, rather than land.

Commenting on this circumstance years later, the Bankers Trust Company of New York observed that "in the first century of our national existence, our producers were primarily concerned with meeting the local demand which steadily increased with our enormous growth in population, and were content to leave the foreign markets to the producers of other countries excepting only those raw materials of which we have always had a surplus. The tremendous development of our manufactures in recent years, however, totally changes the aspect of our trade. . . . The exigencies of foreign trade force us . . . to seek the best methods of stimulating the demand for American products in the markets of South America, Russia and the Orient. . . . Our prosperity will be permanent only when a market can be found for all the goods we produce." The touchstone of policy changed from "land" to "markets."

II

From the onset of the Civil War to the end of the century, therefore, one notes a certain ambivalence in the expansionist goals expressed by key American figures. Territorial acquisition in the old style was still a prime objective of both sides in the War Between the States. The Confederacy, restricted by a porous but nevertheless disturbing blockade of Union war vessels, looked to Mexico as the only neutral country from which it could import lead, tin, sulphur, blankets, tents, coffee, and sugar and receive "contraband" products from Europe and the West Indies. Its envoy, John T. Pickett, a blunt and inept diplomat, at first assured the liberal Mexican government of Pablo Benito Juárez that the South no longer had need to expand into Mexican territory and might even entertain ideas for "retrocession to Mexico of a large portion of the territory hitherto acquired from her by the late United States." But when this ploy failed to win the friendship of a regime that had come to power after a three-year civil war, Pickett urged the Confederate government in Richmond to seize northern Mexico, starting with the provinces of Monterrey and Nuevo León, in order to prevent them from falling into Washington's hands. The Confederacy eventually did set up good relations with the governor of Nuevo León and Coahuila, Santiago Vidaurri, and through those border provinces was able to sell cotton to Europe and buy goods from Europe. Seizing them militarily, however, was deemed unfeasible.

On the other side, the American Secretary of State, William Henry Seward, entertained plans as devious as those of the late James K. Polk. In a memorandum to President Lincoln of April 1, 1861, entitled "Some Thoughts for the President's Consideration," Seward warned that France and Spain had designs on Mexico and suggested that if they did not repudiate those designs the United States immediately declare war against them. Seward evidently nurtured the hope that a foreign war would bind the splintered nation together again, but Lincoln refused to consider the plan. With the outbreak of hostilities at Fort Sumter, Seward dispatched Thomas Corwin as minister to the Juárez government, with instructions to "purchase Lower California or any part of it in preference to seeing it inevitably fall into the hands of the insurrectionary party of this Country by purchase or by conquest." Playing on Juárez's fear that the Confederacy would invade his land and seek to impose slavery on its twenty-two states, and by dangling a $9 to $11 million loan before him, Corwin was able to win Mexico to a pro-Northern policy. But the loan itself was seen by both Corwin and Seward as a prelude to more annexation, for in the proposed treaty, Mexico would pledge "all her public lands and mineral rights in Lower California" and three other provinces as a guarantee for the loan. "This would probably end in the cession of the sovereignty to us . . . if the money were not promptly paid as agreed on," Corwin wrote in

July 1861, and would make up for the loss of the secessionist states. The Senate, after debating this issue a few months, rejected the suggested pact, writing finis to still another plan for gobbling up Mexican territory.

With 900,000 men under arms at the close of the Civil War the United States excited fears in both London and Paris that it might try again to seize Mexico and Canada. But America was tired, and though its leaders sometimes spoke militantly they settled for lesser gains. "Give me fifty, forty, thirty more years of life," Seward told a Boston audience in June 1867, "and I will engage to give you the possession of the American continent and the control of the world." That year Alaska fell into the American lap when the Russian tsar decided it was cheaper to sell it to Uncle Sam for $7.2 million (he would have accepted $5 million, it was later learned) than to take over the obligations of the Russian American Company, which administered the region. This was the first noncontiguous area added to the empire, but the purchase—"Seward's folly," it was called—was made with the expectation that Canada would unite with the United States, thereby attaching a distant limb to the main body.

III

If the advocates of contiguous territorial expansion were the main strain among those who espoused imperialist adventure, however, there was another strain which opted for a strong navy and island bases in the Atlantic (later the Pacific) to encourage American commerce. "To an active external commerce," George Washington said in 1796, "the protection of a naval force is indispensable." In the decades that followed, the navy fought against Tripoli and Algeria to remove restrictions against American shipping, as well as against hundreds of pirate ships in the Caribbean. Naval units landed in Cuba four times between 1822 and 1825 in pursuit of pirates, and in the town of Fajardo, Spanish Puerto Rico, in 1824 to punish pirates who had "insulted" American naval officers. Few years went by without the navy setting anchor unsolicited on foreign shores to effectuate some commercial purpose—in Greece in 1827 to hunt pirates; in the Falkland Islands in 1831–32 to look into the seizure of three American sealing vessels; in Sumatra in 1832 to punish the people of Quallah Battoo for "depredations on American shipping"; in Argentina in 1833; and in Peru in 1835–36 to "protect" American life and property during revolutions; in Sumatra and the Fiji Islands a couple of years later to punish natives for hostile acts against American shippers; in Drummond Island and Samoa in 1841 to avenge the murder of American sailors; and in Africa in 1843 for a variety of reasons including reprisal for attacks on U.S. ships and sailors.

Whether these actions were just or unjust, implicit in them was the notion that strong powers have the right to violate the sovereignty of weak powers when they feel that the interests of their nationals are affected. It was a principle that the United States (or Britain or France) would not accept against itself—that an English warship, for instance, had the right to chase an American privateer into an American port, or to punish an American town because the American navy had imprisoned some English sailors. If the tenets of international law were applied dispassionately one might expect that if Cuba harbored pirates or if Samoa failed to prosecute the murderer of an American seaman, the United States would make diplomatic representations urging a change in attitude, or payment of reparations. It might even suggest arbitration by a third party. But with superior force available the United States lacked restraint; it took matters into its own hands.

Nonetheless the double standard of sovereignty prevailed not only where defensive interests were alleged—protection of American ships and citizens, for instance—but also where clear aggression was concerned. During Mr. Madison's War in 1813, for instance, a naval captain named David Porter occupied one of the islands in the Marquesas group while chasing a British merchantman in the Pacific, and promptly "annexed" it to the United States. On returning home he justified his actions to Madison on the unique theory that the islands in the Pacific "bear the same relation to the northwest coast as those of the West Indies bear to the Atlantic States." They were needed as way stations for shipping and bases of operations. The annexation, of course, was disavowed, since the United States could not possibly have defended a tiny colony deep in the Pacific in 1813.

A couple of decades later the navy took a different kind of action —a prototype of things to come—by prying open the doors of China to American commerce. Following the Anglo-Chinese War of 1839–42, in which the British pierced the walls of Chinese exclusion and gained the rights of trade and residence at five major Chinese cities, the United States sent Caleb Cushing to the land of the Manchus to win the same kind of concessions. Cushing wrote back to Secretary of State John C. Calhoun that since Christians "are utterly excluded" from "the greater part of Asia and Africa," it was necessary to use "fleets and armies" to break the barriers. As a consequence, four warships were sent to the Celestial Empire in 1844 and under the shadow of their guns and Cushing's threats of a second war, the Manchus yielded similar—though lesser—rights to the Americans. The Chinese had followed a policy of keeping their ports closed to foreign trade except during certain months of the year, but Britain, the United States and others—in their own interest—decided to force a change in this policy, and succeeded in doing so through military intervention.

Many years later Senator Everett Dirksen of Illinois entered into the Congressional Record a list of hundreds of incursions by the U.S. military into foreign lands. Included were such items as:

1854—China—April 4 to June 15 or 17—To protect American interests in and near Shanghai during the Chinese civil strife.

1855—China—May 19 to 21—To protect American interests in Shanghai. August 3 to 5—To fight pirates near Hong Kong.

1856—China—October 22 to December 6—To protect American interests at Canton during hostilities between the British and the Chinese, and to avenge an unprovoked assault upon an unarmed boat displaying the United States flag.

As testament to the role of the navy in furthering U.S. trade, the Secretary of the Navy boasted in 1922 that "without the protection of our Navy" the hundreds of millions in commerce handled via the Yangtze River "would be practically nonexistent." The Chinese government did not want such trade, but the navy battered down the doors.

The same technique was used against Japan. In 1846 the Land of the Rising Sun had rejected an American offer for commercial privileges; like China, it considered its policy of exclusion suited to its purposes. But for Commander James Glynn of the *Preble,* an old hand in Eastern waters, the need for a port in Japan loomed so large that he advised President Fillmore to secure it "if not peaceably, then by force." Fillmore obliged in 1852 by sending Commodore Matthew C. Perry, an exponent of empire as well as an able seaman, to "open" Japan. The commodore's arguments for occupying "the principal ports of these islands" sounded much like those of the territorial expansionists who urged seizure of California lest it fall to Britain. "The honor of our nation," he said, "calls for it and the interest of our commerce demands it. When we look at the possessions in the East of our great maritime rival, England . . . we should be admonished of the necessity of prompt action on our part." Fortunately, he pointed out, Japan and many other islands had not yet been annexed by this "annexing" government of Britain. There was still an opportunity for Uncle Sam to make hay. Japan was an ideal spot for a coaling station between San Francisco and Shanghai, and

COMMERCE FOLLOWS THE FLAG 157

an excellent trading prospect in its own right. *De Bow's Review* predicted in 1852 that it would accommodate $200 million in trade each year. To secure this plum Perry arrived with four warships in forbidden Yedo Bay on July 8, 1853, delivered a letter from the American President to the Emperor calling for the establishment of commercial relations—and departed. In the meantime he took the Bonin Islands five hundred miles southeast—which he renamed "Coffin Islands"—setting up coaling stations at Okinawa and the Loo-choos (Ryukyus). He also pressed Washington to establish a protectorate over Formosa, where two Americans in the camphor industry were having difficulties with the native population. The following February, this time with seven ships belching black smoke, Perry returned to Yedo Bay and landed a few hundred men. The Japanese, sorely torn by internal strife between the feudal elements and a rising urban class, got the message and signed a limited treaty opening two minor ports, Shimoda and Hakodate, to American commerce.

The use of military force to gain economic advantage in foreign lands obviously was no alien principle to American statesmen; it was applied as well as threatened repeatedly, to impose Washington's will on weaker peoples. The United States still drew a line, however, at stationing a *permanent* army to rule other nations—in other words, establishing colonies or protectorates. Naval commanders might periodically "annex" a territory and strategically minded men like Perry might urge a policy of annexation, but the American leadership was not yet united on this approach. Somewhere in the mechanism of government—either Congress or the executive, or both—the proposals bogged down. In turning down the plan to take Formosa the Democratic administration in Washington asserted that "the extension of our commercial intercourse must be the work of individual enterprise" rather than the government. This remained official doctrine despite imperialism-minded men like Perry and William H. Seward, and was only to be changed after much travail and inner conflict.

Had the Secretary of State under Lincoln had his way, the United States not only would have established naval bases in the Caribbean and the Pacific but would have added Canada, much of Latin America, and even part of the Arctic region to the empire. "Our population is destined to roll its resistless waves to the icy barriers of the north, and to encounter oriental civilization on the shores of the Pacific," Seward had written in 1846. His acquisition of Alaska in 1867 was part of this grand design. Additionally, Seward sought naval bases in the Dominican Republic's Bay of Samana and tried to purchase the Virgin Islands from Denmark for $7.5 million, but in both instances was rebuffed by a hostile Congress and a lukewarm public. The *Nation* commented that "if the national future be in peril at all, it is not for want of territory but from excess of it," and Bret Harte poked fun at Seward after the Virgin Islands had been hit by earthquake and hurricane:

> *There was not an inch of dry land*
> *Left to mark his recent island.*

Apart from purchased Alaska, the only real estate Seward was permitted to keep during his term as Secretary was the Midway Islands, a thousand miles west of Hawaii. The unpopularity of the Andrew Johnson regime and the tortures of Reconstruction put notions of expansion in limbo.

President Ulysses S. Grant, who replaced Johnson, was presented with a grand opportunity to seize Cuba. A long rebellion against Spain, beginning in October 1868, excited American sympathies and activated Cuban exiles in the United States to undertake filibustering expeditions. Not only did American citizens on the island lose property, but some were executed or jailed. American newspapers in New York beat the drums loudly for military action. Yet such was the mood of the nation that a resolution recognizing Cuban belligerency was turned down in June 1870 by a vote of 101 to 88. Three years later the *Virginius*, a munitions ship owned by Cubans but flying the American flag, was captured by a Spanish warship and fifty-three of its crew and passengers hastily shot as pirates. Here was an instance more flagrant than the future explosion of the *Maine*, directly attributable to Spain, but Grant and his Secretary of State, Hamilton Fish, managed to resolve the problem through diplomatic channels rather than war. The economic panic of 1873 no doubt was a strong dissuading factor, but there was also a matter of habit and tradition that was expressed by Secretary of State Frederick T. Frelinghuysen in the 1880's when he rejected two naval harbors from Haiti. "The policy of this Government . . . ," he said, "has tended toward avoidance of possessions disconnected from the main continent."

IV

The realities of a spiraling industrialism, however, were a more potent factor in determining policy than the abstract rhetoric of isolationists like Frelinghuysen. In the quarter of a century from 1850 through 1875 the United States enjoyed a surplus of trade with foreign nations on only three occasions, and then very small ones. In the twenty-five years that followed, on the other hand, there were hefty surpluses in twenty-two years and deficits—meager ones—in only three. This turnabout was the result, in the first place, as already indicated, of a highly impressive growth of manufacture. A great free market from the Atlantic to the Pacific offered enormous opportunities for expansion. But it was also the result of artificial measures which gave American manufacturers advantage over foreign capital in the internal market, such as the protective tariff, as well as military and political measures to gain foreign markets. The first protective tariff, introduced by William Lowndes of South Carolina, provided for duties on foreign cottons, iron, wollen, and other finished goods of 7.5 to 30 percent of their value, thus giving American "infant industries," still highly inefficient compared to British and European competitors, a great boon. In one form or another this principle of protection has survived to the present. On the other side the United States sought to break down barriers imposed by other nations, such as limitation of trade, quota systems, and tariffs, either through diplomatic means, through naval action, or in some instances by outright occupation. It is this joining of economic, diplomatic, and military action to gain new markets which was to be the essence of the new imperialism.

The most spirited advocate for this form of expansion in the fifteen years after Grant left office was a remarkable man with the morals of a robber baron and the charm of an ancient prince, James G. (Jingo Jim) Blaine—or, as he was otherwise known, the Plumed Knight. Had he not been so blatant an ally of the railroads and profited so handsomely from their favors, he would have been president. Even after a number of scandals had rocked his boat and independent Republicans, known as Mugwumps, deserted him, he came within an eyelash—1,149 votes in New York would have done it—of winning the presidency in 1884.

Blaine of Maine was a fifth-generation American whose Irish-Scotch forebears had migrated to Pennsylvania in 1745. His father, a staunch admirer of Henry Clay, had failed in various business ventures but succeeded moderately in politics. James Gillespie Blaine, born in January 1830, was to be a grand success in both. When he entered Washington and Jefferson College at the age of thirteen, he was tall and gawky, with a prominent nose that gave rise to the nickname "Nosey Blaine" and a speech impediment that marred his oratory. But he made friends easily, was kind, and had the politician's knack for remembering names and details. Unable because of scarce family funds to attend Yale Law School, he migrated to Lexington, Kentucky, home territory of his idol Clay, where he taught school for a few years and married a New England teacher who played a predominant role in his life. Returning to her home, Augusta, Maine, Blaine read law "on the side," then borrowed some money from his brother-in-law to acquire, at the age of twenty-four, half ownership in the Kennebec *Journal*. Journalism was his steppingstone to politics—and wealth.

It was said of Blaine of Maine that "he had the courage of his investments, not his convictions." In the South he had been a secessionist, in the North an abolitionist; in the South an advocate of low tariffs to aid the farmer and frontiersman, in the North of high tariffs to aid the manufacturer and businessman. In one place he was a Greenbacker, urging soft money, in the other a hard-money advocate. As a Whig he joined the Republican Party when it was born, was elected to the Maine Legislature, then to the national House of Representatives, where he served for twelve years. He was by now a man of great poise, his speech impediment virtually licked, tall and broad in figure, with a beard that offset the prominence of his nose, bright brown eyes, and a full head of black and gray hair. Magnetic Blaine, an opponent called him.

By 1876 the charismatic Republican, having spent six years as Speaker of the House, was the party's leading spokesman, a natural for the presidential nomination. He had not only endeared himself to the moneyed classes by advocating hard money and protection, but to the masses of Republicans by opposing the repatriation of Confederate President Jefferson Davis—"the author, knowingly, deliberately, guiltily and willfully, of the gigantic murders and crimes against northern prisoners at Andersonville." But a month later the first of a number of questionable deals with railroads came to light and Blaine's chances for the nomination dwindled apace. After denying he had ever received any money from the Union Pacific, he was forced to admit that he had deposited $32,000 in worthless first-mortgage bonds of a bankrupt road, and been given in return $64,000 cash by Union Pacific. It was all he could do to prevent himself from being expelled from the House, let alone gain the presidential nomination. Subsequently it was learned that Blaine had received stock and money from almost every railroad that sought government land grants or other help in the twelve years he was in the House. Nonetheless, despite these revelations, the Plumed Knight was chosen by the state of Maine for a six-year Senate term and served two stints as Secretary of State, for ten months in 1881 under his close friend James A. Garfield, and for three years, from 1889 to 1892, under Benjamin Harrison. He remained withal the leading figure in his party and had he sought the nomination for president in 1888 he probably would have had it.

Like a musical composer whose opus begins in low key and builds toward a crescendo, Blaine outlined the initial steps for a new expansionism, leaving the final and less savory ones for future discussions. He did not unsheathe the sword; he did not wave the big stick. He spoke only in terms of diplomacy and economic collaboration. "We desire," he wrote, "to extend our commerce, and in an especial degree with our friends and neighbors on this continent. . . . No field promises so much. No field has been cultivated so little." The "Big Sister" policy, as it became known, contemplated using the Monroe Doctrine not merely as a defensive weapon to keep European powers from establishing colonies in the Americas, but as an active instrument to make the United States dominant over the hemisphere. He would tolerate no treaty by European states, he said in 1881, which "impeaches our right and long-established claim to *priority* on the American continent. . . ." (Emphasis added.) He reaffirmed President Hayes's position that any isthmian canal, such as the one projected by the French engineer Ferdinand de Lesseps, must be U.S.-owned and U.S.-run.

The spirit of the United States, as Blaine expressed it in a confidential memo to the American minister in Hawaii, was one "which seeks its outlet in the mines of South America and the railroads of Mexico," a spirit which "would not be slow to avail itself of openings of assured and profitable enterprise even in mid-ocean." It was the government's duty to help this spirit find fruition. At the Pan-American Conference of 1889, which was convoked at his suggestion and over which he presided, Blaine tried to establish a customs union which would lower tariffs between Latin America and the United States, thus increasing Uncle Sam's sale of finished goods below the Rio Grande—and at the expense of Europe. Another proposal called for arbitration of inter-American disputes—such as the war recently concluded between Chile on the one hand and Peru and Bolivia on the other. If Washington was to be paramount on this hemisphere, it would be useful to have an orderly machinery for effectuating peace between its satellites. Ultimately, though it might take years, even generations, the United States would have to annex Cuba, Hawaii, and—yes—Canada, but for the time being the goal was to lay the roots for commercial expansion. Blaine included under the protective shield of the Monroe Doctrine the far-off Hawaiian islands, 2,100 miles from San Francisco, which he said must also be considered part of the "American system."

As a formula for imperialism Blaine's precepts were inade-

quate; in fact they achieved few results. The Latin Americans refused to give up their freedom of maneuver for North American
domination. Senator Roque Sáenz Peña, delegate from Argentina,
explained: "The consumption of the nations of Latin America represented in this conference amounts to $560,000,000, but the United
States shares in these importations to the amount only of $52,000,000,
not being 10 percent of our purchases from Europe." In other words
the southern republics were not so dependent on American commerce that they had to yield to Blaine's nostrums. So that with only
a ragtail navy to impose Washington's will and a lukewarm public
opinion in the States, Jingo Jim's "Big Sister" plan failed of fruition.
America was not yet ready to wage pitched battle for what was
called "Inevitable Destiny"—successor to "Manifest Destiny."

V

Similar difficulties were evident at first in efforts to acquire Hawaii
and Samoa, but were overcome before the end of the century.

When a group of Congregational missionaries from New England
arrived in Hawaii in 1821, its native population was approximately
200,000. Diseases introduced by the English and others, after Captain James Cook had discovered this Pacific real estate in 1778,
however, were rapidly decimating the citizens of the twenty islands.
Venereal disease, measles, whooping cough, influenza, and smallpox
eventually reduced the native strain to 58,000 by 1893, and 22,000
by the 1920's. The slack was taken up by Chinese, Japanese, and
later Filipinos, tens of thousands of whom were imported as contract laborers for as little as three dollars a month (in 1853, for instance).

The New England missionaries who had come to proselytize for
the Lord quickly discovered that there were better prospects in
other endeavors. Exchanging clerical robes for business garb, they
became large landowners, sugar planters, speculators, and, along
with the Honolulu merchants, the political power behind the
Hawaiian throne. Like the Austins of Texas they were loyal to their
new homeland and would have been content to live under an independent flag indefinitely. There were, however, disturbing facts of
life that could not be shunted aside. One was that the great powers
might overrun Hawaii. In 1842 France established a protectorate
over Tahiti, sending shivers down Hawaiian spines that a similar
fate was in store for them. To defend their status they sought treaties of friendship and commerce from Washington, London, and
Paris. The ex-missionaries were further alarmed the next year when

Britain occupied parts of the islands for five months before returning the reins to King Kamehameha.

By this time five out of every six ships setting anchor in the Pacific Shangri-La 2,100 miles from San Francisco flew the American flag. Secretary of State Webster, obviously interested in so fruitful a commercial haven, declared in no uncertain terms, therefore, that while the United States had no intention of annexing Hawaii, it would permit no one else to do so either. When France, evidently unimpressed by Webster's words, temporarily seized Honolulu in 1849, there was a shift in mood in the United States. The cry for annexation became so intense that in 1854 President Franklin Pierce actually negotiated a treaty of acquisition—only to backtrack on it because a provision for immediate statehood stirred so much opposition. A year later Secretary of State William L. Marcy negotiated a pact abolishing duties on goods each country sold the other. But the Senate rejected it because of pressures by Louisiana sugar planters who feared competition from Hawaii. Another such treaty in 1867 also failed to win approval.

By 1875, however, sentiments had changed, and Hawaii and the United States signed a seven-year reciprocity agreement which in addition to economic benefits provided that Hawaii would not "alienate" any port or territory to any foreign power except the United States. If it were to be annexed by anyone it would be by Uncle Sam. The treaty was renegotiated in 1884, this time giving Uncle Sam exclusive control of a harbor on the Pearl River in Oahu for a naval station. Under the spur of these reciprocity arrangements, Hawaiian sugar production quintupled from 1877 to 1887, then doubled again in the next ten years, with 99 percent of Hawaii's exports going to the United States and three fourths of its imports coming from there. From 1877 to 1890 foreign trade quadrupled, the main beneficiaries being the Hawaiians of American descent who owned most of the $33 million investment (as of 1893) in the sugar industry.

From economic dominance and establishment of a naval base it was only a small step to political annexation, though it still had to run the gauntlet of congressional opposition in the United States. The geopolitical logic, as expressed by expansionists, was simple. Acquisition, an American admiral said in 1851, was "intimately connected with our commercial and naval supremacy" in the Pacific. For Blaine, the "gradual and seemingly inevitable decadence and extinction of the native race" posed the danger of colonization by other powers, and hence made it urgent for the United States to impose "an avowedly American solution." When Hawaii seemed disposed in 1881 to give Britain the same reciprocal trade advantages as those contained in the 1875 treaty with Washington, Blaine warned that those islands "cannot be joined to the Asiatic system. If they drift from their independent station, it must be toward assimilation and identification with the American system, to which they belong by the operation of natural laws and must belong by the operation of political necessity." There was no nonsense about this hallowed principle; twice, when there were internal troubles in Hawaii, American troops were landed at Honolulu to "protect life and property."

Many of the American Hawaiians had misgivings about the prospect of annexation because their contract labor laws—virtually a form of peonage—would run afoul of American legislation on the subject, but in the end they had no alternative if they expected the benefits of trade with America. Congress, in 1890, made the import of sugar duty-free to all nations, and decided to pay a bonus of two cents a pound to American sugar producers—thus abolishing the Hawaiian advantage. Then, in 1891, Queen Liliuokalani ascended the throne and attempted to impose an autocratic constitution under which the sugar planters would lose political preponderance. The result was an American-inspired revolution, abetted by one of Blaine's friends, John L. Stevens. U.S. troops were landed from the warship *Boston* to help the rebels. Without this intervention, according to Nicoll Ludlow, commander of another naval ship, "the revolution would not have occurred in the way it did, and at the time it did. . . ." Neither would the American Hawaiians have undertaken it without assurance of "the protection and assistance of the United States forces there."

At any rate, within a month after the Queen's fall, annexation papers were signed and Americans were debating for the first time the virtues and vices of modern imperialism. Unfortunately for the expansionists, the issue coincided with a turnover in administration from Republican Harrison to Democrat Grover Cleveland, who promptly removed the troops, withdrew the treaty of annexation from the Senate, and prevailed on Congress to pass two resolutions on noninterference. The actual annexation would have to wait four more years, to 1898, by which time the imperialist fever had reached the upper tip of the thermometer.

The acquisition of Samoa was similarly protracted, and for much the same reasons. This archipelago, athrust a number of major ocean lanes in the Pacific, had been the object of American attention since 1838, when whaling interests prevailed on the administration to send a scientific expedition there. Nothing much was heard of Samoa until after the Civil War, when it occurred to some people that this might be an excellent stopover for a steamship line on the way from San Francisco to Australia. Commander Richard W. Meade thereupon signed a treaty with a Samoan chief turning over the harbor of Pago Pago—"the most perfectly landlocked harbor that exists in the Pacific Ocean"—to the United States as a naval base and coaling station.

Thus began a comic opera that lasted a quarter of a century. In the meantime Germany and Britain had laid claims to other portions of the archipelago and Germany, the dominant commercial force there at the time, attacked the Polynesian monarch and bombarded some of his villages. In 1889 three American and three German warships, as well as one British, squared away at each other outside the port of Apia and a military confrontation between three great powers seemed likely. By chance, however, a hurricane descended on the area in March, wrecking all the American and German vessels and causing a considerable loss of life. Both Bismarck of Germany and Blaine of the United States decided under the circumstances to be conciliatory with each other, agreeing to a three-power protectorate over Samoa. It was not until 1899, a full decade later, that the island paradise, not far from New Zealand, was finally partitioned between Germany and the United States, with the two largest islands going to the former, and the rest, including Tutuila with the Pago Pago harbor, to Uncle Sam.

VI

If Blaine failed in his specific objectives for creating a U.S. sphere of influence extending throughout the western hemisphere and into the Pacific, it was only a temporary setback along a path whose markings were decisively clear. Henceforth the United States would pay little heed to the principle of contiguity—by the end of the century it had acquired fifty or more specks in the Pacific Ocean, including Wake, Guam, Midway, Howland, Baker. More important, Washington was unceremoniously jettisoning a number of hallowed traditions about "government by consent of the governed." It was now permissible, as in Hawaii, to invade a foreign country without the consent of its people, on the pretext of protecting "American life and property." The native people, it was assumed, did not have to be consulted about the transfer of sovereignty, or given the right to rule themselves afterward.

The justification for all this was that Anglo-Saxons generally and Americans specifically were a superior people chosen by the Almighty to spread their civilization everywhere. The Anglo-Saxon, wrote Congregational minister Josiah Strong in his immensely popular 1885 book, *Our Country*, is the representative of two great ideas, "civil liberty" and "pure *spiritual* Christianity"—the greatest of all human contributions. "It follows, then, that the Anglo-Saxon . . . is divinely commissioned to be, in a peculiar sense, his brother's keeper." For the United States that divine commission was, according to Strong, a mandate to move "down upon Mexico, down upon Central and South America, out upon the islands of the sea, over upon Africa and beyond."

The 1880's and 1890's were a period in which conservative intellectuals invariably used the Darwinian theory of natural selection as justification for their political goals. Nothing should be done for the poor, Herbert Spencer and other Social Darwinists proclaimed, because they had been destined for the scrap heap by the immutable laws of nature. On the other hand, the preeminent Anglo-Saxons were clearly selected for world domination and should accept their assignment with dignity. Such were the views of the historian and philosopher John Fiske, the Boston brahmins Brooks Adams and Henry Cabot Lodge, the senator from Indiana Albert Beveridge, the blustery New Yorker Theodore Roosevelt, and innumerable others.

The mentor of the new imperialism—more thorough than Blaine—was a naval officer undistinguished as a seaman but brilliant and penetrating as a historian and strategist, Alfred T. Mahan. A shy, good-looking man, more than six feet tall, with sandy hair, bright complexion and gray-blue eyes, Mahan was the son of a professor of engineering at the Military Academy in West Point. Until the appearance of his second book, *The Influence of Sea Power upon History, 1660–1783*, his life had been routine and unacclaimed. He had been educated at a private school in Hagerstown, Maryland, attended Columbia University for two years, then entered the Naval Academy at the age of sixteen. He graduated in 1859 with second honors, was made lieutenant during the first months of the Civil War, married a Philadelphia girl when he was almost thirty-two, and rose slowly but steadily to captain in 1885. His only writing to this point was a brief opus on the naval history of the Civil War, published in 1883, that made little impact on the outside world. But in 1885 he was called on to lecture at the new War College in Newport, and after a year of preparation gave the lectures, which were later expanded into a classic work hailed by conservatives in Europe even more than in America. It made an enormous impact on two men who would play major roles in the history of the United States, Senator Henry Cabot Lodge and Theodore Roosevelt.

Mahan's theme, illustrated by prolific historical allusion, was remarkably simple. A nation that aspires to be great, he said, must have not only land power but sea power. The reason is that home trade is only a portion of the trade of a country "bordering on the sea." It is required to import necessities and luxuries to its harbors, and to ship out across the water a commensurate amount of goods. Such shipping must "have secure ports to which to return and must, as far as possible, be followed by the protection of their country throughout the voyage." In time of war this protection "must be extended by armed shipping." Thus the "key to much of the history, as well as of the policy, of nations bordering upon the sea" is to be found in three links of a single chain—production, "with the necessity of exchanging products, shipping, whereby the exchange is carried on, and colonies, which facilitate and enlarge the operations of shipping and tend to protect it by multiplying points of safety. . . ." The United States, he argued, had directed its talents since the Civil War only to the first of these three links, production, and had done little to build a merchant marine and strong navy, or to acquire colonies.

Mahan's prose, didactic but persuasive, emphasized a single theme: America must turn its "eyes outward" and "affirm the importance of distant markets." More than anything else it needed a sizable merchant marine of its own, a powerful navy, coaling stations, safe ports, bases around the world, and colonies. In Mahan's lexicon the word "defense" no longer meant safeguarding one's shores from a foreign attack, but "has its application at points far away from our own coast." In the nationalist view, foreign commerce was the country's lifeblood and to acquire islands and bases for expanding that commerce was in fact a defensive stance. An economist who followed Mahan's line, Charles A. Conant, put it this way: "The United States have actually reached, or are approaching the economic state where . . . outlets are required outside their own boundaries, in order to prevent business depression, idleness, and suffering at home." If all nations practiced "commercial freedom" there would be no need for "the exercise of political and military power" to win outlets; but since they didn't the United States is compelled "by the instinct of self-preservation"—defense—to engage in this game.

Once an opponent of Blaine's imperialism, Mahan now became its most fervid exponent and won disciples in the highest circles. The aristocratic Senator Henry Cabot Lodge, historian turned politician, put the captain's views pithily in his famous phrase, "Commerce follows the flag." Young Teddy Roosevelt, a brash Assistant Secretary of the Navy who had misgivings about McKinley's moderateness, wrote in May 1897: "My dear Captain Mahan: This letter must, of course, be considered as entirely confidential, because in my position I am merely carrying out the policy of the Secretary and the President. I suppose I need not tell you that as regards Hawaii I take your views absolutely, as indeed I do on foreign policy generally." Specifically these men plunked for "a canal through the Central American Isthmus" to ease commerce into the Pacific, a large navy—"we should build a dozen new battleships, half of them on the Pacific Coast," wrote Roosevelt—annexation of Hawaii, Samoa, Cuba, and whatever else was available. Roosevelt, the man of action, suggested that we send two battleships and a coaling ship to Hawaii, "hoist our flag over the island," and leave "all details for after action." Mahan, the theoretician, warned that the great benefits of imperialism might be frustrated by those who clung to the "maxims framed in the infancy of the republic"—in other words by those who still believed in the principles of nonintervention, self-rule, and self-determination.

Mahan need not have worried, however. The propitious rekindling of a revolution a stone's throw from the Florida shores gave the imperialists their grand opportunity.

10

THE FLAG FOLLOWS
COMMERCE

In 1895, after an interval of only seventeen years, rebellion broke out again on the island of Cuba. The worldwide depression that began in 1893, and the restoration of duties on Cuban sugar by the United States the following year, caused economic havoc on the Caribbean island. This rich piece of land about the size of Virginia was, with Puerto Rico, the last vestige of the enormous empire Spain once owned in the western hemisphere—its people having failed to win independence either in the Latin American eruptions of the 1820's or their own uprising of 1868–78. The new revolution, like the old, sputtered along, with the rebels fighting only small harassing actions and the Spaniards, true to form, trying to isolate the *insurrectos* with a massive reign of terror against their rural base. Scores of thousands of peasants and agricultural workers were unceremoniously herded into concentration camps—*reconcentrados*—and considerable numbers left to die of starvation and disease. In the province of Havana alone, it is claimed, 50,000 expired.

Such outrages naturally won the sympathy of the American people for the Cuban cause, especially since the flames were fanned by such sensational yellow journals as Pulitzer's New York *World* and Hearst's New York *Journal*. "Blood on the roadsides," cried the *World*, "blood in the fields, blood on the doorsteps, blood, blood, blood." Such lurid reportage helped galvanize not only Republicans but Democrats and Populists to the side of Cuban liberty. In 1896 Congress voted by a large majority to recognize Cuban belligerency, but the antijingo, muscular 250-pound president, Grover Cleveland, refused to be stampeded into war. At one point he stated that even if the legislature should vote for hostilities "I will not mobilize the army." His position shifted somewhat as he prepared to leave office. Should Spain be unable to exercise its authority in Cuba, he said in his last message to Congress, in December 1896, the United States might be forced to intervene in the interest of its "higher obligations."

President William McKinley, the handsome former congressman from Ohio who had been selected by Mark Hanna and his big-business coterie, ran on a platform calling for, among other things, annexation of Hawaii, purchase of the Danish West Indies, building of a canal in Nicaragua to link the Atlantic and Pacific Oceans, and support for the Cuban revolutionaries. At the urging of his young Assistant Secretary of the Navy, Theodore Roosevelt, he did enter into negotiations to secure Hawaii, but he was no more willing to wage war over Cuba, at first, than his predecessor had been. The corporate trusts whom Senator Mark Hanna represented and who were becoming predominant at this time eschewed war for fear it would cut the ground from economic revival. The severe depression of 1893 had jolted them, and recovery had been inhibited, they believed, first by the war scare over the boundary dispute between Venezuela and British Guiana—in which even Cleveland was prepared to take action if Britain refused to arbitrate—and then by the free-silver candidacy of William Jennings Bryan in 1896. By 1897 the economy was definitely on the upswing, and though big business would eventually profit mammothly from the Spanish-American War, many financial interests feared that such a war would impede the tenuous recovery. The stock market, reflecting those interests, tended to plunge downward every time war seemed probable.

The misgivings of Hanna, McKinley, and a large segment of business, however, were overwhelmed by popular revulsion against Spain, carefully exploited by the Roosevelt-Mahan-Lodge-Beveridge faction and the yellow journals. The situation in Cuba was bad enough, but it was exacerbated by some of the wildest and most dishonest reporting ever known. A correspondent for Hearst's New York *Journal* reported on April 4, 1896, the sensational but entirely mythical capture of Pinar del Río by a group of American volunteers using a battery of Gatling guns. A female reporter for the same paper, hearing noises from what she thought was the Cabanas fortress, wrote a gaudy tale of the execution of native prisoners by "rifle volleys." It raised the Hearst circulation considerably, but it was all fiction. So, typically, was the tale of two women allegedly stripped to the skin by Spanish inspectors on the American ship *Olivette,* and then manhandled. Fairytales, intermixed with true facts of the bestialities committed under General Valeriano

("Butcher") Weyler, evoked enormous sympathy for the Cuban cause and were utilized by Roosevelt and his friends for their own purposes.

In a Western society this is the perfect formula for imperialist intervention: to ride the tide of idealistic popular concern in order to advance the cause of special interests. President Cleveland had stated it with utmost clarity when he pointed out that while Americans sympathized with the victimized Cubans who were trying to establish a "better and freer government," the United States had an interest in the island "which is by no means of a wholly sentimental or philanthropic character." Apart from the strategic setting of this Spanish colony, its "pecuniary interest" for Uncle Sam was second only to that of Spanish businessmen and the Spanish Crown. "It is reasonably estimated," said Cleveland, "that at least from $30 to $50 millions of American capital are invested in the plantations and in railroad, mining, and other business enterprises on the island." Trade between the United States and Cuba, prior to the insurrection, was running at approximately $100 million a year.

While Cleveland did not feel that the "pecuniary" and strategic factors were sufficient cause to impose American rule over foreign territory, Roosevelt, Mahan, and Lodge saw it as a step on the broad path of empire—and they effectively converted a humanistic demand for liberty into the "realistic" advance of empire. The Spaniards in fact were willing to appease the American public's humanitarian sensitivities. In October 1897 a new Spanish premier recalled General Weyler, offered to modify the concentration camp policy, free Americans imprisoned on the island, and grant a certain amount of home rule. This was not enough to win over the *insurrectos,* but it did seem to meet at least some American criticisms. Emotions, however, did not abate. At approximately this time Hearst's *Journal* effected the escape of a Cuban girl, Evangelina Cisneros, from a Havana prison where she was under sentence for treason. It headlined the story: "An American Newspaper Accomplishes at a Single Stroke What the Red Tape of Diplomacy Failed Utterly to Bring About in Many Months." The following January, as rebels turned down the Spanish offer of limited autonomy, and loyalists, on the other side, rioted in the streets of Havana on behalf of Spain, the *Journal* stridently demanded war. Each gaudy headline raised circulation figures so that by 1898 the competitive *World* and *Journal* were each selling 800,000 papers daily. Other journals around the country were buying their copy and using the same techniques to win circulation.

Teddy Roosevelt had been trying persistently but unsuccessfully to get McKinley to act. The President, he confided to intimates, "has no more backbone than a chocolate eclair." But the sustained interventionist mood could not be bypassed indefinitely, and eventually McKinley was caught up in it. In January 1898, against the advice of the American consul in Cuba, the creaky battleship *Maine* was dispatched to the Havana harbor to "protect American life and property." A few weeks later the Hearst press published a sensational letter by the Spanish minister in Washington, Dupuy de Lome, derogating McKinley as "weak," a "bidder for the admiration of the crowd," a "would-be politician who tries to leave a door open behind himself while keeping on good terms with the jingoes of his party." The embarrassed minister resigned his post, while an inflamed American populace refused to forgive his indiscretion. And while the minister's disgrace was still in the headlines another event occurred that raised passions beyond the breaking point: the *Maine* exploded on February 15, killing 258 sailors and two officers.

Inquiries many years later indicated that the tragedy probably resulted from an external mine, but it has never entirely been ruled out that it may have been due to an internal explosion in the ship's own magazine. Four hours after the event, U.S. Captain C. D. Sigsbee wired details to the Secretary of the Navy, John D. Long, urging that "public opinion should be suspended until further report." He also related that a Spanish man-of-war was picking up survivors and that "many Spanish officers, including representatives of General [Ramón] Blanco, now with me to express sympathy." Both Sigsbee and the consul general, Fitzhugh Lee, refused to lay the blame on the Spaniards, and many Americans were convinced that it was illogical for the Madrid government, which was desperately trying to contain hostilities, to engage in an act that curried war with a great power. "Nobody," said the *Nation* of March 3, 1898, "really thinks that the Spanish Government or its military or naval officers caused that disaster or intended that it should take place." The mine, if that is what caused the explosion, might also have been set by a Cuban patriot anxious to embroil the United States, a Cuban loyalist anxious to punish the United States for its sympathies, or even, as the *Nation* speculated at the time, an insane person.

Rational assessment, however, was the furthest thing from the minds of the jingoes, as the drumbeat for reprisal against Spain became deafening. Before the navy had completed its inquiry, Congress voted $50 million for national defense and the armed services began a furious preparation for war. The yellow journals cried for immediate retribution. "The whole country thrills with war fever," said Hearst's *Journal*. If that wasn't exactly true, the slogan "Remember the *Maine!* To hell with Spain!" was on enough lips to raise the nation's fever chart by many degrees. Teddy Roosevelt bellowed at Senator Mark Hanna that "we will have this war for the freedom of Cuba in spite of the timidity of the commercial interests." Henry Cabot Lodge shouted that "this gigantic murder, the last spasm of a corrupt and dying society . . . cries aloud for justice." Mass meetings were held in a number of cities calling for war, and students held drills and carried placards reading "To hell with Spain."

Much of this was genuine revulsion against Spanish rule, but much was camouflage for ulterior motives, especially on the part of Roosevelt and his clique. The Assistant Secretary of the Navy wanted war whatever the excuse. Ten days after the *Maine* was sunk, while he was temporarily in charge of the department, Roosevelt ordered Commodore George Dewey to prepare for an attack on Manila in the Philippines if war should break out. Another cabinet official, it may be recalled, secretly ordered Commodore Sloat, before the Mexican War, to seize California if war should ensue over Texas. Presumably the issue was Cuba and President McKinley was still most anxious to arrive at a diplomatic rather than a military settlement, yet Roosevelt was already widening a war that was not to begin until two months later.

In those two months there were many indications that Spain would accede to whatever the United States demanded. Stewart L. Woodford, U.S. minister in Madrid, informed McKinley at the end of March that in his opinion the Spanish ministry "are ready to go as far and as fast as they can and still save the dynasty here in Spain. They know that Cuba is lost." A few days later he cabled: "I know that the Queen and her present ministry sincerely desire peace and that the Spanish people desire peace, and if you can still give me time and reasonable liberty of action I will get for you the peace you desire so much and for which you have labored so hard." There was fear in Madrid that if the government granted McKinley's request for an armistice with the insurgents it would be toppled by a revolution at home. Nevertheless, by April 9, with the Pope prodding Spain, and six European powers appealing to the American President, Madrid had accepted all the demands of Washington. On that day she agreed to an immediate "suspension of hostilities" with the insurgents. She had already revoked the hated *re-concentrado* policy, freed all American citizens held in prison, offered to arbitrate the dispute over the *Maine* explosion, granted amnesty to rebels, and permitted American relief to enter the island. If humanitarian sympathy for the Cuban people were the basis for intervention, there was no longer any reason for war. Joseph Pulitzer admitted nine years later that "Spain had granted to Cuba all that we had demanded, but passion in Spain and here forced the hands of the government."

The clamor for what John Hay would soon call "a splendid little war" was now irrepressible. Two days after Spain had capitulated, on April 11, McKinley, evidently swayed by the argument that his party would lose the fall elections if he didn't yield to the jingoes, sent a message to Congress proposing "the forcible intervention of the United States as a neutral to stop the war." Among the reasons offered for this step, apart from ending "the barbarities, bloodshed, starvation, and horrible miseries" in Cuba, were "protection and indemnity" for American "life and property" on the island, and the need to prevent "very serious injury to the commerce, trade, and business of our people" there. Eight days later, in a resolution recognizing Cuban independence and demanding Spanish withdrawal, McKinley was authorized to take the proper military steps. A demurrer, tacked on by Senator H. M. Teller, assured the world that the United States had no intention of acquiring Cuba and would "leave the government and control of that Island to its people." After a century of agitation for annexation of Cuba, it was difficult to understand why it was being repudiated, except perhaps that the United States did not want to assume the country's debt of $400 million. Another factor suggested by historian Thomas A. Bailey was that "American sugar interests . . . wanted Cuba to remain outside the tariff wall. . . ." In any event, despite the high-flown rhetoric about Cuba Libre, Cuba would soon become a U.S. colony in all but name.

II

The "little war," or what the New York *Journal* called the "*Journal's* war," was a grand, disorganized coup that lasted only 100 days—not counting the sequel in the Philippines—and cost the United States 385 dead in battle and 2,061 from "other causes," mostly yellow fever. The navy, well nurtured in the previous fifteen years, took only 57 casualties, 10 dead and 47 wounded, while acquitting itself with great distinction both at Manila and Santiago de Cuba. It was a war made for heroes since the opposition, formidable on paper, with 155,000 troops, was in fact poorly led and inept in practice. Teddy Roosevelt, commander of the volunteer Rough Riders, astride his horse, Little Texas, slowly ascended San Juan's hills in "the Charge at San Juan Hill"—to become an American idol drafted for the vice-presidency shortly thereafter. A lieutenant named John Pershing made his mark leading a regiment of dismounted Negro cavalrymen, and another lieutenant, Douglas MacArthur, son of General Arthur MacArthur, won his spurs fighting Filipino *insurrectos*, one of whom shot his hat from his head.

The first surprise of the war, a few days after it was declared, was news that Commodore Dewey, pursuing orders given him by Roosevelt, had swept into Manila Bay with six vessels and annihilated a fleet of seven warships commanded by Rear Admiral Patricio Montojo y Pasaron. The country went wild with joy, but almost no one in Washington knew what Dewey was doing there or what was the political objective of his foray. McKinley's message of April 11, 1898, had mentioned four reasons for war, all of them having to do with conditions in Cuba, none with the Philippines. Nor did he have any prior plans for disposing of them after hostilities. "The truth is," he later confessed to a meeting of Methodists, "I didn't want the Philippines and when they came to us as a gift from the gods, I did not know what to do about them. . . ."

As it happened, here, as in Cuba, a revolt against Spanish rule had broken out in 1896. Dewey evidently intended to fan its flames, for he transported the exiled insurgent leader, Emilio Aguinaldo, from Hong Kong to Manila in May. According to Aguinaldo, who busied himself immediately forming a Filipino resistance army, Dewey advised him that "the United States had come to the Philippines to free the Filipinos from the yoke of Spain. He said furthermore that America was exceedingly well off as regards territory, revenue and resources and needed no colonies. He assured me finally that there was no reason for me to entertain any doubts whatever about the recognition of the independence of the Philippines by the United States." Whether this version is true and Dewey was guilty of a mammoth act of duplicity, or whether Aguinaldo's account is exaggerated, the fact is that with 15,000 loyal Spanish and Filipino troops in Manila and with the arrival of American troops still many weeks off, Dewey could use native allies. Whatever the commodore's on-the-spot promises, however, back in Washington other thoughts were crystallizing. Secretary of the Navy John D. Long cabled the order not to enter into "political alliances with the insurgents . . . that would incur liability to maintain their cause in the future." There was to be no loose talk about helping the Filipinos win independence.

If President McKinley wasn't entirely sure either of the geography or the value of the Philippines, there were more determined men in the United States with a clearer vision. Indiana Senator Albert Beveridge, a friend of Lodge's and a member in good standing of the Roosevelt-Mahan clan, explained it in a speech delivered at Boston

April 21, 1898: "American factories are making more than the American people can use; American soil is producing more than they can consume. Fate has written our policy for us; the trade of the world must and shall be ours. . . . We will cover the ocean with our merchant marine. We will build a navy to the measure of our greatness. . . ." He concluded that "the Philippines are logically our first target." A little later he was even more specific. "Where," he asked, "shall we turn for consumers of our surplus? Geography answers the question. China is our natural customer. . . . The Philippines give us a base at the door of all the East. . . . The power that rules the Pacific . . . is the power that rules the world. And, with the Philippines, that power is and will forever be the American Republic." The American minister to China, E. H. Conger, wrote to Secretary of State William R. Day on August 26, 1898, that the seizure of this island complex in the Pacific "would give a convenient and essential base of supplies, where American trade, capital and brains could and would be massed ready for the commercial conquests, which Americans ought to accomplish in China." Uncle Sam was a Johnny-come-lately to this vast semicontinental market, enjoying only 2 percent of its trade. The Philippines and a strong navy, it was felt, would open the door to expansion in China.

What began, then, as a war to liberate Cuba so as "to put an end to the barbarities, bloodshed, starvation, and horrible miseries now existing there," suddenly disclosed motives of conquest in faraway places not mentioned before.

A new enthusiasm for imperialism flared even among those who had had misgivings that the war would upset economic recovery. Many years before, John Quincy Adams had observed that all wars, including those fought for liberty, excite imperialist lusts. The point was reemphasized by the short but sweet Spanish-American War. "A new consciousness seems to have come upon us," commented the Washington *Post*, "a consciousness of strength—and with it a new appetite. . . . The taste of empire is in the mouth of the people even as the taste of blood in the jungle. It means an imperial policy, the Republic, renascent, taking her place with the armed nations." Brooks Adams, bicycling with Oliver Wendell Holmes, Jr., expressed the jubilant notion that "this war is the first gun in the battle for the ownership of the world"—a view that turned out to be not far off the mark. Businessmen who had been lukewarm to the war suddenly realized that new commercial vistas had been opened for them in the Far East. Financier Frank Vanderlip wrote in the *Century* magazine that half the world could be reached for American trade from the Philippines. Mark Hanna waxed lyrical about possessing "a strategic point" in the Pacific which gave "the American people an opportunity to maintain a foothold in the markets" of China. President McKinley, who had entertained doubts about annexing the Philippines, was now firmly convinced that "the march of events rules and overrules human action."

III

The "march of events" McKinley referred to was, of course, the quick and decisive military success of the armed forces. It gave wings to the jingo spirit, causing many an American to shed inhibitions against naked imperialism and abandon a long-held tradition against colonies and noncontiguous expansion.

This shift in sentiment was made apparent less than two months after hostilities began, when on July 7, 1898, Hawaii, at long last, was annexed to the United States. The year before, McKinley, honoring a campaign pledge, had signed still another treaty of annexation with the pro-American government of the islands, only to have it lapse in the Senate, where it failed to secure the necessary two thirds for ratification. The *Nation* commented, with some exultation, that the issue was now "dead beyond the hope of resurrection." But the notice of death was premature because a year later, when Dewey fired the shot "heard round the world," the expansionists latched their argument onto Dewey's coattails. Hawaii, they said, was needed as a way station to supply the commodore. It was a bastion of defense for the Philippines, a "bridge to the Pacific," as well as a fortress to check would-be invaders who might creep up to the West Coast. It was also, of course, necessary for "the protection and promotion of our commercial interests." In vain did the Democratic opposition argue that American speculators were pushing annexation because they had bought $5 million of Hawaiian bonds at 30 cents to the dollar and were waiting for Uncle Sam to redeem them at 100 cents. "We have gotten along splendidly for one hundred and nine years without these volcanic rocks . . . ," said a Democratic leader. "If we did not need them when we were only three million strong, why are we likely to perish for the want of them now that we are seventy-five million souls?" Again, however, as in 1845, when the United States annexed Texas, the government put the matter to a joint resolution of Congress—requiring a mere majority instead of two thirds—and perseverance was finally rewarded.

Public opinion clearly was being modified in cadence with the easy successes on the battlefields. "The Republican Conventions," Senator Lodge reported to McKinley, "are all declaring that where the flag once goes up it must never come down." Senator Beveridge's impassioned March of the Flag speech, given at Indianapolis in mid-September 1898, was reprinted by the Republican National Committee in an edition of 300,000. "Hawaii," said the Senator, "is ours; Puerto Rico is to be ours; at the prayer of her people Cuba finally will be ours; in the islands of the East, even to the gates of Asia, coaling stations are to be ours at the very least; the flag of a liberal government is to float over the Philippines, and may it be the banner that Taylor unfurled in Texas and Fremont carried to the coast." Having presented this glowing prospect Beveridge next disparaged the notion of the opposition "that we ought not to govern a people without their consent." The "rule of liberty that all just government derives its authority from the consent of the governed," he taunted the other side, "applies only to those who are capable of self-government. We govern the Indians without their consent, we govern our territories without their consent, we govern our children without their consent." Why not the Philippines? Beveridge was remarkably candid about the materialist purposes of the new imperialism: "If any man tells you that trade depends on cheapness [of price] and not on government influence, ask him why England does not abandon South Africa, Egypt, India. . . . The conflicts of the future are to be conflicts of trade—struggles for markets—commercial wars for existence. And the golden rule of peace is impregnability of position and invincibility of preparedness."

By the time the Paris negotiations got under way in October, many top officials who had had reservations about taking the nation on the path of imperialism had become lively enthusiasts. That included those businessmen and their spokesmen, such as Hanna, who had no misgivings about imperialism per se but were concerned that war might undermine a tenuous prosperity; it became clear as the months passed that just the opposite was true. President McKinley himself had abjured "forcible annexation" of Cuba in 1897. "By our code of morality," he said, that "would be criminal aggression." But "criminal aggression" became acceptable a year later at the peace table as the United States directly annexed Puerto Rico, Guam (captured in June by the same convoy which brought General Wesley Merritt's troops to Manila), and the 7,100 islands situated only two hundred miles from Formosa and less than four hundred miles from the China coast, the strategically vital Philippines. The Spaniards resisted this latter cession but were helpless to prevent it. On the other hand they tried to transfer Cuba to American sovereignty but failed because the United States, among other things, did not want to assume the $400 million debt.

The story is told, perhaps apocryphally, how McKinley agonized over making the Philippines an American colony. At first he had thought only of acquiring a coaling station, then of incorporating the largest island, Luzon, into the American empire. Finally, "I went down on my knees and prayed to Almighty God for light and guidance," night after night, until one night it became clear that of the four alternatives annexation was the only sensible one. To give the islands back to Spain would be "cowardly and dishonorable"; to give them to "our commercial rivals in the Orient," France or Germany, "would be bad business and discreditable"; to let the Filipinos have their own rule would soon result in "anarchy and misrule." So there was nothing left "but to take them all, and to educate the Filipinos, and uplift and civilize and Christianize them. . . ." After this sagacious insight McKinley "went to bed, and went to sleep and slept soundly. . . ."

This was a moment of great consequence for the American future, one of those turning points that serve to redefine national purpose and consecrate new tradition. Hitherto, except for Alaska, the United States had always granted self-rule in areas it acquired. It had been imperialist but not colonialist. Its leaders, for the most part, sternly eschewed colonialism as contrary to the principles of the Declaration of Independence and the Constitution. Senator George C. Vest of Missouri defined this doctrine aptly in a December 1898 resolution: "The colonial system of European nations," it said, "cannot be established under our present Constitution, but all the territory acquired by the Government . . . must be acquired and governed with the purpose or intent of organizing such territory into States suitable for admission into the Union." Senator William E. Mason of Illinois, in another resolution a month later, put the theorem in these terms: "That the Government of the United States of America will not attempt to govern the people of any other country in the world without the consent of the people themselves. . . ."

The fundamental issue of self-rule was so deeply emplaced in the national psyche that despite the heartwarming military victories, an anti-imperialist opposition—as bitter and widespread as that against the Vietnam War seven decades later—began to form at the very time Dewey was sweeping into Manila Bay. If the basic doctrine of American democracy, government by consent of the governed, could be shredded to pieces in Cuba, the Philippines, or Puerto Rico, it might need stronger bracing at home. The opposition included such prestigious figures as former president Cleveland and eight members of his cabinet; William Jennings Bryan, Democratic standard-bearer; Senator George F. Hoar; Speaker of the House Thomas B.

Reed; industrialist Andrew Carnegie; AFL President Samuel Gompers. There were also educators such as Charles W. Eliot, president of Harvard, and David Starr Jordan, president of Stanford; writers like Mark Twain, William James, and William Graham Sumner; Carl Schurz, a cabinet member under President Hayes; mugwumps (Republican reformers) like Charles Francis Adams and Moorfield Storey; social workers like Jane Addams; and a shining list of reformers, single taxers, pacifists, prohibitionists, free-traders, and supporters of the Indian cause.

In June 1898 members of the liberal community in Boston came together at Faneuil Hall "to protest the adoption of a so-called imperial policy by the United States." Moorfield Storey, once the president of the American Bar Association, told the audience that "We are not here to oppose the war" against Spain. "We are here . . . to insist that a war begun in the cause of humanity should not be turned into a war for empire." The meeting established a Committee of Correspondence—reminiscent of pre-Revolutionary days—to communicate with like-minded people elsewhere. In November, while Spain and the United States were hammering out a treaty in Paris, an Anti-Imperialist League was formed "to oppose, by every legitimate means, the acquisition of the Philippine Islands, or of *any* colonies away from our shores. . . ." By May 1899 the League had 30,000 members. In October, after a convention attended by 10,000 delegates from thirty states, it formally became the American Anti-Imperialist League with headquarters in Chicago. Eighty-year-old George S. Boutwell, one of the founders of the Republican Party, was its president. Among its endorsers were former president Benjamin Harrison and former president Grover Cleveland, who became one of its forty-one vice-presidents.

Annexation of the Philippines or Cuba, said David Starr Jordan, meant a 180-degree departure from America's "best principles and tradition." We would be "descending," said Senator Hoar, "from the ancient path of republican liberty which the [founding] father trod, down into the modern swamp and cesspool of imperialism." Cleveland and Bryan, though at loggerheads within the Democratic Party, both denounced the exotic notion that overseas expansion was America's "inevitable destiny," and warned that the country could not endure "half republic and half colony." The war, said venerable Professor Charles Eliot Norton, was "a turning-back from the path of civilization to that of barbarism." He advised students not to enlist in the army, because these were hostilities in which "we jettison all that was most precious in our national cargo."

The platform of the American Anti-Imperialist League, which

eventually recruited scores of thousands of members, was as scathing a denunciation of an existing government as the nation had ever read. Written by Carl Schurz and approved in October 1899, it began with the observation that "the policy known as imperialism is hostile to liberty and tends toward militarism, an evil from which it has been our glory to be free." The "subjugation" of the Philippines was "criminal aggression" and "open disloyalty to the distinctive principles of our government." The "destruction of self-government" in the Pacific was a "betrayal of American institutions at home," sparking a "contest that must go on until the Declaration of Independence and the Constitution of the United States are rescued from the hands of their betrayers"—obviously McKinley, Roosevelt, Mahan, Lodge, et al. The platform ended with a quotation from Lincoln that "those who deny freedom to others deserve it not for themselves, and under a just God cannot long retain it."

IV

While this shower of rhetoric, for and against imperialism, fell on the home front, the United States became embroiled in the corollary to modern imperialism, counterrevolution. Senator Beveridge, the nation's most exuberant expansionist, might speak of America's ultimate purpose as "the redemption of the world and the Christianization of mankind," but the "backward" Filipinos showed little enthusiasm for a "Christianization" that robbed them of independence. To acquire the Philippines as a colony, then, the United States had to suppress the revolution of its people.

Philippine nationalism was a relatively new phenomenon—hardly a quarter of a century old—but like American nationalism in 1776 was vibrant and dynamic. It began to manifest itself in 1872 when 200 native troops at the arsenal in Cavite killed their officers and demanded national independence. They intended to spread this revolt to Manila, but the plan went awry and the Spaniards were able to quell the uprising after executing and imprisoning some of its leaders. Two decades later, under the inspiration of a brilliant Chinese mestizo, José Rizal y Mercado, and young associates like Apolinario Mabini, a broad-based organization was formed called Katipunan—"Highest and Most Respectable Society of the Sons of the People"—not much different from the Sons of Liberty during the American Revolution. Its membership was estimated at between 100,000 and 400,000. In August 1896, with the same rhythm of history that was pulsing in Cuba, this movement broke out in a revolt for independence that sputtered along for more than a year until the nationalist leaders accepted 400,000 pesos (with 1.3 million more due them) to terminate the fight and go into exile. In the meantime Rizal had been seized in Barcelona, repatriated to Manila, and executed on December 30, 1896; and Andres Bonifacio, the artisan chief of Katipunan, had been assassinated. The mantle of leadership fell on Emilio Aguinaldo.

Aguinaldo, a remarkable little man, barely 115 pounds, was born near Cavite, Luzon, of Chinese and Tagalog parents, and was educated at the University of St. Thomas. At the time of the insurrection he was a modest landowner and mayor of Cavite. Twenty-seven years old, sharp-eyed, intelligent, he went into exile six or seven weeks before the *Maine* exploded, and was quick to realize that war between the United States and Spain might further Filipino purpose. The idea of a confluence of interests also occurred to some American officials. "At your first gun," cabled consul Oscar Williams in Manila, "there will be 30,000 Filipinos arise." U.S. Consul Spencer Pratt, who contacted Aguinaldo at Singapore, assured him— according to Secretary of State William R. Day—that "the ultimate object of our action is . . . independence of the Philippines," an assurance which caused considerable dismay in Washington. Commodore Dewey wrote his sister from Hong Kong that "the insurgents are ready to rise . . . and long before this reaches you we may be masters of Manila and Philippine cities." Insurrection was still afoot on the islands, despite the pact between the rebel leaders and Spain, so that the notion of parallel action between the *insurrectos* and the Americans must have seemed a natural course for taking the archipelago.

Nonetheless, there were deep suspicions on the Filipino side, even as a measure of collaboration was effected between Aguinaldo and Dewey. Apolinario Mabini, the precocious lawyer who represented the left wing of the revolution, urged his countrymen to give no aid either to the Spaniards or to the Americans, but to concentrate on capturing as much of the islands as possible so that the Americans —who were sure to be the victors—would "become convinced that here we have a strong and organized people that know how to defend their honor. . . ." The rebel committee in exile—in Hong Kong —sought weapons from Uncle Sam's forces, but sent a communiqué to their followers back home, warning "that they are trying to make colonies of us, although they said they would give us independence. The Committee decided to simulate belief at the same time equipping ourselves with arms."

Thus, against a background of distrust, began a tenuous, unofficial, and most temporary partnership. In mid-May, after Dewey had seized control of Manila Bay, General Aguinaldo and seventeen of his officers were taken aboard an American ship at Hong Kong and returned to the Philippines. Dewey himself greeted the Filipino leader at Cavite, gave him weapons and ammunition, and watched approvingly as the rebels—without American ground forces to help them—conquered town after town from the Spaniards. "In my opinion," Dewey reported to Washington, "these people are far superior in their intelligence and more capable of self-government than the natives of Cuba, and I am familiar with both races." The rebels had already cleaned up all of Cavite province and were converging on Manila within weeks after Aguinaldo had landed. In mid-June, the Filipino leader issued a declaration of independence and set up a provisional regime with himself as president—again without a single word from the Americans that he was trampling forbidden territory. In Boston, Moorfield Storey, the anti-imperialist, was thundering at Faneuil Hall: "Why should Cuba with its 1,600,000 people have a right to freedom and self-government and the 8,000,000 of people who dwell in the Philippines be denied the same right?" As yet no one of importance was saying they shouldn't, though the idea was forming in some minds.

A month later, as more Americans were put ashore, against Aguinaldo's wishes, General T. M. Anderson was explaining to the Filipino that "your fine intellect must perceive . . . that I cannot recognize your civil authority." By now Dewey had changed his estimate of Aguinaldo—he was a "big head," said Dewey—and was warning that the *insurrectos* would be General Merritt's "most difficult problem." Merritt himself was poignantly aware of this problem, for he had written to McKinley before shipping out with his troops that "it seems more than probable that we will have the so-called insurgents to fight as well as the Spaniards." He asked for more troops to conquer a people "the majority of whom will regard us with the intense hatred born of race and religion." From week to week the situation became more tense, with Aguinaldo taking the bit in his teeth, setting up a capital at Malolos, and seeking recognition from the world's powers, and Washington sending troop reinforcements to give itself leverage not only against the Spanish army on Philippine soil but against the insurgents as well.

By August, Aguinaldo's Revolutionary Government and 10,000 troops were well on the way toward victory. They controlled fifteen provinces in the key island of Luzon and were prepared to lay siege to Manila. At this point, however, General Merritt arrived with 8,500 American soldiers, and entered into a secret arrangement with the enemy whereby Manila was surrendered to the United States rather than let it fall into the hands of the insurgents. The plan called for a mock battle in which no one would get hurt and Spain could claim it had preserved its "honor." In fact the enraged Filipino forces entered the city from the east, prepared to jointly occupy it, but Merritt and Dewey forced them to withdraw. It was a humiliating moment for the Philippine revolution, as its major target was placed by the terms of the capitulation exclusively "under the special safeguard of the faith and honor of the American army." The *insurrectos* were frozen out.

What happened after this is, in a sense, classic—the scenario would be repeated by imperialist powers in French Indochina, the Dutch East Indies, and elsewhere after World War II. The Filipinos tried with might and main to be conciliatory; the Americans brought in more troops, and became bolder and tougher as each contingent arrived. The declaration of independence issued by Aguinaldo on June 12, 1898, contained the clause "under the protection of the Mighty and Humanitarian North American nation." To appease the moneylenders and landowners, who feared the revolutionaries more than the Americans, Aguinaldo dissolved the nationalist Katipunan. From January 9, 1899, to January 29, 1899, the Filipino government entered into negotiations with General Elwell S. Otis, the military governor, and were ready to accept "independence with limitations." All this while, however, Otis was merely waiting for six regiments of the U.S. army to arrive to supplement his forces against the Filipino army—center of revolutionary resistance. When they did come, in late January, the seventh negotiation session was forthwith called off. Otis was now ready—or so he thought—to carry out the McKinley mandate to move on from Manila to occupy all of the archipelago.

If there was a glimmer of hope that a Filipino-American war could be avoided, it was in that short period after the Treaty of Paris was signed (December 10, 1898) and prior to its ratification by the Senate (February 6, 1899). The outcome was by no means assured. The imperialists, sorely pressed, justified annexation on the grounds that the Filipinos had no capacity for self-government; to which a young congressman from Mississippi, John Sharp Williams, replied: "Who made us God's globe-trotting vice-regents to forestall misgovernment everywhere?" The charge was rebutted too by a number of observers who had had an opportunity to see Aguinaldo's regime in operation. One such man, quoted by Walter Millis, reported that Aguinaldo "had assembled at Malolos a Congress of one hundred men who would compare in behavior, manner, dress, and education with the better classes of other Asiatic nations, possibly including the Japanese." The rebel leader's army, he said, "was the marvel of his achievements. He had over twenty regiments of comparatively well-organized, well-drilled, and well-dressed soldiers carrying modern rifles and ammunition. . . . The people in all the different towns took pride in this army. Nearly every family had a father, son or cousin in it." That the army and the government both acted adroitly was confirmed by an incident on December 27, a couple of weeks after McKinley had ordered General Elwell S. Otis to extend his military authority over the whole archipelago. After the Spaniards had evacuated the city of Iloilo, Otis' troops were sent to occupy it, only to find that the natives had taken the town thirty-nine hours earlier. Otis informed his government on December 30 that the insurgents had seized "all military stations, outside Luzon, with the exception of Zaboanga," and had large numbers throughout Luzon as well.

As the debate in Congress rambled on—mostly in executive session—Senator Lodge realized he was in the "hardest fight I have ever known." To win the support of senators on the fence he shifted ground from a bellicose defense of imperialism per se to a plea that the legislators not humiliate their President by rejecting his treaty. "I want to get this country out of war," he said, "and back to peace. . . . I want to enter upon a policy which shall enable us to give peace and self-government to the natives of those islands. The rejection of the treaty makes all these things impossible."

The expansionists of 1898 might have been dealt a mortal blow at this point if it were not for the bumbling intervention of the 1896 Democratic and Populist standard-bearer, William Jennings Bryan. He was, of course, opposed to annexation on principle, but he arrived in Washington with a devious plan for using annexation as a steppingstone to the presidency in the elections of 1900. The silver plank alone, he was convinced, would not be enough to carry the Democrats through. But, he reasoned, if the treaty were ratified and independence withheld from the Philippines, the ensuing troubles on the islands would keep the issue of imperialism alive and propel the anti-imperialists into the White House. Once in power they would liberate the Philippines and all would be well with the world again. This wild and unprincipled strategy infuriated some of Bryan's supporters—a few suggested that he betake himself back to Omaha. Outside the Senate Andrew Carnegie, who was in the capital lobbying against the treaty, was so incensed that "I could not be cordial to him for years afterwards." One word from Bryan, he felt, "would have saved the country from disaster." Bryan, however, did not backtrack, and though his mission had been no sweeping success, it swayed enough votes to get the treaty approved. On February 6 it squeaked through the Senate by 57 to 27, just 2 votes over the necessary two thirds.

V

McKinley now had his cherished treaty; all he lacked was the Philippines. In the distant land across the international date line, the Americans were still hemmed in to Manila and the Aguinaldists showed no disposition to let them occupy the 7,100 islands without bloodshed. In Cuba, Spanish troops had been successfully replaced by Yankees, with only a few riots and skirmishes, presumably because the Cubans believed they would shortly win their independence. The Filipino nationalists shared no such illusions. On the previous December 21, even before he had submitted the treaty of acquisition to the Senate, McKinley had issued a proclamation, made known to the islanders, that "the future control, disposition, and government of the Philippine Islands" was to be in American hands, and that the military government "is to be extended with all possible dispatch to the whole ceded territory." He sweetened the bitter pill with an assurance that Filipinos would enjoy "individual rights and liberties which is the heritage of free peoples." Washington's policy, he said, was one of "benevolent assimilation." But Aguinaldo put little faith in such music; the reality of the situation was that the Americans were slowly advancing beyond the Manila perimeter, forcing a Filipino retreat.

Two days before the decisive vote in Congress, the issue was sealed. The Philippine-American war broke out, oddly enough, on the very day that the Englishman Rudyard Kipling published his famous poem urging the United States to take up the "White Man's burden":

> Take up the White Man's burden—
> Ye dare not stoop to less—
> Nor call too loud on Freedom
> To cloak your weariness.

At half-past eight on the evening of February 4, an American sentry —a young volunteer from Nebraska—challenged a patrol of four Filipinos in the Manila perimeter. When the first one did not halt he shot him. According to his later report, two others sprang out of the gateway: "Miller fired and dropped one. . . . We retreated to where our six other fellows were and I said, 'Line up, fellows, the niggers are in here and all through these yards.'" Thus began an American war to extinguish the Filipino revolution that was far more costly than the Spanish-American War itself. It lasted almost three and a half years, cost the United States $170 million in cash (plus a billion in soldiers' pensions), committed somewhere between 70,000 and 120,000 American troops in 2,800 actions, and resulted in the death of more than 4,000 Yankees—plus hundreds of thousands of Filipinos. Before it was over the United States was using the same methods as Spanish "Butcher" Weyler had in Cuba, and was perpetrating atrocities that sometimes made Weyler seem like an innocent.

In the initial fighting on February 4, 175 Americans and 500 Filipinos were killed or maimed. Next day, Aguinaldo sent an emissary to General Otis, under a flag of truce, to advise him that the shooting had been against his orders and asking for a cease-fire. Otis replied that the fighting had begun and must now go on "to the grim end." He followed his rhetoric with an attack on Filipino positions which resulted, according to a later congressional hearing, in 3,000 natives being killed or wounded in a single day. Six months later McKinley, in the style of James K. Polk, was still insisting that "the first blow was struck by the inhabitants, they assailed our sovereignty. . . ."

As a reinforced American army advanced, the Filipinos fell back to guerrilla warfare—much like the Minutemen in the American Revolution and the National Liberation Front in Vietnam after 1959. It was the kind of warfare that required popular support, and the Americans found to their dismay that Aguinaldo had that support totally. General Arthur MacArthur reported that when hostilities were initiated he was of the opinion that Aguinaldo represented only a fraction of the people, but "I have been reluctantly compelled to believe that the Filipino masses are loyal to Aguinaldo and the government which he leads." The success of guerrilla activity, he observed in a War Department report of 1900, "depends upon almost complete unity of action of the entire population. That such unity is a fact is too obvious to admit of discussion."

American generals soon learned, as General J. M. Bell put it in his Circular Order 22, that the only way "to combat such a population" was "to make the state of war as insupportable as possible," to keep the people in "such a state of anxiety and apprehension that living under such conditions would soon become unbearable. Little should be said. . . . Let acts, not words, convey the intentions." The kind of war he anticipated was one in which columns of 50 Americans would search "every ravine, valley and mountain peak for insurgents and for food, expecting to destroy everything I find. . . . All able-bodied men will be killed or captured."

Before many months were over it was obvious that American troops were killing wounded enemy soldiers as well as unarmed civilians. Among the first descriptions of what was going on was this report of a returned soldier about what had taken place in the battle near Manila of February 5, 1899: "In the path of the Washington regiment and Battery D of the Sixth Artillery there were 1,008 dead niggers and a great many wounded. We burned all their houses. I don't know how many men, women and children the Tennessee boys did kill. They would not take any prisoners." Official records themselves revealed the extent of the atrocities. Ordinarily there are two to five times as many wounded as killed, but in northern Luzon the records showed, for a given period, 1,013 Filipinos killed, and only 95 wounded; and for southern Luzon, from November 1, 1899, to September 1, 1900, 3,227 killed, 694 wounded. When someone asked MacArthur why there were so many fatalities he replied that his soldiers "are trained in what we call 'fire discipline,' that is, target practice."

On the island of Samar, General "Hell Roaring" Jake Smith issued oral orders: "I want no prisoners. I wish you to kill and burn; the more you kill and burn the better you will please me." Hell Roaring Jake is generally given the credit for having introduced to the Philippines the "reconcentration" system to isolate the populace from the revolutionaries. A prescribed zone was established where people were herded together under guard. All persons outside the zone were then automatically treated as enemies and shot on sight. The crops beyond the zone were left to decay, the homes left deserted. When the Spaniards had used this technique in Cuba, the amiable McKinley bellowed that it was "a new and inhuman phase happily unprecedented in the modern history of civilized Christian people. . . . It was extermination. The only peace it could beget was that of the wilderness and the grave." In the Philippines, under McKinley's tutelage, reconcentration became a widespread fact of life. How many people died in these concentration camps—and outside them —is unknown, but by General Bell's estimate (reported in the New York *Times* of May 3, 1901) one sixth the population of Luzon (about 600,000) was wiped out on that island alone. A Republican congressman called the process "pacification."

The Secretary of War reported on February 17, 1902, that the war "has been conducted by the American army with scrupulous regard for the rules of civilized warfare . . . ," but innumerable correspondents noted the widespread use of a "water cure" to elicit information from prisoners. A reporter for the New York *Evening Post* (April 8, 1902) gave some harrowing details. The native, he said, is thrown on the ground, his arms and legs pinned down, and head partially raised "so as to make pouring in the water an easier matter." If the prisoner tries to keep his mouth closed, his nose is pinched to cut off the air and force him to open his mouth, or a bamboo stick is put in the opening. In this way water is steadily poured in, one, two, three, four, five gallons, until the body becomes an "object frightful to contemplate." In this condition, of course, speech is impossible, so the water is squeezed out of the victim, sometimes naturally, and sometimes—as a young soldier with a smile told the correspondent—"we jump on them to get it out quick." One or two such treatments and the prisoner either talks or dies.

Another indelicate method used on Filipino prisoners was the rope treatment, whereby a man was hanged by the neck "for a period of about ten seconds, more or less." It was not enough to kill him but it inflicted wounds and caused "great bodily pain." Cruel as were these techniques, Americans who were "Christianizing" the natives rationalized them as necessary. The Reverend Homer Stuntz, a Protestant missionary, argued that the water cure "was given only to spies and such captured Filipinos as could give important information as to military movements," and since "the life of the spy is forfeit to his captors" in all countries and all times, there was nothing particularly evil about this practice. Colonel George S. Anderson explained that "many men were shot as they fled, but they probably all deserved it." The word "nigger," he said, was "very often used as applied to the natives, probably correctly."

Commenting on the horrors of Philippine suppression, Mark Twain suggested that the American flag should have "the white stripes painted black and the stars replaced by the skull and crossbones."

VI

All wars, it has been said, finally end at the diplomatic table. So it was that while American troops were brutalizing the Filipino countryside, an American commission was trying to appease the Filipino nationalists with promises of limited concessions. In January 1899, Admiral Dewey had wired McKinley urging that he send "a civilian commission" to the islands, made up of men "skilled in diplomacy and statesmanship." To placate the anti-imperialists the President selected as the chairman of such a commission Jacob Schurman, president of Cornell University, who originally opposed annexation of the Philippines. The other four members, however—General Otis,

Admiral Dewey, Dean C. Worcester, and Charles Denby—were outspoken advocates of imperialism. The commission's powers were limited; it was not to interfere in military policy and its proposals were purely "advisory." By the time the commission landed in the Philippines on March 4, 1899, its role was further restricted by the fact that the war had broken out and the only Filipinos available with whom to hold discussions were the rich moneylenders in Manila who opposed the insurgents.

Schurman, the civilian, and Otis, the military governor, were of different molds. The Cornell president described the general as a man who "repels strangers by the brusqueness of his manner" and concluded that he was definitely "not the man to conquer the Filipinos. . . ." Yet both began with the assumption that the Philippines were to remain an American colony. "Neither the American government nor the American people," read the first draft of a proclamation written by Schurman, "desire anything from the Philippine Islands for themselves." They were holding the archipelago, said the draft, only as a "trust," in the "sole interest of the Philippine people." The final version of this draft promised an "enlightened system of government" but made it clear that this enlightened system would have to be "compatible with those obligations which the United States has assumed." What this meant specifically, as outlined in a report issued by the Philippine Commission on January 31, 1900, was a "territorial government" in which the high offices would be held by Americans, and only the lesser ones by faithful Filipinos. "The United States," the report continued, "cannot withdraw from the Philippines. . . . The Filipinos are wholly unprepared for independence, and if independence were given to them they could not maintain it." This conclusion was not much different from that of General Otis, who considered that the Filipino people "are not fitted for self-government."

In May 1900, Otis was replaced by General Arthur MacArthur, an egotistical figure who, in the opinion of historian Foster Rhea Dulles, "was firmly convinced that the Filipinos needed bayonet treatment for at least a decade." By this time the war had escalated to the point where the general needed 75,000 troops to contain the enemy fighting in the tropical jungle, and would soon be using 126,000 in 639 military posts. Meanwhile a second, civilian, commission was dispatched, with William Howard Taft, an obese judge from Ohio, as its chairman. Taft, like Schurman, was anxious to moderate the excesses of military rule. He called the Filipino "little brown brother"—a reference which raised hackles on the chauvinistic skins of American soldiers at the front, who sang a popular song:

He may be a brother of Big Bill Taft;
But he ain't no brother of mine.

The future President was determined, however, to calm the storm, if only—as his November 1900 report stated—to "afford opportunity to [American] capital to make investment here." At present, the report said, "the only corporations here are of Spanish or English origin . . . and American capital finds itself completely obstructed." This obstruction would be removed if the Taft Commission could be given authority to "pass laws." That authority was not granted until 1902, but the bill to authorize transfer of power from the military to civilians was passed on March 2, 1901, and under it Taft became governor-general four months later with wide powers of administration.

How effective Taft's policies might have been if Aguinaldo had not been captured in March 1901 is a matter of speculation. The Filipino people were certainly tired, but it is worth noting that fighting continued formally until July 1902 and sporadically until October 1911, when the last guerrilla leader was seized and executed. Nonetheless the ruse by which Aguinaldo was taken prisoner was a dispiriting and decisive blow to the nationalists. A short, redheaded brigadier general named Frederick Funston executed a grand coup with the aid of a renegade insurgent and a band of mercenaries. Playing the role of "prisoners," Funston and four other Americans allowed themselves to be dragged along from village to village as presumed "prisoners," until five weeks and 100 miles later they were brought to Aguinaldo's hiding place at Palinan. Here on March 28 the mercenaries attacked the chief's bodyguard and overpowered him. The Filipino leader was brought to Manila and on April 19, convinced that further resistance was futile, took an oath of allegiance to the United States. The war continued for many months, especially among the ferocious Moros on the southern islands, but the insurgent cause was now doomed.

The Philippine Organic Act of 1902—passed under Teddy Roosevelt, after McKinley had been assassinated—promised independence (which was not granted, however, for a half century), and provided for a bicameral legislature and amnesty for insurgents. It limited landownership by corporations to 1,024 hectares and by individuals to 16 hectares, and placed some restrictions on investment. In the ensuing decades American rule was modified further to involve more Filipinos and extend the area of autonomy. That American business gained its objectives through imposition of colonial status on the Philippines, however, is evident from the fact that as of 1920 some 135 U.S. corporations owned $433 million in property on the archipelago.

VII

While the Filipinos were being cut to the American mold, the Cubans were in suspended animation waiting to be showered with the gift of independence promised by the Teller Amendment to the resolution authorizing McKinley to wage war against Spain. Some Americans had second thoughts about this promise, but the Philippine events persuaded them to tread warily. Nonetheless when "independence" was granted, it had stout strings attached to it.

In December 1899, McKinley stated that the new Cuba "must needs be bound to us by ties of singular intimacy. . . ." The man designated to develop this "singular intimacy" was a vigorous, thirty-nine-year-old army doctor who had graduated from Harvard, served in the Indian territory, and, later, acted as the personal physician to Mrs. McKinley. An admirer of Teddy Roosevelt and a dynamo of a man with autocratic tendencies, General Leonard Wood inherited a fiefdom in which the island had been partitioned into military districts, each ruled by an American officer and a contingent of American troops. Among Wood's achievements were the improvement of sanitation, education, health, and efforts to control yellow fever. Wood and Secretary of State Elihu Root—a brilliant lawyer who had initially opposed imperialism—had no intention, however, of withdrawing U.S. troops from Cuba until some mechanism could be forged for tying the island inescapably into the American orbit.

That mechanism proved to be a piece of legislation, formulated by Root, which became known as the Platt Amendment—after Senator Orville Platt of Connecticut. On November 5, 1900, Wood called together a number of Cubans to draw up a constitution and define relations with the United States. There was little difficulty with the first part; a document was written providing for a president, two legislative houses, and a supreme court, much like the North American model. The second part, however, posed serious problems since Wood demanded, as a condition of withdrawing U.S. troops, that the Platt Amendment be incorporated directly into the constitution.

The amendment stipulated that the new Cuba would not enter into treaty with any other foreign power that gave such power any control of the island; that it would not assume too large a burden of debt; and that it would lease to the United States naval and coaling stations (eventually Guantánamo). The Cubans objected to the latter two proposals on the ground that they were offensive to their sovereign rights, but their greatest fury was vented on Section III, which said, "That the government of Cuba consents that the United States may exercise the right to intervene for the preservation of Cuban independence, [and] the maintenance of a government adequate for the protection of life, property, and individual liberty. . . ." Cuban sovereignty, in other words, was to be so restricted as to be meaningless. Whenever the United States, on its own motion, without Cuban consent, concluded that something was awry, it was empowered by the Platt Amendment to intervene with military force, and to take over the administration of Cuba. This was a far cry from the resolution of April 1898 asserting that it was America's intention "to leave the government and control of that Island to its people." The Cubans protested to Root that the United States had obligated itself to make Cuba "independent of every other nation, the great and noble American nation included," but it was a vain plea. On June 12, 1901, the tired nationalists gave up the battle and incorporated the offensive amendment into their constitution. By 1902 most of the American forces had been withdrawn, but as the Paris *Temps* observed, "of the independence of Cuba nothing remains. . . ." The Cubans, it said, had simply "exchanged the yoke of Spain for the tutelage of the United States."

The first American intervention under the Platt Amendment occurred in 1906, when a revolt broke out over the fraudulent reelection of the presidential incumbent. At the urging of Frank Steinhart, the American consul general who had come to Cuba as a sergeant in the war and eventually became head of the $36 million utility company on the island, President Roosevelt sent in warships and troops to "clean up" the situation. Secretary of War William Howard Taft and Assistant Secretary of State Robert Bacon arrived in Havana to set up a provisional government under General Charles E. Magoon that lasted until 1909. According to Cubans, these years were "the most disastrous in the island's history." Magoon succeeded in turning a $13 million surplus in the national treasury into a $12 million deficit. But many an American feathered his nest in this period, including Consul General Steinhart, who was given the concession for extending the lines of the Havana Electric Railway, Light and Power Company, of which he was president. Steinhart also arranged for an American financial company which he represented to put through a $16.5 million loan to Cuba.

In due course elections were held and a new president installed, and the military occupation ended in 1909. Three years later, when race riots occurred on the island, the troops were back again. Secretary of State P. C. Knox's note to the American minister on this occasion was a classic in understatement. The minister was told to advise Havana that if it failed "to protect the lives or property of American citizens in Cuba the Government of the United States . . . will land forces to accord necessary protection." This, the note concluded, "is not intervention." The Cubans protested that they could handle matters on their own, and in fact the rebellion ended in quick order when its leader was killed.

The troops were back again—this time to seize Santiago from a Cuban faction that was contesting election results—in 1917. The "singular intimacy" of Cuban-American relations was so pronounced that an American minister, William E. Gonzales, took it upon himself to issue a proclamation warning the revolutionaries of severe reprisals against them by the United States (not Cuban) government unless they laid down their weapons. Subsequently 2,000 marines were dispatched to the island; Washington explained that they were being prepared for "service in Europe."

By this time the Cubans, of course, had gotten the message. When General Enoch H. Crowder, one of Magoon's assistants, arrived in 1919, the Cuban government was ready to accept his continuous "suggestions" as gospel. American companies received favored concessions; American banks made lucrative—and guaranteed—loans. When J. P. Morgan & Co. issued a $50 million loan in 1923 it was stated quite frankly that it was "with the acquiescence of the United States Government under the provisions of the Treaty dated May 22, 1903"—the treaty which ratified the Platt Amendment.

In 1898 American investments in Cuba were somewhere between $30 and $50 million, and by the mid-1920's somewhere between a billion and a billion and a quarter. As of 1923, more than four fifths of all of Cuba's exports went to the United States and three quarters of her imports came from there. Cuba was the sixth largest export partner of Uncle Sam, quite a role for an island with a few million people.

☆☆☆☆☆

11

☆☆☆☆☆

SUBDUING THE
BANANA REPUBLICS

Woodrow Wilson, who opposed extracontinental expansion prior to the Spanish-American War, later explained why it was necessary. "Since trade ignores national boundaries," he wrote in 1907, "and the manufacturer insists on having the world as a market, the flag of his nation must follow him, and the doors of the nations which are closed against him must be battered down. Concessions obtained by financiers must be safeguarded by ministers of state, even if the sovereignty of unwilling nations be outraged in the process. Colonies must be obtained or planted, in order that no useful corner of the world may be overlooked or left unused." The rationale for modern imperialism has seldom been stated better. Manufacturers and investors need world outlets; the flag—the United States government—must help secure and protect those outlets. If foreign nations close their doors, the doors must be "battered down," and if that means "outraging" the sovereignty of such nations, so be it.

With the victory against Spain and the subjugation of the Philippines, the United States was soon swept up in this pursuit. Having just experienced an unprecedented growth in manufacture and finance, it was ready to batter down as many doors as necessary to find outlets for its surplus goods and capital, as well as sources for raw materials to stoke its factories. Clearly, if commerce follows the flag, the more the potential of commerce the more places the flag should go.

Uncle Sam learned quickly, however, that this was no simple or automatic process. Other great powers had a long head start in outraging "the sovereignty of unwilling nations." By the time America joined in the international rivalry, the colonial standard had been planted through almost all of Africa and most of Asia. As of 1900, for instance, Britain was master of an empire of 11.5 million square miles (125 times its own size) and 305 million subjects, in addition to its "spheres of influence" in China and Latin America. From 1871 to 1900 France added 3.5 million square miles to her possessions, and Germany a million. The newly won American domain, by contrast, totaled—with Cuba included—less than 200,000 square miles. Even in its back yard, Latin America, the U.S. position was not a formidable one. For while the Monroe Doctrine had stopped the European powers from military occupation—"planting" colonies, as Wilson put it—it did not prevent them from economic penetration. As late as 1914, after much headway by Uncle Sam, British investments were still more than twice those of the Colossus of the North, $3.7 billion against $1.7 billion.

The United States, as Walter E. Weyl was to write years later, could not resist "the ubiquitous economic tendency toward expansion," but given the state of affairs in 1900–10 it could not do it in the same way as the Europeans. There were not too many colonies to be had in the old world, and to militarily occupy Argentina, Brazil, Chile, or Peru in the face of British or German economic hegemony was out of the question. The European states would not permit it, and to risk war with them was not a prospect to be taken lightly. Apart from the military inferiority of the United States vis-à-vis Britain, the destructiveness of warfare was escalating in a frightening fashion. In the 1904 fighting between Japan and Russia, battle lines were sometimes forty miles long; single engagements lasted as long as ten days or more; field guns shot four miles distant, and more ammunition was often expended in one day than in the whole Spanish-American War combined.

With few new colonies to conquer, the United States outraged the sovereignty of unwilling nations by means other than annexation. Even the team of Mahan, Roosevelt, and Lodge lost its zeal for occupying "any more islands," a circumstance which led some scholars to conclude that "explosive imperialism" had run its course. But Washington found that weaker nations could be made to serve the American purpose, without the necessity of occupying them— through commercial and financial agreements, through loans with stern conditions attached to them, through training of satellite armies, through the *threat* of military intervention, and, only when other means proved inadequate, by sending in the marines. The end result of this process was a "sphere of influence" which in many respects was a firmer foundation for empire—and cheaper to administer—than a colony.

II

In the two decades from the Spanish-American War to America's entry into World War I, the United States consolidated a sphere of influence near home—in Mexico and the Caribbean—and began a modest penetration outward that would eventually make it a world empire. The policy remained constant under four presidents.

Each of these presidents had his own style, but each pursued the same general goals of expansion. McKinley, an exceptionally handsome man, with high forehead, gray eyes, and Roman nose, who dressed for public occasions in a Prince Albert, seemed to be carried with the tide. Teddy Roosevelt, the Rough Rider, defined his approach in vigorous terms: "I have always been fond," he said, "of the West African proverb: 'Speak softly and carry a big stick; you will go far.'" William Howard Taft, amiable and direct, called for "dollar diplomacy"—substituting "dollars for bullets." It "is an effort," he pointed out, "frankly directed to the increase of American trade upon the axiomatic principle that the Government of the United States shall extend all proper support to every legitimate and beneficial American enterprise abroad." Woodrow Wilson, professorial and complex, sheathed imperial purpose in the verbiage of virtue: "morality and expediency is the thing that must guide us." But there was little to choose between the intervention of McKinley in the Philippines, Roosevelt in Colombia, Taft in Nicaragua, and Wilson in Mexico. Carl Schurz correctly predicted that the government would seek "new conquests to protect that which we already possess"—and it didn't matter much which president was in the saddle.

Early in September 1901, McKinley arrived in Buffalo with his wife and two nieces to attend the Pan-American Exposition. While greeting the public a few days later, he was shot by a boyish-looking man who carried a hidden pistol in a sling around his arm, a self-proclaimed anarchist named Leon Czolgosz. Despite a wound in the abdomen, McKinley seemed to be on his way to recovery—at least that is what the world was told—when on September 14 he took a turn for the worse and died. He was succeeded by the youngest man ever to be president, Teddy Roosevelt.

The hero of San Juan Hill was a complicated man who was sometimes all things to all men. Scion of a New York family which had been prominent in Empire State affairs for six generations, he had been an unvarnished conservative from the time he had taken his place as a state representative at the age of twenty-three. As president, however, he gained the reputation of being a progressive—even a friend of labor when he settled the anthracite miners' strike of 1902. He was the kind of man who could invite a Booker T. Washington to dinner at the White House, then explain privately to friends who questioned such familiarity with the Negro president of Tuskegee that he had done it on impulse. If he spoke repeatedly of righteousness and justice, his contempt for Latin Americans was evident in statements such as the one that he would show "those Dagoes that they will have to behave decently." He might tell the American Peace Society in 1904 that he agreed generally with their objectives "to bring nearer the day when the peace of justice shall obtain throughout the world," but he was always the proponent of the "big stick," and his greatest boast on leaving office was that he had increased the number of battleships in the American navy from nine to twenty-five. His ambivalent rhetoric was so striking that Finley Peter Dunne's Mr. Dooley denied to his friend Mr. Hennessy "th' infamous rayport that th' Prizidint was iver at San Joon Hill. At th' time iv this gloryous an' lamintable performance, th' good man was down with measles conthracted at th' Internaytional Peace Convintion." Mark Hanna called Roosevelt a "madman" in 1900 and detractors of his presidency referred to him as "His Accidency," but he was neither mad nor accidental. He was the spokesman of a nation which had decisively fallen under the sway of the corporate trust and the financial goliath, and for whom commercial and strategic expansion at the expense of weaker powers was to become the way of life.

Roosevelt's first international project was the isthmian canal that would connect the Atlantic with the Pacific and cut the sea distance between the two U.S. coasts by two thirds. It was an idea that had been attracting men for hundreds of years. In the nineteenth century, Colombia and Nicaragua had granted concession after concession for the project, and one company after another had been formed to build it, but without exception had been unable to carry it through. The most noteworthy of these efforts had been undertaken at the initiative of Ferdinand de Lesseps and a multinational group of 135—mostly French but some Americans, Germans, and Britains—who met in Paris in May 1879. Their Panama Canal Company had actually started construction of a sea-level canal at Panama, but the work had to be halted in 1887 when it became obvious that a sea-level waterway could not be built in the allotted time and at a cost the de Lesseps group could afford. A hastily reorganized effort to build a canal with locks foundered when the firm went bankrupt. Meanwhile parallel efforts were going ahead in Nicaragua, where the canal would be longer—156 miles—though the inclusion of Lake Nicaragua in the canal would cut construction by more than a third. An 1884 treaty with the Central American republic calling for the United States to undertake the project at no cost to Nicaragua, the waterway to be jointly owned by the two nations, failed to win ratification in the Senate. Subsequent attempts by private citizens and a company incorporated by Congress also failed to get the plan under way.

The sudden emergence of the United States as both a Caribbean and a Pacific power, however, gave the whole business a new sense of urgency—at least for Americans. In his message to Congress on December 1898, McKinley stated that the annexation of Hawaii and the expected further expansion into the Far East made it "indispensable" to build the "maritime highway" with all due dispatch. There were just two impediments in the way: one was choice of a location —whether to use a route through Nicaragua or through the Colombian province of Panama—the other was an old understanding with Britain, the Clayton-Bulwer Treaty of 1850. Under this pact, the parties agreed that neither would exclusively own or control such a waterway when it was built, or try to fortify it. It was to be "neutral," a truly international waterway. The treaty was one of the least popular the United States ever concluded, since one of its provisions prohibited colonization of Central America. It passed because the project did not loom so large in midcentury as after the Spanish-American War. With victory assured sentiment took a *volte face*, and many Americans insisted that not only should the canal be owned and operated by this country; it should be fortified and under full American domination. If in the process Washington were forced to dishonor its signed word, then, as some Senators put it, "dishonor be damned."

Fortunately, when Secretary Hay approached the British to revise the treaty, he found a receptive mood. Britain was then preoccupied with the Boer War in South Africa, and was feeling the ill will of rivals on the European continent. An initial agreement arrived at with Lord Pauncefote in February 1900—satisfactory to Hay— granted the United States the exclusive right to own, build, and neutralize the "maritime highway," but balked at giving Washington the right to fortify it. Roosevelt pointed out to his friend Hay that failure to win this right "strengthens against us every nation whose fleet is larger than ours," and Senator Lodge wrote defiantly, "The American people mean to have the canal and they mean to control it." As a result of such pressures the Senate tacked on three amendments to the treaty which in effect torpedoed it, or at least so the

British felt. A year later, with the British still involved in the Boer War and relations with Germany deteriorating, London retreated from its adamant stand. It accepted the American terms, including the right of fortification, and signed a treaty which breezed through the Senate by 72 to 6.

With the Clayton-Bulwer obstacle hurdled and Teddy Roosevelt at the tiller in Washington, all that remained was to choose between the Nicaraguan and Colombian (Panamanian) routes—and start building. Each route had its advocates, with Nicaragua seemingly on the inside track because a canal there could be built at sea level, obviating the necessity of locks. The leading figure promoting this pathway was a senator from Alabama, John T. Morgan, who felt that the site would be closer to Southern ports. His adversaries, favoring Panama, were two topnotch salesmen, a wily Frenchman with a full mustache who had been chief engineer for the New Panama Canal Company, Philippe Bunau-Varilla, and a Wall Street lawyer, William N. Cromwell, of the firm of Sullivan and Cromwell, who was the company's attorney. Cromwell's chief asset was the friendship of Mark Hanna and other Republican chieftains, no small advantage as matters turned out. All other things being equal, the Panama route was superior: part of it had already been dug, passage through it would be only 12 hours as against 33 for the Nicaraguan waterway, and construction and maintenance costs considerably smaller. But to counterbalance these advantages the French company wanted $109 million for its concession and there were tricky problems in negotiating arrangements with Colombia, a nation that had been wracked by civil war for the previous three years. The impediments seemed so strong that in January 1902 the House of Representatives voted for Nicaragua, with only two congressmen dissenting.

Congress did not reckon, however, on the resourcefulness of Bunau-Varilla and Cromwell—ably assisted by Senator Hanna. To make the project palatable, the two men reduced their selling price from $109 million to $40 million. Next they began a campaign to discredit the Nicaraguan venture, alleging that the little country was prone to volcanoes and earthquakes that might make the canal unsafe. As luck would have it Nicaragua had issued a postage stamp showing a smoking volcano in the lake through which the canal would pass, and Bunau-Varilla, quick to use an advantage, saw to it that the stamp was placed on the desk of every American senator. Nature itself was even more obliging, for in the midst of the deliberations Mount Momotombo in Nicaragua erupted and an earthquake

destroyed a number of wharves nearby. Duly alarmed by now, the
Senate, on June 19, 1902, approved the Panamanian route by 42 to
34. The House reversed itself a few days later, and Secretary Hay
began negotiations with the Colombian ambassador to Washington,
Tomás Herran.

What ensued was a mixture of confusion, highhandedness, and
brigandage. Under the Hay-Herran Treaty the United States agreed
to pay Colombia $10 million outright plus $250,000 a year rental,
beginning nine years later, in return for a lease on the canal site and
an isthmian zone six miles wide. The treaty included a clause by
which Colombia was precluded from negotiating with the private
canal company to get any part of its $40 million—a strange gesture
of solicitousness by American officials for the private fortunes of
Bunau-Varilla and Cromwell. When these terms were transmitted to
Bogotá—where peace had finally broken out—they were greeted by
a blast of acrimony in the Colombian Senate, followed by a vote of
24 to 0 *against* the treaty.

Presumably matters should have ended there. Colombia, after all,
was a sovereign nation, with the right to dispose of its territory as it
saw fit. But Secretary Hay had no patience for such niceties; he
warned the Latin Americans that if they did not accept the original
treaty, North America would take action "which every friend of Colombia would regret." An infuriated Roosevelt castigated the "con-
temptible little creatures in Bogotá" who were holding up progress.
Outlook magazine, edited by a close friend of the President's, suggested that Panama "might secede" and the Indianapolis *Sentinel,*
echoing the views of many newspapers, suggested: "The simplest
plan of coercing Colombia would be inciting a revolution in Panama . . . and supporting the insurrectionary government." Senator
Lodge, in Paris, expressed "strong hopes" that "by the secession of
the Province of Panama we can get control of what undoubtedly is
the best route." Indeed Roosevelt was so determined to divorce Panama from Colombia that in the first draft of his message to Congress
that year, 1903, he included a passage recommending seizure of the
isthmus "without any further parley with Colombia." Though it was
struck from the final draft, it represented, as he later admitted, his
true views, unembroidered with the typical vagueness of presidential messages.

As it happened, the Rough Rider did not have to take this
precipitous action, for on November 3, 1903, the province of Panama
declared its independence. The plot had been hatched in the offices
of the Panama Railroad, a subsidiary of the New Panama Canal

Company, back in May, and the plotters had received the encouragement of Cromwell and a $100,000 check from Bunau-Varilla. Of even greater importance, the French engineer, in talks with Roosevelt and Hay, had sounded them out as to whether they would prevent Colombia from suppressing a revolution in Panama. And while Roosevelt later denied that any American official "had any part in preparing, inciting, or encouraging the revolution," it is known that Hay wrote the President two months before, urging intervention if an insurrection should break out, and that the day before it took place, orders had been sent the American navy to proceed to both sides of the isthmus.

American ships arrived too late to intercept 400 Colombian soldiers who disembarked at Colón on November 3—they were bought off instead by bribes to their officers, judiciously supplied from Bunau-Varilla's $100,000 fund—but thereafter the U.S. navy effectively stopped Colombia from dealing with its rebels. As a legal figleaf for such brazen interference, the State Department quixotically alluded to an 1846 treaty signed with New Granada (Colombia) that guaranteed the United States the "right of way or transit across the Isthmus of Panama." It stretched matters beyond credibility to claim that a right of transit gave Roosevelt legal sanction to prevent Colombia from using its forces to suppress an internal revolt. But the U.S.S. *Nashville* and other American ships effectively convinced the troops at Colón to reembark for home, and stopped another ship with more Colombian soldiers from landing at Panama. On November 4 the timid revolutionaries, consisting of some 500 mercenaries bought by Bunau-Varilla's money, plus 441 members of the fire department, declared their province an independent republic. Within an hour after receiving this heartwarming news, Roosevelt ordered that the state of Panama be officially recognized. At the twelfth hour, the government at Bogotá offered to accept the American treaty in toto if only the American President would permit it to send troops against the Panamanian rebels. The offer, however, was understandably rejected. Instead, on November 13 Roosevelt formally received the minister of Panama, who turned out to be, by odd happenstance, a Frenchman named Philippe Bunau-Varilla, and within a few days the minister negotiated a treaty with Secretary Hay even more generous than the one rejected by Colombia. The money provisions were identical but the Canal Zone conveyed to the United States was ten miles wide instead of six, and deeded in perpetuity.

As in the case of the treaty with Hawaii in 1893 there was much opposition in the press to the "cooked-up republic" whose independence the United States pledged to guarantee and maintain. The New York *Times* criticized "the heady wine of territorial adventure that now fires the blood of the Administration" and plunges the nation "in the path of scandal, disgrace, and dishonor." Others spoke of "piracy" and called the incident one of the "most discreditable in our history." The *Nation* editorialized that "even the buccaneers who sailed the Spanish Main would have found it too much for them." But a considerable majority of the press and the public endorsed the coup. As *Public Opinion* magazine put it: "No one can deny that the majority opinion of the country approves the course of the administration, little as this course can be justified on moral grounds." The Detroit *News,* with the utmost candor, said: "Let us not be mealy-mouthed about this. We want Panama." That was all there was to it. Roosevelt himself advised all and sundry that his every act had been "carried out in accordance with the highest, finest, and nicest standards of public and governmental ethics." The recognition of Panama, he told Congress, "was an act justified by the interests of collective civilization. If ever a Government could be said to have received a mandate from civilization . . . the United States holds that position with regard to the interoceanic canal." The "cowboy diplomat" never explained why he did not accept Colombia's belated offer, or why he did not come to terms with Nicaragua, which granted more acceptable terms. Foster Rhea Dulles tells the story, perhaps apocryphal, of a cabinet meeting in which Roosevelt asks the cabinet members whether he had defended himself well. "You certainly have, Mr. President," replied Elihu Root. "You have shown that you were accused of seduction and you have conclusively proved that you were guilty of rape."

Work began on the canal almost immediately, and it was completed in 1914 at a cost of $400 million. That same year Secretary of State William Jennings Bryan negotiated a treaty with Colombia expressing regret for all that had happened and offering to assuage its damaged feelings with a payment of $25 million. Roosevelt's friends in the Senate were so outraged they blocked the treaty, but seven years later—two years after the Rough Rider died—the Senate did approve such a treaty but with no apology, and no interest. By now, however, it was only a pittance of money that was involved: the United States had its exclusively owned canal, its exclusively controlled Canal Zone, and its protectorate over another little country, Panama. As the pragmatic Teddy observed in a 1911 speech, "I took the canal zone and let the Congress debate, and while the debate goes on, the Canal does also."

III

The terms "colony" and "protectorate" have never been part of the official American lexicon, for the understandable reason that they clash with the tradition of a nation born in a fight against colonialism. But while the words have been eschewed, the United States did in fact begin its new phase of empire building from 1901 to 1917 by transforming small countries in the Caribbean and Central America into protectorates—their sovereignty effectively curtailed in the interests of the "mother country." The Platt Amendment, giving Washington the unilateral right to occupy Cuba at will, and the leases granted the United States in perpetuity in Panama, as well as guarantees of "maintaining the independence" of that republic, reduced both to protectorate status without using the word. In due course, by treaty, by threat of intervention, and by actual intervention, the United States made of the whole area an American lake, no more independent—as one historian put it—than Long Island or the state of New York.

What began as episodic intervention to expand America's strategic and commercial position was refined by Roosevelt—and his successors—into broad principle. Under the Monroe Doctrine the United States proclaimed that European powers could not occupy any additional territory in the western hemisphere. During a dispute between Germany and Britain against Venezuela in 1901, Roosevelt (then still vice-president) magnanimously conceded to the foreign powers the right to punish small nations that played fast and loose with their investments. "If any South American country misbehaves against any European country," he wrote, "let the European country spank it." "Spanking" in this instance took the form in 1902–03 of a blockade by Germany, Britain, and later Italy; the seizure and sinking of some Venezuelan gunboats; and the naval shelling of Fort San Carlos. But before anyone decided to land occupation troops, Roosevelt—now President—put an end to the dispute by forcing all parties to accept arbitration. Spanking was one thing, landing troops another—and even on the subject of spanking the imperious Roosevelt evidently had second thoughts.

In the course of resolving a crisis in Santo Domingo—the Dominican Republic—shortly thereafter the President decided to modify the Monroe Doctrine by tacking onto it what became known as the Roosevelt Corollary. The Monroe Doctrine had been fashioned against the ambitions of Europe; the corollary refashioned it against the sovereignty of Latin America. In essence it reaffirmed that the United States would not tolerate direct European intervention in Latin America, but added the new feature that since intervention was sometimes necessary, this right was reserved exclusively to the United States of America. As historian Julius W. Pratt defines it: "Uncle Sam now assumed the role of international policeman— kindly to the law-abiding, but apt to lay a stern hand upon little nations that fell into disorder or defaulted on their obligations, since disorder and default . . . might invite intervention from outside the hemisphere."

The events that led to the proclamation of the corollary are as instructive as the corollary itself. The government of Santo Domingo had undergone the usual political tempests since it had secured independence from Haiti in 1844, and by 1902–03 found itself saddled with a debt of $32 million and a bankrupt treasury. The money was owed to capitalists of half a dozen nations, the largest single amount to an American corporation with offices in New York, the San Domingo Improvement Company. In response to intelligence from the company that its holdings were in jeopardy, the State Department arranged for the Dominican regime to purchase its obligations for $4.5 million and a board of arbitrators was chosen to decide how the payments were to be made.

Meanwhile rival factions in the small republic began fighting, and the United States landed some marines in Santo Domingo, Puerto Plata, and Sosua from January 2 to February 11, 1904, ostensibly "to protect American life and property" but actually to put pressure on the faltering regime to place its customhouses in North American hands. In July the arbitrators, as expected, authorized the United States, in case of default by Santo Domingo of its debt to the San Domingo Improvement Company, to install itself as financial agent over the customhouses at Puerto Plata, and if necessary three others. Two months later the inevitable happened and the United States, by odd quirk, chose as collector in Puerto Plata a representative of the very Improvement Company for whom the monies were to be sequestered. Since the move threatened to drain away sums from southern ports, whose customs were pledged to French, Belgian, and Italian bondholders, France and Italy ordered vessels to the island with the same objective in mind as the United States—to do their own collecting. It was in the wake of these events that Teddy Roosevelt, in his annual message to Congress delivered on December 6, 1904, restated the corollary already stated in May, but in more unambiguous language:

"Any country whose people conduct themselves well can count upon our hearty friendship. If a nation shows that it knows how to act with reasonable efficiency and decency in social and political matters, if it keeps order and pays its obligations, it need fear no interference from the United States. Chronic wrongdoing, or an impotence which results in a general loosening of the ties of civilized society, may in America, as elsewhere, ultimately require intervention by some civilized nation, and in the Western Hemisphere, the adherence of the United States to the Monroe Doctrine may force the United States, however reluctantly, in flagrant cases of such wrongdoing or impotence, to the exercise of an international police power."

The idea that the United States had the right to exercise police power against "uncivilized" or "impotent" people had of course been expressed throughout the nineteenth century with respect to Indians, Spaniards, Mexicans. But that right was now being claimed on a broader front. And though the corollary was partly repudiated in 1930, it remained the rationale for dozens of interventions in the western hemisphere and throughout the world.

Early in 1905, then, after a show of military force, the American minister to Santo Domingo, Thomas C. Dawson, was able to "persuade" the Dominican authorities to "invite" the United States to collect customs at all its ports. Forty-five percent of the payments would be turned over to the Dominican government, and the other 55 percent used to service debts to both the San Domingo Improvement Company and the Europeans. The American navy, of course, would stand by and see that everything ran smoothly.

When Dawson's arrangement was transmitted to Washington the outcry was so shrill that the State Department instructed its minister to put the agreement into a formal treaty so it might be debated at home. That treaty was submitted to the Senate in mid-February with a strong statement by Roosevelt that "it is incompatible with international equity for the United States to refuse to allow other powers to take the only means at their disposal of satisfying the claims of their creditors and yet to refuse, itself, to take any such steps." In other words, if Uncle Sam wanted to prevent Europeans from intervening it had to do the intervening itself. The Senate, as it had so often in the past, refused to ratify the treaty, whereupon Roosevelt simply put it into effect by "executive agreement"—or what is called *modus vivendi.*

Simultaneously, with American warships patrolling the area, Roosevelt sent a revealing letter to his Secretary of the Navy: "As to the Santo Domingo matter, tell Admiral Bradford to stop any revolution." To collect a debt for an American company it was necessary to take over the customhouses—lest others take them; to take over the customhouses it was necessary to "stop any revolution." There was an inexorable logic to this process, which would be repeated over and over again in the ensuing decades. Moreover, intervention also brought with it further economic penetration. On Wall Street the firm of Kuhn, Loeb & Company floated a $20 million bond issue to satisfy Dominican creditors, and to undertake long-delayed public works. That loan too was guaranteed by the customs collectors and the American warships.

Both at home and in Latin America there were great misgivings about the expansion of "Monroeism." Not only the anti-imperialist sheets but such fervid Republican papers as the Boston *Transcript* pointed out that the new policy places "us in the unenviable attitude of coercing our Southern neighbors at the behest of Europe. . . . It would be a strange, untoward outcome of eighty years of Monroeism if a secret combination of Latin American countries should be formed in opposition to 'the overlordship of the United States.'" But after the *modus vivendi* had been in effect for more than two years, the Senate in 1907 finally approved a new treaty which was very much like the one rejected, except that it omitted the brash preamble under which the United States could interfere in domestic matters of the Dominican Republic other than the collection of customs. In practice it did not make much difference. In 1911, for instance, the President of Santo Domingo was shot and a provisional government formed to take over the reins. President Taft sent two commissioners to look into the situation, along with a gunboat and 750 marines. At their "suggestion" the provisional president decided to resign. The United States had become an international policeman and would retain that stance wherever and whenever it was disposed to act in that role and strong enough to fill it.

IV

Teddy Roosevelt was an aggressive figure, the master of fire-and-brimstone phrases. In 1904, when a man of doubtful American citizenship named Perdicaris (he may have been a Greek subject) was seized by a Moroccan chieftain named Raisuli, Roosevelt had Secretary Hay send a cable to the U.S. consul general at Tangier demanding "Perdicaris alive or Raisuli dead." He talked of using a "big stick" in international relations, but in truth the cowboy diplomat was a less fierce imperialist than many of his successors. He could have annexed Santo Domingo, as Grant had unsuccessfully tried in 1869 when the Senate rejected a treaty to do so, but the ex-Rough Rider said that "if it is absolutely necessary to do something, then I want to do as little as possible." He wanted to leave the impression that while he himself would have preferred more pleasant alternatives, events had forced him into supporting Panamanian secession and Dominican intervention. Moreover, domestic affairs loomed larger in his purview than foreign issues during his two terms in office, and he worked assiduously, despite a long conservative background, to earn the reputation of being a "progressive."

William Howard Taft, Teddy's corpulent successor and one of the truly reluctant nominees for the presidency, was less blatant and less colorful, but he placed a higher priority on international relations and he propelled the imperialist credo a major step forward. Where Roosevelt was ready to use the navy to defend private American investments *already made,* such as those of the San Domingo Improvement Company, Taft and the corporation lawyer he chose as Secretary of State, Philander C. Knox, actively *sought* outlets for American banking and industrial firms in foreign lands. They came to office at a time when exports were booming and the Panama Canal was nearing completion, and they deemed it the duty of government to grease the way for American dollars and American commerce to penetrate new markets. Their dollar diplomacy was tailored not merely to protect but to encourage foreign investments and foreign trade. That they succeeded mightily is attested to by statistics. As of 1900, private citizens of the United States owned less than half a billion in foreign securities: $150 million in Canada, $185 million in Mexico, $50 million in Cuba, $55 million in other Latin American states, and only $15 million in Europe and the Far East. By 1909, however, the figure had reached $2 billion and by 1913, $2.5 billion, with half of it in Latin America and about a quarter in Canada. Thus investments south of the Rio Grande more than quadrupled in just thirteen years. Jim Blaine's Pan-American dream came true two decades after his death—but not without further and more severe outraging of the sovereignty of Latin America.

"Big Bill" Taft, the architect of dollar diplomacy, was one of the most pleasant and good-natured men to hold the exalted office of president. He was five feet ten and a half inches tall, weighed somewhere between 300 and 350 pounds, and was lethargic and easygoing to a fault. Left to his own devices he would have passed over the presidency, as well as his assignments in the Philippines and Cuba. What he wanted most was to be a justice of the Supreme Court, a position that eluded him until he was appointed by Harding eight years after leaving the White House. But Taft came from a heavy political background, and like a good soldier permitted himself to be driven by an exceptionally capable and ambitious wife, a wealthy brother, and the insistent Roosevelt, into the presidency. For all that, he was a man of some ability, lazy perhaps, but also highly intelligent and deliberate. At Yale he had been second in the graduating class, and at the law school in his home town, Cincinnati, he had shared first prize for scholarly attainments with another young man.

Everybody liked Big Bill Taft, probably because he did not seem to be competing with them, or rubbing them the wrong way. If he was a maverick, it was only in religion, where he was a member of the Unitarian Church and an actor in its amateur theatricals. For the rest he trod a well-worn path. His father, Alphonso Taft, was an established political figure in Cincinnati, not only in local politics but as the Secretary of War in Grant's cabinet and as U.S. minister to Austria and Russia. Even while at law school Young Will worked a ward, "hustling around among good people" to help his father in an unsuccessful effort to win the Republican gubernatorial nomination. On graduation in 1880 he passed the bar but took a job as law reporter for a local newspaper, then moved on easily and naturally to the profession of politician. With his connections it was relatively simple to get appointments as assistant prosecutor, collector of internal revenue, superior court judge, then with the aid of a reactionary and not too savory political figure, Joseph Foraker, Solicitor General of the United States. Two years later, with backing from the same wing of the party, he tried for a Supreme Court appointment but was consoled by President Harrison with a spot in the federal circuit court. In 1900, when McKinley called him to Washington, he nurtured hopes that he would be offered the first vacancy on the Supreme Court. Instead McKinley asked him to head the Philippine Commission, a job that he took on despite misgivings about the whole policy of occupying the islands, and only when the President assured him he would always have a judicial job. Whereas Roosevelt took his first big step to the White House by riding a horse to battle, Taft took it as governor general in Manila trying to moderate some of the military's harshness.

After McKinley's death and the tapering off of the guerrilla war in the Philippines, Taft could have had his Supreme Court appointment, but he was now consumed with the problems of the islands. There was unemployment, as well as terrible epidemics, food shortages, and deep-rooted corruption. He felt he had to stay on for at least a period to mitigate these difficulties, and in so doing detoured his career from the judiciary to the presidency. In 1904, finally, he accepted an offer to come home, as Secretary of War, a post which was more nominal than real since he took on one special assignment after another for Roosevelt. In 1906, on the last of these missions, he went to Cuba to seek a solution for the disorders that broke out after the election of Tomás Estrada Palma. Under the Platt Amendment, Roosevelt was convinced he had to "maintain order," but he was painfully aware that the American people were in no frame of mind for further interventions; he asked Taft to resolve the issue "in as gentle a way as possible." It was Taft, however, who insisted that there was no other solution but immediate occupation, and though he considered the day he made this recommendation "the most unpleasant of my life," temporarily accepted the job as provisional governor of Cuba. He expected to suffer "a great fall" as a result of his role but came off surprisingly well in the public mind back home. For the next two years, then, Taft was in fact if not in name a candidate for president and Roosevelt was in effect his campaign manager. Though a poor speaker and lacking the charisma of his predecessor, he easily defeated the peripatetic William Jennings Bryan, who was making his third and last appearance in a presidential election.

Having won the plaudits of the great corporations by promising "to interfere with legitimate business as little as possible," the corpulent new President espoused an active diplomacy to help financiers and industrialists make their mark in other countries. The United States, Taft insisted, rejected the "outworn dogmas of the past" that diplomacy was "a mere assertion of the right to international existence"; it was to be used now as an active force for commercial expansion. "The diplomacy of the present administration," he would say on December 3, 1912, "has sought to respond to modern ideas of commercial intercourse. This policy has been characterized as substituting dollars for bullets. It is one that appeals alike to idealistic humanitarian sentiments, to the dictates of sound policy and strategy, and to legitimate commercial aims." As historian Thomas A. Bailey summarizes it, "the dollar" became "a diplomat." Typically, when the State Department learned that a consortium of British, French, and German bankers were preparing to build the Hukuang railway in central and southern China, it formed American bankers into a committee, headed by J. P. Morgan, and succeeded in elbowing them into the project. "I have an intense personal interest," Taft wrote the Chinese Prince Regent, "in making the use of American capital in the development of China an instrument for the promotion of the welfare of China. . . ."

Henceforth the diplomatic saga of the United States was to be replete with State Department efforts to promote J. P. Morgan, Kuhn, Loeb & Company, Edward H. Harriman, the First National Bank, the National City Bank, and other financiers in their quest for foreign investments. It was not entirely a new phenomenon. The American Asiatic Association, a group of textile firms with a stake in the cotton-goods market of the Orient, and the American China Development Company, which owned a concession for building a small part of the Peking-to-Canton railroad, had prodded the government to proclaim the Open Door policy in 1899 and expected to profit handsomely from it. But Taft regularized the procedures for aiding American business abroad, and established this objective as clear-cut official policy. Diplomats did the bidding of the corporations, and ex-diplomats, such as Willard Straight, consul general at Mukden from 1906–08, became their agents on retirement. With State Department sponsorship, the trend to insinuate American dollars wherever possible expanded not only in the back yard of Latin America, but in such places as Turkey, where in 1909 Rear Admiral Colby M. Chester secured a preliminary agreement from the government for American capital to operate certain mines and build a port and railways. Subsequently, especially after oil fields became a prime objective of American companies, the State Department's role as an advance agent for big business abroad enlarged immeasurably.

Properly speaking, it was not the dollar that was the diplomat, but diplomacy that pried doors open for the penetration of dollars. And since modern diplomacy is ultimately backed by military might, it was not surprising that the policy which Taft said appealed "to idealist humanitarian sentiments" graduated to military intervention. The first to enjoy this treatment under Taft was Nicaragua, the little republic whose bid for a canal route had been bypassed. From 1893 to 1909 it was ruled by José Santos Zelaya, a dictator no better and no worse than the traditional dictators of Latin America—except that he seems to have manifested little friendship for the United States. He refused its requests for a base at Fonseca Bay and a concession for a second canal route. He turned down proposals for new business opportunities for American firms, threatening to cancel some of the old ones. Zelaya remained a thorn in Washington's side, so much so that in his annual message to Congress, in December 1909, Taft complained that Zelaya "has kept Central America in constant tension and turmoil."

This was the setting for a so-called revolution which broke out against the Nicaraguan chieftain in 1909. It was financed, though this was not known at the time, by Adolfo Díaz, the secretary of an

American firm at Bluefields, Nicaragua, La Luz y Los Angeles Mining Company. Though he earned only $1,000 a year and seemed to have no other wealth to draw on, Díaz somehow scraped together $600,000 for the rebels. He also prevailed on the United Fruit Company and others to use their steamers for transporting troops and supplies to the revolutionaries, all with the assent of the State Department. Washington gave its support to the "rebels" through thick and thin. It broke relations with Zelaya, refused to recognize his successor, Dr. José Madriz—chosen legally by the Nicaraguan Congress—and paid its customs duties to the rump regime established by Díaz and General Juan J. Estrada at Bluefields. Then, when the official government defeated the insurgents, American marines were landed to protect them and permit them to reorganize. Spurred by such aid, the "rebels" finally defeated Madriz and Estrada entered the capital, Managua, at the end of August 1910.

In October 1910 the State Department sent Thomas G. Dawson— the man who had negotiated control of customs in the Dominican Republic—to Managua, to work his magic there. And sixteen days later, aboard an American battleship, appropriately, the leaders of the Díaz-Estrada rebellion signed one of the most interesting agreements ever negotiated between two sovereign states. The first point of the pact provided that a constituent assembly be selected and that it choose Estrada as president and Díaz as vice-president for terms of two years. Why an assembly was needed if the main items on its agenda were already decided was not made clear. The second point called for a mixed commission, satisfactory to the State Department, to settle outstanding financial claims. The third provided that Nicaragua would accept a loan from American bankers, to be secured by part of its customs receipts, which, as in the Santo Domingo convention, would be collected by a U.S. agent. The terms— kept secret at first—were so onerous that when they became known they caused a furor. According to the American minister in Managua in February 1911, "the natural sentiments of an overwhelming majority of Nicaraguans is antagonistic to the United States, and even with some members of Estrada's cabinet I find a decided suspicion, if not distrust, of our motives."

Ramming a loan down the throat of a small nation proved more difficult in this instance than Washington had expected. In a show of independence the National Assembly of Nicaragua decided in April to formulate a constitution that would prevent foreign domination through the mechanism of bank loans. The State Department, of course, opposed this measure, and Estrada, committed bag and baggage to Washington, dissolved the Assembly rather than permit the antiloan provisions of the constitution to stand. Again there was turmoil in the Latin republic and Estrada was forced to resign. The American minister wired the State Department that if it wanted Díaz, the vice-president, confirmed as president by the National Assembly, "a war vessel is necessary for the moral effect." The Liberal Party, he reported, was so incensed that it was planning an uprising and since it constituted "such a majority over the Conservatives" it would be wise to station a war vessel at Corinto "at least until the loan has been put through . . ." Dollar diplomacy it seems was no more considerate of popular sentiment in the countries it was helping to "civilize" than the big stick.

With its puppet, Díaz, in power and a warship standing by, the United States finally had its way. The agreement of June 6, 1911, between Secretary of State Philander C. Knox and a Nicaraguan representative, called for floating a $15 million loan by American financiers, and operation of the customhouses of Nicaragua under American supervision. Simultaneously the State Department worked out the details of the loan with two banking houses, Brown Brothers and J. and W. Seligman. Properly speaking, it was not a loan to Nicaragua, for the government of that country would never see a dime of the money. The two banking firms would simply set up a special account in their own banks for $15 million, out of which they would liquidate claims by Europeans and Americans against Nicaragua; and would allocate monies to improve the national railway, as well as build a new one, both of which would be controlled by them. The arrangement was so blatant that despite President Taft's solemn urging the United States Senate three times refused to ratify it.

In these circumstances both State and the bankers trimmed their sails and came forth with a bizarre loan convention, called the Treasury Bills Agreement. Only $1.5 million would be provided this time, but it would be used to reorganize the Nationl Bank, so that the two American firms would have a 51 percent interest, and Nicaragua was generously permitted to keep 49 percent. Among the other provisions a mere $100,000 would be used as initial capital in the new bank, while $1.4 million would be deposited in the United States Mortgage and Trust Company and be available for "reforming the currency" of Nicaragua. The loan would be secured this time both by a lien on customs and by the liquor tax. This plan was not put before the U.S. Senate; it was instituted by simple executive fiat. An American, Colonel Clifford D. Ham, recommended by the bankers, was placed in charge of customs and remained in that post for seventeen years.

As more loans were pumped into the Central American republic and the straitjacket tightened, resistance to the marionette Díaz increased. His Liberal opponents demanded an election but were sternly advised by the American minister that elections could come only after organization of the National Bank had been completed, not before. Refusing to accept this order of priorities, the Liberals on July 29, 1912, seized a large stock of weapons and several customhouses and ships, occupied part of the railroad, and went over to revolution. Had the United States not intervened they would certainly have won. But when the American manager of the Bank of Nicaragua wired Brown Brothers in New York that he needed "protection," Taft and Knox sent 412 marines immediately, and, later, almost 3,000 troops as well as eight warships to suppress the rebels. They bombarded Managua, assaulted Coyotepe, and took a host of other actions which finally forced the revolutionary leader to surrender aboard the American ship U.S.S. *Cleveland*. After the revolution was defeated the marines finished their job by standing watch over the election booths, to assure Díaz's victory for a new four-year term. Subsequently, at Díaz's request, the United States stationed a contingent of marines as a "legation guard" at Managua. They remained there for thirteen years, from 1912 to 1925. Among the strategical benefits that the United States extorted from Nicaragua in that period—and oddly enough under the "pacifist" Secretary of State William Jennings Bryan and the apostle of the "New Freedom," Woodrow Wilson—were the right to a naval base at the Gulf of Fonseca and a lease for a second canal route "in perpetuity and for all time . . . free from all taxation or other public charge . . . by way of any route over Nicaraguan territory." The concession was undoubtedly worth much more, but with an American "legation guard" at hand it went dirt-cheap, for $3 million.

Reviewing this venture in imperialism, it would be wrong to attribute Washington's interest exclusively to the private American investments in Nicaragua or to the profitable banking loans. Secretary Knox, it is true, had represented Pittsburgh corporations with interests in Nicaragua when he was in private law practice. No doubt this preconditioned him toward the course he and Taft followed, but it is virtually certain that a similar path would have been charted by a Secretary less intimately associated with American corporations in the invaded country. Safeguarding Wall Street's capital was obviously not the only concern, since, as Professor Julius Pratt points out, U.S. investments amounted to only $2.5 million in 1912 and $17 million by 1928. There were at least two other reasons for the intervention. One was that in the process of domesticating Nicaragua,

Knox and Taft were sending messages to the other states of Latin America, in effect warning them not to tamper with Uncle Sam's financial and military position in the whole area. There was to be no Zelaya accepting sizable loans from Europe, or contemplating the grant of canal rights to Britain or Japan. When there was trouble in Ecuador subsequently, the Taft administration also interfered in its affairs "to the end that American interests in Ecuador might be saved from complete extinction." That same year, 1912, the marines landed again in Cuba, and no one in Latin America could have missed the point expressed so poignantly by President Taft: "While our foreign policy should not be turned a hair's breadth from the straight path of justice, it may well be made to include active intervention to secure for our merchandise and our capitalists opportunity for profitable investment. . . ."

When the State Department learned in 1913 that Cuba was on the verge of granting a concession to British capitalists to build a railroad from Nuevitas to Caibarien, the legation in Havana was instructed to urge the Cuban president to postpone action on this bill "emphasizing the burden it would impose on the Cuban Treasury in favor of capital which is neither American nor Cuban." In other words, the Monroe Doctrine, which was originally designed simply to keep Europeans from acquiring new territory in Latin America, was by now interpreted to inhibit their efforts to acquire economic concessions as well. And interventions in places like Nicaragua, Cuba, Honduras, Haiti, etc., made this clear.

Another factor, however, was of a broader strategic nature. The foreign policy of an expansionist nation cannot be gauged by *immediate* commercial and investment benefits. There is also the matter of strategic "security," a factor which may open the door to economic opportunities in other places and other times. Secretary Knox put it crisply when he said that "the logic of political geography and of strategy, and now our tremendous national interest [increased trade, etc.] created by the Panama Canal, make the safety, the peace, and the prosperity of Central America and the zone of the Caribbean of paramount interest to the Government of the United States." If the canal was a maritime highway to the enormous trade potential in the Far East and elsewhere, the United States would have to assert its dominance in all the countries nearby.

Starting from this one pivotal area the American empire would soon expand throughout the western hemisphere and finally—especially after World War II—throughout the world. Secretary Knox may have been technically accurate in 1912 when he said on a good-will tour of the Caribbean nations that "I beg to assure you

. . . that my government does not covet an inch of territory south of the Rio Grande." But he failed to emphasize that it was no longer necessary to annex "an inch of territory" to enjoy the profits of imperialism.

12

THE FINE ART
OF VANDALISM

The first three presidents to adopt the modern imperialist outlook were Republicans who, by party tradition, were close to big business. But Woodrow Wilson, who defeated Taft and Teddy Roosevelt in the three-way race of 1912, was not only a Democrat but an avowed progressive who meant to tame big business. In his first administration, the tariff was substantially cut for the first time in a half century, the currency and banking system was altered to offer a wider dispersal of financial power, a complex antitrust law, the Clayton Act, was put on the books to slow down the march of the trusts (AFL president Samuel Gompers called it "labor's charter of freedom" because it contained a passage that exempted unions from prosecution as "trusts"), and the Federal Trade Commission was created to abolish unfair practices by businessmen. Progressives hailed the La Follette Seaman's Act, the Farm Loan Act, and other bills passed during Wilson's first few years in office as great steps forward for the "little man," and by implication great curbs on the power of the rich. It is a fact nonetheless that the Princeton historian contributed more to America's imperialistic tendencies than both of his predecessors combined, and that he intervened in more places and for longer periods than they did to curb the sovereignty of unfortunate neighbors.

Thomas Woodrow Wilson (the "Thomas" was permitted to atrophy through disuse) has been described by Robert Leckie as "an iceberg needing to be warmed"—by contrast with Roosevelt, who was "a volcano needing to be cooled." He was driven by an inner sense of commitment which by his own admission he could communicate to masses of people collectively but not to a single person directly.

He was the only true scholar to be president in this century—worthy of comparison in that respect to Jefferson or John Quincy Adams— but he often decided issues by intuition, and he was grossly inconsistent. He was not the stuff out of which either heroes or saints are made—an Old Hickory, for instance, or a log-cabin Abe Lincoln —though he was capable of grandeur in planning and idealism in rhetoric.

Wilson was born in Staunton, Virginia, just a few days after Christmas 1856. His "incomparable father," as he called him, was a Presbyterian minister who was reared in Scotland and whose passion was theology. Both the Christian tone and the ability to deal in abstractions were transmitted to young Woodrow and remained a salient characteristic throughout his days. The boy was not a particularly good student; in Augusta, Georgia, where the family migrated, he was usually at the lower end of the scholarship spectrum. When he was fourteen his family moved again, to Columbia, South Carolina, where he developed strong sympathies for the Southern sufferings during Reconstruction. He graduated from Princeton in 1879, an average student with an aptitude for debating and an intense interest in politics. An article he wrote in his senior year on the vicissitudes of the congressional system (he preferred British parliamentarism, he said) was later expanded into a book, *Congressional Government* (published in 1885, it went through 25 editions). After a stint at the University of Virginia Law School, he opened a law office in Atlanta together with a colleague, but clients were few and far between, so after a year the project had to be abandoned in favor of a career in academe.

Considering the low pay of professors it was a step backward, but Wilson persevered to teach history at Bryn Mawr College, take a Ph.D. at Johns Hopkins, and instruct at Wesleyan. Having published a second book, *The State*, before he was thirty, he received many invitations to lecture, and with added status in the profession he was finally offered the job he coveted as professor of jurisprudence and political economy at his alma mater, Princeton. He taught and wrote for twelve years, his best-known work being a five-volume *History of the American People*, which was not particularly outstanding and was so conservative it was called by some "a Tory document." By now, however, he had become an academic luminary and had been offered the presidency of six universities. When a similar bid was tendered him by the trustees of Princeton in 1902, he accepted gratefully, and filled the job for eight years, until a new itch drove him into the political arena.

Wilson at that time was having trouble with the governing board of his university, and the Democratic Party was having trouble between its progressive and conservative wings. To Colonel George Harvey, publisher of *Harper's Weekly*—then financed by J. P. Morgan—and to party bosses in New Jersey, Wilson seemed an excellent counterweight to the wing of the party that leaned toward William Jennings Bryan, considered much too progressive by his peers. The university president by contrast was adjudged conservative to the point of being a near-reactionary. He opposed women's suffrage as well as the regulation of utilities by state or federal authorities. He took the side of the mine operators against the mineworkers in the 1902 strike and as late as 1909 was "a fierce partisan of the Open Shop." He blamed the panic of 1907 on "the aggressive attitude of legislation toward the railroads," and denounced efforts to make corporations disclose all their activities as "socialistic." His early views on foreign policy, as already noted, were that concessions won by financiers must be defended "by ministers of state, even if the sovereignty of unwilling nations be outraged in the process," and that "colonies must be obtained or planted." Walter H. Page correctly described Wilson as "a right-minded man of a safe and conservative political faith." It was this bias which endeared him to Colonel Harvey and the party leaders. Wilson indeed reassured them by publishing an article lauding professional politicians, and pledging that he would do nothing to undercut their power.

Once nominated by the party's state convention at Trenton, however, Wilson began to sing the song of progressivism. He promised to make the Democratic Party "an instrument of justice for the state and for the nation," and he promoted such panaceas as regulation of utilities, direct primaries, referendum and recall, that were high on the agenda of progressives like Robert La Follette. Progressivism was the mood of the country, and Woodrow Wilson, not yet governor, was already running for president. In the next two years his liberalism would deepen as he came into contact with two men who profoundly influenced his style and thinking as president, "Colonel" Edward Mandell House and Louis D. Brandeis. House, son of a rich landowner in Texas, who functioned as the man behind the scenes —or, as he was called, "the silent partner"—for a number of governors in his state (one of whom called him "colonel" of his staff), met Wilson in November 1911 and became his closest associate. "Mr. House is my second half," Wilson was to say of him. "He is myself independent of me, his thoughts and mine are one." House was to play a major part in winning the presidential nomination for Wilson, and subsequently as the major domo of his administration, especially on matters of foreign affairs. Brandeis, an immigrant boy who became a professor at Harvard, a prominent judge, and the avowed enemy of trusts, came onto the scene somewhat later than House, to fortify Wilson's domestic insights, in particular his opposition to "special interests."

By 1912, then, Wilson had a small coterie of friends working to upgrade him and was touring the hustings making his availability known. Speaking in somewhat ministerial fashion and without notes, Wilson's eloquence gave him the aura of an oracle. Even so he would never have been nominated except for the bizarre workings of the political system which produced a coalition that included the progressive Bryan, the machine politicians, and the bourbon supporters of Congressman Oscar W. Underwood of Alabama. When the Democratic convention opened in June Wilson was a dark horse, the favorite being Champ Clark of Missouri, the darling of Hearst and Tammany Hall. It took all of 46 ballots, House's Texas votes, Bryan's support, and a whirlwind of maneuvers that captured Underwood on the final ballot to win Wilson the nomination. Bryan was subsequently rewarded with the post of Secretary of State, where he promptly announced that no liquor would be served at official functions, thus initiating what was called the era of "grape-juice diplomacy."

Wilson's early forays into foreign policy, which he considered distinctly subordinate to domestic concerns, indeed had the moral purity of grape juice. A week after his inauguration he renounced dollar diplomacy and reaffirmed his faith in "government by consent of the governed," even for Latin America. Henceforth, he said, he would not support any "special group of [U.S.] interests" south of the Rio Grande, nor recognize any Latin regime that was not democratically chosen. "The United States," he insisted, "has nothing to gain in Central or South America except the permanent interests of the people of those two continents." When a military group around Victoriano Huerta executed a coup d'état against the revolutionary Madero regime in Mexico, Wilson refused to accredit the new government despite a memorandum from Colonel House that this might mean a surge of English and German influence in that country. The President also sought to make amends to Colombia by tendering "sincere regrets" for the Panama incident and offering $25 million consolation money. At Mobile, Alabama, in an October 1913 speech he told the audience: "I want to take this occasion to say that the United States will never again seek one additional foot of territory by conquest." He pledged that "morality and not expediency" would guide American policy, and observed with characteristic incisiveness that when weak nations "grant concessions . . . foreign interests are apt to dominate their domestic affairs. . . ." There was no misunderstanding this pronouncement: the United States would never again be guided by its own material interests if they violated the rights of foreign countries. Translating this policy for China, Wilson withdrew support from the American bankers whom Taft had edged into the six-power consortium that was making a $125 million loan to that nation, on the grounds that the conditions imposed violated Chinese sovereignty. He also was the first to recognize the Sun Yat-sen revolutionaries after their National Assembly had met in 1913. Meanwhile, on a parallel path, Bryan was advancing the doctrine of pacifying the world through permanent conciliation. The President's Peace Plan, elaborated on by Bryan in April 1914, called for submission of all international disputes that could not be hammered out on the diplomatic anvil to a permanent investigating commission, empowered to make recommendations while the parties kept their swords sheathed. Thirty nations signed agreements with Bryan embodying this "cooling-off" doctrine. Three other states, Italy, Spain, Japan, went further; they signed pacts calling for binding arbitration.

It was all a passing fancy, however. Not only Wilson but Bryan joined the world of *Realpolitik*, intervening in Central America and elsewhere with a fury that make Taft and Roosevelt seem like pacifists. At the behest of President Díaz of Nicaragua, who feared nothing more than an inevitable popular revolution if the U.S. marines left, Bryan wrote into a treaty for a second canal route a provision similar to the Platt Amendment. It gave the United States the unilateral right, in Díaz's own words, "to intervene in our internal affairs in order to maintain peace and the existence of a lawful government." This graceless return to dollar diplomacy caused the New York *Times* to comment that the policies of Wilson and Bryan "more nearly resemble ten-cent diplomacy." Bryan was forced to expunge the intervention section of the treaty because of opposition by the Senate Foreign Relations Committee, but he and Wilson kept the marines in Managua.

The record shows that in the eight years Wilson was in office he dispatched troops, apart from those in World War I, to Mexico, Haiti, the Dominican Republic, Cuba, Panama, Soviet Russia, Honduras, China, and Guatemala. Three of these interventions—in Haiti, Santo Domingo, and Mexico—are highly instructive, for they show how the Roosevelt Corollary and dollar diplomacy were both refined and expanded.

II

Haiti, an impoverished land of 3 million souls, had won its independence from France in 1804 in the first modern revolution led by a black man, Toussaint L'Ouverture. But in ensuing decades, for many reasons, the little nation failed to prosper and her domestic affairs were a seemingly endless train of disorder and strife. None of this affected the United States, for as twenty-four prominent lawyers—including future Supreme Court Justice Felix Frankfurter—pointed out, Haiti "has never manifested hostility to the United States and given no occasion for our intervention in her affairs." Nonetheless Haiti became a target for American imperialists. For one thing, the U.S. navy had been interested in establishing a base at Mole St. Nicholas, on the northwest coast, ever since 1847, and as late as 1891 had sent a small fleet to Port au Prince, capital of the country, to "persuade" the Haitians to cede the harbor. The natives refused but the projected base was now more urgently needed than ever. For another, the National City Bank of New York had designs on Haiti's banking system.

This was at a time when expansionists were less inhibited about expressing their true sentiments than at present. In 1908 Albert Shaw, editor of *Review of Reviews,* inquired of Secretary Root whether he could not "invent a way to put Haiti under bonds," and the secretary replied with candor that "we must wait for the 'psychological moment.'" It was some years before the "psychological moment" arrived. In the meantime, French bankers who in 1881 had founded the National Bank of Haiti, which administered the national treasury, provided the republic with a new loan and reorganized the institution under their continued control. It was at this point, in 1910, that the National City Bank decided there was a future in Haitian banking, and Secretary of State Knox, under the policy of dollar diplomacy, delicately advised the Haitians that "some American banking interests ought to be represented." Both Haiti and France took the hint, with the result that four American firms, including National City, acquired a one-fifth interest in the national bank.

Three years later, with Haitian governments still rising and falling, Secretary Bryan concluded that the American government had an obligation to protect the interests of its bankers on the island of Hispaniola. On six occasions in 1914 and 1915 he demanded that Haiti turn over collection of its customs—its only source of revenue—to the good graces of Uncle Sam. During one of the perennial revolts in the north, Washington advised the beleaguered President of Haiti that it would keep him in power if he agreed to give the United States control of the customhouses. He refused, as did his successor, after he resigned. The "psychological moment" had now arrived. On December 17, 1914, American marines landed at Port au Prince in broad daylight, marched to the vaults of the National Bank, helped themselves to a half million dollars in monies that were security for the national currency, and loaded it on the gunboat *Machias* for delivery to the National City Bank in New York. According to a vice-president of the bank, in testimony before a Senate committee six years later, the purpose of the incredible raid was to force Haiti to accept the usual customhouse arrangement.

Odd as it may seem, the black leaders of the little nation remained obdurate for a number of months, even in the face of such pressure. Negotiations were still going on when another of the ceaseless stream of revolutions broke out in July 1915, ending in the assassination of the country's President. Wilson and Bryan seized on the event to send in troops, even though not a single American or other foreigner had been hurt. On July 28, the very afternoon of the assassination, the U.S.S. *Washington*, under Rear Admiral W. B. Caperton, anchored in the harbor and within a few hours occupied Port au Prince.

The marines were to remain in Haiti for nineteen long years—a year and a half into the Franklin Roosevelt administration—as the only true political power in the country. Theoretically Haiti had its own government, but as Admiral Caperton made clear from the outset, no elections were permitted until a candidate could be found who would "agree to any terms laid down by the United States." The State Department wired its minister at Port au Prince to explain to any candidate "that the United States expects to be entrusted with the practical control of the customs and such financial control over the affairs of the republic of Haiti as the United States may deem necessary for efficient administration." In plain language, Washington was asking for a puppet to present himself, and on that occasion the president of the Haitian Senate, Philippe Sudre Dartiguenave, agreed to serve—and, as Caperton observed, "be sustained by American protection." Tied hand and foot, the National Assembly could hardly do otherwise but accede both to the choice of Dartiguenave—who received 94 votes out of 116—and to the treaty that Secretary of State Robert Lansing, Bryan's successor, imposed on the hapless state. By the time the pact was signed on September 16, 1915, Caperton's marines had taken over the customhouses at the ten major ports, had occupied all the towns and cities needed to establish "order," and declared martial law. Two years later, with the help of the State Department, National City Bank acquired the French shares in the Haitian central bank—the French were divesting themselves of foreign holdings at the time to finance the war—and the American firm became master of the bank, treasury, and, derivatively, the economy.

Despite Wilson's claim to "morality not expediency" as the guideline for American foreign policy, Lansing's treaty had a number of novel features that limited sovereignty even more than Taft and Knox had limited it for Nicaragua. In addition to control of the customs, and a plank similar to the Platt Amendment granting the United States the unilateral right to intervene at will, the pact provided that Washington would select a "financial adviser" to the ministry of finance, as well as engineers to supervise sanitation and public improvements. Another section of the agreement, Article Ten, called for the formation of "an efficient constabulary . . . composed of native Haitians," but "organized and officered by Americans." Thus in addition to its own marines the United States was to have a puppet army, trained by Americans and led by Americans. As of 1917 there were 9 U.S. commissioned officers and 80 noncommissioned officers running the native military force.

That same year Wilson forced the Dominican Republic to dissolve its army because it was "a tool for revolutionists" and replace it with the Policia Nacional Dominicana, also officered by Americans. And when Liberia in far-off Africa relinquished its customhouses to American operation in return for a loan, it too had to agree to a Frontier Force drilled and led by former American army officers working under the supervision of the American military attaché in Monrovia. If Admiral Caperton could wire the Secretary of the Navy in Washington that "next Thursday . . . I will permit Congress to elect a president," there was no reason why the Wilson administration should not also operate the military forces of Haiti, the Dominican Republic, Liberia, and other nations as well.

Some historians, while apologetic about intervention per se, have nevertheless concluded that on the whole the United States did a creditable job in Haiti, building roads, creating political order, and assuring financial stability. Perhaps so, but consider the costs to Haitians in blood and freedom. Conservative estimates are that 2,000 natives were killed by the marines in the course of "pacification." A U.S. Marine Corps report sets the number as 3,250 "killed either by marines or by the person of the gendarmerie of Haiti." In order to recruit labor for building roads, the marines utilized an old road law—corvée—which forced men to work for specified periods or pay a levy in lieu of work. The corvée was implemented with a fervor only American marines can display, with Haitians being seized from their homes and pressed into virtual slavery for months at a time. According to J. W. Johnson, in an article for the *Nation*, "Those who protested or resisted were beaten into submission. . . . Those attempting to escape were shot." One educated Haitian, Charlemagne Peralte, led a revolt against the system when he was impressed for duty, and was killed in the course of fighting. Scott Nearing and Joseph Freeman quote an American in 1920, recently returned from the Black Republic, who said that "if the United States should leave Haiti today, it would leave more than a thousand widows and orphans of its own making, more banditry than has existed for a century, resentment, hatred and despair in the hearts of a whole people, to say nothing of the irreparable injury to its own tradition as the defender of the rights of man."

On the other side, the occupation fully entrenched the National City Bank as the ruler of Haiti's economy. The bank's nominee became the nation's financial adviser. Under another treaty forced on the Haitian administration in 1920, the New York bank became undisputed master of the National Bank of the Republic of Haiti; the national railroad fell into the hands of Roger L. Farnham of National City; the usual loans were floated; and Americans penetrated the sugar and other industries of the island with characteristic vigor. Periodically, when Haitians protested, American military leaders took matters into their own hands, declared martial law and punished those who cast aspersions on American benevolence. In May 1921, for instance, under President Harding, Brigadier General John H. Russell proclaimed an order by which anyone who spoke or wrote anything that reflected "adversely upon the United States forces in Haiti" or stirred agitation against American officials or their Haitian marionettes "will be brought to trial before a military tribunal." Three newsmen were promptly arrested for declaiming against American occupation.

III

Once the bars were let down, the forms of U.S. intervention became as brazen as necessary to effectuate Washington's economic and strategic objectives. The great powers were then in a bitter and brutal competition for markets and spheres of influence, and the Wilson administration had no intention of falling behind—especially in the area it designated as the Panama lifeline. Before coming to office in 1912, Wilson had stated that "our industries have expanded to such a point that they will burst their jackets if they cannot find a free outlet to the markets of the world. . . . Our domestic markets no longer suffice. We need foreign markets." The Caribbean and Central American area, while not the most lucrative (except for Cuba and Mexico) in terms of trade and investment, was nonetheless decisive as a jumping-off point toward the much larger markets of South America and the Far East. Despite lapses of humanitarian rhetoric, therefore, Wilson meant to make this area secure for American material interests no matter what the means.

In the Dominican Republic, which shares the island of Hispaniola with Haiti, the United States showed even less concern for the right of self-determination than in the neighboring republic. Early in the Wilson administration, Secretary Bryan warned Dominican revolutionaries that the United States would not recognize their regime if they won, and would "withhold the portion of the customs collections belonging to Santo Domingo." A warship was sent to emphasize the point. Two years later, in the spring of 1916, an avowed enemy of the United States, Desiderio Arias, initiated a revolt and this time Washington went much further. Marines were landed—under protection by two dozen long-range, big-caliber guns—and the usual demands for a treaty put forth—except that this one included U.S. control not only of customs but of the treasury, police, and army. For a few months there was a stalemate as the legally chosen temporary president, Dr. Henriquez y Caravajal, rallied popular support against the treaty. But Lansing recommended military government and Wilson, concluding that this was "the least of the evils in sight," gave the order.

The Dominican Republic, therefore, was under direct American military dictatorship from 1916 to 1924. Its Congress was suspended, a rear admiral of the U.S. navy became governor with all executive and legislative functions, and the cabinet posts were manned by marine and naval officers of the United States. According to a select committee of the U.S. Congress in 1922, "elections were prohibited; thousands of marines were spread over the country and with unlimited authority over the natives; public meetings were not permitted; . . . destructive bombs were dropped from airplanes upon towns and hamlets; every home was searched for arms, weapons, and implements; homes were burned; natives were killed; tortures and cruelties committed; and 'Butcher' Weyler's horrible concentration camps were established. . . ."

It is a revealing epilogue to the American rule in the Dominican Republic and a subsequent intervention in Nicaragua (1926–33) that these small republics later fell under the iron heel of constabulary commanders who had been trained by the marines. The United States insisted it was training the Central American states in the arts of democracy, but Rafael Trujillo in the Dominican Republic and Anastasio Somoza in Nicaragua, both military men considered friends of the United States, established long military dictatorships and despoiled their countries of hundreds of millions. Haiti did not follow the same route only because the first president elected after intervention, Stenio Vincent, had the foresight to exile the commander of the Garde d'Haïti, but after the long night of occupation the Black Republic remains even today the poorest and most desolate spot in the western hemisphere.

IV

"If America is not to have free enterprise," Woodrow Wilson once said, "then she can have freedom of no sort whatever." Like an almost identical statement by Harry Truman three decades later, this had portentous implications. For if freedom in the United States depended on free enterprise, then the acquisition of markets to dispose of its surpluses, and spheres of influence to facilitate the acquisition of markets, were as vital to freedom as the Bill of Rights itself. At the end of the Spanish-American War the United States was producing $11.4 billion in manufactures; a decade later almost twice that amount, $20.7 billion; and in 1919 almost six times as much, $62.4 billion. Exports and foreign investment, especially in the natural habitat of the western hemisphere, were rising apace. By 1913, with the aid of dollar diplomacy, the United States had gained control of the tin industry in Bolivia, copper in Chile and Peru, and meat packing in Argentina and Paraguay. Its economic role was still distinctly secondary to Britain in that part of the world, but the American star was rising. J. P. Morgan and W. R. Grace operated the Chilean-Andean railroad, and American firms were making inroads into river transportation in Colombia, Argentina, Brazil, Peru. John Bull was already outpaced for the trade of Brazil, Colombia, and Venezuela, and being pressed in Peru and Ecuador. National City Bank would soon open its first branch in South America, to be followed by many other great banking firms, as World War I in Europe began to enervate Uncle Sam's competitors. With a manufacturing plant twice that of Britain or Germany, and a navy that had risen from the sixth largest in the world in 1899 to second in 1911, imperial expansion was clearly on the agenda. If it required military force in the Caribbean or Central America, it proceeded in other places simply through economic penetration—and the political power that came in its wake. Military force was not always necessary. As Willard Straight, the J. P. Morgan advance man in China, observed: "The great lending nations . . . utilize their investing through financial reorganization and the development of its resources, they create for themselves a financial and political influence which they convert to their commercial advantage."

If military intervention was not always needed, however, the threat was ever present, and it could be applied to a greater or lesser degree depending on circumstances. In other words, there was a range of action beginning with trade, loans, and investments, and proceeding through diplomatic pressures toward the ultimate dispatch of marines, which could be interrupted at whatever stage success was assured. The most interesting manifestation of this principle during Wilson's administration was in Washington's relations with Mexico.

"When I go back to England," Sir William Tyrell advised Wilson during a private meeting in November 1913, "I shall be asked to explain your Mexican policy. Can you tell me what it is?" The President replied in uncluttered terms: "I am going to teach the South American Republics to elect good men." Apart from the presumptuousness of this statement, there was much more involved than the selection of "good men" to office. Back in 1867, it will be recalled, the United States forced Napoleon III's cat's-paw, Archduke Maximilian, to relinquish power in Mexico. In 1876 the dictator Porfirio Díaz seized the reins and kept himself in office for thirty-four long years, until he was overthrown by a group of revolutionaries headed by Francisco Madero, and including the dedicated peasant leader Emiliano Zapata.

In this thirty-four-year period American investors had gained one concession after another from Díaz, so that at the end of his reign they owned, according to Marion Letcher, the American consul at Chihuahua, $1,057,770,000 of the nation's capital (as against $321 million for England, and $792 million for native entrepreneurs). They had accumulated silver, gold, and copper mines, oil wells, railroads, ranches. Eighty percent of the railroads were in their hands, 70 percent of the oil was being produced by their companies. When Americans built a railroad from the Texan border to Mexico City they were given free land for the right-of-way as well as a subsidy of $14,000 per square mile in normal terrain, and $35,000 per square mile in "rough country." In 1899 J. P. Morgan floated a $110 million loan for Mexico, to be followed by others, including one to the private railways which the Mexican government had to guarantee.

Of the U.S. investments the most significant were in petroleum, not because they were the largest but because the competition for the world's oil fields was heating up and Mexico was to be the first great battleground in that struggle. The industry had been born in the United States during the Civil War, to provide kerosene for the lamps of America and lubricants for a host of other purposes. For a number of decades the United States enjoyed a near-monopoly of the world trade, and John D. Rockefeller's Standard Oil a near-monopoly of the American industry. By the mid-1890's, however, other titans were moving in to challenge Rockefeller: the Nobel family, of Swedish-Russian extraction, brought in some fields in the Caucasus; the Rothschild bankers gave loans to the Tsar and received concessions in Baku; the Royal Dutch Petroleum Company developed oil fields in the Dutch East Indies. The American lead was not only cut down but wiped out for three years, from 1898 to 1901, as Russia forged ahead.

In this burgeoning competition everyone seemed to get into the act. The Mellons of Pittsburgh formed Gulf Oil, the first integrated company to explore, refine, and market many products, including gasoline, which had once been considered waste. Edward L. Doheny of Los Angeles and some associates bought the 280,000-acre Hacienda del Tulillo in Mexico in 1900, added another 150,000 acres thereafter, and brought in three fabulous strikes, one of which eventually yielded 80 million barrels, and another, at its peak, 260,000 barrels a day. Doheny was followed by Standard Oil, Waters-Pierce Company, and between fifty and a hundred other American prospectors, as well as an English syndicate headed by Lord Cowdray, who secured concessions from Díaz while working to improve Mexico's harbors. The Mexican fields, apart from the fact that their labor costs were cheaper, were in many respects superior to those of the United States. According to one specialist, the oil wells of California, the best in the nation, yielded 100 to 200 barrels a day, whereas Doheny's Juan Casiano No. 7 produced 70,000 barrels on one day in the fall of 1910. By this time the combustion engine and the automobile based on it (there were 619,000 "horseless carriages" in the United States in 1911) were giving the oil industry a new impetus and Mexico a new importance in the quest for petroleum concessions. In 1904 Mexican production had been a mere 220,000 barrels; in 1909 it reached 3.3 million; four years later, 26 million; and by 1920, 157 million—almost a fourth the world's total, making Mexico the second largest producer in the world.

If Mexico was rich in resources, however, its people were poor and landless, beset by a feudal land-holding system, and dominated by a dictatorial government much too long in power. The middle and upper classes, demanding constitutional guarantees, and the lower classes, demanding land, thereupon joined in revolution and Francisco Madero, a reform-minded member of a well-to-do family, was able in May 1911 to drive Díaz into exile. His elected government was quickly recognized by Taft, though it was always under challenge from both the right and the left. Less than a month before Wilson was sworn into office, however, Madero was overthrown and soon executed by General Victoriano Huerta, commander of the federal army. For the American oil interests, Huerta's victory represented a distinct threat, for as one writer for *World's Work* commented, the new Mexican leader manifested an "antagonism to American oil interests and friendship to Lord Cowdray" of Britain. It was "a rich prize for which these American and British capitalists are contending." Doheny pleaded with Washington that "inasmuch as both Germany and Great Britain are seeking and acquiring sources of supply for large quantities of petroleum" the United States should use all its energies to retain dominance in Mexico.

The United States, since Jefferson, had generally recognized any foreign government as long as it effectively held power. Wilson, however, not only withheld recognition from Huerta but demanded that he call elections in which he would "bind himself not to be a candidate." If he accepted this proposal to rule himself out of office, Wilson was ready to mobilize American bankers for an "immediate extension of a loan." From an idealistic point of view there was good reason to oppose a man of Huerta's stripe. Moreover there was still turmoil in the northern part of the country, where Governor Venustiano Carranza of Coahuila, Francisco (Pancho) Villa, and Álvaro Obregón resisted the central regime. But as a leading American journalist, George Harvey, observed: "What legal or moral right has a President of the United States to say who shall or shall not be President of Mexico?" Equally questionable was the threat conveyed through Washington's diplomats on the scene "that any maltreatment of Americans is likely to raise the question of intervention," and the explanation to British officials by the ambassador to London, Walter Hines Page, that if Mexico's internal problems were not resolved "the United States might feel obliged to repeat its dealing with Cuba."

Wilson's "moral" diplomacy might have been more convincing if it were not for the constant gleam of oil in the background. "A large part of our troubles in Mexico," said Wilson's alter ego, Colonel House, was due to Cowdray and to the British minister in Mexico, Sir Lionel Carden, who naturally were seeking concessions for their own nationals. The British, House charged, "had not only obtained concessions from the Huerta government, but expected to obtain others." Presumably this was a cardinal sin, for it quickened American tempers and increased American pressures. Wilson himself adopted a policy of "watchful waiting," hoping that Carranza and Villa would topple Huerta with their own resources. Other Americans pointed to the potential loss to American investors of millions of dollars and stridently called for armed intervention. Among them was Senator Albert B. Fall, an investor in Mexico himself and a close friend of Doheny's. To emphasize the point, a senator from Arkansas warned all and sundry that "those hearing me will live to see the Mexican border pushed to the Panama Canal."

On October 26, 1913, Huerta held elections, defying the United States, and by stacking the ballot boxes had himself chosen president. A month later Secretary Bryan warned that "if General Huerta does not retire by force of circumstances, it will become the duty of the United States to use less peaceful means to put him out. . . ." The existing embargo of arms was lifted so that guns and ammunition could be sent from the United States to Carranza and Villa; and after an interval, during which Washington tried to choke Huerta with a financial blockade, the inevitable pretexts were found for intervention. On April 9, 1914, the paymaster and crew of an American ship in Tampico, the *Dolphin,* were arrested by Mexicans for disembarking "at a place subject to military authority," marched through the streets briefly, and released. The American admiral immediately demanded an apology and punishment of the officer who had perpetrated the arrest; the Mexican commander complied almost at once. Huerta, however, balked at another demand calling on Mexico to salute the American flag with a twenty-one-gun salvo, unless he could be assured that the American battery would return the salute simultaneously. No matter who was right or wrong, the American response to this trivial incident was clearly beyond reason, for five days after the event, on April 14, ten battleships and a regiment of marines were rushed to Tampico. Meanwhile two other minor incidents clouded the horizon: a cable to the U.S. embassy was held up at the cable office by the censor, and an orderly on the U.S.S. *Minnesota* was taken into custody—he was quickly released and apologies tendered—while collecting mail at Vera Cruz. These three occurrences were considered sufficient reason for Wilson to ask Congress for authority to intervene if he saw fit. After Congress voted its approval, Wilson was awakened at 2:30 A.M. on April 21 and informed that a German ship was about to unload arms at Vera Cruz. He thereupon ordered American forces to "take Vera Cruz at once," a task which was completed within a few hours at a cost of the lives of 17 Americans and 200 Mexicans. Even Carranza, who would benefit from this act, bitterly denounced Wilson's violation of his nation's sovereignty and warned that it "may indeed drag us into an unequal war."

For the time being American intervention had to go no further, for despite the efforts at mediation by the "ABC Powers" (Argentina, Brazil, and Chile) between the United States and Huerta, the Mexican leader was in an impossible situation. With his base at Vera Cruz in American hands, he could not resist the troops of Carranza and Villa, which overran Tampico and advanced southward. The Mexican President resigned on July 15, fled the country, and left the door open for Carranza, who was installed as provisional head of the government. American forces could now evacuate Vera Cruz. That American business was also no innocent bystander in effecting this change of government is evident from the testimony of Doheny before the U.S. Congress: "So far as we know, every American corporation doing business in Mexico extended sympathy or aid, or both—and we extended both—to Carranza from the time that President Wilson turned his back on Huerta." Doheny himself had sent a representative to offer Carranza $685,000 worth of oil, and made two other gifts, one for $100,000. American business and the Wilson administration obviously were coordinating their efforts, and toward the same objective—oil.

Unfortunately for both, Carranza's accession to office did not turn out as favorably as expected. Though Wilson did not like Carranza personally—perhaps, as Samuel Eliot Morison suggests, because he was "a man of his own age and similar character: honest, dogmatic, stubborn"—he recognized his regime in October 1915 after it pledged to protect foreign property and pay damages wrought during the fighting. The revolution begun by Madero and his constitutionalists to establish certain democratic safeguards was in the meantime moving beyond these bounds, focusing on basic reforms—land for the peasant, curbs on the power of the church, control of foreign imperialism. Carranza, who paid lip service to land reform before coming to power, was not radical enough for the peasants who fought with Zapata in the south and Pancho Villa in the north. Villa, once favored by Washington and embittered by the fact that Carranza's government had now been recognized, took reprisals against the United States. On January 10, 1916, he removed eighteen American mining engineers from a train at Santa Ysabel and had them executed. Two months later he invaded the town of Columbus, New Mexico, stole some horses, and killed seventeen U.S. citizens. Wilson responded by mobilizing 150,000 militia, and a force of 6,000 under

General John J. (Black Jack) Pershing chased Villa 300 miles into Mexico—without success and at an eventual cost of $130 million. Despite the fact that Villa was his enemy, Carranza sharply assailed this second intervention, as he had the first, and demanded that U.S. troops be withdrawn forthwith. Again war seemed imminent, especially after an engagement at Carrizal, where Carranza's forces killed and captured 17 Americans. Fortunately the captives were released and meetings arranged between the two nations which ended late in 1916 with an order for withdrawal of Pershing's troops.

Nothing, however, had really been settled. Villa was still at large, and when a constitutional convention promulgated a new constitution in 1917, tensions between the United States and Mexico flared again. The constitution was, by any standard, a highly democratic document, calling for popular education, limitations on the power of the church, establishment of peasant freeholds, and the breaking up of large estates. Article 27, however, was considered a threat to "foreign interests," since it vested in the national government "direct ownership of all minerals or substances which in veins, masses, or beds constitute deposits whose nature is different from the components of the land." In simple English this meant that new petroleum fields would now be state-owned, and doled out only under stern restrictions. Any foreigner who might acquire "land or waters" henceforth could not do so in a zone 100 kilometers from the borders of Mexico or 50 kilometers from its seacoasts—precisely where most of the oil lay. Moreover, if the nation did make concessions to foreigners elsewhere, the constitution provided that they had to agree in advance to accept the same legal status as Mexican natives and not to call on their home governments for help if they ran into difficulties. Article 27 was to be a bone of contention between Washington and Mexico for many years. The old oil interests were not touched, but when Carranza imposed a petroleum tax in February 1918, under Article 27, Secretary Lansing protested loud and long that this was virtual confiscation. The Mexican reply was that it had the sovereign right to levy any taxes it pleased to meet its fiscal needs, so long as foreigners and natives were treated alike.

Thus the dispute over oil continued to smolder on into the 1920's. If the United States did not occupy Mexico, as it had done Haiti, the Dominican Republic, Cuba, and Nicaragua, it was for two special reasons: first, Mexico was so much larger than the small republics; and second, the United States by now had greater problems to occupy its attention than getting Congress to declare a second Mexican War. Such a war, said ex-President Taft, "would involve the garrisoning with a sufficient force of every town. It would involve the organization of columns to chase the guerrillas into the mountain fastnesses and across trackless desert plains, and the subjugation of fifteen million people. . . . It would be a drag upon us, and then when we had got the thing done the future would still be doubtful and still be a charge and a burden upon our government and upon our treasury." The Indianapolis *News* added another reason for not going to war, namely that victory would require of the United States that it "absorb into our citizenship fifteen million mongrels." Anyway, in the meantime, as a result of World War I, the Colossus of the North was making a breakthrough in its empire building of more significant dimensions. It was winning markets and spheres of influence so vast, and a position of international power so awesome, that it could deal with the oil problem in Mexico in a more leisurely manner.

V

When Harding succeeded Wilson in March 1921, the new imperialism was an enshrined and virtually unchallenged goal. Its purpose was easily understood: to force other nations, through blandishment or coercion, to grant American business economic advantages against competitors, as well as strategic advantages to the United States government. In the interest of private economic expansion America no longer felt inhibited about "outraging" the sovereignty of weaker states. Intervention into their internal affairs took a variety of forms, some mild, some extreme, running the gamut from soliciting economic concessions for U.S. business—and defending them through diplomatic pressure—to long-term military occupation.

Two examples may perhaps illustrate how this worked on the day-to-day level. When the American China Development Company obtained a concession in 1900 to build a railway from Canton to Hankow, China included a provision that Americans were not to transfer their rights to other nations or "people of other nationality." Nevertheless the company placed its stock on the open market, and most of it was bought by Belgians. When China thereupon annulled the concession, the financiers repurchased their shares and the State Department insisted it would not "tolerate such an act of spoliation." In the end it forced China to pay $6.75 million to the company, which according to one authority was $3.75 million more than it had spent.

In Haiti a foreign firm called the National Railroad Company, largely French-owned, had contracted to build a line with the understanding that Haiti would pay interest on the bonds when the job was finished. The company claimed that Haiti had agreed to make payments after each section had been built. When the Black Republic suspended payments in 1914 because only six sections had been completed in four years, instead of the twenty the company had pledged for that period, the United States protested the forfeiture. After military occupation, the bonds turned up in the hands of the National City Bank of New York and Haiti was forced to resume payments, thus increasing the value of the bonds to the bank by $2 million. In each instance the stronger state was able to gain an economic advantage for its citizens against the sovereign wishes of a native government.

The techniques of imperialism, by the time Wilson left office, had been developed to a fine art. Investment and trade opportunities were solicited by the U.S. government on behalf of private business —then rigorously defended from native laws or decrees that might hamper its operations. Loans were made to governments in economic difficulties, with significant strings attached to them such as employing Americans as financial advisers or overseers of customhouses, and this too made for American trade and investment opportunities. Beyond this a large navy protected American spheres of influence—such as the Caribbean—and acted as a warning to other powers that might have ideas about penetrating these spheres. Only in extreme cases did the United States intervene militarily to enforce its will; usually financial pressure and the *threat* of force was sufficient.

☆☆☆☆☆

13

☆☆☆☆☆

THE BIG LEAP

If the world were limitless and the natives passive, the great powers might have expanded into new colonies and spheres of influence indefinitely, resolving all their differences at the diplomatic table—as they had done, for instance, vis-à-vis China or Africa. But the planet was finite, so that the ever-growing need for world markets caused frictions between the haves and the have-nots that became irrepressible. Britain, the leading have nation, with the strongest navy in the world, an empire on which the sun never set, and $20 billion in foreign investments—an enormous sum in pre-World War I days— retained its position by preventing the others from forming a solid block against her. She lived, so to speak, by maintaining a delicate and precarious balance of power among all her rivals.

Germany, the leading have-not, had begun its industrial and imperialist ascent only after defeating France in the 1870–71 war, and had acquired by 1900 a colonial empire of a million square miles and 15 million people, most of it in Africa. While this was substantial, it was meager compared to the 9.3 million square miles and 309 million people in the British empire, and 3.7 million square miles and 56 million inhabitants in the French empire. This disparity was particularly onerous, in the opinion of Germany's leaders, because their country had forged ahead by leaps and bounds, transforming itself from an agricultural nation into the world's second largest industrial producer in just a few decades. The population grew from 41 million in 1870 to 65 million before World War I; coal production, from 30 million tons to 191 million; and output of pig iron, from 529,000 tons to 15 million. Rich in coal and iron (and the phosphorus of Alsace-Lorraine, acquired from France in 1871), Germany had built an elaborate economic machine, preeminent in chemicals and strong in machine-building, precision instruments, and electrical equipment. As in the United States, its smaller corporations had coalesced under the aegis of the banks and financiers into giant cartels and monopolies. Such an economy inevitably produced surpluses of goods and capital that, under the capitalist system, desperately required foreign outlets.

The fact is that Britain was a power in limbo, marking time, while Germany was a rising star, rapidly achieving dominance over the European continent. Unlike the United States, which also belonged in those days to the have-not classification but threatened neither Britain's precious balance of power nor its Mediterranean-Suez-Indian Ocean lifeline, the Reich had an expansionist blueprint that directly challenged England. Under that plan she would help her ally, Austria-Hungary, consolidate a base in the Balkans, and on her own seek to penetrate into Turkey and the Near East, to the Persian Gulf and beyond. Pivotal to this scheme was the construction of a railroad linking the Bosporus to Baghdad. "The Near East," wrote A. Sprenger, "is the only region in the world not yet appropriated by a Great Power. . . . If Germany does not lose the opportunity . . . she will have acquired the best share in the partition of the world." Turkey in 1901 had granted the Society of Ottoman Railways in Anatolia—founded by two German banks twelve years earlier—a concession to extend its lines from Konia to Baghdad and the Persian Gulf. By building a tunnel under the Bosporus the Berlin-to-Baghdad planners envisioned a rail system that would eventually connect Europe, as far west as Antwerp, with Persia. This would divert large amounts of freight from British shipping companies, make possible development of the thinly populated Mesopotamia, and Asia Minor generally—under German tutelage—and, by running a line south, open the door to Africa. Along this route lay the oil riches of the Near East and the prospect of establishing a land empire that would rival the British and be able, under certain circumstances, to deny Britain access to her colonies.

Linked to Germany was Austria-Hungary, a conglomerate of uneasy minorities attached to Austria, seriously at odds with Russia over the Balkan Peninsula, and Italy, another have-not state, which would eventually desert the Central Powers. The opposing Entente included Britain, France, and Russia. After the Russian Revolution, when the Bolsheviks published many of the secret treaties among the Entente members, it became clear that the cement which held the Allies together was no great principle of civilization but the promise of territorial reward.

France was expecting the return of Alsace-Lorraine, a sphere of influence in the Saar, and a preferred status in the German Rhine, industrial heartland of the Reich. Russia would have its Constantinople; England the oil fields of Persia. The four allies (after Italy changed sides) were, in addition, to divide Asiatic Turkey among them. Italy was also to receive Trieste, parts of the Tyrol, and a few other tidbits. Most important of all, Britain and France were to hang on to their empires—and, as events turned out, to expand them. In this state of tension and expectation the great powers plunged into an arms race, which naturally aggravated the tensions and brought war closer. Germany's navy grew from 85 warships in 1880 to 324 in 1914; Britain's from 248 to 636. The six major powers of Europe, as war impended, had 3,771,000 men under arms and were spending what was then a very substantial sum of money, $1.25 billion, on their armies, and another billion on their navies.

It would be wrong to say, of course, that any of the big states *wanted* war; they would have preferred to achieve their political aspirations without it, and Britain in particular, as the country with the most to lose, tried with might and main to keep the precarious balance of power by a variety of methods. In August 1907 she courted Russia by carving Persia into three zones—the northern one designated as a Russian sphere, the southern one British, and the zone in between neutral. Japan was appeased with an alliance in 1902 that opened the door for her further exploitation of China, and the United States was placated by winking at the Roosevelt Corollary and intervention in Haiti, Nicaragua, the Dominican Republic, and Mexico. Britain also compromised with France vis-à-vis North Africa—with Britain supporting dubious claims of its ally to Morocco and France agreeing to British control of Egypt. For a while it even looked as if an accommodation might be reached with Germany. In 1913 Britain and the Reich came to an understanding that the Berlin-to-Baghdad railway would terminate at Bassora, the southern tip of Mesopotamia (Iraq) and that two British administrators were to be added to the German company's board of administration. In return a petroleum company to exploit Mesopotamia was to be established in which Britain held 75 percent of the shares and Germany 25 percent. France joined the mood of compromise by renouncing any part in the Baghdad rail company as a quid pro quo for control of Syria and for supremacy in a railroad that was to be built in the Black Sea area.

At a minute to midnight, on June 15, 1914, Britain and France tried more magic medicine on Germany, by proposing a secret pact in which all three would gorge themselves on the carcass of a decaying Ottoman empire. Turkey was to be divided so that Britain would receive lower Mesopotamia and Smyrna; France, southern Syria and northern Anatolia; and Germany, the rest of Anatolia, Syria, and Mesopotamia. It was a case, however, of too late and too little. War had been narrowly averted when Austria annexed Bosnia in 1908, and as a result of the Balkan Wars of 1912. By early 1914 many in Germany were preaching, in the words of General Helmuth von Moltke, that "if we delay any longer the chances of success will be diminished." The assassination of Austrian Archduke Franz Ferdinand and his wife in Sarajevo, Bosnia, on June 28, 1914, finally tilted the scale. Obviously it was not the cause of the war, only the last straw or pretext. As Wilson commented to Ambassador Walter Hines Page some time later, it was a case "of England's having the earth and Germany's wanting it."

II

The war in Europe was to result in a quantum jump in America's imperial fortunes, a vast increase in its foreign investments and trade, a mammoth extension of its sphere of influence, and as Frank A. Vanderlip of the National City Bank predicted, "a million new springs of wealth." But its initial effect was a bedlam of confusion, with few people in high places or low aware of its long-term implications. The cataclysm was obviously a surprise to William Jennings Bryan. As late as 1913 he had confidently asserted that "there will be no war while I am Secretary of State, and I believe there will be no war as long as I live." Perhaps he felt that his thirty treaties of conciliation were an effective dike against actual hostilities. Americans, as a whole, though divided in their sympathies, were thankful in August 1914 that they were not directly involved. The *Literary Digest* accurately reflected national sentiment when it wrote: "Our isolated position and freedom from entangling alliances inspire our press with the cheering assurance that we are in no peril of being drawn into the European quarrel." And the Chicago *Herald* tendered "a hearty vote of thanks to Columbus for having discovered America." This did not imply that Americans had no sympathies for the contending sides. There were 92 million people in the country at the time, of whom 13 million were born overseas and 19 million more had one or two parents of foreign stock. Of these 32 million, approximately half were German, Austro-Hungarian, or Irish, mostly ill disposed to the Allies and favorable to the Central Powers. On the other hand, a considerable majority of the population, native and foreign both, identified with Britain and France, especially after the invasion of Belgium by German forces. Yet almost no one wanted the United States to join the fray, and whatever their individual sympathies most people felt that Wilson had struck the right note by urging them "to be impartial in thought as well as in action."

The business community also showed little enthusiasm for the war overseas. The war caught the United States in a depression rivaling the one of 1907 and already a year old. Moreover, any expectation that lush orders from Europe would come pouring in at once to give the economy a needed prod proved optimistic. On the contrary, the instability of Europe seeped through to the United States. The London Stock Exchange, concerned because panic-stricken Europeans were selling off their securities—including American stocks and bonds—to lay their hands on cash, closed its doors on July 31. The New York Stock Exchange followed suit and did not reopen for trading until December 12—and then on a limited basis until the following April. U.S. citizens withdrew so much money from the banks—to hoard in mattresses and strongboxes—that $68 million in new currency had to be printed.

Nor were things any better on the industrial front. The New York *Evening Post* expressed grave doubts at the end of 1914 that American manufacture "could continue even the present activity." Steel production was already down to 50 percent of capacity. As late as May 1915 the New York Chamber of Commerce ruminated dolorously that "the hopes early entertained by American steel manufacturers that they would profit by the conflict through an expansion of exports, were ill-founded." The same could be said of the copper, cotton, meat, chemical, and other branches of enterprise. "Deadening paralysis . . . has settled over many of the country's industries," wrote the New York *Financial Chronicle*.

To make matters worse, American shipping again was forced to operate against a blockade. On August 20, 1914, the British cabinet decided that it would not respect the Declaration of London of 1909, which formulated rules for neutral trading with belligerents during wartime. Under those rules American ships were entitled to dock both at German ports and at neutral ports such as Rotterdam and Genoa to unload cargoes. But the British insisted on searching neutral vessels—including those of the most powerful neutral, the United States—in Allied ports, and preventing them from delivering anything that could be considered helpful to the German war effort. That included foodstuffs, copper, oil, rubber, and various other commodities. The situation deteriorated further when the North Sea was mined by the British in November 1914, and four months later neutrals were forbidden by Britain to engage in any kind of maritime commerce with Germany, whether contraband war matériel or not. To enforce this edict, merchantmen were intercepted on the high seas and brought to Allied ports for minute scrutiny. Thus U.S. foreign trade with the Central Powers, instead of accelerating, slumped from $169 million in 1914 (mostly before war was declared) to $12 million the following year and only $1 million in 1916. The State Department protested repeatedly to the Foreign Office in London about the blockade, but was just as repeatedly rebuffed. These were "exceptional" times, said the British; they had to take drastic measures to deprive the enemy of the matériel of war.

Despite tribulations and obstacles, however, the economic slumber of the United States ended in a flurry of new business from Europe. When Turkey entered the war on the German side in October 1914, it completed the ring around Russia, cutting off Central and Western Europe from a regular supply of 150 million bushels of wheat a year. To fill the gap the Allied powers turned inevitably to the United States, and with demand so much larger than supply the price of wheat in Chicago jumped from 85¢ a bushel in August 1914 to $1.67 in February 1915. Exports of the golden cereal for the fiscal year ending in June were more than a quarter of a billion bushels, as against 92 million in each of the preceding years.

If trade with the Central Powers were reduced to insignificance by the British navy, the booming business with the Allies more than made up for it—and this despite the submarine warfare launched by Germany against enemy ships in February 1915. The United States became the Allied source for food, for raw materials such as copper, iron ore, zinc, cotton, lumber, wool, oil, as well as munitions. From 1914 to 1917 the value of steel exported quadrupled from $.25 billion to $1.1 billion; the value of chemicals, dyes, and drugs rose from $22 million to $181 million. Exports of munitions increased astronomically—from a mere $6 million a year in 1914 to $1.7 billion between January 1916 and March 1917. The firm of E. I. du Pont de Nemours alone supplied the Allies with two fifths of their ammunition during the war and the company's stock rose from $20 a share in 1914 to $1,000 in 1918 when the armistice was signed. The Nye Committee of the U.S. Senate reported in 1934 that du Pont had paid regular and extra dividends between 1915 and 1918 of 458 percent of the par value of its stock.

Never in its history had the United States witnessed such an expansion of its industry, trade, and agriculture. The only limit on exports seemed to be the amount of shipping available. This was remedied by a law of 1914 that permitted 175 foreign vessels to register under the American flag, and the Shipping Act of 1916, which authorized a Shipping Board to buy or build all the vessels needed. For the fiscal year ending June 30, 1914, American exports had exceeded imports by $436 million; three years later the figure was eight times higher, almost $3.6 billion. The boom was so great that while inflation reduced real wages of American workingmen by 7 percent from 1913 to 1918, there were 21,000 new millionaires in the country at the time of the armistice. Even more important were four corollary developments that permanently altered both the economic and imperial status of the United States:

(1) An enormous expansion of domestic industrial facilities.

(2) The liquidation of billions of dollars of foreign holdings in the United States and conversion of the nation from a debtor to a credi- tor.

(3) The emergence of New York on a par with London as the world's leading banking center.

(4) The take-over of British, German, and other investments in South America, to make the United States finally the unchallenged monarch of the western hemisphere.

III

It is impossible to understand this grandiose transformation or the reason why the United States finally entered the war itself in April 1917 without underscoring the role of the banking house of J. P. Morgan & Co. The Morgans, father, son, and partners, were not merely individuals but part of a dynasty; not merely bankers but the epicenter of American capitalism. "Great is Mr. Morgan's power," said a British writer, Maurice Low, in October 1902, "greater in some respects even than that of Presidents and kings." The elder Morgan, referred to by Low, was certainly wooed by many presidents and kings. When Edward VII received him at Windsor Castle, court jesters wondered out loud whether the financier would "take a fancy to Windsor and buy it." When Kaiser Wilhelm dined aboard the Morgan yacht, *Corvair*, he awarded its aristocratic owner the Order of the Red Eagle. A cynical archbishop called the banker "Pierpontifex Maximus."

As great as was the power of the Morgans, however, the war made it far more imposing. The House of Morgan was outspokenly pro-Allies at a time when Wilson was disguising his bias and talking about being neutral in thought as well as in action. Behind closed doors in September 1914, Wilson told the British ambassador that a German victory would force the United States to "give up its present ideals and devote all its energies to defense, which would mean the end of its present system of government." He confided to his secretary, Joseph P. Tumulty, that "England is fighting our fight" and he would do nothing to embarrass her.

Such back-door circumspection was eschewed by the House of Morgan; it made no effort to hide its unneutrality. To be sure, it did not want the United States to become an active belligerent—until its own investments fell into jeopardy in 1916–17—but as the purchasing agent and banker for the Allies it prepared the ground for American entry as surely as if it had fired the first shot. Washington had a choice early in the fray, either of declaring an embargo against trade with Europe, convoying ships through the British blockade with men-of-war, or actively fostering commerce with the Entente at the risk of war with the Central Powers. The first alternative would have meant reduced profits; the second would have led to a clash with Britain, but since the U.S. navy was quite formidable, might either have forced John Bull to retreat or might have plummeted Uncle Sam into the maelstrom; the third—the actual course —was a bonanza, though it also drew Washington into the war. Years later, in May 1935, Admiral William S. Sims correctly summarized the advantages and disadvantages of each alternative: "We cannot," he said, "keep out of a war and at the same time enforce the freedom of the seas. . . . If a war arises, we must therefore choose between two courses: between great profits, with grave risks of war, on the one hand; or smaller profits and less risk, on the other. . . . It is a choice of profits or peace."

The House of Morgan chose profits at the risk of war and in the end made the risk so great that Wilson, despite certain inner doubts, took the final plunge into the European cataclysm. The Morgans did not do it alone, of course—nothing in a complex modern society is ever that simple—but the Wall Street titans who reflected the growth of economic oligarchy were the pivotal force in these developments nonetheless.

The history of the Morgan-Pierpont family is in a sense a microcosm of the nation's own saga. Its roots lay in the same radical-conservative dichotomy which was manifested in the philosophical conflict between Jefferson and Hamilton, the one seeking a measure of egalitarianism, the other a society of, by, and for "the rich and well-born." On the maternal side John Pierpont, born in 1785, was a flaming rebel who took his inspiration from Samuel Adams, the leader of the American Revolution. A teacher, tutor, lawyer, and merchant before being ordained a minister in 1819, he was a leader of the Unitarian Church in Boston and a man of many causes. He fought against imprisonment for debt, one of the social crimes which resulted in 75,000 jailings a year in the United States, and espoused temperance (not prohibition) as a means of alleviating the plight of the workingman. Most of all, he was an unflinching abolitionist, an associate of the radical William Lloyd Garrison and a contributor to his journal, the *Liberator*. When the Fugitive Slave Law was passed, Pierpont denounced it as "a covenant with Judas," and when someone suggested that the law, despite that, was "constitutional," the minister shot back: "What if it is? If the Constitution justifies wrong, I am bound to transgress the Constitution." He helped organize the Liberty Party, which campaigned against slavery, and was its candidate for governor of Massachusetts. At the age of seventy-six he enlisted as a chaplain in the Union army during the Civil War, and four years later on his eightieth birthday was toasted by Garrison as a man "distinguished for independence of thought, boldness of speech, fearlessness of investigation, and an untiring interest in the cause of progress and reform on the broadest scale."

On the paternal side the acquisitive strain in the Morgan family was evident from the outset. When Miles Morgan arrived in Boston in 1636, he joined Colonel William Pynchon to create a new settlement at Springfield on land they bought from the Indians for £30. In executing this "business stroke," Miles hid the fact that he was still a minor, under twenty-one. Later Captain Miles Morgan fought in King Philip's War against the Indians and received as a reward a large tract of additional land. The Morgans, clearly, were never poor, nor did they ever identify with the "injured and oppressed." The elder J. Pierpont Morgan's great-grandfather was a captain in the Continental army during the Revolution, who retired to the ancestral farm after hostilities. His son, Joseph Morgan, born in 1780, shifted from farming, which was becoming unprofitable, to innkeeping and operating a stagecoach. It was at Joseph Morgan's Inn at Hartford that a group of businessmen formed the Aetna Fire Insurance Company in the depression year of 1819, and when its fortunes lapsed Joseph Morgan bought up a large block of shares at a negligible sum to become a major stockholder in a company that soon was capitalized at $3 million. From here he branched out into stage lines and transport. In a couple of generations, then, the Morgan fortune made the transition from agriculture to business. Joseph's son, Junius Spencer Morgan, born in 1809, took a few steps further, into merchandising and banking. A bank clerk at sixteen, he used his father's money to form the New York banking house of Ketchum, Morgan & Co. by the time he was twenty-one. When he dissolved this firm—because his partner had engaged in shady operations—

Junius went into the dry-goods business, and like many merchants of the day, engaged in banking and insurance as lucrative sidelines. Having prospered as a merchant, Junius in 1853 became a partner of George Peabody, an American investment banker in London, and when Peabody retired ten years later, changed the name of the company to J. S. Morgan & Co., the lineal beginning of the House of Morgan. Junius, by all accounts, was a man of high integrity in business relationships, but grim, acquisitive, dignified, pompous, and as conservative as his father-in-law was radical. His aristocratic mien and his contempt for democracy were to become family hallmarks, equally apparent in his son and grandson.

The next and most important figure in this genealogical saga was the first John Pierpont Morgan, the eldest of five children born to Junius Morgan and the daughter of that fiery clergyman reformer, Julia Pierpont. Long afterward the myth was cultivated that J. P. Morgan was a self-made man, a rags-to-riches success story; but in fact he was one of the few buccaneers after the Civil War whose fortune was rooted in hereditary wealth. He had to be prodded by a domineering father to make his start. Large, heavily built, with an oval face and prominent nose, he suffered from lung trouble as a youngster and had to be attended by a physician for a number of years. Until the age of twelve he lived in Hartford, went to high school in Boston, and, still sickly after graduation, was sent to the Azores for his health. Later he made a tour of Europe and wound up at the University of Göttingen for two years. As in high school he was reserved, hostile to others, plodding but not exceptional, except —interestingly—in mathematics. He seemed to have no drive or desire to work, and was a source of constant worry to his father. He must have had a deep romantic reservoir behind his gruff exterior, for at the age of twenty-two he fell in love in Paris with a consumptive young woman, near death, and literally begged her to marry him after she had turned him down. She finally consented but died three months later. This seemed to be J.P.'s last obeisance to romance, for thereafter he "straightened out" and pursued nothing more fiercely than economic power. As biographer Lewis Corey observes, "Morgan overwhelmed his sentimental, almost romantic quality in the masculinity of the strong, silent man wrapt in the ecstasy of business. . . . Power was to be his ideal, its pursuit his romance, love becoming the conquest of women as an appanage of power."

Junius Morgan was elated. The young man, who had lackadaisically gathered some experience in his father's firm as well as independently, was now ready for his destiny. During the Civil War J.P.

distinguished himself by avoiding the army—anyone with $300 those days could hire a substitute to fight for him—and by a small scandal in which he and an associate purchased 5,000 defective carbines from the government at $3.50 apiece and resold them to General J. C. Frémont and the same government at $22 apiece. The guns, Lewis Corey points out in his history of the House of Morgan, were so faulty they "were more dangerous to the Union troops than to the Confederates." J.P. also made a small killing of $160,000, together with Edward Ketchum, by speculating in gold—the type of act which the New York *Times* branded as "unprincipled" and "unscrupulous" and for which the Union League demanded that "Congress at once order the erection of scaffolds for hanging" speculators like Morgan, Ketchum, and others.

By and large, however, the Morgans did not engage in the mammoth corruption, bribery, and swindling that punctuated this era of the robber barons. When they did it was exceptional, such as in the contest with Jay Gould and Jim Fisk for control of the Albany & Susquehanna Railroad, in which each side prevailed on judges they "owned" to issue injunctions (twenty-two in all) against the other, and each used private armies to fight for physical possession of the property. But the Morgans essentially were organizers on a higher level, the men who funneled capital into the right places and made big corporations out of little ones through consolidation. Since they operated investment houses in London and Paris, and, after 1871, when J.P. made an alliance with Drexel & Co., in Philadelphia as well as New York, they were in a unique position to provide foreign capital to finance American business. American corporations that came to the House of Morgan for help were assured a powerful syndicate in Europe to float their securities. At a time when a large part of the economic expansion could not take place without foreign money, this was no small asset.

Until 1879 the House of Morgan, increasingly under the thumb of the truculent son, did a varied but traditional business. It sold corporate stocks and bonds at a commission, handled foreign exchange, and engaged in government financing. All this continued into the 1880's but by the end of the decade, just before old Junius died, J.P. added a new feature to the business which the newspapers called "Morganization." Hitherto the investment bankers had simply acted as middlemen between investors and corporations, without trying to assert any power over the businesses for whom they collected capital. Under Morganization, however, the great financial house gained dominance over the companies that came to it for succor. In return for assuring capital, J.P.'s firm demanded and received places on the board of directors and wound up finally as master of many corporations. It did not build railroads, for instance, as did the leading financier of the day, Jay Cooke, but it used its control of money as a means of securing sway over companies that did build railroads. So successful was this technique that in 1889 Morgan could call together a number of railroad presidents and tell them, more or less in the form of an ultimatum, how they should operate. By 1902, according to financial expert John Moody, Morgan was "identified with" 55,000 miles of railroads, including "rights of way, coal lands, terminals, competing lines, steamship connections and the like." In the marriage of finance and industry the investment banker became the boss, and no one more so than John Pierpont Morgan. After the panic of 1873, when Jay Cooke went bankrupt, J. P. Morgan became the nation's top banker. With the vast sums at his command he was able to enlarge his railroad holdings, then move into other areas. In 1892 he helped organize the General Electric Co. A decade later he effectuated the merger of a number of firms into the International Mercantile Marine Co., which sought to control Atlantic shipping, and of a group of farm equipment companies into the International Harvester Co. The crowning achievement of Morganization was the formation in 1901 of the United States Steel Corporation, the first billion-dollar corporation in the nation's history. Using three companies that he himself controlled as a base, Morgan paid Andrew Carnegie $447 million for a steel company he had been ready to sell for $147 million, and bought out the holdings of the Rockefellers and the Moores (William H. and James H.) to merge them into the mammoth steel trust. If Carnegie's price seems like a vast overcharge, no tears need be shed for either Morgan or U.S. Steel, for in the single year of 1916 its profits were $272 million, and almost a half billion for 1915–17, earned, according to the liberal writer Amos Pinchot, through "cold-blooded extortion in the sale of war supplies to the French and English governments for which J. P. Morgan and Company was the fiscal agent." In any event the House of Morgan, with its great network of Morganized banks and life insurance companies, was perhaps the only capitalist force in the country at the time capable of forming the steel trust.

When the Pujo Committee of the House of Representatives reviewed the power of the Morgan clan in 1912 it found that it held sway over twelve big banks; three insurance firms; eleven major railroads plus the Pullman Company; Adams Express; at least five industrial goliaths, including United States Steel, General Electric, American Telephone & Telegraph, International Harvester, and Western Union; a host of public utilities; and two corporations in

Latin America. The assets of this empire—$10.3 billion—were perhaps small by today's standards, but at a time when the federal government itself took in only $700 million a year they were formidable indeed—so formidable, in fact, that on more than one occasion the regime in Washington had to come to Morgan to be saved from a crisis. On the heels of the 1893 depression, for instance, President Cleveland was forced to negotiate with J. P. Morgan and a group of bankers to buy 3.5 million ounces of gold, when the government's own reserves had dwindled to $41 million. During the crisis of 1907 the Secretary of the Treasury deposited $42 million with the House of Morgan, interest-free, which in turn dispensed it and other sums to banks and corporations to keep them afloat. Sitting in a room adjoining his library, playing solitaire and smoking his inveterate black cigar, the aging majordomo of American finance issued crisp orders and doled out money to the lesser titans he wanted to save. Firms that could not weather the storm such as the Tennessee Coal & Iron Co. were forced by Morgan—with the approval of President Roosevelt—to sell out to U.S. Steel or some other Morgan subsidiary.

Thomas Jefferson, grandpa John Pierpont's hero, had once expressed the hope that America would remain a democratic nation based on small, private entrepreneurs. But for Pierpont's grandson, J. P. Morgan, the byword was centralization of power and money—and devil take those smaller capitalists who could not keep pace. A depression might wipe out the small fry of industry and investment, but for the House of Morgan it was a "readjustment" in which the big fish absorbed the little fish, to become fatter and more arrogant. If this adversely affected society as a whole it was too bad. "I owe the public nothing," said J. P. Morgan. "Men owning property should do what they like with it." This was a counterpart in domestic philosophy to the term used by Woodrow Wilson about "outraging the sovereignty" of foreign nations, and it was no accident therefore that men who paid little heed to public needs at home should be equally unconcerned with the results of their business ventures on peoples abroad.

After the secession of Panama from Colombia, the House of Morgan became the new republic's fiscal agent for the $10 million received from the U.S. government, as well as the fiscal agent for the Panama Canal Co. of France which was paid $40 million for its "assets" and "rights." The Republic of Panama received $4 million outright, but the rest was invested by Morgan in real estate mortgages in New York. The monies accruing to the French company were shrouded in even greater mystery, causing the New York *World* and

the Indianapolis *News* to demand, "Who got the money?" President
Roosevelt was so angered by these charges that he ordered two suits
for criminal libel against the newspapers—in defense of himself,
Morgan, William Nelson Cromwell (of Panama Canal fame), and
three others. The Supreme Court, however, unanimously ruled
against the President, and the question of who got the money was
left unanswered. Just how much Morgan skimmed off from these international transactions is unknown, but step by step the great financial institution began to penetrate outward, using American
money to enter foreign markets. The Morgans participated in floating $130 million in loans to Japan during its war with Russia;
gained control of the American China Development Co. in 1905 (on
which it earned, with President Roosevelt's help, a 100 percent
profit within a short time); invested in railroads in Panama and Bolivia; made a $10 million loan to Argentina; another $10 million to
Honduras (secured by control of its customs by a Morgan agent);
and loans to Haiti and Nicaragua with similar conditions attached.

This massive, integrated financial and industrial empire had
reached a peak of sorts when J. P. Morgan, on a trip to Europe,
passed away in Rome on March 31, 1913. "There will be no successor to Morgan," wrote the *Wall Street Journal* the next day, and the
New York *Times* echoed that "he was the last of his line." The day
Morgan was buried in his native Hartford the choir sang "Asleep
in Jesus," businesses shut their doors in memoriam, and the stock
exchanges of New York and Chicago closed down as well. Pope
Pius X called him "a great and good man," but the laudation testified
more to the ascendancy of finance capital, which Morgan embodied,
than to his personal character. That ascendancy continued and enlarged after his death, for it was not merely Morgan the man but the
Morgan system that captured the American economy. Whether
J. Pierpont Morgan, Jr., who took his father's place as the head of the
House of Morgan, was of equal mettle was irrelevant; the Morgan
system was bigger than any one man.

J. P. Morgan, Jr. looked very much like his father, except that his
eyes did not betray the same fierceness and there were no blemishes
on his face. Born in Irvington, New York, two years after the end of
the Civil War, he went to the usual schools, including Harvard, and
proceeded in his father's footsteps including an eight-year stint with
the London house of J. S. Morgan and Company. His philosophy,
too, paralleled that of his illustrious parent. Asked by the Industrial
Relations Commission in 1915, for instance, whether ten dollars a
week was a fair wage for a worker, he replied: "If that's all he can
get and takes it, I should say that is enough." He did not know, he

told the commission, the number of workers in the corporations in which he was a director—"I have not an idea"—all he knew was the financial details, such as the fact that Pullman Company investors had received regular and special dividends of $398 million on a $33 million investment. He had no views as to either child labor or the workday for children. Like his father he was arrogant, unconcerned with public opinion, appropriately domineering, and seldom gave interviews or made speeches. He denied that his loans to the Allies had anything to do with America's entry into the war, attributing it all to German submarine outrages. But his role was not quite so innocent, for it prodded the United States to take one side against the other, and it propelled her on an irreversible course.

IV

Early in August 1914 the French government approached Morgan, Harjes and Company, the House of Morgan affiliate in Paris, with a request for a $100 million loan. The Morgans were ready to oblige, but they would not do so unless the State Department in Washington approved. Secretary Bryan, in a prophetic letter to President Wilson, pointed out that "money is the worst of all contrabands because it commands everything else." If such loans were authorized, he pointed out, the American citizenry would be divided into groups, "each group loaning money to the country which it favors and this money could not be furnished without expressions of sympathy." The newspapers, pressed by "powerful financial interests," would become aligned to one side or the other, and neutrality would become a fiction. Wilson accepted Bryan's analysis and the Secretary advised the House of Morgan that while a private loan to France—or any of the belligerents—was legal, it was not in accord with the spirit of neutrality. For the time being the great banking firm accepted the restrictions. Within two months, however, under the back-door pressure of the Rockefeller-controlled National City Bank and J. P. Morgan & Co., one of Bryan's subordinates, Robert Lansing, took the issue to Wilson again and convinced him that the policy should be reversed. By referring to the loans as "credits" to finance foreign trade, Wilson absolved his conscience of the charge of unneutrality—but as J. P. Morgan himself observed there was no difference between a loan and a credit. The President requested the bankers not to ask for formal permission from the government, lest this be a source of embarrassment. In fact, until March 1915 the State Department denied that there was any "change of policy in regard to loans to belligerents."

The change, however, was already being implemented with the savage vigor typical of the Morgans and their allies. In January 1915, at the suggestion of a Morgan official, Henry P. Davison, Great Britain designated J. P. Morgan & Co. as its exclusive purchasing agent in the United States. Members of the House of Commons criticized the arrangement as a boon to Morgan's satellite companies—such as du Pont, U.S. Steel, Bethlehem—and an impediment to free competition. But the arrangement stood, as did one with France made subsequently, and by September 1917 the House of Morgan had spent $3 billion of Allied money buying munitions, ships, and other commodities to feed into the British and French war machines. Though the commission for the banking firm was only 1 percent—$30 million—the benefits to the Morgan empire were so immense they promoted the greatest industrial boom the nation had had until that time. So rich were the pickings that du Pont, the munitions supplier, paid a 100 percent dividend for 1916, and Bethlehem Steel a 200 percent dividend in 1917. In 1916, U.S. Steel earned $70 million more than in the three prewar years combined. According to the Federal Trade Commission, such colossal profits reflected an "inordinate greed and barefaced fraud." Many of the corporations, it added, had juggled accounts to indicate a fictitiously greater cost, had padded depreciation allowances, had placed fraudulent values on raw materials, and had engaged in other methods to hide profits considerably greater than those reported. Be that as it may, by tying the American economic kite to the Allied cause, the Morgans helped the basic industries related to war make a quantum jump in profits, size, and power.

Allied purchases in the United States, of course, had to be paid for. Ordinarily England and France would pay for them by their own exports, by shipping charges, and by earnings from capital in America. But in wartime, export industries and surplus capital had to be diverted to military production. The only way to meet obligations therefore was to borrow money, ship sorely needed gold, and sell off foreign stocks and bonds. All of this naturally would weaken the imperial position of the Western European powers—and concomitantly strengthen that of the United States. Whether J. P. Morgan understood this in advance is difficult to tell. Even so sharp a critic as the left-wing socialist Louis C. Fraina was of the opinion that in 1915 the bankers and industrialists were just thinking of making money "hand over fist"—what many people called "blood money." It was only in 1916 that they began to realize, wrote Fraina, that there was an opportunity for achieving "economic and financial supremacy in the world." Hitherto imperialism "was in a

form weak, parochial, without a world-vision" but it was now becoming conscious of a much wider purpose than domination of the
Caribbean or a few bases in the Pacific.

The process was inexorable. The Allies needed credits; the Morgans and their associates in the banking community provided some
$2.5 billion, including one single loan in October 1915 of $500 million. Some of the loans were unsecured; others required collateral.
In July 1915 the Bank of England began to buy American securities
in London, to sell them in New York. Six months later, British insurance and trust firms were requested to submit a list of their holdings
of foreign stocks and bonds and an American Dollar Securities Commission was appointed to buy 909 of these securities, and either
offer them as a collateral or turn them into cash on the American
market. By the end of the war the British stockpile of foreign securities had declined from $3.7 billion to $1.1 billion, the largest liquidation being some $2 billion in railroad stocks. The French also
were forced to give up 70 percent of their holdings in a similar fashion. For all countries combined, ownership of American securities
fell from $5.4 billion in the summer of 1914 to $1.6 billion in 1919.
In addition to converting American stocks and bonds, the Allies also
shipped $907 million in gold to the United States by the beginning
of 1917. From every angle the war became a bonanza for the Morgans and the American establishment. Instead of being in debt to
the rest of the world they found themselves with a healthy surplus
of capital, ready to export to faraway places. And since the British
had suspended gold payments and embargoed loans "for undertak-
ings outside the Empire," Wall Street was now the banking center of
the world.

This concentration of good fortune made it possible for the American colossus to extend its penetration into the underdeveloped
world, especially South America. With Britain and Germany at war,
some of their stock in South American railroads and utilities found
their way into the vaults of downtown Manhattan. Simultaneously,
to finance expanded North American business, the National City
Bank established its first South American affiliate in Buenos Aires in
1914, and other branches of American banks were not slow to follow. A dozen investors, including J. P. Morgan, formed a holding
company—the American International Corporation—to construct
docks, warehouses, and utilities in South America. Two oil concessions owned by Colombian natives were taken over by Standard Oil
of New Jersey and an affiliate of the Mellon-controlled Gulf Oil
when the concessionaires found themselves unable to supply the
capital for exploitation. For the first time American trade outpaced

that of Britain below the Rio Grande. Thus the economic alliance between the American business community and Britain and France had the strange effect of helping the Allies wage their war while undermining, to no small extent, their economic power.

V

Thomas W. Lamont, a Morgan partner, boasted in 1920 that "our firm had never for one moment been neutral; we didn't know how to be." The implication is that the bankers joined the Allied bandwagon quickly out of purely altruistic motives. But in fact there was a recognition in many high places, not excluding Wall Street, that American imperial interests lay in a German defeat. Most of Wilson's advisers believed that there was no danger if Britain won, for it was unthinkable that Britain would invade the western hemisphere or attempt to choke off U.S. expansion. Moreover in an alliance between the British empire and America, said the U.S. ambassador to London, Walter Hines Page, "anything we'd say would go." It would be a partnership in which Uncle Sam would play the unaccustomed role of first fiddle in the orchestra. On the other hand, if British sea power were destroyed and Germany were to achieve hegemony over the European continent, the Reich, said Page, would try to conquer the United States, the Monroe Doctrine "would at once be shot in two, and we should have to get 'out of the sun.'" After a talk with the Kaiser in October 1915, Ambassador James W. Gerard in Berlin cabled the State Department that "if these people win we are next on the list—in some part of South or Central America which is the same thing." In other words, the United States itself might not be attacked but its sphere of influence would be placed under dangerous siege. A half year later Gerard reported that "military and naval people [in Germany] all hope for revenge . . . when they can better arrange their hoped-for revolt in our country and incite the Mexicans and others against us." Colonel House, Wilson's closest confidant, shared the views of Page and Gerard. If the Reich were to win, he wrote in his diary in October 1915, "our turn would come next. . . ."

Such estimates were disputed by antiwar leaders. During a congressional debate in mid-1916, Senator Robert M. La Follette of Wisconsin quoted leading generals and admirals who disagreed with "lurid" suggestions that the United States itself was in danger of invasion. General Erasmus M. Weaver, chief of Coast Artillery and a member of the joint Army and Navy Board, had testified that with the addition of a mere 11,000 troops the American coasts could be made impregnable to attack from anyone—including Britain. General Nelson A. Miles, former commander in chief of the army, and Admiral Frank F. Fletcher, chief of the Atlantic Fleet, had concluded, on evidence from the experience of Alexandria, Port Arthur, and the Dardanelles, that coastal fortifications could easily hold their own against an attack by sea. Moreover the United States was presumably building the strongest navy in the world, adding a second dimension of defense to make America impregnable. According to La Follette, all the panic-mongering was being promoted by du Pont and Bethlehem Steel to immerse the nation in an arms program and a "profiteers' war." Indeed the House of Morgan was accused on the floor of Congress of having welded together a propaganda machine that included 12 publishers and 197 newspapers to "persuade" the American people to join the Allies. But the claims of La Follette and similar men that the nation was safe from invasion were beside the point insofar as the Morgans and the Wilson advisers were concerned. While Teddy Roosevelt was talking of a Pax Anglo-Americana to rule the world, Ambassador Page was speaking about doing "for Europe on a large scale essentially what we did for Cuba on a small scale. . . ." Whether he would impose a Platt Amendment on Europe he did not say, but it is clear that both in the banking community and in the administration the "threat" of Germany was not to the U.S. frontiers but to U.S. designs for empire.

It cannot be proven that Wilson or the House of Morgan wanted to embroil the United States in war from the very outset. But the idea that the United States might join the Allies occurred to many key figures quite early in the war. Secretary of State Robert Lansing, who replaced Bryan in mid-1915, recorded in his diary that eventually the United States would have to enter on the Allied side, and Colonel House, in October 1915, proposed to Wilson that "we should do something decisive now—something that would either end the war in a way to abolish militarism or that would bring us with the Allies to help them do it." As for the Morgans, a French historian, Gabriel Hanotaux, claims that as early as 1914 he and a member of the firm elaborated plans for a war-scare program designed to bring the United States into the conflict. Whether such views and incidents were simply the expression of soul-searching within the American establishment or indicated a tacit decision is beside the point, for the economic alliance with the Allies required a vast propaganda campaign on their behalf, a double standard in diplomacy, a military-preparedness program "just in case," and finally intervention itself.

It is a fundamental principle of democracy that the people must have access to information in order to make intelligent judgments. But the organized distortion of truth in 1914–17 made a shambles of that right. On August 5, 1914, the British cut the international cables linking Germany and the United States, thus eliminating quick communication between those countries and giving censored and colored British "news" the edge in forming American opinion. In addition the British established a War Propaganda Bureau at Wellington House to prepare books and pamphlets for American eyes, to send prominent speakers to the United States to promote the British cause, and to take whatever other measures were needed to convince the American people that Germany was an aggressor guilty of innumerable atrocities, that the Kaiser was the "Beast of Berlin," and that the Germans were losing. Some 260,000 influential citizens, not to mention newspapers, YMCA's, libraries, universities, and clubs, received maps, pictures, diagrams, posters, cartoons, and what have you promoting the Allied side. Scores of prominent lecturers, including Joseph Conrad and Rudyard Kipling, toured the United States for the same purpose. Friendly American correspondents were taken on a trip to the front in order to give the British side of the story. These efforts were supplemented by those of organizations such as the Navy League, whose members included J. P. Morgan, Thomas W. Lamont (a senior Morgan partner), Elbert H. Gary of U.S. Steel, and representatives of a host of Morgan and Rockefeller banks and industries. "What a band of patriots," commented Senator La Follette, "with their business connections owning every financial and industrial center of the United States. Owning newspapers, periodicals, and magazines, and controlling through business relations the editorial good will of many others. . . ." There were also the National Security League, the American Defense Society, and many others. A Morgan partner, Robert Bacon, told Gabriel Hanotaux in 1914 that "in America . . . there are 50,000 people who understand the necessity of the United States entering the war immediately on your side. But there are 100,000,000 Americans who have not even thought of it. Our task is to see that the figures are reversed and that the 50,000 become the 100,000,000." To reverse it, it was necessary to float all kinds of fanciful tales, some of them outright falsehoods —as later admitted by the propagandists themselves—and most of them grossly exaggerated or perverted.

Thus the pro-Allies media—by far the majority—highlighted the invasion of neutral Belgium by the Germans as a dastardly violation of treaties, but underplayed the statement by the King of Greece that Britain and France had occupied a host of similarly neutral

Greek territories. The Allies, said the King, "plead military necessity. It was under constraint of military necessity that Germany invaded Belgium and occupied Luxemburg." The King could not see any difference, but Wellington House and the American press somehow did.

The same was true of freedom of the seas, which neither side respected but which Britain was the first to ignore. Britain enforced a blockade against the Central Powers which included seizure of neutral ships on the high seas that were forced to sail for British ports to be inspected. Germany, unable to challenge the English navy openly, retaliated in February 1915 with a U-boat campaign in the waters around the British Isles, which she designated a war zone. From 1915 to the time the United States entered the war, only one American ship, a tanker called *Gulflight*, suffered any deaths as a result of a German attack, but about 200 Americans lost their lives while traveling on British and Allied ships. In the worst such incident, a British passenger liner, the *Lusitania*, was sunk without warning on May 7, 1915, nine miles from the Irish coast. Of the 1,198 persons who lost their lives, 128 were American, and this caused a tempest in the pro-Allies American press which obscured two simple but basic factors. First, the *Lusitania* was carrying 4,200 cases of rifle cartridges, which were quite clearly contraband of war. Even so fervid an Anglophile as General Leonard Wood commented caustically that "you cannot cover 10,000 tons of ammunition with a petticoat." Secretary of State Bryan, who resigned over Wilson's tough protests to Germany on the *Lusitania* issue, insisted that by all standards of neutrality "Germany has a right to prevent contraband from going to the Allies, and a ship carrying contraband should not rely upon passengers to protect her from attack. . . ." The second was that Americans who traveled on belligerent ships in wartime must have known they were taking a risk, especially since the German ambassador had inserted an ad in New York newspapers warning that such ships "are liable to destruction in those waters. . . ." Even Ambassador Gerard in Berlin was unsympathetic to those who crossed the ocean on British ships to "have a private bathroom." Nonetheless the *Lusitania* sinking was a bonanza for British propaganda, for if neither side respected neutral rights, the British at least had not killed anyone. They spread the word around that there had been two or more torpedoes—against a helpless unarmed ship—where in fact the second explosion was probably the result of munitions aboard the vessel blowing up. They charged, falsely, that the German submarine crew was being awarded medals for their deed, and they left the impression the victims were primarily Americans, when they actually represented only about 10 percent of the casualties.

Five days after the *Lusitania* went down, the British issued the Bryce atrocity report about German inhumanities in Belgium. It included such inflammatory—and imaginary—tidbits as fifteen Belgian women being violated by twelve Germans each, after their menfolk had been killed; a baby whose head was sliced off by two German privates; an enemy soldier who drove his bayonet through a baby; the cutting off of women's breasts, children's hands, and the rape and murder of innocent women. There was also the story of the "crucified Canadian," told in a number of versions, none of them true. One version had "a child—two or three years old—nailed to the door by its hands and feet. . . ." Other stories described how the terrible Huns had shipped dead Allied soldiers back to Germany to be rendered into soap, how exchange prisoners were being shot full of tuberculosis germs, and water wells infected with bacteria. American newsmen who were permitted by the Germans to tour the Belgian front for two weeks wired the Associated Press that "in spirit of fairness we united in declaring German atrocities groundless as far as we were able to observe." Needless to say the Germans, like other belligerents, committed their share of atrocities, but Allied propaganda enlarged them beyond reason.

The Kaiser, of course, had his propaganda machine too, but it could not compete either in quantity or in quality with that of the British, the Morgans, or the munitions makers. It did much the same things as the British machine, but it had been started late, was often crude, and had difficulty with communications. So poor was its counteroffensive that while the German army was battering down one fortress after another in France and Belgium, the newspaper headlines here, as shown in a pamphlet called *A Trip Through Headline Land*, blared almost daily stories of how the German army was being destroyed. Had the Germans enjoyed a stronger base within the American establishment their point of view would have come out with the same vigor, but in the light of conditions it was buried.

The onesidedness that characterized the propaganda war also was apparent in diplomacy. Protests to Germany over the *Lusitania*, for instance, came close to being ultimatums, and when the British passenger vessel *Arabic* was sunk in August 1915, with a loss of two American lives, Secretary Lansing weighed the idea of severing diplomatic relations—a probable precursor to war. The crisis was cooled only when Germany pledged not to sink such liners "without warning and without [considering the] safety of the lives of non-combatants. . . ." When a channel steamer, the *Sussex*, was sunk in March 1916, Wilson sent a furious note to the Kaiser's government threatening "to sever diplomatic relations with the German Empire altogether," even though he was by no means sure that the disaster was the result of a submarine torpedo, and contrary to his charge that Americans had been "killed," no U.S. citizen had perished and only two had been injured. On the other hand, protests about British violations of neutral rights were usually pro forma. Typically, according to Sir Edward Grey, after U.S. Ambassador Page had delivered an official protest to him against the blockade, he concluded with the remark: "I have now read the despatch but I do not agree with it; let us consider how it should be answered." There were in actual fact more reasons for getting tough with the British than with the Central Powers, especially before Germany took to unrestricted submarine warfare in January 1917. The British increasingly imposed rules on neutral ships that virtually made the neutrals part of their own merchant marine. Nonbelligerent vessels were denied bunker coal, blacklisted, and kept in British ports until they agreed that all of their sister ships would not trade with the Central Powers. The British vigorously censored mail going to the United States as a means of cutting communication and trade between Germany and America. In July 1916 they went so far as to prepare a blacklist of eighty-five companies doing business with the Germans and Austrians, and applied pressure on banks and other firms to break off relations with them. Even Wilson and Lansing were so outraged by all this that they considered restricting loans and the export of gasoline to England. But reprisals became impossible, Colonel House told the German Ambassador Count Johann von Bernstorff, because "American commerce was so completely tied up with the interests of the Entente. . . ." The "blood soaked boom," as H. C. Peterson called it, could not be disturbed.

Another effect of the interwoven commercial interests between the U.S. and the Entente was the drive for "preparedness." Wilson—in December 1914—had rejected the idea of escalating military expenditures as an unneeded concession to the "nervous and excited." But the "nervous and excited," such as Teddy Roosevelt, General Leonard Wood, the munitions-minded Navy League, the National Security League, the American Legion, and the National Society for Patriotic Organizations, initiated a campaign to turn the President around. By November 1915 Wilson had reversed himself, and not only was induced to march in the mammoth preparedness parades that the jingoes were organizing, but made a series of addresses in New York, Pittsburgh, Cleveland, Chicago, St. Louis, and other cities justifying his *volte face* with a quotation from Ezekiel that "if the watchman see the sword come, and blow not the trumpet, and the people be not warned . . . his blood will I require at the watchman's hand." A number of measures were taken to enlarge and strengthen the armed forces, the most important being the "Big Navy Act" of August 1916, which contemplated a ten-year plan for making the United States as strong on the seas as any other two navies in the world.

In sum, almost everything that the American administration did from 1914 to 1917 was conditioned not by the empty rhetoric of being "neutral" in thought as well as deed, but by the economic and imperial benefits to be gained from relations with the Entente. It went so far that in 1916, just months before Wilson began his campaign for reelection on the slogan "He kept us out of war," the President sent House to Europe on a "peace" mission that in effect was a demand for German surrender under threat of America entering the war. "President Wilson was ready," read a secret memorandum agreed to between House and Sir Edward Grey, "on hearing from France and England that the moment was opportune, to propose that a Conference should be submitted to put an end to the war. . . . If it failed to secure peace, the United States would leave the Conference as a belligerent on the side of the Allies." In other words, whenever the Entente felt it had Germany on the run, Washington would propose a peace conference to enforce an Allied victory, and, if Germany did not yield, would join the fray on the Entente's side.

Propaganda, one-sided diplomacy, and militarization prepared the way for America's entry into the maelstrom. But the immediate cause was the threatened collapse of the economic partnership with Western Europe. It was threatened, in part, by the German decision at the end of January 1917 to wage unrestricted submarine warfare in the zone around the British Isles, and orders to sink any ship, neutral or not, merchant or passenger. Though the Central Powers were winning on the battlefront, the tightened British blockade, which caused starvation and disease in the German-Austro-Turkish sphere, tended to equalize matters, and the U-boat campaign was conceived as a counterthrust to achieve quick victory for the Central Powers. By sinking 600,000 tons of U.S. and Allied shipping a month (as against previous figures of 350,000) it was hoped to bring the Allies to their knees. This target was actually reached in March and exceeded (900,000 tons) in April, the month that the United States declared war. Obviously, a shortage of merchant vessels was bound to curtail business across the Atlantic highway.

More ominous to the economic partnership, however, was the financial vise that squeezed Britain, France, and their associates. They found themselves more and more in need of loans to make purchases in America, with less and less collateral and gold to secure them. From June to December 1916, the outstanding indebtedness of the Entente in the United States spiraled from $900 million to $1.8 billion. Britain alone borrowed $800 million in this period, for which she put up $960 million in collateral. But Americans were showing a marked reluctance to buy more Allied paper, especially unsecured obligations. "We cannot look to the munitions manufacturers for heavy subscriptions," Thomas W. Lamont, a Morgan partner, cabled London in January 1917. Most of them, he said, "still have on hand the notes of former issues which they have been unable to liquidate at cost." So strapped were the Allies for cash that they were forced to reduce purchases. The House of Morgan found itself with an overdraft of $400 million owed to it by the British, which the American government subsequently underwrote. As of April 1917 the big bankers, not to mention 500,000 individual investors, held a stake of $2.3 billion in notes and bonds which might sink unless Allied credit were buttressed. Even the great House of Morgan was no longer capable of saving it; on March 5, Ambassador Page cabled the State Department urging the United States to undertake the job. "The inquiries which I have made here . . . ," he wrote, "disclose an international situation which is most alarming to the financial and industrial outlook of the United States." There is a danger, he continued, that "Franco-American and Anglo-American exchange will be greatly disturbed; the inevitable consequence will be that orders by all the Allied Governments will be reduced to the lowest possible amount and that trans-Atlantic trade will practically come to an end. The result of such a stoppage will be a panic in the United States. . . . It is not improbable that the only way of maintaining our present preeminent trade position and averting a panic is by declaring war on Germany."

VI

President Wilson's war message of April 2, 1917, emphasized the unrestricted submarine warfare as the *causus belli* for U.S. entry. But the antiwar senator from Nebraska, George W. Norris, insisted that "we are going into war upon the command of gold. We are going to run the risk of sacrificing millions of our countrymen's lives in order that other countrymen may coin their lifeblood into money." At the beginning of 1916 it may have been correct to say, as the British writer Maurice A. Low observed, that the "only statesmanship the [American] public understood was peace with war profits," but by the end of the year it was clear that if America wanted continued war profits it would have to go to war.

As usual Wilson was torn between the "idealistic" and the "practical." He spoke about the need for "peace without victory in Europe." He expressed deep concern, in a chat with Frank Cobb, editor of the New York *World,* the "once lead this people into war and they'll forget there ever was such a thing as tolerance. To fight you must be brutal and ruthless, and the spirit of ruthless brutality will enter into the very fiber of our national life, infecting Congress, the courts, the policeman on the beat, the man on the street." The rights of free speech and assembly, he said, would disappear and the Constitution become a dead letter. Yet in the final analysis it was the mundane that outweighed the idealistic. Wilson himself subsequently admitted to the Senate Foreign Relations Committee that the United States would have become directly embroiled even "if Germany had committed no act of injustice against our citizens. . . ." Anyway, despite the tumult in the press, only 179 Americans had lost their lives through submarine warfare from March 1915 to the time that the United States broke relations with Germany in February 1917—and 128 of these were casualties on the *Lusitania.* Neutral Norway, Denmark, Sweden, and Holland suffered far more —Norway alone lost 247 lives—but were able to avoid direct involvement by being more truly impartial. In the United States, however, tensions had mounted with each incident. Early in March 1917, the first armed U.S. merchant ships went to sea with navy gunners aboard ready to fire at submarines. But on March 12 an unarmed vessel was sunk without notice, and a week later three more were sent to the bottom by U-boats. That same month the British added fuel to the fires by releasing a telegram they had decoded from the German foreign secretary, Arthur Zimmerman, to his minister in Mexico, that in case the United States joined the war the minister was to seek an alliance with Mexico and promise it the reannexation of Texas, New Mexico, and Arizona as her share of the booty. The pressure, especially in the industrial East, was now inexorable. Every time there was a rumor of peace the stock market suffered a sharp decline, reviving only when it became clear that the war would continue.

On April 2, Wilson asked Congress to declare war. "The world," he said, "must be made safe for democracy." The vote in the House of Representatives was 373 to 50, in the Senate 82 to 6; but if there was joy unbounded in Wall Street the average citizen remained lukewarm. Fewer than 200,000 volunteered for the army in the first six months after the declaration—a considerably smaller figure than responded during the Mexican War—forcing the government to resort to the compulsory draft. Though the administration managed eventually to generate enthusiasm for its efforts through the propaganda of the Committee on Public Information, it also found it necessary to initiate a vast campaign of repression against opponents of the war. On September 5, 1917, the Department of Justice descended on the headquarters of the Industrial Workers of the World in fifteen cities from Boston to Los Angeles, arresting all and sundry, and confiscating literature and records. One hundred and sixty-two leading Wobblies (as IWW members were called), including "Big Bill" Haywood, were indicted, and a four-month trial of 113 members before Judge Kenesaw Mountain Landis ended in the conviction of 93, sentenced to terms from 90 days to 20 years and fined a total of $2.3 million. Additionally, 2,000 Wobblies were rounded up in the first two months of 1918, though not all were held. Innumerable foreign-born anarchists and socialists, including Emma Goldman, were arrested and deported. Socialist Kate Richards O'Hare was given five years for an antiwar speech in North Dakota, and Rose Pastor Stokes ten years in prison for writing a letter to the Kansas City *Star* in which she said that "no government which is for the profiteers can also be for the people. . . ." Five members of the Socialist executive committee, including Victor Berger, received sentences up to twenty years from Judge Landis, who later indicated his bias by bemoaning the fact that he could not have been harsher. And the leading figure of the party, Eugene Debs, received a ten-year sentence for making a speech against militarism in Canton, Ohio.

VII

With America's entry into the war, the economic and military balance was tipped in the Allies' favor, and victory over the Central Powers all but assured. On the recommendation of Rear Admiral William S. Sims, president of the Naval War College, Wilson decided to convoy merchant ships with destroyers and other armed vessels, and this scheme plus other measures were so effective that German sinkings fell from a peak of almost 900,000 tons in April to less than 300,000 in November. For the land war, the American army was enlarged as a result of the Selective Service Act of May 1917, which not only brought in conscripted recruits but stimulated volunteers. (Interestingly, 337,649 evaded the draft, about half of whom were caught by the authorities.) General John J. Pershing, famed for his invasion of Mexico, was put in charge of the American Expeditionary Force, and though the Americans reached the front slowly —only 300,000 in France as of March 1918—they made their weight felt in the last half year, when their numbers increased by 263,000 a month.

As important as these military achievements for the Entente— perhaps more so—was the adrenalin of American dollars. Instead of depending on private investment houses like J. P. Morgan & Co., Britain and France were now able to borrow directly from the U.S. government. Under the First Liberty Loan Act of 1917 they received loans of $9.5 billion, most of which filtered back into the U.S. economy in the form of war orders. In addition, from April 1917 to November 1918 the United States itself spent $22.6 billion—three times as much as the federal government had expended in the first 100 years of its existence combined.

The Allied position was desperate in April 1917, when Uncle Sam joined the fray. A revolution had broken out in Russia a month before which could later sweep that country out of the war and permit the Germans to withdraw troops from the eastern front for use on the western front; England was down to a three-week food supply and its credit was shattered; on the battlefront the offensive by the French at Chemin-des-Dames was so inept it resulted in mutinies; and the British Arras venture, which drained the Canadian army, was a similar failure. Without American participation the odds heavily favored a German victory. With America involved, however, the tide turned and the long war moved toward a climax. The "doughboys" helped blunt the last German offensive—at Aisne, Marne, Château-Thierry, Belleau Wood—and then pushed forward with their allies at Meuse, Argonne, Verdun, St.-Mihel, Ypres, to achieve the final victory. In September Bulgaria gave up unconditionally. A month later Austria pleaded for peace and on November 3 put down its arms. After August the German General Erich von Ludendorff realized that the war was lost and a broadened parliamentary government appeared under a tepid liberal, Prince Max of Baden. The Kaiser would have continued the fight but on November 4 the sailors of the imperial fleet mutinied at Kiel and were joined by the very troops sent to put them down. A week later, on November 11, an armistice was proclaimed and the great war had at last ground to a halt.

The question now was how the world would be reorganized. The war had achieved what it was meant to achieve—a redivision of world power—but that redivision had to be ratified in a peace treaty in which the defeated would try to save what they could and the victors seek not only new holdings—but advantages against each other.

The United States, of course, emerged incomparably in the best position. True, the government had spent enormous sums of money and had increased the national debt from a prewar level of a billion dollars to $26.6 billion as of August 1919. But private entrepreneurs had enriched themselves appreciably—and, more important, the structure of American capitalism had been basically modified. The United States, while accounting for only 6 percent of the world's population and occupying 7 percent of its surface, now produced a fifth of its gold; owned nearly a third of its shipping tonnage (only 5 percent before the war); two fifths of its iron, coal, tin, silver; two thirds of its oil; 85 percent of its automobiles. In the six years from 1915 through 1920 the American foreign trade surplus was approximately $16 billion, and most of the trade now was in manufactured goods rather than agricultural products. The United States had been a debtor nation, now it was a creditor with the rest of the world in debt to it to the tune of $12 to $14 billion. Had every nation paid its debt and interest, the treasury in Washington would have been enriched by a half billion a year, or about a fifth of the peacetime budget. Almost half of the world's gold reserve, on which the international monetary system depended, was in the United States. American production of iron and steel in the last war year was higher than that of all the other great powers combined. With surplus money, surplus goods, surplus industrial capacity, the goliath of the western hemisphere was in a position to dominate the world's markets, and, as an adjunct, many of its political decisions. The rest of the capitalist world, except for Japan, was enervated both in manpower and in finances, but America's tribulation had been minimal. In terms of blood, the war had cost 116,516 killed and 204,002 wounded of the nearly 5 million men mobilized, or a total of slightly more than 320,000 casualties; by contrast the comparable figures of dead and wounded for Austria-Hungary were 5 million, Germany 6 million, Britain 3 million, France 5.5 million, and Russia 6.5 million.

On the imperial front the United States forged ahead dramatically. Private American investment abroad rose from $3.5 billion in 1914 to $7 billion by 1919—in Canada alone it went up by almost $1.3 billion from 1915 to 1919. More than that, the United States was now prepared for a major jump, as it planted innumerable banks throughout the world, especially in Latin America. The Pan-

American Financial Conference called by Secretary of the Treasury William G. McAdoo in May 1915 achieved what Secretary Blaine had failed to do three decades before, namely bring together the twenty Latin American governments and U.S. bankers to smooth the way for investment and trade originating in Wall Street. "We have got to finance the world," said Wilson a year later, "and those who finance the world must understand it and rule it with their spirits and with their minds." Our "business hereafter," he said, was "to lend and to help and to promote the great peaceful enterprises of the world. . . ." Banker Paul M. Warburg, a member of the Federal Reserve System, pointed out in 1918 that "if we play our cards right . . . nothing but mismanagement could wrest the financial premiership of the world from us."

To retain "financial premiership" of the world the American establishment needed nothing more than a climate of international tranquillity and an open door. Unlike the powers that were playing for smaller stakes, it did not need outright colonies. With a shattered Europe before it, the United States could conquer market after market—provided there was some machinery for preventing traumatic shocks such as revolutions and wars. It was possible, therefore, to express America's war aims in the rhetoric of idealism, and Wilson did so in a way that captured the imagination of many millions everywhere. The Fourteen Points for a permanent peace he put forth on January 8, 1918, called for an end to secret diplomacy —"open covenants of peace, openly arrived at"—freedom of the seas, limitation of armaments, and the removal "of all economic barriers and the establishment of an equality of trade conditions among the nations. . . ." Point 5 was a fuzzy provision that could be construed as granting the right of self-determination to colonial peoples, though its promise simultaneously to give "equal weight" to "the equitable claims" of the imperial power made it a dead letter. Eight of the points provided for territorial readjustments and protection of national rights—evacuation of Russia, restoration of Belgian independence, return of Alsace-Lorraine taken by Germany in 1871 to France, a "readjustment of the frontiers of Italy . . . along clearly recognizable lines of nationality," "autonomous development" for the peoples in the Austro-Hungarian Empire," guarantees for the Balkan states and Turkish minorities, and an independent Poland. Finally, and pivotal to the whole statement of principles, was the call for a "general association of nations . . . for the purpose of affording mutual guarantees of political independence and territorial integrity to great and small states alike." It was this projected League of Nations that was Wilson's great hope for the future; it would adjust disputes peacefully and create a stable world order presumably under American leadership.

Many historians credit Wilson with pure altruism in promulgating the Fourteen Points. Others assert that it was necessary to codify Western war aims as a means both to unite the Allied peoples and to hold forth the promise of a "just peace" so as to induce the enemy to give up. Leftist writers claim that the Fourteen Points were needed to counter the six-point program proclaimed by Lenin months before for the "liberation of all colonies and all oppressed peoples." It was also required, they say, in order to stifle the criticism that arose as a result of publication by the Bolsheviks of the secret war treaties between the Entente powers, which showed them to be unbridled imperialists interested only in aggrandizement.

Leon Trotsky, speaking to the second congress of the Communist International a couple of years later, expressed prevailing radical opinion (and that of many liberals) when he said: "Under the 'League of Nations' flag, the United States made an attempt to extend to the other side of the ocean its experience with a federated unification of large, multinational masses—an attempt to chain to its chariot of gold the peoples of Europe and other parts of the world, and bring them under Washington's rule. In essence the League of Nations was intended to be a world monopoly corporation, 'Yankee and Co.'" The United States, he said, was supplanting the program of "America for the Americans"—the Monroe Doctrine—to "the program of imperialism: 'The Whole World for the Americans.'"

Whatever Wilson's inner motivations, it is obvious that his blueprint meshed with the imperial needs of the American establishment. Limitations of arms would restrain the power of the British navy. Removal of economic barriers and "equality of trade conditions" would smooth the way for U.S. business overseas. The right of self-determination—if enforced—would contain and weaken the empires of two allies, Britain and France, who were also economic rivals. The dismemberment of the German, Austro-Hungarian, and Turkish empires would be a bonanza to all the victors. And the League would fashion a new balance of power over which the United States would be the main arbiter.

Wilson's plans, however, went awry. Whether or not he thought of himself as altruistic, his associates at the bargaining table considered him naïve. Georges Clemenceau, the "tiger" of France, David Lloyd George of England, and Vittorio Orlando of Italy insisted that peace be made by traditional rules rather than glowing pronouncements of principles. "Mr. Wilson," said Clemenceau, "bores me with his Fourteen Points . . . God Almighty has only ten!" The tiger was ready to accept a League of Nations only if it gave France dominance—"security"—over Europe. And Lloyd George was ready to accept it only if the British empire and the British navy remained undisturbed. Orlando insisted on the acquisition of Fiume and African territories promised Italy in 1915 to bring her into the war. When they were denied him, he skulked away from the peace conference. The Japanese demanded Shantung in far-off China.

When Wilson arrived in Paris in December 1918, he was greeted by delirious crowds and compared to Jesus as the apostle of peace and the tribune of the poor. He came at the head of a five-man delegation, including Colonel House and Secretary Lansing, and with a host of experts on every conceivable subject. But in the months that followed, the Fourteen Points were effectively emasculated by one compromise after another. Peace was to be a continuation of war by other means, and the postwar world, like the prewar world, was to take on all the hues of power politics, imperialism, and intervention. On June 28, 1919, in the Hall of Mirrors at the palace of Versailles, a reluctant Germany was forced to sign a two-hundred-page treaty which stripped her next to naked, and in subsequent months Austria, Hungary, Bulgaria, and Turkey received the same treatment. Under these arrangements the German navy was delivered to the victors. Her merchant marine, foreign property, colonies, and banks in foreign lands were all taken from her, and her future mortgaged by indemnities and reparations that eventually came to the staggering amount of $33 billion. Alsace-Lorraine was given to France permanently; the Saar, with its German population and coal fields, was turned over to France temporarily; and the Rhineland was assigned to occupation by Allied armies for fifteen years. The Chinese province of Shantung, formerly under German control, was taken by Japan but at Wilson's insistence only on condition that it be returned to China ultimately. The Austro-Hungarian empire was dissolved, its component parts being formed into a number of independent states. Italy, Greece, Rumania, Belgium, and Denmark added some territory to their borders, and the colonies of the defeated states were turned over to the victors as "mandates" under the League of Nations. They were to be held, it was said, as "a sacred trust for civilization." The mandate system, suggested by Jan Smuts of the Union of South Africa to appease Wilson's sensitivities, designated "A," "B," and "C" status for the various territories being acquired—depending on how ready they were to "stand by themselves under the strenuous conditions of the modern world. . . ." Only the "A" mandates, such as Syria, Iraq, Palestine, and Transjordan, could expect independence in the near future, and in every one of these instances the right proved devoid of substance. In effect therefore the mandates added 1,607,053 square miles (and 4 million people) to the French empire. Colonialism was continuing under a new name—"mandate."

The ultimate indignity to Wilson's Fourteen Points was the rejection by the United States Senate of the League of Nations, the cornerstone of his program. Under the covenant of the League, incorporated into the Versailles Treaty because Wilson felt the whole peace system was inoperable without it, there was to be a small Secretariat in Geneva, an Assembly of deputies from each nation and self-governing colony, and a Grand Council of nine, made up of the five great powers plus four others periodically selected by the Assembly. All disputes between members were to be submitted to arbitration, with the understanding that neither side would take to arms until at least three months elapsed after a tribunal made a decision; and if that decision were unanimous they were required to live by it, prohibited from going to war. Any state that failed to abide by the covenants was to be considered at war with the League and subject to economic and political sanctions, such as a trade boycott or severance of diplomatic relations, as well as military ones.

Had Wilson been as adroit in political infighting as he was with the pen the League and the Versailles Treaty would have been ratified, though with a number of important modifications. But the Senate was severely fragmented on the issue and the President was unable to find a formula to gain the two-thirds majority necessary to approve the treaty. Thirteen senators, led by William E. Borah, were classed as "irreconcilables" because they were unreservedly opposed to the League. Article 10, they said, made it incumbent on the United States to defend the existing order, including the colonial system of France and Britain. Forty senators, all Democrats, favored the treaty without reservations, and the rest—the "reservationists," led by Senator Lodge—demurred on a number of points, the most important being that it did not guarantee American suzerainty in the western hemisphere, and that it pledged the United States to go to war to defend other nations against aggressors, thus limiting the nation's sovereignty. In the voting that ensued after long debate, the supporters of Wilson, who demanded ratification without change, joined with those at the other end of the pole, the irreconcilables, to torpedo the treaty and the League. Another vote in March 1920 ended with the same result.

VIII

But if Wilson's peace plan was eviscerated by foreign and domestic critics, the American juggernaut was only slightly inhibited in its drive for the world's "premiership." True, the United States, unlike the other powers, received neither territory nor indemnity from anyone. Far from being a symptom of weakness, however, it was a testament to a new strength. In the next decade it covered the earth with loans, private investments, and trade as never before.

An enervated Britain was able to return to the gold standard only in 1925, and France in 1928. Meanwhile American bankers, with the House of Morgan again in the vanguard, floated loans to foreign governments by the hundreds of millions. The demand for such loans exceeded that of the hectic 1915–17 period, with J. P. Morgan & Co. alone floating issues for Belgium, France, England, Italy, Switzerland, Norway, Austria, Germany, Australia, Chile, Japan, and Cuba to the tune of $1.5 billion from 1919 to 1926. From 1919 to 1933 the Morgans hawked $2.2 billion of foreign bonds, or approximately a sixth of all the foreign issues purchased by American investors in that time. Many of these loans had stern conditions: as a result of the $110 million loan to Germany in 1924, for instance, the nationalized railroads were placed under an American commission and three trustees—one of whom was designated by the Morgan firm in Paris. A $50 million loan to Cuba was predicated on certain changes in its fiscal legislation. Often the "exported" monies never even left home, since they were expended on American machinery and capital goods.

Meanwhile, American bankers opened a large number of branches overseas to finance trade and investment of their compatriots. Prior to the war, U.S. traders used British branch banks for their ventures; now they had their own. As of 1926, eight American banks alone had 107 subsidiaries in foreign countries. Moreover, the stability of the dollar and its acceptance as the medium of foreign exchange was an additional advantage for U.S. business, since those entrepreneurs abroad who stockpiled dollars tended, where all other things were equal, to spend them on American commodities rather than those of America's rivals.

Given this favorable set of circumstances, private U.S. investments abroad, including private loans, jumped from $7 billion in 1919 to $16 or $17 billion by 1929. American firms spread across the earth with incredible speed. The copper firms opened subsidiaries in Canada, Chile, Africa. By the mid-1930's more than three fifths of Anaconda's copper was produced in foreign mines and smelters. General Motors established auto factories in Canada and Germany, and eighteen assembly plants in fourteen other countries. Jersey Standard, International Harvester, Armour, Swift, Wilson, United Fruit, International Telephone and Telegraph, Ford, General Electric, purchased existing plants or built new ones in dozens of countries, all through the golden 1920's. American utilities took over vast chunks of the Latin American market, and American aviation—a new industry—set up a virtual world monopoly. Most remarkable was the investment in Europe—about $5 billion just before the Depression, as against $5.6 billion in Latin America and $4 billion in Canada. The billion and a half in Asia, Australia and New Zealand alone was three times as much as American investments throughout the world back in 1900. By 1930 American holdings abroad, which had been only one sixth as much as those of the United Kingdom in 1913, were nearly equal to those of John Bull. In fifteen years the imperial United States had made a qualitative jump in its status as a world power.

In those years, though it did not acquire mandates or colonies, it continued to "outrage the sovereignty" of other nations and peoples. There was never a day from 1919 to 1933 when American marines did not intervene in or occupy the sovereign territory of another country. From 1917 to 1919, U.S. armed forces made themselves at home in Cuba during a period of insurrection. When they left, two companies remained behind to deal with "unsettled" conditions in Camagüey until February 1922. American troops invaded Mexico three times in 1918 and six times in 1919 "in pursuit of bandits." They did "police duty" in Panama "during election disturbances" from 1918 to 1920. They landed in Honduras to keep order in 1919, and in China the following year to "save American lives." In 1921 units of the navy came ashore in Panama and Costa Rica. Marines landed in Honduras and China in 1924, and in both countries again the following year, and in Panama in 1925. American forces occupied Nicaragua for seven long years, from 1926 to 1933, and in the latter year intervened once again in Cuba during a revolution against President Gerardo Machado.

In November 1935, Major General Smedley D. Butler, in an article for *Common Sense* magazine, explained the purpose of these interventions. "I spent thirty-three years and four months," wrote Butler, "in active service as a member of our country's most agile military force—the Marine Corps. . . . And during that period I spent most of my time being a high-class muscle man for Big Business, for Wall Street, and for the bankers. In short, I was a racketeer for capitalism. . . .

"Thus I helped make Mexico and especially Tampico safe for American oil interests in 1914. I helped make Haiti and Cuba a decent place for the National City Bank boys to collect revenues in. . . . I helped purify Nicaragua for the international banking house of Brown Brothers in 1909–1912. I brought light to the Dominican Republic for American sugar interests in 1916. I helped make Honduras 'right' for American fruit companies in 1903. In China in 1927 I helped see to it that Standard Oil went its way unmolested."

IX

The most significant American intervention of this period—as an augury of things to come after World War II—was in the Soviet Union. The Russian Revolution of 1917 was a traumatic shock to western capitalism, its contagious effects being felt in Germany, Austria, Hungary, Bulgaria, Finland, and elsewhere. "The whole of Europe," wrote Lloyd George in a memorandum to the Peace Conference in March 1919, "is filled with the spirit of revolution. . . . If Germany goes over to the Spartacists [a counterpart of the Russian Communists] it is inevitable that she would throw in her lot with the Russian Bolshevists. Once that happens all Eastern Europe will be swept into the orbit of the Bolshevik revolution. . . . Bolshevik imperialism does not merely menace the states on Russia's borders. It threatens the whole of Asia and is as near to America as it is to France. It is idle to think that the Peace Conference can separate, however sound a peace it may have arranged with Germany, if it leaves Russia as it is today." Winston Churchill wrote to Lloyd George that "we may well be within measurable distance of universal collapse and anarchy throughout Europe and Asia." His prescription for the Soviet regime was that "the baby must be strangled in its crib." In this view he was strongly seconded by Clemenceau, who also felt that if Bolshevism were not throttled it would sweep everywhere and endanger the Allied victory in the war. The negotiators at Versailles, in making their compromises and accommodations, always kept one eye focused on developments in the Soviet Union. "The whole of American policy during the liquidation of the Armistice," Herbert Hoover wrote in 1921, "was to contribute everything it could to prevent Europe from going Bolshevik or being overrun by their armies."

The revolution in Russia evolved in two stages; the first, in March 1917, leading to what was for all practical purposes a dual government: a liberal regime coexisting with the councils (soviets) of soldiers and workers; and the second, in November, organized by Lenin's Communists under the slogan "peace, bread, land." The Allies had no fear of the March uprising, in fact welcomed it because it removed the argument that they were fighting to uphold one autocrat, the Tsar, against another, the Kaiser. Moreover, the Kerensky regime that emerged after a short time decided to remain in the war even though Russia had lost so many men—9 million dead, wounded, and captured—that its economy was shattered, its railroads almost inoperative, and its people hungry and war-weary to the point of desperation. Lenin capitalized on the antiwar sentiment and the failure of Kerensky to introduce land reform or solve the hunger problem. His promise of peace and bread and land galvanized the nation behind his revolution, with the Bolsheviks seizing power in Petrograd virtually without bloodshed. The old society just crumbled and the Bolsheviks picked up the pieces. They had not initiated the revolution in March—indeed they were secondary actors in the original drama. For a few months their leaders were in jail or in hiding, as counterrevolutionary forces came to the fore. But they correctly judged the pulse of their people, and rode to power.

Once in power they declared a cessation of fighting and in March 1918, after considerable dispute in their own ranks, accepted the humiliating Brest-Litovsk Treaty from the Germans in which they lost large parts of their territory. Immediately they were confronted with dangers from without and within. At a meeting of the inter-Allied conference to coordinate the war effort, Marshal Ferdinand Foch, Allied commander, proposed intervention in Russia to take over the Trans-Siberian Railway and reestablish a front in the east—though both Colonel House and the English opposed the scheme. Inside the Soviet Union, counterrevolutionary armies under such tsarist military men as General Anton Deniken and Admiral Alexander Kolchak mounted an attack and set up no fewer than eighteen "white" governments on Soviet soil. France and Britain gave these forces large amounts of money, as did private banks in the United States. The U.S. Treasury made available to representatives of the whites $1,239,000 from funds that had been held for the Kerensky regime. Beginning in April 1918, Japanese marines landed in Vladivostok, followed by a small contingent of British troops, and soon by Americans. In late 1918 there were 7,000 U.S. soldiers on Russian soil and eventually the troops of fourteen Allied nations. The original pretext for landing these forces was "to render protection and help" for 45,-000 Czech prisoners, who, it was said, were prevented from moving westward across Siberia by armed German and Austrian troops. In truth, of course, the major aim was to overthrow the Bolshevik regime—a goal which by now Wilson, Lloyd George, and the other Allied leaders embraced in varying degrees.

Time after time the Soviets offered to make peace. In the four months from November 1918 to February 1919 they sent seven notes to the Allied powers, written—as William Henry Chamberlin observes—"in the most conciliatory language." As a result of one of these notes, Wilson sent William C. Bullitt of the State Department and Lincoln Steffens, the well-known journalist, to the Soviet Union to seek a *modus vivendi*. The two negotiators met with Lenin and concluded an agreement highly favorable to the West. The Bolsheviks agreed that all governments in Russia, white as well as red, would retain jurisdiction over the areas they then held. Debts owed the Allies would be honored as a joint obligation by all sides, troops would be demobilized, and a general amnesty offered to political prisoners. In return the West would lift its blockade, withdraw its troops, and reopen communications. Bullitt was joyous, confident he had found the means to end hostilities. But his plan was never considered. As Lloyd George explained to him: in the face of vitriolic attacks by the conservative press "how can you expect us to be sensible about Russia?" President Wilson for some unexplained reason refused even to see Bullitt or to consider his report, perhaps—as the well-known New York *Times* correspondent Walter Duranty suggested—because by this time the white armies were on the march and threatening to end the civil war by military victory. The West refused to be conciliated.

The Allies, including Wilson, conceived of the struggle in purely military terms: if enough soldiers were placed on Russian territory and enough money and arms donated to the counterrevolutionary forces, the Bolshevik regime would collapse. But if such strategy had worked before in India or Haiti, it did not work in the Soviet Union; the Allies grossly miscalculated the inner vitality of a revolution as deep as that of 1917. Trotsky appealed to the patriotism of 30,000 former tsarist officers and was able to mold them into the nucleus of a Red Army. This army scored some successes, but the Bolsheviks did not place their main reliance on military force. They depended much more on propaganda, guerrilla tactics, and world opinion. They rallied innumerable people in and out of Russia who felt that by supporting the Bolsheviks they were supporting an idealistic cause. The Allies and the white Russians, it turned out, were totally unprepared for this kind of conflict (as the United States was to be unprepared for it in Vietnam a half century later) and actually paved the way for the Soviet victory.

Lenin distributed land to poor peasants. The white armies, on the other hand, restored these holdings, wherever they could, to the large landowners who traveled with them. The mass of Russia's peasants thereupon became convinced that a White Guard and Allied success would bring back tsarism or its equivalent—and joined red guerrillas. Lenin also made political and social concessions to the middle peasants and handicraft workers, consolidating them behind his regime. "The rapid collapse of Kolchak and Deniken," writes Walter Duranty, "was greatly aided by guerrilla activities behind their front lines, in which middle peasants and artisans took a vigorous part." The Soviets appealed to foreign soldiers and foreign workers to help them. "Comrades," they said in their leaflets and propaganda, "why are you fighting us? We don't want to fight. We want to be let alone. You go home and we'll go home." Their efforts bore fruit among tired soldiers, sick of war and confused by the realignment of friends and enemies. American troops sang "Home toot sweet" and staged a near-mutiny to force their withdrawal. A mutiny by the French fleet in Odessa caused France to evacuate that key city. All over Europe and America there were demonstrations for "hands off Russia," not only by Communists but by moderate socialists and liberals as well. Longshoremen and sailors refused to load or man ships carrying munitions destined for the enemies of the Soviets. By the end of 1919 the white armies were in retreat. The Red Army chased Kolchak beyond the Urals. Anglo-Russian forces in the north were stymied when their Russian contingent mutinied, killed British and Russian officers—and joined the reds. The pendulum swayed back and forth for a while, but early in the following year, 1920, the Bolsheviks had won their war. Only the Japanese and their puppet regime in Vladivostok remained until 1922.

The intervention was a failure—a rare phenomenon up to that time, particularly when the array of forces are considered. On the other hand, the Communist revolution did not gain the momentum that the capitalist statesmen at first feared it would. A short-lived Communist regime under Béla Kun was overthrown in Hungary. The revolutions that wracked Germany from 1919 to 1924 all failed. Despite revolts and general strikes in other countries the worldwide system of capitalism stabilized itself and returned to the "normalcy" of the prewar era. The confrontation between revolution and militarism, however, would come up again—after World War II. Unfortunately the lessons of the first confrontation were never digested by imperialist leaders, especially in the United States.

14

THE WAR BEFORE THE WAR (I)

"The business of America," said Calvin Coolidge in 1925, "is business." "Silent Cal," who ascended to the presidency on the death of Warren G. Harding in 1923, was in the words of Samuel Morison "a mean, thin-lipped little man, a respectable mediocrity, [who] lived parsimoniously but admired men of wealth. . . ." Nonetheless his notion of the supremacy of business in the affairs of state accurately expressed the growing belief that the nation's destiny and "free enterprise" were one and the same thing. "The driving force of American progress," Coolidge asserted, "has been her industries. They have created the wealth that has wrought our national development." This provincial view during the "golden" 1920's lent credence to the image of an America turned inward, pursuing nothing more vital than the almighty dollar, disengaged from Europe and the world, and, above all, eschewing the game of imperialism played by the other great powers. The mood of America, it was said, was "isolationist," one of "stay at home and mind your own business," and its foreign policy one of "open door," calling simply for equal treatment in commerce and investment. The clear implication was that Uncle Sam no longer violated the sovereignty of other states.

This was not accurate, of course, since American marines were dispatched to foreign soil at least a dozen times during the decade —to China (five times), Russia, Guatemala, Panama, Costa Rica, Turkey, Honduras, Nicaragua. But world capitalism in the 1920's— and America with it—did seem to be reaching toward an era of stability. The Bolshevik revolution, which Winston Churchill feared would bring "universal collapse and anarchy throughout Europe and Asia," had been confined to Russia; rebellions in Germany, Fin-

275

land, Hungary, Bulgaria, Italy, and elsewhere had failed. Uncle Sam's enervated allies in Europe stayed afloat from 1918 to 1929 with $13 billion in loans from American sources. Germany was saved from further chaos and revolution by $2.5 billion, and the paring down of its $33 billion reparations bill through the Dawes and Young Plans. The United States, as the largest beneficiary of the reshuffling of international fortunes, was, by 1929, the master of a sphere of influence comprising half of Latin America. It was investing capital abroad at the rate of more than a billion a year, and its foreign trade, rising steadily, was now almost equal to that of Great Britain. If there were frictions and disputes on the international horizon, they seemed muted, and the prospect of international explosions seemed distant.

Modern imperialism, however, is not a single act such as the occupation of Egypt by Britain, or the seizure of a half million dollars from the Haitian national bank by American marines. It is a complex process that responds to the *internal* requirements of an industrial society. That industrial machine, particularly if it is expanding, needs ever larger amounts of raw materials to stoke its factory fires, and markets for surplus goods and capital. The result is an economic war between the great nations, sometimes mild, sometimes fierce; then a political and diplomatic war in which each power tries to secure concessions, spheres of influence, and colonies; and finally, if these conflicts reach a boiling point, both a military war *between* the great states and "war" against revolutions that usually follow in the wake of traditional wars. This scenario had been played out prior to, during, and after World War I; it was to be played out again prior to, during, and after World War II. What one saw of it in the 1920's was only the mild beginnings of the conflict, before they became exacerbated and irreconcilable. This lent the illusion of stability to international affairs, but it was a synthetic and deceptive stability. For building within it were those subsurface forces that would soon explode into the Great Depression, would unleash a bitter new struggle for earthly spoils, and would lay the groundwork both for the most costly war and the most extensive wave of national revolutions in history. Stability and imperialism proved to be chronically mismated.

II

The objective of America's territorial imperialism in the eighteenth and nineteenth centuries was the acquisition of land. The objective of the new imperialism after 1870 was commercial in nature—access to raw materials and markets. The developed capitalist economy was like a giant bathtub, with a spigot at one end and a drain at the other. Raw materials were tapped in from the spigot and surplus finished goods and capital were carried off through the drain. Close the spigot and there is no water (raw materials) in the bathtub, the economy cannot operate. Close the drain and the bathtub overflows in terrible depression. In the words of Woodrow Wilson, already quoted, "Our industries have expanded to such a point, that they will burst their jackets if they cannot find a free outlet to the markets of the world."

Oddly enough, the richer a nation becomes the more it is dependent on other nations. In the 1920's, for instance, the United States imported almost all of its tin, vanadium, chromium, platinum, nickel, rubber, asbestos, potash, quinine, and certain tropical foods and vegetables. It needed nickel and wood pulp from Canada; manganese and coffee from Brazil; tin from Bolivia; nitrates and copper from Chile; diamonds from South Africa; jute from India; additional petroleum from a dozen areas; rubber from Liberia, Malaya, Ceylon, and the Dutch East Indies; silk from Japan; sisal from Mexico; tea from India; bananas from Central America; and so on. America depended on these nations even though it was itself exceptionally rich in crude materials. It was far better equipped to handle its needs than, say, Japan. Yet as the years went by it found itself less, rather than more, self-sufficient.

At the turn of the century the United States exported more minerals and raw materials than it imported. By 1930 the situation was reversed, and as of 1956 the nation was purchasing from abroad a total of $6.6 billion in primary goods. The prospect was that these figures would double and redouble in ensuing decades. A Senate Committee on Interior and Insular Affairs predicted, July 9, 1954, that if the developing nations should, for one reason or another, withhold supplies of crude commodities "the vital security of this Nation" would be "in serious jeopardy." Industries such as steel, metal cans, copper, petroleum, asbestos, zinc, coffee, sugar, chocolate, would be immeasurably poorer; some might disappear entirely, and certainly the vaunted American standard of living would fall appreciably.

The same sort of interdependence also applied to "exportable surpluses." "Our foreign trade," said Herbert Hoover's Secretary of State, Henry L. Stimson, "has now become an indispensable cog in the economic machinery of our country." His successor, Cordell Hull, believed that "ever increasing surpluses" were America's major economic problem. "All past experience," he said, "teaches us that the power and influence of a nation are judged more by the extent and character of its commerce than by any other standard." The panacea for depression, according to Franklin D. Roosevelt in 1935, was that "foreign markets must be regained. There is no other way if we would avoid painful economic dislocation, social readjustments, and unemployment." Those foreign markets might absorb only 5 or 10 percent of U.S. production, but if they were closed off, the economy back home would choke in gagging depression.

In this scenario of capitalist interdependence, the trouble begins when one nation seeks, or defends, an advantage—at the expense of others. At the beginning of the century, by way of example, the Federated Malay States, owned by Britain, produced 60 percent of the world's tin ore, which was then smelted at a British smelter in Singapore. When the International Tin Company—an American firm—laid plans to build a smelter near New York, the Malayans responded by imposing a prohibitive tax on tin ore going to any place other than Singapore. Thus the cost of production for the New York firm became too high to compete. Conversely, from 1902 to 1913 the United States levied a large tax on all manila hemp produced in the Philippines—except the hemp destined for its own shores—in order to give American fabricators of binder twine an edge against international competitors.

These are but two examples of how nations shut the door in each other's face; there are innumerable others. In the 1920's Canada prohibited the export of pulp wood from its crown lands. It wanted the wood converted to paper in *Canadian* factories, rather than have it sent to the United States—consumer of half the world's paper—and manufactured by American firms. If there had been no such embargo the Canadian industry would probably have disappeared. For the same reason a number of European countries imposed high export taxes on rags—to protect their paper industry—and on bones —to protect their glue industry. To one extent or another all countries, including the United States, restrict and control trade with others through a host of devices—limited only by the human imagination. A government, for instance, will curtail exports of primary goods by requiring that the exports be licensed, by placing an embargo on their sale to others, by setting strict quotas on the amount that can be shipped elsewhere, by forming a marketing monopoly controlled by the government, and even by destroying some of its supply—as Brazil has done frequently with coffee—to keep world prices stable. Insofar as finished goods are concerned, doors are closed through quotas, licenses, monetary controls, and above all through tariffs. If British shoe manufacturers can produce a pair of shoes, delivered in New York, say for $9, while it costs American firms $10 for a comparable pair, the effect of a 20 percent tariff is to raise the price of the English product to $10.80 and thus price it out of the market. In point of fact the United States has been one of the worst practitioners of economic nationalism—closing its doors— through high tariffs. According to Eugene Staley, commenting on the subject in 1937, the United States "has long been one of the outstanding offenders against world trade by reason of . . . high protective duties." Under the reciprocal trade treaty program, initiated by Franklin Roosevelt, the United States did lower tariff walls when other governments gave it a reciprocal benefit of some sort; but generally its duties were above the median of other powers. Insofar as the export of capital is concerned, some nations restrict them through a licensing system, high taxes on profits, or by placing limits on the amount of profits foreign corporations can send home— repatriate, as it is called.

The business of foreign policy and the time of diplomats is preoccupied to a considerable extent with erecting and breaking down barriers of this sort. The most direct way of assuring a supply of raw materials or a market, of course, is by converting a weak nation into a colony, protectorate, or sphere of influence. By acquiring India as a colony, Britain assured itself of a supply of jute and an outlet for its textiles. By making the Caribbean an "American lake" the United States guaranteed its dominance over the banana industry of Panama and Guatemala, the coffee industry of Haiti and El Salvador, the sugar industry of the Dominican Republic.

The United States, as a latecomer on the colonialist scene, however, had a choice either of fighting established empires, such as Britain, for their holdings, or pursuing a more subtle strategy. Historians Henry Bamford Parkes and Vincent P. Carosso assert that "in the 1920's when the chief competitor of the United States was Great Britain, it was sometimes suggested that the two nations would eventually go to war with each other." Their economic battlefront centered, among other things, on the oil of Venezuela, Colombia (won by the Americans), Iran, Iraq, and Mexico. But military war against Britain was not necessary for America's commercial designs; it could accomplish much the same through the euphemistic-sounding strategy of "open door."

Originally proclaimed by Secretary of State John Hay, in September 1899, relative to China, "open door" had the pleasant connotation of anticolonialism and anti-interventionism. But it was nothing of the sort. The United States did not object to the extraterritorial rights established by England, France, Germany, Russia, and Japan;

it only demanded that American businessmen have "equality of opportunity" with these powers in exploiting China. As Woodrow Wilson frankly conceded, it was "not the open door to the rights of China, but the open door to the goods of America." Thomas W. Lamont, senior partner of the House of Morgan, explained that the "open door" was aimed solely at remedying a situation in which China was divided "commercially into almost water-tight compartments, and the nations like the United States which had no compartment could not do much trading." It is instructive that Hay's unilateral proclamation was in considerable measure inspired by the American Asiatic Association, a group of textile firms with a stake in the cotton goods market of the Orient, which accused Europe of a "conscious or an instinctive" drive against the United States "for the markets of the world," and by the American China Development Company, which held a concession for a small part of the Peking-to-Canton railroad—and wanted more. Anticolonialism had nothing to do with the "open door." When Hay spoke of sustaining the "territorial integrity" of the Celestial Empire, it was not because he opposed colonialism per se but because he feared that the division of China would exclude Uncle Sam, that Russia would become sovereign in Manchuria and the territory up to the Great Wall; that Germany would acquire Shantung; France, the three southern provinces; and that Britain would gain the lion's share around the Yangtse basin, as well as Honan and Shansi. Had this happened America's chances of penetrating the Chinese market would have been even less auspicious than under the extraterritorial system, and it was for this reason that Hay became a proponent of "territorial integrity" for China. But this did not prevent the United States from joining four other powers in crushing the Boxer Rebellion of 1900, which would have assured China's national independence. The "open door," then, was simply a specific means by which America, endowed with a highly efficient industrial machine but few colonies or spheres of influence in Asia or Africa, waged economic war against competitors. As the *Nation* pointed out many years later, "Under the Open Door policy . . . we assume that we are giving all countries, and particularly Japan, an equal opportunity to do business in that market. But so vast are our natural resources and so highly developed is our system that the real advantages are all on our side. . . . The Open Door, paradoxically enough, stands in the way of [Japan's] expansion." It was a formula best suited for Uncle Sam's expansion, and highly unsuited for certain other powers.

As practiced in the 1920's, the "open door" was a means of crowning the imperial victory gained by Washington in the First World

War. Using its great economic, diplomatic, and on occasion military power, it pried open many doors closed to American business. Washington protested to Britain in 1920, for instance, that its oil firms were being excluded from any role in the Turkish Petroleum Company—a consortium of British, French, and Dutch interests—which held a concession for the Mosul fields in Mesopotamia. After some years of negotiations, American interests, headed by Standard Oil, received a one-fifth share. When Holland refused to consider an American request for participation in an oil venture by a British-Dutch firm in the Dutch East Indies, the United States retaliated by denying the Dutch-controlled Shell Company of California a lease on public land in Utah. After years of diplomatic exchanges, Holland agreed that U.S. firms would be given some rights in the East Indies.

Behind the schema of "open door" Uncle Sam pursued an aggressive economic and diplomatic "war." Herbert Hoover, as Secretary of Commerce in the Coolidge regime, sent commercial attachés or trade commissioners into "practically every foreign country" searching out opportunities for American business. With the approval of the State Department, mountains of private loans went to foreign countries, usually with specific concessions demanded in return. Loans to Liberia, for instance, were predicated on an exclusive concession for the Firestone rubber interests. On occasion healthy bribes went along with the loans, such as a payment of $415,000 to the son of the president of Peru by J. & W. Seligman and Company, and a payment of a half million dollars plus an annual salary of $19,000 to the son-in-law of the Cuban president by the Chase National Bank. "Many of the Latin American loans," observe Parkes and Carosso, "were not spent on productive economic investments, but helped to keep dictatorial regimes in power." They did, however, augment U.S. trade and did result in mining, petroleum, and many other concessions.

On the other hand, Hoover tried with might and main to weaken the position of countries that supplied rubber, long-staple cotton, iodine, nitrates, potash, mercury, sisal, and other commodites that American manufacturers felt were exorbitantly priced. Representatives of a sisal corporation of Yucatan, Mexico, a Franco-German potash syndicate, a Canadian asbestos firm, and a Dutch quinine company were prosecuted in the United States on charges of combining "in restraint of lawful trade or free competition," or of working "to increase the market price" of these commodities. The State Department refused to sanction loans to the potash syndicate as a reprisal for high prices. Where the shoe was on the other foot, however, Washington winked an eye at monopolistic practices and price fixing. The Copper Export Association, organized by American firms in 1918, under the Webb-Pomerene Act, withheld a considerable amount of the metal from the world market so as to sustain high prices. After this first association passed on, American producers formed Copper Exporters, Inc., and with the help of allies in Europe pushed prices upward, to as high as 24 cents a pound.

Other devices adopted in the worldwide economic war included payments of $2.5 million a year and monopoly rights in carrying mail to Pan American Airways, so that it could dominate the air traffic of Central and South America. According to President Roosevelt these governmental subsidies were necessary to strengthen "trade relations with these [Latin American] countries"; and according to Pan Am's president, Juan Trippe, his firm was the "aerial ambassador of American industry." Just prior to World War II this private corporation was given federal money to build bases in South America, Africa, and certain Pacific Islands, in part for strategic, in part for commercial, purposes. Uncle Sam, notes Benjamin Williams, was "enthusiastic for the open door as a policy for others, while it has maintained the closed door for itself."

III

Few people in the "golden" 1920's realized there was something foreboding in the economic aggression practiced by the United States and all great powers—or anything synthetic about their prosperity. Three months before he left office Coolidge proclaimed that "the country is in the midst of an era of prosperity more extensive and of peace more permanent that it has ever before experienced." A half year later Hoover played the same tune, noting exuberantly that "we in America today are nearer the final triumph over poverty than ever before in our land. The poorhouse is vanishing among us." Cold statistics showed an increase in the gross national product, that ultimate materialist measurement of national greatness, from $70 billion in the depression year 1921 to $103 billion in 1929—with prices fairly stable. Government data on per capita earnings showed that they had risen by almost a fifth; others placed it at a third.

On the international front too, there was that comfortable feeling that America had found its place in the sun and that its supremacy in world affairs was—in the words of Max Weber—"as inevitable as that of Rome in the ancient world after the Punic War." The nation thought of itself as isolationist and refused to enter into alliances with other powers, but it was nonetheless the epicenter of the international community. At the Washington Conference of November 1921, called by Secretary of State Charles Evans Hughes, three interrelated treaties were concluded to nurture the stability sought by Washington. The Four-power Treaty, between the United States, Britain, France, and Japan, guaranteed respect for each other's island possessions in the Pacific. The Five-power Treaty—with Italy added—limited naval strength to 525,000 tons each for Britain and America; 315,000 tons for Japan; and 172,000 each for France and Italy. The Nine-power Treaty sanctified the open-door principle and agreed to the territorial integrity of China. Under severe American —and British—pressure Japan was forced to evacuate Siberia and Shantung, return a railroad to China, and grant Uncle Sam cable rights on the island of Yap. The Japanese yielded grudgingly, but their need for American economic aid—and for the friendship of Britain—evidently outweighed other considerations. It was a feather in the American cap too when Secretary of State Frank Kellogg and French Foreign Minister Aristide Briand signed the Kellogg-Briand Treaty—concurred in by fifteen other states—renouncing "war as an instrument of national policy" and agreeing to solve any and all disputes between nations by "pacific means."

The United States seemed to be reaching a zenith of power, capable of bending others to its will—and it was doing it with only minimal recourse to military force. Its most formidable weapon for expansion was again, as under Taft, the dollar—"the Dollar Decade," James Warren Prothro called it. American banking firms, under a pledge given by J. P. Morgan to Harding in 1921, made no foreign investments without approval by the State Department and were thereby able to punish America's "enemies" and reward its "friends." Thus a projected loan to France in 1921 by J. P. Morgan was vetoed pending payment of part of $400 million owed the United States for military supplies. When Italy applied for financing from the same House of Morgan in 1925, it was hastily forced to sign a war-debts agreement before the State Department would let down the bars. Japan, which did not enjoy prosperity equal to that of other great powers in the 1920's, was denied a loan by the Oriental Development Company (guaranteed by the National City Company) because the State Department considered her activities in Manchuria a breach of the open door. Only a few *short-term* credits (by General Motors, General Electric, etc.) were permitted to the Soviet Union, on the theory that she was an avowed enemy of "world order." The large loans made to Germany made their way back to New York for the most part, through a circuitous route by which the Reich used them to pay reparations to the Allies, the Allies in turn paid some of their war debts to Uncle Sam and bought some of his goods.

The flaws in this Dollar Decade did not become evident until the stock market crash of 1929, which inaugurated the Great Depression, and sharpened international rivalries that a decade later led to war. In subsequent years it became fashionable to blame these catastrophes on the foibles of myopic leaders. But at the tiller in October 1929 was a man of stature and depth, Herbert Clark Hoover. If Harding, an amiable journalist from Marion, Ohio, was of limited education and even more limited vision, and Coolidge a "respectable mediocrity," Hoover was a man of considerable attainments and intellect. He was not, as commonly believed, an extreme reactionary; he was considered, in fact, the most "liberal" member of the Harding-Coolidge cabinets. Mary Elizabeth Lease, the Populist agitator of the 1890's, called him "one sent by God." He had flirted with the Bull Moosers in 1912 and later tried to buy into the *New Republic* magazine, then and now the voice of liberalism. If the image he projected in the 1930's was of a dour, unconcerned, heartless representative of Wall Street, no one can disparage his work as a humanitarian after World War I. He may be criticized for seeking to use food as a political weapon—particularly against the Bolsheviks—but his relief work throughout Europe was impressive nonetheless. John Maynard Keynes, to whose economic views Hoover was titanically opposed, said of Hoover's activities with the American Relief Administration that "never was a nobler work of disinterested goodwill carried through with more tenacity and sincerity and skill, and with less thanks either asked or given."

Hoover was the self-made man personified. His father, a devout Quaker and village blacksmith in West Branch, Iowa, where Herbert was born, died when he was six; his mother, a gifted woman, also a Quaker and well known as a preacher, died three years later. The three orphaned children were divided among relatives; Herbert, the middle one, went to an uncle on his mother's side—a doctor and land speculator who was moderately well-to-do. Herbert acquired an education at a small Quaker academy, then at the newly opened Stanford University in California, where he worked part time and summers to pay his own way. At college he associated with and helped organize the poorer students, and, in the only other job besides president to which he was elected, was chosen treasurer of the school body in 1893. He graduated with an engineering diploma two years later in the midst of another terrible depression, so that instead of working at his profession, he was forced to take on a common laborer's job in a Nevada mine, shoveling ore at $2.50 a day.

It was not long, however, before he had become assistant to a prominent San Francisco engineer and from there moved along to his first foreign assignment as an engineer for British gold mines in Australia. At twenty-four he was earning $7,500 a year; at forty, after marriage and a host of jobs in China, Italy, Central America, Russia, Burma, and elsewhere, he was linked with a couple of dozen mining companies and was a millionaire.

Perhaps it was Hoover's Quaker background or his knack for administration, but when he found himself stranded in Europe at the outbreak of World War I, he organized a private relief agency for tens of thousands of fellow Americans similarly unable to get home. Before he had completed this task he was called on to perform the same kind of duties for 10 million starving Belgians and Frenchmen. With the approval of the American ambassador to London, Walter Hines Page, Hoover formed the Commission for Relief in Belgium and distributed to the needy 5 million tons of food and clothing valued at a billion dollars—no mean task considering the blockade that hampered shipments. When the United States entered the fray, President Wilson called on Hoover to act as food administrator back home, and again he acquitted himself well. After the war, duty called him once more to Europe, this time to provide food for relief in twenty-three countries.

Hoover was no innocent dispensing food for its own sake; it was for him, as for Wilson, part of a program for rebuilding the old continent as a liberal capitalist haven, secure from the virus of Bolshevism. "My job," he later asserted, "was to nurture the frail plants of democracy in Europe against . . . anarchy or Communism. And Communism was the pit into which all governments were in danger of falling when frantic peoples were driven by the Horsemen of Famine and Pestilence." The same motivation undoubtedly caused him to assume another relief project in the fall of 1921, when he was Secretary of Commerce, to feed 10 million Russians in the Volga Valley.

Like General Eisenhower three decades later, Hoover the humanitarian seemed to be a man above politics, with no known affiliations. He had been an advocate of Wilson's Fourteen Points and, with reservations, of the League of Nations; when asked in 1920 to define his political philosophy he described himself as "an independent progressive." When he announced his availability for the Republican presidential nomination soon thereafter, it was as "a forward-looking liberal," a designation that no doubt contributed to the fact that the old guard passed him over, despite his immense national following, for the nondescript Harding. By 1928 he was the party's natural and overwhelming choice, and he ran off with the election with 444 electoral votes against a mere 87 for the colorful Alfred E. Smith of New York. He was, as the campaign showed, a poor orator and something less than dynamic in his public stance, but he was neither incompetent nor base, and though he believed in individualism, it was with certain qualifications to protect the weak from the strong.

If the economy came apart at the seams during Hoover's presidency, then, it was not because of his ineptness—though he undoubtedly could have administered first aid quicker and more effectively—but because of inherent weaknesses in the system over which he presided. Franklin D. Roosevelt put his finger on one of the major difficulties during the 1932 election campaign, when he told the story of *Alice in Wonderland* and the Republican leader, Humpty Dumpty:

"What if we produce a surplus?" Alice asked.

"Oh, we can sell it to foreign consumers," replied Humpty Dumpty.

"How can the foreigners pay for it?"

"Why, we will lend them the money."

"I see," said Alice, "they will buy our surplus with our money. Of course, they will pay us back by selling us their goods?"

"Oh, not at all. We set up a high wall called the tariff."

"And how will the foreigners pay off these loans?"

"That is easy," said Humpty Dumpty. "Did you ever hear of a moratorium?"

Be that as it may, the Depression simply overwhelmed Hoover, the nation, and indeed the rest of the world, which suffered under its backlash. Within a few weeks after Black Thursday on the stock market, $30 billion of paper value, a sum larger than the national debt, had "vanished into thin air." As the banks began calling in loans to stock speculators, thousands were wiped out, hundreds committed suicide. From October 1, 1929, to August 31, 1932, 4,835 banks failed, costing depositors more than $3.25 billion. The value of all stocks listed on the stock exchange fell from ninety to sixteen billion. The consequence was a merry-go-round of economic tragedy, loans called in where falling stocks had been put up as collateral, curtailment of business spending, reduction in manufacture, layoff of workers, further cuts in spending, further loans called in. The full effects were not felt immediately, but by late 1932 and early 1933 industrial production had fallen by one half, construction by six sevenths, and farm prices, already depressed, by three fifths. A million agricultural families had abandoned their homesteads and 13 million workers were without jobs, with at least an equal number working only short hours. "This depression," commented Colonel Leonard Ayres in *The Economics of Recovery*, "has been far more severe than any of the 20 depressions that we have experienced in this country since 1790."

IV

If international rivalry is sharp in good times, it is bound to be intensified in bad ones, when world markets contract and "exportable surpluses" glut the home economy. The Great Depression, which soon engulfed all the major nations, caused each one to severely readjust relations with rivals and led, in the end, to an irreconcilable impasse between them—and to war. There were, of course, other factors, rooted in tradition and national psychology, but as the Office of Naval Intelligence has observed, "all wars have been for economic reasons." The one that began in 1939 was no exception. Again, it was the have-not nations, so-called, which seemed to be on the offensive, but in fact all the powers were involved in the continuing battle, each one taking different measures of defense depending on its needs and inner reserves.

Hoover's response to the crisis in the United States, after a few reassuring speeches about having "turned the corner" and the need for "confidence," changed little in either the tone or the structure of society. Like Grover Cleveland before the turn of the century, he operated on the thesis that while "the people support the government, the government should not support the people." He had used government funds for relief in Europe, and during a drought in Arkansas in December 1930 urged Congress to allocate $45 million to save the animals, but he opposed government relief to human beings at home. Instead, under the directorship of Walter S. Gifford of the American Telephone and Telegraph Company, an attempt was made to raise $175 million from voluntary private sources to feed the 20 million people estimated then to need help. Hoover's primary counterattack against the Depression was the passage in January 1932 of a bill for a Reconstruction Finance Corporation, which provided $3.5 billion for loans to banks, insurance companies, and similar institutions. Cynics called it a "breadline for big business." The only concession to the indigent was a rider to the RFC bill, making $300 million available to the states after July 1932 to finance relief for the poor. Thus, despite a harrowing slump, the old establishment felt itself sufficiently secure to make little modification in its structure. Laissez-faire continued to dominate economic habits and rugged individualism the minds of social philosophers.

In the area of international affairs Hoover's reactions had that same lackluster and unimaginative quality, centering on old-style economic nationalism. The total foreign trade of all nations was on the downswing—from almost $70 billion in 1929 to $25 billion in 1932; that of the United States from $9.6 billion to $2.9 billion. Enormous "exportable surpluses" piled up everywhere, with no place to export them. The same was true of exportable capital; foreign issues on the New York Stock Exchange fell from a billion dollars in 1928 to $229 million in 1931, and zero in 1932. In the words of two economists, Howard C. Hill and Rexford G. Tugwell, "we ceased to be able to lend money to buy our own goods."

In this dolorous situation Hoover had a choice of lowering tariffs so as to permit foreign powers to sell more in the United States—to pay for what they might buy *from* the United States, or raising the barriers to choke off imports, thereby protecting American producers. He chose the latter course. In June 1930 the Hawley-Smoot Act increased duties on 890 products while lowering them on only 235. Since the American tariff was already much higher than those of other nations—34 percent of the value of manufactured goods, as against 20 percent for Germany and 21 percent for France—the effect was not only to curtail trade further but to bring on a host of retaliatory measures. Twenty-nine governments expressed their disenchantment with American policy by sending notes of protest to Washington. Canada adopted rules that gave preference to British trade over American. Argentina entered into a reciprocal agreement with England, to exchange raw materials and manufactured goods, the effect of which was to enhance British trade and further depress Uncle Sam's business with the Argentines. France, Spain, and some smaller European nations imposed quotas on foreign goods, ten countries required importers to secure licenses before they could buy from abroad, and twenty nations established controls over currency to stop the flight of money and to limit imports. Late in 1931, nineteen nations went off the gold standard, thus reducing purchases from places like the United States, which required a settlement of accounts in gold. Most important, Britain jettisoned its long-standing free-trade policy, and levied a 10 percent duty on many commodities. In view of the fact that, as Sir Norman Angell once noted, wealth under capitalism depends on "keeping the traffic moving," measures which slowed the traffic simply pyramided crisis on crisis. That was especially true of the weaker links on the capitalist chain—such as Japan.

The land of Nippon had joined the industrial revolution late in history, and was still woefully backward in heavy industry. As of

1929 its steel production was a mere 2.5 million tons; two thirds of its exports were in soft goods—textiles and silk. According to a survey by Sir Thomas Holland, of the twenty-five raw materials indispensable for a modern economy, Japan had an adequate supply only of three and no supply at all of seventeen—as against the British empire which had adequate amounts of eighteen and the American empire of sixteen. Since almost all of its silk and nearly half of its exports went to the United States, the effect of the slump in America on the relatively fragile Japanese system was direct and traumatic. Japanese capitalists moved hastily to develop a rayon industry as a substitute for silk, but this did little to assuage the circumstances of hundreds of thousands of farmers who depended on silk for a living. It was apparent that if Japan wanted to offset the effects of the Depression and keep up industrially with the other great powers she would have to take measures much more drastic than those adopted, say, by Hoover.

To leading figures in Japan, the indicated path out of their dilemma was one of colonial expansion abroad and the garrison state at home—long advocated by such military-minded organizations as the Kokuryukai. Formed in 1901, often called the Black Dragon Society, this group proposed to "renovate the present system, foster a foreign policy aiming at expansion overseas . . . and establish a social policy that will settle problems between labor and capital." In America, where the economy was severely stalled but where there were large reserves to fall back on, the Hoover regime was replaced by a government of reform; in Japan, where the reserves were meager, ultranationalist regimes emerged—after a series of political assassinations—dominated by the military. Their first step toward colonial expansion was the conversion of the Chinese province of Manchuria—500,000 square miles, or one sixth the size of continental United States—into a puppet state. On September 18, 1931, using the pretext that vandals had slightly damaged their railroad line near Mukden, the Japanese attacked a nearby group of Chinese soldiers and moved from there to overwhelm the whole province. Some months later a vassal regime declared its independence of China and Pu Yi, last of a line of old Manchu emperors, was installed as the figurehead leader of a new "country," Manchukuo, totally under the Nipponese thumb.

The United States, in the person of Secretary of State Henry Stimson, refused to recognize this new state, for it had been born in direct violation not only of the Kellogg-Briand pact, but, even more, of the open-door policy. It was the first important step toward a reshuffling of world power, and the have nations, in particular the

United States, saw it as a direct threat to their own status. The economic results were also unacceptable, for while Japan's share of exports to Manchuria (Manchukuo) rose from 36 percent of the total in 1930 to 72 percent in 1936, America's share fell from 7 percent to 3.5. Within a few years almost every foreign firm—other than Japanese—had been forced to withdraw from Manchukuo. Symbolic of the puppet regime's attitude was the formation of a national oil monopoly which effectively froze out British and American petroleum interests. Moreover, the Japanese seemed intent on continuing their military offensive into China—they attacked Shanghai in January 1932, seized Jehol in 1933, Inner Mongolia and Northern China in 1935–36—until all of China, Manchukuo and Japan were welded into a single economic bloc. This would, of course, seriously reduce the trade and investment of other powers in the Far East.

If these steps seemed ominous, illegal, and indecent to Washington, they were for Tokyo only an expression of "manifest destiny"— and there were many throughout the world who considered it justified. "Japan," said former British Labor Minister H. B. Lees-Smith in March 1932, "had an undoubted case against the rest of the world, which we must now admit. She could not support her population without foreign trade, which would bring her the food and raw materials without which she could not live. . . . She was desperate. If we were in her position we should not die quietly, but we should undoubtedly burst out somewhere, as she has done in Manchuria and Shanghai." Writing more dispassionately, American Professor Charles S. Tippetts predicted that "those nations which have already cornered 'enough' of the world's resources will become the object of jealousy and hatred of those who are not so fortunate. Those countries which have almost 'enough' will try to grab more territory so that they will have what they need." Many Americans believed (Franklin Roosevelt among them) that Japan would not stop until she controlled "all of Asia including India," a prospect that have nations would not tolerate indefinitely.

As of the middle of the decade 51.5 percent of raw materials imported into the United States came from Asia. Malaya and the Dutch East Indies provided 86 percent of the crude rubber and 87 percent of the tin bought from the outside. From Asia too came 87 percent of the tungsten, 99 percent of the jute, 98 percent of the shellac, and one third of the mica. The danger of cutting off access to these commodities was enough to send shivers down Washington's back.

Herbert Hoover pointed out just before he left office in 1933, that "the American people will soon be at the fork of three roads." The first option open to them was "cooperation among nations . . . to re-move the obstructions to world consumption and rising prices." The second was "to rely upon our high degree of national self-contain-ment, to increase our tariffs, to create quotas and discriminations, and to engage in definite methods of curtailment of agricultural and other products and thus to secure a larger measure of economic iso-lation from world influence." The third was to "inflate our currency, consequently abandoning the gold standard, and with our depre-ciated currency attempt to enter a world economic war; with the certainty that it leads to complete destruction both at home and abroad." There were other possibilities as well. One of them, put forward by historian Charles Beard and philosopher John Dewey, called for the establishment of a planned economy that would set America's course toward democratic socialism. The government would fix a desired national standard of living, and plan production so that this standard was met. By controlling both production and consumption the United States could adjust to whatever resources were available and reduce its reliance on world markets.

In a highly competitive capitalist world, however, with frictions intensified by the Depression, the trend of events was toward nei-ther international cooperation nor internal planning, but toward economic war, as Hoover had predicted, and toward territorial ex-pansion and martial holocaust.

☆☆☆☆☆

15

☆☆☆☆☆

THE WAR BEFORE THE
WAR (II)

On January 30, 1933, Adolf Hitler was appointed chancellor of Germany. The Depression that originated in New York had taken an extraordinary toll on the Reich. Loans from America had sustained it in the 1920's and saved it from revolution, but with America itself now in difficulties no new loans were available. The moratorium on war debts, including German reparations, effected by President Hoover in 1931 ameliorated the crisis slightly, but the economy was much too sick for mere palliatives. Exports had fallen from 13 billion reichsmarks in 1929 to 5 billion in 1933; thousands of small businesses had folded; and perhaps as many as 6 million proletarians were without jobs. In July 1931, one of the Reich's largest banks, the Darmstaedter und Nationalbank, collapsed, causing the government temporarily to shut down all the others lest there be a run on their deposits. Though Germany's economic machine was much more advanced than, say, Japan's, the depression of foreign markets and the shortage of foreign exchange with which to buy raw materials was bound to have a harrowing effect nonetheless. The country was in desperate need of cash or credit to buy silk, rubber, manganese, nickel, tungsten, tin, copper, petroleum, chromium, iron ore. With many people starving and a few skinning cats for food, a drastic political change, either rightist or leftist, was inevitable. When the socialists, Communists, and trade union leaders were unable or unwilling to form a united front against the tide of National Socialism, Hitler's Nazis rode to power. With them came not only anti-Semitism and a new approach to domestic problems, but a foreign policy, like Japan's, oriented on expansion.

A month after Hitler's success, Franklin D. Roosevelt, having defeated the incumbent Hoover by the lopsided score of 472 electoral votes to 59, was sworn in as President of the United States. The history of the next decade would pivot around these two self-assured but totally different men, Hitler and Roosevelt.

The squire of Hyde Park, New York, came to office at a time when everything seemed to be falling apart and not a few citizens were beginning to discuss the possibility of revolution. As president, FDR sired a host of alphabetical agencies—AAA, NRA, FERA, CWA, TVA, CCC, WPA, FHA, NLRB, SEC, REA, to name some—which gave his administration a magical luster in the folklore of America, and he showed a facility for experimentation unmatched by any other president of this century. Roosevelt was an empiricist who sought class peace and was willing to discipline his own capitalist class to get it. Given the reserves of vitality still hidden in the system he presided over, and given his own background and disposition, the former New York governor was able to prescribe his nostrums within, rather than outside, the framework of parliamentary democracy. But on second sight these nostrums were closer to the traditionalism of his upbringing than the encompassing panaceas of many of his supporters.

Unlike Hoover, the self-made man, Roosevelt was a patrician, born with a gold spoon that never wore thin. His family tree on the paternal side was American back to the 1640's, when Claes Martenszen Van Rosenvelt came to Nieuw Amsterdam from Holland; and on his mother's side to 1621, when the French-Dutch Delano family (originally De La Noye) set foot on Plymouth Rock. Genealogists claim he was distantly related to eleven American presidents, including Teddy Roosevelt, his fifth cousin.

The only son of a second marriage by James Roosevelt, fifty-two at the time, and Sara Delano, a twenty-six-year-old former debutante, Franklin lived in a milieu that was, if not flamboyantly rich, considerably better than comfortable. He was educated by governesses and tutors, had his own pony and sailboat, and had been taken on pilgrimages to Europe eight times before he had learned how to shave properly. School meant Groton, the elite haven run by the Reverend Endicott Peabody; Harvard, the mecca of so many upper-class youngsters; and a stint at Columbia Law School. Though he failed to finish his law studies—because of poor grades—he passed a subsequent bar examination and went on to a desultory career with a New York law firm, meanwhile dabbling in sundry public and charitable activities which gave the Roosevelts a reputation for *noblesse oblige*. The salaries he earned, in this and other jobs, were frosting to a cake already sufficiently sweet. While he was in

Washington, as Assistant Secretary of the Navy under Wilson, ten
servants manned his household. When he died he left a fortune of $2
million, plus a half million in insurance, twice as much as the legacies left by Coolidge, Wilson, and Taft combined.

Franklin Roosevelt's liberalism, then, was a branch grafted to a
root of conservative background. It was enriched by his marriage to
Eleanor Roosevelt, niece of Teddy, and also a remote cousin, who
was more advanced in this respect than FDR. As a New York State
senator from the district around Hyde Park, he made a good but not
remarkable record as a progressive—he favored social legislation,
women's suffrage, direct election of senators, party primaries. After
a visit to Woodrow Wilson in 1911, he campaigned hard for the
New Freedom candidate (against his fifth cousin, Teddy), and as a
sign of his predilections was rewarded not with a post to challenge
his social values but with one in the Navy Department. In 1920 he
was chosen vice-presidential candidate on the Democratic slate,
then lapsed into obscurity after August 1921, when he was caught in
a siege of infantile paralysis. Friendly biographers insist that the experience of living in a wheelchair and wearing braces (for the rest
of his life) tempered his spirit. Nonetheless when he returned to politics, under the encouragement of his wife and his close associate
Louis Howe, to win the state governorship in 1928, he still lacked
that zeal for innovation that was to characterize his first five and a
half years at the White House. He was a likable man, warm, with a
dazzling smile visible behind the long cigarette holder that he held
at a jaunty angle, an excellent mixer, charmingly impulsive. Yet, as
Walter Lippmann observed, he was neither a "crusader," a "tribune
of the people," nor an "enemy of entrenched privilege." His New
Deal, William E. Leuchtenberg wrote, "never demonstrated that it
could achieve prosperity in peacetime." Without World War II and
the postwar military expenditures that absorbed the unemployed,
the Roosevelt bundle of experiments would today appear much less
glossy.

What distinguished Roosevelt from another wartime president,
Wilson, was a much keener recognition—perhaps intuitive—that in
addition to free access to the world's markets, American capitalism
needed an international climate of social stability. Revolution was a
threat equal to or greater than the closed door, and unless the two
were dealt with as interrelated phenomena America had no future
as a great empire. When Roosevelt recognized the Soviet Union on
November 16, 1933—after four American presidents had refused to
deal with it for sixteen years—he did it in part because he felt that
a *modus vivendi* with the Communists would result in muting their

propaganda for class struggle and revolution. He was rewarded handsomely during the next few years. Stalinist agitation for a revolution in Cuba, previously high on the Russian agenda, ceased without notice. Roosevelt himself, charged by the American Communists with "carrying out more thoroughly, more brutally than Hoover, the capitalist attack against the living standards of the masses" was soon hailed as a "middle of the roader" who merited support; and the Communist Party, which had been calling the President a "reactionary," declared itself "fully prepared to continue and develop our united front relations with those who support Roosevelt." Backhanded endorsement of the New Deal by the Soviet-oriented segment of the left was an important factor in stilling the militant storms within the United States in the 1930's, and though Roosevelt did not avow a formal alliance with the Communists he refrained from red-baiting and he gave jobs to many people who sympathized with the Soviet cause. During World War II he evolved the strategy of "coexistence," by which the United States and the Soviet Union would collaborate on a world scale so that the colonial revolution then rising to the surface would be guided to "safe" and peaceful channels, undisturbing to America's needs for markets and raw materials.

Quite naturally Roosevelt's first preoccupation was in plugging a leaking ship foundering badly at home. On that fateful Saturday when he took the oath of office, Governor Herbert H. Lehman of New York had put an executive padlock on the state's banks in order to avoid a run. Nine other states had already declared a bank holiday, including California and Michigan—and the New York Stock Exchange, as well as the Chicago Board of Trade and a half dozen commodity markets, shut their doors. Millions of people and innumerable communities found themselves penniless. Added to the unemployment of a quarter of the working class (another fourth was working only part time) and the mammoth decline in production, this represented the nadir of the Depression.

Roosevelt responded with one hundred days of the most frenzied legislative and executive activity in American history. Invoking an old Trading with the Enemy Act, he forbade trade in foreign exchange, or the export of gold. He declared a four-day national bank holiday during which no currency or gold could be paid depositors. Many had expected that FDR would nationalize the credit institutions, but the banking bill, hastily passed at a special session, used more traditional techniques, such as the printing of more money. A Federal Deposit Insurance Corporation was formed to guarantee individual bank deposits up to $5,000, and a Federal Emergency Relief Administration was set up to dole out a half billion dollars to the states for direct relief to the jobless and poor. As an offshoot of FERA, the Civil Works Administration initiated 180,000 "made-work" projects within four months, repairing schools, cleaning playgrounds, improving roads, beautifying parks, operating a pest- and erosion-control program. A Public Works Administration, with a $3.3 billion budget, was mandated to revive the construction industry, and a Civilian Conservation Corps to make jobs for young people at $30 a month, plus food, lodging, and uniforms. All of this, and other measures, fitted a new nomenclature called "pump priming," and a new economic philosophy designed by the English economist John Maynard Keynes, which held that in a crisis the government itself must take over the task of stimulating demand for goods, even if it meant large budgetary deficits.

To set the wheels of agricultural and industrial production turning, Roosevelt took two shaky steps toward national planning. The Agricultural Adjustment Administration paid farmers hundreds of millions of dollars from the federal treasury to kill 6 million pigs, plow under 10 million acres of cotton, as well as other crops. The purpose obviously was to reduce supply, raise prices and profits, and thereby encourage the agricultural community to plow its curtailed acreage. The National Industrial Recovery Act authorized businessmen in each industry to establish associations and draw up codes of fair practices, dealing with prices, wages, hours, exchange of information, etc., subject to presidential approval.

NRA—the National Recovery Administration—was not empowered to do national planning, as men like Rexford Tugwell urged, but solely to help each segment of industry recover separately. In essence, what it amounted to was a pledge by government that if industry raised wages and reduced hours, thereby increasing the demand for goods, it would be allowed to set prices for its products without antitrust prosecution. A blanket code was proclaimed setting a 35-hour week for blue-collar workers and 40 hours for white-collar employees, with a 40-cent-an-hour minimum for the former and $12 to $15 a week for the latter. Since the code was not enforceable by law it was enforced by appeals to the public not to buy the goods of any producer who failed to display the Blue Eagle symbol, showing that he had complied. In all, 576 basic and 189 supplementary codes were drawn up by industrialists. The codes had the basic weakness, as a Rooseveltian review board stated in 1934, that they "offered an opportunity for the more powerful and more profitable interests to seize control of an industry or to augment and extend a control already obtained." But the wheels did begin to turn: the gross national product rose from $56 billion in 1933 to $72.5 billion in 1935 and $100.6 billion in 1940—almost as much as in 1929. Unemployment fell from 25 percent of the labor force in the former year to 15 percent in the latter. If this was not the grandiose achievement that the New Deal image has evoked in popular minds, it nonetheless was a precondition for coming to grips with external problems.

On that score—external problems—the President was of a mind with his predecessors of the previous half century, that overseas economic expansion was a *sine qua non* for survival. "Foreign markets must be regained," he argued. "There is no other way if we would avoid painful economic dislocation, social readjustments, and unemployment." Secretary of Agriculture Henry A. Wallace called foreign economic expansion vital if the United States were not to lapse into fascism or socialism. Leon Trotsky, the exiled leader of the Russian Revolution, assessing New Deal prospects, put the matter more aggressively in an April 1934 article: "Sooner or later American capitalism must open up ways for itself throughout the length and breadth of our entire planet. By what methods? By *all* methods. A high coefficient of productivity denotes also a high coefficient of destructive force." Historian Beard insisted that endless expansion abroad, even if only economic, was a sure-fire formula for imperialism and war, and suggested that America adopt instead a Five-year Plan that would organize the corporate economy, control surpluses, and introduce a measure of self-containment.

But the New Deal and its brain trust of intellectual advisers, knowingly or unknowingly, were headed in the path that Trotsky outlined and that would eventually blend into global imperialism. Whether the methods they used to increase foreign markets were fair or unfair, moral or immoral, compared to those of Germany, Japan, and Italy, is a moot and irrelevant question, for it was the *intensification* of the world economic war that tipped the scales toward military solutions. In a hundred different ways every government was subsidizing its exporters, so that a clash between private businessmen inevitably became a clash between governments.

One method for "regaining foreign markets" was to establish normal trade relations with the Soviet Union. It was a notion championed not merely by so-called fellow travelers but by such sound business institutions as the General Motors Export Corporation, hoping for a new market of 160 million people. At the London Economic Conference, which convened in June 1933, Soviet Foreign Minister Maxim Litvinov held forth the prospect of a billion dollars a year in trade between his country and America—no mean sum at a time when total U.S. commerce with foreign powers was in the neighborhood of $3–$4 billion a year. Even before recognition, the Reconstruction Finance Corporation issued a multimillion-dollar credit for Russia to buy American cotton. Once recognition was accorded, the administration set up an Export-Import Bank to provide loans on a more systematized basis. Such a government agency was something new in peacetime, but according to the corporation lawyer and future Secretary of State, John Foster Dulles, private loans could no longer sustain international markets. It was necessary for the government to supply the dollars for "foreigners to acquire goods for which domestic consumers would otherwise have to be found." In that way the "risk would be placed upon the taxpayers as a whole rather than upon individual investors." Each citizen, in other words, rich or poor, was subsidizing the private exporters in order to improve the general economic climate.

Hopes for enlarged trade with the Soviet Union foundered when Secretary Cordell Hull and Litvinov quarreled over how much of the tsarist war debts were due the United States; and Litvinov asked for a loan which could be spent anywhere in the world rather than exclusively in the United States. Washington lost interest in Soviet trade and turned instead to other devices. One was the manipulation of currency and gold so as to make the purchase of American goods more attractive. The dollar was devalued to 59.06 cents, making it possible for foreigners to buy more goods with the same amount of their own currency. And dollars were pumped into the international bloodstream in exchange for gold bullion, until the United States owned $16 billion of the precious metal—more than half the world's supply. The dollars of course tended to come back as orders for American goods. Hoover had warned that this kind of artificial inflation would lead "to complete destruction both at home and abroad," but for the time being its effect was salutary.

Another device to secure what Roosevelt called "a lowering of foreign walls [so] that a larger measure of our suplus may be admitted abroad" was the reciprocal trade agreement. The idea of lowering an American tariff in exchange for another nation giving the United States a reciprocal benefit was an old one going back to 1890. It was fervidly supported by such organizations as the National Association of Manufacturers and its satellite American Manufacturers Export Association, as well as many other business groups which had tried to press this panacea on Hoover. The fly in the ointment was that each such pact had to run the gamut of Senate perusal, long debate, and a two-thirds vote. Under the Reciprocal Trade Agreements Act of 1934 Roosevelt was empowered to enter into such covenants without submitting them to Congress. He was authorized to raise or lower tariffs by as much as 50 percent in favor of those nations who were willing to make concessions to Uncle Sam. A reciprocal trade agreement with Brazil, for instance, called for the United States to cut tariffs on manganese, nuts, and castor beans, and keep coffee and cacao on the free list; Brazil in return reduced tariffs on autos, radios, electric batteries, cement, paints, fruit, fish, and other commodities. The agreement prohibited import quotas or a licensing system—except for sanitary purposes—and contained a "most-favored nation" clause, so that if greater concessions were made by Brazil to a third country they would automatically apply to the United States as well. In effect, writes economic expert Eugene Staley, the trade agreement was a "program of economic disarmament" for the weaker countries. When they imported American trucks, pork, chemicals, etc. instead of subsidizing such industries at home, they inhibited their own development and made themselves vulnerable in case of war. Evidently, however, their short-term needs were too pressing to permit concentration on their long-term ones. As of 1939 the Roosevelt administration had concluded reciprocal trade agreements with twenty-one nations, accounting for two thirds of America's foreign business. How much all this improved Uncle Sam's position has been a subject of dispute, but statistics show that exports to trade-agreement nations rose 63 percent from 1934–35 to 1938–39, while those with non-trade-agreement states went up only half as fast, 32 percent.

Reciprocity combined with loans were America's primary means of warding off competitors in the 1930's. For instance, when Brazil flirted with the idea of a large barter deal with Germany in mid-decade, Washington cut the ground from under it by offering Brazil a trade agreement and sweetening it with a $60 million loan. It was a policy designed to meet new challenges, and based on the theorem that since American technology exceeded the efficiency levels of other powers all that was needed for American commercial success was "equality of opportunity." Given that equality it could undersell and outfinance its rivals.

Needless to say, other nations fashioned instruments of economic warfare to suit *their* purposes. England, for instance, also went off the gold standard and entered into "trade agreements containing quota and preferential clauses." The most extreme measures of course were taken by the have-not nations, and in particular Germany. With 6 million—perhaps 8 million—unemployed, with exports reduced from 13 billion reichsmarks a year to less than five, and with little gold reserves (77 million reichsmarks as of June 1934), the

Reich under Hitler adopted a policy of "autarchy" or "self-suffi-ciency." It was a complicated but well-planned system, engineered by a financial wizard named Hjalmar Schacht, which reduced the un-employed to fewer than 2 million by 1936–37 and doubled both pro-duction and national income. At its core was the revival of the econ-omy, through government-provided adrenalin—in this instance a massive rearmament program that would propel Germany toward the levels of Britain and France. The Reich was soon spending what was then the staggering sum of $4 billion a year on military prepar-edness. Since there was no money in the treasury to pay for this "work creation," the Schacht team floated short-term bonds and per-formed such sleight-of-hand as printing "Mefo" bills, which had nothing behind them but a government prayer. Normally this in-crease of credit and money supply would have pushed both prices and wages skyward, but the Nazis took care of the wage problem by abolishing trade unions and setting pay scales at the lowest level possible to keep body and soul together. Prices too were controlled by decree, and taxes were boosted from a total of 6.5 billion marks in 1932–33 to 17 billion for 1938–39, so as to drain off excess money. The free market was replaced by state guidance of all economic ac-tivity.

Such a system obviously required equally stringent state supervi-sion of international commerce. The Reich, like Japan, was woefully short of raw materials: of the twenty-five basic commodities needed for an advanced capitalist economy it had an adequate supply only of four, a partial supply of two, and no supply at all of the remain-ing nineteen. If the Nazis had had enough money they could have bought "when and where they pleased," but they had little hard cur-rency. Exports which would have earned foreign exchange were, as already noted, precipitously reduced, and loans from other nations unavailable. In this state of affairs the Nazis adopted measures which made a shambles of Adam Smith's theories of the free market. In order to husband whatever foreign exchange there was, imports were cut back to the bone, except for items needed for the arms pro-gram. And as a substitute for the curtailed raw materials usually purchased abroad, the Hitler regime encouraged and subsidized pri-vate firms to produce ersatz. Large factories were outfitted to manu-facture synthetic rubber, textiles, fuel, saltpeter (from nitrogen). The massive Hermann Goering Works was built to fabricate steel from low-grade ore locally supplied rather than the higher grades that could be imported. All of this raised costs and would have perverted the price system, except that the state spread the burden onto the backs of workers forced to labor ten and twelve hours a day for real wages below those of 1932.

"Self-sufficiency" required desperate and unorthodox innovations. Foreign firms, for instance, were forced to convert their profits to *blocked* marks, which could be neither sent home nor exchanged for francs, dollars, or pounds. They had to be spent within the Reich. Thus, one American oil company, after buying a few ships with its surplus money, acquired 40 million mouth organs for which it obviously had no need. Yugoslavia bought enough drugs on one occasion to last for many years.

Dr. Schacht's most noteworthy achievement was the barter deals —which obviated the need. for money or gold changing hands. Under this arrangement the Reich exchanged a certain number of locomotives, say, for an equal value in Brazilian coffee, or German drilling equipment for Mexican oil, German typewriters for Turkish tobacco. Often the coffee, oil, tobacco, cotton, or what have you never came to the Reich but was reexported to other European nations such as Holland for hard currency. With this foreign exchange Schacht was then able to buy goods from those countries that refused to make barter deals, such as the United States. Admittedly this was a bizarre system, a throwback to ancient times before capitalism, but it worked—to an extent. By subsidizing exports, Germany was frequently able to undersell its competitors by a wide margin. German entrepreneurs, according to W. T. Moran, quoted prices on many items for the Latin American market 20 percent below those of the United States—the difference being made up by the Nazi government. Schacht was able to increase exports to Latin America by 178 percent from 1932 to 1937, and dramatically to improve Germany's trade with nearby countries such as Rumania, Turkey, and Greece. For a brief moment the Reich outranked both the United States and Britain as Brazil's leading commercial partner. On the whole, however, despite Schacht's amazing jugglery, the Nazis increased exports from its low point in 1934 by only a third. Economic war by itself was clearly indecisive.

II

Those who sit astride the status quo can make themselves appear defenders, while those who seek to upset the status quo appear as aggressors. During a labor strike the employer may seem to be the beleaguered party, while the unionists on the picket line may seem to be on the offensive. Yet the strike in most cases would not have occurred in the first place if the employer had not held wages low or continued poor working conditions. The parallel with World War II is not exact, since strikers normally eschew violence and are never bestial, whereas the three Axis powers—Germany, Italy, and Japan—committed savage crimes against human beings that stagger the imagination. From Mussolini's castor oil treatment of political prisoners to Japan's militarist repression and "thought control," to Hitler's extermination of six million Jews, the record is an affront to all that ordinary men consider decent. Yet the emergence of fascism and militarism was linked with the international economic anarchy for which the have nations were mostly responsible, and was considered by many leaders in the "democratic" West as an important and useful countervailing force to communism.

The West was disingenuous in opposing the expansion of the Axis powers, said the Archbishop of York in a September 1935 broadcast. "Before there was any thought of a League of Nations we [the British] had ourselves occupied a great part of the earth and the supply of raw materials. . . . If we now say to those who have need of expansion, 'In the name of love and brotherhood—hands off!' we shall be convicted of hypocrisy. If we really believe in the community of nations we must be ready, and obviously ready, to start the work of arranging for the nations which lack outlet the means of satisfying their need."

The New York *Times* (March 26, 1940) ruefully admitted that the underlying cause for Germany's descent to Nazism was its loss of foreign markets—the same kind of phenomenon which had driven the United States to the less drastic experiments of NRA and AAA. Innumerable leaders in the democracies found considerable good in fascism, militarism, and Nazism—until they went "too far." "Do not forget," asserted Alvin Owsley, commander of the American Legion in 1923, "that the Fascisti are to Italy what the American Legion is to the United States. . . . If ever needed, the American Legion stands ready to protect the country's institutions and ideals as the Fascisti dealt with obstructionists who menaced Italy." "If I had been an Italian," Winston Churchill said in 1927, "I am sure that I should have been wholeheartedly with you [Mussolini] from the start to finish in your triumphant struggle against the bestial appetites and passions of Leninism." Churchill, David Lloyd George, and Lord Halifax, among others, advised Hitler in November 1937 that they "were fully aware that the Fuehrer had not only achieved a great deal inside Germany herself, but that, by destroying Communism in his country, he had barred its road to Western Europe, and that Germany could rightly be regarded as a bulwark of the West against Bolshevism." At the Brussels conference called late in 1937 to consider the Far Eastern situation, the Soviet Union offered to fight Japan provided the United States and Britain would guarantee the Soviets from attack in Europe. The suggestion was firmly rebuffed by the American delegation, indicating the ambivalence of the Western democracies. On the one hand they feared that the Axis powers would upset the delicate balance in economic markets and political spheres of influence; on the other they feared the Soviet Union as a potential moral and material support to revolution, which would also upset the status quo. Many Western leaders sincerely hoped that Germany would declare war on the Soviet Union so that the two would bleed each other to death. Not a few were pleased with passages in Hitler's book *Mein Kampf* which demanded *Lebensraum*—living space—for the Reich, that "could be obtained by and large only at the expense of Russia. . . ."

At any rate, whatever the appearances and realities of aggression, the world of the 1930's was divided between those great powers who defended the status quo—though willing to make some concessions in order to save it—and those who sought to topple it. Superimposed on the economic war was a political-military war for colonies and spheres of influence, as well as an arms race—all of which finally coagulated into World War II. The Japanese doctrine of a "new order" in East Asia, calling for an economic alliance between Japan, China, and Manchukuo, was expanded into the more ambitious goal of a Greater East Asia Coprosperity Sphere, which included Southeast Asia under Japanese tutelage as well. As one right-wing publicist, Hashimoto Kingoro, put it, there were only three ways for "Japan to escape from the pressure of surplus population . . . namely emigration, advance into world markets, and expansion of territory." Emigration was foreclosed by "the anti-Japanese immigration policies of other countries"—including the United States. Penetration of world markets was hampered "by tariff barriers and the abrogation of commercial treaties." The only alternative therefore was territorial expansion.

Many years later Robert Leckie, in his classic book *The Wars of America*, expressed the view that "in fairness to Japan, it is not easy to see how she could have followed anything other than an imperialist course." She had already acquired a small empire—the Kurile, Bonin, and Ryukyu Islands, the Volcano group, Formosa, and the Pescadores before the end of the old century; Port Arthur, half of the island of Sakhalin, and Korea in 1910, and a mandate power over the Marshall, Caroline, and Marianas Islands after World War I. Much of this brigandage had the support of Great Britain, which for a long time maintained a military alliance with the Nipponese. From 1931 to 1937 the minions of the Rising Sun captured Manchuria, Jehol, Inner Mongolia, and the provinces of northern China—an area larger than Britain, France, Italy, Spain, and Germany combined, and with a population of 100 million. Then, during the night of July 7, 1937, at the Marco Polo Bridge near Peking, the Japanese provoked another little incident, as pretext for initiating a full-scale campaign for the conquest of the whole of China. With more than 150,000 troops deployed, the bone-crushing Japanese machine steadily marched forward, seizing Tientsin, Peking, Nanking, Hankow, Canton, and the richest and most heavily populated areas of China except for Szechwan. It was during this campaign that Roosevelt made his dramatic—but for the time being empty—"quarantine the aggressor" speech, and warned that "war is a contagion. . . ."

"To have not and want to have," wrote political analyst Hu Shih in July 1938, "the only way is by the use of military force." This was in fact not only the course of Japan but of the two allies who had joined with her in 1936 in an anti-Comintern axis, Italy and Germany. Though the least significant of these allies, Mussolini's Italy had an appetite equal to the others. Il Duce, the turncoat socialist whose father had named him after the Mexican revolutionary Benito Juárez, insisted that "our future lies to the east and south, in Asia and Africa." Self-imposed leader of a nation of 42 million people, lacking rubber, tin, nickel, tungsten, and a host of other materials, still only partially industrialized, and with 21 percent of the nation illiterate—Mussolini established a sphere of influence in Austria and Hungary, but had little luck in penetrating the Balkans, and was blocked by the French and Russians from seizing either Tunis in North Africa or Anatolia in Turkey. He settled finally on Abyssinia in Africa, the only remaining unconquered territory on that continent (unless one counts Liberia, an American client state). Using almost a half million troops, not to speak of poison gas, in 1935–36, Il Duce subdued Haile Selassie's Ethiopia and made himself ruler of its 10 million people. While the League of Nations debated the issue, eventually imposing mild sanctions which did not include the key commodity, oil, Mussolini told a reporter: "We are on the march. It is too late now to tell us to stop. . . . Look at Portugal, and Belgium, and Holland. They all have fruitful colonies. Surely, Italy must have fruitful colonies, too. As soon as we get such colonies, Italy will become conservative, like all colonial powers." Mussolini's achievements, alas, did not match his lust. Austria, which he considered an Italian bailiwick, went to Nazi Germany in Hitler's lightning *Anschluss* in 1938, and it was only as war approached that Il Duce overwhelmed Albania, across the Adriatic Sea.

The one plan designed to rupture most quickly the vaunted balance of power that underlay British, French, and to some extent American policy was Hitler's blueprint for expanding in the heartland of the planet—Europe. "Territorial policy," he wrote in *Mein Kampf*, "cannot be fulfilled in the Cameroons but today almost exclusively in Europe." In his schema of the future, Germany would first have to destroy France in order "to give our people the expansion made possible elsewhere"—to the East—at the expense of Russia. Sitting athrust such a land empire, with hundreds of millions of people and untold resources at its disposal, the Reich would of course write finis in quick order to the British and French empires—just as it had hoped to do a generation before with the Berlin-Baghdad strategy. While Schacht, therefore, was experimenting with barter deals and *aski* marks (which could be spent only in Germany), more exciting activities were taking place at the diplomatic and military front. Under the Versailles Treaty, Germany's army was limited to 100,000 long-term volunteers and was prohibited from acquiring tanks or planes. In addition parcels of land were returned to their presumed original owners, such as Alsace-Lorraine to France, and other sections to Poland, Denmark, and Belgium; and the Rhineland and the Saar Valley were placed under French occupation for fifteen years, with the latter to hold a plebiscite at that time to determine whether it should be reincorporated into Germany. Before he could make a "final active reckoning with France" and undertake his *Drang nach Osten*—drive into the East, the Soviet Union—Hitler first had to destroy this Versailles system. He did it methodically and adroitly, avoiding a general war for more than six years, leading one writer to conclude that "the Germans do not want a war; all they want are the rewards of victory."

Rearmament began secretly—with the army instructed to triple its manpower from 100,000 to 300,000 by October 1934 and the navy to construct U-boats and two battle cruisers considerably above the 10,000-ton limit set by Versailles. In March 1935, Hitler repudiated the military clauses of the peace pact entirely, decreeing universal military service and expansion of the army to 36 divisions—a half million men. An air force, soon to have 3,000 planes, was initiated under Hermann Goering, and pilots, disguised as members of the League for Air Sports, trained to fly them. Some 240,000 factories were told to be ready to accept war orders. The victors of World War I, of course, could have stopped the Hitler steamroller at its inception simply by reoccupying the Reich, but there were too many people in high places who regarded Nazism as a proper "bulwark" against Bolshevism. The British government, in particular, was willing to agree to German rearmament and to the establishment of a

German navy one third the size of the British, all in the hopes that Hitler would endorse a general European settlement preserving the balance of power.

In this circumstance the German Fuehrer, covering his advance with saccharine phrases about his love for peace, marched forward toward the new empire. In 1935, the year that Mussolini invaded Ethiopia, Germany regained the Saar, in a peaceful plebiscite, by the overwhelming vote of 477,000 to 48,000. In 1936 its troops reoccupied the demilitarized Rhineland—without a sign of French resistance—and together with Italy supplied planes and men to General Francisco Franco in Spain to wage war against the ill-fated Spanish republic. Again the West stood by idly, immobilized by its fears of communism and its strange pretensions at neutrality. In 1938 the Nazi steamroller rolled over Austria and incorporated it directly into greater Germany. Late that September Hitler presented demands for amalgamation with the Reich of the Sudetenland, the German-speaking section of Czechoslovakia, bringing the world close to the abyss of war. President Roosevelt kept the international wires humming with appeals for a peaceful resolution, and it was partly as a result of his initiative that Prime Minister Neville Chamberlain of Britain and Premier Edouard Daladier of France met with Hitler at Munich to negotiate a *modus vivendi*. The two leaders agreed to give the Chancellor his Sudetenland on the promise that he would make no further land grabs in Europe, and Chamberlain announced to a happy crowd in London that "I believe it is peace for our time." Less than a half year later, in violation of the pledge, German armies forcibly seized the rest of hapless Czechoslovakia. In April 1939 Roosevelt again pleaded with Hitler and Mussolini to pledge that they would take no action against thirty specific states for the next ten years, in return for which an international conference would be held to adjust trade problems and disarmament. The heady effects of gaining the "rewards of victory" without war, however, disposed the two dictators to reject the proposal, and in August, when Hitler demanded "return" of the Polish Corridor and Danzig—stripped from Germany at Versailles—the day of reckoning was at hand.

III

In the great power conflicts of the present century, euphemistic terms have sometimes been as vital as bayonets. The Nazis proclaimed that they wanted nothing more than justified "living space," and the Japanese militarists promised on their honor to seek nothing more than "coprosperity" for the area they were plundering. The United States, responding to the crisis of the 1930's and the pressures of three nations trying to sunder the status quo, also had its euphemisms—"open door" and "good neighbor." With great resources in gold, surplus capital, and industrial efficiency, far outstripping its competitors, it could dominate weaker nations with an *economic* big stick as much as or more than the military big stick. The United States became, as Lloyd C. Gardner notes, "less and less interested in formal colonial empire and . . . dedicated to the expansion of the Open Door Policy instead. Washington believed that this approach would yield the United States all the advantages an empire might bring yet force upon it no binding responsibilities or dangerous political involvements." American exports to China, for instance, rose under the open-door policy from 6 percent of that nation's total imports to 15 percent, and by the end of the 1930's to about one quarter. Concurrently, the British share—almost half in 1913—fell steadily so that at the end of the critical decade before the war it was considerably below that of Uncle Sam. "We feel," said the Standard Oil Company of New York, "that the strict maintenance of the 'Open Door' policy is the only hope for the protection of American interests in Manchuria." And what disturbed the State Department most was not the plight of the people in such places as Manchuria but "that Japanese superiority in the Far East would definitely mean the closing of the Open Door. . . ."

The good-neighbor policy for Latin America, corollary to the open door, also placed a veneer of compassion around a hard core of self-interest. Early in the decade Hoover and Stimson, as well as many financial leaders, concluded that haphazard military intervention had more drawbacks than benefits. "The theory of collecting debts by gunboats," declaimed Thomas P. Lamont, senior J. P. Morgan partner, "is unrighteous, unworkable, and obsolete." If Latin America were to be aligned with the United States in what Stimson and Sumner Welles called "a common bloc for the purpose of furthering trade and stimulating recovery," it was necessary to reassure the nations south of the Rio Grande that they were not living under the permanent threat of North American gunboats. To make the idea credible, Hoover and Stimson entered into a treaty with Haiti in 1932 for withdrawing the marines, and saw to it that the last American forces in Nicaragua boarded ship for home early the following year. Washington found that there were means of guaranteeing American investments in the hemisphere other than by dispatching the marines. In Haiti and Nicaragua, for instance, the United States trained a puppet militia—*Guardia*—which defended American commercial interests as well as or better than the marines did, and without generating the same hatred for the United States. These were the prototypes of a large number of puppet armies that served American interests after World War II.

Franklin Roosevelt, in his first inaugural address, March 4, 1933, reaffirmed support "to the policy of the good neighbor." His reasoning was perhaps best expressed by his friend Sumner Welles: "If the United States . . . is to maintain itself as one of the greatest forces in the world of the future . . . it must reach the conviction that in the Western Hemisphere lies its strength and support. . . . A policy which consists in cooperation with the peoples . . . in removing the motive and the contributing factors of revolution . . . will be of far greater benefit to the United States, as well as to the Republics concerned, than a policy which will permit the culmination of the causes for revolution and anarchy and then attempt to cure them through the exercise of force." An ounce of prevention against revolution, in other words, was worth a pound of cure. Evaluating Welles's good neighborliness in a 1939 article, Blair Bolles observed that nothing had changed in basic aims—only the means were different: "actually the American policy always calls for dominating Latin America from the Rio Grande to the Tierra del Fuego. It remained for Welles to evolve a methodology which would camouflage the United States policy as a hemisphere excursion into higher cooperation."

The somber realities of the policy were illustrated by Welles's own role in "saving" Cuba. With sugar prices dropping drastically as a result of the Depression and popular unrest against the dictatorship of Gerardo Machado rising apace, Cuba was near turmoil when the White House in Washington changed residents. Though his predecessor's secretary of state, Stimson, concluded that Machado could "hold the country safe and suppress revolutions," Roosevelt decided to offer an increase in Cuba's sugar quota as a reward, if the Havana regime would institute reforms. Welles was sent to the scene and reported optimistically that "a fair commercial agreement" would distract "the attention of the [Cuban] public from politics" and simultaneously assure Washington of "practical control of a market it has been steadily losing for the past ten years." Unfortunately, while Welles was dangling the extra plum of a larger sugar quota, the proletarians of Havana called a general strike that drove Machado into retirement. A moderate regime, largely the work of Welles's backstage management, took the reins, but lasted only two weeks. It was replaced by a left-of-center regime under Ramón Grau San Martín which Welles considered inimical to the billion dollars or more in American investments on the island. He refused to recognize Grau on the ground that this would be "political intervention," and on three occasions during September 1933 recommended that Roosevelt send in the marines. The President refused to heed this advice but he did dispatch "several small warships and Coast Guard vessels" to Cuban waters—allegedly to defend American lives—and four American planes were ordered to sweep the skies over the island to remind Grau where the power lay.

Finally, after Welles had departed and been replaced by his close friend Jefferson Caffery, Uncle Sam found its man on horseback in the person of an army sergeant named Fulgencio Batista. After a considerable amount of flattery and encouragement by Caffery, Batista duly executed the bloodless coup which toppled Grau from power. Diplomatic recognition—considered "political intervention" shortly before—was immediately conferred on Batista and his government, nominally headed by Carlos Mendieta, and the sugar quota was raised from 1.7 million to 2 million tons. To tide the new regime over the critical period before export monies would be forthcoming, Roosevelt and Hull accorded it a generous Export-Import Bank loan. Thus by a combination of military and economic threats on the one side, and the alluring bait of more sugar sales and a much-needed loan, Washington had its puppet in office without having to resort to direct intervention.

If the Cuban incident was atypical it was only in the sense that warships and planes were used as a backup to economic pressure. This approach was not repeated by Roosevelt. At the Seventh International Conference of American States at Montevideo toward the end of 1933, Secretary Hull pleasantly agreed to a pact that "no state has the right to intervene in the internal or external affairs of another," and Roosevelt, in Washington, assured Latin America that "the definite policy of the United States from now on is one opposed to armed intervention." In the whole decade there was not one instance of U.S. troops landing on foreign soil. Moreover the Platt Amendment, which gave Washington the unilateral right to intervene in Cuba, and a similar arrangement with Panama were abrogated in 1934 and 1936. The customs receivership in the Dominican Republic, always linked with military pressures, was terminated in April 1941. It was the last relic of the Big Stick prior to the war.

Nonetheless, the good neighbor did not eschew using other levers against the weaker inhabitants of this hemisphere—and FDR applied them with remarkable consistency. When Bolivia nationalized the Standard Oil Company, Washington held up loans and technical assistance until La Paz came to terms. When Axis-controlled airlines began to threaten the Pan American Airways monopoly in Latin America, Roosevelt not only granted Pan American $12 million to build landing fields on the hemisphere, but offered $8 million to South American countries that would put German lines out of business. They responded by such tactics as withholding gasoline from Pan Am's German competitors, and in one instance, Colombia used troops to physically prevent their pilots from flying. Special measures were also taken to push U.S. munitions sales and to train Latin American officers in American army schools.

As historian Arthur S. Link points out, the "Roosevelt administration was not motivated by sentimental altruism. . . ."

In 1936 when American bondholders were at odds with Mexico over payments, Welles threatened to stop financing a section of the Pan American Highway until an agreement was reached. In 1939 a $120 million authorization to stabilize the currency of Brazil and finance its exports undercut German influence. To help achieve New World Solidarity against the Axis, Roosevelt in 1938 established an Interdepartmental Committee of Cooperation with American Republics to provide technical aid for the Latin states. He encouraged U.S. firms to invest in neighboring nations in order, as he said, "to develop sources of raw materials needed in the United States," and in the fall of 1940 increased the Export-Import Bank's funds from $100 to $700 million so as to finance a host of projects in Latin America—$45 million for the steel industry in Brazil, $40 million for roads in Mexico, $30 million for Colombia's factory program, $25 million for Cuba, $20 million for Chile.

A particularly revealing insight into good-neighbor techniques was the vain effort to bring Mexico to its knees following the nationalization of foreign oil companies in March 1938. Apart from the fact that a half billion or more in property was at stake, the measure by Mexican President Lázaro Cárdenas might prove to be contagious, not only affecting other foreign property in Mexico, but encouraging Venezuela, Ecuador, Peru, and Colombia to follow the Mexican example. Hull was furious. However, having committed himself not to use the mailed fist, the only recourse was to economic pressure. Mexico then enjoyed a special arrangement for selling silver to the United States above the world market price. That was revoked. With State Department support, a boycott was declared against Mexican oil, and both European and Latin American nations were solicited to adhere to that boycott. The result of the silver and oil policies was a decline in the value of the peso by a staggering 28 percent. Had Mexico not been able to turn to Germany and Japan to sell its oil, Cárdenas might have been forced to yield. As it was, his term in office expired with the 1940 elections, and the new president, Manuel Ávila Camacho, proved more tractable to American blandishments. He did not denationalize the oil or pay the companies what they wanted, but he committed himself to work with Uncle Sam in the "defense" of the hemisphere. Washington patched up relations by agreeing to a $30 million Export-Import Bank loan, and by pledging to continue buying Mexican minerals. Mexico at least was "saved" from falling into Axis clutches, or turning neutral.

On balance the good-neighbor policy paid dividends at least as substantial as Axis autarchy. Though U.S. trade with Latin America in the 1930's did not reach 1929 levels, it did go up by 236 percent from 1933 to 1937—a higher climb than even Germany enjoyed. "Viewed as a way to develop an informal empire, or sphere of influence," Lloyd C. Gardner writes, "the Good Neighbor Policy was an advance over anything that had gone before." It not only contained and rolled back the Axis, but it laid the groundwork in the future for capturing the British holdings in the hemisphere as well. Speaking to a press conference in January 1940, Roosevelt contemplated the rosy prospects: "As you know," he said, "the British need money in this war. They own lots of things all over the world . . . such as tramways and electric light companies. Well, in carrying on this war, the British may have to part with that control and we, perhaps, can step in or arrange—make the financial arrangements for eventual local ownership. It is a terribly interesting thing and one of the most important things for our future trade is to study it in that light."

IV

The American success in Latin America was not matched by success for the open door worldwide; on the contrary, the have nations, including the United States, saw their empires rolled back or placed in jeopardy. "We do not maintain," Roosevelt told an audience at Chautauqua, New York, in 1936, "that a more liberal international trade will stop war, but we fear that without a more liberal international trade, war is a natural sequence." The economic and political interests of the Axis and the Western democracies were at loggerheads, hurtling them toward the total war they all wanted to avoid. For a time Roosevelt felt that economic sanctions would force the miscreant powers to compromise. A "moral embargo" on exports to Italy and Germany was proclaimed in 1935, and expanded to include Japan in 1937–38. In July 1939 Washington advised Japan that it was revoking its commercial treaty with that country, and in September 1940 it placed an embargo on shipment of aviation gasoline and scrap iron to Tokyo.

Neither sanctions, moral or otherwise, nor diplomatic appeasements, however, could head off the martial engagement. All the powers were now in an arms race—in January 1938 Roosevelt requested a billion dollars to build a "two-ocean" navy. "Incidents," such as the bombing by Japan in Chinse waters of an American river gunboat, the *Panay*, with casualties of two dead, 30 wounded, and the sinking of three Standard Oil tankers, inflamed passions. And the insistent German demand for more territory, after Munich, sponsored belief that war was inevitable. Finally, in August 1939, the shocking word was flashed that Stalin and Hitler had joined in a pact. According to the Soviet dictator, in a speech the previous March, the "nonaggressive states, primarily England, France and the United States of America," had watched Japan seize "a vast stretch of territory in China"; Italy take Abyssinia; Germany, Austria and the Sudetenland; Germany and Italy together, Spain—and yet had done nothing but "draw back and retreat, making concession after concession to the aggressors." The chief reason for this lassitude, he concluded, was that they wanted to place no obstacles in the path of the Axis powers "in order that they might become embroiled with others, especially the Soviet Union." To forestall this prospect Stalin himself came to terms with the German chancellor, presumably to gain time. Whatever the reasons, however, Hitler was assured that he would not have to fight a simultaneous war on two fronts, and on September 1 ordered his legions into Poland. Britain and France came to the aid of their ally, and the war was on.

For the United States this was to be both a moment of peril and the prelude for its greatest imperial victory: the attainment of a full-fledged global empire.

☆☆☆☆☆

16

☆☆☆☆☆

AGAINST FRIEND
AND FOE

On September 3, 1939, the day Britain and France declared war on Germany, Franklin Roosevelt told the American people: "I hope the United States will keep out of this war. I believe that it will. And I give you assurances that every effort of your government will be directed toward that end." The Democratic platform on which he ran for an unprecedented third term was even more forthright: "We will not participate in foreign wars, and we will not send our Army, naval, or air forces to fight in foreign lands, outside of the Americas, except in case of attack. . . . The direction and aim of our foreign policy has been, and will continue to be, the security and defense of our own land. . . ." Speaking at Boston during that campaign, Roosevelt repeated a theme he referred to often: "I have said this before, but I shall say it again and again and again: Your boys are not going to be sent into any foreign wars. . . . The purpose of our defense is defense."

In the light of what happened subsequently some historians have questioned Roosevelt's sincerity, as they were later to question that of Lyndon Johnson in respect to the Vietnam War. But there was an economic and political logic to events that transcended the wishes of mortals—a logic rooted in industrialism, private profit, and competition, which literally drove the great nations against each other, and all of them against the weaker states. The capitalist system subsists on markets and access to raw materials; and if those should be cut off abroad through political or economic manipulation, the home country is enervated by the social diseases of unemployment and economic stagnation. Subsidized competition in Latin America by Germany and Japan, for instance, caused Secretary of the Treasury

Henry Morgenthau to record in his diary of December 16, 1937, the alarming possibility that "we're just going to wake up and find inside of a year that Italy, Germany, and Japan have taken over Mexico." Should Germany establish its suzerainty over Europe it would have both the economic and military wherewithal to whittle the U.S. sphere of influence in Latin America toward oblivion; and should Japan forge an empire that included China, Southeast Asia, Singapore, and the Dutch East Indies, half the world's raw materials would become inaccessible to other powers. Disruption of the status quo would have dire economic consequences as well as dire strategic ones for the have nations.

This is not to say that no alternatives to war existed in 1939, that the march toward conflict could not have been slowed down, that a *modus vivendi* could not have been reached for a few more years. Just prior to Hitler's invasion of Sudetenland, for instance, a group of German generals led by Ludwig Beck and Franz Halder plotted to arrest Hitler and establish a military regime to prevent a general war. Their plot, alas, depended on Britain and France manifesting a will to resist the Fuehrer, and when this failed to eventuate the generals drew back. There were to be other plots in the coming years, and no one can tell for sure what might have happened had the Allies given them more concrete support. Similarly, the government of Japan under Fumimaro Konoye was slightly more tractable than the one that followed his resignation, headed by General Hideki Tojo. Whether judicious concessions to Konoye's regime might have cut the ground out from under the militarists—at least for some years— is one of those historical "if's" whose answer can only be guessed. In either case, however, peace might have been preserved for a period.

But the war did start in 1939 and Roosevelt cast his lot with the nations that were least inimical to the interests of the American establishment, Britain and France, against those most inimical, the Axis powers. Unlike Wilson, who called on his fellow citizens to be "impartial in thought as well as in action," Roosevelt was openly disposed toward the Allies both in spirit and in performance. There were at the time a number of neutrality laws on the books prohibiting sale and transport of munitions to belligerents, or floating loans on their behalf. Within three weeks FDR had called Congress into special session to revise these acts so that the combatants could buy what they wanted as long as they paid cash and carried away the ordnance on their own ships—"cash and carry," it was called. In theory, both sides could buy in the United States, but in practice, since Britannia ruled the waves, the benefits of the bill were confined to England and France. So blatantly unneutral was FDR's bill that, even though the vast majority of Americans wanted the Allies to win, the debate in Congress lasted six acrimonious weeks.

Concurrent with the lifting of the arms embargo, the Roosevelt administration prevailed on the Latin American republics to issue the Declaration of Panama, which delineated a "safety belt" around the Americas 300 to 1,000 miles wide. Combatants were warned not to engage in any naval activity in this zone, and the declaration, though it turned out to be a dead letter, was the first of a number of steps toward "regional security" that welded the hemisphere behind Big Brother in the north.

Once again, because of the benevolence of geography, the United States was able, despite its partiality, to stay out of the shooting for a relatively long period—two years and three months—and once again it benefited handsomely while the resources of Britain and France were dissipated. During the Depression years, many leading figures had feared that full employment would never again return. Senator Hugo L. Black, a future Supreme Court justice, had thrown a bill into the hopper reducing the work week from forty-eight to thirty hours, so that the permanent army of jobless could be absorbed by sharing the work. Senator James F. Byrnes, a future secretary of state, urged that "we accept the inevitable, that we are now in a new normal" with millions doomed to unemployment to the end of their days. Harry Hopkins, often referred to as the Assistant President, as late as 1937 argued that it was "reasonable to expect a probably minimum of 4,000,000 to 5,000,000 unemployed in future 'prosperity' periods." But as the war orders came in and as Washington itself enlarged its military budget, the 9 to 10 million idle hands, as of 1939, were reincorporated into the productive process. In the first two years alone the factories doubled their output, almost 6 million workers were added to the nonagricultural payroll, and exports climbed from $3.2 billion to $5.1 billion. The war put America back to work, where CWA, NRA, PWA, and WPA failed. The cold war that followed kept it at the workbench thereafter.

Had hostilities lapsed into a stalemate, America might have stayed out of the fray even longer. But Germany had perfected a new strategy of warfare—the blitzkrieg, a war of movement in which tanks and planes were used to overrun or encircle enemy positions quickly—that gave Hitler a series of unparalleled victories. In two weeks the 800,000 German invaders, in mechanized divisions, with 1,400 planes at their disposal, decimated a Polish army twice as large and captured 150,000 square miles of territory, including Poland's richest mines, most productive plants, about 22 million of the nation's 35 million population. Simultaneously the Soviets, under the Hitler-Stalin agreements, took the eastern portion of Poland, completing the obliteration of that nation. After this initial thrust came a lull in hostilities while the French army and the British Expeditionary Force sat snugly behind the concrete and steel fortifications called the Maginot Line, and the Germans bivouacked behind their recently finished Siegfried Line, neither side peppering each other with anything more lethal than propaganda leaflets. The only fighting was in Finland, which the Soviet army invaded at the end of November, but this like the subsequent seizures of Latvia, Estonia, Lithuania, Bessarabia, and Bukovina by the Kremlin, were sideshows to the main event. Three months after the onset of war the British had not suffered a single casualty; Senator William Borah called it a "phony war," others called it a "sitzkrieg." Hitler seemed willing to wait, on the theory that his enemies would once again accept a *fait accompli* and come to terms; the Allies, on the other hand, were now convinced that a settlement was impossible, that a combination of the "impregnable" Maginot Line and the British blockade would bring the Nazis to brook.

Soon, however, the "phony war" became dramatically real again —and American aid began to accelerate in cadence with the Allies' adversity. In April 1940, Hitler's legions occupied Denmark— despite a recently signed nonaggression pact—and marched into Norway, where their Norwegian agent, Vidkun Quisling, had tried to prepare the way. The British mobilized a small force to defend the small state and sent some ships to challenge the invaders, but the German steamroller could not be stopped. In May it rolled into Belgium; neutral Holland was devastated and conquered in five short days. The Maginot Line, behind which the French hoped to wage a "war of position" similar to the type of fighting that prevailed in the First World War, was neutralized by the simple device of sending Panzer divisions around it in the north.

In less than two weeks the German troops were at the English Channel and the British were forced into the humiliating—though successful—evacuation of 338,000 men at Dunkirk. Simultaneously Belgium surrendered, and on June 10, Mussolini, sensing a "quasi-mathematical certainty of winning," declared his nation at war with France. A few days later as the French army continued to reel backward, Paris fell. Thus within a month Hitler had achieved what the Kaiser had been unable to do in four years. The newly installed British prime minister, Winston Churchill, pleaded with France to continue fighting and offered political union of the two countries as an incentive, but except for Charles de Gaulle, who preserved the flame of resistance in his London exile, the ancient nation was a

psychological shambles. On June 22, 1940, at the Forest of Com-
piègne, and in the same railway carriage in which Germany had
surrendered twenty-two years earlier, Hitler imposed an armistice
whereby the Nazis occupied half of France; the other half was left
to a puppet regime in Vichy, under Marshal Henri Pétain and
Pierre Laval. England was now alone, battered by Goering's Luft-
waffe, awaiting an amphibious invasion—if Hitler could assemble
the necessary landing craft. "The winter of illusion," as Churchill
had called the sitzkrieg, had passed into a summer of furious conquest, with the British leader promising his countrymen nothing but
"blood, toil, tears, and sweat" for the immediate future.

II

"The American people," according to Sherry Mangam in a November 1943 *Fortune* article, "were eased into the war by a process of
discreet gradualism and manufactured inevitability. . . . Pearl Harbor merely legalized the accomplished fact." The manufacture of
inevitability was accelerated by Roosevelt when the European
house of cards began to topple. On May 16, 1940, as he asked for
$1.2 billion more in defense money, he drew a harsh picture of what
lay in store for the American people. With air power at its present
technological levels, he said, the United States was no longer safe
behind its two oceans: New England could be attacked from bases
in Greenland; New York from airfields in Bermuda; and Seattle from
stations in Alaska if the Japanese were to conquer it. To counter
such gruesome possibilities he urged that "this nation [be] geared
up to the ability to turn out at least 50,000 planes a year."

Three weeks later FDR began to supply England with military
equipment in direct contravention of international law, which holds
that it is an act of war for a neutral to give weapons to a belligerent.
Brushing aside old restrictions on the sale of weapons, he shipped
rifles, machine guns, and other matériel to the British. In August he
exchanged 50 mothballed destroyers with Britain in return for nine-
ty-nine-year leases on naval and air bases in Newfoundland, Bermuda, the West Indies, and British Guiana. Theoretically such an
arrangement required, under the U.S. Constitution, a two-thirds vote
of the Senate, but the President took action by executive fiat—a precedent which would become commonplace in the turbulent 1960's.
Meanwhile, Roosevelt also asked for, and received, authorization to
spend $4 billion more for a two-ocean navy; added two venerable
Republicans to his cabinet, Henry M. Stimson and Frank Knox, to
give it the flavor of national unity; set up a Joint Board of Defense

with Canada, and concluded an agreement with the Latin American nations at a meeting in Havana, affirming that all of them would stand as one to protect "the integrity or political independence of an American state." Most important was the passage of the first Selective Service Act in peacetime history, allowing for the immediate draft of 800,000 men between twenty-one and thirty-five. It was coupled with assurances that it was only for "hemispheric defense," and "your boys are not going to be sent into any foreign wars. They are going into training to form a force so strong that, by its very existence, it will keep the threat of war far away from our shores."

Roosevelt's own steamroller was slow to start but it gained momentum, especially after the 1940 elections, which he won with 449 electoral votes, compared to 82 for Wendell Willkie. America clearly was now in a "war short of war." When Congress convened in January 1941, the President urged it to support all nations which upheld, in his historic phrase, the "Four Freedoms"—freedom of speech, freedom of religion, freedom from want, freedom from fear. And a few days later he proposed a far-reaching and unique method for financing Britain and the various governments in exile—such as de Gaulle's Free French—which was to be five times as costly as the loans made by Uncle Sam in World War I. Under the Lend-Lease Act, passed after bitter debate in March 1941, the chief executive was authorized to "sell, transfer, exchange, lease, lend" any war matériel to any government that "the President deems vital to the defense of the United States." This was without question a flagrant violation of international dictum, but it was approved in spite of bitter debate and strong opposition from Republicans (135 against, 24 for). "Never before," declared antiwar critic Senator Burton K. Wheeler, "has the Congress of the United States been asked by any President to violate international law. Never before has this nation resorted to duplicity in the conduct of its foreign affairs. . . . Never before has a Congress boldly and flatly been asked to abdicate." The bill, he predicted, "will plow under every fourth American boy." Nevertheless it passed, and in the next four and a half years $49.1 billion in munitions, food, goods, and services were doled out to U.S. allies, about three fifths to Britain and about one fifth to the Soviet Union, after it was attacked by Hitler. The recipients "paid back" in *reverse* lend-lease about $8 billion; that is, they made available airfields, hospitals, depots, barracks, food, and oil, for America's own armies overseas.

Churchill called America's effort "the most unsordid act in the history of any nation," but it was in truth indispensable for Washington's goals as well. Hundreds of thousands—perhaps millions—of additional American "boys" would have died on the western front if the $11 billion in aid (427,000 trucks, 13,000 combat vehicles, 2,000 locomotives, 11,000 railroad cars, 35,000 motorcycles, 4.5 million tons of food, 4 million pairs of army shoes, tanks, planes, oil, etc.— 15 million tons of supplies altogether) had not been delivered to the Soviet Union to help it contain, then roll back, Hitler on the eastern front. Though American goods in each category were ordinarily only 5 to 10 percent of the total used by Stalin's forces, they were a decisive and vital part, without which—locomotives, for instance— Soviet armies would have been too poorly supplied to defeat the Germans. Insofar as Britain was concerned, by December 1940, after paying out $4.5 billion for foreign purchases, mostly American, she was starved for dollars and had to suspend all but a few munitions orders. Without lend-lease her effort too would have faltered, again forcing U.S. soldiers eventually to fight more of the war. In effect, the Roosevelt administration substituted dollars for casualties.

After lend-lease there was nothing either discreet or gradual about America's plunge toward the maelstrom. It was no longer a question of whether but of how. Within a few weeks all Axis vessels in American harbors were sequestered for the duration. In April, Greenland was occupied for "hemispheric defense." In May the President ordered 50 oil tankers transferred to British use, and after a freighter had been sunk by a German U-boat, declared a state of "unlimited national emergency." By now Roosevelt was no longer talking about solely defending the United States. "Our Bunker Hill of tomorrow," he said, "will be several thousand miles from Boston," perhaps in Iceland, Greenland, the Azores, or the Cape Verde Islands. In June, Axis consulates in the United States were padlocked and the assets of the three countries—with none of whom America was yet formally at war—frozen. A new selective service bill extended the service of drafted men from a year to eighteen months and removed the limit on the number of men that might be in training at any one time—previously set at 900,000. Despite the popular feeling that America was headed for battle, hostility to conscription was still so great that this bill carried the House by only a single vote.

By the summer of 1941 it was obvious that there were no limits to the war—that the stakes were the whole planet, and that this was, in fact, a Second World War. This was clear not only to the Axis nations, which had joined in a formal Tripartite Pact in September 1940 to help each other in case any of them became engaged with the United States, but to Churchill and Roosevelt as well. Even be-

fore he became head of the British government, Churchill had cabled FDR: "I am half American, and the natural person to work
with you. It is evident we see eye to eye. Were I to become Prime
Minister we could control the world." Roosevelt had other ideas on
how the world should be controlled—with Britain as junior, not senior, partner—but it was evident that the martial confrontation had
total, rather than limited, objectives. It became more evident on June
22, 1941, when Hitler turned his Panzers loose on his erstwhile nonaggression partner, the Soviet Union. Taking Stalin completely by
surprise, he unleashed 150 divisions and 2,400 planes on the eastern
front, and within ten days had temporarily immobilized the Soviet
air force and captured 150,000 Russian soldiers. The buffer zone that
Stalin had so meticulously established melted like butter before the
advance, and by October, as the Nazi legions battered at Moscow
itself, the Soviet Union had lost a half million square miles of its
richest industrial territory and 1.7 million men. Only the Russian
winter, for which the Germans were badly prepared, stalled their
drive.

In the face of the attack on the Soviet Union the pace of America's undeclared war became even more feverish. On June 24, Roosevelt announced he was making lend-lease supplies available to Moscow. On July 7, Iceland, a Danish colony that had cut loose from its
mother country, was occupied by American forces and used as an
intermediate base for ships and planes headed for England. This
was a major step toward hostilities because Roosevelt simultaneously
ordered American destroyers to escort merchantmen carrying lend-
lease goods as far as the island—where the British would take over
—and to drop depth charges when they suspected the presence of
German submarines. Until then the President had held off on convoying ships because he feared public opinion was not yet ready for
what was so patently a war measure. Caution, however, was out of
style.

In September, after a German U-boat fired two torpedoes at the
U.S.S. *Greer* and two merchantmen were sunk, the chief executive
proclaimed a "shoot on sight" policy against enemy submarines. In a
Navy Day address that month the President proclaimed that "America has been attacked" by "rattlesnakes of the sea. . . . The shooting
war has started." He raised hackles on many skins by stating that he
possessed a secret map to prove that the Nazis planned to divide
South America into "five vassal states." They were also determined,
he said, to "abolish all existing religions." International law was now
a dead letter, the only relevant law remaining was that of "self-defense," in whose interests he asked Congress for two major modifica-

tions of the neutrality laws. One called for putting guns on merchant vessels, the other for lifting the restriction on going into combat zones. "I consider the pending Senate decision," said Senator Arthur Vandenberg, a Republican leader, in discussing the FDR proposals, "as substantially settling the question whether America deliberately and consciously shall go all the way into a shooting war, probably upon two oceans. The ultimate acknowledgment by Congress of a state of war, I fear, will be a mere formality. . . ." Nothing more was needed to trigger the explosion but an "incident" that would unite the American people.

That incident occurred at 7:55 A.M. on Sunday, December 7—not in Europe or the Atlantic but on the other side of the world, in the Pacific. The Japanese attacked Pearl Harbor, Hawaii, with 135 bombers and a flotilla of ships, killing 2,403 Americans, destroying 149 planes on the ground, and shattering 6 battleships and various other vessels in less than two hours. Roosevelt described the attack as "sudden" and it galvanized the American people behind their government as in no other war. Almost everyone believed that the Japanese had perpetrated a "sneak" assault, without warning, and many were convinced that had it not been for this treachery war might have been avoided.

Pearl Harbor, however, was merely the exclamation point to a very long sentence. In July 1940, Roosevelt cut off the supply of oil, scrap iron, and aviation gasoline to Japan—all vital to its economy. The Nipponese responded by moving into Indochina (with the begrudging approval of Vichy), consolidating their influence in Thailand, and threatening the Dutch East Indies and Singapore. Washington countered by making some loans to China to buttress its defense and demanding ever more vigorously that Japan respect the open door. There was no reconciling these two approaches—to expand economically, Japan felt she needed to control additional territory, while the United States opposed further territorial expansion by anyone since it inevitably would close what might be, or might become, an open door.

Both governments knew, weeks or months before Pearl Harbor, that they were headed for war. The Japanese had completed their plans on September 18. Secretary Stimson recorded in his diary for November 25, 1941, that Hull, Frank Knox, General George Marshall, Admiral Harold I. Stark, Roosevelt, and himself met at the White House that day and discussed "how we should maneuver them [the Japanese] into the position of firing the first shot without allowing too much danger to ourselves." Testifying before a congressional committee on Pearl Harbor five years later, he reminisced that "one problem troubled us very much. If you know that your enemy is going to strike you, it is not usually wise to wait until he gets the jump on you by taking the initiative. In spite of the risk involved, however, in letting the Japanese fire the first shot, we realized that *in order to have the full support of the American people* it was desirable to make sure that the Japanese be the ones to do this so that there should remain no doubt in anyone's mind as to who were the aggressors." (Emphasis added.)

According to Oliver Lyttelton, British Minister of Production, "Japan was provoked into attacking Pearl Harbor. It is a travesty on history even to say that America was forced into the war. It is incorrect to say that America ever was truly neutral even before America came into the war on an all-out fighting basis." And according to Arthur Sulzberger, publisher of the prowar New York *Times*, "we did not go to war because we were attacked at Pearl Harbor. I hold rather that we were attacked at Pearl Harbor because we had gone to war. . . ." War, in other words, was expected and considered inevitable by both sides; Roosevelt simply wanted the other side to perform the first overt act so that he could consolidate public opinion behind him. That the strategy worked is evident from the vote on the war resolution December 8th—82 to 0 in the Senate, 388 to 1 (Representative Jeanette Rankin of Montana, a pacifist) in the House.

III

The prologue to Pearl Harbor, apart from indicating the irreconcilable economic and political motives of the belligerents, reveals a key aspect of America's transition to global imperialism—the centralization of power in the presidency.

The Second World War generated only meager opposition—from a few leftist groups such as the Trotskyites (the Stalin Communists, of course, had become the most fervid supporters of the war after Hitler's invasion of Russia), the diehard isolationists, and some small numbers in the German-American and Italian-American communities. Victory was won, despite a high cost in dollars—$330 billion, exclusive of subsequent payments for pensions, veterans' aid, and interest on loans—with a relatively low cost in blood compared to other nations, 292,000 dead in battle, 671,000 wounded (as against 6 million killed and 14 million injured for the Soviet Union). Despite controls on wages, prices, rents, materials, and job transfers, civilian life was disturbed only minimally, and not a single American city or building was touched by a foreign bomb. Under the circumstances there has been little disposition to castigate Roosevelt for transforming a government theoretically based on popular and congressional "consent" to a vassal run by executive fiat. Yet he reshaped the process as no president before him had done, and developed a credibility gap at least as ominous as the one created by Lyndon Johnson a quarter of a century later during the Vietnam War. He made innumerable treaties and arrangements, both for execution of the war and for shaping the postwar world, without seeking approval of the Senate as provided in the Constitution or invoking popular discussion, as provided by a higher concept of democracy. He did not *follow* popular will, but manipulated it toward goals he had already determined on, including entry into the conflagration itself.

Alden Hatch, in his sympathetic book *Franklin D. Roosevelt: An Informal Biography* (1947), asked FDR's closest associates—including Mrs. Roosevelt, Admiral William D. Leahy, Samuel L. Rosenman, Justice Felix Frankfurter, Ernest K. Lindley, and others —"When do you think that the President decided that the United States would probably have to enter the war?" In every instance, he records, "the reply fixed the time within a few weeks" of the Hitler-Stalin Pact. Adolf Berle, Assistant Secretary of State from 1938 to 1944, said in 1946 that "the date when war was considered probable rather than remotely possible was shortly after the Munich conferences. . . ." In his memorial address at Harvard, April 1945, Justice Frankfurter stated that Roosevelt made the decision "for the utter defeat of Nazism" as "essential to the survival of our institutions" not "later than when Mr. Sumner Welles reported on his mission to Europe," in March 1940. For one or two years at least, while the American people were being assured by their President that he was trying with might and main to stay out of war, he had already decided that entry was inevitable—and was proceeding accordingly.

He engaged in a host of actions that were either violations of international law, such as supplying weapons to a belligerent, or violations of the U.S. Constitution, such as failure to seek Senate approval for the agreement exchanging 50 destroyers for British bases, or the occupation of Greenland and Iceland. By misrepresenting what he fully expected he would have to do—go to war—the President was able to acquire authority far beyond what he was entitled under the basic law of the land. Under the Lend-Lease Act he could designate whether a nation was a friend or a foe, and in effect enter into binding war alliances that should have been the prerogative of Congress, or at least a joint prerogative, not an exclusive one of the President's. Whether the American people did or did not want an alliance with Britain or the Soviets is beside the point;

what is pertinent here is that Roosevelt accrued to himself the right to determine what his people "wanted" or were entitled to, *without* their actual consent. Roosevelt, to be sure, was an instrument of the social system he served; he moved in accord with the economic and political necessities of that system. But within prescribed limits he could act decisively or phlegmatically, and in this situation his direction was firmly fixed. Each single step he took may not have been conclusive in itself, but cumulatively they headed the nation as inexorably into war as if a favorable vote had been taken in September 1939 rather than December 1941. The logic of each move led to another, so that in reality the decision on war or peace was predetermined. The only real questions were when, where, and under what conditions. It is significant that the war resolution of December 8, 1941, was not on the question of "declaring" war, but simply "recognizing" that a state of war already existed. Having set this precedent it was to be expected that future presidents would similarly bypass the mechanism for "consent of the governed" and catapult the nation into all kinds of adventures about which it was uninformed, unprepared, and unconsulted.

It soon became commonplace for the President to arrive at secret understandings with the heads of foreign governments that were of the utmost significance for the future, and normally should have been placed before Congress. By way of example, in August 1941—four months before the United States formally entered the war—Roosevelt held a historic meeting with Churchill off the coast of Newfoundland, at which the famous Atlantic Charter was drafted. Apart from the fact that it was somewhat unorthodox, as the Chicago *Tribune* observed, for the head of a nation *not* at war to be discussing common strategy with the head of a nation at war, there were other, equally disconcerting, features. On his return Roosevelt told the press that no new commitments had been made, when in fact agreement had been reached on the broad strategy not only for the war in Europe but the impending one in Asia. The two political titans, moreover, had concurred on a number of specific items, ranging from the relatively minor one of occupying the Azores to the grandiose one of setting up, in the future, a machinery for policing the world.

In the subsequent meetings with Churchill and Stalin, especially at Yalta, all kinds of agreements were concluded over the disposition of territory and spheres of influence in Europe and Asia (that Greece, for instance, would be a British sphere, Bulgaria a Russian sphere, or that half of Sakhalin Island would go to the Soviet Union in return for her secret pledge to enter the war against Japan), and all of this without Congress or the American people even knowing about it. Thus in rapid order the mechanism for government by consent of the governed was dismantled in favor of a mechanism by which the executive arrogated the broadest power of peace and war, of life and death, to himself. This helped pave the way for a dramatic transformation not only of the style but of the essence of government.

IV

Of the war itself the military aspects are the least pertinent, for once the vast resources of Uncle Sam had been thrown on the scales, the result was never in doubt. In the five years from July 1, 1940, to July 31, 1945, the United States spent $186 billion on munitions alone. At the time of Pearl Harbor there were barely a thousand planes and a thousand tanks ready for combat, but American factories fabricated 297,000 additional planes and 86,338 tanks; 17.4 million rifles, carbines, and sidearms; 64,500 landing vessels; 5,000 cargo ships and transports; 6,000 naval vessels, and 2.5 million machine guns. The federal government built $16 billion in war plants to be used by private entrepreneurs—five sixths of all the factory construction in this period. The merchant fleet was quadrupled and naval fire power increased by ten times. By mid-1944 the war production of the Allies —United States, Britain, Canada—was four times as great as that of the Axis, which negated the initial successes of the other side on the battlefield.

Within a few months of Pearl Harbor the Japanese flag flew over most of Asia up to the Indian border, including the Philippines, evacuated just after Christmas. In the Atlantic theater England was on the defensive against Nazi bombing raids, and German submarines took a fearful toll of Allied shipping—700,000 tons a month as of mid-1942. Some of the vessels were torpedoed only thirty miles from New York City. In the midst of setbacks, however, the tide began to turn, beginning with the heroic defense of Stalingrad by the Russians late that year. On November 8 an amphibious force of Americans and some British troops—under a then unknown lieutenant general, Dwight D. Eisenhower—landed in North Africa. Together with a British army moving eastward across Tripoli, it inflicted a heavy defeat by May 1943 on the Germans and Italians, taking a quarter of a million prisoners. In July Sicily was invaded and the Allies moved slowly toward Rome. The trend was also reversed on the sea, where submarine losses were reduced appreciably, and in the air, where 27,000 American and British bombers rained 2.5 million tons of munitions on German positions, destroying 57,000 of the enemy's planes, devastating cities like Hamburg and Dresden, and killing hundreds of thousands—250,000 to 400,000 in Dresden alone. The end came in sight with Operation Overlord beginning on June 6, 1944 (D-Day), when 326,000 men and 54,000 vehicles were transported across the English Channel and landed on the Normandy coast. Paris was liberated in August. Rumania surrendered to the Russians. American soldiers landed in Southern France and seized Marseilles. In September the stalled offensive in Italy was resumed, headed toward Pisa; Brussels, Liège, and Luxembourg were retaken. The last sweep began in February 1945 and ended with Hitler's suicide and the German surrender, May 7.

In the Pacific the Japanese also crumbled before the enormous superiority of matériel produced in American factories; toward the end the Japanese air force and navy were virtually destroyed and the country was naked to attack by air or sea. All through 1944 the forces of General Douglas MacArthur continued jumping from one strategic island to another; toward the end of the year the Philippines were reconquered. In March 1945, one third of Tokyo was burned to the ground by American-dropped incendiary bombs. The seizure of Iwo Jima and Okinawa, before and after this bombardment, for all practical purposes sealed Japan's fate. Her oil supplies were now cut off, her planes driven from the skies, her fleet from the oceans. A few days before she surrendered in August the Soviet Union—in accordance with understandings concluded at Yalta—entered the war in Asia, making the odds still more adverse. The end came after the atom bomb was dropped on Hiroshima on August 6, and on Nagasaki on August 9. On September 2, aboard the battleship *Missouri*, representatives of Emperor Hirohito formally signed the documents of capitulation. "Today the guns are silent," exclaimed MacArthur in a broadcast to the American people. "A great tragedy has ended. A great victory has been won. . . . A new era is upon us."

V

Unfortunately, each of the victors had a different vision of the "new era." The Allies had been united on seeking military defeat of the Axis, but not on the political and economic purposes for which they fought. For Churchill, the aim was to restore the old order and the old colonial empires, with as little modification as possible. He and his successors reimposed monarchies on Greece, Belgium, and Italy, and helped restore French rule in Indochina and Dutch rule in Indonesia. As a corollary to preserving the status quo, Churchill felt it necessary to contain the Soviet Union—so that its moral and material aid would not be used on behalf of postwar revolutions. Churchill, since 1917, had been and remained a fervid anti-Communist, determined to hold off the Bolsheviks. He considered this goal as compelling indeed—though not as immediate—as defeating Nazism. Parenthetically, it should be stressed, this was the thesis that America adopted after Roosevelt's death—and still lives by.

For Stalin, the purpose of the war was precisely the opposite; he wished to demolish the old order and the old balance of power which Churchill so avidly cherished. He expected at last to break out of the *cordon sanitaire* that the West had forged around his nation, and to establish a buffer zone—Rumania, Bulgaria, Yugoslavia, Albania, Czechoslovakia, Poland, Hungary—between Russia and Anglo-French Europe. Although, as events soon proved, he would happily have come to terms with a liberal capitalism in return for material aid for his own semidestroyed nation, Stalin nonetheless understood that if the defeat of the Axis should result in fragmentation of the established empires and a surge of revolutionary nationalism, the results would not be unfavorable for his cause.

For Roosevelt, the "new era" meant a shift from the imperialism of the past, in which Britain and France ruled great colonial empires, to a softer imperialism, in which the United States was predominant. He articulated his particular vision of the future on many occasions. Commenting on the good-neighbor policy in 1940, for instance, FDR defined a new approach to underdeveloped countries—"give them a share"—while simultaneously expressing the opinion that it was "a terribly interesting idea" that Britain would have to sell much of its holdings in Latin America to finance its war—holdings of course that would end up in the hands of American entrepreneurs. "We've got to make clear to the British from the very outset," Roosevelt remarked to his son Elliott, "that we don't intend to be simply a good-time Charlie who can be used to help the British empire out of a tight spot, and then be forgotten forever." His bias against the old colonialism was so evident that during an informal dinner at the Atlantic Conference in August 1941, Churchill pointed a stubby finger at the American chief executive and exclaimed: "Mr. President, I believe you are trying to do away with the British empire. Every idea you entertain about the structure of the postwar world demonstrates it."

Yet, Roosevelt's opposition to the old imperial system was not predicated on idealism but on the practical and materialistic desire to enhance American trade and investment. As Richard Hofstadter

observes in his *American Political Tradition,* it "was not simply altruistic; American commercial interests—for instance the vast oil
concessions that had been made to American companies in Saudi
Arabia—were much on his mind. . . . Roosevelt appears to have believed that the ruthless imperialism of the older colonial powers
might be replaced by a liberal and benevolent American penetration that would be of advantage both to the natives and to American commerce. He believed that British and German bankers had
had world trade 'pretty well sewn up in their pockets for a long
time,' to the disadvantage of the United States. Arguing that 'equality of people involved the utmost freedom of competitive trade' he
appealed to Churchill to open markets 'for healthy competition' and
to dissolve the British Empire trade agreements."

Here again was the old open door—but with one distinguishable
difference, both from the policy of Roosevelt's predecessors and
those who followed him. The wartime President was convinced that
if the postwar world were to be "stable"—free from uncontrolled rebellions and revolutions—it would be necessary to collaborate with
the Soviet Union. He disliked Stalin's communism, of course, but he
had no pathological fear of it. He recognized its pliability. The
American Communists, for instance, had once called him a reactionary but after his recognition of the Soviet Union in 1933 they looked
upon him as a progressive, meriting support. After Hitler invaded
the Soviet Union in June 1941, American Communists became the
most fervid advocates of labor's no-strike pledge, of national unity,
and class peace. The chances were good that if Russia were offered
a measure of security and material aid, it would evolve a soft Communist line directing discontent around the world into reformist
rather than revolutionary channels. This was not as farfetched as it
sounds today, after a quarter of a century of cold war, for the socialists of the Second International had frequently defended the empires
of their "bourgeois governments," and the Communist Parties
around the world had throughout the 1930's muted their criticism of
capitalist regimes when the foreign policies of those regimes meshed
with that of the Soviet Union. It was not inconceivable, then, that
the Communists could be transformed into good social democrats
and live as a left opposition *within* the established system. "We
really believed in our hearts," said Harry Hopkins, FDR's closest
adviser, "that this was the dawn of the new day we had all been
praying for and talking about for so many years. . . . The Russians
had proved that they could be reasonable and far-seeing, and there
wasn't any doubt in the minds of the President or any of us that we

could live with them and get along with them peacefully for as far into the future as any of us could imagine."

The divergences in the Allied camp over the shape of tomorrow's world were kept in rein during the fighting but were hinted at on many occasions. Four months before Pearl Harbor, as already noted, Churchill and FDR met secretly "somewhere in the Atlantic," and proclaimed a statement of their postwar goals. Point 3, by far the most important of the eight points in the Atlantic Charter, stated that the two leaders, speaking for their countries, "respect the right of all peoples to choose the form of government under which they will live; and they wish to see sovereign rights and self-government restored to those who have been forcibly deprived of them." Seemingly, this was an unequivocal promise to "all people," as Roosevelt later explained to the Sultan of Morocco, that the colonial nations could have their independence after the war, if they wanted it.

On Churchill's part, however, as Robert Sherwood noted, the document was "not much more than a publicity handout." All through Africa and Asia young men joined the Allied colors believing they were fighting not merely against Nazism—which they knew only slightly and indifferently—but for the final liberation of their own countries from imperialism. Churchill dashed cold water on their aspirations. In a speech to the House of Commons "clarifying" the Atlantic Charter, he explained that the promise of self-government was limited solely to "the states and nations of Europe now under Nazi yoke. . . . That is quite a separate problem from the progressive evolution of self-governing institutions in the regions, and people, which owe allegiance to the British Crown." Austria and Greece, in other words, would regain their independence, but India and Kenya would have to be content with a few reforms—"the progressive evolution of self-governing institutions." Under this interpretation, the Atlantic Charter, a document of high resolve, saturated with nobility, and promising a beautiful tomorrow dramatically different from the grim present, was rendered meaningless—even though Britain was eventually forced to give up her empire by other circumstances.

The divergent political strategies were reflected occasionally in differences over military strategy. The Soviets, who were doing by far the major share of the fighting and suffering the most casualties, wanted Britain and the United States to mount a second front across the English Channel as early as 1942. General George C. Marshall also favored making such a thrust as soon as possible. But Churchill was able to postpone it for two years, arguing that the main campaign should proceed up through Sicily and Italy into Central Eu-

rope, the Balkans, and finally Germany. The political advantages of
this course for those who wanted to "contain" the Kremlin were obvious. If the British and American armies could be placed flat
against Soviet borders—or near them—the Russians would be held
in check and confined primarily to their old domain. On the other
hand, an assault from the west, across the Channel, made it easier
for the Red Army to overrun Eastern and Central Europe. Though
Churchill was later forced to yield to Marshall's strategy, it was only
out of recognition that he was the junior partner in the alliance.

Still another source of discord was what to do about such countries as Italy, Belgium, and Greece, where British troops had been
assigned the major responsibility for maintaining order. After the
collapse of Mussolini in June 1943, Churchill insisted that King Victor Emmanuel be returned to his throne. Later, under severe pressure, the King was replaced by a regency under Crown Prince Umberto. But reforms were held in abeyance, and resistance fighters in
the north were disarmed without any concessions to their political
demands. "It seemed," writes Robert Sherwood, "that Britain was
backing the most conservative elements . . . as opposed to the liberals or leftists who had been the most aggressive in resistance to the
Germans and Fascists." The English government argued that its actions were predicated on military necessity, "but American liberal
opinion . . . was becoming increasingly suspicious of Churchill's apparent determination to restore the unsavory status quo ante in Europe." Some time later Britain vetoed Count Sforza, a leading liberal
who had lived in exile during Mussolini's tenure, for membership in
the Italian cabinet. Relations between Churchill and Roosevelt, says
Sherwood, "were more strained than they had ever been before," because of such machinations, but this did not deter Churchill from
continuing to restore the past.

In Belgium and in Greece, he resuscitated discredited monarchs
and conservative politicians. British troops mercilessly battered the
leftist EAM (National Liberation Front) out of Athens, even though
EAM had been the backbone of resistance to Hitler and Mussolini.
It "represented the people of Greece," according to Professor L. S.
Stavrianos of Northwestern University, "as much as any organization
could during the period of occupation. . . . Under it for the first
time the average Greek felt a sense of belonging, a sense of working
toward a common goal." For four years EAM and its military arm,
ELAS, had fought with vigor against the Nazis and fascists, only to
be greeted by Churchill's soldiers with sixty-three days of machine-
gun terror. Elliott Roosevelt reports that his father was appalled by
this development: "How the British can dare such a thing! The

lengths to which they will go to hang on to the past!" But Churchill was single-minded; in the process, thousands of Greeks were killed, a quarter of a billion dollars of property destroyed.

Another sign of the times, as portentous as Churchill's acts in Europe, was the suppression of nationalism in Madagascar, an island in the Indian Ocean that belonged to France. Britain had occupied Madagascar at the outset of the war to prevent it from falling into the hands of the Nazis, or the Nazi-controlled government at Vichy. But in 1943, by agreement with de Gaulle, Free French troops replaced the British. The Malagasy nationalists demanded independence; de Gaulle merely offered to continue colonialism in a more moderate form. Madagascar was to become part of a "French union," with the 4 million Malagasy represented by three elected members in the French Parliament, and the 50,000 French colonists also allotted three members. The native delegates arrived in liberated Paris sometime later, and, instead of taking their seats, denounced the plan as a sham. It was not the "sovereign rights and self-government" promised by the Atlantic Charter, they said, but a ruse for colonialism. Quai d'Orsay rejected the pleas of the Malagasy. Tempers flared, "incidents" occurred. The Malagasy attacked a military camp at Mouramanja, the French reestablished "order." When the smoke had lifted, the three native members of parliament and thousands of others were in jail, and by official figures 80,000 Malagasy and 200 French had been killed in bitter fighting. The nationalist council claimed that 220,000 had died, some thrown from airplanes without benefit of parachute, others buried alive. Similar outbursts occurred in Algeria, Tunisia, and Morocco, for the same reasons and with the same results. The native peoples demanded independence; de Gaulle, with the assent of Churchill, answered with machine-gun fire. Forty-five thousand Moslems died in Algeria in 1945; 7,000 in Tunisia.

Wars are fought not simply for "victory," as General MacArthur once said, but for economic and political objectives. In that sense each of the Big Three was precociously clear about what it wanted: Churchill, to hold the old empire; Roosevelt, extension of the American empire; Stalin, to break out of isolation and build a Soviet sphere of influence. It is certain, however, that none of them foresaw the tornado of national revolutions that would sweep the planet after hostilities, or calculated their impact on the "new era." At the Yalta Conference early in 1945, during the discussion of the projected United Nations Security Council, Churchill explained how the Council would deal with a Chinese demand for the return to her of Hong Kong or an Egyptian request for the return of the Suez

Canal. In each case, he said, the grieving country would be given an opportunity "to make a broad submission to the opinion of the world"—the UN—but Britain would not be obligated "to give Hong Kong back to the Chinese," or the Suez to Egypt, "if we did not feel that was the right thing to do." Suppose, Stalin asked Churchill, the Chinese or Egyptians were not placated "only with expressing opinion"? Suppose they demanded that a decision be made? There were no answers to these questions in the seventeen wartime conferences, from Argentia Bay to Potsdam. Roosevelt evidently believed they could be dealt with on an ad hoc basis, as each crisis came up, provided the Soviet Union and the United States (plus the three lesser victorious powers, Britain, France, and China) could coexist. Peace and stability could be assured only if harmony could be sustained between Washington and Moscow. Churchill presumably believed that the British could handle their own revolutionary problems as they had in the past, by military suppression; this was the same folly he had advocated against the Soviet Union after its revolution. The United States was able to organize most of the non-Communist world into a relatively stable *Pax Americana,* with an open-door economic policy, held together by enormous U.S. loans, and sheltered under an American military umbrella. But the schism between the United States and the Soviet Union after Roosevelt's death, and the turbulence of national revolutions that swept five dozen countries, wracked that stability and fathered a cold war more ominous to the future of humanity than Hitler's offensive in World War II.

★★★★★

17

★★★★★

GLOBAL
IMPERIALISM

While sitting for a portrait in Warm Springs, Georgia, where he had gone to rest a few months after being inaugurated for a fourth term, Franklin Roosevelt collapsed and was dead within two hours. The massive cerebral hemorrhage which took his life on April 12, 1945, was a traumatic shock to the nation, for though he had been stricken with polio in the 1920's and had carried himself clumsily on metal braces, he seemed to be an enduring fixture in a tumultuous era. Now at sixty-three, after twelve years of leading the nation through depression, recovery, and war, he was gone, his mantle falling to a little man, little known and little tested, from Independence, Missouri, Harry S Truman.

Whether Roosevelt's sophisticated imperialism, based on coexistence with the Soviet Union, would have survived the political torrents of the postwar world is a debatable question. The inherent expansiveness of a swelling capitalist economy would have pushed Roosevelt to seek additional spheres of influence, as it pushed Truman. The dozens of revolutions that shook the status quo would have forced Roosevelt to some kind of drastic response, as it forced Truman. It may be that with FDR's policy the Soviets, under the balm of coexistence, would have guided the revolutions along more moderate channels; it may also be, on the other hand, that if they tried to do so they would have lost their influence in the third world and perhaps among Communists in other countries. It can only be said that Roosevelt and Henry A. Wallace, who was his vice-president from 1941 until just before his death, would have tried harder to avoid a rupture with Moscow. But short of making the structural changes toward a planned economy that Charles Beard and John

Dewey advocated in the 1930's—or more radical ones—it is unlikely that either Roosevelt or Wallace would have forestalled a cold war of some kind. The question, however, is moot, since Roosevelt was dead, and Wallace had been bypassed by the big-city bosses in the nominations of 1944 because they didn't want a man so consistently liberal; they wanted someone closer to their own background and philosophy—Truman. Roosevelt had yielded to them, thus opening the door for Truman to become president three months after he himself was sworn in for the fourth time.

Already sixty-one, lean, gray-haired, with thick spectacles, the best that could be said for Harry S Truman was that he was a simple man, with laconic and simple answers to complex problems. Shortly after the Nazi armies invaded the Soviet Union he offered the strategical suggestion that "if we see that Germany is winning the war we ought to help Russia, and if Russia is winning we ought to help Germany, and in that way let them kill as many as possible." The first time he met Molotov, eleven days after becoming president, Truman dressed him down in what columnist Drew Pearson called "Missouri mule-driver's language," and when the Soviet foreign minister complained, he snapped back: "Carry out your agreements and you won't get talked to like that." Such rudeness could be explained only as the provincialism of a man who saw things as either black or white. "I'm tired of babying the Soviets," he wrote to Secretary of State James F. Byrnes some months later. The only language the Russians understood, Truman said, was "How many divisions have you?" A nation was either all good or all bad, to be babied or terrorized; the shading of gray was outside the purview of the haberdasher from Independence.

Until he became president, Truman could have melted into any crowd without being visible. Born in Lamar, Missouri, on May 8, 1884, he spent his first six years on a farmstead in commonplace fashion, much like his none too prosperous ancestors. At six the family moved to Independence, where Harry's father worked as a laborer and Harry finished grade school and high school. Afterward he tried to enter both West Point and Annapolis, but was turned down because of defective eyesight. Dispirited by the rejection, he worked at mundane jobs until 1906, when the family returned to the land, operating a six-hundred-acre farm as a partnership among his father, his brother, and himself. Here, too, the results were not pleasing, for the farm was always in debt and eventually the brother moved off on his own and the father died. Harry was at sixes and sevens until World War I gave him the opportunity to find himself. He had already served in the National Guard while in Independence. He now accepted active duty, rose to First Lieutenant, in charge of a field artillery battery in France. Mustered out after two years in military service he joined with an old army buddy in a haberdashery business that turned out disastrously and saddled him with debts he would be paying for many years.

At thirty-eight, married only three years before to a onetime schoolmate, Bess Wallace, Truman was at the nadir of his fortunes, with no visible means of filling the family larder. Luckily, however, some army friends recommended him to the political boss of Missouri, Tom Pendergast, an unsavory figure who was later to go to jail for his transgressions; and Pendergast helped Truman to a county administrative post, which for some vague reason was designated a judgeship. "Judge" Truman served his constituency well, was trustworthy and honest, but neither then nor later did he forget or cross his sponsor. In 1926 and again in 1930 he was elected presiding judge of Jackson County, and four years later to the United States Senate, where he served in effect as Boss Pendergast's delegate. Though he was moderately well read in American history, the panaceas of the New Deal bewildered Truman; it was an enormous jump from Jackson County to Washington. Yet he was a good party regular. He seldom spoke, and he voted consistently as he was supposed to, except on two occasions when he kicked the traces—once for an army bonus bill, and another time to support a reactionary for the majority leadership in the Senate. His party regularity paid off in handsome dividends to the machine back home, which received more than its share in money for relief, public works, and contracts for the favored few.

Truman was a humble man who often spoke of his limitations and seldom rubbed people the wrong way. Vice-president Garner and Senate Secretary Leslie Biffle were happy to accept him on the informal "boards of education" which mapped party strategy. As the scion of small business he disliked Wall Street intensely; yet he had little love for organized labor, on the other side, and his liberalism was of the milk-and-water variety—in 1936, for instance, he voted against a low-cost housing program and in 1939 in favor of reducing relief appropriations. Nonetheless, in 1940, when he ran again for the Senate, it was organized labor (the railroad unions especially) that helped Truman to a narrow victory in the primaries and reelection in November. By now Pendergast was in jail and it was the union movement that filled the gap, rewarding the senator for quiet loyalty to Franklin Roosevelt. During this second term in office Truman gained a national reputation as chairman of a committee to investigate the defense program—though the research and reports were done by a brilliant young man named Hugh Fulton—and it was this more than anything else that suddenly made him vice-presidential material. The chairman of the Democratic Party's National Committee, Robert Hannegan of Kansas City, was an old Pendergast hand who knew Truman well and pushed his candidacy avidly. When FDR was forced to drop Wallace, the big-city bosses in the party rallied to Hannegan's suggestion of Truman.

Truman eventually gained the reputation of being a liberal, primarily because as an underdog in the 1948 election campaign he turned left to wean away some of the supporters of third-party candidate Henry Wallace. But in 1945, though he pledged "to continue both the foreign and domestic policies of the Roosevelt administration," he swept out most of the New Deal cadre and replaced them with men of more conservative mien. Of the 125 major appointments he made in his first two years, 49 were bankers or industrialists, 31 military men, and 17 lawyers for the most part related to big business. It was under this leadership that the postwar global imperialism was carried forth.

II

Apart from the influence of these men—and of Winston Churchill —three decisive developments shaped Truman's policy. One was the engineering of a new type of explosive, based on nuclear fission— the atom bomb. The second was the consolidation of what Dwight Eisenhower would later call the military-industrial complex. The third, undergirding the others and by far the most important, was the enormous growth of America's economic power and the concomitant decline of the economic power of both its allies and its enemies. Between 1940 and 1945 national income in the United States more than doubled, from $81.6 billion to $181.2 billion (and as of 1950, $241.9 billion). Bank deposits, exclusive of vast sums plowed into government war bonds, jumped from $41 billion in the prewar year of 1938 to $83 billion in 1944. The National Planning Association estimated that the capital equipment industry had expanded to the point where it was "nearly twice the size which would be needed domestically under the most fortuitous conditions of full employment and nearly equal to the task of supplying world needs." American exports during the war averaged about $10 billion a year (more than three times prewar figures) and imports $3.5 billion, leaving the rest of the world with a disheartening dollar deficit running into many billions. The balance of payments was so heavily weighted in favor of Uncle Sam that by the end of the war America had accumulated a stockpile of $29 billion in gold—77 percent of the world's reserves. Summarizing the American position early in the postwar era, James McMillan and Bernard Harris in *The American Take-Over of Britain* record that "on the production side the U.S., with six and a half percent of the world's population, harvested one-third of the world's grain; half its cotton; smelted 55 percent of its steel and other basic metals; pumped 70 percent of the world's oil; used 50 percent of its rubber; generated 45 percent of its mechanical energy; produced 60 percent of its manufactured goods and enjoyed 45 percent of the entire annual income of humanity. On the consumption side—the U.S. owned 50 percent of the world's telephones; 50 percent of its radios; 75 percent of its baths; 70 percent of motor cars; 84 percent of civil aircraft and 85 percent of refrigerators and washing machines." It was an awesome economic mechanism that would need foreign markets more desperately than ever.

By contrast, British wealth plunged downward 30 percent. Britain was forced to sell off much of her investments in the United States, South America, and Asia to amass dollars for imports and for aid to her allies. As early as 1941 her exports, on which she depended to survive, had fallen by half; her gold drained away to the point where in 1945 the reserve was a mere $12 *million.* Before the war Britain imported 80 percent of her raw materials and half her food, paying for them in three ways: from income on foreign investments, from earnings of her merchant ships, and from the sale of industrial goods. At that time the British held a portfolio of half the foreign investments in the world. But after selling much of it and borrowing from the empire, their position was reversed: instead of being a lender of $16 billion, Britain was now a borrower of $12 billion. The merchant marine had been depleted by about a fourth, and as for industry the British lion was past his prime, the nation's coal mines misused and worn out, factory equipment ancient and sadly in need of replacement. Thus, despite an austerity program meant to save valuable dollars, the British balance of payments was now severely in the red. Surveying the situation in a debate before the House of Lords, Lord Woolton, a big, jovial businessman, commented, "The war has left us poor. It has left us the largest debtor nation in history. America, on the other hand, has been left by the war rich beyond her dreams."

Since wealth begets power, it was inevitable that Uncle Sam would use his wealth to mold the world to his own image. The lend-lease agreement with Britain, for instance, was conditioned on Churchill's acceptance of a provision, section VII, "against discrimination in either the United States or the United Kingdom against the importation of any product originating in the other country." What this cumbersome sentence meant was that England would have to open a door she had partly closed a decade before. In 1930 the United States had raised its tariffs precipitously; Britain responded in 1932 with the Ottawa agreements whereby members of the British empire gave each other tariff "preference"—lower rates than those for outside powers. Now Roosevelt, Secretary Hull, Dean Acheson, et al. were using the lure of planes, tanks, and dollars to drive a wedge into that imperial preference system, thereby assuring deeper American penetration into Commonwealth trade. The British argued valiantly against section VII for a number of months, even though they desperately needed lend-lease, but in the end had to give up part of their protective system.

After hostilities ended and Truman had abruptly terminated lend-lease the British were again in Washington, hat in hand, pleading for a loan to tide them over. Once more Uncle Sam demanded that imperial preferences be abolished, a demand which Howard K. Smith says "would have opened the Empire to irresistible American production, swamped British produce, and ruined the island." Another condition, the "convertibility" clause, required that foreign purchases made with an American loan be paid for in dollars, if so requested, rather than British pounds. In effect this meant that third nations which received those dollars would buy goods in America rather than Britain. These terms, even when ameliorated, were so onerous that almost a hundred members of Parliament voted against taking the loan. A Tory named Robert Boothby said of it that "comparable terms have never hitherto been imposed on a country that has not been defeated in war. . . . This is our economic Munich." As finally concluded the agreement for $3.75 billion called for Britain to spend at least $930 million of that money in the United States; to pay for imports with dollars or gold; to refuse loans from Commonwealth states if they offered better terms than Uncle Sam had given; and to "establish the same quotas on goods coming from the Empire as on those coming from the United States."

Throughout the war and the postwar period the dollar was wielded like a club to make nations, big and small, conform to the Pax Americana. When lend-lease aid was given to Ethiopia it carried the proviso that the African regime would not grant England "exclusive" air bases, but would hold the door open for the United States. Aid to Egypt eventually brought alteration of that nation's investment laws, so as to encourage joint stock companies, and concessions to American airline companies to ply the route between Cairo and Europe. On the other hand planned credits for Poland in

1945–46 were suspended because the Boleslaw Bierut regime refused to revive free trade, hold "free elections," or join in the American system for the "expansion of world trade and employment." A
$50 million credit for Czechoslovakia to buy surplus property was
unceremoniously cut off by Secretary of State James F. Byrnes because, as he told Jan Masaryk, Czech officials had applauded "a denunciation of the United States as a government seeking to dominate the world by 'hand-outs.'"

The same attitude prevailed toward the Soviet Union. Secretary
Hull decided back in 1943 that he would make it clear to the Russians that their chances of obtaining postwar loans depended on accepting his foreign trade program. Later there were specific plans to
grant the Soviets a postwar credit of $10 billion at 2 percent a year
interest, provided that the Kremlin committed itself to supply strategic raw materials to the United States and to "normalize" economic relations. All this, however, was in the planning stage, before
Roosevelt died and while the Soviet Union was still receiving lend-
lease. On May 8, 1945, Truman abruptly ended lend-lease shipments, but while the British were fortified with other monies, no
credits or loans were offered the Soviet Union to replace the wartime grants. The President decided that before the Russians would
receive American help they would have to show by good deeds that
they deserved them—such as agreeing to free elections in Poland or
honoring property rights of American corporations in Eastern Europe and the Soviet zone of Germany. The Kremlin paid a heavy
price for refusing to align itself with the American system. Denied
aid from the only country that could provide it, the Soviet Union
tried to make up for it by exacting all the reparations it could from
Germany and by exploiting the countries it occupied in Eastern Europe. Subsequently, when Washington went further and punished
the Soviets by withholding strategic materials, the Russians were
forced to introduce innumerable innovations and tighten their belts
to make their economy work.

From lend-lease to the Marshall Plan to the Alliance for Progress
and beyond, recipients of American dollars had to accept political
and economic conditions dictated by Washington before the money
was forthcoming. Sometimes those conditions involved general principle or broad objectives—for instance, under the Economic Cooperation Act every nation that received Marshall Plan aid had to cer-
tify each month that it had not exported to the Soviet Union and
other Communist countries any arms, strategic material, or other
goods on which the United States had placed an embargo. Sometimes
the terms were specific—one of the conditions for an ECA loan to

Britain in 1948, according to Senator Arthur Vandenberg, "was that the United States be given a bigger share in the uranium development in the Congo." In line with this understanding a group of American companies, associated with the Rockefeller interests, were permitted to buy 600,000 shares of Tanganyika Concessions, the largest financial holding company in sub-Sahara Africa. "Tanks," as it was called, held a controlling interest in Union Minière du Haut Katanga, from which the United States was then receiving 90 percent of its uranium. Another ECA loan of $24 million to improve railways in Northern and Southern Rhodesia was predicated on repayment in strategic raw materials such as copper, cobalt, tungsten, and chrome. Understandably, then, when Britain contemplated uniting the two Rhodesias and Nyasaland into a federation more easily controlled by the white settlers, it sought and received American approval for its action.

"America," wrote Howard K. Smith in *The State of Europe,* "truly possesses the whip-hand over the world. For America, becoming 'imperialist' is as easy as rolling off a log. With this preponderance of power, and most of the rest of the world in a crisis of scarcity, there need be no crude conquests; they can be carried out gently, invisibly, by the almost surreptitious means of wealth, by investments that bring silent control, and by aid-grants accompanied by polite hints regarding the direction of the receiving nation's policy." When Russia "extends her security zone," Smith observed, it "requires an overthrow of the status quo, for the status quo of the world is capitalist; which means a lot of noise and ugly scenes." When America does it, however, "it involves only supporting the status quo: no scenes, no noise. It can be done under the aegis of fair-sounding arrangements like 'equality of trade.'"

One of the first crises in which "no noise" imperialism showed its effectiveness was the postwar struggle for Iranian oil. The ancient kingdom of Persia had been taken over by Britain and the Soviets in 1941, when it appeared that its ruler, Reza Shah, was prepared to join the Axis. Since this would cut off an important supply route into the Soviet Union, the Russians occupied the northern part of the country while the British took over the central and southern sections, in which their oil fields lay. According to the Tripartite Treaty of Alliance, the foreign forces (including Americans, who came in later) were to be withdrawn no later than six months after the war. But when the time came, March 2, 1946, and after Britain and America had evacuated Persia, the Soviets balked. In the meantime they had encouraged a revolt in the province of Azerbaijan, installed a pro-Communist government under Jafar Pishevari, and secured a temporary concession for oil exploration to compensate for their heavy losses in the Caucasus. Legally, of course, the Soviets were in the wrong, but British and other Allied troops were still in Greece, Syria, Lebanon, Indochina, the Dutch East Indies, and elsewhere; in such circumstances, the Soviets considered it unfair that they were being pressured to give up an area that had been a Russian sphere of influence before 1918 and whose oil was so vital now to her reconstruction. Nevertheless, under American pressure, the Soviet troops were withdrawn, the Pishevari regime collapsed, and the oil agreement was canceled. Persia was saved from "Soviet imperialism"! The story, however, does not end there, for as the Russians moved out the Americans moved in. In May 1947 Washington supplied $25 million in arms to the Iranian army and the Iranian gendarmerie—headed by an American general. Before long, the Asian state had become a satellite of the United States, complete with military bases and economic and military advisers. And in August 1953, when the Central Intelligence Agency overthrew the government of Mohammed Mossadegh, five American companies were assigned 40 percent of Iran's petroleum riches. What the Russians had failed to achieve with their occupation, the Americans achieved through dollars, advisers, and military support for a coup d'état.

III

The conflict between the United States and the Soviet Union, from the time of Truman's accession to power to the present, has obscured the imperialist intent of American policy behind a veil of ideology. But even had Roosevelt lived, Washington would still have tried to organize the world around its own needs. The result might have been less raucous, but the goals would have been much the same. There still would have been a dollar gap between what the world sold the United States and what it bought from it. America would still have demanded the open door as a means of gaining outlets for its surpluses, would still have dominated the seas and sought hundreds of bases in foreign lands to protect its prerogatives. "My contention is that we cannot have full employment and prosperity in the United States," said Assistant Secretary of State Dean Acheson in November 1944, "without the foreign markets." Donald M. Nelson, head of the War Production Board, predicted on June 7, 1944, that "unless we can develop a broad export market, for capital goods, I do not see the chance in the reconversion period for the capital goods industries [the heart of the American economy] to be prosperous." Echoing such sentiments, Roosevelt emphasized in a letter to Foreign Economic Administrator Leo Crowley that every worker, farmer, and businessman "has a stake in the production and flow of manufactured goods, agricultural products, and other supplies to all other countries of the world." Without that flow the system could not work.

What Truman changed in the Roosevelt strategy was not objectives but methods. In that sense, the conflict with the Kremlin was not the cause of American behavior in the cold-war period, but an effect of it: To get what it wanted—a Pax Americana—the American establishment decided it had to curb, contain, and isolate the Soviet Union. For the neoimperialists, writes Howard K. Smith, "containment" of Marxist Russia was "an excellent excuse for extending American control everywhere by establishing military bases, financing and thereby dominating threatened governments, and tying down other nations' power by standardized arms agreements."

Truman had been at his White House desk only eleven days when he told Charles E. Bohlen that "if the Russians did not wish to join us they could go to hell." That day he met with Molotov to discuss the Polish question and dressed him down, as already noted, in "Missouri mule-driver's language." Bohlen, who was present and acted as interpreter, later commented that "he had never heard a top official get such a scolding." Two weeks later Truman signed an order ending lend-lease even though the Russians were secretly committed to enter the war against Japan and needed that aid not only for reconstruction but for their pending military effort. Why the new President decided to take the "tough" line, and take it so quickly after Roosevelt's death, is a subject of considerable speculation. "Harry Truman," *Time* magazine wrote, "has never pretended to a great grasp of foreign affairs. Unlike his predecessors, he depended heavily on his advisers." Among those advisers was Fleet Admiral William D. Leahy, Chairman of the Joint Chiefs of Staff and Chief of Staff to the President, who briefed Truman every morning and who was perhaps the principal architect of the "tough" policy. It was Leahy, according to a *Collier's* article, "Watchdog in the White House," who "tutored Truman on what happened at all of the Big Four conferences" and "coached Roosevelt's inexperienced successor on the significance of Russia's emergence as a major power at the end of World War II. . . ." There were also a number of leading investment bankers such as James V. Forrestal, former president of Dillon, Read & Co.; General William H. Draper, former vice-president of the same company; W. Averell Harriman of Brown Bros., Harriman & Co.; Robert A. Lovett of the same firm; Paul Hoffman of Studebaker; and others. Most of these men had links to the status quo in Europe, through financial arrangements with leading corporations on both sides of the war, and carried a strong anti-Communist bias.

More important than the predilections of the advisers or Truman himself, however, was a feeling that the United States was now so strong no nation could long hold out against it, including the Soviet Union. In part this sense of power derived from economic reality, but in part also from the atom bomb. An hour after he had been sworn in and held his first brief cabinet meeting, Truman was called aside by Secretary of War Stimson and given his first clue that scientists were at work on "a new explosive of almost unbelievable destructive power." The atomic bomb, Stimson recorded, gave Truman "an entirely new feeling of confidence." It changed "a lot of ideas," said Admiral Leahy, "including my own. . . ." The administration, to be sure, intended to be "firm" toward the Russians anyway, but as Gar Alperovitz points out in his *Atomic Diplomacy: Hiroshima and Potsdam*, "Western policy makers harbored very grave doubts that Britain and America could challenge Soviet predominance in Eastern Europe. . . . It may well be that, had there been no atomic bomb, Truman would have been forced to reconsider the basic direction of his policy. . . ." Such a bomb was in the making, however, and it encouraged the Americans "to demand more at Potsdam than they had asked at Yalta." Churchill, who had been pessimistic about containing Soviet power, felt that "we now had something in our hands which would redress the balance with the Russians." James F. Byrnes, Director of War Mobilization under Roosevelt and Secretary of State after July 1945, had already advised Truman "that in his belief the bomb might well put us in a position to dictate our own terms at the end of the war." This was a position with universal appeal for American policy makers—then, and for years thereafter. Bernard Baruch expressed it with ultimate forthrightness: "America can get what she wants if she insists on it. After all, we've got it—the bomb—and they haven't and won't have it for a long time to come."

With "The Bomb" in the American arsenal, Byrnes was confident that the Soviets could be forced to "retire in a very decent manner" from their dominant position in Eastern Europe, and could be kept from playing a serious role in the Far East. In later years, as the cold war evolved its own myths, it was said that the conflict began, among other reasons, because the Kremlin had violated pledges given at the Yalta Big Three conference in February 1945. It refused to hold "free and unfettered" elections in Poland, and it imposed puppet governments in its sphere of influence. Most of these charges were true, of course, but distorted in the sense that while the Soviets were trying to hold on to a relatively small sphere of influence in Eastern Europe, the United States was seeking both to roll back the Soviets and to expand its own sphere on a vastly wider front.

In October 1944, Churchill and Stalin had arrived at a secret agreement over the Balkans, in which, by the Prime Minister's own account, the Soviets were to have a "90 percent predominance in Rumania," 75 percent predominance in Bulgaria (and 25 percent for other powers), and 50–50 in Hungary and Yugoslavia; Britain would have full sway in Greece. Though Roosevelt disapproved of this understanding, and Yalta did speak of free elections, Uncle Sam and John Bull were generally reconciled—before the bomb began to loom large in their thinking—to Soviet prevalence in Eastern Europe. "It was not a question of what we would *let* the Russians do," Byrnes observed early in 1945, "but what we could *get* them to do." According to Churchill, "the arrangements made about the Balkans were, I was sure, the best possible." What was remarkable, in retrospect, was not Stalin's bellicosity, but contrariwise, his steadfast compliance to so many accords. Churchill alluded to it in discussing the British repression in Greece. "We have been hampered in our protests against elections in Eastern Europe," he wrote, "by the fact that in order to have freedom to save Greece, [Anthony] Eden and I at Moscow in October recognized that Russia should have a largely preponderant voice in Rumania and Bulgaria while we took the lead in Greece. Stalin adhered very strictly to this understanding during the thirty days fighting against the communists and ELAS in the city of Athens, in spite of the fact that all this was most disagreeable to him and those around him." Not one word of criticism appeared in Soviet newspapers against the use of British troops in Greece.

There is something synthetic about the contention that Stalin refused to compromise on anything and everything. The Red Army did withdraw from Iran, Manchuria, Hungary, and Czechoslovakia. Though the Soviets refused American-style elections in Bulgaria and Rumania, they did permit such elections in Hungary, where the Communists were beaten by 59 percent for the Small Landholders' Party to 17 percent for themselves. Free speech, free press, free elections, and a moderately independent coalition government were permitted to prevail in Czechoslovakia until February 1948, when the Communists overturned the regime and seized full control. The record shows that until the cold war heated up, the Soviet Union and Communist Parties in most places worked feverishly to sustain the very status quo that Washington cherished.

"Near the end of the war," writes historian D. F. Fleming, "Stalin scoffed at communism in Germany, urged the Italian Reds to make peace with the monarchy, did his best to induce Mao Tse-tung to come to terms with the Kuomintang and angrily demanded of Tito that he back the monarchy, thus fulfilling his [Stalin's] bargain with Churchill." In France and Italy, on the morrow of liberation—while de Gaulle was still in Algiers and Italy was in gross confusion—the Communist-controlled partisans and *garibaldini* took over the factories in both countries. With their stockpile of armaments and their mass followings they might have gone further—to revolution. But General de Gaulle took a plane to Moscow, talked with Stalin, and French Communists evacuated the factories and disarmed the partisans. Another word from Moscow and revolutionary danger in Italy abated. So moderate was Communist policy that French Communists refused to endorse nationalist movements in the colonies; the events in Madagascar, Tunisia, Algeria, and Morocco occurred despite them, not because of them.

Communists also entered "bourgeois governments" throughout Europe—willingly, even enthusiastically. For almost two years, Maurice Thorez, veteran Communist leader, was vice-premier of France, and Palmiro Togliatti held similar status in Italy. As late as 1947 Europe was distressingly vulnerable to internal revolt—yet the followers of the Kremlin seized no factories, armed no guerrilla detachments, engineered no revolutions. As a matter of fact they worked avidly to revive capitalism. Joseph Alsop, writing in the New York *Herald Tribune* in July 1946 was struck by the cooperation Jean Monnet was getting from the Communists in reconstructing France: "The key to the success of the plan to date, which has been considerable, is the enthusiastic collaboration of the French Communist Party. The communists control the most important unions. . . . Communist leadership has been responsible for such surprising steps as acceptance by the key unions of a kind of modified piecework system. . . . Reconstruction come first, is the Party line."

Not only was there no social threat from the Stalinists, but, if the word of leading American figures is to be credited, no military one either. James Forrestal was convinced in June 1946 that the Russians "would not move this summer—in fact, at any time," and General Walter Bedell Smith, ambassador to Moscow, reported in August 1948 to the War Council "that the Russians do not want war." "I do not know any responsible official, military or civilian, in this government or any government," declared John Foster Dulles in March 1949, "who believes that the Soviet government now plans conquest by open military aggression." George Kennan, author of the containment policy and at one time an ambassador to the Soviet Union, recorded in a 1965 lecture, "It was perfectly clear to anyone with even a rudimentary knowledge of the Russia of that day that the Soviet leaders had no intention of attempting to advance their cause by launching military attacks with their own armed forces across frontiers."

No, it was not the Kremlin that was on the offensive in 1945–47, trying to uproot the old world, but an American leadership, goaded by its new economic power and by the bomb, that tried to force the Soviets and their satellites into the Pax Americana. "The Americans and the British," said de Gaulle in summarizing the results of the 1945 Potsdam Conference, "hoped to recover by application what they had conceded in principle." The rapid Sovietization of Eastern Europe, de Gaulle pointed out "was only the inevitable result of what had been agreed upon at the Crimea [Yalta] Conference. . . . The regrets the British and Americans now expressed [at Potsdam] were quite uncalled for." Secretary of State Byrnes was convinced, however, that the atom bomb—successfully tested at the time of Potsdam—gave Uncle Sam the necessary leverage to dilute Soviet power. It was certainly incongruous, to say the least, for Byrnes and Truman, while condoning the British intervention in Greece and the fake elections there, to demand that Russia agree to a three-power reorganization "of Bulgaria and Rumania to permit participation of all democratic groups there," or a similar policy for Poland. Through such "reorganizations" the Americans hoped to keep their foot in the East European door, whereas the Russians saw it as a vital threat to their sphere of influence.

Byrnes went further: if the Kremlin did not toe the line he was ready to mount a "preventative war" against it. In his *Speaking Frankly*, published in 1947, he expressed the view that Moscow would not "try to hold permanently all of eastern Germany. However, if I misjudge them, and they do go to the point of holding eastern Germany and vetoing a Security Council directive to withdraw occupation forces, we . . . must make it clear to all that we are willing to adopt *those measures of last resort* [i.e., an atomic war] if, for the peace of the world, we are forced to do so." (Emphasis added). He prayed that the Russians would "never force us to this course of last resort. But they must learn what Hitler learned—that the world is not going to permit one nation to veto peace on earth." When he left office it was with disappointment that he had not forced the Russians to withdraw from Eastern Europe, and the chastened thought that they "don't scare."

There is reason to believe that the atom bomb would not have been used in 1945 except for the desire to threaten the Soviet Union. The first such bomb employed against people was dropped by an American B-29, christened the *Enola Gay*, on Hiroshima at 9:15 A.M. August 6, 1945. Within a few minutes the city of 300,000, considered the second most important military center in Japan, was a flaming ruin—80,000 dead, an equal number wounded, 62,000 buildings destroyed, a great fire storm raging. Fire raids in the past had killed as many as 125,000 people in Tokyo, but this was a *single* bomb, 20 kilotons—equivalent to 20,000 tons of dynamite. As he was handed the message about the bomb's "success," aboard the *Augusta*, which was taking him home from Potsdam, an ebullient Truman told the sailors around him: "This is the greatest thing in history." To this day there is a vehement dispute even among establishment figures as to whether the bomb should have been dropped. Did it really save "millions of lives," as Truman first stated, or even the "lives of 200,000 American soldiers," in his revised estimate of 1949? Or was it delivered on two hapless cities simply as an illustration of American power, and as a warning, above all, to the Soviet Union?

"Before the atom bomb was used," said General Dwight D. Eisenhower during a triumphal trip to Moscow, "I would have said, yes, I was sure we could keep the peace with Russia. Now I don't know. . . . People are frightened and disturbed all over. Everyone feels insecure again." On another occasion he commented: "I must say that personally I am not at all sure that we were well advised to use it." Secretary Stimson, one of those who did advise its use, admitted only a month later that "I was wrong." Every one of the Joint Chiefs of Staff stated before the bombings that Japan was bound to surrender unconditionally, without the bomb, even without an invasion. "It is my opinion," said Admiral Leahy afterward, "that the use of this barbarous weapon at Hiroshima and Nagasaki was of no material assistance in our war against Japan. The Japanese were already defeated and ready to surrender."

As early as July 12, 1945, Forrestal recorded in his diary, "The first real evidence of a Japanese desire to get out of the war came today through intercepted messages from Togo, Foreign Minister, to Sato, Jap Ambassador to Moscow, instructing the latter to see Molotov . . . to lay before him the Emperor's strong desire to secure a termination of the war." Since the invasion of the Japanese islands was not scheduled until November 1945, there was obviously plenty of time to probe this peace feeler. "Certainly prior to December 31, 1945," reads the U.S. Strategic Bomber Survey No. 4, "Japan would have surrendered, even if the atom bombs had not been dropped, even if Russia had not entered the war, and even if no invasion had been planned or contemplated." The Land of the Rising Sun after all was helpless and prostrate, its air force and navy shattered, 40 percent of its 66 major cities destroyed, its harbors mined and block-aded.

The full story as to why the bomb was dropped will someday be known, but it is quite clear even now that the Truman administration expected more political dividends than military dividends from its use. When Roosevelt, Stalin, and Churchill met at Yalta in February 1945, the bomb had not yet been tested, and it was felt that Soviet ground troops would be urgently needed to win in Asia. In return for Stalin's pledge that his nation would declare war on the Nipponese three months after European hostilities had ended, the others agreed that the southern half of the island of Sakhalin, taken from Russia after the Russo-Japanese War of 1904, would be re-turned; that the Kurile Islands would be assigned to Moscow; that the Manchurian port of Dairen would be internationalized, and Russia's "preeminent interests" there recognized; that Port Arthur would be leased to the Soviet Union as a naval base; and that cer-tain railroads with an outlet to Dairen would be operated by a Soviet-Chinese company. Fighting in Europe ended May 8, so that Rus-sian entry into the Asian phase of hostilities was scheduled no later than August 8 (when it actually did take place). By that time, however, Byrnes had serious misgivings about the concessions that had been made to Stalin. He "would have been satisfied," he tells us in *Speaking Frankly*, "had the Russians determined not to enter the war. . . . I believed the atomic bomb would be successful and would force the Japanese to accept surrender on our terms. I feared what would happen when the Red Army entered Manchuria." Spe-cifically, he very much wanted to upset the agreements vis-à-vis the two ports. Forrestal records in his diary for July 28 that year that "Byrnes said he was most anxious to get the Japanese affair over with before the Russians get in, with particular reference to Dairen and Port Arthur. Once in there, he felt, it would not be easy to get them out. . . ." The British author P. M. S. Blackett, winner of the Nobel Prize for Physics and holder of the U.S. Order of Merit for his help to Allied defense in World War II, concluded in retrospect that the main reason the bombs were dropped on Hiroshima and Naga-saki was to keep the Soviet Union out of that phase of the war and thereby to minimize its role in the Far East. Stimson, who later—to repeat—changed his mind, thought of the bombs in even broader context: it would be a matter of the "greatest complication," he said, if Truman negotiated with Stalin *before* the bomb had been "laid on

Japan." The bomb, in other words, was to act as a prime diplomatic threat to the Soviets, and not only in Asia but Europe. Vannevar Bush, director of the Office of Scientific Research and Development and adviser to Stimson on atomic matters, proclaimed that the new terror weapon was "delivered on time so that there was no necessity for any concessions to Russia at the end of the war." Finally there is the revealing statement by Byrnes to Leo Szilard, a leading scientific figure in developing the bomb. As Szilard reports it, "Mr. Byrnes did not argue that it was necessary to use the bomb against the cities of Japan in order to win the war. . . . Mr. Byrnes' . . . view [was] that our possessing and demonstrating the bomb would make Russia more manageable in Europe."

IV

The quarrel with the Soviet Union—it cannot be affirmed too often —was not the *cause* of America's imperial policy, but an *effect* of it. Washington was determined to organize the world to its ends; Moscow simply refused to be molded and manipulated like Britain or France. At a time when its losses included 15 to 20 million dead; 15 large cities, 1,710 towns, 70,000 villages partly or wholly destroyed; 6 million buildings demolished; 10,000 power stations ruined, etc., etc., etc.—the Soviet Union was certainly no military threat. But it stood in the way of America's thrust to fashion the world in its image, since it sealed off a substantial part of the globe to the open door; and it stood in the way of what is euphemistically called "international stability," since it could become a bastion to which revolutionary nationalists in the underdeveloped countries looked to for aid to their revolutions. Neither Communist ideology nor Stalinist tyranny (most of America's allies outside the advanced nations were ruled by tyrannical governments) had anything to do with it. What was at stake was the imposition of a Pax Americana, and those who opposed it, whether Communists or "neutralists," leftists or rightists, dictators or saints, would be the butts of American ire if they continued opposition.

Pax Americana—more properly, global imperialism—unfolded from the inner logic of America's new status. There were no *a priori* plans or blueprints, simply an impulse that guided the policy makers. As it evolved, it manifested a number of similarities to, and some features quite different from, the Pax Britannica that England had fashioned for the nineteenth-century world. Under Pax Britannica, John Bull and his navy guaranteed the colonies and spheres of influence of the great powers, and kept the capitalist states from clawing at each other. Under Pax Americana, Uncle Sam organized the great powers into a consortium dedicated to a certain economic way of life, the open door, and developed a military machine to uphold the status quo against revolutions and revolutionaries. The older imperialism feasted on the carcasses of dying empires—the Ottomans, the Moguls, the Manchus, the Spaniards; so too the global imperialism of Uncle Sam watched with unabated satisfaction the decimation of the British, French, Dutch, and other empires—except in those instances where the Communists or other radical forces threatened to replace them. In both cases, a new status quo emerged which Britain in the nineteenth century and America in the twentieth century defended avidly. The one great difference between the two imperialisms and the two periods was that for the most part the "enemy" in the nineteenth century was usually external—a foreign power— whereas the "enemy" in the mid-twentieth century was usually internal—revolution.

It was assumed by America's leadership at first that a Pax Americana could be arranged with a modest effort, involving only monetary measures, international relief, a mechanism for resolving disputes—the United Nations—and judiciously placed loans. At Bretton Woods, New Hampshire, delegates of forty-four nations met in the summer of 1944, and adopted two proposals to facilitate trade and development. The International Bank of Reconstruction and Development was chartered to grant loans for reconstruction in areas devastated by the war and to underdeveloped countries, as well as to guarantee certain private and public loans. As of 1946 this World Bank was hobbled by the circumstance that only the United States had made available its share of the subscription ($635 million). The International Monetary Fund, with $8.8 billion, one third of it subscribed by America, was to be a clearing union for international payments, so that nations with adverse balance of payments could weather the storm by purchasing the currency of other nations.

These two institutions have never had overriding importance in themselves, but like the subsequent loan to Britain, they were indicative of the intense economic aggressiveness of the United States. To become part of the Bretton Woods system a nation had to agree to conduct trade along standard capitalist lines—which meant that nations such as the Soviet Union which had nationalized foreign trade were excluded. On a number of occasions the Kremlin was asked to join the IMF, but to do so would have meant jettisoning the socialist economic order. In March 1946 the Soviets were advised that Washington might consider a $1 billion credit if the Kremlin would settle its lend-lease account, join the IMF and World Bank, and live up to their rules against discrimination in international trade. This, of course, would have forced not only Russia but its Eastern European sphere into the "American system" and would have meant, as well, that Eastern Europe (except for Czechoslovakia) would remain a raw-material-producing area, since these countries needed protection (tariffs and quotas and other devices) for their nascent industries, rather than free trade. The United States itself in a comparable period, after the Civil War, had insisted on high tariffs to protect its new industrial machine. Soviet specialists expressed the view to an American in London that the "real object . . . in advocating freer trade was to hold the markets for manufactured goods in the less developed countries and to check their industrialization." The Russians argued that "protection was necessary for the industrialization of Eastern European countries, and their industrialization was necessary to free them from economic domination by the capitalist countries."

If one examines the economic offensive of the United States at Bretton Woods and thereafter, its aim seems to have been to force all nations to give up those devices they felt protected them. Britain was made to give up empire preferences ultimately, as a result of the 1946 loan and the Marshall Plan, and reduced to a second-rate power subordinate to Uncle Sam. Had she kept the preference system—giving her advantages within the Commonwealth against outsiders—and entered into "bilateral" trade agreements rather than the American "multilateralism," she might have become the center of a third configuration of power. In 1945–48, however, she was in little position to talk back to Uncle Sam. Multilateralism doomed the weaker countries, inside and outside the Soviet bloc, to nonindustrial economies; and had the Soviets accepted it, would have reversed the whole purpose of the Russian Revolution. But Bretton Woods and later the Marshall Plan, Point 4, Mutual Security, Alliance for Progress, and all other aid were fashioned to incorporate other countries into the "American system"—whether it was good for their long-term interests or not.

There was never any doubt in the minds of Washington's policy makers that aid was a political weapon. America, said Forrestal in a memo to Byrnes, must receive "considerations" for everything it does to help others. In that respect, he wanted to know: "What is our policy as regards British loans to South American countries? . . . To what extent shall we permit the British to finance the Argentine, Brazil and Chile in an effort to re-establish the dominance of the Pound Sterling in the South American market?" With that arrogance so typical of power he assumed that Washington had the right to permit or not permit another nation to do certain things. When the Marshall Plan was being discussed, William L. Clayton, Undersecretary of State for Economic Affairs, pointed out that "we will hold in our hands the powerful weapon of *discontinuance of aid* if contrary to our expectations any country fails to live up to our expectations." (Emphasis added.)

The only exception to this purposive policy was war relief—and then only for a short time. To alleviate hunger and resettle refugees (in Europe alone there were ten million people who had been driven from their homes) the Allies in 1943 established what was later known as the United Nations Relief and Rehabilitation Administration (UNRRA). Headed first by Herbert H. Lehman, then by the peppery mayor of New York, Fiorello La Guardia, it dispensed about a billion a year, more than two thirds of which was donated by the United States. There were many who hoped that UNRRA would be the model for future economic aid, since it was a collective project of many nations and thus exercised few political controls over recipients. Moreover it gave help to all that needed it, whether in or out of the Soviet orbit. But the planet was in the process of being polarized, and the men in Washington decided that multilateral aid did not give them the leverage they wanted to make other nations do their bidding. UNRRA, in spite of La Guardia's objections, went out of business early in the postwar period. American aid in the future would be primarily bilateral, with precise conditions to the receiving nation, and outside the frame of the United Nations.

V

What stiffened American policy and officially inaugurated the cold war was not that the Russians were making any further penetrations beyond Eastern Europe, but that the sector of the world under American overlordship began to founder. The new status quo was in jeopardy.

As of war's end the United States was suddenly master of a vast empire. To be sure, it added only small pieces of territory to its suzerainty—Micronesia, Okinawa, etc.—but its control of the "free world" was exercised in three other ways. Japan was now directly occupied by General MacArthur's troops, and the general was busy recasting its political structure to conform to the American pattern. One zone of Western Germany plus a sector of Berlin was under a U.S. military government—and on critical matters the British and

French zones were also subordinate to Washington's wishes. Beyond that, many countries were tied hand and foot to Uncle Sam through grants and loans. Through such grants and loans, writes Howard K. Smith, "the economic veins of a large part of the world have been connected to America's pumping industrial and agricultural heart. Many of them depend on America not merely for aid without which they would be worse off; they depend on the heart's regular pumping for naked survival. By a decision on whatever grounds to reduce or cut off the flow, America could stop factories, cause riots and upheaval, break governments." The United States had replaced Britain as master of the seas, including even the eastern Mediterranean which had been a decisive part of John Bull's lifeline; and it was ensconced in 400 naval and air bases throughout the world, so that existing empires and existing trade depended on American sufferance.

Symptomatic of how the United States was reorganizing the world to its own ends, even before the crisis of 1947, was the reinvestment of the old power elite in Germany. The Allies had pledged to "eliminate or control all German industry that could be used for German military production. . . ." In the opinion of Great Britain this meant that the Ruhr factories, heart of the German military economy, should be nationalized. Labor's foreign minister, Ernest Bevin, argued in October 1946 that Germany's heavy industries "were previously in the hands of magnates who were closely allied to the German military machine, who financed Hitler, and who in two wars were part and parcel of Germany's aggressive policy. We have no desire to see those gentlemen or their like return to a position which they have abused with such tragic results." The London *Economist*, authoritative conservative weekly, counseled that conditions in the Ruhr "make far-reaching socialist experiments a necessity. . . ." In Germany itself not only the Social Democrats and Communists favored nationalization, but many Christian Democrats, as well as the Parliament of North Rhine Westphalia.

Under American pressure, however, the core of West Germany's economy went back to the very men who used it to support the Nazis. "We do not propose to endorse socialization in Germany under any circumstances," recorded Secretary of the Navy James Forrestal in his diary of May 7, 1947. "At some point it would have to be made clear to the British at the highest levels that they were operating their economy on three and a quarter billion capital obtained from this country, and that they would probably need additional working capital, and that we did not propose to have our money used to implement a German system contrary to our own ideas. . . ." When the German government in the Ruhr finally voted a socialization law by parliamentary majority, the British, under American pressure, vetoed it. The American military government, under General Lucius Clay and General William H. Draper —whose business training had been with Forrestal's investment firm of Dillon, Read & Company—refused to allow nationalization. Before U.S. entry into the war there were 316 German firms, worth more than a billion dollars, in which Americans had a controlling share—$105 million belonging to Dillon, Read & Company. Thus, instead of socialists and unionists coming to power in postwar Germany, as most observers agree they would have had elections been held promptly, it was the big businessmen and financiers. The first postwar German Chancellor, Konrad Adenauer, was, according to John Gunther, "on terms of intimate personal friendship with the Ruhr magnates and their bankers." Yet he was the hand-picked candidate of the American government. Moreover he was elected by the margin of a single Bundestag vote, after a systematic decimation of socialist strength by the United States in the first four years of occupation.

MacArthur, though he followed an enlightened policy on land reform, similarly reestablished the power of the old industrial and banking classes in Japan. It turned out, however, that not only in these former enemy countries but elsewhere the capitalist system was more fragile than had been expected. The multibillion-dollar loan to Britain, which was expected to last four years, was drained away in less than half that time because of the "convertibility" clause which forced the English to pay dollars to her trading partners. Added to this man-made catastrophe was one inflicted by nature. In January 1947 a great snowstorm, the worst since 1894, hit Britain like an avalanche, leaving as much as twenty feet of snow in some places and, after a thaw, blocks of ice. By February more than half the factories were out of production. The coal pits were shut, electricity cut off to industrial consumers for several days, and to the population at large for three hours daily. Before it was over the nation had lost $800 million in export sales and the drive to close the "dollar gap" had collapsed. In the words of the financial editor of Reuters, "the biggest crash since the fall of Constantinople—the collapse of the heart of an Empire—impends." The cause, he said, was not a few snowstorms but an "awful debility in which a couple of snowstorms could have such effects." Millions were out of work, demoralized, disillusioned.

It became obvious, with thunderbolt impact, that England could no longer support a large navy, 1.4 million troops around the world, and police an empire with its reduced resources—especially if it hoped to silence working-class clamor for higher living standards and such social reforms as national health insurance. Part of the empire, at least, had to be cut adrift. The first bastion to go was Greece, on which London had spent $760 million to buttress a monarchist dictatorship and to suppress the EAM. The former guerrillas had been brought to their knees on February 12, 1945, by overwhelming British force, including two divisions transferred from North Africa. But a reign of terror resulted in 258 killed and 13,000 imprisoned almost immediately after "peace" broke out. The New York *Herald Tribune* of September 17, 1946, reported "a pitiless war on scores of thousands of women and children in a desperate effort to halt a growing rebellion and wipe out not only communists but all democratic, liberal and republican elements." The trade-union movement, which had swept in a leftist leadership on elections held under the eyes of British laborites, was "reorganized" by the royalist government and placed under a quisling who had served the Axis during the war, Fotis Makris. Half of the budget by the regime of Constantine Tsaldaris was being spent on police and army, only 6 percent on reconstruction. Under this severe repression the Communists and their allies in EAM, who had expected to function within a legal, parliamentary system, saw no recourse but to retreat again to the mountains. From September 1946 to February 1947 their ranks grew from 3,000 to 13,000 guerrillas, with very sizable popular support behind them. This was the "free Greece" that the British now abandoned and Harry Truman decided to shelter under the American umbrella.

The British Foreign Office advised the State Department that it would have to withdraw all troops from Greece by mid-February 1947, and end all military and economic aid to both Greece and Turkey (also part of the British sphere of influence and also a dictatorship) by the end of March. On March 12, therefore, President Truman asked Congress for $400 million for the two nations, and gave a long dissertation on the need "to insure the peaceful development of nations, free from coercion," which became known as the Truman Doctrine. It takes no divine insight to recognize that what the President was defending was not "freedom" or "free societies," but a sector of the world which was in danger of slipping from Western control and adopting another form of government, either Communist or neutralist.

Six days before proclaiming his famous doctrine, Truman had delivered a speech at Baylor University which gave some frank insights into America's new global imperialism. Freedom, said the President, was more important than peace, and freedom—of speech, press, worship—was not possible unless there was "free enterprise." In those nations where industry and foreign trade were under government control, the "governments make all the important choices and he (the trader) adjusts to them as best he can." Unless the United States checkmated this pattern of regimented economies it would "be under pressure, sooner or later, to use these same devices to fight for markets and for raw materials." It would become a regimented society itself. Indeed "the American system could survive in America only if it became a world system." That was the essence of the Truman Doctrine and of Washington's policy ever since—to make the American free-enterprise system and "free international trade" the "world system." As Dr. Herbert I. Schiller, editor of the *Quarterly Review of Economics and Business*, observed years later: "The association of the objectives of American expansionism with the concept of freedom, in which the former are obscured and the latter is emphasized, has been a brilliant achievement in American policy. Rarely has the word 'freedom' produced so much confusion and obtained so much misdirected endorsement."

VI

The sickness of Europe in 1947 was not confined to Greece and Turkey. In addition to the blizzard there was the painful reality that if British citizens were to enjoy 1939 living standards, the country's exports would have to rise by 75 percent. In fact they had fallen by two thirds. Each day Britain was losing precious dollars to the United States, and the dollar gap again threatened her with bankruptcy. Conditions elsewhere were even worse. France was producing only half as much iron and steel as before the war. Germany lay in rubble; its major cities—Cologne, Essen, Berlin, Frankfurt, Hamburg, Munich, Mannheim—immobilized. Food was scarce, money almost worthless. There were no apartments to be had and few jobs. As Dean Acheson, Undersecretary of State, summarized the economic facts of life, "the world needed and should receive in 1947 exports from the United States—the only source—of sixteen billion dollars (four times our prewar exports), and could find imports to the United States with which to pay for them of only half that sum." A balance-of-payments deficit of $5 billion faced Britain, France, Italy, and the U.S.-British zones of Germany. "It is now obvious," said William Clayton, Undersecretary of State for Economic Affairs, "that we have grossly underestimated the destruction to the European economy by the war." Unless something was done and done quickly, disaster was imminent. The very Communists from whom America was protecting the world would absorb a disoriented Europe—and with it Asia and Africa as well. It would not be a matter of Soviet "expansionism," but an unavoidable coefficient of social decay.

To save Europe for the American system, Secretary of State George Marshall formulated a plan for massive economic aid—originally $17 billion over a four-year period. In the self-serving rhetoric of the cold war, the Marshall Plan was later extolled as a simple exercise in philanthropy, but American policy makers were under no such illusions. Clayton told a New York audience in December 1947 that if Washington did not provide such aid "the Iron Curtain would then move westward at least to the English Channel." Europe, in other words, would fall to communism or some other leftist leadership, and this in turn would mean "a blackout of the European market [that] could compel radical readjustments in our entire economic structure . . . changes which could hardly be made under our democratic free-enterprise system." "The real argument for the Marshall Plan," said Chester Bowles, chief of the Economic Stabilization Bureau, "is a bolstering of the American system for future years." A Brookings Institution paper set the goal for foreign aid as the creation of "political stability and the acceptance of international financial integrity that would be conducive to foreign investment." "Political stability," "financial integrity," "foreign investment"—these are the related facets of the "American system" that Truman wanted to establish worldwide. Molotov, in criticizing Marshall's proposal, called it an extension of Truman's "plan for political pressures with dollars and a program for interference in the internal affairs of other states." Western Europe was forced to make innumerable adjustments it would not otherwise have made, and to live under a system it might otherwise have changed. In March 1948, Secretary of State Marshall warned categorically that aid "will come to an abrupt end in any country that votes [sic] communism into power."

Under the Marshall Plan, participating nations were asked to submit a common plan for recovery and were promised $17 billion in grants ($12.3 billion was actually spent) over a four-year period. Unlike UNRRA, this was not a joint project by the world community. It was totally controlled by Washington—"The United States," said Clayton, "must run this show," and it did. A central command, called the Economic Cooperation Administration (ECA), operated from Washington and from the Hotel Talleyrand in Paris. Sizable missions of Americans also functioned in every one of the 17 nations which comprised the Organization of European Economic Cooperation (OEEC). These missions, made up of finance, trade, agriculture, labor, and public-relations specialists, kept a wary eye on every penny spent. A Program Review Division studied all requests and made recommendations for approval or rejection of projects. In addition Americans held veto power over the "counterpart" funds—monies put aside in native currency to partly match the dollar grant. Uncle Sam had the last word on how these "counterpart" monies could be spent, so that there was no paucity of levers to force OEEC states into the required directions—or at least prevent them from going in other directions.

For its $12.3 billion—of which $5.25 billion was for food, $5.5 billion for industrial products, almost a billion for shipping, and $360 million for the European Payments Union—the United States exacted a variety of concessions and imposed a host of conditions. Both the European states and their colonies were opened to American investors on an equal basis with their own nationals, a prize of no mean importance, allowing for mammoth financial penetration by U.S. business. At almost every session of OEEC, the representatives of Washington prodded member nations to abolish quota restrictions on trade, until fully three quarters were dropped. Trade generally was liberalized, and raw materials were made available to the United States through a provision which required that 5 percent of counterpart funds be exchanged for prime commodities to go to the United States. Stabilization loans to increase the supply of gold and dollars were predicated on European pledges to balance their budgets. In addition there were innumerable specific understandings by which American firms bought their way into European and other firms—such as the one already mentioned, according to which the Rockefeller interests were allowed to purchase 600,000 shares of Tanganyika Concessions. Finally, there was the section of the act, incorporated through an amendment in 1949, which threatened to cut off aid to any OEEC country that traded in arms, military matériel, or other strategic commodities to the Soviet Union or its satellites.

Not only was Europe remade to American "free enterprise" specifications, but its political mold was also recast. As in Germany, American aid became a mechanism for pushing the political center of gravity to the right. Just before the Marshall Plan was outlined, Stuart Gelder, New York correspondent of the London *News Chronicle*, wrote: "I am informed on high authority that the State Department policy is that 'it is in the interests of America to see the establishment of an independent democratic moderate Government in France.' It was expected that very substantial aid would have to be given during the next two years." That very month, May 1947, the Ramadier government suddenly dismissed the Communists—who had been part of a coalition since the end of the war—from the cabinet.

Joseph and Stewart Alsop, writing in the *Saturday Evening Post* nine months later, related that Italian Prime Minister Alcide de Gasperi pleaded with the American ambassador in Rome that "without your help we have only a few weeks to last. . . ." The United States responded to this appeal, but officials warned they "would find it hard to do so as long as the Italian Government included Togliatti and his Communists." There was no outright deal, said the Alsops, "But there was at least a shadow of a hint of an outline of a tacit understanding." De Gasperi went home, another government crisis ensued, and a new cabinet emerged with the Communists, second largest party in Italy, expelled. In the 1948 elections, which Western observers felt might go to the Communist-Socialist bloc, American intervention on behalf of the pro-Western Christian Democrats was more direct. It ranged all the way from promises to return Trieste to Italy, the gift of 29 merchant ships, and return of gold taken from Italy by the Nazis, to the threat that Italians who voted Communist would be denied the right to emigrate to the United States. A private campaign with government encouragement was organized for Italo-Americans to send 10 million letters and telegrams to friends and relatives in Italy, urging them to vote against the Communists. An issue of *Time*, widely distributed in Italy, counseled, "The U.S. should make it clear that it will use force, if necessary to prevent Italy from going Communist." It should use such force, said *Time*, even if the people of Italy "freely" chose communism in elections. In the 1953 elections Ambassador Clare Booth Luce publicly called for a de Gasperi victory, almost as if she were a citizen of Italy. That same year Secretary of State John Foster Dulles warned Germans, on the eve of their elections, that a defeat for America's friend Adenauer would upset hopes for German unity.

VII

Both the dispensation of aid with strings attached and persistent interference into the internal affairs of foreign nations—sometimes openly, sometimes subtly—were to become fixtures of America's global imperialism, developed and refined to a point of high science. They replaced the military occupation technique of British imperialism a few generations before—not because the United States was averse to military occupation, but because it had become impossible to police the world with a few million American troops. In the nineteenth century Britain was able to pacify the subcontinent of India with only 50,000 soldiers. The French subdued large parts of Indochina with only 2,000 troops. China's Boxer Rebellion at the beginning of the twentieth century was suppressed with only 20,000 Western fighting men. But after World War II, when nationalist revolutions broke out in dozens of countries, the scale of military force needed rose by geometric progression. In Malaya, Britain had to use 40,000 of its own troops, 100,000 police, and 200,000 home guards to hold in check a nationalist and Communist guerrilla force varying from 1,800 to 12,000 men—and it took twelve long years to complete the job. Britain deployed 50,000 soldiers, police, and home guards against a ragged group of 14,000 Mau Mau in Kenya and were able to bring them to brook only after five years of fighting. France commanded 500,000 troops against a mere 45,000 Algerian guerrillas, spent $3 million a day, $1 billion a year, but was unable to subdue the native revolutionaries after seven years—and in 1962 had to grant independence. A French force of 116,000 was ignominiously defeated by the Vietminh in Indochina in 1954, and an American force that reached a peak of 540,000, supplemented by a million puppet troops, armed and trained by the Pentagon, has as yet been unable to defeat the so-called Vietcong and North Vietnamese, despite an expenditure of more than a hundred billion dollars. Had the United States intervened in China to directly help Chiang Kai-shek against the Maoist guerrillas, it would have had to dispatch an army considerably larger than was used in Europe and Asia during World War II—and even then would not have been assured of "victory." In these circumstances the Washington establishment could only depend on puppet armies or, in the case of advanced countries, armies subordinate to its controls, to carry out its plans for Pax Americana.

General Maxwell D. Taylor, chairman of the Joint Chiefs of Staff, reported on April 8, 1963, that in the previous year alone the Pentagon had trained and graduated 27,830 officers of foreign nations—almost all of whom, it may be safely assumed, were ready to follow an anti-Communist, pro-U.S. line. For the coming year, Taylor announced, the United States would supply $1.4 billion in military aid to "friendly countries who are maintaining ground forces of about 4 million men, some 8,000 operational aircraft, and about 1,900 naval craft." Thus for the relatively small sum of $1.4 billion the Pentagon could rely on the allegiance of military forces larger than its own. That the purposes of this program were essentially to protect against an "internal" rather than "external" threat can be adduced from the two examples Taylor gave of its "success." "For the first time in fifteen years," he said, "the people of Vietnam, with our military assistance started winning instead of losing their fight to protect their freedom. In Thailand, the government, with our assistance, is effectively pursuing a broad program to train and equip regular and paramilitary forces to combat infiltration and subversion." Satellite armies became an adjunct to the American empire, often policing it in ways preferable to the use of U.S. troops.

VIII

Concurrent with the debate over the Marshall Plan, America was cranking up a motor for sterner forms of intervention into the internal affairs of foreign states. That intervention was to be military and nonmilitary, overt and covert, directed by the government or instituted through such private organizations as the American Federation of Labor. Even before the Marshall Plan became law, the National Security Act of 1947 brought into being the Central Intelligence Agency as an institution for coordinating intelligence—and "other functions." Among these "other functions" have been the subsidizing of right-wing groups in innumerable countries, sabotage, assassination, fomenting of revolt and invasion against neutralist or Communist governments. The agency, which has a headquarters covering nine acres and 1.6 million square feet of floor space at Langley, Virginia, twenty minutes from the White House, is the only one in American history that does not have to make its budget public; its expenditures are held in absolute secrecy, known only to itself and a few members of Congress. The number of its employees are variously estimated at between 10,000 (Andrew Tulley in his *CIA: The Inside Story*) and 200,000 (David Wise and Thomas B. Ross in *The Invisible Government*), "spending several billion dollars a year." The CIA's shadowy activities, most of which are still unknown, include the overthrow of governments in Guatemala, Iran, Bolivia, British Guiana, perhaps Brazil, Cambodia, and Indonesia, the attempted invasion of Cuba, clandestine support for the conservative governments in the Congo, Thailand, Vietnam, Laos, Ethiopia, subsidies to subvert labor movements and other organizations in scores of places, and all kinds of mischief to disrupt life in the Communist countries. Tully, a sympathetic chronicler with obvious access to some of the CIA's mysteries, reports the following CIA exploit with the strong implication that it is a daily chore: "In one satellite, for instance, factory workers were griping about Communist pay cuts. A CIA agent trained in the technique of labor organiza-

tions infiltrated the workers' ranks and promoted work slowdowns."
Presumably the CIA sees nothing wrong in promoting slowdowns
in "enemy" countries, or breaking strikes in "friendly" ones. At any
rate, with a budget of a few billion a year the CIA can and does
alter the political physiognomy of many nations—particularly the
weaker ones—to make them conform to the "American system."

That same year, 1947, the United States finally welded Latin
America into a military bloc with the signing of the Inter-American
Treaty of Reciprocal Assistance. It provided, in a formula that was
to become classic for all the other regional pacts (NATO, SEATO,
CENTO), that an attack against the territory or sovereignty or political independence of any of the twenty-one states (twenty in Latin
America plus the United States) would be deemed an attack against
all. Since the United States was the only one likely to be embroiled
in foreign ventures—say in Formosa, Indochina, Germany, Korea—
this was in fact a pledge to aid Washington in whatever travail
might confront it. The sardines, wrote former Guatemalan president
Juan José Arevalo, were merely being swallowed by the shark. "So
we want to Rio de Janeiro," he recalls, "and we installed ourselves
in Petropolis. The papers were all ready, drawn up in advance" by
the State Department. The sardines had only to sign and later—
most of them—to conclude bilateral military pacts with Washington: Uruguay in 1952; Nicaragua in 1953; Honduras in 1954;
Guatemala and Costa Rica in 1955; etc.

These pacts, in addition to expected provisions on gifts of American military hardware and advice by American personnel, also carried promises to cooperate with Uncle Sam "in measures designed to
control trade with nations which threaten the security of the Western Hemisphere," and "to facilitate the production and transfer to
the Government of the United States . . . of raw and semi-processed
materials required by the United States of America. . . ." As a result
of the Rio Pact, military aid to Latin America rose from $200,000 in
1952 to $11 million in 1953 and $92 million in 1961. From 1953 to
1966 the total was $1.136 billion, 10 or 15 percent for training of na-
tive personnel, most of the rest for arms acquisition. It is conceded,
wrote James Reston of the New York Times, that little of this can be
used for "hemispheric defense." "Our arms are now intended to
maintain internal order, [and] President Kennedy has formally authorized their use in that way." Miguel Ydigoras, former president of
Guatemala, who was himself jettisoned by a military coup in 1963,
says of American military aid that "generally speaking modern
weapons are not used by the military to defend the territorial integrity of their respective countries, but to repress popular aspirations

and undermine democratic institutions." American weapons, almost always used with approval from the American military and the CIA, made it possible for military coups to occur in Paraguay, Brazil, Bolivia, Peru, Colombia, the Dominican Republic, Argentina, and other places. The Bogotá Inter-American Conference of 1948 stated categorically in article 15, "No State or group of States has the right to intervene, directly or indirectly, for any reason whatever, in the internal or external affairs of any other state." But military assistance and training, added to economic aid, has converted this idealistic statement into a sanctimonious dead letter: the United States has intervened daily, making Latin America as much a satellite of Washington as India and Egypt used to be of Great Britain.

The third instrument of global imperialism that had its inception in 1947 was the North Atlantic Treaty Organization (NATO). The treaty actually was not signed until April 1949, but it grew from a conversation in December 1947 between Ernest Bevin and General Marshall. After an abortive meeting of the Council of Foreign Ministers which failed to bring an understanding with Molotov, Bevin suggested to Marshall that Western Europe could survive only if it evolved some kind of political union backed by the military force of the United States and Canada. Marshall was receptive to this line of reasoning, since economic integration was a major objective of his Marshall Plan, and the Western Union, as it was to be called, only a hop, skip away. Thus in two stages was born a military grouping which for the first time (another first) committed the United States to an alliance with European nations in *peacetime*. In the spring of 1948, France, England, and the Low Countries, prodded by the State Department and alarmed by the Communist take-over in Czechoslovakia the month before, signed a pact of collective defense which historian John W. Spanier calls the "military counterpart of OEEC." President Truman quickly gave the agreement his blessings and a year later, in April 1949, twelve nations (later fifteen), including the United States and Canada, signed the North Atlantic Treaty, agreeing that "an armed attack against one or more of them in Europe or North America shall be considered an attack against them all." Article 2 committed the parties to strengthen "their free institutions," to "eliminate conflict in their international economic policies," and to "encourage economic collaboration between any or all of them." In sum the signators tied themselves both economically and militarily to the "American system," under American leadership. General Eisenhower, not surprisingly, was appointed first supreme commander of NATO.

The Atlantic Alliance has often been called a response to Soviet "aggression." Certainly there were many sources of friction and concern between West and East. While the United States was joining Greece to its expanding sphere of influence, the Kremlin tightened its hold on Hungary. In late February 1948 Czech Communists executed a revolt against President Eduard Beneš and Jan Masaryk. The Americans and British introduced currency reform in West Germany; the Russians responded with harassment of transportation in the corridor between West Germany and Berlin, causing the United States to mount a great airlift to bring in supplies to the beleaguered city. But NATO was much more than a response to these episodic events; it was, as Truman himself writes, "one more step in the evolution of our foreign policy." It was indissolubly linked to the Marshall Plan as part of a continuing process to bring Western Europe under Pax Americana. "The first postwar step toward a union of the North Atlantic . . . ," said Thomas K. Finletter, an official in the Truman regime, "was economic. . . . NATO came soon afterwards; NATO might never have been born if the Marshall Plan had not come first." Finletter adds "that foreign policy and military policy cannot be thought of separately."

To organize the world for American imperialism it was necessary to preserve the social status quo; to preserve that status quo it was necessary to contain revolution; to contain revolution it was necessary first of all to stabilize Europe through economic aid and to exert pressure on the Soviet Union, which might give aid and comfort to revolution; and to exert pressure on the Soviet Union it was deemed indispensable to have a large military force at home, more troops in Europe, the atom bomb, and the hydrogen bomb (decided on in 1949).

Under NATO, America's allies were required to increase their military production, in return for which Uncle Sam "would transfer to them some essential items of military equipment . . . [and] send some of our experts abroad to help train and equip their military forces." From the spring of 1949 to January 1953, the United States shipped 4 million tons of war matériel to its NATO allies, including 503 planes and 82 warships. From 1945 to 1965, Europe was to receive the respectable sum of $16 billion in military gifts, and the world as a whole twice that much. He who pays the piper calls the tune, and the United States sometimes called it with unsubtle severity. A few months after the Korean War began, Washington advised Marshall Plan recipients that henceforth they would receive aid to the extent that they contributed to the Western defense effort. By 1952, most American aid to Europe had become military. Similarly in December 1953 Dulles warned that unless the Allies accepted an

American version of the European Defense Community the American government would have to make an "agonizing reappraisal" of its aid program.

Through NATO, then, the United States stationed a permanent force of hundreds of thousands of its own men flush against the Soviet empire, and acquired control over another force made up of Europeans and Canadians. By 1949 it had 400 military bases around the Soviet perimeter, to contain a Russian bear who, as Dulles pointed out that same year, had no intentions of expanding through military advance—only through revolution.

The antirevolutionary character of military assistance to Europe is not as evident as that to Latin America. In large measure that was due to the impact of the Marshall Plan, which began operations in June 1948. Despite the fact that living standards failed to reach pre-war levels in France and elsewhere, by 1950 production in Western Europe exceeded pre-1939 totals by as much as 25 percent. This was enough to put a damper on revolution in France, Italy, or Germany. Yet, as the interdepartmental foreign military assistance coordinating committee of the U.S. government stated it, the Atlantic Pact had a "two-fold objective . . . first to protect the North Atlantic Pact Countries against *internal* aggression inspired from abroad," and secondly to "deter aggression." (Emphasis added.) Moreover, American guns were undoubtedly all that stood between the conservative Greek governments and perdition, and played no small part in the military coup of Colonel George Papadopoulos in April 1967. The American-subsidized rearmament helped France combat the Indochinese revolution, and Britain to fight the people of Malaya. In any case NATO was part of a grand design to contain and roll back—through aid and military force—inimical elements that threatened the American status quo.

☆☆☆☆☆

18

☆☆☆☆☆

THE ECSTASY AND
THE AGONY

The stabilization of Western Europe was the bedrock on which the American establishment built a new form of imperialism. Uncle Sam became Big Brother to advanced nations (including Japan) with 350 million people, and in the process vastly enlarged its pockets of economic penetration. From 1950, the year that stability was assured, to 1965, American exports to Europe grew from less than $3 billion to $9.5 billion; the direct private investment of American entrepreneurs in Europe rose from almost $2 billion to almost $14 billion. In Britain the figure in 1950 was less than $1 billion, in 1965 more than $5 billion; in France a mere $217 million and fifteen years later more than $1.5 billion; in Germany $204 million in 1950, almost $2.5 billion in 1965.

As of 1966, according to a summary by Amaury de Riencourt, "one third of all automobiles manufactured in Europe are built in American-owned or -controlled plants; American firms control between a quarter and a third of the oil industry's market in Britain and the Common Market. In tires, earth-moving equipment, razor blades, sewing machines, and countless other industries, their share is even larger. By 1967, American firms had a stake of almost $6 billion in Britain alone, produced 10 percent of its manufacturing output, 17 percent of its exports, employed already one out of sixteen British workers, controlled about 7 percent of the country's total industrial assets—and at the present rate of growth, would control one quarter of Britain's entire economy by 1980." Direct private investments in Japan zoomed as a result of the occupation from a negligible $19 million in 1950 to $676 million a decade and a half later. In Australia it grew from $201 million to $1.7 billion.

These statistics confirm the remarkable success of the new imperialism. "A serious and explicit purpose of our foreign policy," Dwight Eisenhower was to say in his 1953 State of the Union Message, is "the encouragement of a hospitable climate for investment in foreign countries." That goal certainly was achieved in Europe as a result of the Marshall Plan aid and the North Atlantic Treaty. "Foreign aid," John F. Kennedy noted still later, "is a method by which the United States maintains a position of influence and control around the world. . . ." It cannot be said that Western Europe is controlled by Washington in the same way that England used to control India when it was a colony, but the "influence and control" was overwhelming at the time of the Marshall Plan and has been substantial enough ever since to place these nations firmly within Pax Americana.

Duplicating the European experience outside Europe, however, was impossible. The nations of Asia, for instance, simply could not be welded into an economic union or a military alliance similar to OEEC or NATO. With few exceptions they had been colonies; most were in the process of nationalist revolutions, their internal lives polarized between leftists dedicated to the overthrow of imperialism and its replacement by some form of socialism, and rightists anxious to find a *modus vivendi* with imperialism—old or new—in order to keep or win power. There was little of what Arthur Schlesinger Jr. has called the "vital center." Moreover there was no common cultural or economic tradition as in Europe. The result was that such regional alliances as the Southeast Asia Treaty Organization (SEATO) or the Central Treaty Organization (CENTO) were empty shadows. SEATO, formed in 1954, for instance, includes Britain, France, Australia, New Zealand, the United States, the Philippines, Pakistan, and Thailand—in other words five non-Asian countries and only three Asian ones, one of whom (Pakistan) has for all practical purposes withdrawn. The American establishment, therefore, has had to tailor its tactics outside Europe to every specific situation, the only common thread being a desire to make the American system into the worldwide system.

Generally, the Washington strategy for Asia, Africa, and Latin America was:

1) To establish the open door and multinational trade as the pillars of economic policy.

2) To weaken, isolate, and set back those political forces that arrayed themselves against the open door. These included on the one side the old British, French, Dutch, Belgian, and other empires—since they denied the open door except to the mother country; and

on the other, the revolutionary nationalists and Communists who also rejected the open door, because it inhibited industrial development of new nations. (Where the *only* choice was between the old colonialism and either communism or revolutionary nationalism, as in Indochina or the Belgian Congo, the United States usually chose colonialism, however.)

3) To gain, in Kennedy's words, "influence and control" over pliable governments—mostly rightist—through much the same techniques as were used in Europe. These included grants and loans with conditions attached to them, military aid, equipment and training of puppet armies, military pacts, CIA-sponsored revolts, and on occasion, when these other methods were inadequate (as in Korea and Indochina), direct intervention by U.S. armed forces themselves.

II

It would require many volumes to record the minute details by which the American elite tried to organize dozens of countries into the American system, but a few illustrations shed some light on the process.

Consider the Philippines. In line with its anticolonialist protestations, the United States granted independence to the islands on July 4, 1946, amid much pomp and ceremony, and with an assurance of $380 million to rebuild the new nation's war-torn economy. Both independence and aid were conditional, however, on acceptance of the Philippine Trade Act passed by the U.S. Congress. Under section 341 of the act, the Filipinos were required to grant American businessmen the same rights as native entrepreneurs. Moreover, the Philippine constitutional stricture against foreigners owning more than 40 percent of any local company was changed so that it did not apply to capitalists from the States. The Trade Act also tied Philippine currency to the dollar until 1974, and allotted export quotas to American (and native) firms that had been in foreign trade before the war.

In practice all this meant that American corporations would continue to dominate the economy. Undersecretary of State William L. Clayton conceded that the Trade Act deprived "the Philippine government of a sovereign prerogative. . . ." The Manila *Daily Standard* compared it to the harsh twenty-one demands imposed on China by Japan. *Business Week* referred to independence as "nominal." "Indorsement of the Philippine Trade Act," it said, "gives American business a preferential position to exploit Philippine resources." Not surprisingly, the men who agreed to such terms included President Manuel Roxas—whose election the magazine called a "political farce"—and members of his government, who like himself had played double roles during the war, sending intelligence to MacArthur while also collaborating with the Japanese. Roxas granted the United States ninty-nine-year leases on various naval and military bases—increasing its "influence and control." Washington showed its gratitude in the next two decades by giving the native governments a billion dollars in grants alone and a half billion of military assistance. Whether this was a profitable arrangement for the American taxpayer is a moot question; it certainly was highly advantageous to the American businessman, whose direct investments in the archipelago rose from $149 million to $529 million, or about three and a half times.

The old colonialism was collapsing of its own dead weight; if the Marshall Plan was saving capitalism in Western Europe, the empires of European capitalism were beyond help. Britain, strained to the breaking point at home, could not spare the money or the troops to counter Mahatma Gandhi's agitation in India. It granted that subcontinent independence in 1947, though severing two Moslem sections and forming them into Pakistan. Ceylon also gained its sovereignty in 1947, and freedom for Burma followed in 1948. The Netherlands tried strenuously to hang on to the Dutch East Indies, one of the richest areas of the world, and fought the nationalists under Sukarno and Hatta so vigorously that 100,000 people died and tens of millions of dollars in property were destroyed. But the prospect of keeping 125,000 troops tied down indefinitely, as well as the threat by the United States to cut off aid to the mother country, forced the Dutch to yield independence to Indonesia in August 1950. The momentum of revolt accelerated throughout the 1950's, as five dozen former colonies or spheres of influence broke the shackles. In some instances the imperial power withdrew before being enveloped by chaos, in others, especially in the French domain, it had to be pushed out by force and violence. But in each instance the United States was Johnny-on-the-Spot with Point 4 technical aid, grants, loans, offers of military help, and other means that prepared the way for eventual prevalence.

If there was any distinction between American policy in the developing world from that in Europe it was that intervention into the internal affairs of the former was, if anything, more brazen. As of June 25, 1950, the day that the Korean War broke out, the American colossus was embroiled in four civil wars simultaneously—in the Philippines, Indochina, China, and Korea—and except for the Philippines all had been outside its sphere of influence prior to World

War II. In every one Washington was the handmaiden of rightists and reactionaries—seemingly the only "safe" allies for global imperialism. Indeed the "American system" as applied to the third world became synonymous with counterrevolution.

While President Roxas of the Philippines was serving the Japanese during the war, the Hukbalahap (National Anti-Japanese Army), dominated by the Communists, was one of the major guerrilla movements resisting Nipponese rule and, as such, a recipient of American aid. In that respect it was like the EAM in Greece and the Vietminh in Indochina, and it suffered a similar fate. After MacArthur returned to Manila the Huks dispersed and disarmed, contenting themselves with legal political activity through the Democratic Alliance. In the elections of 1946 the Alliance won six congressional seats in central Luzon by large margins and, though only a minority party nationally, it held the balance of power. Conceivably, it might have blocked pro-American legislation, as well as acceptance of the Philippine Trade Act. Roxas, therefore, used the army—still commanded by American officers—to suppress the movement, remove the six congressmen from office, and outlaw Huk-controlled peasant and labor organizations. Confronted by the iron fist the leftists returned to guerrilla activity and at the peak of their successes, according to Lieutenant Colonel Tomás C. Tirena of the Philippine air force, commanded 15,000 armed men, plus "80,000 active HMB's [National Army of Liberation], with a mass support of 500,000." Against them were arrayed 54,000 government troops, including the navy and air force—trained, equipped, and advised by the Joint U.S. Military Advisory Group (JUSMAG). Approximately the same number of men were organized into "civilian guards" who also took to the field. Despite this superior fire power, innumerable Huk mistakes, and the expenditure of a billion dollars of American money, there were still 300 Huks underground during 1962, sixteen years after the fighting began. In March 1964 the government was forced to undertake division-sized operations (still under the guidance of JUSMAG) against the Huks in Pampanga and other sections of central Luzon, and as late as 1971 there was still a residual force of unconquered rebels. The American system could not have prevailed in the Philippines without this help in defeating the Huks. Nor could its Congress have remained "largely in the hands of big landlords and industrialists," as Alex Campbell points out in a *New Republic* article, or unemployment at the staggering figure of "almost two million, in a labor force of just over ten million."

Intervention in Indochina was even more high-handed, for while the Huks represented only a minority in the Philippines, the Viet-minh of Indochina undoubtedly articulated aspirations of the vast majority. When Japan seized Indochina toward the end of World War II she was met by a guerrilla band of 10,000 men determined, in their words, to smash both "French imperialism and Japanese fascism." The most forceful of two guerrilla groups was the Vietminh (national front), composed of the Democratic Party, a creation of the nonpolitical student movement at Hanoi University; the Socialist Party, with a philosophy akin to that of the social democrats in the Second International; the Communists; and various other groups. Directed by Ho Chi Minh, a Communist who had led an abortive nationalist revolt in 1930, the Vietminh liberated six northern provinces and established a national government which received support even from Chiang Kai-shek in China. On September 2, 1945, Ho's national congress issued a Declaration of Independence modeled on the American prototype of 1776. According to Ellen J. Hammer, in *The Struggle for Indo-China,* the Vietminh coalition had become "a broad national movement uniting large numbers of Vietnamese regardless of their politics, and reaching down into the masses"—a view confirmed by Edwin O. Reischauer, Asian expert and U.S. ambassador to Japan under President Kennedy. On March 6, 1946, France itself recognized the regime as "a free state with its own government, parliament, army and finances, forming part of the Indochinese Federation of the French Union." The honeymoon, however, was doomed from the start. The major share of French investments were in the South, in the Saigon area, and Paris was determined to sever this section from Ho's control by establishing a separate administration. In four months of negotiations, France refused to relinquish authority over the army, diplomatic functions, currency, and the economy. The formula for a "free state within the French Union" turned out to be a euphemism for continued domination.

The usual incidents occurred as popular wrath mounted. At Haiphong on November 23, 1946, the French cruiser *Suffern* fired on the Vietnamese section of town, killing 6,000 people. This was the signal for French seizure of all of Indochina and the installation of a discredited former emperor, Bao Dai, who had also been the puppet for Japan, as the head of government. Before long guerrilla warfare again erupted in full fury, as the Vietminh General Vo Nguyen Giap mobilized 70,000 irregulars to fight 166,000 French troops. There was no question as to who had the people on their side. In 1951 Senator John F. Kennedy made a tour of the Far East and on his return wrote, "In Indochina we have allied ourselves to the desperate effort of a French regime to hang on to the remnants of empire.

There is no broad, general support of the native Vietnam Government [of Bao Dai] among the people of that area." Yet so fearful was Washington that Indochina would be divorced from the American system that as of 1952 it had shipped 100,000 tons of supplies to the French forces, and as of 1954 was paying 78 percent of French military costs. Without U.S. intervention the war would have ended much sooner, and the second phase of the war, after 1954, would never have been started. But, as in the Philippines, the United States was involved in another nation's internal affairs up to its neckbone, and refused to withdraw even after the French were defeated. Its war by proxy was a prelude to the direct war it would wage under Kennedy, who apparently had forgotten what he said as senator in 1951, and under Lyndon B. Johnson and Richard Nixon.

A third war by proxy, and the worst defeat inflicted on the American system in the postwar period, was conducted in China. As of V-J Day the United States was within an eyelash of what was potentially the greatest of all imperial prizes. With the defeat of Japan and the enervation of Britain, the United States had an open field. But there was a civil war in China that had been held in abeyance during the common defense against Japan and was now aflame once again. The Chiang Kai-shek regime was obviously corrupt and tyrannical—according to General Joseph Stilwell it was "a one-party government supported by a Gestapo. . . ." Roosevelt had demanded that Chiang introduce reforms, but in vain. General Marshall, as Truman's emissary, tried for thirteen months to edge Chiang's Kuomintang and the Communists into a coalition that would assure change and stability—again in vain. The landlords and businessmen who supported Chiang felt they did not have to make any concessions either to Mao's Communists or to the common man of China. Chiang understood clearly that the Truman government could not seek to organize the world in the American image and yet permit China to fall to the Communist guerrillas.

Despite the fact that the Kuomintang, according to a subsequent admission by Secretary of State Dean Acheson, suffered from a "total lack of support both in the armies and in the country," Washington gave the Chiang government $3 billion in aid, plus weapons from a million disarmed Japanese soldiers. In addition, the United States garrisoned troops in a number of cities to hold them for the Kuomintang, flew Kuomintang troops into battle zones with American air force planes, and sent large military missions to advise Chiang and his military leaders. The Soviets did none of this; their aid to Mao was minuscule, consisting only of a small number of weapons captured in Manchuria. Indeed, Stalin opposed Mao's final drive to power. During the war he sent all his military aid to Chiang; none to Mao. And after the war, as he told a delegation of Yugoslav Communists in 1948, he advised "the Chinese comrades . . . [to] join the Chiang Kai-shek government and dissolve their army."

But Mao decided to continue the civil war and won a sensational victory against both Chiang and the United States. Of the 4 million men in Chiang's army, 1,690,000 defected or were lost from July 1946 to November 1947 alone, and mountains of American weapons fell into rebel hands. In an appraisal of the Kuomintang defeat, Acheson put it as well as anybody: "Nobody, I think, says that the Nationalist Government fell because it was confronted by overwhelming military force which it could not resist. Certainly no one in his right mind suggests that. . . . The broad picture is that after the war, Chiang Kai-shek emerged as the undisputed leader of the Chinese people. Only one faction, the Communists, up in the hills, ill-equipped, ragged, a very small military force, was determinedly opposed to his position. He had overwhelming military power, greater military power than any ruler had ever had in the entire history of China. He had tremendous economic and military support and backing from the United States. . . . No one says that vast armies moved out of the hills and defeated him. . . . What has happened in my judgement is that the almost inexhaustible patience of the Chinese people in their misery ended. They did not bother to overthrow this government. There was really nothing to overthrow. They simply ignored it throughout the country. . . ." The United States had intervened on the losing and unpopular side. Moreover, after Mao came to power Washington continued to help Chiang from his retreat in Formosa, even though it had pledged unequivocally that Formosa would be reunited with China. It interposed its Seventh Fleet between the two forces, and the CIA gave sizable material support to 12,000 of Chiang's troops who fled to the northeastern section of Burma in 1948 and stayed there until January 1961. David Wise and Thomas B. Ross report in *The Invisible Government* that, with CIA aid, these "troops made one concerted effort to return by force to Yunnan, their native province in China. But they were easily turned back, and settled down in Burma to a life of banditry and opium-running."

III

A fourth U.S. intervention in a civil war took place in Korea, this time leading not to a war by proxy as in China, but to the fifth most costly martial engagement in American history. Korea, a six-hundred-mile peninsula jutting out of the Chinese province of Manchuria, had been annexed to Japan in 1910 and treated with harsh severity. The occupiers took over the richest resources, forbade the Korean language, taught Japanese in the schools, outlawed opposition, and held women in textile plants as virtual slave laborers. Hostility to Nipponese rule was endemic and guerrilla harassment by such legendary figures as Kim Il Sung (whose name was borrowed by the present head of North Korea) became a constant feature of Korean life. By the end of World War II there was a small resistance force within the country, and three exile movements outside —the Korean Provisional Government, established in 1919 and operating from China; the Korean Commission, headed by Dr. Syngman Rhee in Washington; and the Korean Communists, based in China and Manchuria. As the Russians occupied the northern (and industrial) half of the Land of the Morning Calm and the Americans the southern (and agricultural) half below the 38th parallel, all these groups were jockeying for position in the revolutionary committees that emerged in the last days of Japanese rule. Many of these revolutionary committees were led by Communists, but not a few were under non-Communist leadership. In the important province of Cholla Nam Do the committee was headed by a pro-American Christian pastor, and the executive council was fairly conservative. Two days before General John R. Hodge landed to assume command of Korean occupation for the United States, Committees of Preparation for National Independence held an assembly and formed a national government for *all* Korea. The People's Republic was headed by a much-respected non-Communist who had been associated with the Korean Provisional Government in Shanghai, Woon Hyung Lyuh, and his regime, according to New York *Times* reporter Foster Hailey, "was as representative of Korea as any group that could have been quickly organized." It was leftist-inclined, but as E. Grant Meade wrote in *American Military Government in Korea*, "it only reflected with reasonable accuracy the views of the Korean majority."

Under similar circumstances in Indochina the French had recognized Ho Chi Minh and in Indonesia the Dutch had recognized Sukarno and Hatta—though in both cases the honeymoons were brief. But in South Korea General Hodge was so obsessed with the dangers of radicalism that he refused to deal with Lyuh or the provisional regime. Instead he imposed direct military rule, dissolved a congress of the People's Republic in November 1945, and three months later sponsored the Representative Democratic Council under Syngman Rhee. Rhee's greatest virtue, apart from the fact that he had spent thirty-seven of his seventy years in the United States and spoke English, was his rightist philosophy, which attracted landlords and reactionaries to his banner. Since the Soviets would not accept Rhee and Hodge would not accept the northern radicals, there were soon two Koreas—South Korea becoming an independent republic in August 1948. The difference in approach between the United States and the Soviet Union was prophetic. In the North, the Soviets attached themselves to nationalism, using the revolutionary committees as the kernel of government; in the South, Hodge placed his reliance on Rhee and his band of conservatives.

Owen Lattimore, a much-maligned expert on Asian affairs, correctly predicted in a 1949 book, *The Situation in Asia,* what the results of this policy would be. The South Korean army, he wrote, "cannot be trusted to fight; the people do not trust the government; the government cannot be depended on and does not depend on itself; it appeals for continued American occupation and protection. If there is to be a civil war, South Korea would not be able to subdue North Korea without a good deal more American help than is now available . . . [whereas] North Korea would be able to overrun South Korea without Russian help, unless stopped by American combat troops." Lattimore's explanation for this disparity was that "in South Korea the Americans organized not a national army, but a constabulary, the backbone of which consists of men who served in the police under the Japanese—the most hated of all who collaborated with the Japanese. There has already been one serious mutiny in this force, and there will be more. Syngman Rhee, a returned exile, is at the head of the political structure. He has completely tainted himself by his wholehearted association with the relatively prosperous, crooked, and pliable Koreans who collaborated with the Japanese. . . . Peasant dissatisfaction has already been shown in a number of risings; there will be more."

In June 1950, a year after these words were written, South Korea was in a civil war with the North, and Truman was sending scores of thousands of American troops to fight on their terrain. How the war began and who was the "aggressor" make intriguing speculation for historians. Rhee charged that the Northerners had crossed the 38th parallel without provocation. Kim Il Sung, on the other hand, claimed that Rhee had started hostilities because he had been overwhelmingly swamped in recent elections that reduced his strength in the assembly to only 47 members out of 210. Rhee needed a war, said the North Korean leader, to maintain his hold on the South, where unity sentiment was growing. He had rejected all proposals for unification, therefore; had arrested (and probably executed) three emissaries from Pyongyang sent to negotiate at Seoul; and had "drowned [his] iniquity by launching an invasion from across the parallel."

Whatever the truth of these claims, the salient point is that the United States intervened in a purely internal conflict to defend its imperial prerogatives. Korea was not considered strategically important; in fact, American troops had already been withdrawn, as were Soviet troops from the North. But China had fallen to Mao the year before and Truman was determined that no other nation in America's sphere of influence would be permitted to leave the fold. It is significant that on June 27, 1950, the day Truman ordered American air and naval support for the Rhee regime, he also instructed the Seventh Fleet to place itself between Formosa and China in support of Chiang Kai-shek's rump regime on the island, and greatly increased aid to the French in their war in Indochina. The United States was drawing taut a line of containment against those who would upset the American system. General MacArthur had been most explicit in an earlier speech at Seoul in which he expressed hope that "this barrier [between South and North] must and will be torn down," so as to promote "not only the unity and well being of your own people *but also the future stability of the continent of Asia.*" (Emphasis added.)

The Korean War illustrated with remarkable poignancy the major problem Uncle Sam would have shielding the empire outside of Western Europe. North Korea had only 9 million people, South Korea 21 million, yet the latter's army was defeated within weeks and the Northerners—without any foreign troops or air support of any kind—would undoubtedly have taken all the country in short order if American forces had not intervened. A frequent explanation for the debacle suffered by Rhee's army was that the North Koreans had executed a *surprise* attack with 70,000 troops and 70 tanks. It was certainly a surprise in the sense that the public in the West was not prepared for it. But Rhee had been boasting for a couple of years about the strength of his army, saying it would be easy for his troops to seize the North. In Tokyo on October 31, 1949, his Minister of Defense declared that "we are strong enough to march up and take Pyongyang [the Northern capital] within a few days."

Washington evidently was not swayed by this braggadocio, for on the first day of the civil war Truman—vacationing in Independence —decided to take military action. He wanted, he said, to "move with United Nations support," but he was seemingly determined to move regardless. Fortunately for Truman's plans, the Soviet delegate to the UN Security Council was then boycotting its sessions because of the United Nations' refusal to seat Maoist China. The delegate was not present to veto the American resolution—hastily passed without hearing the North Korean side—on the very day hostilities began. The resolution demanded that the invaders withdraw to the 38th parallel and urged UN members to give South Korea their blessings and help. Two days later Truman ordered the air force and navy to provide Rhee's troops with "cover and support," and three days later instructed MacArthur to land combat soldiers as soon as possible. What followed was a game of seesaw. The Communists first seized most of the South, even isolating a UN contingent at Pusan, the major seaport at the tip of the peninsula.

Alfred Crofts, a member of the American Military Government, in an article for the *Nation* ten years later, explained the causes of this debacle. After only a few weeks of fighting, he noted, "three-fourths of South Korea was overrun. The invaders' Russian tanks could easily have been stopped in the hills by a resolute defense. . . . Communist doctrine had little appeal to a population familiar with the grim reports of Northern refugees. But millions of South Koreans welcomed the prospect of unification, even on Communist terms. They had suffered police brutality, intellectual repression, and political purge. Few felt much incentive to fight for profiteers or to die for Syngman Rhee." By contrast, in the words of General MacArthur himself, the North Korean army was "as smart, as efficient and as able a force as I have ever seen in the field."

It was only when American troops were deployed on a large scale that the tide began to turn. On September 15, MacArthur, in a daring foray, put ashore an army at the west coast port of Inchon—outside Seoul—far behind North Korean lines. By September 25, Seoul, the Republic of Korea's capital, had been recaptured, cutting the lines of supply between the Communist army and its bases in the North, and by the 30th the enemy was hastily fleeing north. The UN objective—to "repel" aggression—presumably had been achieved.

Truman and his advisers, however, were not content with the status quo ante. There was now a chance to quickly "liberate" the other half of Korea as well—doing, in other words, what the Communists had been accused of, namely, trying to unite Korea by force of arms. In the brash overconfidence that almost all American generals have had in dealing with people in the underdeveloped areas, MacArthur assured Truman that the coup could be brought off before Thanksgiving—late November. He brushed aside the danger of Chinese intervention as an impotent bluff—even though Premier

Chou En-lai had warned that Peking would not "supinely tolerate seeing their neighbors being savagely invaded by imperialists." At best, MacArthur said, the Chinese could send only "50,000 to 60,000" men across the Yalu River, the border between China and Korea, and if they "tried to get down to Pyongyang there would be the greatest slaughter." Heartened by the quick victory in the first phase of hostilities, Washington secured a mandate from the American-controlled UN on October 7 to invade North Korea and set up "a unified, independent and democratic government in the sovereign state of Korea."

At first it seemed that the subjugation of North Korea would be as easy as the campaign in the South. By mid-October the Republic of Korea army was a hundred miles across the 38th parallel, and General Walton Walker's Eighth Army was confidently advancing. On October 19 the first segments of the Eighth Army entered Pyongyang to find that it had been abandoned by Kim Il Sung and his government, who had left behind huge amounts of supplies. The Chinese threat, however, proved more substantive than MacArthur had anticipated—and more formidable. Chinese leaders were convinced that the seizure of the Korean Democratic People's Republic was but a prelude to attack on China itself and part of a plan to dominate Asia and "conquer the whole world." The Americans were "copying the old trick of the Japanese bandits—first invading Korea and then China." Therefore, early in November Peking began to filter into Korea the first of 320,000 "volunteers." Within two weeks there were 200,000 Chinese across the Yalu—not "50,000 or 60,000"—and MacArthur's divided forces were in serious jeopardy. By the end of the month they were in bitter retreat through mountain passes and valleys, in deep snow. The Eighth Army was forced back 300 miles in three weeks; X Corps, with 105,000 men fighting on the East Coast, had to be evacuated by the U.S. navy all the way back to Pusan. As of December 15 the American troops were again below the 38th parallel.

The Korean War unveiled the ambivalency with which America has waged its global imperialism. Truman, though he refused to rule out use of the atom bomb, nonetheless wanted the war limited to Korea. A war with China, and perhaps Russia as well, was much more than he had bargained for, especially since the situation in Europe remained precarious and the Russians now also had the bomb. The dozen other nations that had token forces in the UN contingent were even more edgy about the prospects of an expanded war, and Britain in particular made this known to Washington in the most urgent terms. To enlarge the war might make it a world war, and no one could foretell, in an era of nuclear weaponry, where that would end. MacArthur, the supremely capable—and supremely egotistic —man on the scene, however, felt the attack could be widened without risk. He proposed that simultaneous with the advance into North Korea, a naval blockade be established off the Chinese coast and that the major industrial cities, supply depots, and other military centers in China be bombarded from the air. In addition, Chiang Kai-shek in Formosa was to be reinforced and encouraged to take "diversionary action possibly leading to counterinvasion" of China proper. In a letter to Congressman Joseph Martin, Republican leader of the House, MacArthur alleged that Korea was the pivot point of the struggle for global supremacy, the place where "we fight Europe's war with arms while the diplomats there still fight it with words." The Joint Chiefs of Staff rejected the general's plan as militarily unfeasible and Truman turned it down as politically impractical. America was to face the same dilemma in other situations: whether to enlarge a conflict and invite Russian intervention, or to keep the scope of battle limited but often indecisive. In this instance the decision was for a limited war, and MacArthur, the man who appealed to the public over the President's head for extending the limits still further, was removed from his post in April 1951. Though immensely popular back home, he was replaced by Major General Matthew B. Ridgway, and in July negotiations began for an armistice.

The war had been fought to a bitter stalemate, and at heavy cost. According to General Emmet O'Donnell, chief of the Bomber Command in the Far East, "the entire, almost the entire Korean peninsula is just a terrible mess. Everything is destroyed. There is nothing standing worthy of the name." The United States had lost 54,246 men dead and 103,284 wounded, four fifths of them after North Korea had been invaded; including the Korean losses, somewhere between 2.5 million and 4 million casualties had been suffered. The empire had been defended, but no new gains made.

IV

Despite setbacks such as China and stalemates such as Korea, by the time Dwight D. Eisenhower was sworn in as president early in 1953, America's global imperialism had become institutionalized— imperialism was to remain a fixed and unyielding policy, modified only in details during the next four administrations. Equally important, an institutional mechanism with incredible power in its hands had crystallized to advance imperialism. Eisenhower, in his last public statement as president eight years later, called it the military-industrial complex.

The complex evolved inexorably out of America's newly militarized society, a society that had been militarized in order to achieve global imperialism. Thus, the end created the means, as those segments of the establishment which for reasons of money or reasons of ideology accepted that goal formed a new configuration of power which has ruled the United States for more than a quarter of a century. At one time in the past it had been the commercial elite that predominated within the ruling class, later the industrialists, then the bankers. After World War II, it was a complex of military officials, plus civilian militarists in the legislature, the executive, business and industry, the labor hierarchy, and academia. From 1945 to 1970 the military spent $1.25 trillion on bases, research and development, weaponry, manpower, and fighting "little" wars. Any institution that had at its disposal such incredible sums was bound not only to reshape many other institutions in its own image, but to generate additional momentum for its objective—global imperialism.

The military, supported by large industrialists, tried as early as World War II to take charge of the American economy. Donald Nelson, head of the War Production Board, records in *Arsenal of Democracy* that "from 1942 onward the Army people, in order to get control of our national economy, did their best to make an errand boy of the WPB." A Bureau of the Budget document published in 1946, *The United States at War*, alleges that the army tried to gain "total control of the nation, its manpower, its facilities, its economy," and when Roosevelt or Nelson thwarted their scheme temporarily, the military leaders refused to take no for an answer, making further attempts throughout the war. Since war expenditures accounted for more than one out of every three dollars of gross national product in 1945, the men who were spending the money—the military—felt they had a right to run things.

Innumerable business leaders supported the military view. What the nation needed, said Charles Wilson of General Electric in January 1944, was "a permanent war economy." If this was to be, as Henry Luce, publisher of *Time* and *Life*, called it, "the American Century," and if the United States deemed it its "duty" to "exert upon the world the full impact of our influence, for such purposes as we see fit and by such means as we see fit," then the military machine was bound to become the central feature of American life. Wilson suggested that every large corporation designate a liaison man with the armed forces—to be commissioned a colonel in the reserves—because military preparedness "must be, once and for all, a continuing program and not the creature of an emergency." Congress, under this scheme, would be "limited to voting the needed funds" while the armed services and big business decided how they would be spent.

America did not go as far as Wilson wanted, but at the onset of the cold war it was obvious that the military had massively infiltrated civilian government and, together with civilian militarist allies, was running the show. "Today," boasted the *Army and Navy Bulletin* of January 18, 1947, "the Army has virtual control of foreign affairs. . . . The chain of control in diplomatic hot spots, both in the execution of basic policy and in the formulation of ad hoc arrangements, lies almost totally in the hands of military authorities." General MacArthur ruled Japan, Lieutenant General Lucius D. Clay ruled the American sector of Germany, and Lieutenant General Geoffrey Keyes the American sector of Austria. General of the Army George C. Marshall was appointed Secretary of State, and ten of the twenty executive officers in the department were transferees from the military services. In due course the generals and admirals departed, but their influence on foreign affairs was guaranteed in another manner. Under the National Security Act of 1947 they were to play a formal role, through the National Security Council, in advising the President'on international policy. How extensive had become the Pentagon influence was illustrated by its widened role in foreign trade. A New York *Times* story of August 4, 1947, reported that the armed services have been represented at all "major international trade conferences to 'see that the interests of national defense are fully considered in determining the trade policy of the United States.'" As a footnote to the military's incursion into politics it is worth noting that as of 1953, 9 army generals and 58 colonels, on leave or retired, were working for civilian agencies of government; and as of 1957, 200 generals and admirals, plus 1,300 colonels or navy officers of similar rank and 6,000 of lower grade.

Conversely, leaders of industry and banking have shifted from private business to key posts at the Pentagon. The first Secretary of Defense, James Forrestal, was a former president of the Dillon, Read investment firm; another secretary, Charles E. Wilson (not to be confused with the Wilson from General Electric), came from General Motors; Secretary Neil H. McElroy from Proctor and Gamble; Secretary Robert S. McNamara from Ford; Secretary Clark Clifford from a law firm which included du Pont, RCA, General Electric, and Philips Petroleum as clients. David Packard, Deputy Secretary of Defense under Nixon, the richest man ever to serve in this post, was the cofounder of Hewlett-Packard, a Palo Alto electronics and computer firm that did more than $100 million in government work in 1968. Willis Hawkins, vice-president of Lockheed, later turned his talents to the army as Assistant Secretary for Research and Development.

Over the years, then, there coagulated in America a complex of many specific interests—e.g., those who were solely concerned with getting war orders or subsidies for a supersonic plane, as well as those who sought markets or sites for their factories overseas—but all related and tied in to a common imperialist objective. The complex was made up of the following, often overlapping, elements:

1) A civilian militarist faction in Congress. According to a tally made by two Chicago *Daily News* reporters, William McGaffin and Robert Gruenberg, in 1969, 100 of the 435 congressmen and 30 of the 100 senators carried officer ranks—active, inactive, or retired—in the military forces. Two members of the Senate Armed Services Committee, Democrat Howard Cannon of Nevada and Republican Strom Thurmond of South Carolina, were major generals, and one other, Republican Jack Miller of Iowa, was a brigadier general. Representative Robert Sikes of Florida, a leading Democrat on the House Military Appropriations Committee, who usually wrote its military construction bills, was also a major general of the army reserve.

2) The large corporate contractors who did business with the Pentagon, a kind of Who's Who of American Industry. Significantly, as of fiscal 1968, according to Senator William Proxmire of Wisconsin, the 100 companies that did more than two thirds of the prime military work held on their payrolls "2,072 retired military officers of the rank of colonel or Navy captain or above." Lockheed Aircraft, the largest recipient of military orders, led the pack with 210; Boeing came next with 169.

3) A selected group of organizations that acted as liaison between industry and the military, such as the American Ordnance Association and the National Security Industrial Association.

4) Sixteen Department of Defense-subsidized research organizations, popularly called "think tanks," such as the Rand Corporation and the Institute for Defense Analysis. These were headed for the most part by former defense officials: H. S. Rowen, president of Rand, was formerly Deputy Assistant Secretary of Defense; General Maxwell D. Taylor, president of IDA, was at one time chairman of the Joint Chiefs of Staff. The purpose of the think tanks was to research problems in a host of areas, including the social sciences, and to formulate strategies for the Pentagon.

5) A considerable number of private research and educational or-

ganizations, such as the Hoover Institution on War, Revolution, and Peace; the American Security Council; the Center for Strategic Studies; the American Enterprise Institute for Public Policy Research. These institutions, financed by and large by civilian militarists, prepared position papers—on the antiballistic missile, for instance—that in one way or another percolated down to the mass of America as hard-line propaganda.

6) The leadership of the AFL-CIO, especially in the international affairs department, headed by Jay Lovestone; as well as a number of satellite organizations under the control of leading union officials—e.g., the American Institute for Free Labor Development.

7) The section of the academic community whose fate was tied to the Pentagon, including such prominent professors as Edward Teller, such schools as the Massachusetts Institute of Technology (MIT) and Johns Hopkins, and the "contract centers" run by elite universities. Almost $1.25 billion a year was funneled to the schools of higher education from the Pentagon, the Atomic Energy Commission, and the National Aeronautics and Space Administration. The research-and-development budget of MIT in 1967–68 was $174 million, 95 percent of which came from federal government coffers, $120 million from defense sources alone. MIT, of course, was the ne plus ultra of academic collaboration with the military, but Michigan received $20 million in 1967 from these sources, Harvard $9 million, the California network more than $70 million, Illinois $18 million, Yale $7 million, Columbia $18 million, Princeton $11 million.

Towering over everything, of course, was the Pentagon—and such related institutions as the Central Intelligence Agency. By the end of the 1960's the Department of Defense estimated its assets as $202.5 billion. This was more than the value of the twenty-five largest private corporations combined, but even this figure was on the low side because, as a Senate subcommittee researcher, Richard F. Kaufman, points out, it "greatly underestimated" the value of land and other items kept on the books at *acquisition costs* of years before when prices were much lower. The Pentagon owned 29 million acres of land—almost the size of New York State—plus another 9.7 million acres under control of the Army Civil Works division, valued, all told, at $47.7 billion. It was custodian of $100 billion worth of weaponry and $55.6 billion in supplies and plant equipment. It was spending $70 to $80 billion a year, as against $1.3 billion in 1939 on the eve of World War II and $10 billion in 1950 on the eve of Korea. It was procuring $44 billion in goods from 22,000 prime contractors and 100,000 subcontractors. It had 3.5 million troops under its command, and operated 470 major domestic bases, camps, and installations, together with 5,000 lesser ones, as well as 429 major foreign bases and 2,972 minor ones. Its expenditure of some $8 billion a year for research and development made it "the largest consumer of research output in the nation." Thus, argued Senator J. William Fulbright, chairman of the Senate Foreign Relations Committee, "millions of Americans whose only interest is in making a decent living have acquired a vested interest in an economy geared to war. Those benefits, once obtained, are not easily parted with. Every new weapons system or military installation soon acquires a constituency."

The internal effects of this vast machine were, of course, also mammoth—undermining the civilian role in government. The Pentagon has engaged in propaganda and lobbying in direct violation of section 201, title 18, of the United States Code, and spying on dissenters. In 1948, when it was plunking for universal military training (UMT), the War Department, according to Fred J. Cook in the *Nation* of October 28, 1968, enlisted the support of 370 national organizations "including the U.S. Chamber of Commerce and the American Legion; it . . . contacted 351 mayors in the principal cities of the land; it . . . promoted at least 591 articles and editorials in the press." Assistant Secretary of War Howard C. Peterson frankly conceded that government money was being used for propaganda "to sell the program to the public with the hope that the public would sell it to Congress." The military financed scores of social research projects with the same purpose, to put itself and its programs in a favorable light for the citizenry. Thus, for instance, Douglas Aircraft was paid $89,500 by the army to do a study called "Pax Americana," outlining world political patterns through 1985. It concluded that "the United States is not an imperialistic nation," but that it has "acquired imperial responsibilities"—a curious way of denying the existence of an American empire while asserting that the United States has to maintain the apparatus traditionally used to support one, including contingency forces, bases around the world, and a substantial enough military army for any "emergency."

As of the late 1960's the Pentagon employed 339 full time lobbyists (there were five at the end of the World War II) to plead its case, and many thousands on a part time basis.

Early in 1969 the Department of Defense began equipping a multimillion dollar army operations center in the Pentagon basement, 400 feet long and 250 feet wide, as a "war room" for the "dispatch and coordination of military troops in the event of urban riots. . . ." It was prepared to handle 25 major riots simultaneously—virtually a revolution.

In 1970 it was learned that the army operated a spy network against civilian critics; in Chicago alone it spied on 800 people, including Representative Abner Mikva, the future senator Adlai Stevenson III, former governor Otto Kerner, and the nationally known black leader Reverend Jesse Jackson.

Most important, however, was the transformation of "government by consent of the governed" into "government by the executive branch"—at least insofar as foreign affairs were concerned. The complete story of the machinations of the CIA in dozens of countries, including many attempts at coups, has never been made public, and may never be—their occurrence becoming known in a small number of instances only by accident or by leaks from inside the government. Facts about secret pacts, contingency arrangements, and innumerable other matters were studiously kept from the citizenry, or distorted. "I think that any people will support their government in not putting out information that is going to help the enemy," said Arthur Sylvester, Pentagon information chief, in December 1962. There was nothing wrong, "if necessary," in "misleading" the American people. "There are times when lying is justified," Malcolm Kilduff, assistant press secretary for Presidents Kennedy and Johnson, told the Texas Public Relations Association on September 9, 1966.

Withholding information and "lying" significantly whittled away countervailing power in the area of foreign policy and left matters almost exclusively with the executive. When the U-2, piloted by Gary Powers, disappeared over Soviet territory in 1960, the administration said that the plane had been lost while "gathering weather information." In fact it was on a spy mission, as President Eisenhower himself admitted later. This "small" incident may have had an important impact on history since it scuttled a scheduled meeting between Eisenhower and the Soviet leader, Nikita Khrushchev. The training of exiles for the invasion of Cuba was kept secret from the American people until the invasion was under way. President Kennedy himself later admitted to Turner Catledge, executive editor of the New York Times, that "if you had printed more about the [planned] invasion you would have saved us from a mistake." The Times had dug out the story on its own but did not publish it lest it be castigated for breaking government secrecy. On April 28, 1965, President Johnson advised the American people on television that he was sending marines to the Dominican Republic "in order to give protection to hundreds of Americans . . . and to escort them safely back to this country." In fact, of course, the marines were sent to suppress a revolution against an American-supported junta. These and hundreds of other instances emphasized the strange state of affairs whereby a military-minded government, by secrecy, distortion, and deception, made it impossible for its citizens and its legislature to make intelligent judgments on the most important issue confronting them—war and peace. They were neither given the requisite information nor consulted on scores of secret decisions that might have led—and in some cases did—to limited wars or to nuclear incineration.

V

The internal transformation of America by the military-industrial complex, as significant as it has been, however, was simply a by-product of an external purpose—global imperialism. It did not hang in midair, for no such complex of power would have evolved in the first place if there had been no external function to perform—to make the American system, in Truman's words, into the world system. The hundreds of foreign bases that would have gladdened Admiral Mahan's heart, the more than 3.5 million men under arms, the industry to back them up, the labor and academic allies, the attempts to whittle dissent through such institutions as the Eastland Subcommittee in the Senate and the House Committee on Un-American Activities (HUAC), were all part of a global design for imperial advancement. The four presidents after Truman furthered this design with equal avidity, even though they were men of widely different character and of both political affiliations.

Dwight D. ("Ike") Eisenhower, the first of these four, was at sixty-two everybody's father image—a genial man with wide mouth and bald head, self-assured, athletic-looking, the kind of person who seemed ready at the drop of a hat to tell Junior about his days as a star quarterback. According to Rexford Tugwell, he was "obviously unfitted" for office, but to the average man he was the symbol of victory in World War II, the typical American hero who had risen from poverty to greatness. His father had been a failure in business and the six sons had to be reared on a family income of fifty dollars a month. Dwight had gone off to West Point after graduation from high school in Abilene, Kansas, after a few years at odd jobs—no doubt to the dismay of his pacifist mother. He was popular, charming, and almost became a great football star—until he injured a knee—but he was no sensation in his studies; and after graduation in 1915 moved up the military ladder with painful slowness. He was still a major when shipped off to the Philippines in 1935 to serve under MacArthur. After 1939, however, he moved to staff positions under General Marshall and when the United States entered the war, in one of those Cinderella stories, he was promoted over 300 men his senior to be commander in chief of the Allied forces in North Africa. He was no military genius, but his gregariousness and ability to hold people together commended him to Roosevelt when the choice was made for Supreme Allied Commander to direct the storming of Europe in 1944. FDR would have preferred Marshall but he was reluctant to spare him from Washington. Thus it was that Ike went off to glory and eight years later became Republican standard bearer. Though he was president of Columbia University for two and a half years, he was no searing intellectual—his knowledge of history was mostly confined to military lore. He had a penchant for golf and Western stories, but no real experience in politics. Yet he was for America in 1952 the man of the hour who would bring peace and calmness after the turbulent Truman years, with its inflation, Korean War, influence-peddling scandals, and anti-Communist hysteria.

Eisenhower did in fact end Korean hostilities—only a few months after inauguration. Thirteen years later he revealed that he had effected the compromise by threatening to use nuclear bombs: "I let it be known," he said, "that if there was not going to be an armistice . . . we were not going to be bound by the kind of weapons that we would use. . . . I don't mean to say that we'd have used those great big things and destroyed cities, but we would use them enough to win and we, of course, would have tried to keep them on military targets, not civil targets." The public naturally was not informed of this threat, but it was happy to disentangle itself from what everyone conceded was a mess. A host of generals concluded that it would be folly for America ever again to involve itself in a land war in Asia.

Despite the quick settlement in Korea, however, Ike's tenure was punctuated by continuing intervention of the military and the CIA into one country after another. The ink was hardly dry on the Korean pact when the Eisenhower regime decided to topple the government of Mohammed Mossadegh in oil-rich Iran. John Foster Dulles, a senior partner in the prestigious Wall Street firm of Sullivan and Cromwell, and a long associate of the big bankers, was now Secretary of State; and his brother Allen W. Dulles, who had served as a supersleuth with the Office of Strategic Services during the war, had just been promoted to director of the CIA. Between them they decided that Mossadegh represented a threat to Pax Americana.

The Iranian leader's transgression, it seems, was that he had nationalized the British-owned Anglo-Iranian Oil Company, as well as the large refinery in Abadan. Surveying the situation in once-proud Persia—80 percent of the population living on the land and almost all of them at a mere subsistence level, 50 percent of the people suffering from trachoma and other diseases, three of every ten children dying at birth—Mossadegh concluded there could be no progress without land reform, and no true land reform unless there was money for roads, cooperatives, credits, electrification, dams. The only place such money was available was in the British oil concessions. In seizing them, Mossadegh, a fervid nationalist but non-Communist, was motivated not by ideology but by the pragmatic fact that it would take an annual sale of 8 million tons of oil to provide the funds for social change in his country. He found to his consternation, however, that when private property rights were jeopardized, the great powers were ready to act as one. A world boycott was declared on Iranian petroleum and Mossedegh could find neither tankers to transport his oil nor customers to buy it.

The United States as yet had no stake in the oil fields, but Eisenhower and the Dulles brothers were fearful that the virus of nationalization might become contagious. They not only joined the boycott but instructed the CIA to get rid of Mossadegh. The man placed in charge of this delicate task was the grandson of Teddy Roosevelt, and the seventh cousin of FDR, Kermit (Kim) Roosevelt. Then thirty-seven years old, Kim Roosevelt, like Allen Dulles, had served with OSS during the Second World War and later had become a CIA Middle East specialist. With a half dozen assistants, and in collusion with Fazollah Zahedi, a six-foot-two Iranian general suspected by the British of wartime collaboration with the Nazis, he began his operations from a basement office in Tehran. Also on the team was H. Norman Schwarzkopf, who had helped solve the Lindbergh kidnapping case in 1932, and had trained a police force for the Shah of Iran in the 1940's. He, too, was close to Zahedi, and according to Andrew Tully, a semiofficial chronicler of CIA history, "supervised the careful spending of more than ten million of CIA dollars," as a result of which "Mossadegh suddenly lost a great many supporters."

The plans went poorly at first. On August 13, 1953, the Shah issued a decree replacing Mossadegh with Zahedi, but the aging prime minister arrested the colonel who brought him notice of the decree and refused to budge. Masses of people, friendly to Mossadegh and to the Communist-dominated Tudeh, took to the streets; the thirty-three-year-old Shah and his queen, Soraya, fled to the safe confines of Baghdad, then to Rome. A few days later, however, Roosevelt's CIA money began to work its magic. Countermobs took the streets, beat up demonstrators, and paved the way for Zahedi to seize the reins. Summarizing events later, the director of the U.S. Military Assistance Mission, Major General George C. Stewart, noted that the coup was "about to collapse" when Uncle Sam began supplying "the [Iranian] army . . . on an emergency basis—blankets, boots, uniforms, electric generators, and medical supplies that permitted and created an atmosphere in which they could support the Shah. . . . The guns that they had in their hands, the trucks that they rode in, the armored cars that they drove through the streets, and the radio communications that permitted their control, were all furnished through the military defense assistance program. . . ." He concluded that "had it not been for this program a government unfriendly to the United States probably would now be in power."

Mossadegh was defeated and jailed, the oil properties were denationalized, and five years later American corporations reaped the bonanza. The British oil monopoly was superseded by a consortium in which Anglo-Iranian received 40 percent, five U.S. corporations —Gulf Oil, Standard of New Jersey, Standard of California, Texas, and Socony-Mobil—another 40 percent, the rest going to Royal Dutch Shell and a French firm.

A second subversion of an "unfriendly" government engineered by the Dulles brothers, with Eisenhower's approval, took place in Guatemala the following year. Here too there was a regime that menaced the American empire, in this instance closer to home. The "menace" traced back to a revolution in 1944 against General Jorge Ubico, who boasted of political kinship to Adolf Hitler and claimed that "I execute first and give trial afterward." After the overthrow, a former schoolteacher named Juan José Arevalo was elected president by a large margin and proceeded to legalize unions, raise minimum pay (to 26 cents a day), and reclaim his country's economy from the United Fruit Company and other foreign firms. When he introduced social security reforms that cost United Fruit $200,000 a year (bananas constituted about two fifths of the nation's exports), the company reduced its production by 80 percent, and W. R. Grace and Pan American actively discouraged the vital tourist trade. Arevalo was succeeded, after six years, by Jacobo Arbenz, who if anything was considered by Washington to be worse. He too was no Communist, but as American pressures tightened he leaned on the Communists more and more until they became a decisive force in his regime.

Arbenz's most significant act was the introduction of an extensive land-reform act (2 percent of the population owned 70 percent of the land) which distributed tracts to 85,000 peasant families. In the

process, however, the Guatemalan regime took over 234,000 unculti-
vated acres from United Fruit. The company demanded $16 million
for its lands, the government offered $600,000 in twenty-five-year
bonds. This was the setting when—in the words of a conservative
Guatemalan, Miguel Ydigoras Fuentes, as quoted in Richard J. Barnet's *Intervention and Revolution*—"a former executive of the
United Fruit Company, now retired, Mr. Walter Turnbull, came to
see me with two gentlemen whom he introduced as agents of the CIA.
They said that I was a popular figure in Guatemala and that they
wanted to lend their assistance to overthrow Arbenz. When I asked
their conditions for the assistance I found them unacceptable.
Among other things, I was to promise to favor the United Fruit
Company and the International Railways of Central America; to destroy the railroad workers labor union; : . . to establish a strong-
arm government, on the style of Ubico. Further, I was to pay back
every cent that was involved in the undertaking."

Rebuffed by Ydigoras, the CIA fastened its hopes on Colonel Carlos Castillo Armas, who had been trained in a military school at
Fort Leavenworth. Late in 1953, then, John E. (Smilin' Jack) Peurifoy, an old diplomatic hand with experience in the Greek insurgency, was dispatched as ambassador to Guatemala City for the
purpose of coordinating a revolt against the government to which he
was accredited. A few months later Operation el Diablo was
launched. The CIA established a headquarters for Castillo at Tegu-
cigalpa, Honduras, and not long thereafter a training camp at Mom-
otobito, a volcanic island belonging to Nicaragua. Meanwhile Arbenz discovered the plot through intercepted correspondence
between Castillo and Ydigoras, and applied to the Soviet Union to
buy $10 million of small arms. A shipment of Czech weapons aboard
a Swedish ship, *Alfhem,* in mid-May brought charges from Secretary
Dulles that Arbenz might be planning to attack the Panama Canal a
thousand miles away, and served as a pretext for more or less open
support to Castillo's invaders. On June 18 the American-inspired
colonel led a band of 150 exile mercenaries over the border from
Honduras, while four P-47 Thunderbolts, flown by U.S. pilots,
bombed the Guatemalan capital. The mercenaries settled six miles
across the border, waiting for the planes to wreak enough havoc for
Arbenz to collapse. Unfortunately one bomber was shot full of holes
and another crashed, thus hobbling the operation. But while the ambassador to the United Nations, Henry Cabot Lodge, was denying
that any American planes or fliers were involved, Eisenhower made
the decision to send in more. These were enough to tip the scales.
Though Castillo did not get as far as the capital, he didn't have to.

Arbenz, fearful of provoking a bloodbath and deserted by old friends in the army, refused to distribute arms to the unions and peasant organizations clamoring for them. To this day Arbenz is accused in radical Guatemalan circles of having lost his nerve. While he pondered, the bombing continued and on June 27 he simply gave up.

The epilogue to this story is as interesting as the main act. United Fruit lands were promptly restored to the company and a tax on interest and dividends for foreigners abrogated, saving the company a healthy $11 million. All unions were disbanded temporarily on the grounds that they were "political," and then, after being permitted to reorganize, were harried to the point where their membership fell to 16,000 (it had been 107,000). The right to strike was abolished, and wage increases—in a nation where two thirds of those employed earned less than $30 a month—held up. The 85,000 parcels of land distributed to peasants were returned to the *finca* owners, some of whom went on a rampage, burning the crops of their serfs. In the next seven years, the Guatemalan dictators distributed land to only 4,078 peasants—in a country where 70 percent of the rural population was landless. Upwards of 5,000 people were arrested by Castillo, and the election law was modified so that illiterates—70 percent of the population—were denied the vote. In a one-candidate election that followed, Castillo was confirmed by what Eisenhower called a "thundering majority." If there was any "improvement" in the situation it was that the annual rate of foreign—i.e., North American—investments went up dramatically, and economic aid from Washington skyrocketed as well.

VI

From the CIA coup in Guatemala to the invasion of Cambodia under President Nixon in 1970—and beyond—the United States intervened on scores of fronts to defend and build its empire. It intervened through exaction of concessions for economic aid—for instance, through Point 4, the Alliance for Progress, or the PL-480 food-assistance program. It intervened by supplying and training satellite armies in dozens of countries. It intervened through the CIA. It intervened through the Lovestone apparatus in the American Federation of Labor, and AFL-CIO—in British Guiana, for instance. And on occasion, when other methods proved insufficient, it intervened by landing its own troops on foreign soil—for example, in Lebanon, Vietnam, the Dominican Republic. The imperial drive was never checked. "Americans," wrote Harvard's political scientist Samuel P. Huntington, "devoted much attention to the expansion of communism (which, in fact, expanded very little after 1949) and in the process they tended to ignore the expansion of the United States influence and presence throughout much of the world."

Each breakdown in the old empires found the American establishment trying to wedge its way into a new area. The great wave of national uprisings that began in Asia in the late 1940's moved on into Africa in 1952, beginning with a revolt by Mohammed Naguib and Gamal Abdel Nasser against the British and their vassal in Egypt, King Farouk. The two rebel leaders, seeking to break the British shackles once and for all, demanded that Britain relinquish the enormous military base on the west bank of the Suez Canal—65 miles long, three miles wide—which was the core of its might in the Middle East. With American diplomatic help, they succeeded. A couple of years later, in 1956, Nasser went one step further, nationalizing the Suez Canal, long owned and operated by Anglo-French interests. This was the *cause célèbre* which led the two European powers to invade the ancient land on the Nile—in conjunction with and parallel to an invasion by Israel. Militarily, of course, this force was unassailable. But the Eisenhower administration, for reasons of its own, demanded withdrawal, and when the Soviets—then occupied in suppressing a democratic revolution in Hungary—threatened "to crush the aggressors and restore peace in the Middle East through the use of force," the invasion collapsed.

The State Department for some time had wanted to lay an American claim for the Middle East. Years before, Dean Acheson had made plans to establish a Middle East Defense Command, and in November 1955 the State Department grouped Turkey, Iran, Britain, Pakistan, and Iraq (but not Egypt) into a Baghdad Pact (later called the Central Treaty Organization, or CENTO). But CENTO, like SEATO, was an empty shell, and in any case an inadequate means for asserting an American presence in the Middle East. With Britain's eclipse after the Suez debacle, the opportunity was at hand for Washington to fill the breach.

Thus it was that on January 5, 1957, in an address to Congress, Eisenhower proclaimed protection for fourteen countries in the Middle East, covering 5 million square miles of territory and embracing a population of 125 million. Without consulting any of them he offered military assistance, economic grants, and the use of America's own armed forces, if so requested, "against overt armed aggression from any nation controlled by international communism." With this Eisenhower Doctrine, as with the Truman Doctrine, Washington sought to take from the faltering hands of British and French imperialism a sphere of influence for itself. Henceforth, it hoped, the Middle East would become an American bailiwick, the Mediterranean an American lake.

In point of fact the Doctrine failed of its purpose. Despite Eisenhower's offer of help to ward off the international enemy, Egypt, Syria, Iraq, Libya, and others drew away from the Western orbit and entered into closer ties with the Soviet Union. In the case of Egypt, John Foster Dulles in July 1956 withdrew an offer of aid to build the High Dam at Aswan, because the Egyptians were purchasing arms from the Communist bloc and had just recognized China. The Soviets jumped into the breach and with their aid the dam was completed in 1970. Presumably Dulles felt that a little more pressure on Nasser would make the Egyptian president more pliant; but it was a prize miscalculation, which the Eisenhower Doctrine in subsequent years could not modify. Without the support of Egypt, the most populous country in the area, the Doctrine was an empty gesture insofar as assuring American control of the whole Middle East was concerned. It did, however, result in one threatened intervention and one actual one.

A couple of months after it was promulgated King Hussein of Jordan charged that "international communism" was trying to overthrow his government. Hussein did not formally ask for U.S. aid, but Eisenhower nonetheless ordered the supercarrier *Forrestal*, two cruisers, and fifteen destroyers into the troubled area. No intervention took place, however.

A year later another armada sped to the Middle East, dropped anchor at the port of Beirut, Lebanon, and this time did land a contingent of 10,000 men. The landing was precipitated by a small civil war against Camille Chamoun, pro-American president of Lebanon, who had come to power a year before in what his opponents said was a rigged election. Before long a big oil pipeline was cut, the United States Information Library burned, and the rebels were in possession of half of the country. If this were not enough, the crisis in Lebanon was soon coupled with something more serious, a revolution in Iraq—the cornerstone of the Baghdad Pact. Neutralist Colonel Karim Kassem overthrew the regime of a man who had served the British for many years, Nuri es-Said. The revolt and the subsequent murder of King Feisal and Nuri jeopardized not only the Western strategic position but its oil holdings. Both in Lebanon, where Uncle Sam's troops landed, and in Jordan, where a British force was waiting, the word went forth that there would be an invasion of Iraq if it failed to "respect Western oil interests." The American ambassador in Baghdad was advised from Washington that "marines, starting to land in Lebanon, might be used to aid loyal Iraqi troops to counterattack." American officials, the New York *Herald Tribune* reported, gave "strong consideration" to "military intervention to undo the coup in Iraq." But no "loyal" Iraqi force could be found to undertake the defense of the feudal sheiks and aghas against the revolution. An uproar in the Arab world and elsewhere, plus the calming of the internal storms in the afflicted countries, caused the United States finally to withdraw its forces in November 1958. An agreement with Kassem saved Iraqi—and Middle Eastern—oil for the West. Four and a half years later, after Kassem announced formation of a national company to exploit the oil fields, he was overthrown by another putsch. This time, however, there were no troop landings or invocation of the Eisenhower Doctrine. As *Le Monde* reported, "the present coup is not regarded as a menace to U.S. interests; on the contrary, it is regarded as a pro-Western reorientation in the Middle East."

☆☆☆☆☆

19

☆☆☆☆☆

CLOSING THE
CIRCLE

When the United States was being born, its leaders defended their revolution by trying to spread the virus of revolt to Canada and Ireland. Two decades later the Jeffersonians expressed passionate sympathy for the French Revolution, and still later the American people warmly applauded the uprisings of Hidalgo, Bolívar, and San Martín in Latin America. Men like Prince Metternich who fought the nationalist upheaval wherever it reared its head found little patronage in the United States. But by the time Eisenhower turned over the mantle to young John F. Kennedy at the dawn of the 1960's, it was abundantly clear that defense of empire and containment—or suppression—of national revolution were two sides of the same coin. What Metternich did for the first half of the nineteenth century, the presidents of the United States did for the second half of the twentieth, except on a grander and larger scale.

To be sure the Pentagon was geared to two kinds of "defense": its "strategic forces" were designed to fight an all-out nuclear war, and its "general-purpose forces" to wage "two and a half wars" simultaneously, including a NATO war in Europe, a war against China in Southeast Asia, and a minor war in Latin America with a small nation like the Dominican Republic. But nuclear defense was the inactive part of the program, in the sense that no nuclear war, major or minor, took place in this period. Counterinsurgency, on the other hand, was the active part of Pentagon and CIA activities, in the forefront of their concerns. From 1949 to mid-1966, by official figures, the Pentagon sold $16 billion of weapons to foreign governments, and gave away $30 billion more. The true figures were doubtless much higher—according to Senator Fulbright they could have been as much as $175 billion from 1945 to 1970. Deputy Assistant Secretary of Defense Armistead I. Selden Jr. conceded in a congressional hearing that military assistance to foreign nations in fiscal 1970 was $4.9 billion rather than the $545 million estimate in the federal budget—or eight times more than admitted. The General Accounting Office disclosed that even the Food for Peace Law—known as Public Law 480—was used as a device for buying arms. The countries that received the food deposited local currency with the United States, which in turn often permitted them to buy weapons for that money. At one time the Pentagon was supplying military hardware to 69 nations, almost half the sovereign states in the world. The chief advantage of these grants and sales, as Amaury de Riencourt has observed, lay "in binding to the Pentagon satellite military establishments in Latin America, the Far East, and Europe. . . ." All in all, he wrote, the United States had assumed a "protectorate" over "more than 40 nations covering some 15 million square miles with populations amounting to over 600 million human beings." Not infrequently, the Pentagon and CIA were able to induce satellite military establishments to overthrow leftist governments hostile to the American system.

So extensive had this operation become that both the civilian and military arms of government took intervention into the affairs of other nations as a natural right. A Pentagon lecturer at one of its national security seminars, according to testimony before the Senate Foreign Relations Committee (February 1969), listed four "U.S. options in insurgency situations":

"1. Military advice and assistance to the country's military establishment.

"2. Training by American officers and enlisted men.

"3. Adequate and suitable matériel for this kind of war.

"4. If necessary, direct support by U.S. forces of combat missions launched by government troops, and *unilateral U.S. operations against the insurgents.*" (Emphasis added.)

From 1953 to 1966, official reports show $1.1 billion in military aid was supplied to Latin America, even though, as former defense secretary Robert McNamara admitted, there was no "threat of significant overt external aggression." Ydigoras, the Guatemalan who was approached by the CIA in 1953 and later became president of his country only to fall in a 1963 military coup, ruefully pointed out that this sort of aid was not used "to defend the territorial integrity of their respective countries, but to repress popular aspirations and undermine democratic institutions." Thousands of Latin Americans were trained in counterinsurgency at such places as Fort Gulick in

Panama or Fort McNair in Washington; facilities for thousands of Asians and Africans were provided elsewhere. These officers were taught, according to General Robert W. Porter Jr., head of the Southern Command at Balboa in the Canal Zone, "to control disorders and riots," and discourage "those elements which are tempted to resort to violence to overthrow the government." And the Pentagon was evidently prepared to go further. In the summer of 1965 it was revealed that the army had sponsored a secret study called Project Camelot. The project, undertaken by the American University beginning in 1962, focused on "turmoil-ridden areas" such as Chile, Quebec, Brazil, and a dozen others, with a view toward influencing their internal politics. A Chicago labor expert was approached by an American University professor and asked to prepare a plan for the *American* army on "how to deal with the Brazilian labor movement if a state of insurgency should develop there." What right the American army had to suppress a general strike in Brazil was not made clear, but since the army was preparing for it, it evidently assumed it did have such rights.

To formalize arrangements for American intervention, the Department of Defense, and occasionally the State Department, entered into secret agreements with a host of countries that were in effect treaties of alliance and therefore should have had Senate approval. No one outside the cloistered official family knew how many such understandings existed or what they encompassed. *U.S. News & World Report* (July 21, 1969) claimed there were "at least 24" with nations such as Spain, Iran, Jordan, Congo Republic (Leopoldville), Ethiopia, Tunisia, etc. How much the United States was committed in each case was not clear. A representative of the Congo in Washington, for instance, denied that there was a permanent military agreement, but acknowledged that ad hoc arrangements had been made from 1964 to 1967 for "logistical support" to put down "mercenaries." Such support included, according to the New York *Times,* transport planes and bombers flown by Americans.

In 1962 Secretary of State Dean Rusk signed a pact with the foreign minister of Thailand, Thanat Khoman, pledging that the United States would defend ancient Siam not only from outside aggression but from civil war. "Under the secret agreement," wrote columnist Flora Lewis, who helped uncover the details, "the United States has been providing Thailand with something between $175 million and $250 million a year for Thai forces. The aid has been hidden in the defense budget under other programs so that Congress never knew what the money was going for." When the Vietnam War heated up in 1965, Washington built air bases in Thailand and sent

48,000 soldiers to the country. Lieutenant General Richard G. Still-well, an old CIA hand then in charge of the troops, signed a secret military agreement with the Thai called a "contingency agreement." It was detailed enough, according to senators who finally saw a copy, to spell out the number of American soldiers to be sent to Thailand and the theaters of operation for which they were to be responsible in case of combat. The Department of Defense and the State Department both refused in 1969 to release the text of the agreement on the ground that the plans were only of a *contingency* nature. But back in 1967 Graham Martin, U.S. ambassador to Thailand, told author Louis Lomax that "our commitment to Thailand is total and irrevocable." Lomax asked: "Does that mean our men will die, if necessary, to defend the current government in Bangkok?" The answer was an unequivocal yes.

In the summer of 1969, congressional investigators uncovered a similar contingency agreement which bound the United States to defend the Falangist government in Spain. Indeed, it was revealed that U.S. troops had engaged in two major joint maneuvers with Francisco Franco's army and a number of minor ones "to practice suppressing a theoretical rebellion against the Spanish government." Almost invariably the secret understandings were entered into with rightist regimes on a quid pro quo basis: Uncle Sam agreed to defend the regimes from their people, the rightist leaders agreed to help America extend its empire. By way of example, on May 22, 1953, Emperor Haile Selassie of Ethiopia came to terms with Washington, permitting it the use of the Kagnew Station, the largest military base in sub-Sahara Africa, for twenty-five years. On the same day another pact was signed providing military assistance for Ethiopia—in addition to the economic aid already agreed to. Seven years later a supplementary understanding was reached—the details of which were kept secret until accidentally disclosed—to equip and train the army, as well as paramilitary and police forces. Through June 1970, Ethiopia received almost $400 million in military and economic help, the largest such program in Africa. Additionally 2,800 Ethiopian officers were trained in the United States. "Our program," said George W. Bader, director of the Africa region of the Defense Department, "is authorized for and keyed to their *internal security problems.*" (Emphasis added.)

II

Since it had no occupation troops to man the dozens of countries that constituted its empire, the American establishment, as already noted, had to resort to other means to assure that the "right" men were in power and the "wrong" ones kept out. It achieved this in large measure through economic aid, the creation of satellite military establishments, and the CIA. But in addition it utilized the talents of the American labor leadership to guarantee a pro-American and "anti-Communist" trade-union movement in many places. This was a highly necessary feature of global imperialism, since unions of workers and peasants are often the key element in a revolution.

The labor adjunct of the military-industrial complex, like the complex itself, emerged first as improvisation, then as an institution. In 1940 David Dubinsky, president of the International Ladies Garment Workers Union, and Matthew Woll, president of the International Photo-Engravers' Union of North America, established the Labor League for Human Rights to help European unionists involved in resisting Hitler's advance on the Continent. In 1944 the same men, with the aid of AFL president William Green and then secretary-treasurer George Meany, set up the Free Trade Union Committee to revive unions in Europe and Japan, and "to help such unions . . . to resist the new drives of totalitarian [i.e., Communist] forces." They were ahead of the cold war by a couple of years. As their executive secretary they chose, ironically, a former head of the Communist Party, Jay Lovestone. Then in his mid-forties, a vigorous and intelligent man, he spoke the language of European Marxists— a language alien to most labor leaders and to the State Department —and he commanded a small band of associates, including Irving Brown, a unionist and former radical who was to be his closest collaborator throughout the next quarter of a century. In a short while, these men and women were covering the globe trying to win unionists to an anti-Communist position, and passing out money to those who followed their thinking. Apart from strident anticommunism, money was their magic weapon—money that came from the AFL in small part (later the AFL-CIO), but mostly from government sources including the CIA and the Agency for International Development.

The ongoing activities of the Meany-Lovestone-Brown team are too extensive to chronicle. Among their achievements, however, was the isolation of the Communists in the union movement of West Germany and the splitting of the official federations of labor in France and Italy. Had it not been for the AFL group, said Dubinsky in January 1949, "the Communists . . . might by now have seized control of the reviving German trade unions." The Brown-engineered split-offs in France and Italy were small and impotent compared to the Communist-controlled unions, but they cost large sums of money to effectuate. Thomas W. Braden, assistant to CIA chief Allen Dulles from 1950 to 1954, claimed that the agency, through him and others, paid out $2 million a year to the Lovestone people for their work in France and Italy alone. In Greece, Brown helped build a little empire around the rightist Fotis Makris, who took over the unions after the government had purged them of Communists. A Free Trade Union Center in Exile was formed in Paris made up of laborite refugees from Communist lands. According to the New York *Times* October 5, 1947, this center, with few members, "appears to have at its disposal a working intelligence division." Gathering intelligence and setting up "an undercover organization" in East Germany also seems to have been an occupation of the leader of the German railroad union, who admitted to Donald Robinson, according to a *Reader's Digest* article, that "Irving Brown helped us."

The American labor representatives supplied food, paper, mimeograph machines, and autos to their counterparts in Europe and Japan. They financed educational programs, subsidized friendly factions against unfriendly ones in many countries, and on at least one occasion underwrote a band of strikebreakers. In 1949–50, Communist trade unionists refused to unload American arms at Marseilles. Whether they were right or wrong is beside the point; it was something for *French* labor and the *French* government to handle. But Brown paid the bills for a man named Pierre Ferri-Pisani to form a "Mediterranean committee" to get the weapons unloaded. Thereupon Ferri-Pisani's hired strong-arm men went on the rampage, beating up and even killing dockworkers and Communists, until they cleared the waterfront. According to a British magazine, *Private Eye*, Brown spent $225,000 for this and similar work in Italy and North Africa.

A particularly blatant intervention into the internal affairs of a foreign state by the U.S. labor hierarchy was the 1963 effort to overthrow the government of Cheddi Jagan, an independent Marxist, in British Guiana. Since the colony was awaiting independence from the mother country there was much anxiety in Washington and London about a "second Cuba." It was no secret that Washington was exerting pressure on London to delay independence until Jagan could be replaced. The golden opportunity came when the Prime Minister introduced a new labor-relations law (modeled on the American Wagner Act) which caused fears among Guianese union leaders that they might lose control of their largest affiliate, the sugar union, to Jagan's followers. To forestall this possibility they called a general strike, which, according to Neil Sheehan of the New York *Times,* received support from "the Central Intelligence Agency, working under cover of an American labor union." Before the eighty-day walkout was over the pro-American unionists were calling not merely for revocation of the new labor law but for the ouster of Jagan and his party from government.

A dozen important American union officials descended on Guiana, a nation of only 600,000 souls, to give succor to the strike. Included among them were Meany's son-in-law, Ernest S. Lee, and Andrew McClellan, Latin American chieftain of the AFL-CIO international affairs department. A strike leader in Georgetown admitted that the strike benefits for the 25,000 men on the picket lines were all paid for from American sources, something between $700,000 and $850,-000. Jagan put the figure at $1.2 million, plus another $2 million for a union housing scheme financed by an AFL-CIO agency, the American Institute for Free Labor Development (AIFLD). AIFLD also paid the salaries of six union leaders for the duration of the strike. In addition, according to a secret report by the British police superintendent on the scene—quoted by Susanne Bodenheimer in the *Progressive* (November 1967)—one AFL-CIO leader financed "the activities of the 'security force' (organized gangs) . . . including assassinations and destruction of public buildings with 'explosives and arson.'" Others concentrated on training, advice, and passing out money.

The AFL-CIO officialdom denied at the time that their operations in Guiana were in collusion with the CIA, but four years later some of the people and organizations involved in this incident admitted receiving CIA money regularly. The American Newspaper Guild conceded it had taken a million dollars from CIA foundations. Arnold Zander, then the head of the American Federation of State, County, and Municipal Employees, put the sum he got from the CIA at $12,000 to $15,000 a year, but *New Politics* magazine put it at $100,000 and "considerably greater sums" for one of his associates who had been in Guiana, William Howard McCabe. O. A. (Jack) Knight, former president of the oil workers' union, was also known to have collected large sums from CIA conduits for the petroleum union's activity around the world.

After President Johnson in 1967 ordered the CIA to stop the practice of secretly financing student, labor, and similar organizations, the Agency for International Development (AID) evidently took over. By this time collaboration with the government by many AFL-CIO leaders had become fairly open. In 1961, together with business leaders from W. R. Grace, the Rockefeller interests, Anaconda Copper, and Pan American Airways, the unionists formed the American Institute for Free Labor Development. Meany was its president and Joseph Beirne of the Communications Workers of America was its secretary-treasurer. Subsequently two similar groups were organized—though without management representatives—for Africa and Asia; the African-American Labor Center, headed by Irving Brown, and the Asian-American Free Labor Institute, headed by Gerard P. O'Keefe.

The major activities of the three groups were "education" and "social projects." Meany reported in August 1969 that 100,000 unionists in twenty Latin American countries had gone through AIFLD's educational mill in their native surroundings, and 730 of the most promising had been brought to the United States for extended studies at Front Royal, Virginia. They were indoctrinated with a rabid anticommunism and taught to eschew left-wing politics—like the American unions. The kind of people trained can be gauged from some of the resulting activity, as reported in AIFLD's bulletin: "Former AIFLD students help oust Reds from Uruguay Port Union"; "Two institute graduates challenge communist control of Honduran union." Student Hugo Solon Acero of the Confederation of Colombian Workers (CTC), it was reported, eliminated "the last vestiges of communist influence in the regional federation of Cundinamarca." AIFLD trainees "were so active" in the 1964 military coup in Brazil, that according to William C. Doherty Jr., AIFLD's director, "they became intimately involved in some of the clandestine operations" that preceded the coup. Hundreds of former AIFLD students were assigned by General Humberto Castelo Branco to "reorganize" militant unions whose leaders were ousted by the dictatorship.

The social projects division built housing programs, formed credit unions, gave legal assistance and other services to unions that were pro-American. The objective of the latter-day Lovestone program remained the same as before: to build pockets of support within the laboring classes for anticommunism and on behalf of the American position in the cold war. The only significant difference was that the financing was now provided openly from the U.S. budget, rather than disguised. Ninety percent of the monies of the three institutes was contributed by AID.

The AFL-CIO leadership was no puppet manipulated by the government. But with infrequent exceptions its policy meshed with that of the White House and the Pentagon, and its collaboration became a day-to-day affair. George P. (Phil) Delaney was designated a special assistant in the State Department to act as the AFL-CIO liaison man, and in that capacity sat in on high-level departmental and interdepartmental meetings. Appointments for labor attachés in overseas embassies, it was generally conceded, had to be approved by Lovestone. A Labor Advisory Committee on Foreign Assistance, including high officials of AID, the Departments of State and Labor, and AFL-CIO representatives, met in Washington every two months. The minutes of these meetings revealed the close rapport between labor's hierarchy and the government. The March 11, 1968, record showed that "as a result of the request from Secretary Rusk" the AFL-CIO had made a contribution to the Vietnamese Confederation of Labor—the union movement closest to the American-supported Thieu regime—of $35,000. At the November 12, 1968, meeting a report was given that Irving Brown had arranged to train drivers for the Nigerian army at an AID-supported drivers' school. At the January 8, 1969, meeting Assistant Secretary of State William Bundy "thanked Mr. Meany for the strong resolution of support for U.S. policy in Vietnam. . . ."

On the domestic front the top labor brass—with some notable exceptions such as Frank Rosenblum, Pat Gorman, Harold Gibbons, Jerry Wurf, Emil Mazey—sold the hawkish position of the government on foreign policy; on the foreign front it implemented part of it.

III

Quietly but persistently, then, in the quarter of a century after World War II global imperialism became the American way of life and the machinery for pursuing it fixed facets of daily endeavor. The 1960's illustrated the enormous benefits of Pax Americana to the establishment, as well as the enormous pitfalls that faced it.

"Our influence," said Secretary of State Dean Rusk in 1962, "is used wherever it can be and persistently, through our Embassies on a day-to-day basis, in our aid discussion and in direct aid negotiation, to underline the importance of private investment." He might have alluded also to the military programs and the CIA, but the results were certainly pleasing for the establishment. From 1950 to 1970, private American investments abroad pyramided from $11.8 billion to $71 billion. In Latin America corporate investments rose from $4.5 billion in 1950 to $10.3 billion in 1965; and just to indicate how lucrative they were, in that same period profits transferred home were larger than the total investment—$11.3 billion. Following a similar pattern, U.S. exports climbed from $4 billion in 1940 to $10.5 billion in 1945 and $33 billion in 1968. Much of this rise was due to the provisions in the aid programs that foreign countries must buy all or a substantial part of the goods purchased with aid money in the United States. As of 1965, almost a quarter of the iron and steel exports, 30 percent of the fertilizer, 30 percent of the railroad equipment, and about the same percentage of agricultural products, were generated through foreign aid. Even more sensational were the production figures of American companies abroad. Judd Polk of the U.S. Council of the International Chamber of Commerce reported in December 1970 that "the output of goods and services by U.S. business abroad is well over $200 billion annually now. . . ." That was more than the whole gross national product of any other country in the world except the Soviet Union.

Yet despite this impressive success—perhaps because of it—the empire was harried constantly during the 1960's.

One of the first points on the agenda of John F. Kennedy, after he defeated Richard Nixon in 1960, was what to do about the Fidelista revolution in Cuba. The youthful and handsome thirty-fourth President, a man of charisma and literacy, seemed like a fitting antidote to the gruff, antirevolutionary administrators of the previous fifteen years. The first Catholic to hold this office, scion of a closely knit Irish family from Boston, his accession to the presidency in 1961 coincided with the student surge that crystallized into freedom rides, demonstrations against the House Committee on Un-American Activities, the formation of the Students for a Democratic Society and the Student Non-violent Coordinating Committee—a mood and a movement that C. Wright Mills in a 1960 article called the "new left." Kennedy's style—buoyant, vigorous, poetical in its prose—catered to the disaffection of this new generation without embracing its radical implications. His inaugural address rang with idealistic intonations—"If a free society cannot help the many who are poor, it cannot save the few who are rich"—and urged Americans to "ask not what your country can do for you. Ask what you can do for your country." Where Eisenhower was a father image, Kennedy was the symbol of youth, the herald of a new day for a new generation. Eisenhower rose from poverty; Kennedy was born to wealth and politics, the grandson of Honey Fitz Fitzgerald and Pat Kennedy, both known to everyone in Boston, and the son of a self-made capitalist who served Roosevelt as ambassador to Great Britain. Eisenhower was a military hero for having led the armies of World War II; Kennedy for his authentic courage when a Japanese destroyer sank the PT boat he commanded. Eisenhower had a limited knowledge of history; Kennedy was sufficiently versed in American history to write a book, *Profiles in Courage*. He was so unlike his two predecessors, so much more dynamic and innovative, that he seemed to embody a new approach. In his inaugural address he promised the Latin American people he would help them make a peaceful revolution. "To our sister republics south of our border," he said, "we offer a special pledge—to convert our good words into good deeds—in a new alliance for progress, to assist free men and free governments in casting off the chains of poverty."

Yet, while these lofty words were being spoken, the CIA was secretly training a group of exiles on a coffee ranch fifteen miles from Retalhuleu, Guatemala, to invade Cuba and overthrow its government. The United States presumably was going to repeat in Cuba what it had done in Guatemala six years before. The enemy this time was Fidel Castro, a handsome young Havana lawyer who had been jailed in 1953 for leading an assault on the Moncada barracks in Oriente, then been amnestied only to organize another attack, on the dictatorship of Fulgencio Batista. Landing from Mexico aboard an overcrowded 58-foot yacht in December 1956, Castro's 82 men were decimated to a mere dozen before they reached the Sierra Maestra. Nonetheless, with a fighting force that never numbered more than 1,200 they defeated the American-trained Batistiano army of 43,000 men and rode to power on New Year's Day 1959. More properly, the dictatorship collapsed under the weight of its own corruption—embezzlement of hundreds of millions of dollars, the killing of thousands of opponents who like Castro demanded honest elections, unemployment of one third of the working class, 40 percent illiteracy, poverty, tuberculosis, parasitic diseases that infected most of the children in rural areas, and a lopsided land distribution by which 1.5 percent of the landowners controlled almost half the land.

Castro, like Arbenz, was a leftist but no Communist—a fact attested to by Deputy CIA Director General C. P. Cabell in testimony before the Senate Internal Security Committee on November 5, 1959. The Communists, in fact, did not join the revolution until a few months before it succeeded. But Washington was prejudiced against this young rebel, just as it had been against Arbenz, because he threatened to bolt the American system. Batista, after all, had been —in the words of former ambassador Arthur Gardner—America's "best friend," and had permitted North American firms to dominate 40 percent of the sugar industry, 90 percent of the electric and telephone utilities, a quarter of all banking, 90 percent of the cattle ranches, 90 percent of the mines, almost all the oil refining industry —investments of about a billion dollars.

When it became clear that Batista would fall, Washington sent William D. Pawley, a former U.S. diplomat, to urge the dictator "to capitulate to a caretaker government unfriendly to him but satisfactory to us, which we could immediately recognize and give military assistance to in order that Fidel Castro not come to power." On the very day that Batista was preparing to flee, U.S. Ambassador Earl E. T. Smith was still trying to form a military junta to forestall Castro. It was, however, much too late. Once in Havana, Castro attempted to reach an understanding with Uncle Sam: he requested a $4 million loan for road building equipment and a $1 million barter exchange of Cuban chrome for American corn to meet a food shortage. Both were turned down. The United States was willing to provide military advisers but no aid as long as Castro talked of land reform. Small planes, piloted by Cuban exiles and based in Florida, made repeated raids on Cuba's cities and sugarfields, but the State Department offered no apologies and the Justice Department took no steps to enforce the neutrality laws which specifically forbade such acts. Pedro Díaz Lanz, an ex-major in the Cuban Air Force, publicly boasted that he had taken part in attacks over Cuba that originated on American soil, but the American government neither arrested him nor stopped him.

In April 1959, Castro came to the United States to speak at a meeting of newsmen. Eisenhower refused to see him. The State Department did, but in order not to dignify his status, the meeting was held in a hotel room. According to the Cubans, Castro told Secretary of State Christian Herter that while other governments had promised land reform, he intended to carry it out. This would mean that hundreds of millions of dollars in American properties would be nationalized. Castro offered to pay for them in twenty-year bonds at 4.5 percent interest. With cash reserves of only a few million dollars in the national treasury ($49.4 million as of December 26 that year), and with a large accumulation of unmet social needs such as housing and health care, it was clearly impossible to do better. But Washington demanded that seizure "be accompanied by payment of prompt, adequate and effective compensation." In a similar situation twenty-two years before, Roosevelt had accepted bonds from Mexico for U.S. oil holdings; Eisenhower rejected such a solution, and his vice-president, Richard M. Nixon, after a private meeting with Castro, recommended military action.

Negotiations with the United States having failed, Castro went ahead with his Agrarian Reform Law anyway. If this were, as American newspapers and politicians charged, a "Communist" measure it did not seem to foster harmony between the Communists and the Fidelistas; a month later the traditional leftists demonstrated in front of the offices of *Revolución* charging the Castroist paper with being anti-Communist. And the newspaper responded with a stern lecture to the Communists. "In reality," write Maurice Zeitlin and Robert Scheer, "at the time social reforms were introduced, the Communist Party had no influence on the Revolutionary Government, was not respected, and on some issues was at odds with it. . . . The 'Communist threat' was a figment of the imagination of those preoccupied with their own economic interests." Edwin Lieuwen, one of the leading experts in the United States on Latin American affairs, concluded that "during the first six months of the Castro regime, little trace of Communism was detectable in the revolutionary coalition." In March the Communists suffered an overwhelming defeat in elections to 3,800 trade-union posts, losing to slates backed by David Salvador of the July 26th movement. Even a year later, when Anastas Mikoyan was in Havana to negotiate a trade agreement, he was roundly taken to task by Cuban officials and by radio commentators for Russia's intervention in Hungary in 1956. The bitterness between Washington and Havana could not be explained by ideological simplicities such as America's "hostility to communism." There was a more meaty economic issue, and above all the fate of Pax Americana in the hemisphere at stake.

In any event the dispute continued to escalate. In the next year Cuba began to take over ranches and sugar lands owned by private Americans. Washington responded by threatening to reduce the sugar quota by which Havana was permitted to sell millions of tons of sugar in the United States somewhat above the world market price. In February 1960 the Cubans turned to Moscow for succor, signing an agreement with Mikoyan to sell 5 million tons of sugar to the Soviets in the next five years. As a corollary to this agreement the Revolutionary Government also began to import oil from the Soviet Union, which American firms—contrary to a long-held agreement—refused to refine. Thereupon the foreign-owned oil industry, like the foreign-owned sugar industry, was also nationalized. In late June 1960, Congress authorized the President to curtail sugar quotas, and on July 6 Eisenhower cut the Cuban quota by the unfulfilled balance for that year, 700,000 tons. Meanwhile planes from Florida continued to bomb selected targets in Cuba; on March 4, 1960, the French ship *La Coubre*, was blown up in Havana harbor, killing 75 and injuring 300; and on June 28 another explosion took place at an army munitions dump, killing two and wounding 200 others. The Cubans believed that this mischief was the work either of Americans or of CIA-supported Cuban exiles. No one has been able to prove that this was so, but it is worth emphasizing that Eisenhower had approved plans for an invasion on March 17, 1960; it is not outside the realm of possibility, therefore, that those who were preparing a military attack also engaged in, or sanctioned, preliminary sabotage as well.

To prepare the invasion, the CIA united five exile groups into a common—though uneasy—*frente*, with Manuel Antonio de Varona, a former premier of Cuba, as coordinator, and in May began shipping exile recruits to Retalhuleu to be trained under the watchful eye of a CIA agent who went by the cover name Frank Bender. In July the agency started building an airstrip to accommodate C-46's, C-54's, and B-26's, and was soon recruiting pilots for eventual missions over Cuba. On November 13, 1960, the whole project almost came apart when a portion of the Guatemalan army rebelled against the Ydigoras regime and seized Puerto Barrios, a banana port on the Caribbean. If the rebels had succeeded, the secret training agreement might have been canceled and certainly the cover would have been blown. The CIA solved the dilemma by dispatching American B26's, with Cuban and American pilots, to bomb the airport at Puerto Barrios. C-46's were used to transport loyal troops to the scene, and in short order the rebellion was suppressed. The operation continued without an inkling except for reports in three small publications, including the *Nation*.

This was the situation when Kennedy was elected. On November 29, 1960, Allen Dulles of the CIA gave the forty-three-year-old President-elect a briefing on the Cuban project and was told to continue preparations. Whatever doubts JFK had were not over whether it was right or wrong to intervene with arms to overthrow a sovereign government—he accepted that as a natural American right just as had Truman and Eisenhower—but over the composition of the exile leadership, which he found too heavily weighted with Batistianos, and over pragmatic military problems. Historian Arthur Schlesinger Jr., who was on Kennedy's staff and who opposed the action, offers as extenuation for the President's decision to go ahead with the invasion "the fact that he had been in office only seventy-seven days. He had not had time or opportunity to test the inherited instrumentalities of government. He could not know which of his advisers were competent and which were not." But all of this bears only on whether the project was destined for success or failure, not on the basic question as to whether the United States had a *right* to intervene on its own or through mercenaries. On that score Kennedy seems to have had few misgivings; before he was assassinated in November 1963 he had sent 22,000 American "advisers" to South Vietnam in another intervention.

The Bay of Pigs invasion proved to be an undiluted disaster, indicating that Uncle Sam, despite unparalleled might, was not invincible. Later Kennedy was castigated by disaffected Cubans and some Americans for failing to provide U.S. air cover for Operation Pluto, and for failing to send in American troops once the assault had failed. Actually, the United States had secretly given air cover —six "unmarked" jets from the *Essex*, piloted by Americans, and, according to Schlesinger, a few planes flown by "some American civilian pilots, under contract to the CIA." But whether more cover or an American follow-up would have saved the day was subject to dispute. No one questioned that the marines would have captured the major cities in quick order; after that, however, they might have confronted a long guerrilla war in the rural hinterland, as in Vietnam four years later. Moreover an American landing would have complicated the task of winning friends in Latin America, where Fidel Castro was the greatest hero since Simón Bolívar. Kennedy refused to expand the war on the theory, as he told a group of editors immediately after the defeat, that unilateral intervention violated tradition and flaunted international obligations. It was permissible, evidently, to intervene through an American-financed puppet army with American logistical support, but no more.

The puppet army was singularly ineffective. The CIA discovered quickly that Castro was no Arbenz. Where the Guatemalan had refused to arm workers and peasants, the Cuban leader was prepared not only with the regular army but a popular militia of 300,000 to 400,000 men and women. When four cargo ships and a dozen smaller craft, accompanied by trim U.S. destroyers, approached Playa Larga and Playa Girón with their 1,400 men aboard, the Cuban forces were ready for them. A ship carrying the main ammunition supplies was grounded by fire from a Castro plane. Five of the U.S.-donated B-26's were destroyed in a single twenty-four-hour period. A contingent of 152 exiles, disguised as Fidelistas, headed for another beach as a diversionary measure, found the Castroites waiting for them. The exiles failed to take a single objective or spark a single revolt within the population. Their Operation Pluto, in preparation for thirteen months at a cost of $45 million to the United States, collapsed within three days.

Eighteen months after this debacle, and as a sequel to it, the United States almost became embroiled in a worldwide nuclear war. In the year and a half between the Bay of Pigs and the October 1962 missile crisis, the taste of defeat remained strong and sour with both the citizenry and the official family. Many regarded it as a temporary setback. Richard Nixon urged the administration to "find a proper legal cover and . . . go in." Senator Kenneth Keating of

New York, within days of the fiasco, proposed a naval blockade and a trade embargo to "isolate Cuba from its sources of supply and reduce Castro's military machine, his iron grip on the Cuban population—to impotence." Kennedy seemed to be following this course. In January 1962, under Washington's prodding, the Organization of American States excluded Cuba from membership—though six nations with two-thirds Latin America's population voted against the resolution or abstained. Step by step thereafter, with Uncle Sam wielding the pressure, the governments of the Hemisphere suspended diplomatic and commercial relations with Cuba. The U.S. embargo on shipments to the Caribbean island included everything but food and drugs, badly crippling an economy that had been overwhelmingly dependent on its northern neighbor. Meanwhile Washington continued a $2.4 million a year subsidy to the Cuban Revolutionary Council and tolerated air drops to anti-Castro guerrillas, sabotage, infiltration, and boat raids which either originated in Florida or were directed from there. As late as September 1962 a group of exiles known as Alpha 66 attacked three ships along the Cuban coast, including a British freighter. The following month it conducted another foray, claiming to have killed 20 Cubans and Russians.

Both in Havana and in Moscow all this was viewed as preliminary to a second invasion, and a decision was made to emplace Russian nuclear missiles on the island—according to Castro, as a *deterrent*. "Six months before these missiles were installed in Cuba," Castro later told French newspaperman Jean Daniel, "we had received an accumulation of information warning us that a new invasion of the island was being prepared under the sponsorship of the Central Intelligence Agency." Castro personally doubted that Kennedy would endorse another venture of this sort, but in a meeting between Khrushchev's son-in-law, Alexei Adzhubei, and Kennedy these doubts were dispelled. According to Castro the President said that "the new situation in Cuba was intolerable for the United States," that it jeopardized peaceful coexistence because Soviet influence in Cuba "altered the balance of strength." He reminded Adzhubei that "the United States had not intervened in Hungary [during the 1956 Hungarian Revolution], which was obviously a way of demanding Russian nonintervention in the event of a possible invasion." After the Adzhubei interview the Soviets and Cuba agreed on the missiles; and it was the discovery by American intelligence sources that missile sites were being built that triggered the confrontation between the world's two strongest powers.

Thus it was that during the last week of October 1962 the world came as close to an all-out nuclear holocaust as it has ever been before or since. Crews of 144 intercontinental ballistic missiles were put on special alert in the United States. One hundred and eighty-three naval ships with 110,000 men, including 8 aircraft carriers, were deployed around Cuba; 1,000 planes of the Tactical Air Command were placed "on the ready" in Southeastern U.S. bases; and 100,000 soldiers (with 200,000 more available if needed) were poised, according to *Army Times,* for a possible invasion that would "secure" the island within 48 to 72 hours. Had the war broken out, Kennedy later said, the two nations would have suffered "150 million fatalities in the first 18 hours." The total after a few days would, of course, have been far higher, and the number of wounded, as well as the property damage, incalculable. Oswald Spengler's prediction of the decline of the West would have become a gruesome reality, reflected in hundreds of atomic mushrooms from San Francisco to the Urals. In Kennedy's words: "Even the fruits of victory would be ashes in our mouths." That fateful week the world waited with bated breath while Soviet ships moved toward the blockade lines established by the United States in the Caribbean. Finally, Khrushchev backed down on October 28, agreeing to withdraw the missiles in return for a secret pledge—later confirmed by President Nixon in 1970—that the United States would not invade Cuba or permit hostile actions against it to originate from North American soil.

IV

The October missile crisis, more than any other event of the era, highlighted the strange circumstance that conflict over a small prize can escalate into a worldwide emergency of vast consequences. The Fidelista revolution, with all its side effects, convinced Kennedy that while Uncle Sam was busy assuring "stability" in Europe, Asia, and Africa, the heart of its empire—in the western hemisphere—was in serious jeopardy. Truman and Eisenhower had virtually disregarded the area. The United States, wrote Professor Robert J. Alexander, "supported virtually every military tyrant who came upon the scene (or was already there) between 1945 and 1960." Less economic aid was given to Latin America in this period than to Falangist Spain in the first twelve years of the mutual security program. Cuba was one result of this myopia; there was a danger other nations might follow it out of the "American system." In a discussion with Jean Daniel, Kennedy admitted in 1963 that there was no country in which "economic colonization, humiliation, and exploitation were worse than in Cuba, partly as a consequence of U.S. policy during the Batista regime. . . . I also believe that this accumulation of errors has put all Latin America in danger."

The area was certainly in an economic crisis, registering an annual rate of growth in 1960–61 of only 1 percent (in 1940–50 it had been 3.5 percent), while population increased 2.8 percent. Raw material prices, on which Latin America depended for its income, had been falling steadily since 1952—coffee, for instance, was down by half as of 1963. Thus, the prices of what Latin America sold *to* the United States went down, while the prices of the finished goods she bought *from* the United States went up. A tractor made by Ford, the Major, could be bought in 1954 for the equivalent of 22 Uruguayan young bulls, but cost the equivalent of 42 such bulls in 1963. It was estimated by one official inter-American agency that as a result of these unfavorable terms of trade the area was losing $1.5 billion annually. In human terms the situation was even worse. Statistics recorded an average income (including the relatively high ones in Argentina and the incredibly low ones in Haiti) of $200 a year per capita. Tens of millions lived on half or a quarter of that. One of every two Latin American adults was illiterate. The daily intake of food for 52 percent of the 200 million inhabitants at the time was 500 calories, as against 3,100 in the United States. In Brazil three of every ten children died before they reached the age of one. Venezuela and Panama had eight times more tuberculosis per capita than the United States; Brazil, fifteen times more. According to John Gerassi, former *Time* correspondent, a million people annually died of starvation or lack of proper nutrition. Three of five people never drank a glass of potable water, and 1,000 children a day died because of this deficiency. Worst of all was the maldistribution of land —typically, in Brazil the richest 5 percent of the rural population owned 95 percent of the land, in Venezuela 2 percent owned 74 percent of the acreage, while 300,000 families were landless. Of the 28.5 million agrarian families, 18 million had no holdings at all and 5.5 million insufficient acreage to keep body and soul together. Clearly only a match was needed to set the whole hemisphere ablaze, especially with the example of Cuba to guide it.

To cope with this problem Kennedy spelled out an Alliance for Progress in March 1961 "to transform the 1960's into an historic decade of democratic progress." It was ratified by the nineteen republics (exclusive of Cuba) at Punta del Este on August 17, 1961. The United States promised "to furnish development loans on a long-term basis, where appropriate, running up to fifty years and at very low or zero rates of interest." In return, the Latin American coun-

tries agreed "to devote a rapidly increasing share of their own resources to economic and social development and to make the reforms necessary to assure that all share fully in the fruits of the
Alliance for Progress." This emphasis on social justice was an important departure from the practice of the previous decade. According
to Howard Rusk in the New York *Times* of April 5, 1963, $30 billion
of the $50 billion in total foreign aid during the previous decade
had been in "military" aid, and of the remaining $20 billion, "about
85 percent was also military in that these funds were made available
to support the budgets of nations mainly on the periphery of the
Iron Curtain that have undertaken a scale of military effort far
greater than they can afford. Korea, Taiwan, Pakistan and Turkey
are examples." For Latin America Kennedy was now reversing this
trend. Under the Alliance $20 billion would flow in to the nineteen
republics in the ensuing ten years: a half billion or so in loans each
year from such agencies as the Export-Import Bank, a half billion
more from the U.S. government, and a billion a year in private investments, mostly from American entrepreneurs. The Latins themselves were to scrape up another $80 billion, so as to assure a rate of
economic growth of 2.5 percent per capita a year.

Unlike the Marshall Plan, most of the Alliance for Progress money
was in the form of loans, not gifts. The 1966 "aid" to Chile, for instance, was listed by the U.S. embassy as consisting of "loans of over
$100 million, technical assistance of $3.5 million," the sale of nearly
$20 million in agricultural commodities, and the donation of another
$13.5 million. If the food sales of $20 million are deducted, loans accounted for five sixths of the $140 million "aid." But as with the
Marshall Plan there were strings attached to Alliance aid. President
Kennedy may sincerely have hoped for major changes south of the
border, but had no intention of forgetting American commercial and
business interests—or imperial control. In return for the loans—
usually at 1 percent interest a year for the first ten years and 2.5
percent thereafter—the recipient nation agreed to buy an equal
amount of imports from the United States. It agreed to earmark half
or more of the loans for purchase of equipment from North America,
using the other half for native labor and supplies at home. Though
it might buy a tractor, say, much cheaper from Japan than from
Ford or International Harvester, it was required to purchase only an
American product. To illustrate the effect of this provision: in 1968
Bolivia received a $4.5 million budget-support loan, in return for
which Washington demanded that she buy American ore carts at
three times the price they could be had from Belgium, and oil well
casing at 60 percent more than it could be bought from nearby Ar-

gentina. Moreover, the United States could invoke the principle of "additionality," according to which the Latin states were required to spend the *total* amount of their loans on American products, not just half. As of 1969, Bolivia had $65 million in authorized loans which it could not afford to accept because of the purchasing provisions. A third condition was that at least half of what the recipient nation purchased be shipped in American boats, at much higher freight rates. A fourth was that Washington not only approve the specific projects, but check the country's budget to satisfy itself as to the recipient's "fiscal responsibility." It is difficult to conceive of a government being independent if its budget is subject to veto by a foreign power, or capable of rapid development if it is constantly pressed to balance its budget and pay off old loans which sop up a third or half of the monies earned from exports (as in Colombia or Chile). Moreover U.S. experts were placed in the ministries of the Latin American states to oversee what happened to the loan money. In the Dominican Republic at mid-decade there were eighty such officials operating out of thirty Dominican offices. Finally, there was the Hickenlooper Amendment, according to which aid was terminated if a southern republic expropriated an American firm without paying what Washington considered a "fair" price.

Like that of the Marshall Plan, the Alliance for Progress aid was wielded with deliberate design to further American business. Bolivia was denied loans to build a tin smelter for a dozen years because it refused to agree to private instead of public ownership. Peru saw its loans severely reduced for almost three years, according to the American Embassy itself, in order to exert pressure on it to come to terms with a Standard Oil of New Jersey subsidiary. When Argentina nationalized Standard Oil it lost the right to receive aid. The government in Brazil was granted only a pittance while João Goulart was in power, but when he was succeeded by the Castelo Branco dictatorship, aid skyrocketed to $234.8 million in the first year.

The Alliance for Progress, unlike the Marshall Plan, was ineffective. "Latin America's balance of payments deficit," said a report of the Special Coordinating Commission for Latin America at a meeting in Buenos Aires, "has soared alarmingly. From $558 million in 1946–50, it shot up to $5,488 million in 1961–65." The 2.5 percent rise in per capita income was never met. Much of the money that was to have been assigned to development had to be used to prop up collapsing currencies. In the first two years, for instance, $345 million of the $700 million committed to Mexico was put aside as a credit to shore up the weakening peso. Of the billion and a half dollars disbursed by the Alliance for the whole hemisphere, $600 million were loans from the Export-Import Bank, used to finance American sales into the southern republics. The Alliance did help in the construction of homes, schools, hospitals, water supply systems—on a modest scale—but it made little headway in land reform or in changing the atavistic social systems.

Land reform proved to be a meaningless gesture in most countries, with only a few thousand families resettled on unused and undeveloped land, while the power of the old aristocracy stood undisturbed. In Venezuela, where the broadest such reform took place under the Alliance, 50,000 families were given small holdings in the first three years. But of the 1.5 million hectares distributed, only a half million came from the large landowners, who continued to work 21.5 million hectares—three quarters of the tilled acreage of the nation. In Brazil there was much talk of reform, as there had been for decades, but no action. Toward the middle of the decade more meaningful steps were taken in Chile under the Christian Democratic government of Eduardo Frei. But by and large the old landlord structure survived the Alliance for Progress "reforms."

Tax reform too was usually symbolic and often redistributed income the wrong way—in favor of the rich. In Guatemala, for instance, a tax law passed in 1962 replaced a business tax of 44 percent with an income tax that rose to 48 percent. The latter, however, was so full of loopholes that in 1963, according to an American expert, the rich were paying fewer taxes, the middle class much more. Teodoro Moscoso, Alliance administrator, had assured the oligarchs of Latin America that "in supporting the alliance members of the traditional ruling class will have nothing to fear. [It is] their very means of defense." If there were any in the Kennedy administration who believed that a "democratic revolution" could be made from the top down—that the oligarchs, in other words, would commit economic suicide in order to help the poor—they were to be disillusioned. The Alliance made no revolution. At the end of the decade, in fact, there were far more people living under military or authoritarian regimes than at the beginning.

But along with the military assistance program, its inevitable adjunct, the Alliance did preserve the U.S. empire in this hemisphere and did profit American business handsomely. In a single decade, by the statistics of the Economic Commission for Latin America, $5.5 billion private U.S. money was invested in the nineteen republics, while $9.5 billion was earned as profits and dividends, mostly repatriated to New York. This favorable result for the American establishment was in no small measure due to the concessions gained in return for Alliance loans, and equally to the "stability" achieved as a result of the military program.

Officially admitted military aid for Latin America rose from $200,000 in 1952 to $11 million in 1953 and $92 million in 1961. The weaponry and training was supplied, said Defense Secretary McNamara, not to meet outside aggression, but to improve "internal security capabilities for use against Communist-inspired subversion or overt aggression. . . ." "Our arms," wrote James Reston of the New York *Times*, "are now intended to maintain internal order, [and] President Kennedy has formally authorized their use in that way." What the generals in Latin America considered "internal order" was abundantly evident as they toppled one regime after another. Thus, on March 30, 1963, Colonel Enrique Peralta seized the reins of government in Guatemala because it was obvious that former president Arevalo, a moderate socialist hated in Washington, would easily defeat his rivals in the impending election. The Argentine military vitiated elections and placed President Arturo Frondizi under house arrest, because the Peronistas had gained too many seats in the legislature. Later in the decade, in June 1966, an elected president, Arturo Illia, was overthrown by another military clique under General Juan Carlos Ongania. In the Dominican Republic, Juan Bosch, the first democratically elected chief of state in almost four decades, was removed by the army in 1963 after only six months in office, because he refused to denationalize property seized from the long-time dictator Rafael Trujillo. None of these shifts from civilian to military government could have taken place without North American weapons and training; and most of them were probably approved by Washington beforehand, as suggested by the circumstances surrounding coups in Bolivia and Brazil.

Bolivia, as a result of its 1952 revolution, had virtually dissolved the regular army in favor of workers' and peasants' militia. For years Washington pressed the little land-locked state to liquidate the militia in favor of an enlarged conventional force. Finally, during one of the perennial crises, President Victor Paz Estenssoro yielded, increasing the regular force from 4,000 to 20,000 men. Not long thereafter—1964—General Rene Barrientos and the army overthrew Paz. Bolivian opponents of Barrientos charged that the coup was executed under U.S. orders. They pointed out that the general was a friend and protégé of the American General Curtis LeMay, that prior to these events a U.S. ambassador friendly to Paz was replaced by another one who had in his youth been associated with the Bolivian oligarchy, and that a certain Colonel Fox, an expert in anti-guerrilla warfare, was dispatched by Washington to La Paz around the time of the upheaval.

In Brazil, on April 1, 1964, General Humberto Castelo Branco seized power from João Goulart. The first person he had lunch with the following day was an American officer, Vern Walters. Sometime later the former governor of Guanabara, Carlos Lacerda—who had been a leading figure in the coup—revealed that American authorities had come to him and the governors of São Paulo and Minas Gerais with an offer of military and economic aid if they would declare a state of insurgency against the elected national government. Significantly American warships were off Rio de Janeiro's shore during the crisis, just as they were to be a year later off the shore of Santo Domingo, and with the same excuse that they were there to "protect American lives." Had Goulart decided to resist—he had the support of the working class and segments of the army and air force —something akin to the guerrilla war in Vietnam might have exploded in Brazil. Washington made little effort to hide its delight over Castelo's coup.

V

Until the end of the 1960's, when the military of Peru and Bolivia turned to what has been called "Nasserism," and Chile voted in a Marxist government, the satellite military establishments of Latin America adequately preserved Pax Americana. Only once was the United States forced to intervene with its own troops—after a puppet military leadership in the Dominican Republic had failed to hold the fort. On April 24, 1965, young officers under Lieutenant Colonel Francisco Caamaño Deñó arrested their superiors and seized two camps near Santo Domingo. The "Constitutionalists," as they called themselves, proposed to restore the democratically elected Juan Bosch to the presidency, from which he had been ousted by a military coup in 1963. On the next day, as police stations were invaded, guns distributed to 20,000 civilians, and as filling stations handed out free gasoline for Molotov cocktails, the government of Donald Reid Cabral disintegrated.

Four days later, on the evening of Wednesday April 28, President Johnson announced in a special television address that he had ordered marines into the troubled Caribbean nation "in order to give protection to hundreds of Americans who are still in the Dominican Republic and to escort them safely back to this country." The statement was deceptive, for in fact, as events proved, the marines were being sent in to prevent Bosch from regaining power. Resistance to the rebels was organized by General Elias Wessin y Wessin, a hard-line friend of the United States. A junta was established under Colonel Pedro Bartolome Benoit, "visibly sponsored," according to Tad Szulc of the New York *Times*, by the American embassy. Benoit, in his first telephonic talk with the embassy early on April 28, asked Washington to land 1,200 troops "to help restore peace." Later in the day, as the situation deteriorated, he asked—this time in writing—for "unlimited and immediate military assistance" to prevent the Communists from converting "the country into another Cuba." The colonel was advised, according to a subsequent report of the Senate Foreign Relations Committee, that President Johnson would order the marines to land "if he [Benoit] said American lives were in danger. . . ." The President evidently was loath to make the invasion seem like naked aggression; saving lives was a more palatable pretext to be sold to the American public. In fact, of course, not a single American had been hurt, let alone killed, and the rebels, as former ambassador John Bartlow Martin states in his book *Overtaken by Events*, had "agreed to cooperate fully" in evacuating 1,000 U.S. citizens.

Later, on May 2, the President explained that he had landed 22,-000 troops because what began "as a popular democratic revolution" had been "taken over and really seized and placed into the hands of a band of Communist conspirators." A list of 53 alleged Communists, later enlarged to 77, was produced to justify the attack. But the charge had little credibility since none of the Communists held any positions of command. "Little awareness has been shown by the United States," said the New York *Times*, "that the Dominican people—not just a handful of Communists—were fighting and dying for social justice and constitutionalism."

Actually the marine invasion was designed, says Philip Geyelin of the *Wall Street Journal*, "to checkmate the rebel movement by whatever means and whatever cost." Wessin's troops were beaten. As he himself said in testimony before the U.S. Senate Internal Security Committee five months later, "The chiefs of the army who were not in the conspiracy were on the run. . . . The Navy, with the exception of nine of its more than 30 ships of all types, was totally on the other side. Indecision continued at air force headquarters. The police force's chiefs were indecisive and vacillating." Air Force General Juan de los Santos Cespedes had in fact urged Wessin to "surrender." This estimate was confirmed by John Bartlow Martin, who was sent to the scene by President Johnson on April 30: "I learned that the Dominican Armed Forces had virtually disintegrated. Of the nearly 30,000 men who had been under arms in my time, the San Isidro generals now could command the loyalty of no more than 1,500 Army, 900 Air, and probably 150 tankers, plus part of the Navy, several thousand virtually useless soldiers scattered in garrisons around the country, and about a thousand police. The generals themselves were demoralized." Without American intervention the Constitutionalists would have won easily. But the U.S. forces landed, hemmed in the rebels to certain areas of Santo Domingo, and patrolled the streets side by side with the troops of General Wessin. The rebels were stymied, and an arrangement was eventually made for elections on June 1, 1966, in which a former leading associate of Trujillo, Joaquin Balaguer, defeated Juan Bosch. The Constitutionalists attributed their leader's defeat to a reign of terror against their followers and Bosch's failure to leave his home to conduct an active campaign, for fear of being assassinated.

On June 24, 1969, Senator Frank Church denounced the American policy in Latin America as one of "extreme imperialism" and, with Senator Fulbright, demanded that military aid be terminated and the training of tens of thousands of Latin officers be stopped. Despite all the aid and the interventions, direct and indirect, there was a note of malaise and instability as the decade ended. There were city guerrillas, called Tupamaros in Uruguay and Marighellistas in Brazil, conducting arson, kidnaping, and other violent activities in those countries. There were rural guerrilla activities in Guatemala, Colombia, Venezuela; urban terror in Argentina; student riots in Mexico. Military regimes with radical philosophies akin to that of the late President Nasser in Egypt were installed in Peru and Bolivia, both showing signs of anti-Americanism. Even more, a Marxist government, including Communists, was elected in Chile in 1970. The President, a left-wing socialist named Salvador Allende, was undoing Chile's ties to the American system, recognizing Cuba and China, and nationalizing American copper firms. The empire in Latin America was not yet in jeopardy, but it was beginning to show significant weaknesses here and there.

VI

The most dogged and the most costly—probably, in the long run, the most futile—defense of the postwar American empire took place in Southeast Asia. The Dominican intervention was estimated to cost $150 million, the Korean War $18 billion, the Vietnam (Laotian and

Cambodian) War, as of 1970, $125 billion—and still rising. Though undeclared, it was, in terms of casualties, the fourth biggest war in American history.

Every American president since 1945 had a hand in seeding the so-called Vietnam War—Truman in aiding France, Kennedy in sending in "advisers"—but it was Lyndon B. Johnson who crossed the threshold to full hostilities. The tall Texan, first Southern president in a century, was more chameleon than crusader. He had none of the warmth of an Eisenhower or the appeal to youth of a Kennedy; his image while in the Senate was that of the wheeler-dealer, the backroom compromiser, and all efforts by public-relations men to convert him into a popular figure failed. Johnson had come to Washington originally in 1931 at the age of twenty-three, as secretary to a rich Texan congressman whose social views were as backward as those of an Indian maharajah. After four years he passed over to the New Deal, serving as state director of the National Youth Administration under left-of-center Aubrey Williams. Then, hitching his star to that of Congressman Sam Rayburn, at that time considered a liberal, Johnson ran in Texas' Tenth District as a New Dealer against six opponents who considered Franklin Roosevelt anathema, and beat them all. In Washington he drew the attention of political potentates, including FDR, who treated him like an adopted son.

Following Roosevelt's death, however, Johnson shifted severely rightward. He cozied to the oil and construction interests of his home state, especially Brown & Root Inc., and was rewarded by generous donations to his campaign chests. Though he did not move into the ranks of reaction, lest he sever links with the national party, Johnson displayed an aptitude for caution, compromise, and conservatism consonant with postwar America. In August 1948 he won a primary fight for the Senate by the shaky margin of 87 votes, after the mysterious appearance of 202 additional ballots from a remote precinct. Two years later, mainly through the efforts of Senator Robert Kerr, the oilman from Oklahoma, Johnson was installed as whip for the Democrats, and when the floor leader, Senator Ernest McFarland of Arizona, lost his seat to Barry Goldwater in 1952, LBJ rose to the top post at the youngish age of forty-four.

As Democratic leader Johnson worked closely with Republican President Eisenhower, as well as the Southern powerhouse, Senator Richard B. Russell. He would have liked the 1960 nomination for president, but could not dent Kennedy's lead. When he was chosen for the second post, organized labor, and in particular the auto union chief, Walter Reuther, were so horrified they considered bolting the Democratic ticket. Yet in his first year as president, after Kennedy was assassinated in Dallas, Johnson compiled a credible liberal record in civil rights and antipoverty legislation. When he ran on his own in 1964—against Senator Goldwater—most liberals and not a few radicals considered him the "peace" candidate. "I have had advice," he said, "to load our planes with bombs and to drop them on certain areas that I think would enlarge the war, and result in our committing a good many American boys to fighting a war that I think ought to be fought by the boys of Asia to help protect their own land. And for that reason, I haven't chosen to enlarge the war." A few weeks before the polling, on October 21, he stated unequivocally: "We are not about to send American boys 9,000 or 10,000 miles away from home to do what Asian boys ought to be doing for themselves." He painted a gruesome picture of what might happen if this occurred: "Losing 190 American lives in the period that we have been out there is bad, but it is not like 190,000 that we might lose the first month, if we escalated the war." Within a month after inauguration, however, American planes were dropping bombs on Vietnamese soil, and a few months later "American boys" were indeed "fighting a war" that "ought to be fought by the boys of Asia."

Why Johnson should have embarked on this venture was obscure to most people. To be sure the National Liberation Front (NLF) and its so-called Vietcong guerrillas were within months of victory at the end of 1964. But the economic stake of the American power elite in Indochina was negligible—as of 1950, exports to its three component parts combined were less than $10 million, and imports from them only $11 million; a decade later exports to Indochina had risen to $60 million—still a small figure—and imports remained the same. There were important raw materials in the country: "If Indochina goes," President Eisenhower had said, "the tin and tungsten that we so greatly value from that area would cease coming."

But tin and tungsten could not justify the enormous commitment Johnson was making. The explanation seems to lie in two directions: first, the fear that a successful revolt against Pax Americana in one place would give it wings elsewhere; and second, the economic potential of the area for the future. Secretary Dulles expressed anxiety in March 1954 that "if the Communist forces won uncontested control over Indochina or any substantial part thereof, they would surely resume the same pattern of aggression against other free peoples in the area." This was the "domino theory," which would be heard unceasingly thereafter: that if Indochina fell the nations around it—Burma, Thailand, Indonesia, Malaya, Singapore, etc.—

would fall like dominoes almost automatically. Put another way, as Henry Cabot Lodge did on February 28, 1965: "He who holds or has influence in Vietnam can affect the future of the Philippines and Formosa to the east, Thailand and Burma with their huge rice surpluses to the west, and Malaysia and Indonesia with their rubber, ore, and tin to the south."

The long-term financial benefits in Indochina proper were expressed by Henry M. Sperry, vice-president of the First National City Bank in 1965: "We believe that we're going to win this war. Afterwards you'll have a major job of reconstruction on your hands. That will take financing and financing means banks. . . . It would be illogical to permit the English and French to monopolize the banking business because South Vietnam's economy is becoming more and more United States oriented." Alfred Wentworth, vice-president of Chase Manhattan, was even more outspoken in an interview the same year: "In the past, foreign investors have been somewhat wary of the over-all political prospect for the [Southeast Asia] region. I must say, though, that the U.S. actions in Vietnam this year . . . have considerably reassured both Asian and Western investors. In fact, I see some reason for hope that the same sort of economic growth may take place in the free economies of Asia that took place in Europe after the Truman Doctrine and after NATO provided a protective shield. The same thing also took place in Japan after the U.S. intervention in Korea removed investor doubts."

With such objectives—both strategic and economic—in mind, the United States stepped deeper into the quicksand with each passing year. The full chronicle of this war has been told many times: how the United States air-dropped arms to the Vietminh toward the end of World War II to fight the Japanese, and the intelligence work done for the Office of Strategic Services by the Vietminh; how Washington turned full circle against the Vietminh and supplied France with billions from 1950 to 1954; how Dulles and Admiral Arthur Radford, chairman of the Joint Chiefs of Staff, proposed, on the eve of France's defeat at Dienbienphu, a joint U.S.-French-British offensive that would include air strikes by 200 U.S. planes and, according to French Foreign Minister Georges Bidault, the possible "use of . . . one or more nuclear weapons near the Chinese border against supply lines," and two against the Vietminh at Dienbienphu—and how this plan was vetoed by Eisenhower only because Britain refused to participate and leading figures in Congress, among them Lyndon Johnson, gave it a lukewarm reception.

Accords signed at Geneva by the Vietminh and France on July 20, 1954, ended hostilities, and the country was temporarily divided at the 17th parallel pending all-Vietnam elections in 1956. The Vietminh, according to French Prime Minister Pierre Mendès-France, gave up large sections of the Mekong Delta in the South and a great stretch between the 13th and 17th parallels to win the concession of elections, but the elections were never held—primarily because Ngo Dinh Diem, installed as premier by the French at the behest of the United States, and then as president in the rigged referendum of October 1955, which gave Diem 98.2 percent of the vote, could not win. Diem refused to discuss elections, columnist Joseph Alsop wrote, because "outside the feudal domains of the military religious sects, anywhere from 50 to 70 percent of the southern Indochina villages are subject to Vietminh influence or control. French experts give still higher percentages, between 60 to 90."

Fortified by hundreds of millions of U.S. dollars and American training of his troops and police, Diem turned to repression as the only means of staying in power. In 1956 he eliminated the elected village councils, substituting his own appointees. In 1959 he introduced a decree to regroup peasants into "relocation centers," or "agrovilles"—complete with forced labor, barbed wire, spiked moats, and military control. Manhunts against Communists and anyone else who had previously opposed French rule began in 1956, according to France's leading expert on Indochina, Philippe Devillers. As many as 75,000 people may have been killed in this campaign. Presidential Ordinance No. 6, signed in January 1956, gave Diem the right to imprison in concentration camps anyone "considered dangerous to national defense and common security." According to the figures of Diem's own Ministry of Information, 48,250 dissidents were so incarcerated from 1954 to 1960.

In the face of such repression, tribesmen and former Vietminh fighters began to retreat to the forests for new guerrilla wars, and in December 1960 they grouped together into the National Liberation Front of South Vietnam. From then until Diem fell from power in 1963 the situation deteriorated steadily as the NLF killed appointed village chiefs and drove informers and landlords from the rural areas. Land was distributed to the peasants—according to an NLF claim of 1964, 3.2 million acres of the 8.6 million cultivable acres in South Vietnam—and a solid base built for the new insurgency. As of late 1961, according to Jerry A. Rose, a former *Time* correspondent, "in one degree or another, seventy to ninety percent of the entire peasant population now leans toward the Viet Cong." Max Clos, a writer for the conservative French newspaper *Le Figaro,* reported, "The South Vietnam rice granary is politically controlled by the Vietminh [Vietcong]. . . . The national army [of Diem] is in exactly the same situation as the French expeditionary corps in 1950, and for exactly the same reasons. It holds the main roadways and the important towns, but the very substance of the country—the men and the rice—have escaped it."

By May 1963, even Washington was convinced that Diem could not prevail. That month government troops fired on Buddhists in the old imperial capital, Hue, killing nine and unleashing riots and demonstrations in many other places. As the turmoil continued a number of monks burned themselves alive, dramatizing for a shocked world opinion the terrible state of affairs in South Vietnam. Finally, with the silent assent of Ambassador Henry Cabot Lodge, three generals on November 1 executed a coup d'état. Diem and his brother Ngo Dinh Nhu were murdered. As General Duong Van Minh took over the government, the NLF controlled considerably more than half the country, and according to a report of the United States Operations Mission in Saigon were levying taxes in forty-one of the forty-four provinces.

President Kennedy was assassinated a few weeks after the change-over in Saigon; Vice-president Johnson took his place. In the next nineteen months there was an endless train of coups and changes in government in South Vietnam—four under military leaders, three under civilians. As of the time President Johnson ordered the bombing of North Vietnam, the war had once again been lost—for the third time in one decade. Whatever Secretary McNamara might say publicly about the war's going well, General Maxwell Taylor reported on returning from Vietnam in September 1964 that Saigon ruled no more than 30 percent of the country, with 20 percent in the hands of the Vietcong and 50 percent contested. Soon thereafter a rising of Montagnard tribes further reduced Saigon's territory. On December 1 Taylor portrayed the situation to a cabinet meeting in such dire terms that his appearance at a press conference had to be canceled, because, as McNamara told President Johnson, "it would be impossible for Max to talk to these people without leaving the impression the situation is going to hell." All of this and more, incidentally, were confirmed by a study made by the Defense Department itself and subsequently published by *The New York Times* in the summer of 1971.

Unwilling to let the puppet regime in Saigon collapse, and unwilling to negotiate with the NLF—except on subtly put terms of surrender—Johnson took the only other path possible. He made it an American war. Using the legal cover of a resolution passed after an incident in the Tonkin Gulf on August 2, 1964, which gave him authority to "take all necessary measures to repel any armed attack against the forces of the United States and to prevent further aggression," LBJ ordered the bombing of North Vietnam and later the landing of troops in the South. The Tonkin Gulf incident is still clouded in controversy, with critics claiming that the two American destroyers which were allegedly attacked by North Vietnamese PT boats—though undamaged—were acting as cover for a South Vietnamese assault on two North Vietnamese islands. In the heat of national outrage, however, the vote in the House was 466 to nothing, in the Senate 88 to 2; and subsequently an administration official, Nicholas de B. Katzenbach called the resolution the "functional equivalent" of a declaration of war, giving the President virtually unlimited powers to escalate.

This was the easiest war in American history to get into, the hardest one to terminate. Since North Vietnam had virtually no defense against aerial bombardment it was felt she would soon be brought to her knees, leaving the local guerrillas in the South—still doing almost all of the fighting—isolated. In June 1965 a "stable" government, under Air Force Vice-marshal Nguyen Cao Ky, was installed in Saigon and there were no coups thereafter, even when Ky's right-hand man, General Nguyen Van Thieu, replaced Ky and demoted him to vice-president in the carefully managed—rigged—elections of 1967. Nonetheless, America's overwhelming superiority in men and firepower, as well as the supposed political "stability" of the South, were inadequate to win.

The 23,000 U.S. troops in South Vietnam in 1964 rose to 185,000 the next year, 385,000 in 1966, 485,000 in 1967, and a peak of 542,000 in 1968. From 1965 to early 1970, 4.5 million tons of dynamite were dropped on Vietnam—plus additional tonnage on Laos and later on Cambodia—or five hundred times as much as the tonnage used by the other side, and far more than dropped by the United States in World War II. In addition to a half million American troops, there were 65,000 from South Korea (for which the Korean government was paid $150 to $200 million a year), a contingent of Thais (for which Thailand received $50 million a year), a small number of Filipinos (also subsidized by Washington), Australians, and New Zealanders, plus the nearly 1 million in the armed services and auxiliaries of South Vietnam. Yet this massive force was unable to defeat a quarter of a million Vietcong and North Vietnamese. The Vietnamese suffered incredible losses—a million civilian casualties alone, 2 to 6 million made refugees—but they also made the war costly to America—50,000 killed and 300,000 wounded by the end of 1970. Above all they made the war unwinnable, despite the soporific statements from Washington—such as the one by General Earle G.

Wheeler, chairman of the Joint Chiefs of Staff, in August 1968, that "our forces have achieved an unbroken string of victories which, in the aggregate, is something new in our military history."

Just when there seemed to be a lull in the war, in February 1968, and when the "pacification" of Vietnamese villages was reported to be proceeding smoothly, 50,000 to 60,000 NLF soldiers launched the Tet (Vietnamese New Year) offensive—with the aid of urban sympathizers. The Vietcong and the North Vietnamese attacked thirty-six of the forty-four provincial capitals and held large sections of both Saigon and Hue for an extended period. To root out the enemy from its entrenchments, American planes bombed and destroyed portions—sometimes as much as half—of the built-up areas. American forces had to destroy one city, commented a U.S. officer, "in order to save it."

VII

A month and a half after the Tet offensive, even as administration leaders were claiming it was a stunning defeat for the Communists, President Johnson announced that he had ordered all bombing of North Vietnam ended above the 20th parallel (leaving the area from the 17th to the 20th for continued attack), and took himself out of the presidential race. Both revelations were startling, the only explanation for them being the upsurge of massive antiwar sentiment.

In June 1965 the octogenarian pacifist A. J. Muste had led a band of 200 men and women to the Pentagon to distribute 30,000 circulars to the less than sympathetic military men, and to hold a speak-out within the building. Two months later Muste, David Dellinger, Staughton Lynd and SNCC leader Robert (Moses) Parris, led another demonstration in Washington in which hundreds were arrested in the shadow of the Capitol. Out of this evolved the National Coordinating Committee to End the War in Vietnam and parades in ninety-three cities in October. A year later, on the initiative of professors Robert Greenblatt and Sidney Peck, with Muste again as chairman, was born a new committee which eventually was known as the New Mobilization Committee to End the War in Vietnam (New Mobe). Two antiwar parades and rallies in New York and San Francisco in April 1967 drew between a quarter and a half million people. A "confront the warmakers" demonstration at the Pentagon that October was more militant and resulted in 800 arrests and hundreds of injuries as the government brought out troops to defend the five-sided structure. In August 1968, during the Democratic Party convention in Chicago, a smaller crowd—only 12,000 to

15,000—made headlines as a result of an orgy of violence by the city police which was duly recorded on the television screens of the nation. The following October 15, 1969, literally millions declared a "moratorium" from work and school, under the auspices of the Vietnam Moratorium Committee, to be followed a month later by the largest protest in American history, somewhere between 400,000 and 800,000 in Washington and about half that number in San Francisco —this time under the leadership of the New Mobe.

Slower to develop than the outpourings of students in campuses and on the streets, and the draft card burnings, vigils, draft refusals, and other activities that complemented them, was the emergence of opposition in Congress. But like the opposition to the Mexican War a century before, it appeared late in the day, especially after Tet, to harry the administration and question its credibility. A new name was coined—"dove"—for senators like Wayne Morse, Ernest Gruening, Stephen Young, Fulbright, Edward M. Kennedy, Albert Gore, George McGovern, Charles Goodell, and their counterparts in the House, who urged withdrawal from the Indochinese morass. The Vietnam War became the most unpopular one in American annals, and the President accused of a "credibility gap." Citizens were shocked by revelations of scores of villages being burned to the ground by American soldiers (much of which could be seen on the TV tube) and by tales of torture and killing. The nation learned of such things as "free-fire zones," in which the bombing and killing of all living things, including children and animals, was both permitted and encouraged. Not only was the war not being won, but America's morality was being stretched to the point where its leaders were charged by leftists and some liberals with being war criminals under the principles laid down during the postwar trial of Nazis in Nuremburg.

Such protests account for the reduction of bombings over North Vietnam and Johnson's decision not to run again. Peace talks with Hanoi began in Paris shortly thereafter, and under further popular pressures, LBJ on October 31, 1968, stopped the bombing of North Vietnam entirely, including the area between the 17th and 20th parallels. There was some speculation that had he taken this step a few weeks or months earlier he might have assured the victory of Democratic standard-bearer Hubert H. Humphrey in that year's presidential race. As it was, Richard M. Nixon squeaked through by a mere half million votes—out of 73 million.

Nixon, born in Yorba Linda, California, of Quaker parents, was a man of considerable malleability, but at the right wing end of the political spectrum. A lawyer by profession, a good debater when he attended Whittier College and Duke University Law School, a navy veteran who served as an air transport officer in the Pacific and a legal officer in the States, he ran for Congress for the first time in 1946. Arrayed against an outspoken liberal, Jerry Voorhis, seeking his sixth term, Nixon red-baited him into defeat by a 15,000-vote margin. Later he won national acclaim as a member of the House Committee on Un-American Activities for laying low a prominent State Department official under Roosevelt, Alger Hiss. Hiss was sent to jail for perjury; Nixon climbed the ladder to his next niche, as senator. Once again red-baiting was his stock in trade, this time against a Democratic congresswoman, Helen Gahagan Douglas. Eisenhower chose him as his vice-presidential running mate and stood by him after he was charged with impropriety for accepting funds from businessmen. Defending himself over television in his famous Checkers Speech, Nixon won the plaudits of his audience, and was swept into office both in 1952 and again, with Eisenhower, in 1956.

In 1960 television was Nixon's undoing, for in four televised debates with John F. Kennedy he was an obvious loser. Kennedy barely made it, by a margin of 119,450 votes. Undaunted, Nixon began to rebuild his fortunes by running for governor of California. The campaign, however, turned out to be a disaster and seemed to end his career. Ploddingly, he returned to the political wars, worked hard for Barry Goldwater and other candidates in 1964 and 1966, was given another whirl in 1968, and emerged victorious. The sobriquet applied to Nixon by those who disliked him was "Tricky Dick." He spoke fluently but lacked charisma. Many suspected that he also lacked depth. He had supported Johnson throughout on the war in Vietnam, but he said during the 1968 campaign that he had a plan for ending the war, though he refused to explain exactly what it was. When he became president, he also promised to bring a divided nation together, all of which sounded heartening to a people emotionally exhausted by far away hostilities and the tumult on the campuses at home.

With the help of his key adviser, Harvard professor Henry Kissinger, Nixon altered the policy of his predecessor in two respects. Stopping at Guam on a tour of the world in July 1969, he announced a "Nixon Doctrine" for Asia. The United States, he said, "would furnish military and economic assistance when requested in accordance with our treaty commitments. But we shall look to the nation directly threatened to assume the primary responsibility for its defense." The United States would continue to supply matériel and money to its allies, but it would "disengage" itself from ground combat. Any ally in difficulties would receive American help only if it was willing to help itself, i.e., do its own fighting. In a sense Nixon was returning to the strategical guideposts of Harry Truman in Greece: Uncle Sam supplied the weapons and the finances, the Greeks did the fighting and dying. Under the Nixon Doctrine some soldiers were withdrawn from Japan, Thailand, the Philippines, South Korea. Most important, by August 1971, the troop level in Indochina was reduced by 300,000 men. Administration officials assured the public they were "winding down" the war in Vietnam, that the United States was slowly "getting out."

The second policy modification was elaborated by the President on November 3, 1969—midway between the antiwar tumult of the October 15 "moratorium" and the November 15 "mobilization." "In the previous administration," said Nixon, "we Americanized the war in Vietnam. In this administration, we are Vietnamizing the search for peace." Under Vietnamization the Pentagon planned to phase out its ground combat and as much of air and naval support as was feasible, leaving those tasks to the natives. Cynics called it substituting yellow casualties for white; indeed, killed-in-action figures for American forces fell from about 200 a week in 1969 to a third that average in the first four months of 1970, and as low as a dozen by summer 1971.

If the President, however, was disengaging from ground combat, he did not end intervention or the war. On the contrary the war widened appreciably and the Pentagon's air and logistical activity became substantially greater. In Laos, where a second Geneva Accord had been signed by Kennedy in July 1962, temporarily ending the fighting between American-supported rightists and the Communist-led Pathet Lao, the secret war going on there took a big leap forward. Bombing sorties by U.S. planes over the Ho Chi Minh Trail—used by the North Vietnamese to transport supplies to Vietnam—grew, from 1964 on, until they reached 12,500 a month and had fanned out far beyond the trail deep into the interior, where the Pathet Lao held two thirds of the territory. After Johnson's bombing halt in North Vietnam, the planes were freed for use elsewhere and the number of sorties over Laos rose to 17,000 to 27,000 monthly. As of 1970 more dynamite had fallen on this tiny nation of three million people than on both Vietnams combined. Seven hundred thousand of its citizens—one of four—had been made refugees. The saturation bombing of 1970—particularly in the contested Plain of Jars, resulted in a situation—according to a U.S. AID official—where "most villages and fields are now almost completely ruined." In addition the CIA's clandestine army of 15,000

Meo tribesmen, based at a headquarters in Long Cheng, had been so heavily engaged in battle that two fifths of the men among the Meo population of 400,000 and a quarter of the women and children were casualties.

The Indochina War took another quantum jump under Nixon when on April 30, 1970, the President announced that American and South Vietnamese forces had launched an attack into Cambodia. The invasion was explained as an effort to wipe out "Communist sanctuaries" in that land, which "clearly endanger the lives of Americans who are in Vietnam"; and to destroy the central headquarters of the NLF (referred to as COSVN—Communist Operations in South Vietnam), which allegedly was on Cambodian soil. The invaders destroyed considerable stocks of rice (some of which may have belonged to rubber plantations in the area) and weapons caches, but they never found COSVN—disappointing those hawks who hoped that the whole Provisional Revolutionary Government might be captured in one fell swoop. Nixon, nonetheless, claimed that the invasion was a great success, making it possible to withdraw additional troops from Vietnam and protecting the Vietnamization program.

The uproar at home, however, was more bitter than any since the Indochina War had begun. Students at hundreds of universities demonstrated and scores of schools were closed down to the end of the semester. Tempers flared when four students at Kent State College in Ohio were killed by the National Guard during a protest action on May 4. One hundred and fifty thousand people were brought to Washington in a hastily organized action called by the New Mobe on May 9, and for a time it appeared there would be a major confrontation between police and demonstrators. One dovish senator and congressman after another denounced the action in Cambodia, and President Nixon was so concerned about the disaffected youth protesting all over the nation that he rose early on the morning of May 9 to talk with young dissidents at the Lincoln Memorial. To allay public opinion, the chief executive announced on the day before the big action that the 50,000 allied troops would penetrate no deeper than 21 miles into Cambodia and that all forces would be withdrawn by June 30 at the latest. He seemed to promise too that South Vietnamese forces would not return either, "because when we come out our logistical and air support will also come out with them."

Subsequent events proved that this initial foray was only a beginning. Once again Washington—ineptly but with terrible determination—was embarked on extending its empire. At the Geneva Conference in 1954 the Vietminh had agreed to evacuate Cambodia; an independent and neutral government was established in that ancient land of 6 million people under Prince Norodom Sihanouk. For the next fifteen years Sihanouk balanced himself adroitly between East and West, seeking United States aid on occasion, breaking off with Washington when he felt it was trying to assert dominance over his nation. Dulles promised that he would protect Cambodia under the provisions of the SEATO treaty, even though Sihanouk protested that "we want absolutely nothing to do with SEATO or any other military pact. . . ." An attempt was made to overthrow Sihanouk in 1959, an attempt ascribed by Pnompenh to the CIA. As evidence Sihanouk's followers produced a letter purportedly written by Eisenhower to a Khmer general "pledging full support to a projected coup and to a reversal of Cambodian neutrality." Early in the next decade, the CIA formed a contingent of rightists called Khmer Serai and trained it militarily for fighting Sihanouk. On March 18, 1970—just forty-three days before the U.S. invasion—while Sihanouk was in Moscow on his way back from Paris for a health cure, General Lon Nol in Pnompenh deposed him as the nation's ruler. What role the CIA played in this, if any, is still unknown; but there was no question of Washington's sympathies.

Sihanouk flew to Peking from Moscow to organize the opposition. If he was a neutralist before, he was now leaning almost entirely on the Communists from Peking and Hanoi. By the end of 1970, North Vietnamese, Vietcong, and native sympathizers of Sihanouk were in possession of two thirds of the country and had cut the major lines of communication to Pnompenh, including its link to the sea. In the face of this adversity Nixon asked for a quarter of a billion dollars in aid for Lon Nol's regime and was granted it by a grudging Congress with the proviso that no American forces would be used in ground combat or as advisers in Cambodia. There were also public assurances from the administration that bombing of the country would be limited to "air interdiction missions against the enemy efforts to move supplies and personnel through Cambodia *toward South Vietnam and to reestablish base areas relative to the war in Vietnam.*" (Emphasis added.) In fact, however, the Pentagon was flying support missions for the Cambodian army in its efforts to dislodge the other side. Late in January 1971, while South Vietnamese and Lon Nol's Cambodian troops were trying to reopen Highway Four, which connected Pnompenh to the sea, it was discovered that U.S. planes and helicopters were engaged in the battle and that American advisers were flying with South Vietnamese officers in helicopters over the battlefront. Senate Majority Leader Mike

Mansfield, among others, castigated the action as a violation of the spirit of Congress's edict.

There was now a pro-American government in Pnompenh, but it was unable to stay afloat for more than a few weeks without some form of U.S. intervention. And there was no doubt that Washington intended to go further with that intervention. A subcommittee of the Senate reported in September 1970 that since May the invasion of Cambodia had caused one and a half million refugees, and that 200,000 of the 400,000 Vietnamese living in the country had been deported, while thousands of other Vietnamese had been killed or placed in government camps. The rubber plantations had been shattered to the point where rubber exports, which produced $20 million in foreign exchange—one half the normal total—were down to zero. And agricultural production had been so discommoded that international relief agencies in Geneva were expecting a famine the following year.

The American-sponsored invasion of Laos in 1971 by South Vietnamese forces, though a military debacle, indicated that the Nixon regime would continue with might and main its efforts to control as much of Southeast Asia as it possibly could.

VIII

The defeat of the United States in Vietnam—its glaring inability to cope with revolution and civil war in a small, seemingly impotent nation—punctuated the fact that imperial ascendancy is not limitless. An empire that confronts revolution ceaselessly and must balance itself between counterrevolution and nuclear war lives a precarious existence, to say the least. Was it possible that the American colossus, at the zenith of its power, was beginning that long descent that had caught up with Britain, France, Spain, Arabia, Rome, Greece, Macedonia, Persia, Mesopotamia, and so many others? Arnold Toynbee reminds us that great nations often are eclipsed at the pinnacle of their success, challenged from without and corrupted from within by forces they do not understand or correctly evaluate.

Can global imperialism, of the present American variety, survive in an age of revolution?

Pax Americana certainly could credit itself with many successes in the quarter of a century after World War II. From World War I to World War II there had been an interval of twenty-one years without a new large-scale engagement; under Pax Americana a world war had already been averted for a longer period. Moreover, during

Pax Americana the United States and its economically advanced allies had enjoyed extremely high standards of living. The gross national product at home had climbed to the phenomenal figure of a trillion dollars a year, and though there had been five "recessions," none had even remotely approached in intensity the depression of the 1930's.

Yet there were danger signals all around, flashing from three quarters. The tide of national revolution, unlike the revolutionary wave that followed World War I from 1917 to 1924, showed no signs of abating. Properly speaking, it was a double revolution, its first phase centering on independence from imperialism, its second on building viable economic structures—usually along socialist lines. If the revolutionary tide continued or accelerated there would be many countries trying to escape Pax Americana, each one posing problems for the empire. Vietnams seemed to be endemic to the situation. There might have been one in Brazil in April 1964, or the Congo in 1964, or the Dominican Republic in 1965, or in other places at other times. Each crisis held within it the seed of a Bay of Pigs, an October missile crisis, or an Indochina. One of these conflicts, in the end, might escalate to total war with China, the Soviet Union, or both.

A second set of difficulties emanated from the advanced countries. Ever since the end of the Second World War, they had accepted, almost unquestioningly, American leadership—for three reasons: first, that Uncle Sam supplied the dollars for economic revival; second, that the United States opened the door to trade and investment for its major allies while opening the door into new markets for itself; and third, that it offered a military shield for sustaining the desired internal and external status quo. It was not outside the realm of possibility, however, that Japan, Germany, France, and Britain might loosen or break their ties with the American goliath once they could stand on their own economic feet. France had already withdrawn its troops from NATO and was pursuing a semi-independent foreign policy. Japan was making overtures to China and might soon strike out on its own to consolidate an independent base in Asia. There was friction with the United States, where the textile industry, oblivious to the risk of starting a trade war, sought to have quotas imposed on low-cost Japanese imports.

Germany was coming to terms with the Eastern European countries and the Soviet Union, opening the way to trade realignments and perhaps political ones. Increasingly, Western Europe seemed to fear American commercial and financial competition more than it feared a Soviet military thrust. Once Europe and Japan began to feel independent of Washington for aid, trade, and military defense, many things might change. The other capitalist states now had it within their power to tighten the economic vise against the United States—if they saw fit. "Someday uncomfortably soon," Gaylord A. Freeman, chairman of the First National Bank of Chicago, told 1,200 bankers in November 1970, Uncle Sam may be asked to make good on claims against its gold reserves—"and we don't have it." Because the United States had been spending so much overseas in the previous twenty years—on wars, bases, etc.—"the foreign nations," he said, "have the right to ask us to pay $44.5 billion in gold. We don't have the gold. Our country cannot pay its short-term debts." So long as the international ship stayed at even keel, with America at the tiller, there was no prospect that the dollar would be undermined. But if international tensions grew, the danger could become acute. The seeds of the tension were just beginning to sprout, and indeed there was a serious dollar crisis in mid-1971 that forced Nixon to cancel the dollar's relationship to gold and let it float substantially below its former value. Moreover, the unfavorable balance of trade in the first nine months of 1971 (first since the 1890's) led the President to impose a 10% surcharge on imports, and invited foreign retaliation.

The gold problem, incidentally, revealed one of the paradoxes of global imperialism, namely that the costs to the American people *as a whole* are many times greater than the benefits reaped by the establishment. Private American investment overseas might go up six or seven times—to $70 billion—and trade by three or four times, but these sums are far smaller than what it has cost to build and run the military machine that preserves imperialism—about a trillion dollars in the same two decades. In theory it would seem wiser for the American government to pay $50 or $100 million in outright subsidies to American corporations that seek investment in Vietnam than to spend $125 *billion* to fight a war there. In this sense, the taxes of a great many Americans are being used uneconomically for the benefit of one small group of Americans—the so-called establishment. However, it is not just the few million in investments or trade that is at stake, but the functioning of a whole capitalistic system. Take away the opportunities to increase foreign investment and trade, or to gain access to raw materials, and the domestic economy can do nothing else but choke. Gorged with unsalable surpluses, which under capitalism are distributed not on the basis of need but only in exchange for money, the system founders. Thus it is the *domestic* economy itself that is "saved" by imperialism, not merely the export and investment industries; and that is why the government considers it feasible to expend such vast sums on the instruments of imperialism. Yet there must eventually be a day of reckoning, as the dollar becomes "softer" and inflation chips away at stability. That is what Freeman was hinting at.

A third set of problems was of course domestic. The American economy was not as stable as it appeared. In 1969–71 the United States witnessed its first serious recession during a war period, with unemployment reaching 6 percent of the work force while prices, flouting the classical theory that they should go down when people are out of work and reduce their purchases—actually rose about 6 percent a year. The national debt—$257 billion in 1950—had jumped to $383 billion twenty years later. Deficit financing, resulting from the government's repeatedly spending more than it took in, was no longer an ogre that terrified people; President Nixon, though a conservative, in fact planned a large deficit for the fiscal 1972 budget to reinvigorate the lagging economy. By the pumping of additional billions into the system it was hoped that jobs would be made available to some of the unemployed and a higher plateau of prosperity attained. But this was all well and good only so long as there was no international trade war and "exportable surpluses" could be exported in ever larger quantities. It was all well and good, in other words, so long as Pax Americana prevailed. If, however, the fabric of Pax Americana should begin to shred and the great capitalist nations again declare economic war against each other, the results might be disastrous. Whatever traditionalist economists might say, an international trade war might very well bring on a deep depression.

Equally ominous for the pursuit of empire was the disaffection within the home population. From 1945 to 1955 there was virtually no resistance to the establishment; a synthetic "Americanism" ran rampant. From 1955 on, however, the mood of radicalism grew by geometric progression, and the war in Vietnam gave it additional stimulus. A large portion of teenagers and those in their early twenties had lost faith in the "system" in varying degrees. A Gallup poll of January 1971 indicated that 50 percent of college students felt that change might come by "peaceful means," but 42 percent believed that America could be saved only through a "revolution." Forty-four percent believed that "violence is sometimes justified." The young people of college and high-school age had developed a new radical life-style, veering sharply from the values of yesteryear. Many were burning draft cards and thousands were avoiding the draft. In Illinois, it was reported, the draft boards had to call twice as many youth to the colors as were needed for their quota—the rest did not show up. This generation refused to become excited over charges of "communism" or "Communist dupes" as the older generation had in the early 1950's. Indeed, it brushed aside such things with contempt; at any university on any day students could be seen reading Marx, Lenin, Mao, Castro, Che Guevara, even Kim Il Sung and books on anarchism.

The armed forces, for the first time since the Revolutionary War, were beset with serious desertion problems, and, in Vietnam itself, refusal to obey orders. "The difficulties that face the U.S. Army in Vietnam today," reported *Newsweek* (January 11, 1971), "are much more serious than the withdrawal pains suffered in any previous American conflict." "Drugs and racial tensions," said the magazine, "are becoming more prevalent . . . and the men who soldier with frontline infantry battalions are increasingly unwilling to risk their lives in combat." American soldiers, like the South Vietnamese, whose morale was exceptionally low, were now pursuing "search and evade" rather than "search and destroy" tactics. "In a few cases, groups of American soldiers have flatly refused to go into action, and some of these 'combat refusals' have even managed temporarily to tie up entire fighting units. In many more cases, young lieutenants and noncoms have simply failed to carry out their orders." A new pastime, "fragging"—throwing fragmentation bombs at hated officers—was becoming much too popular for comfort. Antiwar newspapers were sprouting among troops not only at home but on foreign bases and in Vietnam.

Disaffection in the black and Spanish-speaking communities rose and fell, but in general was on the upswing. The steady increase in crime not only among the poor but in the middle class suburbs mirrored a rise in national frustration. In a country which did not seem to be solving its problems, some youth turned to radicalism, a few turned to crime.

None of the dangers confronting Pax Americana were as yet so dire that they brought America to the brink of disintegration. It would be unwise to exaggerate. But these dangers did exist and they were neither episodic nor insignificant. Given time, they could be overwhelming.

Global imperialism might yet do for the United States what another type of imperialism had done for Rome a long time ago.

SELECTED
BIBLIOGRAPHY

Following the pattern of my *Radicalism in America* and *Poverty: America's Enduring Paradox,* the two earlier books in this series, I have omitted footnotes. Wherever feasible, however, I have tried to include the source in the text itself. For the reader who intends to do further research in this field, the following bibliography will serve, I believe, as an adequate beginning. The book titles and the authors will give a clue as to the most useful references for each specific subject.

I do not include in this bibliography original sources such as the Annals of Congress or American State Papers—to which I refer frequently, especially in the early chapters. Nor have I tried to list magazine articles, except in a few instances where they had some special significance, or newspaper stories. A number of general works in history, economics, biography, and diplomacy are set down as "General" because they were reference sources for a variety of subjects throughout the period covered.

GENERAL

Bailey, Thomas A. *Diplomatic History of the American People.* Crofts. 1945.

Beard, Charles A. and Mary B. *The Rise of American Civilization.* Macmillan. 1927.

Bemis, Samuel Flagg. *A Diplomatic History of the United States.* Holt, Rinehart & Winston. 1965.

Divine, Robert A., ed. *American Foreign Policy.* Meridian. 1960.

Faulkner, Harold U. *Economic History of the United States.* Macmillan. 1928.

Leckie, Robert. *The Wars of America.* 2 volumes. Harper & Row. 1968.

Morison, Samuel Eliot. *The Oxford History of the American People.* Oxford. 1965.

Morris, Richard B., ed. *Encyclopedia of American History.* Harper. 1953.

Tugwell, Rexford Guy. *How They Became President.* Simon & Schuster. 1964.

1. THE MYTH OF MORALITY

Allen, Devere. *The Fight for Peace.* Macmillan. 1930.

Beard, Charles A. *The Idea of National Interest.* Quadrangle Paperbooks. 1966.

Curti, Merle E. *Peace or War, The American Struggle 1636–1936.* W. W. Norton. 1936.

Clarkson, Jesse D., and Cochran, Thomas C., eds. *War as a Social Institution.* Columbia University Press. 1941.

Dupuy, R. Ernest. *Compact History of the United States Army.* Hawthorn. 1961.

Dupuy, R. Ernest, and Trevor, N. *Military Heritage of America.* McGraw-Hill. 1956.

Ekirch, Arthur A., Jr. *The Civilian and the Military.* Oxford. 1956.

Ganoe, William Addleman. *The History of the United States Army.* D. Appleton-Century. 1924.

Hamlin, C. H. *The War Myth in United States History.* Pamphlet. Fellowship Publications. 1948.

Lea, Homer. *The Valor of Ignorance.* Harper. 1942.

Mahan, Alfred T. *The Influence of Sea Power on History, 1660–1783.* Little, Brown. 1890.

Mead, Edwin D. *Washington, Jefferson and Franklin on War.* World Peace Foundation Pamphlet Series, Vol. 3, No. 5.

Meyer, Peter. *The Pacifist Conscience.* Regnery. 1967.

Millis, Walter. *Arms and Men.* Putnam's. 1956.

Nettels, Curtis P. *The Roots of American Civilization.* Appleton-Century-Crofts. 1963.

Palmer, John McAuley. *The Experience of the United States with Military Organization.* Yale University Press. 1941.

Vagts, Alfred. *A History of Militarism.* W. W. Norton. 1937.

Van Alstyne, R. W. *The Rising American Empire.* Oxford. 1960.

Weinberg, Albert K. *Manifest Destiny.* Quadrangle. 1963.

Weinberg, Arthur and Lila. *Instead of Violence.* Grossman. 1963.

Wells, Donald A. *The War Myth.* Pegasus. 1967.

Williams, William Appleman. *The Tragedy of American Diplomacy.* World Publishing Company. 1959.

Wright, Quincy. *A Study of War.* 2 volumes. University of Chicago Press. 1942.

2. FORGOTTEN ALLY

Adams, Henry. *The Formative Years.* Houghton Mifflin. 1947.

Allen, Gardner W. *Our Naval War With France.* Houghton Mifflin. 1909.

———. *Our Navy and the Barbary Corsairs.* Houghton Mifflin. 1905.

Bemis, Samuel Flagg. *Jay's Treaty.* Yale University Press. 1962.

———. "The London Mission of Thomas Pinckney 1792–1796." *American Historical Review.* Vol. 28.

Blyth, Stephen C. *History of the War Between the United States and Tripoli & Other Barbary Powers.* Salem Gazette Office. 1806.

Bowers, Claude G. *Jefferson and Hamilton.* Houghton Mifflin. 1925.

Channing, Edward. *A History of the United States.* Vol. 4. Macmillan. 1917.

Davis, W. W. H. *The Fries Rebellion, 1798–1799.* Doylestown, Pa. 1899.

Dunaway, Wayland F. *A History of Pennsylvania.* Prentice-Hall. 1948.

Felton, Cornelius G. *Life of William Eaton.* Hilliard, Gray and Co. 1837.

Genet, George Clinton. "Beaumarchais' Plan to Aid the Colonies." *Magazine of American History.* Vol. 2, No. 11.

Gerard, James G. "French Spoliations Before 1801." *Magazine of American History.* Vol. 12.

Goldsborough, Charles W. *The United States Naval Chronicle.* Printed by James Wilson, Washington, D.C. 1824.

Hamilton, J. G. de Roulhac. "The Pacifism of Thomas Jefferson." *Virginia Quarterly Review.* Vol. 31.

James, James A. "French Opinion as a Factor in Preventing War Between France and the United States, 1795–1800." *American Historical Review.* Vol. 30.

Knox, Dudley W. *A History of the United States Navy.* Putnam's. 1948.

Levy, Leonard W., and Peterson, Merrill D. *Major Crises in American History.* Harcourt, Brace & World. 1962.

Lincoln, Charles H., ed. *Hull-Eaton Correspondence, 1804–1805.* American Antiquarian Society. 1911.

Lisitzky, Gene. *Thomas Jefferson.* Viking. 1935.

Logan, Deborah Norris. *Memoir of Dr. George Logan.* Historical Society of Pennsylvania. 1899.

Metcalf, Clyde H. *A History of the United States Marine Corps.* Putnam's. 1939.

Pease, Theodore Calvin, and Roberts, A. Sellew. *Selected Readings in American History.* Harcourt, Brace. 1929.

Prentiss, Charles. *The Life of the Late General William Eaton.* Brookfield. 1813.

Shachner, Nathan. *Alexander Hamilton.* Appleton-Century. 1946.

——. *Thomas Jefferson: A Biography.* Appleton-Century-Crofts. 1951.

Smelser, Marshall. *The Democratic Republic, 1801–1815.* Harper Torchbooks. 1968.

Tolles, Frederick B. *George Logan of Philadelphia.* Oxford University Press. 1953.

Turner, Frederick J. "The Origin of Genet's Projected Attack on Louisiana and the Floridas." *American Historical Review.* Vol. 3.

Wright, Louis B., and MacLeod, Julia H. "First American Campaign in North Africa." *Huntington Library Quarterly.* Vol. 7.

3. FALLEN STAR

Abel, Annie Heloise. *The History of Events Resulting in Indian Consolidation West of the Mis-*

sissippi River. Annual Report of the American Historical Association. Vol. 1. 1906.

——. *Proposals for an Indian State, 1778–1878*. Annual Report of the American Historical Association. Vol. 1. 1907.

Adams, Henry. *War of 1812*. Scribner's. 1891.

Adams, James Truslow, ed. *Dictionary of American History*. Scribner's. 1940.

Aptheker, Herbert. *The Colonial Era*. International Publishers. 1959.

Britt, Albert. *Great Indian Chiefs*. Whittlesey House. 1938.

Butterfield, Roger. *The American Past*. Simon & Schuster. 1957.

Fey, Harold E., and McNickle, D'Arcy. *Indians and Other Americans*. Harper & Brothers. 1959.

Halbert, H. S., and Bell, T. H. *The Creek War of 1813 and 1814*. Donahue and Henneberry. 1895.

Harlow, Ralph Volney. *The Growth of the United States*. Vol. 1. Holt. 1943.

Jackson, Helen Hunt. *A Century of Dishonor*. Harper. 1881.

James, Marquis. *Andrew Jackson, the Border Captain*. Grossett & Dunlap. 1933.

Josephy, Alvin M. *The Patriot Chiefs*. Viking. 1961.

McNickle, D'Arcy. *They Came Here First*. Lippincott. 1949.

Moore, William V. (pseudonym of John Frost). *Indian Wars of the United States from the Discovery to the Present Time*. R. W. Pomeroy. 1941.

Ogg, Frederic Austin. *The Old Northwest*. Yale University Press. 1921.

Oskison, John M. *Tecumseh and His Times*. Putnam's. 1938.

Peithmann, Irvin M. *Broken Peace Pipes*. Charles C Thomas. 1964.

Philbrick, Francis S. *The Rise of the West 1754–1830*. Harper Torchbooks. 1965.

Royce, Charles C. *Indian Land Cessions in the United States*. U.S. Bureau of American Ethnology. 18th Annual Report. 1896–97.

St. Clair, Arthur. *A Narrative of the Campaign Against the Indians*. Printed by Jane Aitken, 1812.

Smelser, Marshall. *The Democratic Republic 1801–1815*. Harper Torchbooks. 1968.

Tucker, Glenn. *Poltroons and Patriots*. 2 volumes. Bobbs-Merrill. 1954.

Underhill, Ruth Murray. *Red Man's America*. University of Chicago Press. 1953.

Vogel, Virgil. *The Indian in American History*. Pamphlet. Integrated Education Associates. 1968.

Wellman, Paul I. *The House Divides*. Doubleday. 1966.

4. On to Canada

Adams, Henry. *The Formative Years*. Vol. 2. Houghton Mifflin. 1947.

——. *The War of 1812*. Scribner's. 1891.

Allen, Devere. *The Fight for Peace*. Macmillan. 1930.

Bartlett, Ruhl J. *The Record of American Diplomacy*. Knopf. 1960.

Brown, Roger H. "The War Hawks of 1812: An Historical

Myth." *Indiana Magazine of History*. Vol. 60.

Butterfield, Roger. *The American Past*. Simon & Schuster. 1957.

Carey, Matthew. *The Olive Branch*. Published by the author. Sept. 1815.

Cox, Isaac Joslin. "The American Intervention in West Florida." *American Historical Review*. Vol. 17.

Eaton, Clement. *Henry Clay and the Art of American Politics*. Little, Brown. 1957.

Hacker, Louis M. "The West and the War of 1812." *Mississippi Valley Historical Review*. Vol. 10.

Hart, Albert Bushnell, ed. *American History Told by Contemporaries*. Macmillan. 1896.

Horseman, Reginald. *The Causes of the War of 1812*. University of Pennsylvania Press. 1962.

———. "The War Hawks and the War of 1812." *Indiana Magazine of History*. Vol. 60.

James, Marquis. *Andrew Jackson, the Border Captain*. Grossett & Dunlap. 1933.

Jones, Wilbur Devereux, ed. "A British View of the War of 1812." *Mississippi Valley Historical Review*. Vol. 45.

Lord, John. *Beacon Lights of History*. Fords, Howard, and Hulbert. 1898.

Padgett, James A., ed. "The West Florida Revolution of 1810, as Told in the Letters of John Rhea, Fulwar Skipwith, Reuben Kemper, and others." *Louisiana Historical Review*. Vol. 21.

Paine, Ralph D. *The Fight for a Free Sea*. Yale University Press. 1920.

Perkins, Bradford. *Prologue to War, England and the United States, 1805–1812*. University of California Press. 1961.

Philbrick, Francis S. *The Rise of the West*. Harper Torchbooks. 1965.

Pratt, Julius W. *Expansionists of 1812*. Macmillan. 1925.

Schachner, Nathan. *Alexander Hamilton*. Appleton-Century. 1946.

Schurz, Carl. *Henry Clay*. 2 volumes. Houghton, Mifflin. 1899.

Sears, Louis Martin. *Jefferson and the Embargo*. Farrar, Straus, & Giroux. 1967.

Smelser, Marshall. *The Democratic Republic, 1801–1815*. Harper Torchbooks. 1968.

Taylor, George Rogers, ed. *The War of 1812*. D. C. Heath. 1963.

Tucker, Glenn. *Poltroons and Patriots*. 2 volumes. Bobbs-Merrill. 1954.

Usher, Roland G. *The Rise of the American People*. Garden City Publishing Co. 1926.

Van Alstyne, R. W. *The Rising American Empire*. Oxford University Press. 1960.

Wecter, Dixon. *The Hero in America*. Scribner's. 1941.

5. PICKING THE SPANISH BONE

Adams, Henry. *The Formative Years*. Vol. 2. Houghton Mifflin. 1947.

Barker, Eugene C. *Mexico and Texas 1821–1835*. P. L. Turner. 1928.

Beals, Carleton. *America South*. Lippincott. 1938.

Cunliffe, Marcus. *Soldiers and Civilians*. Little, Brown. 1968.

Frank, Waldo. *Birth of a World.* Houghton, Mifflin. 1951.

Griffin. C. C. *The United States and the Disruption of the Spanish Empire 1810–1822.* Columbia University Press. 1937.

James, Marquis. *Andrew Jackson, Border Ruffian.* Grosset & Dunlap. 1933.

LaFeber, Walter, ed. *John Quincy Adams and American Continental Empire.* Quadrangle. 1965.

Pease, Theodore Calvin, and Roberts, A. Sellew. *Selected Readings in American History.* Harcourt, Brace. 1928.

Tyler, Alice Felt. *Freedom's Ferment.* Harper Torchbooks. 1962.

Williams, William Appleman. *Contours of American History.* World. 1961.

6. MEXICO FOR AMERICANS

Barker, Eugene C. *Mexico and Texas 1821–1835.* P. L. Turner Co. 1928.

——. "President Jackson and the Texas Revolution." *American Historical Review.* Vol. 12.

Garrison, George Pierce. *Westward Expansion 1841–1850.* Harper. 1937.

James, Marquis. *The Raven, A Biography of Sam Houston.* Bobbs-Merrill. 1929.

Merk, Frederick. *Manifest Destiny and Mission in American History.* Knopf. 1963.

Morison, Samuel Eliot; Merk, Frederick; and Freidel, Frank. *Dissent in Three American Wars.* Harvard University Press. 1970.

Stephenson, Nathaniel W. *Texas and the Mexican War.* Yale University Press. 1921.

Weinberg, Albert K. *Manifest Destiny.* Quadrangle. 1963.

7. TRANSCONTINENTAL CONQUEST

Allen, Devere. *The Fight for Peace.* Macmillan. 1930.

Barker, Charles A. "Another American Dilemma." *Virginia Quarterly Review.* Spring. 1969.

Beveridge, Albert J. *Abraham Lincoln, 1809–1858.* 4 volumes. Houghton Mifflin. 1938.

Brock, Peter. *Radical Pacifists in Antebellum America.* Princeton University Press. 1968.

Cunliffe, Marcus. *Soldiers and Civilians.* Little, Brown. 1968.

Curti, Merle Eugene. *The American Peace Crusade.* Duke University. 1929.

Ekirch, Arthur A. Jr. *The Civilian and the Military.* Oxford. 1956.

Foner, Philip S. *History of the Labor Movement of the United States.* Vol. 1. International Publishers. 1962.

Fuller, John Douglas Pitts. *The Movement for the Acquisition of All Mexico, 1846–1848.* Johns Hopkins Press (brochure). 1936.

Garrison, George Pierce. *Westward Expansion, 1841–1850.* Harper. 1937.

Graebner, Norman A. *Empire on the Pacific.* Ronald Press. 1955.

Hart, Albert Bushnell, ed. *American History Told by Contemporaries.* Vol. 3. Macmillan. 1968.

Hofstadter, Richard. *Great Issues in American History.* Vol. 1. Vintage. 1958.

Latane, John Holladay. *A History of American Foreign Policy.* Doubleday, Page. 1927.

McMaster, J. B. *A History of the People of the United States.* Vol. 7. Appleton-Century. 1938.

Merk, Frederick. *The Monroe Doctrine and American Expansionism.* Knopf. 1967.

——. "The Oregon Pioneers and the Boundary." *American Historical Review.* Vol. 29.

Mexican War Speeches. Representative Columbus Delano of Ohio. February 2, 1847.

Morison, Samuel Eliot; Merk, Frederick; and Freidel, Frank. *Dissent in Three American Wars.* Harvard University Press. 1970.

Morrel, Martha McBridge. *Young Hickory, the Life and Times of President James K. Polk.* Dutton. 1949.

Nevins, Allan, ed. *Polk, the Diary of a President, 1845–1849.* Longmans, Green. 1952.

Singletary, Otis A. *The Mexican War.* University of Chicago Press. 1960.

Smith, Justin H. *The War with Mexico.* 2 volumes. Macmillan. 1919.

Stenberg, Richard R. "The Failure of Polk's Mexican War Intrigue." *Pacific Historical Review.* Vol. 4.

——. "Polk and Fremont, 1845–1846." *Pacific Historical Review.* Vol. 7.

Stephenson, Nathaniel W. *Texas and the Mexican War.* Yale University Press. 1921.

Tarbell, Ida. *The Life of Abraham Lincoln.* Vol. 2. Macmillan. 1923.

8. THE BRAVE BRAVES

Adams, James Truslow. *Epic of America.* Little, Brown. 1931.

Baldwin, Leland D. *The Stream of American History.* American Book Company. 1952.

Cotner, Robert C., Ezell, John S., and Fite, Gilbert C. *Readings in American History—Vol. 2—1865 to the Present.* Houghton Mifflin. 1964.

Ganoe, William Addleman. *The History of the United States Army.* D. Appleton-Century. 1924.

Haines, Francis. *The Buffalo.* Thomas Y. Crowell Company. 1970.

Jackson, Helen Hunt. *A Century of Dishonor.* Harper. 1881.

Josephy, Alvin M., Jr. *Patriot Chiefs.* Viking. 1961.

LaFarge, Oliver. *As Long as the Grass Shall Grow.* Longmans, Green. 1940.

Meadowcroft, Enid La Monte. *The Story of Crazy Horse.* Grosset & Dunlap. 1954.

Peithmann, Irvin M. *Broken Peace Pipes.* Charles C Thomas. 1964.

Powers, Mable. *The Indian as Peace Maker.* Fleming H. Revell Co. 1932.

Schlesinger, Arthur M. *Political and Social Growth of the American People, 1865–1940.* Macmillan. 1941.

Vestal, Stanley. *Sitting Bull, Champion of the Sioux.* University of Oklahoma Press. 1957.

9. COMMERCE FOLLOWS THE FLAG

Baldwin, Leland D. *The Stream of American History.* Vol. 2. American Book Company. 1952.

Beard, Charles A. *The Idea of National Interest.* Quadrangle Paperbooks. 1966.

Craven, Avery; Johnson, Walter; and Dunn, F. Roger. *A Documentary History of the American People.* Ginn. 1951.

De Riencourt, Amaury. *The American Empire*. Dial. 1968.

Dulles, Foster Rhea. *Imperial Years*. Thomas Y. Crowell Company. 1956.

Ekirch, Arthur A., Jr. *The Civilian and the Military*. Oxford. 1956.

Graber, D. A. *Crisis Diplomacy*. Public Affairs Press. 1959.

Hacker, Louis M. *The United States, a Graphic History*. Modern Age. 1937.

Johnson, Willis Fletcher. *A Century of Expansion*. Macmillan. 1903.

Lothrop, Thornton Kirkland. *William Henry Seward*. Houghton Mifflin. 1899.

Mahan, Alfred T. *The Influence of Sea Power Upon History, 1660–1783*. Little, Brown. 1890.

Nearing, Scott, and Freeman, Joseph. *Dollar Diplomacy*. Monthly Review Press. 1966.

Owsley, Frank Lawrence. *King Cotton Diplomacy*. University of Chicago Press. 1959.

Perkins, Dexter. *The Monroe Doctrine, 1867–1907*. The Johns Hopkins Press. 1937.

Pratt, Julius W. *Expansionists of 1898*. The Johns Hopkins Press. 1936.

Schlesinger, Arthur M. *Political and Social Growth of the American People*. Macmillan. 1941.

Stone, Irving. *They Also Ran*. Doubleday, Doran. 1943.

Storey, Moorfield, and Lichauco, Marcial P. *The Conquest of the Philippines by the U.S., 1898–1925*. Putnam's. 1926.

Tyler, Alice Felt. *The Foreign Policy of James G. Blaine*. University of Minnesota Press. 1927.

United States Navy in Peace Time, The. United States Government Printing Office. 1931.

Van Alstyne, R. W. *The Rising American Empire*. Oxford. 1960.

Weinberg, Albert K. *Manifest Destiny*. Quadrangle. 1963.

Weinman, Samuel. *Hawaii, A Story of Imperialist Plunder*. International Pamphlets. Labor Research Association. 1934.

10. THE FLAG FOLLOWS COMMERCE

Beard, Charles A. *The Idea of National Interest*. Quadrangle Paperbooks. 1966.

Bicknell, Edward. *The Territorial Acquisitions of the United States*. Small, Maynard. 1899.

Cotner, Robert C.; Ezell, John S.; and Fite, Gilbert C. *Readings in American History—Vol. 2: 1865 to the present*. Houghton Mifflin. 1964.

Craven, Avery; Johnson, Walter; and Dunn, F. Roger. *A Documentary History of the American People*. Ginn. 1951.

Dulles, Foster Rhea. *America's Rise to World Power— 1898–1954*. Harper Torchbooks. 1963.

——. *The Imperial Years*. Thomas Y. Crowell Company. 1956.

Earle, Edward Mead. "The Navy's Influence on Our Foreign Policy." *Current History*. Vol. 23.

Harrington, Fred H. "The Anti-Imperialist Movement in the United States 1898–1900." *Mississippi Valley Historical Review*. Vol. 22.

Mahan, Alfred T. *The Influence of*

Sea Power upon History, 1660–1783. Little, Brown. 1890.

Millis, Walter. *The Martial Spirit*. Literary Guild of America. 1931.

Morison, Samuel E.; Merk, Frederick; and Freidal, Frank. *Dissent in Three American Wars*. Harvard University Press. 1970.

Nearing, Scott, and Freeman, Joseph. *Dollar Diplomacy*. Monthly Review Press. 1966.

Pease, Theodore Calvin, and Roberts, A. Sellew. *Selected Readings in American History*. Harcourt, Brace. 1928.

Pomeroy, William J. *American Neo-Colonialism*. International Publishers. 1970.

Pratt, Julius W. *Expansionists of 1898*. The Johns Hopkins Press. 1936.

Schlesinger, Arthur M. *Political and Social Growth of the American People, 1865–1940*. Macmillan. 1941.

Storey, Moorfield, and Lichauco, Marcial P. *The Conquest of the Philippines by the United States, 1898–1925*. Putnam's. 1926.

United States Navy in Peace Time, The. United States Government Printing Office. 1931.

Van Alstyne, R. W. *The Rising American Empire*. Oxford. 1960.

Weinberg, Albert K. *Manifest Destiny*. Quadrangle. 1963.

11. Subduing the Banana Republics

Beard, Charles A. *The Idea of National Interest*. Quadrangle Paperbooks. 1966.

Corey, Lewis. *The House of Morgan*. Grosset & Dunlap. 1930.

Cotner, Robert C.; Ezell, John S.; and Fite, Gilbert C. *Readings in American History—Vol. 2: 1865 to the present*. Houghton Mifflin. 1964.

De Riencourt, Amaury. *The American Empire*. Dial. 1968.

Dos Passos, John. *Mr. Wilson's War*. Doubleday. 1962.

Dulles, Foster Rhea. *America's Rise to World Power, 1898–1954*. Harper Torchbooks. 1963.
——. *The Imperial Years*. Thomas Y. Crowell Company. 1956.

Duroselle, Jean-Baptiste. *From Wilson to Roosevelt*. Harper Torchbooks. 1948.

Fleming, D. F. *The Origins and Legacies of World War I*. Doubleday. 1968.

Graber, D. A. *Crisis Diplomacy*. Public Affairs Press. 1959.

Horowitz, David, ed. *Corporations and the Cold War*. Monthly Review Press. 1969.

Mowry, George E. *The Era of Theodore Roosevelt*. Harper Torchbooks. 1962.

Nearing, Scott, and Freeman, Joseph. *Dollar Diplomacy*. Monthly Review Press. 1966.

Pratt, Julius W. *America's Colonial Experiment*. Prentice-Hall. 1950.

Stuart, Graham H. *Latin America and the United States*. Appleton-Century-Crofts. 1955.

Van Alstyne, R. W. *The Rising American Empire*. Oxford. 1961.

Viallate, Achille. *Economic Imperialism and International Relations During the Last Fifty Years*. Macmillan. 1923.

12. THE FINE ART OF VANDALISM

Barnes, Harry Elmer. *The Genesis of the World War*. Knopf. 1929.

Corey, Lewis. *The House of Morgan*. Grosset & Dunlap. 1930.

Duroselle, Jean-Baptiste. *From Wilson to Roosevelt*. Harper Torchbooks. 1948.

Gerassi, John. *The Great Fear*. Macmillan. 1963.

Gibbon, Thomas Edward. *Mexico Under Carranza*. Doubleday, Page. 1919.

Horowitz, David. *Empire and Revolution*. Random House. 1969.

Lewis, Cleona. *America's Stake in International Investments*. Brookings. 1938.

Nearing, Scott, and Freeman, Joseph. *Dollar Diplomacy*. Monthly Review Press. 1966.

Noyes, Alexander D. *The War Period of American Finance, 1908–1925*. Putnam's. 1926.

Osgood, Robert Endicott. *Ideals and Self-Interest in America's Foreign Relations*. University of Chicago Press. 1953.

Peterson, H. C. *Propaganda for War*. University of Oklahoma Press. 1939.

Pratt, Julius W. *America's Colonial Experiment*. Prentice-Hall. 1950.

Rochester, Anna. *Rulers of America*. International Publishers. 1936.

Stuart, Graham H. *Latin America and the United States*. Appleton-Century-Crofts. 1955.

Viallate, Achille. *Economic Imperialism and International Relations During the Last Fifty Years*. Macmillan. 1923.

Williams, Benjamin H. *Economic Foreign Policy of the United States*. McGraw-Hill. 1929.

Williams, William Appleman. *The Tragedy of American Diplomacy*. World. 1959.

13. THE BIG LEAP

Bining, Arthur Cecil. *The Rise of American Economic Life*. Scribner's. 1943.

Corey, Lewis. *The House of Morgan*. Crosset & Dunlap. 1930.

Cotner, Robert C.; Ezell, John S.; and Fite, Gilbert C. *Readings in American History*. Houghton Mifflin Company. 1964.

De Riencourt, Amaury. *The American Empire*. Dial. 1968.

Dulles, Foster Rhea. *America's Rise to World Power 1898–1954*. Harper Torchbooks. 1963.

Duranty, Walter. *USSR, The Story of Soviet Russia*. Lippincott. 1944.

Duroselle, Jean-Baptist. *From Wilson to Roosevelt*. Harper Torchbooks. 1963.

Dutt, R. Palme. *World Politics 1918–1936*. International Publishers. 1936.

Englebrecht, H. C., and Hanighen, F. C. *Merchants of Death*. Dodd, Mead. 1934.

Foner, Philip S. *The Bolshevik Revolution*. International Publishers. 1967.

Fraina, Louis C. "The War and America." *The Class Struggle*. May–June 1917. Vol. 1.

Goshal, Kumar. *People in Colonies*. Sheridan House. 1948.

Kennan, George F. *Russia and the West Under Lenin and Stalin*. Little, Brown and Co. 1960.

Lewis, Cleona. *America's Stake in International Investments*. Brookings. 1938.

Minton, Bruce, and Stuart, John. *The Fat Years and the Lean.* International Publishers. 1940.

Myers, Gustavus. *History of the Great American Fortunes.* Random House. 1937.

Nearing, Scott, and Freeman, Joseph. *Dollar Diplomacy.* Monthly Review Press. 1966.

Noyes, Alexander D. *The War Period of American Finance, 1908–1925.* Putnam's. 1926.

Osgood, Robert Endicott. *Ideals and Self-Interest in America's Foreign Relations.* University of Chicago Press. 1953.

Parkes, Henry Bamford, and Carosso, Vincent P. *Recent America—Book One: 1900–1933.* Thomas Y. Crowell Company. 1963.

Peterson, H. C. *Propaganda for War.* University of Oklahoma Press. 1939.

Rochester, Anna. *Rulers of America.* International Publishers. 1936.

Rossenbrook and Others. *Development of Contemporary Civilization.* D. C. Heath. 1940.

Trotsky, Leon. *Five Years of the Communist International.* Vol. 1. Pioneer Publishers. 1945.

Viallate, Achille. *Economic Imperialism and International Relations During the Last Fifty Years.* Macmillan. 1923.

Weisbord, Albert. *The Conquest of Power.* 2 volumes. Covici-Friede. 1937.

14. THE WAR BEFORE
THE WAR (I)

Beals, Carleton. "Cash for Brazil's Good-Will." *Current History.* April 1939.

Beard, Charles A. *The Open Door at Home.* Macmillan. 1935.

Beasley, W. G. *The Modern History of Japan.* Macmillan. 1957.

Clark, Lewis B. "Competing for Latin American Markets." *Annals of the American Academy.* September 1940.

De Riencourt, Amaury. *The American Empire.* Dial. 1968.

Dulles, Foster Rhea. *America's Rise to World Power 1898–1954.* Harper Torchbooks. 1963.

Duroselle, Jean-Baptiste. *From Wilson to Roosevelt.* Harper Torchbooks. 1968.

Dutt, R. Palme. *World Politics, 1919–1936.* International Publishers. 1936.

Feis, Herbert. *Diplomacy of the Dollar.* The Johns Hopkins Press. 1950.

Gardner, Lloyd C. *Economic Aspects of New Deal Diplomacy.* University of Wisconsin Press. 1964.

Gerassi, John. *The Great Fear.* Macmillan. 1963.

Grebler, Leo. "Self-Sufficiency and Imperialism." *Annals of the American Academy.* Vol. 198.

Hill, Howard C., and Tugwell, Rexford Guy. *Our Economic Society and Its Problems.* Harcourt, Brace. 1934.

Horowitz, David, ed. *Containment and Revolution.* Beacon. 1967.

Kolko, Gabriel. *The Roots of American Foreign Policy.* Beacon. 1969.

Latourette, Kenneth Scott. *The History of Japan.* Macmillan. 1957.

Link, Arthur S. *American Epoch, A History of the United States Since the 1890's.* Knopf. 1955.

Moran, W. T. "Our Latin American Trade Faces Financial Difficulties." *Annals of the American*

Academy. September 1940.

Nearing, Scott, and Freeman, Joseph. *Dollar Diplomacy.* Monthly Review Press. 1966.

Parkes, Henry Bamford, and Carosso, Vincent P. *Recent America—Book One: 1900–1933.* Thomas Y. Crowell Company. 1963.

Peffer, Nathaniel. "Would Japan Shut the Open Door in China?" *Foreign Affairs Quarterly.* Vol. 17.

Peterson, A. D. C. *The Far East.* Funk & Wagnalls. 1950.

Schroeder, Paul W. *The Axis Alliance and Japanese-American Relations.* Cornell University Press. 1958.

Staley, Eugene. *Raw Materials in Peace and War.* Council on Foreign Relations. 1937.

Strachey, John. "From Isolation to Empire." *The Forum.* Vol. 91.

Stuart, Graham H. *Latin America and the United States.* D. Appleton-Century. 1938.

Walter, K. "Italian Housekeeping: A Study in Autarchy." *Fortnightly.* Vol. 43.

Williams, Benjamin H. *Economic Foreign Policy of the United States.* McGraw-Hill. 1929.

Williams, William Appleman. *The Contours of American History.* World. 1961.

Young, Ralph A. "An American Foreign Investment Policy." *Annals of the American Academy.* Vol. 174.

15. The War Before
the War (II)

Beals, Carleton. *The Coming Struggle for Latin America.* Halcyon House. 1940.

Beard, Charles A. *The Idea of National Interest.* Quadrangle Paperbooks. 1966.

Beasely, W. G. *The Modern History of Japan.* Macmillan. 1957.

Bining, Arthur Cecil. *The Rise of American Economic Life.* Scribner's. 1943.

Borkenau, Franz. *The New German Empire.* Viking. 1939.

Dutt, R. Palme. *World Politics, 1919–1936.* International Publishers. 1936.

Feis, Herbert. *The Road to Pearl Harbor.* Atheneum. 1966.

Fleming, D. F. *The Cold War and Its Origins 1917–1950.* 2 volumes. Doubleday. 1961.

Gardner, Lloyd C. *Economic Aspects of New Deal Diplomacy.* University of Wisconsin Press. 1964.

Gerassi, John. *The Great Fear.* Macmillan. 1963.

Grebler, Leo. "Self-Sufficiency and Imperialism." *Annals of the American Academy.* Vol. 198.

Gunther, John. *Inside Europe.* Harper. 1938.

Hamlin, C. H. *The War Myth in United States History.* Pamphlet. Fellowship Publications. 1948.

Hofstadter, Richard. *The American Political Tradition.* Vintage. 1954.

Horowitz, David. ed. *Containment and Revolution.* Beacon. 1967.

Leuchtenberg, William E. *Franklin Roosevelt and the New Deal.* Harper Torchbooks. 1965.

Link, Arthur S. *American Epoch, A History of the United States Since the 1890's.* Knopf. 1955.

Moran, W. T. "Our Latin American Trade Faces Financial Difficulties." *Annals of the American Academy*. September 1940.

Olden, Herman. *U.S. Over Latin America*. Pamphlet. International Publishers. 1955.

Shih, Hu. "To Have Not and Want to Have." *Annals of the American Academy*. Vol. 198.

Shirer, William L. *The Rise and Fall of the Third Reich*. Simon & Schuster. 1960.

Stolper, Gustav. *German Economy 1870–1940*. Reynal & Hitchcock. 1940.

Stuart, Graham H. *Latin America and the United States*. D. Appleton-Century. 1938.

Williams, William Appleman. *The Contours of American History*. World. 1961.

———. *The Tragedy of American Diplomacy*. World. 1959.

Wolfe, Henry C., and Strauz-Hupe, Robert. "Bargains by Barter." *Current History*. April 1939.

16. AGAINST FRIEND AND FOE

Baldwin, Leland D. *The Stream of American History*. Vol. 2. American Book. 1952.

Beard, Charles A. *President Roosevelt and the Coming of the War 1941*. Yale University Press. 1948.

Broad, Lewis. *Winston Churchill, A Biography*. Hawthorn Books. 1958.

Duroselle, Jean-Baptiste. *From Wilson to Roosevelt*. Harper Torchbooks. 1948.

Fleming, D. F. *The Cold War and Its Origins 1917–1950*. 2 volumes. Doubleday. 1961.

Hamlin, C. H. *The War Myth in United States History*. Pamphlet. Fellowship Publications. 1948.

Hatch, Alden. *Franklin D. Roosevelt: An Informal Biography*. Holt. 1947.

Hofstadter, Richard. *American Political Tradition*. Vintage. 1948.

Nevins, Allan. *The New Deal and World Affairs*. Yale University Press. 1950.

Rollins, Alfred B., Jr., ed. *Franklin D. Roosevelt and the Age of Action*. Dell. 1960.

Roosevelt, Elliot. *As He Saw It*. Duell, Sloan and Pearce. 1946.

Sherwood, Robert E. *Roosevelt and Hopkins*. 2 volumes. Bantam. 1950.

Shirer, William L. *The Rise and Fall of the Third Reich*. Simon & Schuster. 1960.

Spanier, John W. *American Foreign Policy Since World War II*. Praeger. 1960.

Stavrianos, L. S. *Greece, American Dilemma and Opportunity*. Regnery. 1952.

Williams, William Appleman. *The Contours of American History*. World. 1961.

Young, Peter. *World War 1939–1945*. Thomas Y. Crowell Company. 1966.

17. GLOBAL IMPERIALISM

Acheson, Dean. *Present at the Creation*. Norton. 1969.

Alperovitz, Gar. *Atomic Diplomacy: Hiroshima and Potsdam*. Secker & Warburg. 1965.

Arevalo, Juan José. *The Shark and the Sardines*. Lyle Stuart. 1961.

Bernstein, Barton J., and Matusow, Allen J., eds. *The Truman Administration, A Documentary*

History. Harper Torchbooks. 1968.

Byrnes, James F. *Speaking Frankly.* Harper. 1947.

Craven, Avery; Johnson, Walter; and Dunn, F. Roger. *A Documentary History of the American People.* Ginn. 1951.

Davidson, Basil. "Cashing in on Old Imperialisms." *The Nation.* Sept. 13, 1952.

Fleming, D. F. *The Cold War and Its Origins 1917–1950.* 2 volumes. Doubleday. 1961.

Gardner, Lloyd C. *Architects of Illusion.* Quadrangle. 1970.

——. *Economic Aspects of New Deal Diplomacy.* University of Wisconsin Press. 1964.

Graber, D. A. *Crisis Diplomacy.* Public Affairs Press. 1959.

Horowitz, David, ed. *Corporations and the Cold War.* Monthly Review Press. 1969.

——. *The Free World Colossus.* Hill & Wang. 1965.

Kolko, Gabriel. *The Roots of American Foreign Policy.* Beacon. 1969.

McMillan, James, and Harris, Bernard. *The American Take-Over of Britain.* Hart Publishing Co. 1968.

Millis, Walter, ed. *The Forrestal Diaries.* Viking. 1951.

O'Connor, Harvey. *The Empire of Oil.* Monthly Review Press. 1955.

Ransom, Harry Howe. *Central Intelligence and National Security.* Harvard University Press. 1958.

Rollins, Alfred B., Jr., ed. *Franklin D. Roosevelt and the Age of Action.* Dell. 1960.

Smith, Howard K. *The State of Europe.* Knopf. 1949.

Spanier, John W. *American Foreign Policy Since World War II.* Praeger. 1960.

Stone, I. F. *The Hidden Story of the Korean War.* Monthly Review Press. 1952.

——. *The Truman Era.* Monthly Review Press. 1953.

Truman, Harry S. *Memoirs.* 2 volumes. Doubleday. 1955–1956.

Tully, Andrew. *CIA: The Inside Story.* Morrow. 1962.

White, Theodore H. *Fire in the Ashes.* William Sloane Associates. 1953.

Wise, David, and Ross, Thomas B. *The Invisible Government.* Random House. 1964.

18. THE ECSTASY
AND THE AGONY

Barnet, Richard J. *Intervention and Revolution.* World. 1968.

Cook, Fred J. "Juggernaut, The Warfare State." *The Nation.* October 28, 1961.

Dedijer, Vladimir. *Tito.* Simon & Schuster. 1953.

De Riencourt, Amaury. *The American Empire.* Dial. 1968.

Eisenhower, Dwight D. *Mandate for Change.* Doubleday. 1963.

——. *Waging Peace.* Doubleday. 1965.

Fischer, John. *Master Plan U.S.A.* Harper. 1951.

Fleming, D. F. *The Cold War and Its Origins 1917–1950.* 2 volumes. Doubleday. 1961.

Goshal, Kumar. *People in Colonies.* Sheridan House. 1948.

Graber, D. A. *Crisis Diplomacy.* Public Affairs Press. 1959.

Hailey, Foster. *Half of One World.* Macmillan. 1950.

Hammer, Ellen. *The Struggle for*

Indo-China, 1940–1955. Stanford University Press. 1966.

Horowitz, David. *The Free World Colossus.* Hill and Wang. 1965.

Houghton, N. D., ed. *Struggle Against History.* Simon and Schuster. 1968.

Lattimore, Owen. *The Situation in Asia.* Little, Brown. 1949.

———. *Solution in Asia.* Little, Brown. 1945.

Magdoff, Harry. *The Age of Imperialism.* Monthly Review Press. 1969.

Millis, Walter, ed. *The Forrestal Diaries.* Viking. 1951.

Morris, Christopher. *The Day They Lost the H-Bomb.* Coward-McCann. 1966.

Mowrer, Edgar Ansel. *The Nightmare of American Foreign Policy.* Knopf. 1948.

Peffer, Nathaniel. "Close-up of China in Travail." *New York Times Magazine.* May 4, 1947.

Pomeroy, William J. *Guerrilla and Counter-Guerrilla Warfare.* International Publishers. 1964.

Ransom, Harry Howe. *Central Intelligence and National Security.* Harvard University Press. 1958.

Shoup, David M. "The New American Militarism." *Atlantic Monthly.* April 1969.

Smith, Howard K. *The State of Europe.* Knopf. 1949.

Spanier, John W. *American Foreign Policy Since World War II.* Praeger. 1960.

Swomley, John M., Jr. *The Military Establishment.* Beacon. 1964.

Tully, Andrew. *CIA, The Inside Story.* Morrow. 1962.

Warburg, James P. *The United States in a Changing World.* Putnam's. 1954.

White, Theodore H. *Fire in the Ashes.* William Sloane Associates. 1953.

Wise, David, and Ross, Thomas B. *The Invisible Government.* Random House. 1964.

Zeitlin, Maurice, and Scheer, Robert. *Cuba: Tragedy in Our Hemisphere.* Grove Press. 1963.

19. CLOSING THE CIRCLE

Barnet, Richard J. *Intervention and Revolution.* World. 1968.

Committee of Concerned Asian Scholars. *The Indochina Story.* Bantam. 1970.

Cook, Fred J. "Juggernaut, The Warfare State." *The Nation.* October 22, 1968.

De Riencourt, Amaury. *The American Empire.* Dial. 1968.

Drummond, Roscoe, and Coblentz, Gaston. *Duel at the Brink.* Doubleday. 1960.

Eisenhower, Milton S. *The Wine Is Bitter.* Doubleday. 1963.

Evans, Rowland, and Novak, Robert. *Lyndon B. Johnson, the Exercise of Power.* New American Library. 1966.

Fleming, D. F. *The Cold War and Its Origins 1917–1950.* 2 volumes. Doubleday. 1961.

Gettleman, Marvin E., ed. *Viet Nam.* Fawcett. 1965.

Hersh, Seymour M. *Chemical and Biological Warfare, America's Hidden Arsenal.* Doubleday. 1969.

Horowitz, David. *The Free World Colossus.* Hill & Wang. 1965.

Houghton, N. D., ed. *The Struggle Against History.* Simon & Schuster. 1968.

Huberman, Leo, and Sweezey, Paul M. *Anatomy of a Revolu-*

tion. Monthly Review Press. 1960.

Kahin, George McTurnan, and Lewis, John W. *The United States in Vietnam*. Delta. 1967.

Kennedy, Robert. "Thirteen Days, a Personal Story About How the World Almost Ended." *McCall's*. November 1968.

Knoll, Erwin. "The Military Establishment Rides High." *Progressive*. February 1969.

Kolko, Gabriel. *The Roots of American Foreign Policy*. Beacon. 1969.

Kondracke, Morton. "Washington's Whispered Issue: Our First Strike Capability." *The Washington Monthly*. June 1969.

Lacouture, Jean. *Vietnam: Between Two Truces*. Random House. 1966.

Lukacs, John. *A New History of the Cold War*. Doubleday. 1962.

Matthews, Herbert. *The Cuban Story*. Braziller. 1961.

Rice, Berkeley. "The Cold-War College Think Tanks." *The Washington Monthly*. June 1969.

Ridgeway, James. *The Closed Corporation, America's Universities in Crisis*. Ballantine. 1969.

Schlesinger, Arthur Jr. *A Thousand Days*. Houghton Mifflin. 1965.

Sorenson, Theodore C. *Kennedy*. Harper. 1965.

Szulc, Tad. *Dominican Diary*. Farrar, Straus & Giroux. 1966.

Szulc, Tad, and Meyer, Karl E. *The Cuban Invasion*. Ballantine. 1962.

Wise, David, and Ross, Thomas B. *The Invisible Government*. Random House. 1964.

Woytinsky, W. S. "The United States and Latin America's Economy." *New Leader Supplement*. November 24, 1958.

Zeitlin, Maurice, and Scheer, Robert. *Cuba: Tragedy in Our Hemisphere*. Grove Press. 1963.

INDEX

Abel, Annie H., 43
Aberdeen, Lord, 119
Acheson, Dean, 6, 338, 341, 356, 372, 373, 392
Adams, Abigail, 90
Adams, Brooks, 166, 176
Adams, Charles Francis, 129, 180
Adams, Henry, 84, 86
Adams, James Truslow, 138
Adams, John, 2, 24-26, 28, 32-34, 40, 73
Adams, John Quincy, 3, 44, 89-91, 93-98, 105, 112, 113, 116, 123, 129, 176
Adams, Samuel, 2, 11, 16, 54
Addams, Jane, 180
Adenauer, Konrad, 354, 359
Adzhubei, Alexei, 410
Aguinaldo, Emilio, 175, 182-184, 186, 187, 191
Alexander, Robert J., 411
Alien and Sedition Acts, 17, 29-31, 34, 76
Allen, Gardner W., 18, 35
Allende, Salvador, 419
Alliance for Progress, 339, 351, 391, 405, 412-416
Alperovitz, Gar, 343
Alsop, Joseph, 345, 359, 423
Alsop, Stewart, 359
American Anti-Imperialist League, 12, 180
American Federation of Labor, 361, 391, 399
American Federation of Labor–Congress of Industrial Organizations, 383, 391, 399, 401-403
American Institute for Free Labor Development, 383, 401, 402
Ames, Fisher, 29
Ampudia, Pedro de, 125, 128
Anderson, George S., 189

Anderson, T. M., 183
Angell, Norman, 288
Appleton, Nathan, 129
Arbenz, Jacobo, 389-391, 405, 409
Arbuthnot, Alexander, 93
Arevalo, Juan José, 362, 389, 416
Arias, Desiderio, 226
Arista, Mariano, 125
Ashmun, George, 131
Atchison, David R., 101
Atlantic Charter, 324, 329, 331
Austin, Moses, 103
Austin, Stephen F., 103, 106-108, 119
Ayres, Leonard, 287

Bache, Benjamin F., 28
Bacon, Ezekiel, 78
Bacon, Robert, 193, 255
Bader, George W., 398
Bao Dai, 371, 372
Bailey, Thomas A., 70, 73, 174, 210
Bancroft, George, 101, 120, 125
Balaguer, Joaquin, 419
Barnet, Richard J., 390
Barrientos, Rene, 416
Baruch, Bernard, 343
Batista, Fulgencio, 309, 405, 412
Beard, Charles, 291, 297, 333
Beard, Charles and Mary, 16, 44, 78, 105
Beck, Ludwig, 314
Beirne, Joseph, 402
Bell, J. M., 187, 188
Bender, Frank, 408
Beneš, Eduard, 364
Benezet, Anthony, 10
Benoit, Pedro Bartolome, 418
Bent, Charles, 128
Benton, Thomas Hart, 100, 105, 119, 120, 124, 128
Berger, Victor, 262

453

Berle, Adolf, 323
Bernstorff, Johann von, 258
Beveridge, Albert, 166, 170, 175, 178, 181
Bevin, Ernest, 353, 363
Bidault, Georges, 422
Bidwell, John, 121
Bierut, Boleslaw, 339
Biffle, Leslie, 335
Birney, James Gillespie, 117, 118
Bismarck, Otto von, 165
Black, Hugo L., 315
Black Dragon Society, 289
Black, P. M. S., 348
Blaine, James G., 159-163, 165, 167, 265
Blount, William, 70
Bodenheimer, Susanne, 401
Bohlen, Charles E., 342
Bolivar, Simón, 88, 89, 91, 95, 395, 409
Bolles, Blair, 308
Bonaparte, Joseph, 64
Bonaparte, Napoleon, 34, 35, 64, 66, 68, 74, 88, 89, 96
Bonifacio, Andres, 182
Boone, Daniel, 50, 51
Boothby, Robert, 338
Borah, William E., 268, 316
Bosch, Juan, 416-419
Boudinot, Elias, 45
Boutwell, George S., 180
Bowles, Chester, 357
Braden, Thomas W., 400
Bradford, William, 42
Brandeis, Louis D., 219
Briand, Aristide, 283
Brock, Isaac, 59, 60, 81
Brown, David, 30
Brown, Irving, 399, 400, 402, 403
Bryan, William Jennings, 6, 170, 179, 180, 185, 203, 210, 214, 220-223, 226, 231, 239, 250, 256
Bryant, William Cullen, 101
Buchanan, James, 122, 127, 132, 133
Bullitt, William C., 273
Bunau-Varilla, Philippe, 200-202
Bundy, William, 403
Burnet, David G., 103
Burr, Aaron, 34, 71, 76, 102, 103
Burritt, Elihu, 12, 130
Bush, Vannevar, 349
Butler, Anthony, 105
Butler, Smedley D., 270
Byrnes, James F., 315, 334, 339, 343, 344, 346, 348, 349, 351

Caamaño Deño, Francisco, 417
Cabell, C. P., 405

Caffery, Jefferson, 309
Calhoun, John C., 75, 80, 92, 93, 107, 114, 119, 123, 126, 129, 130, 133, 134, 155
Callender, James Thomas, 30
Camacho, Manuel Ávila, 311
Campbell, Alex, 370
Canning, George, 97
Cannon, Howard, 382
Caperton, W. B., 223, 224
Carden, Lionel, 230
Cárdenas, Lázaro, 310, 311
Carnegie, Andrew, 12, 180, 185, 247
Carosso, Vincent P., 279, 281
Carranza, Venustiano, 230-233
Carson, Kit, 143
Cass, Lewis, 132
Castelo Branco, Humberto, 402, 414, 417
Castillo Armas, Carlos, 390, 391
Castlereagh, Lord, 69, 80
Castro, Fidel, 405, 406, 409, 410, 436
Catledge, Turner, 385
Central Intelligence Agency, 5, 341, 361-363, 368, 373, 383, 385, 387, 388, 390, 391, 395, 396, 398-401, 403, 405, 408-410, 429, 431, 432
Central Treaty Organization (CENTO), 362, 367, 392
Cespedes, Juan de los Santos, 418
Chamberlain, Neville, 306
Chamberlin, William Henry, 273
Chamoun, Camille, 393
Channing, Edward, 35
Cheesekau, 51, 52
Chester, Colby M., 211
Cheves, Langdon, 78
Chiang Kai-shek, 360, 371-373, 376, 379
Chipman, John S., 101
Chivington, J. M., 143
Chou En-lai, 378
Church, Frank, 419
Churchill, Winston, 271, 275, 302, 316-320, 324, 326-332, 336, 337, 343-345, 348
Clark, Champ, 220
Clark, Dan E., 41
Clark, George Rogers, 19, 51
Clay, Henry, 65, 75-80, 84, 89, 93, 96, 101, 105, 115-118, 134, 159
Clay, Lucius D., 354, 381
Clayton, William L., 352, 356, 357, 368
Clemenceau, Georges, 266, 271
Cleveland, Grover, 10, 12, 164, 169-171, 179, 180, 248, 287
Clifford, Clark, 381

Clos, Max, 423
Cobbett, William, 29, 33
Cochise, 146, 148
Cody, William F., 136
Coffee, John, 61
Conant, Charles A., 167
Conger, E. H., 176
Conquering Bear, 141, 142
Conrad, Joseph, 255
Cook, Fred J., 384
Cook, James, 162
Cooke, Jay, 247
Coolidge, Calvin, 275, 281, 282, 294
Cooper, Thomas, 30
Corey, Lewis, 245, 246
Cornstalk, 51
Corwin, Thomas, 126, 153
Cowdray, Lord, 229, 230
Craig, James, 78, 79
Craig, William, 79
Crazy Horse, 40, 138, 141-146, 148
Crockett, Davy, 103, 108
Crofts, Alfred, 377
Cromwell, William Nelson, 200-202, 249
Crook, George, 138, 144, 145
Crowder, Enoch H., 194
Crowley, Leo, 342
Cushing, Caleb, 155, 156
Custer, George A., 41, 135, 138, 144, 145
Czolgosz, Leon, 197

Daladier, Edouard, 306
Daniel, Jean, 410, 411
Dartiguenave, Philippe Sudre, 223
Davis, Garrett, 125
Davis, Hart, 86
Davis, Jefferson, 160
Davison, Henry P., 251
Dawson, Thomas C., 206, 212
Day, William R., 176, 182
Dearborn, Henry, 81
Debs, Eugene, 262
Decatur, Stephen, 82
de Gasperi, Alcide, 359
de Gaulle, Charles, 316, 318, 331, 345, 346
Delaney, George P., 402
Delano, Columbus, 126, 130
Dellinger, David, 426
Denby, Charles, 190
Deniken, Anton, 272, 274
de Riencourt, Amaury, 366, 396
Devillers, Philippe, 423
Dewey, George, 173, 175, 177, 179, 182-184, 189, 190
Dewey, John, 291, 334

Díaz, Adolfo, 211-214, 221
Díaz, Porfirio, 228-230
Díaz Lanz, Pedro, 406
Dickinson, Daniel S., 132
Diem, Ngo Dinh, 423, 424
Dirksen, Everett, 7, 156
Dix, John A., 125
Doheny, Edward L., 229-232
Doherty, William C., Jr., 402
Douglas, Helen Gahagan, 428
Douglas, Stephen A., 126
Draper, William H., 342, 354
Dubinsky, David, 399
Dulles, Allen W., 387, 388, 400, 408
Dulles, Foster Rhea, 190, 203, 298
Dulles, John Foster, 345, 359, 364, 387, 390, 393, 421, 422
Dunmore, Lord, 50, 51
Dupuy, R. Ernest, 7
Duranty, Walter, 273, 274
Dwight, Timothy, 16

EAM (National Liberation Front of Greece), 330, 355, 370
Eastland Subcommittee, 386
Eaton, William, 36-39
Eden, Anthony, 344
Edwards, Hayden, 104, 107
Eisenhower, Dwight D., 12, 285, 325, 336, 347, 363, 367, 379, 385-393, 395, 404, 406-408, 411, 420-422, 428, 431
Eisenhower Doctrine, 392-394
Eliot, Charles W., 180
Emerson, Ralph Waldo, 101
Erskine, David, 73, 74
Estrada, Juan J., 212, 213
Estrada Palma, Tomás, 210
Export-Import Bank, 298, 309-311, 413, 415

Fall, Albert B., 231
Farnham, Roger L., 225
Farouk, King, 392
Faulkner, Harold G., 66, 152
Franklin, Benjamin, 11, 17, 28, 41
Feisal, King, 393
Ferdinand, Archduke Franz, 239
Ferdinand VII, King, 88, 96
Ferri-Pisani, Pierre, 400
Fillmore, Millard, 156
Finletter, Thomas K., 364
Fish, Hamilton, 158
Fisk, Jim, 246
Fiske, John, 166
Fleming, D. F., 345
Fletcher, Frank F., 254
Foch, Ferdinand, 272

Foraker, Joseph, 209
Forrestal, James V., 342, 345, 347, 348, 351, 353, 354, 381
Fourteen Points, 265-268, 285
Fraina, Louis C., 251
Franco, Francisco, 306, 398
Frank, Waldo, 88
Frankfurter, Felix, 222, 323
Franklin, Benjamin, 147
Freeman, Gaylord A., 434
Freeman, Joseph, 225
Frei, Eduardo, 415
Frelinghuysen, Frederick T., 158
Frémont, John C., 120, 127, 128, 178, 246
Fries Rebellion, 17, 31, 32
Frondizi, Arturo, 416
Frost, John, 52
Fulbright, J. William, 7, 384, 395, 419, 427
Fulton, Hugh, 336
Funston, Frederick, 191

Gaines, Edmund P., 92, 110, 113
Gall, 145, 148
Gallatin, Albert, 30, 64, 83, 129
Gandhi, Mahatma, 369
Ganoe, William Addleman, 7
Gardner, Arthur, 405
Gardner, Lloyd C., 307, 311
Garfield, James A., 12, 160
Garner, John Nance, 335
Garrison, William Lloyd, 244
Gary, Elbert H., 255
Gelder, Stuart, 358
Genêt, Edmond Charles, 18, 19
Gerard, James W., 253, 256
Gerassi, John, 412
Geronimo, 146, 148
Gerry, Elbridge, 25, 32, 33, 70
Geyelin, Philip, 418
Giap, Vo Nguyen, 371
Gibbons, Harold, 403
Giddings, Joshua R., 126, 130
Gifford, Walter S., 287
Giles, William Branch, 71
Glynn, James, 156
Goering, Hermann, 305, 317
Goldman, Emma, 262
Goldwater, Barry, 420, 421, 428
Gompers, Samuel, 180, 217
Gonzales, William E., 194
Goodell, Charles, 427
Gore, Albert, 427
Gorman, Pat, 403
Goulart, João, 414, 417
Goulburn, Henry, 82

Gould, Jay, 246
Grace, W. R., 227
Grant, Ulysses S., 12, 129, 147, 158, 208, 209
Grattan, J. L., 142
Grau San Martin, Ramón, 308, 309
Greeley, Horace, 147
Green, Duff, 114
Green, William, 399
Greenblatt, Robert, 426
Grenville, Lord, 23, 24
Grey, Edward, 258, 259
Grouard, Frank, 140
Gruenberg, Robert, 382
Gruening, Ernest, 427
Grundy, Felix, 75, 77-79, 116
Guerrero, Vicente, 104
Gunther, John, 354

Haile Selassie, 304, 398
Hailey, Foster, 374
Haines, Francis, 137
Halder, Franz, 314
Halifax, Lord, 302
Hamilton, Alexander, 14, 16, 17, 19-27, 29, 31, 32, 34, 35, 71, 88, 243
Hammer, Ellen J., 371
Hanna, Mark, 170, 173, 176, 178, 198, 200
Hannegan, Robert, 336
Hanotaux, Gabriel, 254, 255
Harding, Warren G., 225, 234, 275, 283-285
Harmar, Josiah, 52
Harney, William S., 141
Harriman, W. Averell, 342
Harrison, Benjamin, 160, 180
Harrison, William Henry, 12, 49, 54, 56-58, 60, 78, 81, 114, 135
Hart, Thomas, 76
Harte, Bret, 158
Harvey, George, 219, 230
Hatch, Alden, 323
Hatta, Mohammed, 369, 374
Hawkins, Willis, 382
Hawthorne, Nathaniel, 147
Hay, John, 174, 199, 201, 202, 207, 279, 280
Hayes, Rutherford B., 12, 136, 161
Haywood, William D., 262
Henry, John, 78, 79
Henry, Patrick, 45
Henry, T. C., 138
Herran, Tomás, 201
Herrera, José, 122
Herter, Christian, 406
Hidalgo, Miguel, 64, 89, 102, 103, 395

Hill, Howard C., 288
Hirohito, Emperor, 326
Hiss, Alger, 428
Hitler, Adolf, 13, 292, 293, 300, 302, 304-306, 314-320, 322, 323, 326, 328, 330, 332, 353, 399
Hoar, George F., 179, 180
Ho Chi Minh, 371, 374
Hodge, John R., 374, 375
Hoffman, Paul, 342
Hofstadter, Richard, 327
Holland, Thomas, 289
Holy Alliance, 96-98
Hoover, Herbert Clark, 271, 281, 282, 284-293, 295, 298, 307
Hopkins, Harry, 328, 315
Hopkins, Samuel, 81
House, Edward Mandell, 219, 220, 230, 253, 254, 258, 259, 267, 272
House Committee on Un-American Activities (HUAC), 386, 404, 428
Houston, Sam, 60, 105-111, 114, 120
Howe, Louis, 294
Hu Shih, 304
Hudson, Charles, 130, 131
Huerta, Victoriano, 220, 230, 232
Hughes, Charles Evans, 283
Hukbalahap, 370, 371
Hull, Cordell, 277, 298, 309, 310, 321, 338, 339
Hull, Isaac, 82
Hull, William, 59, 81
Humphrey, Hubert H., 427
Huntington, Samuel P., 392
Hussein, King, 393

Illia, Arturo, 416
Irving, Washington, 73, 107
Iturbide, Agustín de, 103

Jackson, Andrew, 12, 44-51, 60-62, 65, 81, 90, 92, 94, 100, 105, 107-113, 115-117, 119-121
Jackson, Helen Hunt, 139, 147
Jackson, Jesse, 385
Jagan, Cheddi, 400, 401
James, Marquis, 48, 103
James, William, 180
Jay, John, 13, 23, 24
Jefferson, Thomas, 2, 3, 11, 14, 19, 20, 22, 23, 28, 30, 31, 33, 34, 36, 37, 40, 43, 56, 63, 64, 70-73, 90, 97, 99, 100, 139, 150, 243, 248
Johnson, Andrew, 158
Johnson, J. W., 225
Johnson, Lyndon B., 14, 313, 323, 372, 385, 401, 417, 418, 420-422, 422-428

Johnson, Richard M., 65, 75
Jones, Anson, 119
Jones, Thomas Ap Catesby, 122
Jordan, David Starr, 180
Joseph, Chief, 146, 148
Juárez, Pablo Benito, 153
Junaluska, 48

Kamehameha, King, 163
Karamanli, Hamet, 37-39
Karamanli, Yusuf, 36, 38, 39
Kassem, Karim, 393, 394
Katzenbach, Nicolas de B., 425
Kaufman, Richard F., 383
Kearney, Stephen W., 127, 128
Keating, Kenneth, 409
Kellogg, Frank, 283
Kennan, George, 346
Kennedy, Edward M., 427
Kennedy, John F., 362, 367, 371, 372, 385, 395, 404, 408-413, 415, 416, 420, 421, 424, 428, 429
Kerensky, Alexander, 272
Kerner, Otto, 385
Kerr, Robert, 420
Key, Francis Scott, 81
Keyes, Geoffrey, 381
Keynes, John Maynard, 284, 296
Khoman, Thanat, 397
Khrushchev, Nikita, 385, 410, 411
Kilduff, Malcolm, 385
King, Preston, 129
King, Rufus, 27
Kingoro, Hashimoto, 303
Kipling, Rudyard, 186, 255
Kissinger, Henry, 428
Knight, O. A., 401
Knox, Frank, 317, 321
Knox, Henry, 27, 42
Knox, Philander C., 194, 208, 213-215, 222, 224
Kolchak, Alexander, 272, 274
Kun, Béla, 274
Konoye, Fumimaro, 314
Ky, Nguyen Cao, 425

Lacerda, Carlos, 417
Ladd, William, 11
Lafayette, Marquis de, 89
LeFeber, Walter, 94
Laffite, Jean, 103
La Follette, Robert M., 10, 217, 219, 253-255
La Guardia, Fiorello, 352
Lamar, Mirabeau B., 113
Lamont, Thomas W., 253, 255, 260, 280, 307

Landis, Kenesaw Mountain, 262
Lansing, Robert, 4, 6, 223, 224, 226, 233, 250, 254, 257, 258, 267
Lattimore, Owen, 375
Laulewasika, "the Prophet," 55, 56, 58
Laval, Pierre, 317
Lawrence, James, 81
Lea, Homer, 13
Leahy, William D., 323, 342, 343, 347
Lear, Tobias, 38
Lease, Mary Elizabeth, 284
Leckie, Robert, 217, 303
Lee, Ernest S., 401
Lee, Fitzhugh, 172
Lee, Robert E., 129
Lees-Smith, H. B., 290
Lehman, Herbert H., 295, 352
LeMay, Curtis, 416
Lend-Lease, 318, 320, 323, 337-339, 343, 351
Lenin, V. I., 271-274, 436
Lesseps, Ferdinand de, 161, 198
Letcher, Marion, 228
Leuchtenberg, William E., 294
Lewis, Flora, 397
Lieuwen, Edwin, 407
Liliuokalani, Queen, 164
Lincoln, Abraham, 131, 181
Lindley, Ernest K., 323
Link, Arthur S., 310
Lippmann, Walter, 294
Little Crow, 142
Litvinov, Maxim, 297, 298
Lloyd George, David, 266, 267, 271-273, 302
Lodge, Henry Cabot, 6, 166, 167, 170, 171, 173, 177, 185, 196, 199, 201, 268
Lodge, Henry Cabot, Jr., 390, 422, 424
Logan, George, 33
Lomax, Louis, 398
Lome, Dupuy de, 172
Lon Nol, 431
Long, James, 102, 103
Long, John D., 172, 175
Lovestone, Jay, 383, 391, 399, 400, 402, 403
Louis XVI, 15-17, 24
Louisiana Purchase, 2, 35, 64, 99
L'Ouverture, Toussaint, 29, 222
Lovejoy, Elijah, 113
Lovett, Robert A., 342
Low, Maurice A., 261
Lowell, James Russell, 131
Lowell, John, 84
Lowndes, William, 159
Luce, Clare Booth, 359

Luce, Henry, 380
Ludlow, Nicoll, 164
Ludendorff, Erich von, 263
Lundy, Benjamin, 112
Lynd, Staughton, 426
Lyttelton, Oliver, 322
Lyuh, Woon Hyung, 374

Mabini, Apolinario, 181, 182
McAdoo, William G., 265
MacArthur, Arthur, 187, 188, 190
MacArthur, Douglas, 175, 326, 331, 352, 354, 369, 370, 376-379, 381, 386
Macay, Spruce, 47
McCabe, William Howard, 401
McCarthy, Eugene, 10
McClellan, Andrew, 401
McClellan, George B., 129
McElroy, Neil H., 381
McFarland, Ernest, 420
McGaffin, William, 382
McGillivray, Alexander, 43
McGovern, George, 10, 427
MacGregor, Gregor, 92
Machado, Gerardo, 270, 308
McHenry, James, 25, 26
McKinley, William, 14, 170-175, 177-179, 183, 185-187, 188, 189, 191, 192, 197, 209
McMillan, James, 337
McNairy, John, 47, 48
McNamara, Robert S., 381, 396, 416, 424
McNickle, D'Arcy, 42
Macon, Nathaniel, 63
Macon's Bill No. 2, 72, 74
Madero, Francisco, 220, 228, 230, 232
Madison, Dolly, 73, 82
Madison, James, 10, 14, 23, 36, 37, 59, 62, 64, 68, 70, 73, 74, 77-79, 82, 84, 91, 97
Madriz, José, 212
Magee, Augustus, 102
Magoon, Charles E., 193
Mahan, Alfred T., 13, 166-168, 170, 171, 196, 386
Makris, Fotis, 400
Mangam, Sherry, 317
Mansfield, Mike, 432
Manypenny, G. W., 147
Mao Tse-tung, 345, 372, 373, 376, 436
Marcy, William L., 163
Marshall, George C., 321, 329, 330, 357, 363, 372, 381, 387
Marshall, John, 15, 25, 43, 44

Marshall Plan, 339, 351, 352, 357, 358, 361, 363-367, 369, 413, 414
Martin, Graham, 398
Martin, John Bartlow, 418
Martin, Joseph, 379
Masaryk, Jan, 339, 364
Mason, William E., 179
Massachusetts Peace Society, 11
Mather, Cotton, 42
Mathews, George, 65, 79
Mazey, Emil, 403
Meade, E. Grant, 374
Meade, Richard W., 165
Meany, George, 399, 401, 403
Mendès-France, Pierre, 423
Mendieta, Carlos, 309
Merritt, Wesley, 178, 183, 184
Metternich, Prince Clemens von, 96, 97, 395
Mier y Terán, Don Manuel de, 104, 105, 107
Mikoyan, Anastas, 407
Mikva, Abner, 385
Miles, Nelson A., 145, 254
Miller, Jack, 382
Millis, Walter, 184
Mills, C. Wright, 404
Minh, Duong Van, 424
Miranda, Sebastian Francisco de, 27, 88, 103
Molotov, Vyacheslav M., 334, 342, 347, 357, 363
Moltke, Helmuth von, 239
Monnet, Jean, 345
Monroe, James, 70, 83, 89, 91, 94, 96-98, 100
Monroe Doctrine, 88, 95, 97, 98, 204, 206, 215, 253, 266
Montojo y Pasaron, Patricio, 175
Moody, John, 247
Moran, W. T., 301
Morelos, José María, 89
Morfit, Henry M., 111
Morgan, John Pierpont, 210, 227, 228, 242, 245-249
Morgan, J. Pierpont, Jr., 249-252, 255, 283
Morgan, John T., 200
Morgan, Joseph, 244
Morgan, Junius Spencer, 244-246
Morgan, Miles, 244
Morgenthau, Henry, 314
Morison, Samuel Eliot, 24, 72, 134, 146, 147, 232, 275
Morris, Thomas, 112
Morse, Jedidiah, 43
Morse, Wayne, 10, 427

Moscoso, Teodore, 415
Mossadegh, Mohammed, 341, 387-389
Murray, William Vans, 33, 34
Mussolini, Benito, 302, 304, 306, 316, 330
Muste, A. J., 10, 426

Naguib, Mohammed, 392
Nasser, Gamal Abdel, 392, 393, 419
National Liberation Front of South Vietnam, 421, 423, 424, 426, 430
Nearing, Scott, 225
Nelson, Donald M., 341, 380
Nelson, Lord, 69
Nevins, Allan, 115
Nhu, Ngo Dinh, 424
Nicholas, Tsar, 272
Nicola, Lewis, 10
Niles, Hezekiah, 84
Nixon, Richard M., 12, 372, 391, 404, 406, 409, 411, 427-429, 431, 435
Nixon Doctrine, 429, 430
Nolan, Philip, 102
Norris, George W., 10, 260
North Atlantic Treaty Organization (NATO), 362-365, 367, 395, 422, 433
Norton, Charles Eliot, 180
Nuri es-Said, 393

Obregón, Alvaro, 230
O'Donnell, Emmet, 379
O'Hare, Kate Richards, 262
O'Higgins, Bernardo, 91, 95
O'Keefe, Gerard P., 402
Olney, Richard, 12
Ongonia, Juan Carlos, 416
Onis, Luis de, 91, 92, 94
Orlando, Vittorio, 266, 267
Oskison, John M., 59
O'Sullivan, John L., 3, 101, 102
Otis, Elwell S., 184, 185, 187, 189, 190
Overton, John, 48
Owsley, Alvin, 302

Packard, David, 381
Page, Walter Hines, 219, 230, 239, 253, 254, 258, 260, 285
Papadopoulos, George, 365
Paredes, Mariano, 122
Parkes, Henry Bamford, 279, 281
Parris, Robert, 426
Parrott, William, 122
Pauncefote, Lord, 12, 199
Pawley, William D., 405
Paz Estenssoro, Victor, 416
Peabody, George, 245
Pearl Harbor, 321, 322, 325, 329

Pearson, Drew, 334
Peck, Sidney, 426
Peithmann, Irvin M., 45
Peña, Roque Sáenz, 162
Pendergast, Tom, 335, 336
Penn, William, 41
Peralta, Enrique, 416
Peralte, Charlemagne, 225
Perry, Matthew C., 156, 157
Perry, Oliver H., 60, 81
Pershing, John J., 174, 233, 263
Pétain, Henri, 317
Peterson, Howard C., 258, 384
Peurifoy, John E., 390
Pickering, Timothy, 25, 29, 33, 34, 38, 71, 84
Pickett, John T., 153
Pierce, Franklin, 12, 163
Pierpont, John, 243, 244
Pinchot, Amos, 247
Pinckney, Charles C., 24-26, 34
Pishevari, Jafar, 340, 341
Platt Amendment, 8, 192, 193, 204, 210, 224, 254, 309
Plummer, William, 76
Polk, James K., 3, 14, 113, 115-130, 132, 133, 136
Polk, Judd, 404
Pontiac, 50, 54
Porter, David, 155
Porter, Peter B., 65, 75, 78
Porter, Robert W., Jr., 397
Potsdam Conference, 343, 346
Powers, Gary, 385
Pratt, Julius W., 205, 214
Pratt, Spencer, 182
Prentiss, Charles, 63
Prevost, George, 82
Price, Sterling, 128
Proctor, Henry, 59, 60
Prothro, James Warren, 283
Proxmire, William, 382
Puckeshinwa, 50, 51
Pulitzer, Joseph, 173
Pu Yi, 289

Quincy, Josiah, 75
Quisling, Vidkun, 316

Radford, Arthur, 422
Ramadier, Paul, 359
Randolph, John, 80
Rankin, Jeanette, 322
Rayburn, Sam, 420
Reed, Thomas B., 180
Reid, Cabral Donald, 417
Reischauer, Edwin O., 371

Reston, James, 362, 416
Reuther, Walter, 420
Reza, Shah, 340, 388, 389
Rhee, Syngman, 374-377
Ridgway, Matthew B., 379
Rizal y Mercado, José, 181, 182
Robinson, Donald, 5, 400
Rockefeller, John D., 229, 282
Roosevelt, Eleanor, 294, 323
Roosevelt, Elliott, 327, 330
Roosevelt, Franklin Delano, 14, 278, 279, 286, 290, 292-296, 298, 299, 304, 306, 308-315, 317-324, 327-336, 338, 339, 341, 342, 344, 348, 372, 380, 387, 406, 420
Roosevelt, Kermit, 388
Roosevelt, Theodore, 3, 4, 12, 166, 168, 170, 171, 173, 174, 191-193, 196-210, 217, 248, 249, 254, 258
Roosevelt Corollary, 204-206, 221
Root, Elihu, 192, 193, 222
Rose, Jerry A., 423
Rosenblum, Frank, 403
Rosenman, Samuel L., 323
Ross, Thomas B., 373
Rowen, H. S., 382
Roxas, Manuel, 369, 370
Royce, Charles C., 41
Ruddell, Stephen, 49
Rush, Richard, 97
Rusk, Dean, 397, 403
Rusk, Howard, 413
Russell, John H., 225
Russell, Richard B., 420

Salvador, David, 407
San Martin, José de, 91, 95, 395
Santa Anna, Antonio López de, 106-110, 121, 132, 134
Sato, Eisaku, 347
Schachner, Nathan, 16
Schacht, Hjalmar, 300, 301, 305
Scheer, Robert, 407
Schiller, Herbert I., 356
Schlesinger, Arthur, Jr., 367, 408, 409
Schneider, Jacob, 30
Schurman, Jacob, 189, 190
Schurz, Carl, 180, 181, 197
Schwarzkopf, H. Norman, 388
Scott, Winfield, 128, 129, 131-133
Sears, Louis Martin, 73
Selden, Armistead I., Jr., 396
Serra, Junipero, 120
Seward, William Henry, 153, 154, 157
Sforza, Count, 330
Shaw, Albert, 222
Sheehan, Neil, 400

Sheridan, Philip H., 136
Sherwood, Robert, 329, 330
Sibley, Henry, 143
Sigsbee, C. D., 172
Sihanouk, Norodom, 431
Sikes, Robert, 382
Sims, William S., 262
Sitting Bull, 138, 140, 141, 144, 146, 148
Slidell, John, 118, 124
Sloat, John D., 120, 127, 173
Smith, Caleb B., 129
Smelser, Marshall, 67, 68
Smith, Alfred E., 286
Smith, E. T., 406
Smith, Howard K., 338, 340, 342, 353
Smith, Jake, 188
Smith, Robert, 38
Smith, Walter Bedell, 345
Smith, William, 25, 70
Smuts, Jan, 267
Smyth, Alexander, 81
Somoza, Anastasio, 227
Southeast Asia Treaty Organization (SEATO), 362, 367, 392, 431
Spanier, John W., 363
Spencer, Herbert, 166
Sperry, Henry M., 422
Sprenger, A., 237
Staley, Eugene, 279, 299
Stalin, Joseph, 312, 316, 319, 320, 323, 324, 327, 328, 331, 332, 344, 345, 348, 372
Stark, Harold I., 321
Stavrianos, L. S., 330
St. Clair, Arthur, 14, 40, 44, 52
Steffens, Lincoln, 273
Steinhart, Frank, 193
Stephen, James, 68
Stevens, John L., 164
Stevenson, Adlai, III, 385
Stewart, George C., 389
Stillwell, Richard G., 398
Stilwell, Joseph, 372
Stimson, Henry L., 277, 289, 307, 308, 317, 321, 343, 347, 348
Stockton, Robert F., 127
Stokes, Rose Pastor, 262
Storey, Moorfield, 180, 183
Straight, Willard, 211, 228
Strong, Josiah, 166
Stuntz, Homer, 189
Sukarno, Achmed, 369, 374
Sulzberger, Arthur, 322
Sumner, Charles E., 129, 130
Sumner, William Graham, 180
Sun Yat-sen, 221

Sung, Kim Il, 375, 378, 436
Sylvester, Arthur, 385
Szilard, Leo, 349
Szulc, Tad, 418

Taft, Alphonso, 209
Taft, William Howard, 4, 190, 191, 193, 197, 207-211, 214, 215, 217, 221, 224, 230, 233, 283, 294
Talleyrand, Charles Maurice de, 25, 32, 33
Taylor, Maxwell D., 360, 361, 382, 424
Taylor, Zachary, 12, 124, 125, 128, 130-132, 178
Tecumseh, 47, 49-60, 62, 74, 81, 138, 146
Teller, Edward, 383
Teller, H. M., 174
Thieu, Nguyen Van, 425
Thompson, Waddy, 121
Thoreau, Henry David, 10, 86, 131
Thorez, Maurice, 345
Thornton, William, 83
Thurmond, Strom, 382
Tippetts, Charles S., 290
Tirena, Tomás C., 370
Togliatti, Palmiro, 345, 359
Togo, Heihachiro, 347
Tojo, Hideki, 314
Toombs, Robert, 129
Tracy, Uriah, 25, 70
Travis, William Barret, 108
Treaty of Ghent, 80
Treaty of Guadalupe Hidalgo, 133
Treaty of Greenville, 41, 53
Treaty of Vincennes, 41
Trippe, Juan, 282
Trist, Nicholas P., 133
Trotsky, Leon, 266, 273, 297
Trujillo, Rafael, 227, 416, 419
Truman, Harry, 14, 333-336, 338, 339, 341-343, 346-348, 355, 357, 363, 372, 375-379, 386, 387, 408, 411, 420
Truman Doctrine, 355, 356, 422
Tsaldaris, Constantine, 355
Tugwell, Rexford G., 288, 296, 386
Tulley, Andrew, 361, 388
Tumulty, Joseph P., 243
Turnbull, Walter, 390
Twain, Mark, 12, 180, 189
Tyler, John, 114, 117, 119
Tyrell, Sir William, 228

Ubico, Jorge, 389, 390
Umberto, Crown Prince, 330
Underwood, Oscar W., 220

United Nations, 331, 332, 352, 376-
378, 390
United Nations Relief and Rehabilitation Administration (UNRRA),
352, 357
Upshur, Abel P., 114

Van Buren, Martin, 45, 112-115, 119,
125
Vandenberg, Arthur, 321, 340
Vanderlip, Frank A., 176, 239
Varona, Manuel Antoniode, 408
Vest, George C., 179
Victor Emmanuel, 330
Vidaurri, Santiago, 153
Vietminh, 370, 371, 422, 423, 431
Villa, Francisco, 230-233
Vincent, Stenio, 227
Voltaire, E. M. A. de, 41
Voorhis, Jerry, 428

Walker, Francis A., 147
Walker, Robert J., 132
Walker, Walton, 378
Wallace, Henry A., 297, 333, 334, 336
Warburg, Paul M., 265
Washington, Booker T., 198
Washington, George, 2, 9-12, 14, 15,
17-21, 24-26, 33, 34, 42, 48, 52, 90,
154
Wayne, Anthony, 14, 53, 54
Weathford, Billy (Red Eagle), 60
Weaver, Erasmus M., 253
Weber, Max, 283
Webster, Daniel, 10, 83, 121, 129, 130,
163
Weinberg, Albert K., 4
Welles, Sumner, 307-310, 323
Wentworth, Alfred, 422
Wessin y Wessin, Elias, 418
Weyl, Walter E., 196
Weyler, Valeriano, 171, 187, 226
Wharton, William F., 112, 113
Wheeler, Burton K., 318
Wheeler, Earle G., 426
White Antelope, 143
Whitman, Walt, 101
Wilhelm, Kaiser, 257, 258, 263, 272

Wilkinson, James, 27, 70, 81
Williams, Aubrey, 420
Williams, Benjamin, 282
Williams, David R., 78
Williams, John Sharp, 184
Williams, Oscar, 182
Williams, Roger, 41
Williams, William Appleman, 95
Willkie, Wendell L., 318
Wilmot, David, 129, 134
Wilson, Charles E. (of General Elec-
tric), 380, 381
Wilson, Charles E. (of General Mo-
tors), 381
Wilson, Woodrow, 4, 6, 14, 195-197,
214, 217-221, 223-228, 230-232,
235, 239, 240, 242, 243, 248, 250,
256, 258-262, 265-268, 272, 273,
280, 285, 294, 314
Winchester, James, 59
Winthrop, John, 9
Winthrop, Robert, 101
Wise, David, 373
Wolcott, Oliver, 25
Woll, Matthew, 399
Wood, Leonard, 192, 256, 258
Woodford, Stewart L., 173
Wool, John E., 81
Woolman, John, 10
Woolton, Lord, 337
Worcester, Dean C., 190
Worchester, Noah, 10, 11, 13
Wright, Quincy, 7
Wurf, Jerry, 403

Yalta Conference, 331, 343, 344, 346,
348
Ydigoras Fuentes, Miguel, 362, 390,
396, 408
Young, Stephen, 427
Yrujo, Marquis de, 70

Zahedi, Fazollah, 388, 389
Zander, Arnold, 401
Zapata, Emiliano, 228, 232
Zeitlin, Maurice, 407
Zelaya, José Santos, 211, 212, 215
Zimmerman, Arthur, 261